MICROPROCESSORS/MICROCOMPUTERS

ARCHITECTURE, SOFTWARE, AND SYSTEMS

MICROPROCESSORS/ MICROCOMPUTERS

ARCHITECTURE, SOFTWARE, AND SYSTEMS

ADI J. KHAMBATA

ST. PAUL TECHNICAL-VOCATIONAL INSTITUTE

JOHN WILEY & SONS

NEW YORK   CHICHESTER   BRISBANE   TORONTO   SINGAPORE

Library of Congress Cataloging in Publication Data:
Khambata, Adi J.
    Microprocessors/microcomputers.

    Includes indexes.
    1. Microprocessors. 2. Microcomputers.
I. Title.
QA76.5.K43   001.64'04   81-11360
ISBN 0-471-06490-4   AACR2

Printed in the United States of America

10 9 8 7 6 5 4 3 2 1

To my granddaughter Barbra Ann
and my grandson Jimmy, Jr.

PREFACE

Advances in semiconductor technology have revolutionized the computer field; this is impacting many aspects of American life and industrial activities. The availability of inexpensive computing capability permits applications that were not considered potential candidates for computerization a few years ago. Microprocessors/microcomputers appear in many consumer products, from computer games and kitchen appliances to automobiles. The advent of these low-cost computing systems has led to the development of still another field, until now completely unknown and foreign to the traditional computer industry: computer hobbyists and home computer use.

Understandably, this has created a voracious appetite for microcomputer education. Many segments of industry that were previously not concerned with computers are in the midst of a digital world, requiring personnel trained in the field of microcomputers. Several companies have set up specialized, in-house, microcomputer training courses. Others are relying on established educational institutions to supply them with trained graduates in this field. The major academic problem encountered by most educational institutions is the formation of the required curriculum and the availability of the appropriate teaching materials. The literature abounds with excellent books and other publications on microprocessors/microcomputers; however, most of them are not suitable for classroom use, nor can curriculum be developed around them. This book, based on microcomputer courses that I designed and taught at the St. Paul Technical-Vocational Institute, St. Paul, Minnesota, and at local industries over the past several years, will fill this need.

This book satisfies the requirements of four distinct user groups. First, it can be used in community colleges, vocational schools, and other two-year educational institutions. A group of microprocessor courses can be designed around the basic material in the book. Product supplements to the basic textbook provide sufficient background for the practical application of specific microcomputer systems in the laboratory. Second, each topic starts out at a very fundamental level; the presentations and discussions proceed to greater depth and higher levels, so it could also be used at institutions of higher learning such as four-year colleges and universities. Third, many persons working in industry need and desire to learn about and use microcomputers. Unfortunately, not all of these people can attend courses offered by educational institutions. Self-study may be their only option, and the reasonably detailed explanations and worked-out examples in this book will be helpful to these people. Finally, hobbyists will find this book useful because it is written so that they can scan a subject lightly or pursue it in greater depth, depending on desire and requirements.

It is assumed that students who use this book have some prior knowledge of digital logic and basic logic functions such as AND gates, OR gates, flip-flops, and logic blocks (registers, counters, etc.). These items are not included here, since they are adequately covered in many other excellent publications. The book is divided into two sections. The first covers the hardware aspects of microcomputers, including the central processor (CPU) and the commonly used schemes for interfacing the CPU with the outside world. The second section covers the software aspects of microcomputers. This includes a chapter on BASIC, which is presently the most popular higher-level language used in microcomputer systems.

Chapter One is a fundamental review of digital computers. The architecture of the CPU and the sequence of basic operations are covered here. Number systems and binary data coding are discussed in Chapter Two. The pure binary system, the octal system, the binary-coded-decimal system (BCD), and the hexadecimal system are included. The CPU architecture is the topic of Chapter Three. Busses, which are an important feature of microprocessors, are covered along with machine and instruction cycles. The principal registers and counters of the CPU and their respective functions are then presented. Chapter Four deals with microprocessor instructions. The basic instruction formats for both the memory-reference and the nonmemory-reference instructions are treated. The various addressing modes are presented in Chapter Five. Special attention is given to the indirect addressing mode, which is troublesome to some students. Chapter Six discusses how instructions are executed by the CPU, the microsteps or microinstructions that comprise a macroinstruction are shown, and the basic concept of a microprogrammable microprocessor is introduced. Memory chips, which are used in microcomputer systems, are briefly presented in Chapter Seven. Programmed I/O transfers (both conditional and unconditional) are the subject of Chapter Eight. Chapter Nine describes the interrupt I/O. The vectored interrupt, the software-polled interrupt, and the popular daisy-chained interrupt are examined. Multi-level priority interrupts are also included. Direct Memory Access (DMA) is described in Chapter Ten. Serial I/O transfers are the subject of Chapter Eleven; conversion and synchronization logic and the problems of data identification in serial bit streams are studied in this chapter. Programmable I/O interfaces are described in Chapter Twelve; programmable interfaces for both serial and parallel transfers are included. Chapter Thirteen analyzes D/A and A/D converters. Many microprocessors are required to interface with equipments that have nondigital signals, and so appropriate D/A and A/D interfaces are required.

Chapter Fourteen (which begins the software section) introduces the microcomputer software development cycle. Problem definition and flowcharting are the subject of Chapter Fifteen. Chapter Sixteen shows how to organize the data for processing purposes; exponential notation, the sign convention, and floating-point operations are also presented. The data transformation process is the subject of Chapter Seventeen, which also describes the fundamental functional statements. Chapter Eighteen is entirely devoted to BASIC (Beginner's All-Purpose Symbolic Instruction Code), the higher-level language widely used in microcomputer systems today. Assemblers and interpreters are dealt with in Chapter Nineteen. Interpreters are used frequently in home computers, so this chapter is of special interest to hobbyists. Chapter Twenty briefly describes operating systems and systems software.

To aid readers in learning the material, several chapter elements have been incorporated into the text. These include numerous worked-out examples and figures, end-of-chapter summaries, review questions, and problems. Three appendixes are also included. Appendix A gives the popular ASCII character set and the associated codes. The subject of system testing and checkout and the various testing approaches, commonly used with microcomputer systems, is examined in Appendix B. The logic analyzer, briefly treated in Appendix C, is the most powerful microcomputer trouble-shooting tool available today. A glossary of important terms follows the appendixes.

In addition to offering theoretical descriptions and discussions, it is desirable to describe at least one real, existing microcomputer system. However, including a description of any one product in this book would immediately have dated the publication and also made it unacceptable to other users who may be committed to another product. This dilemma was resolved by adopting a unique approach. A series of separate, soft-cover, supplements, each covering a popular microcomputer system, will accompany the basic text. Four such supplements are presently planned. They will cover the Zilog Z-80, the popular Intel 8080 series, the Motorola MC6800, and the 6502 by MOS Technology. This approach will enable us to introduce additional supplements on future products that find acceptance in educational institutions as well as update existing supplements as needed. It also allows users of this book to purchase only the supplements that are of direct use for their specific needs. In addition to the paperback supplements, separate laboratory manuals—on the most popular microcomputers—will also be published.

When writing a book such as this, it often becomes necessary to borrow some material from prior publications of computer manufacturers and other publishers. I wish to express my appreciation and thanks to the following for giving me permission to use material from their respective publications in this textbook: McGraw-Hill Book Company, New York, Intel Corporation, Santa Clara, California, Prentice-Hall, Inc., Englewood Cliffs, New Jersey, and John Wiley & Sons, Inc., Publishers, New York.

I would like to thank the many people who helped me during the writing and publication of this book. First, Irving L. Kosow, Series Editor at Wiley, meticulously edited the original manuscript and helped me transform it into a finished product. Judy Green, Engineering Technology Editor, and her staff were extremely helpful during the publication process. Their efforts and cooperation are most appreciated. Dr. George Richter, Technical Division Manager at St. Paul Technical-Vocational Institute, constantly encouraged and supported me. Several of my students and former engineering colleagues at Sperry Univac reviewed parts of the manuscript and offered many valuable comments and suggestions; special contributions were made by Philip Gaines, Walter Knights, and Richard Paske. I would also like to thank the following reviewers, whose comments and suggestions were invaluable in preparing the final version of the manuscript: Louis Gross, Columbus Technical Institute; James King, Joliet Junior College; Arthur Seidman, Pratt Institute; Dave Terrell, ITT Technical Institute; J.W. Toliver, University of Houston; and Charles Van Buren, DeVry Technical Institute.

This book is a Khambata family project: my wife Ruth and daughter Pixie typed the manuscript; my son Danny, assisted by his wife Renee, drew the diagrams; and my son Jim and his wife Shelly did all the proofreading. I thank all of them.

Adi J. Khambata

CONTENTS

MICROPROCESSORS/MICROCOMPUTERS

ARCHITECTURE, SOFTWARE, AND SYSTEMS

ONE

MICROCOMPUTER ARCHITECTURE

1
FUNDAMENTALS OF DIGITAL COMPUTERS

1-1 INTRODUCTORY REMARKS

In the electronics field of the 1970s there have been major advances in the applications of silicon technology in the form of microprocessors/microcomputers. It all started in 1948 with the transistor. The early and middle 1950s saw a trend toward replacement of the vacuum tube by semiconductor devices, mainly in digital computers. The maturing of the semiconductor processes, particularly the silicon planar technology, led to the emergence of the silicon integrated circuit in the late 1950s and early 1960s. It then became possible to put a complex circuit on a single silicon chip. Encouraged by the wide acceptance of such devices, called integrated circuits or ICs, it was only a matter of time before several such circuits were put on the same chip and interconnected right on the chip itself to provide more complex logic blocks such as registers, counters, and adders. Thus medium-scale integration (MSI) came into its own during the late 1960s. Once again the computer industry was the principal beneficiary as well as the primary catalyst for further advancements. The much talked about and sought after goal of a "computer-on-a-slice" or "computer-on-a-chip" was no longer just a dream. In 1971 the Intel 8008, the first microprocessor in industry, appeared; it was developed primarily for electronic calculator-oriented applications. The 8008 is on a single silicon chip and uses LSI (large-scale-integration) techniques and MOS (metal-oxide-semiconductor) circuitry. The success of the 8008 prompted other major semiconductor manufacturers to introduce microprocessors of their own. Thus, in the middle and late 1970s, a variety of microcomputer products became available at attractive prices and with ever-increasing performance and capabilities.

The impact of microprocessors/microcomputers on the traditional and well-established large-computers industry is significant, but its impact on the entire

5

field of electronics is no less dramatic. The availability of low-cost, low-power, and small weight/volume computing capability reveals many applications in defense, industrial, and consumer products that were not even considered for computerization just a few short years ago. As prices continue to spiral downward, microcomputers will undoubtedly find more applications, particularly in consumer products. Because of the anticipated widespread use of microcomputers in the near future, it is apparent that a working knowledge of these devices is desirable and perhaps is even an indispensable tool for people in the electronics field. For persons already in the computer field the transition into microprocessors/microcomputers will be relatively simple although, in some instances, it might perhaps be quite demanding. For those not acquainted with computers things may be different. This chapter provides a brief, simple introduction to digital computers and to microprocessors/microcomputers.

1-2 INTRODUCTION TO THE DIGITAL COMPUTER

1-2.1 The Typical System

In the most basic terms a computer is a device or machine that automatically executes a sequence of operations upon given data. The purpose of such operations may be the solution of mathematical problems, the control of certain functions of other devices or, quite often, a combination of the two. In digital computers the data are expressed in discrete, binary form, in analog computers the data are expressed in continuous or analog forms.

In electronic digital computers numerical quantities are represented by voltage levels of electrical pulses. The presence or absence of a single pulse, or of the appropriate voltages, defines a bit, which is a contraction for a *binary digit*. A group of bits, which are considered and handled together, is called a *word*. A word consists of the binary digits or bits, which are expressed as either 1 or 0, and these are represented by appropriately defined electrical signal pulses.

A word may represent a numerical quantity, called the operand, or it may represent a directive, called an instruction, which commands the machine to operate on the given operands in a specified manner. The group or set of instructions presented to the computer is called a *program*. The process or procedure by which the mathematical calculations or logical operations are performed by the machine is called an *algorithm*.

To compute or control automatically, the computer must perform several fundamental internal functions. Some of the most basic functions are arithmetic operations such as addition and subtraction, to be performed on two operands. Even simple processes involve several functions that are performed by different sections of the computer system. Figure 1-1 is a block diagram of the major functional blocks of any digital computer.

1-2.2 The Memory System

In a computer the memory system is used primarily for two purposes.

- To provide a storage system for the data or the operands.
- To provide a facility for storing the program, (i.e., a group of commands or instructions.

The portion of the memory that stores the operands is called data memory, and we will refer to it as such. This memory stores the data that will be utilized by the computer during execution of the program. The operating portion of the computer can call out (or read out, as it is called) a certain desired operand from any part of the data memory. Likewise, it can insert, or write, a word in any location in the data memory. The data memory is designed so that the computer can access any location within the memory randomly. For this reason the data memory is often referred to as random-access memory (RAM). For certain applications the internal data memory of the computer may not be large enough to hold all the required data. In such situations the computer could acquire data from auxiliary external storage sources such as magnetic tapes, bubble memories or disks via the input port of the system. Thus the computer could process large volumes of data at high speeds.

The part of the memory that stores the commands or the instructions is called the program memory. Each instruction from this memory is supplied to the computer in a certain preestablished sequence. The computer then decodes each instruction and initiates the specific process, which is called out.

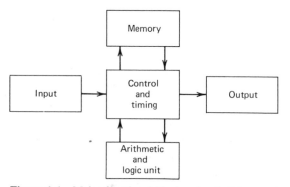

Figure 1-1 Major functional blocks of a digital computer.

Unlike the data memory, where data could be written into certain locations during the execution of the program, normally no write-in operations are involved in the program memory. The instructions are loaded into the program memory prior to the execution of the program. For this reason the program memory is sometimes referred to as read-only memory (ROM).

The internal memory of a computer is sometimes called the mainframe memory. This term includes both the data and the program memories. Mainframes in today's computers can be the semiconductor types or the magnetic types such as magnetic cores, magnetic films, or plated magnetic wires. Furthermore, memories can be the random-access, read/write types or the read-only types or, more likely, a combination of the two. The mainframe memories in microcomputers are generally the semiconductor chip types. It should be noted that the ROMs, although referred to as such, can also be accessed randomly.

1-2.3 The Central Processing Unit (CPU)

Central processing unit is the term applied to two of the functional blocks of Fig. 1-1. The CPU includes the arithmetic and logic unit (ALU) and the control and timing block. The CPU is the heart of the computing system. It controls all the other functions performed by the system. The CPU calls for instructions from the memory, decodes them, and executes them. It references the memory and the various input-output ports as required for the execution of the various instructions. The CPU also recognizes and responds to several external request signals such as *"interrupts,"* which will be described later in the book.

The ALU performs the arithmetical operations on the operands. The various logical processes are also performed by this section. The operations performed by the ALU may provide either complete results or only partial or intermediate results, depending on the problems solved. Partial results are utilized within the computer itself and are seldom presented to the outside world unless specifically instructed to do so.

The control unit controls and coordinates all other functional units of the computer in a timed, logical sequence. An accurately controlled central clock provides the basic clock pulses. All other working circuits are then synchronized with these pulses. The control unit receives the instructions from the program stored in the program memory, decodes them, and directs the functional subsystem units of the system to execute those commands. The control signals generated by the control unit and the memory cycle time are closely synchronized. Generally, the time required for the execution of each fixed instruction is a multiple of the memory speed.

1-2.4 The Input-Output Ports (I/O)

This unit provides a vehicle for the computer to communicate with several types of devices called peripherals or I/O devices. The input port permits the CPU to acquire the data from other external devices or external memory banks. The output port enables the CPU to communicate the results of its computations or logical processing to the external peripherals. The output port can also be used to communicate process control signals that may direct the operation of other external systems such as an instrumentation system. Most computing systems contain more than one I/O port, and these are addressable, meaning that they can be selectively activated under program control.

1-3 THE CPU ARCHITECTURE

1-3.1 The Functional Subsystems

The CPU in any computer system contains the following groups of interconnected functional units.

- Registers and counters.
- Arithmetic logic unit (ALU).
- Timing and control circuitry.

The general characteristics of each of these are now considered. Remember that no two computers are exactly alike even if the functions they perform are similar, and the design of each unit will be different in different machines even though they may be performing similar functions.

1-3.2 Registers and Counters

Registers and counters are basic to all computers and are some of the fundamental building blocks of computing systems. Registers are used for temporary storage of binary bits within the CPU. Binary data can be input and output into registers serially (i.e., one bit at a time). As each bit is input serially, the previously loaded bits are shifted one place. Figure 1-2a shows how the bits can be loaded and serially shifted to the right. They can also be loaded and serially shifted left (Fig. 1-2b).

In the 8-bit registers in Fig. 1-2, during serial shift output the original 8 bits of the register are no longer there. This may be acceptable in some cases but, in other applications, it may be necessary to retain the original 8 bits in the register even after the serial readout. This can be accomplished by feeding

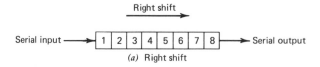

(a) Right shift

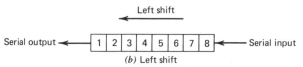

(b) Left shift

Figure 1-2   Serial input/serial output shift register.

the serially output bits back into the input (Fig. 1-3). Such registers are called recirculating registers, and the process is often called rotation right or rotation left. It is possible to design serial registers so that the recirculation path can be either opened or closed upon appropriate command or instruction.

Registers are also designed to have parallel inputs and parallel outputs. Here all 8 bits are input and output simultaneously on command (Fig. 1-4). In serially shifted registers, each shift can destroy or alter the previously stored bit in the flip-flop. Thus, in a noncirculating type serial shift register, all 8 bits are essentially destroyed. On the other hand, in parallel output registers, the output of each flip-flop is sampled but not altered. Thus, regardless of the number of readouts, the register would still contain the original 8 bits. It is possible to design a register such that the same register could perform any or all of the various just mentioned functions.

- Serial input/serial output (right or left).
- Right/left rotate.
- Parallel input/parallel output.

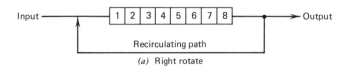

(a) Right rotate

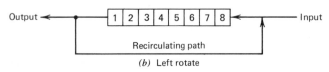

(b) Left rotate

Figure 1-3   Circulating registers.

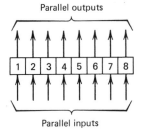

Parallel outputs

Parallel inputs

Figure 1-4   Parallel input/parallel output register.

- Serial input/parallel output.
- Parallel input/serial output.

In digital systems registers could be either general-purpose or dedicated. General-purpose registers can be used for several functions under program control. Dedicated registers perform certain functions only. They are hard-wired into the machine to perform these functions and are not under the control of the program. Registers are generally cleared to all zeros at the start of a program.

Counters are devices that record and hold a count of the number of input pulses or bits. A counter may count up or down. The up counter is cleared to all zeros; it is updated every time a bit is input into it. All ones are first inserted in down counters (i.e., the maximum count capability of the unit), and then, with every input, the count is lowered by one. The up counter is incremented with each input and the down counter is decremented with each input. Instead of clearing the counter to all zeros or setting it to all ones, it is possible to load any number into the counter first and then, under program control, increment or decrement it from this point on. Counter readout is always parallel and never serial. Thus the original bits in the counter are never destroyed during readout. Finally, it is possible to design a combination register/counter unit that can perform any of the functions under program control.

1-3.2.1 The Accumulator Generally, the accumulator is the principal working register in the microprocessor and frequently is the I/O port to the CPU. In many microprocessors the results of either the arithmetical or logical operations performed by the ALU are transferred to and stored in the accumulator.

Usually the accumulator is considered to be a general-purpose register in most microprocessors and stores one of the operands to be used by the ALU in performing arithmetic or logical operations. The accumulator can function both as a source register and as a destination register. For example, the program may call for the contents of a certain memory location to be added to the contents of the *accumulator* and the resulting sum to be stored in the same, or some other, memory location. In this case the accumulator functions as a source register. But, if the program calls for the contents of the memory location to be added to the contents of the accumulator and the result to be stored in the same accumulator, the accumulator becomes both a source and a destination register.

Sometimes a group of general-purpose accumulators are used for temporary storage of operands or of intermediate or partial results of computations or logical processes. Such a group of accumulators, located in the CPU, is called a scratch-pad memory.

Many times the principal accumulator in the computer is designed to perform several other functions such as complementing the contents, right or left shifting the number, and right or left rotating the number. Also, the accumulator is often designed to store a cumulative or progressive total of the numbers transferred into it. Each successive operand or number transferred into it is added to the previous sum. Accumulators can also be designed so that, under program control, the quantity transferred into it is subtracted from the previous quantity.

1-3.2.2 The Program Counter The instructions that comprise the program are stored in consecutive locations within the program memory, which may consist of several ROM chips in microcomputers. Each memory location is assigned a unique code or number, called the address. In order to execute the program in the properly assigned sequence, the CPU must know what location in the program memory it should go to fetch the instruction. The program counter is the vehicle by which this is accomplished. It contains the address of the next instruction to be fetched. The CPU updates or increments the program counter every time it fetches the instruction.

When a JUMP instruction is inserted in the main program, the normal sequence of the program is suspended. That instruction directs the program counter to some address within the main program other than the next sequential address. The JUMP instruction contains the address of the instruction to which the program is directed, and this address is automatically inserted in the program counter. This then provides logical continuity to the program. Note that a JUMP can be either a jump forward or a jump backward, but always within the main program.

Subroutines are programs within a program. During the execution of a program, a certain group of instructions are often used over and over again. Of course, it is possible to repeat these instructions every time they are needed in the main program. Such a procedure would use up many memory locations in the program memory. They could be written and stored in the memory as a subroutine only once and then called out by the main program when needed. A special JUMP instruction, called the BRANCH, in the main program calls out a subroutine. The BRANCH instruction contains the starting address of the subroutine, and this is automatically inserted in the program counter.

To insure an orderly return to the main program after completion of the subroutine, it is necessary that the address of the next sequential instruction in the main program, following the BRANCH instruction, be saved somewhere. Prior to the branching and execution of the subroutine, the CPU increments the program counter and stores this in a special group of registers or memory area known as the stack. The program counter is thus released for keeping track of the addresses in the subroutine.

The last instruction in the subroutine is a BRANCH BACK or RETURN instruction that returns control back to the main program. The CPU simply inserts the address at the top of the stack into the program counter, and the main program is resumed at the address immediately following the BRANCH instruction.

Nesting is the process by which one subroutine can call out a second subroutine, that, in turn, may call out a third subroutine, and so on. The number of subroutines that can be nested depends on the number of return addresses that can be saved by the CPU. In other words, the depth of nesting is determined by the depth of the stack.

1-3.2.3 The Instruction Register and Decoder The computer's word length in bits is usually established by the size of the internal storage elements such as registers, other component subsystems such as counters and accumulators, and internal data transmission paths called busses. A word is the basic unit of bits that the machine handles as a group. In today's computers, including microprocessors, 4-bit word lengths, or multiples of 4, are commonly used. In microcomputers a 4-bit field is called a nibble and an 8-bit field is a byte. Each operation performed by the CPU is identified by a unique group of bits called instruction codes. Eight-bit instruction codes are used in most microcomputers, although 16 bits are also becoming very common. If an 8-bit instruction is used, it is possible for that system to have up to 256 unique instructions ($2^8 = 256$).

Fetching the instruction from the program memory involves two separate operations. First, the CPU transmits the address of the instruction in the program counter to the memory. The memory then transmits the contents of the addressed location to the CPU, where it is temporarily stored in a dedicated register called the instruction register. The contents of the instruction register are then decoded by the decoder and, in association with the timed clock pulses, establish the appropriate data transfer paths within the system and execute the various other electrical activities called out by that particular instruction.

Although 8 bits are adequate for instruction codes in most microcomputers, there are cases where more than 8 bits may be required, for example, instruction that references a fairly large data memory. Here, the 8-bit instruction can identify the operation to be performed but not the operand location. A 2-byte or even a 3-byte instruction is the answer. Such multibyte instructions are stored in adjacent memory locations. The CPU then performs two or three fetches in succession, as appropriate, to acquire the full instruction. Where multibyte instructions are involved, the first byte, which contains the operation code of the instruction, is transferred into the instruction register. The remaining byte or bytes are placed in temporary or auxiliary registers.

1-3.2.4 The Address Register/Counter The address register (which may be a register pair) is a temporary storage device for holding the address of the location to be accessed for either a readout or a write-in of data in the data memory. In some more sophisticated microprocessors the address register is programmable where instructions are available to the programmer to modify the contents of this register. Then the program can be designed so that it can build or generate an address in this register prior to executing a memory reference instruction. Even further sophistication is available in some systems where the address register is provided with additional up/down counter capabilities. This feature is especially useful in applications where large blocks of data that are sequentially stored in the data memory are required to be accessed.

1-3.3 The Arithmetic/Logic Unit (ALU)

All computers have an ALU where the arithmetic computations and various logical (Boolean) operations are performed. The ALU, which can perhaps be thought of as an electronically controlled calculator, uses binary and not decimal methods to represent and operate on numbers. The ALU contains an adder that fundamentally performs only binary additions (subtraction is performed by complement addition) on two operands that may be supplied by any components of the system such as internal registers, accumulators, data memories, or I/O devices.

ALUs also contain status *flags* or *status bits* that register and indicate certain specific conditions that could arise during certain manipulations (mostly arithmetic). These flags or status bits are indicated by the state of simple R/S flip-flops. A micro-processor may have as few as 1 status flag or as many as 16. Most systems have 4 to 8 flags. Status conditions are generally stored in a special dedicated register called the *status register*. Some typical conditions indicated by these flags are:

- Overflow.
- Zero.
- Negative sign.
- Carry.

In the CPU, flags are used to perform conditional JUMPS or conditional BRANCHES to subroutines; they are occasionally used to handle special or unusual situations.

1-3.4 Timing and Control

Using the clock inputs, the CPU insures the proper execution and sequencing of events required to process the specific instruction. Depending on the instruction involved, the control circuitry will issue the appropriate signals to units internal and external to the CPU for initiating the processing actions.

1-4 THE SEQUENCE OF BASIC OPERATIONS

1-4.1 The Basic Timing Sequence

The CPU operates in a cyclical manner; that is, it fetches an instruction from the program memory, decodes it, and executes the particular operations specified by the instruction. The next instruction is then fetched, and the process is repeated until the entire program is executed. This entire sequence is synchronized by a timing clock. In early microcomputers this clocking system was physically located on a chip separate from the CPU chip, although there are a few microcomputers available where the clock is included on the CPU chip. In either case the fundamental clock frequency is provided by some external source, generally an accurately controlled crystal. Some microcomputers also provide other means of fundamental frequency sources such as external RC circuits or synchronization by a master system clock. The clock could supply a single stream of pulses (the clock is then called a single-phase clock) (Fig. 1-5*a*) [the Greek letter Φ (phi) is generally used to denote clock phases], or it could supply two phases (Fig. 1-5*b*). The number of clock phases used depends primarily on the type of circuitry employed in the system. It is, of course, possible to have more than two phases in the clocking system. A 2-phase clock could have either nonoverlapping pulse streams (Fig. 1-5*b*) or overlapping streams (Fig. 1-5*c*). Although $\Phi2$ pulses are shown enveloping $\Phi1$, it is possible to have $\Phi1$ enveloping $\Phi2$. It is possible to have one of the

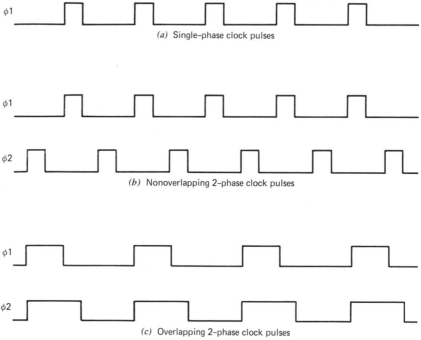

(a) Single-phase clock pulses

(b) Nonoverlapping 2-phase clock pulses

(c) Overlapping 2-phase clock pulses

Figure 1-5   Typical microcomputer clock pulses and phases.

phase pulses only partially overlapping the other instead of completely overlapping it (Fig. 1-5c).

The time interval between identical points on two adjacent clock pulses of the same clock phase is called the *clock period*. The time involved in the combined fetch and execution processes of a single instruction is called a *machine cycle*. Any portion of a machine cycle that is identified with a clearly defined activity is called a phase of the machine cycle (not to be confused with clock phase or phases). At least one, and usually more, clock periods are necessary for completion of a phase, and several phases make up a machine cycle.

1-4.2 Instruction Fetch/Execution Sequence

The first phase of a machine cycle fetches the instruction. The contents of the program counter are sent to the program memory to be used as the address of the instruction. The program memory then transmits the instruction to the CPU. The first word (or byte) of the instruction is loaded into the instruction register. If the instruction is a multiword or multibyte instruction, additional machine cycles will be required to fetch the rest of it. The program counter is then incremented in preparation for fetching the next instruction. Finally, the CPU executes the operation specified in the instruction.

1-4.3 Data Memory Read Operation

Suppose a particular instruction calls for data to be read from the data memory into the CPU. The CPU would receive the instruction and hold it in the instruction register. Computers employ different addressing schemes; these will be discussed in detail in a later chapter. One of these schemes is the indexed addressing mode. If the particular instruction calls out the indexed addressing mode then, prior to the execution of the instruction, the contents of the index register (sometimes called the B register) are added to the address specified in the instruction, thereby modifying the address.

In machines that incorporate the *interrupt* capabilities, the contents of the index register are stored in a separate register or memory location that holds this value during the execution of the instruction, in case an interrupt comes along during this time. This procedure allows the program to be automatically resumed at the proper point when a return from interrupt is made.

Upon receipt of the proper or effective address and the readout command signal from the CPU, the memory responds by transferring the contents of the addressed location to the CPU I/O, usually the accumulator, through the data bus.

1-4.4 Data Memory Write Operation

This is very similar to the read operation except for the direction of the data flow. As before, the appropriate instruction is held in the instruction register and modified by the contents of the index register if this mode of addressing is specified. The CPU then transmits the address to the data memory. This is followed by the proper write command to the memory and the transfer of data bits from the CPU, usually the accumulator, into the addressed location in the memory.

1-4.5 Input/Output Operations

In microcomputers, I/O operations are very similar to the data memory read/write operations except that a peripheral I/O port is addressed instead of a memory location. The instruction is received from the program memory, stored, and executed in the same manner as that previously described for memory read/write. (The CPU then outputs the data to the I/O device or receives data from it, as appropriate.)

Depending on the particular application involved, the I/O data transfer could be in either serial or parallel form. Serial data transfers occur over a single line, are slow, but require comparatively less hardware. Parallel transfers take place over several lines, depending on the number of bits in the word to be transferred, are much faster than serial transfers, but generally require more hardware.

1-4.6 Interrupts

In computers, interrupt capabilities are provided to increase the system's efficiency by reducing the idle time of the CPU. Very often the CPU has to suspend its normal operations and remain idle while waiting for a slower peripheral to catch up. If interrupt capability is provided, the peripheral sends an *interrupt request* signal to the CPU when it is ready to be serviced, that is when it is either ready to accept data from or send data to the CPU. Until such time, the CPU continues to execute other tasks as dictated by the program. After receiving the interrupt request, the CPU suspends operation of the main program and automatically branches off to the appropriate subroutine to service that particular I/O device. After completing the subroutine, the CPU resumes execution of the main program. Interrupt servicing is very similar to subroutine calls except that the entire operation is initiated by an external I/O device, not by an instruction in the main program.

Note The explanations provided up to this point are oversimplifications intended to introduce students to the fundamentals, principles, and concepts of digital computers. Each machine will, of course, be different and will have its own unique features. In many cases the same results could be obtained by different approaches. Each item described in this chapter will be discussed in greater detail in subsequent chapters.

1-5 DIGITAL COMPUTER IN BLOCK DIAGRAM FORM

1-5.1 Realistic Organization

Figure 1-1 is a generalized block diagram of a digital computer system intended to introduce students to the major functional blocks only; it is unrealistic. When a computer solves a given problem, regardless of whether it is a mathematical problem or a logical process for control purposes, the CPU must follow a specific, predetermined sequence of operations. In other words, the CPU must be controlled according to the preestablished program. This sequencing of the different operations is provided by the program stored in the program memory in conjunction with the timing and control unit in the CPU.

A general-purpose (GP) computer must be capable of handling several different problems for different customer applications, as opposed to a special-purpose (SP) machine, which is designed specifically to handle one particular application or a certain category of applications only. Commercially available microcomputers are generally of the GP variety.

The control unit of any computer senses the various commands presented to it by the program and then issues appropriate control signals to various parts of the computer. We have also seen that the CPU responds to signals from external devices, such as interrupt requests. Furthermore, the control unit would also receive external signals from the human operator. Typical signals would be start and stop commands. Also, a temporary or scratch-pad memory is always required to store the intermediate result of computations or logical processes. Operator communications with the computer is generally through an operator console that may contain a CRT-type display and a type-writer-type keyboard, or it could be through a front panel that has light displays and push buttons for inputs. If these features are included a more realistic computer organization results (Fig. 1-6).

Note that in Fig. 1-6 some busses are unidirectional while some are bidirectional. Also notice that for the simplification of the diagram, only two blocks are shown in the CPU, which is indicated by the dotted lines. Of course, the CPU contains more than just the ALU and the timing and control unit. For this reason all the busses, with the exception of that between the ALU and the scratch-pad memory, are shown going to or from the CPU only. In other words, it is shown that way in Fig. 1-6 to indicate that the major functional blocks of the system communicate with functional blocks within the CPU other than the ALU and the timing and control unit.

1-5.2 The Microcomputer Organization

Microprocessors and microcomputers came about because of major advances in semiconductor technology. Figure 1-6 illustrates the traditional organization of the digital computer but, because of these technological advances, some changes in this organization are necessary. For example, for organizational and addressing purposes, it is possible to combine the program and the data memories into one single mainframe memory that could contain both RAM and ROM chips. The different parts of the mainframe memory can be assigned to data or operand storage and to program storage functions. Likewise, both input and output functions could be combined on one chip and into a single I/O unit. The resulting configuration is shown in Fig. 1-7. It is the very basic configuration of today's microcomputers. For simplicity, only the data busses and control lines are shown in Fig. 1-7.

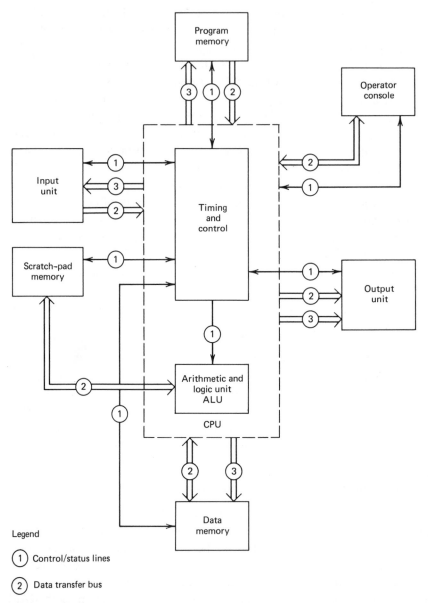

Legend

① Control/status lines

② Data transfer bus

③ Address bus

Figure 1-6   Realistic computer organization.

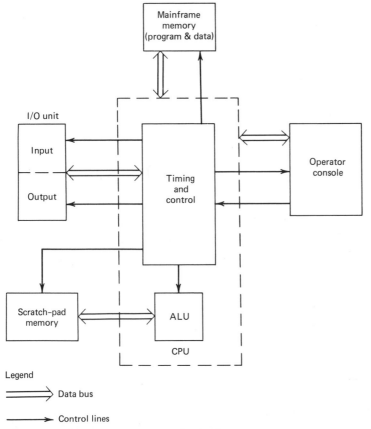

Figure 1-7 Basic microcomputer organization.

1-6 THE MICROCOMPUTER STRUCTURE

Advances in semiconductor technology have made it possible to include some degree of memory capabilities on the same LSI chip that contains the ALU portion of the system. The scratch-pad memory shown in Fig. 1-7 usually consists of several registers that have shift-in/shift-out capabilities. When the scratch-pad memory is included on the ALU chip, that chip is referred to as the *register and arithmetic/logic unit* (RALU). As further advances were made in LSI technology, it became possible to include even the timing and control circuitry on the RALU chip. The resulting chip is what is now referred to as *the microprocessor,* which is one chip in a microcomputer configuration. Figure 1-8 shows the basic chips in a simple microcomputer system. The operator console is also included.

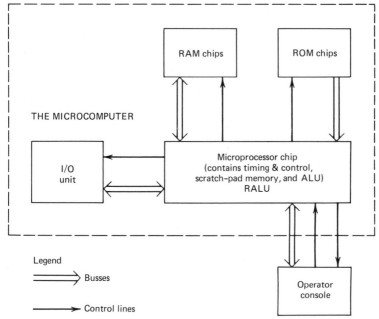

Figure 1-8 The microcomputer.

1-7 SUMMARY

This chapter had three objectives: first, to introduce students to the major functional blocks in today's digital computers; second, to present the principal functional blocks in the CPU such as the accumulator, the program counter, and the instruction register and to explain the sequence of basic operations; and third, to show how the present microprocessor chip evolved and how it fits into the system of chips that we call the microcomputer.

1-8 REVIEW QUESTIONS

1-1   What are the two principal functions of the memory system in a digital computer?

1-2   In what order are the instructions from the program memory supplied to the CPU? Are there any exceptions? If so, explain.

1-3   Are the operands stored sequentially in the data memory? If not, are there any exceptions? How are the operands accessed? Explain.

1-4   Explain why semiconductor read/write memories are called RAMS but semiconductor read-only memories are not referred to as random access memories.

1-5   State the (four) basic functions performed by the CPU of a digital computer.

1-6   What are I/O ports? Why are they necessary in a system? How are they accessed? How many I/O ports can a typical microcomputer have?

1-7   The following questions relate to shift registers.
(a) The data bits in an 8-bit serial shift register are shifted right eight times. Will the register still contain the original data? Explain.
(b) An 8-bit shift register has the recirculating capability. What will happen to the most significant bit if the bits are shifted left once?
(c) What will happen to the original data bits in an 8-bit parallel input/parallel output shift register after eight consecutive readouts?

1-8   What is the difference between an up counter and a down counter? Is is possible to have the same counter with both the up and down counting capabilities?

1-9   A 6-bit up/down counter contains the binary count 110101.
(a) What will the counter contain after it is incremented twice?
(b) What will it contain if it is now decremented once?
(c) What would the counter have contained if the original binary quantity had been decremented once instead of incremented twice, as in Question 1-9a?

1-10   Explain how an accumulator differs from an adder.

1-11   How are the addresses for the instructions in a program generated by the CPU? Explain.

1-12   Explain how a JUMP instruction is executed. How is the nonsequential address of the instruction generated?

1-13   Describe how control is returned to the main program when a subroutine (initiated by a BRANCH instruction) is completed.

1-14   How many subroutines can be *nested* in the CPU of a μP?

1-15   Describe the function of the instruction decoder in the CPU of a μP.

1-16   What is the advantage of providing an up/down counting capability in an address register?

1-17   Name the (four) most common status flags found in most μPs.

1-18   What circuit (or component) provides the fundamental clock frequency to the clocking system of a μC?

1-19   Define the following:
(a) Clock period.
(b) Machine cycle.
(c) Nonoverlapping clock pulses.

2

NUMBER SYSTEMS AND BINARY DATA CODING IN MICROCOMPUTERS

2-1 BINARY DATA AND NUMBER SYSTEMS

All digital computers operate on electrical signals that are defined as 1s and 0s in a system of binary numbers. In any computer, a fixed number of bits comprise a word, and the machine is designed to operate on this word. For example, a word could be consistently 8 bits long, 16 bits long, or any other number of bits long.

A computer word, consisting of a pattern of 1s and 0s, can by definition be coded so that it could represent a numerical quantity, an alphabetical character, or a computer instruction. Data words and instructions can be stored in the mainframe memory, and each memory location is always identified by a unique address. This address can also be coded in a binary manner (i.e., by means of 1s and 0s).

Two fundamental elements are basic to all numbering systems.

- The base or the radix of the system.
- The value assigned to the position of a digit.

Our familiar decimal system of numbers uses the base 10; that is, 10 unique symbols are used to represent 10 different conditions. The ten symbols are 0, 1, 2, 3, 4, 5, 6, 7, 8, and 9.

Each position in a given number is indicative of the particular coefficient multiplied by a power of 10. Thus the system of numerical notation is basically a kind of shorthand system. Also, it is common to denote the base or radix of the system used by means of a subscript. The following examples demonstrate how this system works.

Example 2-1

Explain what the shorthand representation 381_{10} means in the decimal system.

Solution

The position each coefficient occupies is the power to which base 10 is raised and then multiplied by that particular coefficient, starting with the rightmost position. (*Note:* $10^0 = 1$.)

$1 \times 10^0 = 1 \times 1 = 1$
$8 \times 10^1 = 8 \times 10 = 80$
$3 \times 10^2 = 3 \times 100 = 300$

Therefore, 381_{10} really is the sum of these quantities; that is:

$(3 \times 10^2) + (8 \times 10^1) + (1 \times 10^0)$
$= 300 + 80 + 1$
$= 381$ ■

Notice that in the base 10 system, there are 10 and only 10 unique coefficients. We can likewise represent numbers in any base system, as shown in the following examples.

Example 2-2

Explain what the shorthand representation 403_5 means in the decimal system.

Solution

In the base 5 or quinary system there can only be five unique coefficients and no more. They are:

0, 1, 2, 3, and 4 (not 5)

Therefore 403_5 means:

$(4 \times 5^2) + (0 \times 5^1) + (3 \times 5^0)$
$= (4 \times 25) + (0 \times 5) + (3 \times 1)$
$= 100 + 0 + 3$
$= 103$ ■

Example 2-3

Explain what the shorthand representation 2841_7 means in the familiar decimal system.

Solution

This is nonsense. The digit 8 is meaningless here because in a number system to the base 7 there can only be seven coefficients (i.e., 0 to 6).   ■

Remember that our digital computers work only with the binary number system, so there are only two coefficients involved: 0 and 1.

Example 2-4

Explain what the shorthand representation 1101_2 means in the decimal system.

Solution

The decimal representation of 1101_2 is:

$$
\begin{aligned}
(1 \times 2^3) + (1 \times 2^2) &+ (0 \times 2^1) + (1 \times 2^0) \\
= (1 \times 8) + (1 \times 4) &+ (0 \times 2) + (1 \times 1) \\
= \quad 8 + 4 &+ 0 + 1 \\
= \quad 13
\end{aligned}
$$

Therefore $1101_2 = 13_{10}$.   ■

2-2 THE PURE BINARY NUMBERS

A group of binary bits without any prior, preestablished pattern or definition can represent a number, depending on the number of bits and the combination of 1s and 0s in the group.

For example, a 4-bit word can represent $2^4 = 16$ unique values. Similarly, an 8-bit word can represent up to $2^8 = 256$ unique values. Very often confusion arises because of the following situation. Notice that in a 4-bit word the maximum number represented is 1111. The decimal equivalent of this is:

$$
\begin{aligned}
(1 \times 2^3) &+ (1 \times 2^2) + (1 \times 2^1) + (1 \times 2^0) \\
= (1 \times 8) &+ (1 \times 4) + (1 \times 2) + (\times 1) \\
= \quad 8 \quad &+ \quad 4 \quad + \quad 2 \quad + \quad 1 \\
= \quad 15
\end{aligned}
$$

But we just said that a 4-bit word can give us unique values up to 16. This apparent discrepancy is explained by the fact that all four zeros (i.e., 0000) is the sixteenth possible combination of 4 bits. Likewise, in an 8-bit word the combination of 11111111 gives us 255. When the code combination of

00000000 is also included, we get $2^8 = 256$ possible combinations of 1s and 0s. A few examples will show what binary number codes look like.

Example 2-5

Write the binary equivalents of decimal 0, 2, 5, 8, 12, and 14 for 4-bit words.

Solution

Decimal	Four-bit Binary Equivalents
0	0 0 0 0
2	0 0 1 0
5	0 1 0 1
8	1 0 0 0
12	1 1 0 0
14	1 1 1 0

Example 2-6

Write the binary equivalents of decimal 3, 6, 8, 17, 24, 31, and 46 for 6-bit words.

Solution

Decimal	Six-bit Binary Equivalents
3	0 0 0 0 1 1
6	0 0 0 1 1 0
8	0 0 1 0 0 0
17	0 1 0 0 0 1
24	0 1 1 0 0 0
31	0 1 1 1 1 1
46	1 0 1 1 1 0

Example 2-7

Write the binary equivalents of decimal 0, 17, 36, and 147 for 8-bit words.

Solution

Decimal	Eight-bit Binary Equivalents
0	0 0 0 0 0 0 0 0
17	0 0 0 1 0 0 0 1
36	0 0 1 0 0 1 0 0
147	1 0 0 1 0 0 1 1

Using this binary system, it is possible to do various arithmetic operations such as addition, subtraction, multiplication, and division. Such a binary system is often referred to as the pure binary data system or a stand-alone binary system. Note that the relative position of the binary bits (from the right) determines its appropriate weight in the system. No grouping of bits or bit positions are involved. We will now describe how simple binary addition and subtraction are performed. We will not discuss multiplication or division at this stage, since they involve complex logical operations that have not yet been explained.

2-2.1 Binary Addition

Addition of numbers in the binary system is very similar to decimal addition in some respects. In decimal addition a carryout of 1 can result, as in 28 + 16 = 44. Here we add 8 and 6 first, which gives us 14. A carryout of 1 must then be added to the sum of the two digits in the next higher position, thereby giving us 44. Of course, it is possible to have a carry that could conceivably be propagated through all possible positions and even result in an additional or extra carry digit, as shown here. Also observe that although both numerical quantities A and B each had only three digits, the result of the addition, R, has one extra digit.

$$
\begin{array}{rl}
A & \rightarrow 898 \\
B & \rightarrow \underline{643} \\
R = A + B & \rightarrow 1541
\end{array}
$$

The same basic principles apply to addition in the binary system, but there are only two coefficients. The rules for binary addition are easy and are summarized for two bits, A and B, and all their possible combinations along with their results and carry bits in Table 2-1.

Table 2-1   TRUTH TABLE FOR BINARY ADDITION.

A	B	Result R	Carry C
0	0	0	0
1	0	1	0
0	1	1	0
1	1	0	1

Let us try a few examples in binary addition. Refer to Table 2-1 and follow the carries as they happen. Remember that a carry from a previous pair of bits must be added to the sum of the next pair of bits.

Example 2-8

Perform the addition of A and B in the binary system for $A = 5_{10}$ and $B = 2_{10}$. Use 4-bit words only.

Solution

	Decimal	Four-bit binary equivalent
A	5	0 1 0 1
B	2	0 0 1 0
$R = A + B$	7	0 1 1 1

Note that no carries are involved in this example.   ■

Example 2-9

Add $A = 29_{10}$ and $B = 9_{10}$ in binary and 6-bit word format.

Solution

	Decimal	Six-bit Binary Equivalent
A	29	0 1 1 1 0 1
B	9	0 0 1 0 0 1
$R = A + B$	38	1 0 0 1 1 0

Notice the carries from the fourth and fifth pair of bits.   ■

Example 2-10

Add $A = 171_{10}$ and $B = 202_{10}$ in binary and 8-bit word format.

Solution

	Decimal	Eight-bit Binary Equivalent
A	171	1 0 1 0 1 0 1 1
B	202	1 1 0 0 1 0 1 0
$R = A + B$	373	(1) 0 1 1 1 0 1 0 1

Here a ninth bit position is required for the extra carry bit.   ■

2-2.2 Binary Subtraction in Ones Complement

Just like addition, subtraction in the binary system can also be performed using basically the same rules of borrow as in decimal subtraction. It is possible to design and build a subtractor similar to an adder. In today's microprocessors this is not done. Fortunately, techniques are available that make it possible to use the adder for the subtraction functions even though the adder can only perform additions. Through complementation, subtraction can be converted into a simple problem of addition.

2-2.2.1 The Sign Convention Before we can describe the binary subtraction process we must establish some method of identifying positive and negative quantities. The generally accepted convention is to use a 0 in the most significant bit position to indicate a positive quantity and a 1 in the same position to indicate a negative quantity.

Since it is always possible that an extra carry bit could result from an addition, an extra bit position is provided between the highest-order bit position of the operand and the sign bit position. Also, in order to identify the sign bit, it is commonly separated from the other bits by a period. Thus, using a 4-bit basic word length, here is how $+13_{10}$ and -10_{10} would look in the conventional binary notation system.

$$\left.\begin{array}{l} +13_{10} = 0.01101 \\ -10_{10} = 1.01010 \end{array}\right\} \leftarrow \textit{Note.} \text{ The period (.) indicated here is } \textit{not} \text{ a radix point.}$$

2-2.2.2 The Complement Method In the binary system the complement of a 1 is a 0 and the complement of a 0 is a 1. To perform subtraction in the binary system, the quantity with the negative sign (subtrahend) is complemented with the exception of the sign bit and then added to the quantity with the positive sign (minuend). However, some unusual conditions arise that may require further steps in the process. Also, depending on the relative magnitude of the minuend and subtrahend and their respective sign bits involved, some additional steps may be required. These are best explained by taking actual examples for various conditions.

Example 2-11

Using the ones complement method, perform binary subtraction for $A = 11_{10}$ and $B = -6_{10}$.

Solution

To simplify the solution, we will first write out both the minuend and the subtrahend in binary forms, using the previously mentioned sign and format conventions. The subtrahend will then be complemented and added to the minuend.

Binary Form

$A = +11_{10} = 0.01011$
$B = - 6_{10} = 1.00110$

Ones Complement Addition

$$
\begin{array}{ll}
0.01011 & \\
1.11001 & \\
\hline
(1)\ 0.00100 & \text{Intermediate Result} \\
\ \longrightarrow +1 & \\
\hline
0.00101 & \text{Final Result}
\end{array}
$$

The first addition of the two quantities gives an extra carry bit and an incomplete result. This is corrected by taking the extra carry bit, called the *end-around carry,* and adding it to the partial result to give the true final result.   ∎

From Example 2-11 we can formulate the first rule for subtraction by ones complement.

Rule 1 If the minuend is a positive quantity and larger than the subtrahend, which is a negative quantity, the true result is obtained by complementing the subtrahend (except the sign bit), adding it to the minuend, and adding a binary 1 to this partial result.

Example 2-12

Using the ones complement method, perform the binary operation for $A = -13_{10}$ and $B = +10_{10}$.

Solution

Binary Form

$A = -13_{10} = 1.01101$
$B = +10_{10} = 0.01010$

Ones Complement Addition

$$
\begin{array}{ll}
1.10010 & \\
0.01010 & \\
\hline
1.11100 & \text{Intermediate Result}
\end{array}
$$

$$\text{Complement} \rightarrow \quad 1.00011 \quad \text{True Result}$$

Notice that in this case there was no additional carry bit from the partial result, and the true result is the complement of the partial or intermediate result.   ∎

Example 2-12 leads us to the second rule for subtraction by ones complement.

Rule 2 If the minuend is negative and the subtrahend is positive and smaller than the minuend, an intermediate result is obtained by complementing the subtrahend (except the sign bit) and adding it to the minuend. The true result is then obtained by complementing the intermediate result except the sign bit.

Example 2-13

Using the ones complement method, perform the binary operation for $A = -13_{10}$ and $B = -10_{10}$.

Solution

Binary Form

$A = -13_{10} = 1.01101$
$B = -10_{10} = 1.01010$

Ones Complement Addition

$$\begin{array}{ll} & 1.10010 \\ & \underline{1.10101} \\ (1) & 1.00111 \quad \text{Partial result} \\ & \!\!\longrightarrow +1 \\ & 1.01000 \quad \text{Partial result} \\ \text{Complement} \rightarrow & 1.10111 \quad \text{True result} \end{array}$$

In this example both the subtrahend and the minued are negative, so both are complemented and then added. This gives the first intermediate result; the end-around carry is added to this, giving the second intermediate result. The final result is then obtained by complementing the second intermediate result. ■

Example 2-13 leads us to the third rule for ones complement subtraction.

Rule 3 If both the minuend and the subtrahend are negative, both quantities are complemented (except their sign bits) and added. The end-around carry is then added, and the resulting quantity is complemented (except the sign bit) to give the true result.

2-2.3 Binary Subtraction in Twos Complement

The ones complement method has been used in many computers. Another version of this approach, called the twos complement method, is also used extensively, including in most microprocessors. If offers certain advantages in implementation with hardware.

In twos complement representation the quantity with the negative sign is first complemented exactly as in the ones complement system with the exception of the sign bit. Then a 1 is added to this quantity. This gives us the twos complement, which is then added to the other quantity or operand. The same procedure is followed if both operands have negative signs. Twos complement operations also have certain rules, just like those presented for ones complement arithmetic. To explain and illustrate these rules, we will use the same quantities and signs as we did for Examples 2-11, 2-12, and 2-13, and we will follow the same format for presentation of the solutions. Compare these solutions with the corresponding solutions for the same problem in the ones complement method, noting the similarities and dissimilarities between various steps of the two processes.

Example 2-14

Using the twos complement method, perform the binary operations for $A = +11_{10}$ and $B = -6_{10}$.

Solution

Binary Form   **Twos Complement Addition**
$A = +11_{10} = 0.01011$ 0.01011
$B = - 6_{10} = 1.00110$ $\underline{1.11010}$ ← Twos complement
          Discarded ← $(1)\ 0.00101$ ← True result

In this case the true result is obtained without requiring any further process steps. The overflow bit 1 beyond the normal sign bit is ignored or discarded.   ■

Example 2-14 enables us to write down the following first generalized rule for subtraction using the twos complement method.

Rule 1 If the minuend is positive and larger than the subtrahend, which is a negative quantity, the true result is obtained by adding the twos complement of the subtrahend (without changing the sign bit) to the minuend and discarding the overflow bit beyond the normal sign bit position.

Example 2-15

Using the twos complement system, perform the binary operation for $A = -13_{10}$ and $B = +10_{10}$.

Solution

Binary Form   **Twos Complement Addition**
$A = -13_{10} = 1.01101$ 1.10011← Twos complement
$B = +10_{10} = 0.01010$ $\underline{0.01010}$
          1.11101← Intermediate result in twos
                    complement form
          1.00011← True result

In this case the intermediate result is in twos complement form. The true result is then obtained by converting the intermediate result to its twos complement form.   ■

From this example we are able to formulate the second generalized rule for subtraction by the twos complement method.

Rule 2 If the minuend is negative and larger than the subtrahend, which is positive, the twos complement of the minuend (except the sign bit) is added to the subtrahend to give an intermediate result, which is in twos complement form. The final, true result is then obtained by converting the intermediate result into its twos complement form.

Example 2-16

Using the twos complement method, perform the binary operation for $A = -13_{10}$ and $B = -10_{10}$.

Solution

Binary Form

$A = -13_{10} = 1.01101$
$B = -10_{10} = 1.01010$

Twos Complement Addition

$$\left.\begin{array}{l} 1.10011 \\ 1.10110 \end{array}\right\} \text{ Twos complement}$$

Discard ← (1) 1.01001 ← Intermediate result in twos complement form

1.10111 ← True result

In this case, also, the intermediate result is in twos complement form. The true result is then obtained by converting the intermediate result into its twos complement form. Note that the overflow bit is discarded.   ∎

From Example 2-16 we can now write down the third generalized rule for subtraction by the twos complement method.

Rule 3 If both the minuend and the subtrahend are negative (regardless which of the two is larger), the twos complement of both quantities are added to give an intermediate result that is in twos complement form. The true final result is then obtained by converting the intermediate result into its twos complement form and ignoring the overflow bit from the normal sign bit position.

2-3 THE OCTAL SYSTEM

2-3.1 Why the Octal System?

Compared to the decimal system, the binary system of number representation requires many more digits to represent a given number. For instance, the number 250 requires only three digits in the decimal system. On the other hand, it requires eight digits in the pure binary system (i.e., 11111010). The large number of ones and zeros required in the binary system makes it cumbersome and susceptible to errors when human beings are involved. Since human-machine interfaces and communications are unavoidable, the need for a simpler system with which the human operator can be comfortable is obvious. The octal system is one such system, and it is being used in many machines.

2-3.2 Notation in the Octal System

Although the base of the binary system is 2 and the base of the octal system is 8, it is possible to utilize binary bits to represent numbers in the octal system. How this is done will be shown shortly.

Remember that there are only eight digits in the octal system. They are 0 to 7. Table 2-2 shows the decimal numbers and the corresponding pure binary numbers and what their octal equivalent representations are.

Table 2-2   DECIMAL/PURE BINARY/OCTAL EQUIVALENTS

Decimal	Pure Binary	Octal Representation
0	0 0 0 0 0	0
1	0 0 0 0 1	1
2	0 0 0 1 0	2
3	0 0 0 1 1	3
4	0 0 1 0 0	4
5	0 0 1 0 1	5
6	0 0 1 1 0	6
7	0 0 1 1 1	7
8	0 1 0 0 0	10
9	0 1 0 0 1	11
10	0 1 0 1 0	12
11	0 1 0 1 1	13
12	0 1 1 0 0	14
13	0 1 1 0 1	15
14	0 1 1 1 0	16
15	0 1 1 1 1	17
16	1 0 0 0 0	20
17	1 0 0 0 1	21
↓	↓	↓

In table 2-2 notice how the octal representation proceeds. Notice that 18, 19, 28, 29, and so on are illegitimate in this system. Since octal notation can only go up to 7, it becomes very simple to represent octal coefficients with 3 binary bits. It other words, a group of 3 binary bits is all that is necessary to define octal coefficients, as shown here.

Binary	Octal
0 0 0	0
0 0 1	1
0 1 0	2
0 1 1	3
1 0 0	4
1 0 1	5
1 1 0	6
1 1 1	7

Conversion of pure binary numbers into octal numbers is simple and is readily accomplished by separating the binary string of bits into groups of 3 bits each and then assigning their respective octal equivalents as previously indicated. Examples 2-17 and 2-18 demonstrate how this is done.

Example 2-17

Write down the octal equivalent of the following pure binary bits.

1 0 1 0 0 1 1 1 1 0 1 0

Solution

The binary bit stream is divided into groups of 3 bits as follows.

1 0 1   0 0 1   1 1 1   0 1 0

Equivalent octal numbers are then assigned.

5   1   7   2

Thus $(101001111010)_2 = (5172)_8$.   ∎

In Example 2-17 the binary bit stream contained 12 bits which, of course, is convenient for segregating the bits in groups of 3 bits. If the number of bits in the binary stream are such that they are not divisible by three, then either one or two zeros can be added to the left of the most significant bit of the binary stream to complete the group of three. This is illustrated by Example 2-18.

Example 2-18

Convert the following bit stream into its octal equivalent.

1 0 0 1 1 0 1

Solution

Since there are only 7 bits here, we will complete the bit stream of 9 bits by adding two zeros to the left so that the total bits can be divided into groups of 3 bits.

0 0 1   0 0 1   1 0 1

The octal equivalent is 1 1 5.

Thus $(1001101)_2 = (115)_8$.   ■

2-3.3 Decimal-to-Octal Conversion

It is often necessary to convert a decimal number into its octal equivalent. This is easily accomplished by dividing the decimal number by eight and noting the remainder. The quotient of this process is then again divided by eight and the remainder again noted. This division of the quotient is repeated until the quotient is reduced to a zero. The remainders are then grouped from the last one (most significant digit) to the first one (least significant digit), and this gives the desired octal equivalent. The following examples show how this is done.

Example 2-19

What is the octal equivalent of decimal 683?

Solution

Successive Division	Successive Remainders
683/8 = 85	3 (LSD)
85/8 = 10	5
10/8 = 1	2
1/8 = 0	1 (MSD)

Thus $(683)_{10} = (1253)_8$.   ■

Example 2-20

What is the octal equivalent of decimal 7348?

Solution

Successive Division	Successive Remainders
7348/8 = 918	4 (LSD)
918/8 = 114	6
114/8 = 14	2
14/8 = 1	6
1/8 = 0	1 (MSD)

Thus $(7348)_{10} = (16264)_8$.   ■

2-3.4 Octal-to-Decimal Conversion

The simplest way to convert octal codes to decimal is by a two-step process. The octal number is first converted into its binary equivalent by writing down 3 binary bits for each octal digit. The binary bits are then treated as a group of pure binary numbers and, the decimal equivalent of that is obtained by inspection based on the positions of the various 1s and 0s. Example 2-21 shows how this is done.

Example 2-21

What is the decimal equivalent of octal 432?

Solution

Step 1: Convert octal into binary groups of 3 bits each.

Octal	$\rightarrow$	4	3	2
Binary	$\rightarrow$	100	011	010

Step 2: Convert binary bits into their decimal equivalents.

Binary $\rightarrow$ 1   0   0   0   1   1   0   1   0
                      256   16   8   2
Decimal $\rightarrow$ 256 + 16 + 8 + 2 = 282

Thus $(432)_8 = (282)_{10}$.   ■

2-4 THE BINARY-CODED-DECIMAL SYSTEM (BCD)

2-4.1 Why the BCD System?

Human beings who work with computers can work best with the familiar decimal system. The computer, on the other hand, works only with numbers in the binary system. Various input-output devices, which provide interfaces between the computer and the human operator, can be designed so that on the human side of it they receive and transmit data in the decimal system and on the computer side in the binary system. However, such systems usually require more electronics and are more complex. Most of them would also require more time to perform these conversions. The binary-coded-decimal system of numerical representation is a simple compromise to this problem that works quite well.

2-4.2 Notation in the BCD System

In the BCD system each decimal digit is represented by a group of 4 binary bits. This code is really the pure binary code, limited to only 4 bits per decimal digit. Table 2-3 illustrates this.

2-4.3 Decimal-to-BCD Conversion

The conversion of decimal numbers to BCD is simple. Each decimal digit is replaced by its equivalent 4-bit code, as shown in Table 2-3. Example 2-22 illustrates this. Note that the resulting string of binary bits *are not* the pure binary equivalent of the decimal code.

Example 2-22

Convert the following decimal codes into their equivalent BCD codes.

1.   36
2.   108
3.   3792
4.   92536

Table 2-3   THE BCD CODE SYSTEM

Decimal	Pure Binary	BCD Code
0	0	0 0 0 0
1	0 1	0 0 0 1
2	1 0	0 0 1 0
3	1 1	0 0 1 1
4	1 0 0	0 1 0 0
5	1 0 1	0 1 0 1
6	1 1 0	0 1 1 0
7	1 1 1	0 1 1 1
8	1 0 0 0	1 0 0 0
9	1 0 0 1	1 0 0 1

Solution

1. $(36)_{10} = 0011\ 0110$
      $= (0011\ 0110)_{BCD}$

2. $(108)_{10} = 0001\ 0000\ 10000$
      $= (0001\ 0000\ 1000)_{BCD}$

3. $(3792)_{10} = 0011\ 0111\ 1001\ 0010$
      $= (0011\ 0111\ 1001\ 0010)_{BCD}$

4. $(92536)_{10} = 1001\ 0010\ 0101\ 0011\ 0110$
      $= (1001\ 0010\ 0101\ 0011\ 0110)_{BCD}$ ■

2-4.4 BCD-to-Pure Binary Conversion

The conversion of BCD code to a stream of pure binary bits is complex and requires additional steps. Remember that a simple conversion of each BCD digit results in a 4-bit binary representation of that particular digit only. The relative position of that digit in the decimal number and, consequently, its weight in that particular number is not reflected in the simple digits-to-binary bits conversion. This weighting can be easily included by a simple procedure that can be best understood by Examples 2-23 and 2-24.

Example 2-23

Convert $(0011\ 0110)_{BCD}$ to a straight or pure binary bit stream.
(Note that the BCD number is 36_{10}.)

Solution

Notice that the digit 6 in this number carries a weight of 1 and the digit 3 a weight of 10. Since these two decimal digits are represented by 4 binary bits in the BCD system, which assigns the weights 8, 4, 2, 1 to the bits, the proper weights can be assigned as follows.

$$(3 \times 10) + (6 \times 1)$$
$$= [(0011) \times 10] + [(0110) \times 1]$$

To simplify the multiplication of binary 0011 by decimal 10, we simply split 10 such that $10 = 8 + 2$. Multiplying any binary quantity by 2 involves nothing more than shifting it left one place, just as we multiply a decimal quantity by 10 simply by shifting it left one place. Therefore our BCD number here can be expressed as

$$(0011) \times (8 + 2) + (0110) \times 1$$

Also note that to multiply a binary quantity by 8 requires shifting it left three places.

The pure binary equivalent of $(0011\ 0110)_{BCD}$ is then obtained by simple multiplication and addition.

```
      0 1 1 0   × 1
      0 0 1 1   × 2
  0 0 1 1       × 8
  0 1 0 0 1 0 0
```

Thus $(0011\ 0110)_{BCD} = (0100100)_2$.   ■

This works well for two decimal digits such as 3 and 6 as in Example 2-23. What happens if 3 or more decimal digits are involved? How do we handle those? We will demonstrate it by using a 3-digit number in Example 2-24. A similar procedure can be followed for numbers with additional digits.

Example 2-24

Convert $(0001\ 0011\ 0110)_{BCD}$ to a pure binary bit stream. (Note that the BCD number is 136_{10}.)

Solution

The BCD codes can be represented as follows.

$$(0001) \times 100 + (0011) \times 10 + (0110) \times 1$$
$$= [(001) \times (32 + 32 + 32 + 4)] + [(0011) \times (8 + 2)] + [(0110) \times 1]$$

To simplify the multiplication and the addition process, we will fill in the blanks created by left shifts with dashes. Examine the process one step at a time.

```
              0 1 1 0   × 1  ⎫ 6
            0 0 1 1 −   × 2  ⎬ 30
        0 0 1 1 − − −   × 8  ⎭
          0 0 0 1 − −   × 4  ⎫
    0 0 0 1 − − − − −   × 32 ⎬ 100
    0 0 0 1 − − − − −   × 32 ⎪
    0 0 0 1 − − − − −   × 32 ⎭
    0 1 0 0 0 1 0 0 0
```

Thus $(000100110110)_{BCD} = (010001000)_2$.

Suggestion In this example we are performing seven binary additions. Keeping track of carry bits becomes cumbersome and is subject to errors. The process can be greatly simplified by adding only two quantities at a time, starting with the first two and then adding each succeeding line to the progressive sum. We suggest that you follow this procedure (as shown next) for this example. The blanks that were formerly filled with dashes are now replaced with 0s to avoid confusion in addition.

```
          0 1 1 0
        0 0 1 1 0
        0 1 1 0 0
      0 0 1 1 0 0 0
      0 1 0 0 1 0 0
        0 0 0 1 0 0
      0 1 0 1 0 0 0
    0 0 0 1 0 0 0 0 0
    0 0 1 0 0 1 0 0 0
    0 0 0 1 0 0 0 0 0
    0 0 1 1 0 1 0 0 0
    0 0 0 1 0 0 0 0 0
    0 1 0 0 0 1 0 0 0
```

■

2-4.5 BCD Addition

In BCD arithmetic an unusual problem comes up because the adder performs additions in pure binary fashion only. A carry is generated when a pair of 1s are added. If we utilize the BCD system, the adder still functions in a normal binary manner. In our decimal operation, if we add 7 and 6, a carry is generated when the sum exceeds 9. Since BCD notation uses 4 binary bits, a carry into the fifth bit position will occur only when the 4 bits are greater than 1111 or 15. But BCD notation goes only up to 9, which is represented by 1001, thereby creating a situation where a legitimate carry would require an addition of a further decimal 6 number. The following examples illustrate this problem and how it can be corrected. This process is often referred to as decimal arithmetic adjust (DAA) in computer literature.

Example 2-25

Perform $(7 + 6)_{10}$ in BCD notation.

Solution

$$7_{10} = 0111_{BCD}$$
$$6_{10} = 0110_{BCD}$$

The adder performs this operation as follows.

```
    0 1 1 1
+   0 1 1 0
  ─────────
    1 1 0 1
```

This is correct in pure binary because $(1101)_2 = 13_{10}$, but it makes no sense in BCD notation because anything over 1001 is unacceptable in BCD. The proper BCD representation for this is

$13_{10} = (0001\ 0011)_{BCD}$

This can be readily corrected by adding 6 to the incorrect sum generated by the adder.

```
      1 1 0 1  ←Code generated by the binary adder
    + 0 1 1 0  ←Add 6 for BCD correction
0 0 0 1   0 0 1 1  ←Correct BCD notation is obtained
```

Example 2-26

Perform $(17 + 24)_{10}$ in BCD notation.

Solution

```
17₁₀ →  0 0 0 1 0 1 1 1
                          in BCD
24₁₀ →  0 0 1 0 0 1 0 0
        0 0 1 1 1 0 1 1  ←Generated by adder
            + 0 1 1 0  ←Add 6 for correction
        0 1 0 0 0 0 0 1  ←Correct answer
```

Thus $(17 + 24)_{10} = (0100\ 0001)_{BCD}$

In these examples the correction 6 is added whenever the BCD sum exceeds 9. If the decimal quantities involved are such that more than one pair of digits results in a sum over 9, the 6 will have to be added to each pair, as shown in Example 2-27. In BCD 6 codes that are possible with 4 bits are not used (i.e., from 1010 to 1111). Therefore this extra factor of 6 must be added when the sum of two BCD digits is 10 or more in order to obtain the correct answer. The correction factor is also added if there is a carry into a higher-order digit.

Example 2-27

Perform $(342 + 739)_{10}$ in BCD notation.

Solution

```
342₁₀   →              0 0 1 1  0 1 0 0  0 0 1 0
739₁₀   →              0 1 1 1  0 0 1 1  1 0 0 1
                       1 0 1 0  0 1 1 1  1 0 1 1  ←Adder generated
                      +0 1 1 0            +0 1 1 0  ←Correction 6s
                0 0 0 1  0 0 0 0  1 0 0 0  0 0 0 1  ←Correct answer
```

$342 + 739 = 1081$

Thus $(342 + 739)_{10} = (0001\ 0000\ 1000\ 0001)_{BCD}$.

2-4.6 BCD Subtraction

Subtraction in the BCD system is very similar to the addition process and has similar problems with borrow that the addition process has with the carry. The negative quantity is subtracted utilizing the twos complement method. Also, when the twos complement addition results in a BCD code of 9 or more, a 6 must be subtracted using the twos complement method. This means adding 10 or 1010. Any carry into the fifth bit position resulting from this addition is discarded. The carry from the most significant bit position is likewise ignored. The following examples cover these situations and how they are handled.

Example 2-28

Perform $(12 - 8)_{10}$ in BCD notation.

Solution

$$
\begin{matrix}
+12_{10} \rightarrow \\
- 8_{10} \rightarrow
\end{matrix}
\left.
\begin{matrix}
0\ 0\ 0\ 1\ \ 0\ 0\ 1\ 0 \\
0\ 0\ 0\ 0\ \ 1\ 0\ 0\ 0
\end{matrix}
\right\}
\text{ in BCD}
$$

```
                0 0 0 1  0 0 1 0
                1 1 1 1  1 0 0 0  ←Twos complement
            (1) 0 0 0 0  1 0 1 0  ←Addition
Discarded                1 0 1 0
                0 0 0 0(1)0 1 0 0  ←Correct answer
                         ↓
                     Discarded
```

Thus $(12 - 8)_{10} = (0000\ 0100)_{BCD}$.
Note that a borrow did result from the first pair of decimal digits, so a correction of -6 was necessary. ∎

Example 2-29

Perform $(93 - 61)_{10}$ in BCD notation.

Solution

$$
\begin{matrix}
+93_{10} \rightarrow \\
-61_{10} \rightarrow
\end{matrix}
\left.
\begin{matrix}
1\ 0\ 0\ 1\ \ 0\ 0\ 1\ 1 \\
0\ 1\ 1\ 0\ \ 0\ 0\ 0\ 1
\end{matrix}
\right\}
\text{ in BCD}
$$

```
                1 0 0 1  0 0 1 1
                1 0 0 1  1 1 1 1  ←Twos complement
            (1) 0 0 1 1  0 0 1 0  ←Correct answer
Discarded
```

Note that since there were no borrows involved, correction by subtracting by 6 was not necessary. ∎

Example 2-30

Perform $(71 - 28)_{10}$ in BCD notation.

Solution

$$+71_{10} \rightarrow \quad 0\ 1\ 1\ 1 \quad 0\ 0\ 0\ 1 \left.\right\} \text{ in BCD}$$
$$-28_{10} \rightarrow \quad 0\ 0\ 1\ 0 \quad 1\ 0\ 0\ 0$$

$$
\begin{array}{ll}
 & 0\ 1\ 1\ 1 \quad 0\ 0\ 0\ 1 \\
 & 1\ 1\ 0\ 1 \quad 1\ 0\ 0\ 0 \leftarrow \text{Twos complement} \\
\text{Discard (1)} & \overline{0\ 1\ 0\ 0 \quad 1\ 0\ 0\ 1} \\
 & \qquad\qquad\quad 1\ 0\ 1\ 0 \leftarrow \text{6 in Twos complement} \\
 & \overline{0\ 1\ 0\ 0(1)1\ 0\ 1\ 1} \leftarrow \text{Correct answer} \\
 & \qquad \swarrow \\
 & \text{Discard}
\end{array}
$$

Note that a subtraction of 6 is required here because of the borrow. ∎

2-4.7 Character Representation in BCD

It is possible to encode alphabetical characters and other symbols (such as +, /, %, \$, @, *, etc.) by using 2 BCD digits. One common way to do this is to have 2-digit decimal numbers 00, 01, 02, . . . 09 to represent numerals 0 to 9. Then the 2-digit decimal numbers from 10 to 99 can be used to represent alphabetical characters or any other desired symbols.

2-5 THE HEXADECIMAL SYSTEM

Each decimal digit in the BCD system is represented by a group of 4 binary bits, thereby giving us a capability of up to 16 different bit combinations or codes. The last 6 bit combinations, (i.e., from 1010 to 1111) are not used. In fact, in the BCD system, they are illegal, so these codes are wasted. The hexadecimal system is really an extension of the BCD system, which utilizes these wasted 6 combinations to represent some specific characters or symbols. It is, of course, possible to use these combinations in any way we desire. In most applications today they are used to represent the first six letters of the alphabet (A to F). Table 2-4 shows this system, which is extensively used in today's microcomputers.

Table 2-4   THE HEXADECIMAL CODE SYSTEM

Decimal	Binary Code	Hexadecimal
0	0 0 0 0	0
1	0 0 0 1	1
2	0 0 1 0	2
3	0 0 1 1	3
4	0 1 0 0	4
5	0 1 0 1	5
6	0 1 1 0	6
7	0 1 1 1	7
8	1 0 0 0	8
9	1 0 0 1	9
10	1 0 1 0	A
11	1 0 1 1	B
12	1 1 0 0	C
13	1 1 0 1	D
14	1 1 1 0	E
15	1 1 1 1	F

2-6 INTERPRETED BINARY DATA

The pure binary data could be a word in the computer that can stand alone by itself. It could also be a part of a larger word. It is possible to divide up a word into two or more groups of bits where each group would be assigned a distinctly separate or unique function within the computer system. Furthermore, it is possible to concatenate (link or connect in a serial fashion, like a chain) two or more computer words to generate larger operands or larger memory addresses.

Consecutive bits within a word that are usually handled or processed by the computer as a group is called a byte. In microcomputers an 8-bit group is referred to as a byte and a 4-bit group as a nibble. A byte consists of 2 nibbles.

Binary arithmetic operations are possible using multiple bytes. Such bytes may or may not be contiguous (i.e., they may or may not be located, say in the data memory, in adjacent locations). Multibyte quantities can also be signed to indicate positive or negative quantities, and they could be utilized using the rules and conventions of signs that were covered earlier in this chapter. It is not unusual to see two 8-bit words combined in a microprocessor to give a 16-bit word. Arithmetic operations performed by such words are called *double-precision* arithmetic, and the words themselves are referred to as double-length words. Double-length words are also used to generate complex instructions. A multiword or a multibyte operand or instruction could be composed of more than two words or bytes. The computer, however, still operates on only one word at a time.

2-7 CHARACTER CODES

Human-machine interaction requires that the computer be capable of handling text material that may include numerics, alphabetics, and other special symbols. The binary codes that represent numerical data can also be used to represent such alphabetical and special symbols, provided the program properly recognizes and interprets these bits.

Most microcomputer systems provide an adequate set of character coding capabilities that approximates the standard typewriter keyboard quite closely. These coding capabilities usually are divided as follows.

- Ten numerical digits 0 to 9.
- Twenty-six lowercase alphabetical letters.
- Twenty-six uppercase alphabetical letters.
- Twenty to twenty-five special symbols such as #, +, /, @, %, and *.

The previously mentioned codes thus require a coding capability of 82 to 87 characters. A 6-bit binary word would give 64 possible combinations or codes and would not be adequate for the job. A 7-bit word, giving 128 possible codes ($2^7 = 128$), would be quite adequate. Today the 8-bit byte is generally accepted as an industry standard for representing character codes. The coding systems most widely used in the United States are ASCII (American Standard Code for Information Interchange) and EBCDIC (Extended Binary Coded Decimal Interchange Code). ASCII is used in all microcomputers and minicomputers; it is described in Appendix A, which also includes a chart for this code.

Since only 7 bits are needed for character codes but the 8-bit byte is used most of the time, the eighth bit is often used as a parity bit for detecting errors in transmission of words. The parity bit could be either a 1 or a 0 and is used along with the other 7 bits so that the number of 1 bits in the byte is either always odd or always even.

2-8 SUMMARY

The various number systems generally used in today's computers, including microcomputers, were introduced. Familiarity with the binary system is required for anybody intending to work in the computer field. Students should acquire some proficiency in working with pure binary numbers and also subtractions in the ones and twos complement systems. Knowing the sign conventions and the various rules of subtraction is essential. To facilitate the learning process, several typical examples were presented with their solutions. The octal and the binary-coded-decimal (BCD) systems were discussed. The principles underlying the conversion processes that students are most likely to encounter in their work with microcomputers were presented along with typical examples. Particular attention should be given to various examples in this chapter. Students are likely to run into them frequently. The concept of representing alphabetical characters and symbols in BCD notation was discussed. The hexadecimal system was then presented. The chapter concluded with a discussion of interpreted binary data and character codes. The concept of the parity bit was also introduced.

2-9 PROBLEMS AND EXERCISES

2-1   The following 8-bit words represent pure binary numbers. What are their decimal equivalents?
  (a) 0 0 0 0 0 1 0 1
  (b) 0 0 0 1 0 0 0 0
  (c) 0 1 0 0 0 0 0 1
  (d) 1 0 1 0 0 1 1 0
  (e) 1 1 0 0 0 0 0 1

2-2   Up to what numerical value can an 8-bit word represent?

2-3   Write down the octal equivalents of the following binary numbers:
  (a) 0 0 1 0
  (b) 0 1 1 0
  (c) 1 0 0 1
  (d) 1 1 0 1

2-4   What are the binary equivalents of the following octal numbers?
  (a) 4
  (b) 7
  (c) 14
  (d) 12
  (e) 17

2-5   What are the octal equivalents of the following binary numbers?
  (a) 1 0 1 0 0 1
  (b) 1 1 0 1 1 0
  (c) 0 0 0 1 0 1 1 0 1
  (d) 1 0 0 0 1 1 0 0 1
  (e) 1 1 0 0 1 1 1

2-6   What is the octal equivalent of decimal 523?

2-7   What are the HEX equivalents of the following?
  (a) Decimal 6.
  (b) Decimal 11.
  (c) BCD code 1110.
  (d) Decimal 16.

2-8   Operands A and B are given below in pure binary forms. Perform the addition $A + B$ and give the result, also in pure binary form.

	A	B
(a)	0 1 0 1	0 0 1 1
(b)	0 1 1 1 0 1	0 0 1 0 0 0
(c)	1 0 1 0 1 0 1 0	1 1 0 0 1 0 0 1

2-9   Using the ones complement method, perform the binary subtraction for $A = +11_{10}$ and $B = -5_{10}$.

2-10   Using the ones complement method, perform the binary subtraction for $A = -14_{10}$ and $B = +12_{10}$.

2-11   Using the ones complement method, perform the binary subtraction for $A = -10_{10}$ and $B = -15_{10}$.

2-12   Using the twos complement method, perform the binary subtraction for $A = +11_{10}$ and $B = -4_{10}$.

2-13   Using the twos complement method, perform the binary subtraction for $A = -8_{10}$ and $B = -6_{10}$.

2-14   Convert the following decimal codes into their equivalent BCD codes.
   (a) 487.
   (b) 9301.
   (c) 78,656.

2-15   Convert $(0100\ 0011\ 0101)_{BCD}$ to a pure binary bit stream.

2-16   Perform $(23 + 7)_{10}$ in BCD notation.

2-17   Perform $(168 + 250)_{10}$ in BCD notation.

2-18   Perform $(13 - 7)_{10}$ in BCD notation.

2-19   Perform $(86 - 46)_{10}$ in BCD notation.

2-20   Perform $(93 - 56)_{10}$ in BCD notation.

3

THE MICROPROCESSOR ARCHITECTURE

3-1 MICROPROCESSOR INTERNAL BUS STRUCTURES

3-1.1 What are Busses?

Busses are groups of lines used for interconnecting various building blocks within a computing system. These lines transmit electrical signals over them and provide a common means of communication between these blocks. Each line is capable of transmitting one electrical pulse, representing a binary bit, at any one time, but the same line can transmit a series of several such bits in a timed sequence. A single transmission line such as this could, therefore, be used for serial transmission of binary bits. If several bits are to be transferred simultaneously in a parallel fashion, a separate line must be provided for each bit. A scheme for serial transmission of bits from block P to block Q is shown in Fig. 3-1a. A scheme for parallel transfer from block R to block S is shown in Fig. 3-1b. The number of lines in a bus is established by the number of bits to be transferred. Generally, in microprocessors the width of the internal bus or busses will be determined by the word length of that particular microprocessor.

Busses may be unidirectional (the information flow is in one direction only, as shown in Fig. 3-1) or bidirectional (bits can flow in either direction, as shown in Fig. 3-2). Since busses are nothing more than lines utilized for conducting electrical pulses, students might wonder what makes them conductive in one direction only in one case and conductive in both directions in other cases. The lines themselves are always capable of transmitting bits in both directions, but the circuits connected on either end of the line may be capable of either unidirectional or bidirectional transfers. Most microprocessors will have both types of busses.

50   Busses can be dedicated (i.e., used for transfer of information) only from

(a) Bus for serial bit transmission

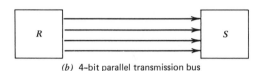

(b) 4–bit parallel transmission bus

Figure 3-1 Unidirectional bus structures for binary transmissions.

a certain block *A* to another specific block *B* (or from *B* to *A*, also, if it happens to be a bidirectional bus). They could also be *multipurpose* for transferring various types of information to *different* functional blocks within the system. Such multipurpose busses are often referred to as universal busses. Both types are used in microprocessors. From this point on we will show busses in our diagrams as enlarged lines, both for unidirectional and bidirectional busses (Fig. 3-3). The number of bits involved in a particular bus will be indicated by a number in the bus, as indicated for an 8-bit bus in Fig. 3-3. Also, the words microprocessors and microcomputers will be abbreviated as μPs and μCs, respectively, to conform to the current popular use in the literature. (μ is the Greek letter *mu,* commonly used in science and engineering to represent the English prefix *micro-.*)

In a μP, the bus structure connecting various functional blocks can be shown as in Fig. 3-4. Generally, a common bus called the internal data bus

(a) Bus for serial bit transmission

(b) 4–bit parallel transmission bus

Figure 3-2 Bidirectional bus structures for binary transmissions.

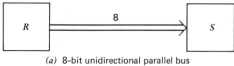

(a) 8-bit unidirectional parallel bus

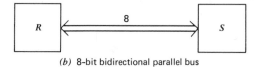

(b) 8-bit bidirectional parallel bus

Figure 3-3   Unidirectional/bidirectional parallel bus representation.

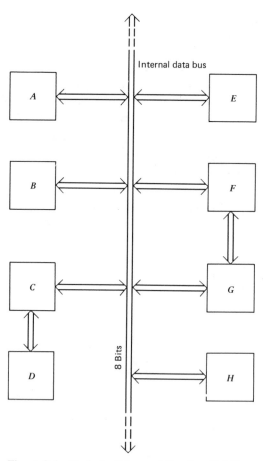

Figure 3-4   Typical μP bus and functional block representation.

(or busses, in some cases) provides a single pathway for binary information transfers to which the various functional blocks are connected. The internal data bus is bidirectional, but the dedicated branch busses could be unidirectional or bidirectional. Also, it is possible to have special dedicated busses between certain functional blocks that could completely bypass the internal data bus. This is shown in Fig. 3-4 for blocks *C* and *D* and blocks *F* and *G*.

3-1.2 The Memory Busses

In this section we extend the concept of the bus to provide communication between the CPU and the program and data memories, which may consist of several chips. In order to access any location within the memory, the CPU must first identify the desired location by means of an *address*. The address must be capable of first selecting one of the several chips. In μCs each memory chip is sometimes (but not always) referred to as a *memory page*. So the portion of the address that identifies the page can be designated as the CS bits or lines (where CS refers to chip select). The remaining portion of the address must identify the exact location of the desired page. This part of the address is often referred to as the *local address*. The address is transmitted to all memory chips through a common, unidirectional bus called the memory address bus (Fig. 3-5). Once the desired location in the particular chip is identified, transfer of data takes place between the chip and the CPU through the

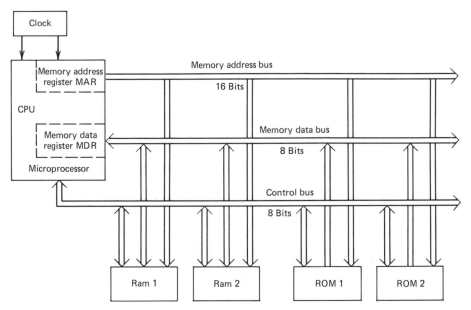

Figure 3-5 Microcomputer dedicated memory bus structure.

external, bidirectional data bus, which is also shown in Fig. 3-5. Notice that the bidirectional capabilities of this bus are used only by the RAM chips. The ROM chips will be involved only in unidirectional transfer of information (i.e., from the chip to the CPU).

Additionally, it is necessary that the CPU chip inform the particular memory chip whether the information is to be read from the memory or written into it. In most μCs this is accomplished by the READ and $\overline{\text{WRITE}}$ signals on two separate control lines from the CPU to the memories. (In some μCs these two signals are transmitted on the same line. In that case they are generally labeled READ/$\overline{\text{WRITE}}$ signal.) The inversion bars on these signals indicate that they are only active (i.e., ON) when driven low by the CPU. The memory chips and the transfer of data must be properly synchronized with the rest of the system. The necessary clock pulse lines and the previously mentioned READ and $\overline{\text{WRITE}}$ lines will usually be a part of another bus that is usually called the control bus. The control bus is not limited to these lines only. This bus includes other lines such as INTERRUPT REQUEST and INTERRUPT ACKNOWLEDGE. These controls and others will be discussed later in the appropriate chapters. Some lines in the control bus will be unidirectional, such as the previously mentioned READ or $\overline{\text{WRITE}}$ lines, and others could be bidirectional.

Within the CPU the address of the memory location is held in a dedicated register called the memory address register, or simply the address register. Regardless of where the address came from or how it was generated, its ultimate destination in the CPU is always the address register before it is gated on to the memory address bus. The address register generally consists of D-type flip-flops that hold this address for a predefined period of time. Usually the *memory* chips are *slower* in operation than the CPU. Holding the address in this register for a longer period of time makes it possible to use memory chips with several different speeds in a system. Likewise, the data word is also held in a dedicated register within the CPU (Fig. 3-5). However, there are some differences here that should be pointed out. Although Fig. 3-5 shows only one memory data register, there is more involved in it.

The memory data bus is shown as bidirectional bus. This means that any one line on this bus can be driven by several of the RAM chips but by only one chip at a time. This requirement is readily implemented with chips that have three-state or tristate outputs driving the bus. The tristate capability thus effectively isolates all other chips from the memory data bus *except* the particular *chip* that is *addressed*. On the CPU side of the bus, the input port likewise contains tristate buffers. The output port, in addition to the tristate buffers (or gates) contains *latches* that are again D-type flip-flops. These latches are used to reconcile speed and timing differences between the CPU and the slower memory chips. Latches are not needed on the input side to the

CPU because the CPU is faster than the memroy chips and is able to catch and process the information sent out by the memory chips. The CPU can thus be completely isolated from the rest of the system by means of the tristate buffers. The tristate capabilities allow us to *float* the data bus.

3-1.3 The I/O Busses

In addition to the memory chips, the CPU must also communicate with various peripheral or I/O devices. These devices could be input devices such as keyboards, output devices such as CRT displays, or devices capable of both input and output capabilities such as floppy disks or magnetic tape cassettes. Such I/O devices are also addressable by the μP and they transfer data over the I/O data bus (Fig. 3-6). Like the memory chips, the I/O devices also require control lines and various request and acknowledge lines that usually become an integral part of the control bus. It is possible that a dedicated I/O address register may be provided within the CPU (Fig. 3-6). More likely, however, this could be the same register as the memory address register whose capabilities would be time-shared for both the memory and the I/O addressing functions. The data word is held either in a dedicated I/O data register or in one of the accumulators in the CPU. In many μPs the accumulator is used as the primary I/O port of the CPU.

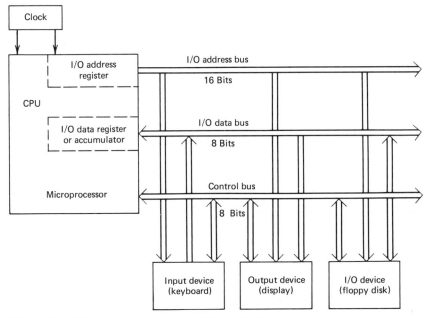

Figure 3-6   Microcomputer dedicated I/O bus structure.

3-1.4 The Memory-I/O Shared Busses

From the previous discussion it is apparent that both the memory chips and the I/O devices use the unidirectional address bus and the bidirectional data bus. It is obviously advantageous to provide one address bus and one data bus and have both the memory chips and the I/O devices use them on a *shared* basis. Likewise, a common control bus could be used. Such a configuration is shown in Fig. 3-7. *Space* on a silicon chip, often called the *real estate,* is always scarce and at a premium. Because of this a common address register and a common I/O port (which could be the accumulator) for both the memory chips and the I/O devices is used (Fig. 3-7).

3-1.5 Multiplexed Bus System Configuration

Some μCs do not provide a separate address bus. Instead, they use the existing data bus for transmission of the address. This is shown for an 8-bit data bus in Fig. 3-8. For example, assume that the total memory and the I/O address capabilities of this system is 65,536. A 16-bit address (2^{16}) would be required

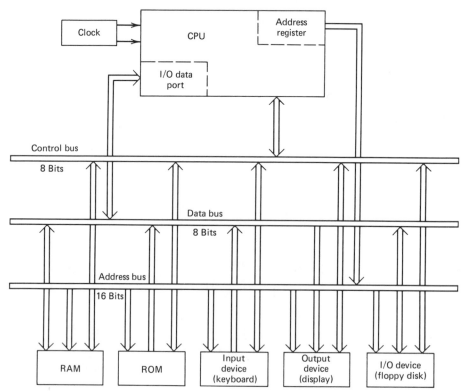

Figure 3-7 Microcomputer with shared memory-I/O bus structure.

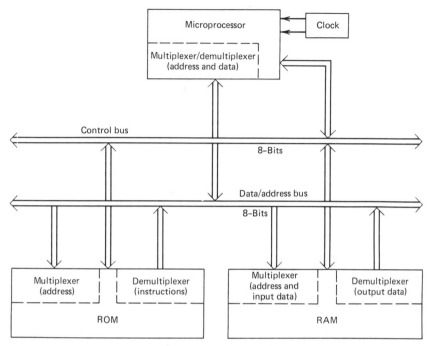

Figure 3-8 Microcomputer common data/address bus configuration.

to access all of these locations directly. Also assume that we are going to fetch and execute an instruction from the ROM and that this is a 3-byte instruction. An operation such as this takes five discrete steps:

1. The first byte of the address would be sent out by the CPU on the common data bus and received and held by the selected ROM chip.
2. The second byte of the address would be sent by the CPU and received and held by the ROM chip.
3. The multiplexing circuits in the ROM would then combine these 2 bytes into a single meaningful address and access the specific locations on that particular chip.
4. The ROM would then send out the first byte of the instruction to the CPU on the data bus. The second and the third byte would then be sent out by the ROM to the CPU in two more steps.
5. Finally, the multiplexing circuits within the CPU would combine these 3 bytes into a single 3-byte instruction.

In both cases multiplexing and demultiplexing circuits are employed in both the μP and the ROM chip. First, the CPU demultiplexes the 2-byte address into 2 single bytes and sends them over the data bus. On the receiving end, the ROM chip multiplexes them into a single address. Likewise, the ROM demultiplexes the instruction into 3 separate bytes and transmits them individually to the CPU. The CPU then multiplexes them into a single, 3-byte instruction. The other chips in the system will have similar multiplexer/demultiplexer circuits. (*Note:* These are special ROMs designed for use in multiplexing systems.)

For the RAM chip the incoming bits are first multiplexed for the multibyte address. If the particular operation is a write-into-RAM operation, the next multibyte group of bits would again be multiplexed and stored in appropriately addressed locations. If it is a read-from-ROM operation, the multibyte data word would be demultiplexed and put on the common data/address bus.

3-2 THE MACHINE AND INSTRUCTION CYCLES

3-2.1 The Clocking System and Sync Pulse

The computer system's operation is closely synchronized with and by an accurate central clock. This clock could be a free-running multivibrator, but almost always the fundamental frequency is generated by a crystal-controlled oscillator. Depending on the type of circuitry used in the system, the clock may be required to supply either a single stream of pulses or multiple streams of pulses that are accurately timed and spaced. Two-phase clock systems are common in μCs. Review section 1-4.1, which describes the basic timing sequence.

When power is applied, the clocking system starts putting out its stream(s) of clock pulses. This does not by itself initiate operations within the μP or the other chips within the system. A stream of clock pulses is meaningless unless a well-defined starting point is provided for all operations to all the chips in the system. This is explained next.

1. An external signal is applied to the μP. This signal may be generated by the human operator pushing a START button, or a similar signal could automatically be applied by some other piece of equipment.
2. The CPU generates a pulse called the SYNC pulse, which defines the start of a specific computer operation. The SYNC pulse is periodically generated after a specific number of clock pulses have been counted.
3. The SYNC pulse for a two-phase clocking system is shown in Fig. 3-9. In this example, the SYNC pulse is generated every 8 clock pulses.
4. Notice that in this particular example the SYNC pulse is generated by and synchronized with $\Phi2$ of the clocking system. It could have been synchronized by $\Phi1$.

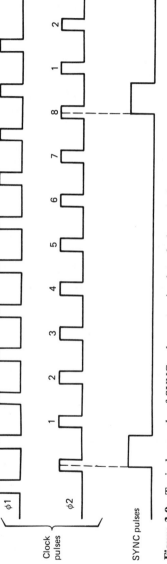

Figure 3-9 Typical example of SYNC pulse generation by a 2-phase clock system.

3-2.2 The Machine Cycle

The computer only performs what it is commanded to do by an instruction. A certain number of operations or activities must take place in the CPU in connection with each instruction in the program. A time duration covering several clock periods would be required for this. This time span is called the *machine cycle*. In Fig. 3-9 the machine cycle is the time interval between 2 consecutive SYNC pulses and covers a time span of 8 clock periods. In some μPs the time duration for this basic machine cycle is fixed for a certain, defined clock frequency. There are machines where the time span for the machine cycle is variable, depending on the design of the CPU and the particular operation involved. In most computers, during one machine cycle one of the following three events takes place:

1. An address can be sent to the program memory and the instruction could be fetched.
2. The fetched instruction could be executed.
3. An address can be sent to the data memory and a data word can be read from or written into this memory.

In some μPs, steps 1 and 2 are combined into one subcycle, called the fetch subcycle or, simply, the fetch cycle. The machine cycle in such a machine could consist of the fetch and execute cycles (Fig. 3-10).

3-2.3 The Instruction Cycle

3-2.3.1 The Fixed Instruction Cycle An instruction cycle is defined as the time duration required to fetch an instruction from the program memory, decode it, and execute it. In some μPs the time duration and the actual actions that take place during an instruction cycle are fixed by design. In such a situation it is possible that the instruction cycle and the basic machine cycle

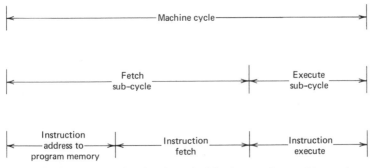

Figure 3-10 Phases (subcycles) in typical fetch/executive machine cycle.

are the same. The machine cycle of Fig. 3-10 then becomes the instruction cycle of such a μP.

During each clock period of a fixed instruction cycle, one (or sometimes more) specific event takes place in the CPU. This event can be best explained by describing a typical fixed instruction cycle of a simple μP. Because of its simplicity, we will consider our μP to be a 4-bit machine. (Note that 4-bit μPs are being rapidly replaced with μPs of longer word lengths.)

Before explaining the fixed instruction cycle, we make the following assumptions for the hypothetical μP:

1. Although the data word is 4 bits long, the basic instruction word is 8 bits long.
2. The instruction word's upper nibble (the upper 4 bits) will be called UNI (upper nibble of instruction) and the lower 4 bits will be called LNI (lower nibble of instruction).
3. The instruction set consists of 1-word, or 8-bit, instructions and 2-word, or 16-bit, instructions.
4. There are 4096 words of ROM memory locations available, thereby requiring 12-bit addresses for directly accessing the entire program memory.
5. The required 12-bit ROM addresses are obtained by concatenating two 8-bit instructions where the UNI of the first word contains the operation code and the 12-bit address is formed by the LNI of the first word and the upper and lower nibbles of the second word.

A simplified timing diagram for this μP is shown in Fig. 3-11. The instruction cycle shows the various CPU activities associated with it, and it takes 8 clock periods for completion. The instruction cycle is initiated by the SYNC pulse, which is generated by the μP and sent out to the ROM and RAM chips. The instruction cycle is divided into three major subcycles. The following operations are performed during each clock period.

1. During the first 3 clock periods labeled A_1, A_2, and A_3, the 12-bit address is sent out to the ROM chips in three successive upper, middle, and lower nibbles, respectively.
2. During the next 2 clock periods labeled M_1 and M_2, the ROM chips send out the 8-bit instruction to the μP as UNI and LNI nibbles, respectively. Also during this time frame the instruction is decoded in the CPU.
3. During the last 3 clock periods, labeled X_1, X_2, and X_3, the instruction is executed. Depending on the particular instruction involved, one of the following three actions will be taken by the CPU:
   (a) The CPU may operate on the data within it.
   (b) Data or address information may be sent to or received from the RAM chips.
   (c) Data or address information may be sent to or received from the I/O ports.

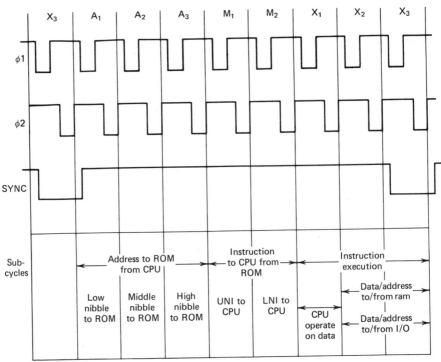

Figure 3-11 Simplified timing and instruction cycle of a typical microprocessor. Reprinted by permission of Intel Corporation, copyright © 1974. A few minor modifications have been made to conform to the material in this text.

3-2.3.2 The Variable Instruction Cycle

There are computers where the time duration of the instruction cycle is not fixed but varies, the actual time required depending on the particular instruction being executed and the different CPU activities being called out by that instruction. Once again this concept will be illustrated by describing a real μP. The popular 8008/8080 μPs by Intel Corporation, which is an 8-bit machine, is selected for this purpose. The 8080 is an enhanced version of the earlier 8008.

The 8008/8080 system is synchronized by two nonoverlapping clock pulses, Φ1 and Φ2. Notice that these are positive-going pulses, where +1.0 V represents a logic 0 and a +8.0 V represents a logic 1. The internal logic in the CPU utilizes the 2 input clock phases to generate a SYNC pulse that is then used to indicate the beginning of a machine cycle. In this system a *machine state* is defined as the "smallest unit of processing activity" and is the time interval between two successive positive-going transitions of the Φ1 clock pulse. The machine state then is the familiar clock period which, in this case, is measured from the 10% rise time point of the first Φ1 pulse to the 10% rise time point of the next Φ1 pulse. Note that only the Φ1 clock pulse and not the Φ2 pulse identifies the machine state.

The time duration of the machine state is fixed for all cases except three conditions: WAIT, HOLD, and HALT. These three functions are generated external to the CPU and are therefore of *indeterminate* time duration. They can last from a minimum of 1 clock period to an indefinite length of time. Machine states are designated as $T_1, T_2 \ldots T_5$ in timing charts. The WAIT state is represented by T_W.

In the 8008/8080 a machine cycle consists of a minimum of three machine states and a maximum of five. Machine cycles are sometimes referred to as memory cycles because every instruction has at least one memory reference: fetching the instruction from the program memory. The machine cycles are designated as $M_1, M_2, \ldots M_5$. The M_1 machine cycle is always involved with the operation code fetch cycle. It requires either four or five machine states. Machine cycles $M_2 \ldots M_5$ normally require three machine states each. Like most μPs, the 8008/8080 can transmit only one address per machine cycle. If the fetch and execution of a certain instruction calls for more than one memory reference, the instruction cycle will require a correspondingly larger number of machine cycles.

The instruction cycle is made up of one or more machine cycles up to a possible maximum of five, depending on the particular instruction involved. There are 10 different types of machine cycles that could occur within one instruction cycle. Thus each instruction cycle will be different, and its composition will depend on the content of the instruction. All instructions will, however, have one common machine cycle: the fetch machine cycle M_1.

Figure 3-12 shows the basic 8008/8080 instruction cycle in a simplified form. In this case, for brevity, only the M_1 machine cycle is shown. The operations that take place during each state are briefly described here. Note that M_1, in this case, contains five states and T_W as applicable.

1. *During T_1.* The SYNC pulse identifies the start of M_1. The contents of the program counter (i.e., the address of the next instruction to be fetched from the program memory) are placed on the address bus. This address remains stable to give the CPU sufficient time to read the bits received from memory. The CPU identifies the current machine cycle to the external chips in the system by means of an 8-bit status code. These signals, which provide control for the circuitry external to the CPU, are placed on the data bus during the SYNC pulse time.

2. *During T_2.* The CPU tests or samples the status of the READY, HOLD, and HALT signals. If READY is indicated, the CPU will proceed to the next normal machine state, T_3. If either HOLD or HALT is indicated, the CPU will go into the WAIT state, T_W, and stay in this mode until the READY condition is indicated. This feature makes it possible for this CPU to be synchronized with a memory of virtually any access time.

3. *During T_3.* The instruction is available from the program memory on the data bus.

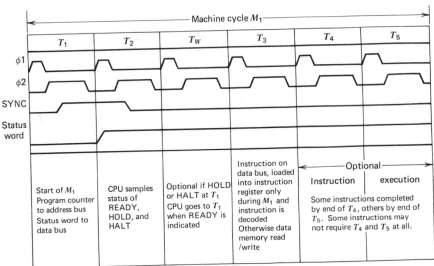

Figure 3-12 Basic Intel 8008/8080 timing for machine cycle M_1 of the instruction cycle. Reprinted by permission of Intel Corporation, copyright © 1976. A few minor modifications have been made to conform to the material in this text.

It is then transferred into the instruction register in the CPU. From there the instruction is decoded, and the control section generates the appropriate electrical signals for the execution of the instruction. Note that the preceding sequence of events takes place only during T_3 of the M_1 machine cycle. For machine cycles other than M_1, data transfer either to or from the memory will take place during T_3.

4. *During T_4 and T_5 (Optional).* The instruction will be executed. Some instructions may be completely executed by the end of T_4, while others may be completed by the end of T_5. It is possible that some instructions may not require T_4 and T_5 at all.

At the end of M_1, the CPU will enter the T_1 state of the next machine cycle M_2, depending on the instruction involved. If the instruction in question requires only one machine cycle, the CPU will start with the T_1 state of the new M_2 cycle. The preceding sequence of steps will then be repeated as often as required by that instruction. During the last state of the last machine cycle, the CPU will test the interrupt request line. If an interrupt is indicated, the CPU will enter a special M_1 cycle, an interrupt acknowledge signal will be sent, and the program counter will be prevented from being incremented.

In the 8008/8080 simple instructions may require as few as 4 machine states while more complex instructions could require up to 18 machine states. If a minimum clock frequency of 2 MHz is used, an instruction cycle could vary from 2 to 9μs in time duration.

3-3 INSTRUCTION FLOW IN THE CPU

In Section 3-2 the various activities that take place in the CPU during the machine cycle and the instruction cycle were presented. At this stage, we will not attempt to understand how each step is implemented in the μP. It is, however, important to see how the instruction and the data words flow through the CPU while performing their respective functions and processes.

During the machine cycle, an instruction or a data word could be processed by the μP. Figure 3-13 shows how the instruction word is processed in a typical μC. At the start of the machine cycle the contents of the program counter, which contains the address of the next instruction to be fetched, are transferred to the memory address register. This is the incremented or updated address, which specifies the location of the next instruction in the program memory. It is not the address of the current instruction being processed. This updated address is then put on the address bus if one is used, or on the time-shared data/address bus if that is the case, and sent to the ROM chips. In the selected ROM chip the local address is decoded, and the circuitry is activated to allow the information stored in the location to be accessed. When the appropriate READ signal is sent from timing and control in the CPU to the ROM, the instruction bits from this location are put on the data bus and sent to the memory data register in the μP. From here the instruction word is

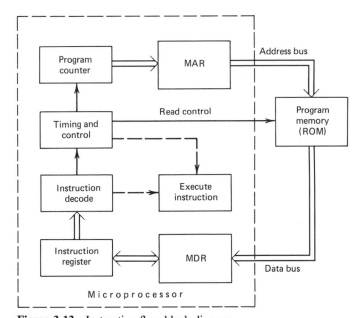

Figure 3-13   Instruction flow block diagram.

transferred to the instruction register where it is held usually until the end of that particular machine cycle or the instruction cycle.

The instruction is then decoded into the appropriate electrical signals and, under control of the timing and control section of the μP, the appropriate commands are executed by the various functional blocks within the μP and the different subsystems in the μC system. Finally, the program counter is incremented by one if the memory location to be accessed is the next higher address number in the normal operation of the program. It is quite possible that the program counter may not be incremented at all. The current instruction could be such that it may reset the program counter to some other specified address, as in JUMP or BRANCH operations, which will be described in a later chapter.

3-4 DATA FLOW IN THE MICROCOMPUTER

Regarding the just described instruction flow, the instruction is always fetched from the program memory. In the case of data word retrieval, the source could be either the data memory or one of the I/O devices. Similarly, a data word processed by the CPU could be transferred to either the data memory or to an I/O device. In either case the address of the data memory or the I/O device must first be sent out by the CPU from the address register (Fig. 3-14).

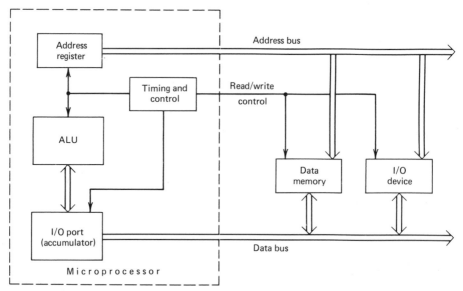

Figure 3-14   Data flow block diagram.

In most of today's μCs the point of entry and exit from the μP takes place by way of the I/O port, which is a special register called the accumulator. In many μPs the accumulator is the ultimate destination for all the data processed by the CPU. All operations on data words that are specified in a particular instruction take place during the *execute* subcycle of the machine cycle.

3-5 REGISTERS AND COUNTERS

3-5.1 General Comments

In any digital computer the CPU contains several subsystems that can be broadly categorized as follows.

1. Counters.
2. Adder.
3. Registers, including accumulators and both dedicated and general-purpose registers.
4. Circuitry for control and timing.

In Chapter 1 we briefly discussed the following registers and counters.

1. The accumulator (Section 1-3.2.1).
2. The program counter (Section 1-3.2.2).
3. The instruction register and decoder (Section 1-3.2.3).
4. The address register/counter (Section 1-3.2.4).

We will not repeat them here, but students should review these sections to refresh their memory. There are other registers/counters that we did not cover in Chapter one that will be briefly described next.

3-5.2 The Stack

In Section 1-3.2.2 we briefly mentioned the stack and its functions. There are two types of stacks widely used in μPs: the cascade and the pointer.

3-5.2.1 The Cascade Stack The need for the stack arises because it is necessary to *save* the *last* updated address of the next instruction in the main program whenever a branch to a subroutine is called out. Saving this address makes it possible to resume the main program at the proper address of the next instruction after *completion* of the subroutine.

The cascade stack is a group of parallel-input/parallel-output shift registers where the contents of the register group are accessed on a last-in/first-out (LIFO) basis. When a branch instruction is executed, the following events take place.

1. The contents of the program counter are incremented as usual.
2. The contents of the program counter are transferred into the top register of the stack.
3. The starting address of the subroutine, which is contained in the branch instruction itself, is transferred to the program counter.
4. The subroutine is executed.
5. After completion of the subroutine, control is returned to the main program by transferring the contents of the top register of the stack back into the program counter.
6. The main program resumes its normal operation.

If the first subroutine A calls out a second, nested subroutine B, *two* return addresses must be saved. The return address to the *main* program from subroutine A would be saved first in the top register of the stack. When the second branch to subroutine B takes place, the return address to subroutine A will be inserted in the top register of the stack, and the first return address to the main program will be cascaded down to the next highest register in the stack. This process is called the *push* or *push down* operation.

When subroutine B is completed, the return to subroutine A is accomplished by transferring the contents of the top register of the stack into the program counter. Simultaneously, the contents of the next higher register will be cascaded into the top register of the stack. This process is called the *pop* or *pop up* operation. After completing subroutine A, the contents of the top register of the stack will be transferred into the program counter and the main program will be resumed. The following examples graphically illustrate the push-pop operation.

The number of registers in the stack is called the depth of the stack. In today's µPs, the cascade stacks run from 3 to 16 deep. The push-pop operation is automatic, and programmers will not be required to insert special instructions for either operation. However, users must be careful in the use of the cascade stack to make sure that they do not attempt to store more return addresses than available in the depth of the stack. If the stack is full and one more address is pushed into it, the contents of the bottom register are destroyed. In such a situation, control will never return to the main program.

Example 3-1

Microprocessor X has a 16-bit program counter, and all addresses are expressed in hexadecimal, 4-digit codes. The main program is stored from address 1200 to address 13FF. The instruction at address 1254 is a branch instruction to subroutine A, whose starting address is 1418 and ending address is 14C0. A 4-deep stack is used in this μP. Graphically show the push-pop operation of the stack and the contents of the program counter for the call subroutine and the return operation.

Solution

The graphical representation is shown in Fig. 3-15.

The main program addresses are first shown at the point where a branch instruction comes along (address 1254). The updated address (1255) in the program counter is pushed and saved in the stack. The starting address (1418) of subroutine A is inserted in the program counter. When subroutine A is completed, the stack is popped and address 1255 is inserted in the program counter. The main program then resumes with the instruction stored in address 1255.   ■

Example 3-2

The main program of microprocessor Y runs from address 2611 to 30AA. Subroutine C is nested in subroutine B, and subroutine B is nested in subroutine A. The starting and ending addresses are as follows.

Subroutine A → 34B1 to 3500
Subroutine B → 370D to 3711
Subroutine C → 3911 to 394C

The addresses of the branch instructions in the programs are:

Subroutine A → 2734
Subroutine B → 34BD
Subroutine C → 37C8

Graphically show what the stack will contain after each push and each pop operation.

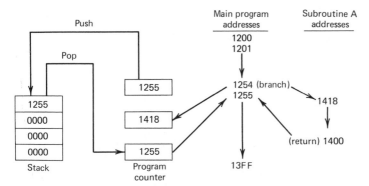

Figure 3-15 Graphical representation for Example 3-1.

Solution

This can be easily displayed in tabular form (Table 3-1). Remember that during the BRANCH operation (push), the stack contains the return address, which is the address containing the BRANCH instruction incremented by 1.   ■

3-5.2.2 The Stack Pointer The cascade stack has limitations that make it unsuitable in some applications. Its susceptibility to lose the addresses at the bottom (if the stack depth limitation is not strictly observed) is a definite shortcoming. Also, the number of subroutines that can be nested is severely limited by the depth of the stack.

It is possible to designate a certain portion of the read/write (R/W) memory as a stack and use those memory locations for storing return addresses from the branching operations. Such a scheme requires the use of a separate address register called the stack pointer (SP). The SP register is really an up/down counter that holds the address of the memory location that holds the last inserted word in the stack. Unlike the cascade stack, where the first return address is inserted in the top register of the stack with the highest address, the first return address is stored in the lowest address in the area of the RAM designated as the stack.

The operation of this stack and the SP register is shown by a simple example in Fig. 3-16. The following steps will explain the workings of this system before the push, after the push, and after the pop operations.

1. During a push operation, the contents of the pointer are incremented by one and the incremented quantity is the next address in the RAM location, which is blank and available for the insertion of the next address. In Fig. 3-16 the pointer contains

Table 3-1

Register number in stack	Push Operation			Pop Operation		
	Branch to Subroutine			Return to:		
	A	B	C	B	A	Main Program
4	2735	34BE	37C9	34BE	2735	0000
3	0000	2735	34BE	2735	0000	0000
2	0000	0000	2735	0000	0000	0000
1	0000	0000	0000	0000	0000	0000

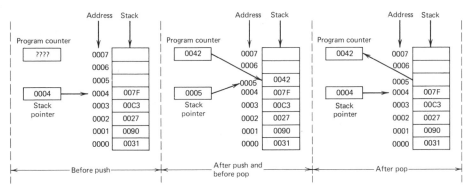

Figure 3-16   Push-pop operations of the pointer-type stack.

the address 0004, which is the last location in the stack where a return address is stored. This is before the next push operation.

2. Now a BRANCH operation requires that the return address in the program counter (i.e., 0042) be saved in the stack. The contents of the stack pointer are now incremented to 0005, which is the next empty location in the stack.

3. The contents of the program counter (i.e., 0042) are now pushed into location 0005 of the stack, as shown in the center diagram of Fig. 3-16.

4. After completion of the subroutine, control is returned to the main program by popping the stack. The contents of the RAM location addressed by the stack pointer (address 0005 in this case) are transferred into the program counter, which will now contain 0042.

5. As soon as the preceding transfer is completed, the contents of the stack pointer will be decremented by one (i.e., it will now contain 0004). This is shown in the rightmost diagram of Fig. 3-16.

Example 3-3

The main program in a μP runs from address B3A1 to B3BB. Three nested subroutines have their addresses as follows.

Subroutine A → C300 to C327
Subroutine B → C6A1 to C6A9
Subroutine C → C801 to C8A1

The BRANCH instructions are at the following addresses.

Subroutine A → B3A6
Subroutine B → C315
Subroutine C → C6A4

The stack is 6 deep, and its addresses run from EE03 to EE08. Graphically show the contents of the stack, the stack pointer, and the program counter after all the addresses for all three subroutines are pushed into the stack (see Fig. 3-16).

Solution

The graphical representation of the solution is shown in Fig. 3-17.   ■

Example 3-4

Refer to the solution for Example 3-3 after all the return addresses have been pushed into the stack. Graphically show the contents of the stack, the stack pointer, and the program counter immediately after two addresses are popped from the stack.

Solution

The graphical representation of the solution is shown in Fig. 3-18.   ■

3-5.3 The Status Register

In every digital computer, during some arithmetic or logic operations, certain specific conditions arise that may require some unusual handling. It is important to recognize such conditions and temporarily hold indications of these conditions for a certain period of time. This is needed because succeeding operations in that program may be determined by these conditions.

In a typical program these conditions reflect decision points that result in program JUMP or BRANCH to subroutines. Each of these conditions resulting from ALU operations is stored in a specific, preestablished flip-flop called a *flag*. Each flag is part of a common register called the status register, and the bits contained in this register are often referred to as the status word. In μPs the status register's size can range from 1 bit in the simplest μP to as many as 16 bits in some of the more sophisticated units. The great majority of μPs today contain some or all of the following 5 flags, so we will briefly describe them.

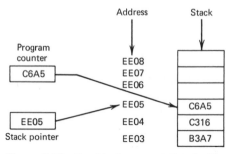

Figure 3-17 Graphical representation for Example 3-3.

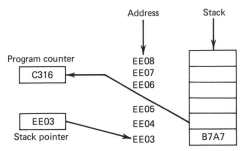

Figure 3-18 Graphical representation for Example 3-4.

3-5.3.1 The Sign Flag We have already described how indicating and manipulating signed operands in arithmetic operations is handled by the μP. (Review Sections 2-2.2.1 and 2-2.2.2.) The sign of the operand is always the *highest* or the most significant bit (MSB) of the word, regardless of whether it is a single-byte or multibyte operand. The sign flag in the status register simply reflects this sign bit, which results from any particular ALU operation. Keep in mind that the μP will tend to treat the most significant bit of every word as a sign bit unless something within the instruction directs it to ignore it and treat it as a nonsigned quantity or operand. Also remember that a *positive* sign is indicated by a 0 bit and a *negative* sign by a 1.

3-5.3.2 The Overflow Flag The CPU in μP performs addition of two quantities by treating them as pure binary numbers. Subtraction is handled similarly, since it is also performed by complementing either one or both operands and adding them. A peculiar problem arises when adding multibyte operands. If both operands consist of only 2 bytes, an overflow carry resulting from the addition of the 2 low-order bytes is legitimate and simply needs to be added to the sum of the high-order byte pair as a normal carry bit. The situation is different for the high-order bytes because the highest-order bits of these bytes are sign bits. A legitimate carry resulting from the addition of the 2 bits next to the sign bits, sometimes called the *penultimate bits,* creates a problem of becoming a resulting quantity that is 1 bit larger than the normal bit spaces allowed in the CPU. If such a carry bit is allowed to be propagated and added to the sign bits, an erroneous result will be obtained, as shown in Example 3-5.

Example 3-5

Operands $A = +74$ and $B = +45$. Express these in BCD codes with the highest-order bits showing the proper signs. Show how the computer will add them and whether or not the result is correct.

Solution

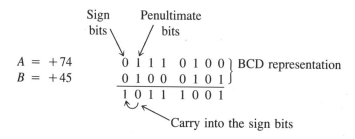

The ALU treats both operands as pure binary numbers and produces the preceding binary bits.

$(1011\ 1001)_{BCD} = -39$, which is obviously not correct, since $+74 +45 = +11$ ■

Example 3-5 shows that a carryout from the penultimate bits (which are the highest-order bits of the data word) results in a quantity that is too big for the 8-bit space allocated in the CPU and, when permitted to be added to the sign bits, ends up with a completely erroneous result. Such a situation must be recognized by the program, and appropriate action, as specified by the computer designer or the programmer, should be initiated. Based on Example 3-5, we might be tempted to make a generalized statement that a carry from penultimate bits *always* indicates an error. This is not true, as shown by Example 3-6.

Example 3-6

Operands $A = -3$ and $B = -4$. Express them in BCD codes with the highest order bits showing the proper signs. Show how the computer will handle these and whether the result is correct or not.

Solution

$A = -3$ 1 0 0 0   0 0 1 1 ⎫
$B = -4$ 1 0 0 0 0 1 0 0 ⎬ BCD representation

$A = -3$ 1 1 1 1   1 1 0 1 ⎫
$B = -4$ 1 1 1 1   1 1 0 0 ⎬ In twos complement
      (1)   1 1 1 1   1 0 0 1 ←Intermediate result

Carry from sign bits   Carry into the sign bits

           1 0 0 0   1 1 1 ←True result obtained by taking the two complement of the intermediate result

$(1\ 0 0 0 \quad 0\ 1\ 1\ 1)_{BCD} = -7$, which is the correct answer. ■

Notice that in Example 3-6 there was a carryout from both the penultimate bits and the sign bits and the final result obtained was correct. On the other hand, in Example 3-5 only a carry from the penultimate bits was obtained, and the final result was erroneous. There are two more situations that wind up with different possible combinations of carries from the sign and the penultimate bits that give different results. The two combinations are (1) no carry from either the penultimate or the sign bits, and (2) a carry from the sign bits but none from the penultimate bits. The final results obtained from these two situations are shown in Examples 3-7 and 3-8.

Example 3-7

Operands $A = +4A$ and $B = +1A$. Express these in HEX codes with the highest-order bits showing the proper signs. Show how the computer will handle these and whether the result is correct or not.

Solution

$$
\begin{array}{ll}
A = +4A & 0\ 1\ 0\ 0\quad 1\ 0\ 1\ 0 \\
B = +1A & \underline{0\ 0\ 0\ 1\quad 1\ 0\ 1\ 0} \\
R = +64 & 0\ 1\ 1\ 0\quad 0\ 1\ 0\ 0
\end{array}
$$

$(0\ 1\ 1\ 0\quad 0\ 1\ 0\ 0)_{HEX} = +64$, which is correct.

There were no carries from either the sign or the penultimate bits.   ■

Example 3-8

Operands $A = -65$ and $B = -56$. Express these in HEX codes with the highest-order bits showing the proper signs. Show how the computer will handle these and whether the result is correct or not.

Solution

$$
\begin{array}{ll}
A = -65 & 1\ 1\ 0\ 1\quad 0\ 1\ 1\ 1 \\
B = -56 & 1\ 1\ 0\ 1\quad 0\ 1\ 1\ 1
\end{array}\Bigg\} \text{in HEX codes}
$$

$$
\begin{array}{ll}
A = -65 & 1\ 0\ 0\ 1\quad 1\ 0\ 1\ 1 \\
B = -65 & \underline{1\ 0\ 1\ 0\quad 1\ 0\ 1\ 0}
\end{array}\Bigg\} \text{in two complements}
$$

$$
\begin{array}{l}
(1)\quad 0\ 1\ 0\ 0\quad 0\ 1\ 0\ 1 \leftarrow\text{Intermediate result} \\
\quad 0\ 0\ 1\ 1\ \cdot 1\ 0\ 1\ 1 \leftarrow\text{Final result (twos complement of the} \\
\text{intermediate result)}
\end{array}
$$

$(0\ 0\ 1\ 1\quad 1\ 0\ 1\ 0) = +3B_{HEX}$, which is an incorrect result, since $-65 - 56 = -121$.   ■

From Examples 3-7 and 3-8 we can now state the following general rule for these overflow situaitons.

Rule If the carries from both the penultimate and the sign bits are the same (i.e., either a 0 or a 1), the final result obtained is a true result. If the carry from the penultimate bits is different fromt he carry from the sign bits (i.e., if one of them is a 0 and the other is a 1), the final result obtained is erroneous.

This rule can be graphically illustrated by a simple truth table where a 1 would represent a true final result and a 0 an erroneous result for all possible carry situations.

Students should recognize this table as the truth table for the familiar exclusive-OR function. These overflow situations can be easily identified by a simple R-S flip-flop and an exclusive-OR circuit connected as shown in Fig. 3-19.

3-5.3.3 The Carry Flag In Chapter 2 in our discussions on BCD additions (Section 2-4.5) and BCD subtractions (Section 2-4.6) we encountered some unusual problems regarding carry from a low-order BCD digit into the next-higher-order BCD digit in the case of an addition or a borrow in the case of a subtraction. This intermediate carry/borrow had to be recognized by the ALU to initiate the appropriate corrective steps. Likewise, it was also shown that a carry resulting from the highest-order BCD digit had to be taken into consideration to yield the proper result in BCD. The carry flag in the status register indicates these conditions and initiates the necessary logical steps in the ALU. A word of caution is in order at this point. Many students confuse the carry flag with the overflow flag, and some even wonder why we need two flags to indicate essentially the same conditions. To make matters worse, not all computer manufacturers use the same terminology or are consistent in their use of whatever they use. Students should be thoroughly familiar with the functions associated with both these flags and how they are different from each other. When working with a certain μP, first acquaint yourself thoroughly with the particular unit, how flags are defined in the manufacturer's literature, and what precise functions they perform before attempting to use them in your programs.

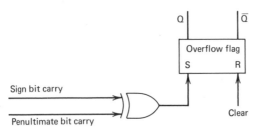

Figure 3-19 The overflow status indication.

3-5.3.4 The Zero Flag This flag is normally in the 0 state but is set to the 1 state when the result of a *data manipulation* operation goes to 0. This convention is generally accepted as standard by virtually all μP manufacturers. Notice one peculiarity of this flag. If the just cited convention is used, the zero status flag, at any time, indicates the *complement* of the condition resulting from a *data manipulation* operation.

3-5.3.5 The Parity Flag This flag is used only in situations where a parity bit is used in conjunction with data transfers within the system. This flag is set to the 1 state if the number of 1 bits in the byte (either odd or even, as specified by the manufacturer) conflicts with the indication of the parity bit.

3-5.4 General-Purpose Registers (Scratch pad)

Most computations and logical processes require that intermediate or partial results are temporarily stored and readily available to the CPU. In most μPs one or more registers are provided for these scratch-pad operations. The number of such registers, their *access times,* and their *flexibility* vary with each μP. These three parameters of the scratch pad are significant in determining the computing power and capabilities of the μP.

3-5.5 Other ALU Registers

Two other registers in the ALU require brief discussions. Regardless of the number system used, we have seen that binary subtraction is performed in an indirect manner (i.e., by *complement addition*). This means that the operand in question must be first complemented before loading it into the adder. In μPs this is generally accomplished by means of a complementing register that is often called the complementer. The operand in question is loaded into this register; then, upon command, the states of all of the flip-flops are complemented (i.e., all 1s are changed to 0s and 0s to 1s). The outputs of the complementer are then loaded into the adder. The complementer uses the familiar toggle-type flip-flop, which is often called the R-T-S or trigger flip-flop.

Many arithmetic operations require bits to be shifted right or left a certain number of times or *rotated* right or left (review Section 1-3.2 for these functions). For this purpose a separate shift register, or shifter, is often provided in the ALU. Usually this is a single register having both shift/rotate, right/left capabilities. In microcomputers these capabilities are almost always provided in the accumulators.

3-6 SUMMARY

As the title of this chapter indicates, the basic hardware architectural features of the μP were presented here. Unidirectional and bidirectional concepts of busses were introduced along with the information that some busses are dedicated to transfers between certain specific blocks only while other general-purpose busses are shared by several functional blocks within the μP. The concept of time-shared busses between the memory and the input-output devices was also presented. The presentation on busses concluded with a discussion on the multiplexed bus system configuration frequently used in μPs for transmission of both the data and the address words on the same bus.

Machine and instruction cycles of both the fixed and variable time spans were discussed and illustrated by examples from existing μPs, specifically the Intel 8008/8080. The flow of instructions and data words within the μC system were then briefly presented. The rest of the chapter dealt with registers/counters in the μP, which were not covered in previous chapters. The cascade and the pointer stacks were described in sufficient detail with several examples to enable students to clearly grasp their functions and their respective operations. Students should go through each example carefully to understand stack operations thoroughly. Since the similarity between the carry and the overflow flags causes confusion among some students, special emphasis was placed on clarification of these flags through examples.

3-7 REVIEW QUESTIONS

3-1   Explain how data bits are transferred from one functional block to another within the μP. What determines the number of lines in an internal bus, or busses, on the μP chip?

3-2   What is the difference between unidirectional busses and bidirectional busses? Explain what makes one bus unidirectional and another bidirectional. Are the internal busses of a μP CPU unidirectional or bidirectional?

3-3   In your own words, briefly explain the scheme that is most commonly used in the CPUs of today's μPs for the internal, parallel transfer of data bits.

3-4   In μCs each memory chip is commonly referred to as a memory page. The portion of the address that identifies this page is usually designated as the CS bit or CS line. What does the remaining portion of the address identify and what is it called?

3-5   Refer to the dedicated memory bus structure in Fig. 3-5. Both the control bus and the memory data bus are shown as bidirectional, but the memory address bus is shown as unidirectional. Is this correct? Explain why.

3-6 As far as the operating speeds are concerned, are the memory chips usually faster or slower than the CPU chips? Explain.

3-7 Is it possible to use memory chips with different access times in the same μC system? If so, explain how.

3-8 Is it possible to isolate effectively all chips from the memory data bus except the particular chip that is addressed? If so, how?

3-9 In Question 3-5 we established that the address bus must be unidirectional. Looking at Fig. 3-8, we find that the data/address bus here is *bidirectional*. Is Fig. 3-8 correct? If so, explain why this discrepancy between Figs. 3-5 and 3-8 exists.

3-10 The clocking system in a μC puts out string, or strings, of pulses. How does the CPU know where a certain machine cycle starts and when the next machine cycle begins? Explain.

3-11 In a μC with a fixed-time machine cycle what event (or events) takes place during the fetch subcycle of an instruction cycle?

3-12 In the fixed-time instruction cycle discussed in Section 3-2.3.1, how many clock periods are required to send the address of the instruction to the ROM? Explain what each such clock period accomplishes.

3-13 The following questions relate to the fixed-time machine cycle discussed in Section 3-2.3.1.
  (a) During what portion of the instruction cycle is the 8-bit instruction, or other fixed binary information, received by the CPU?
  (b) During what portion of the instruction cycle does the CPU operate on the data presented to it?
  (c) During what portion of the instruction cycle are the contents of the program counter sent out to the ROM chips?
  (d) During what portion of the instruction cycle are the addresses, or the data, sent to or received from the I/O ports?
  (e) When is the instruction decoded?
  (f) During what clock period(s) are the data or the addresses sent to or received from the RAM chips?

3-14 The following questions apply to the machine cycle of the Intel 8080 μP.
  (a) How many machine states are involved in the machine cycle?
  (b) How many machine states are involved in the M_1 machine cycle?
  (c) For how many machine states do machine cycles M_2 to M_5 normally last?

3-15 Refer to the basic Intel 8080 timing chart of Fig. 3-12 and answer the following questions.
  (a) Is the instruction execution during T_4 and T_5 mandatory or optional?
  (b) At the end of the M_1 machine cycle does the CPU have to enter the T_1 state of M_2?

(c) During what machine cycle and its machine state will the CPU test or sample the interrupt request line?

(d) How many machine states are required in the instructions?

3-8 PROBLEMS AND EXERCISES

3-1 Microprocessor ARIES has a 16-bit program counter, and all addresses are in hexadecimal codes. The main program is stored from address 0008 to 0134. ARIES uses a 4-deep cascade stack. The instruction address 0019 is a branch-to-subroutine A whose starting address is 1418 and the ending address is 14C0. Graphically show the push-pop operation of the stack and the contents of the program counter for the call subroutine and the return operations.

3-2 ARIES is now loaded with another main program that runs from address 0736 to 31AB. Subroutine C is nested in subroutine B, which is nested in subroutine A; their starting and ending addresses are shown here:
Subroutine A → 3782 to 3888
Subroutine B → 0611 to 0639
Subroutine C → 4A30 to 4A3D

The addresses of the branch instructions in the programs are:
Subroutine A → 094B
Subroutine B → 37CB
Subroutine C → 0630

Graphically show what the stack registers will contain after each push and pop operation.

3-3 The μP TAURUS uses a memory-type stack whose addresses run from B038 to B03D. It is a 6-deep stack. Three respectively nested subroutines have their start and end addresses as follows.
Subroutine A → A200 to A235
Subroutine B → A239 to A258
Subroutine C → C1A1 to C1A9

The main program runs from address D110 to D193, and the BRANCH instructions are at the following addresses.
Subroutine A → D122
Subroutine B → A222
Subroutine C → A244

Graphically show the contents of the stack, the stack pointer, and the program counter after the return addresses for all three subroutines are pushed into the stack.

3-4 Refer to TAURUS again and the completion of Problem 3-3. Graphically show the contents of the stack, the stack pointer, and the program counter immediately after the first address is popped from the stack.

3-5 Two operands, $A = +65$ and $B = +36$, are expressed in BCD codes and added in the TAURUS μP. Will the addition, as performed by the adder, be correct? Will the overflow flag be set? Explain why.

3-6 Operands $A = -7$ and $B = -D$. These are expressed in HEX codes and handled by the adder in the TAURUS μP.
  (a) Will conversion into twos complement be required for either A or B? If so, explain why.
  (b) Will the addition of twos complements of A and B give the final true result?
  (c) How is it possible to perform an arithmetic operation on two operands, one of which is an alphabetical character?
  (d) Will there be a carryout from the sign bits?
  (e) Will there be a carryout from the penultimate bits?
  (f) Will the twos complement of the intermediate result give us the true answer? If yes, what number system will the correct answer be in after conversion?

3-7 Operands $A = +6B3$ and $B = +10F$ are expressed in HEX codes. The adder in the TAURUS μP adds these.
  (a) Will there be a carryout from the penultimate bits?
  (b) Will there be a carryout from the sign bits?
  (c) Will the overflow flag be set?
  (d) Will the answer obtained by direct addition of A and B be correct or erroneous?

3-8 Operands $A = -53$ and $B = -74$ are in HEX codes. Show how the TAURUS μP adder will handle them, and answer the following questions.
  (a) Will the final answer in the adder be correct?
  (b) Will the overflow flag be set?

3-9 The adder of the TAURUS μP is required to handle $R = (M + N) - P$, where $M = +62$, $N = +06$, and $P = +26$ in HEX codes. Show how the adder will handle this equation and answer the following questions.
  (a) Is the partial result (i.e., the result obtained by adding M and N) correct?
  (b) Is the final result in the adder correct? Explain why.
  (c) Will the overflow flag be set?

3-10 $R_O = M - N - P - Q$ is to be handled by the TAURUS μP. Here $M = +12$, $N = -22$, $P = -3$, and $Q = +2$ in BCD codes. Show how the TAURUS adder will handle this and answer the following questions.
  (a) Are the partial results that are obtained correct? If so, why?
  (b) Does subtracting Q from the previous partial result give an incorrect answer? Why? Explain.

3-11 Operands $M = +3$, $N = +5$, $P = +2$, and $Q = +7$ in BCD codes. Show how the adder of the TAURUS μP will solve the equation $R_O = (M - N) + (P - Q)$ and answer the following questions.
  (a) Are the two partial results positive or negative?
  (b) Will the two partial results be added or subtracted? Explain.

4

MICROPROCESSOR INSTRUCTIONS

4-1 WHAT ARE INSTRUCTIONS?

Digital computers are designed and built to perform only one specific task at a time. The computer is fed that task by a human being, the programmer, before it can accomplish anything. The programmer tells the computer the various tasks or activities to be performed by means of a series of *instructions*. An instruction therefore can be defined as a *command* directing the CPU to perform a certain *specified* task or *activity*. A *series* of such instructions comprises a *program*. The specific set or series of instructions available in a certain computer is referred to as the *set of instructions, repertoire of instructions,* or *instruction set*. Therefore, when designing a program, the programmer is restricted to using only the instructions in the set provided for that particular machine. Each digital computer has its own unique set of instructions (instruction set), and no two computers have exactly the same set of instructions. Many manufacturers of μCs, however, have done an acceptable job of providing reasonably similar and compatible sets of instructions for their product lines.

The speed or rapidity with which the computer executes the tasks given in the instructions is one factor determining the computing power of that machine. Another factor is the number of instructions required to complete a given task. It would be safe to say it is possible to write a program for a given task using the instruction set of any existing μCs on the market. However, the number of instructions needed and the time required to perform that particular task would be different in each case.

The commonly used terms "a 4-bit μP or an 8-bit μP" refer to the number of bits in the data word handled by that particular machine. They do not indicate the number of bits used in the instruction word. The interpretation given to the bits in a word, as determined by their relative positions or locations, is different in data and instruction words. This is shown in Fig. 4-1, where the number of bits in both words are the same and where the minimum number of fields are shown in the instruction word.

In most μPs 4 bits or even 8 bits are hardly adequate for the coding requirements of most instructions. In μPs, 8-bit instruction words are common, but many instructions require more than 8 bits to do the job. This problem is then handled by designing multiword or multibyte instructions into the instruction set. A certain μP could have a basic instruction word length of 8 bits but could use 16-bit or 24-bit instructions by concatenating (joining together) 2 or 3 instruction words or bytes to come up with a single instruction of the desired length, as shown in Fig. 4-2 for a basic 8-bit instruction word. Such concatenation is usually done to accommodate a larger number of bits in the address field of the instruction word.

An 8-bit instruction does *not* necessarily imply that the μP also uses an 8-bit basic instruction word. Many instructions require 2 bytes, or 16 bits.

Instructions are stored in sequential locations in the program memory, which can consist of several ROM chips in a typical μC system. It is also possible to store the program in RAM chips. This is often done when new programs are first developed because it simplifies the task of changing or modifying erroneous instructions. Within the program memory, the instructions are stored in sequential locations whose addresses are automatically incremented by 1 after the execution of a single-word instruction. But what happens if a particular instruction requires 2 or 3 words? For proper interpretation and execution of the entire instruction, it becomes necessary to read and load the outputs from the two or three consecutive locations in the ROM into the CPU. Furthermore, the CPU must recognize that the second and third words, where applicable, are *not* new instructions but parts of the *same* instruction as the first word. This problem is handled as follows in the CPU.

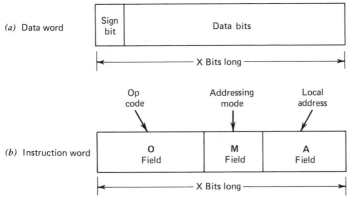

Figure 4-1 Data and instruction words using the same number of bits.

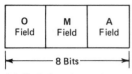

(a) Single-byte instruction

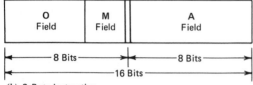

(b) 2-Byte instruction

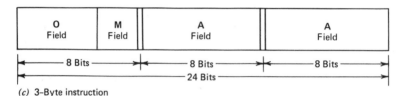

(c) 3-Byte instruction

Figure 4-2   Instructions using 8 bits per byte.

1. The starting address of the first instruction of a program is inserted in the program counter. This can be done either manually by the operator or automatically by the CPU.
2. A certain code in the first word of the instruction will inform the CPU whether it is a 1-word, 2-word, or 3-word instruction.
3. If it happens to be a 1-word instruction, the CPU executes the operation specified in that instruction. The contents of the program counter are incremented, and the next instruction will be fetched from the ROM.
4. If it happens to be a 2- or 3-word instruction, the program counter is incremented once to fetch the second word and incremented again to fetch the third word, if required, before executing the operation called out in the first word of the instruction.
5. After completing these steps, the program counter is incremented once again, and the next instruction will be fetched from the ROM.

4-2 THE INSTRUCTION SET

4-2.1 Introductory Remarks

We have seen that each computer has its own unique set of instructions. Computer manufacturers provide the instruction sets for their respective product lines in slightly different forms. Generally, the instructions are categorized or grouped in a certain way to simplify their use by programmers. In this chapter we will discuss the various groupings commonly used and present some typical instructions in each category. This will introduce students to some of the types of instructions that they will use later on with an actual μP. The final section of this book (published separately as softcover supplements) describes the more popular μCs, and the complete instruction set for each μP is presented and discussed in detail.

4-2.1.1 Categorization by Computer Section Computer instructions can be categorized either by the section of the computer that is referenced or by the function that the instructions perform. The first category generally consists of the following three instruction types.

1. Memory reference instructions.
2. I/O reference instructions.
3. ALU reference instructions, usually called register reference instructions.

Memory reference instructions command the CPU to go to a certain location in the data memory either for reading from or writing into that particular location. The address of the desired memory location is specified in the instruction itself. A typical example of such an instruction is:

1. Operand A is in the accumulator.
2. Fetch operand B from address XXXX of the data memory.
3. Add operands A and B and store the result in the accumulator.

I/O reference instructions direct the transfer of data between the CPU and peripheral devices such as printers and displays or between the CPU and auxiliary memory devices such as magnetic tapes, disks, and drums.

Register reference instructions perform several operations that do not require reference to either the data memory, the I/O devices, or the auxiliary memory devices. These instructions usually deal with only one operand. In μPs instructions in this group are:

1. Clear the accumulator to zero.
2. Rotate the specified operand one place either right or left.
3. Obtain the complement of a certain operand.

4-2.1.2 Categorization by Functions Performed Computer instructions can also be categorized by the function they perform. In most computers the grouping of functions is usually along the following lines.

1. Transfer data, arithmetic, and logic instructions.
2. Control instructions.
3. Subroutine linking instructions.
4. Operation instructions.
5. I/O instructions.

This method of grouping, or something similar to it, is widely used in μPs, so we will describe each group and also describe typical instructions in each group.

4-2.2 Transfer Data, Arithmetic and Logic Instructions.

4-2.2.1 Transfer Data Instructions The instructions in this subgroup are those that are involved in the movement of data words within the μC system. The transfer of data could be internally within the μP chip, between the memory chip and the CPU, or between different locations in the memory. These instructions must specify the direction of transfer in each case; that is, each instruction must identify the originating source of the data word and the final destination to which it must be transferred. Figure 4-3 identifies the three most commonly used terms with regard to transfers involving CPU registers. They are:

- Load into a CPU register.
- Store in a memory location.
- Transfer or move from one register to another.

Data moves or transfers can also be represented symbolically. In the literature provided by μC manufacturers, it is common practice to include symbolic representation of each instruction in the instruction set. By convention, parentheses are used to indicate the contents of either a register or a memory location. An arrow is used to show the direction of the transfer. Thus (A) → (B) means that the contents of register A are transferred into register B. In either case, A, B, or both could also be specific memory locations.

A word of caution is necessary here. In most instruction sets for symbolic representation, the destination location is shown first or on the left. In other words, the transfer of the contents of A to B would be shown as (B) ← (A). (*Note.* Original contents of A are not lost.)

Some of the typical transfer instructions are shown and explained next.

1. *Register-to-Register Transfer*
   MOV (SSSS) → (DDDD)
   This is a typical register-to-register transfer internally within the CPU. The instruc-

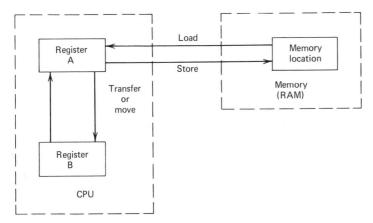

Figure 4-3 CPU-memory transfers and moves.

tion is a command to transfer the contents of the register identified by address SSSS into the destination register identified by the address DDDD.

2. *Store, CPU-to-Memory Transfer*

(A) → (MMMM)

This instruction says that the contents of the accumulator (A) are transferred and stored in the memory location identified by address MMMM. This instruction assumes that the CPU contains only one accumulator. There are μPs that have more than one accumulator in their CPUs. For such machines, the same instruction could be shown as

(AAAA) → (MMMM)

where AAAA gives the address of the particular accumulator.

3. *Load, Memory-to-CPU Transfer*

(MMMM) → (A)

(MMMM) → (AAAA)

(MMMM) → (DDDD)

Three possible situations are shown for transferring the contents of the addressed memory location into the CPU register. The first shows the transfer into the CPU that has only one accumulator. The second would identify the desired accumulator if the CPU contains more than one accumulator. In some machines it is possible to transfer from the memory into a CPU register other than an accumulator. The third shows this situation and identifies the particular register by address DDDD.

4. *Exchange, Register-to-Register, Register-to-Memory, and Memory-to-Memory Transfer*

There are three types of data exchanges possible, and each is shown here. Notice the two heads on the arrows used for symbolic exchange representation.

(IR) ↔ (AAAA)

This represents the case where two internal registers in the CPU are involved. The instruction in this case transfers the contents of the index register (IR) into the accumulator (identified by the address AAAA) and simultaneously loads the contents of the accumulator into the index register.

(AAAA) $\leftrightarrow$ (MMMM)

This instruction transfers the contents of the memory location MMMM into the accumulator (identified by the address AAAA), and vice versa.

$(M_1M_1M_1M_1) \leftrightarrow (M_2M_2M_2M_2)$

In this case the contents of two memory locations, identified by $M_1M_1M_1M_1$ and $M_2M_2M_2M_2$ respectively, are exchanged. This exchange mode is not used in the μPs as extensively as the first two simultaneous exchanges. It is, however, an important feature, and it is reasonable to expect that it would be used more in future μPs.

In several existing μPs the exchange instructions have additional features included in them. For example, the Rockwell PPS-8 μP has an instruction that says:

(A) $\leftrightarrow$ (M)

(X) $\leftarrow$ (X + 1),   skip if X = 0

This instruction exchanges the contents of the accumulator with those of the memory location M. The contents of the memory address register, identified as X, are incremented. The next instruction is skipped if X = 0.

4-2.2.2 Arithmetic Instructions These instructions generally involve simple additions and subtractions. In most μPs one operand is generally called out from the memory while the other operand is usually the contents of the accumulator. The accumulator link flip-flop may (or may not) be involved in case of a carry or a borrow resulting from the addition or subtraction. If it is involved, it is generally complemented (i.e., it changes its prior state whenever a carry/borrow occurs). In most cases the result of the operation will be loaded into the accumulator.

(A) ADD (MMMM) $\rightarrow$ A,   if C = 1, complement ACC link

This instruction transfers the contents of the memory location MMMM into the accumulator and adds it to the operand already sitting in the accumulator. The result of the addition is stored in the accumulator, and the accumulator link flip-flop is complemented if the addition process results in a carry bit.

(A) SUB (MMMM) $\rightarrow$ A,   if B = 1, complement ACC link

This instruction is very similar to the previously described add operation except that the contents of the memory location are subtracted from the contents of the accumulator, and the link flip-flop is complemented whenever a borrow occurs.

4-2.2.3 Logic Instructions The logic instructions perform a bit-by-bit Boolean operation between two operands. These operands are usually the contents of the accumulator and some memory location. The result of such an operation is generally left in the accumulator. For example:

$$(AAAA) \bullet (MMMM) \rightarrow AAAA$$

This instruction will perform a logical AND operation between the contents of the memory location MMMM and the accumulator AAAA. Note that neither the contents of the memory location nor the accumulator link flip-flop are affected by this operation in any way. There are computers, however, where the link flip-flop is involved and specifically instructed to do something. For example:

$$(A) \oplus (MMMM) \rightarrow A, 0 \rightarrow L$$

In this instruction the contents of the memory location MMMM are Exclusive-0Red with the contents of the accumulator, and the result is left in the accumulator. Regardless of what was in the link flip-flop prior to this operation, a zero (0) is inserted in it (i.e., it is cleared).

4-2.3 Transfer of Control Instructions

In the normal operation of a program, the program counter determines and establishes the address of the next instruction to be fetched and executed. Since the instructions are stored in the program memory in consecutively increasing addresses, the addressing operation is performed by simply incrementing the program counter. While small, simple programs, consisting of just a few instructions, could be straightforward and readily stored in consecutive memory locations, most programs are fairly complex and have several decision points in them. This is particularly true of programs solving scientific and engineering problems. The result of some calculation or operation (just prior to reaching the decision point) determines how the rest of the program proceeds from this point on and which one of the (two or more possible) branches the program proceeds on.

Decisions and branching are performed in the CPU by transfer of control instructions. These instructions could be either unconditional or conditional.

In the case of an unconditional BRANCH instruction, control of the program is automatically transferred to a subroutine. After completion of the subroutine, control is returned to the main program. Students might wonder what purpose is served by such an unconditional branch. In many programs there are situations where a certain group of instructions is used several times in the main program. Of course, it is possible to rewrite these instructions in the main program each time they are needed. Such repetition is very inefficient because it makes the main program longer (thereby requiring more space in the program memory to store it). A much more efficient method would be to write such specific instructions only once as a subroutine. This subroutine is called out by means of an unconditional branch instruction every time these instructions are needed in the main program.

The conditional instructions are generally governed by the status of one of the status flip-flops. In most μPs it is the SIGN, CARRY, or zero flip-flop that is sampled. The conditional instruction will check the status of the specified flip-flop and branch to a subroutine, depending on whether or not the flip-flop is set. The transfer of control instructions most often used in μPs are briefly described next.

4-2.3.1 The HALT Instruction This is the simplest control instruction. Although generally initiated by the operator or programmer, in some applications it could be initiated by other external equipment that could actuate it automatically under abnormal conditions. This instruction does the following.

1. It inhibits the program counter from incrementing or advancing.
2. The program is therefore stopped, and further execution is suspended.

The program can be restarted only by the operator pushing the START button or by the external equipment accomplishing essentially the same thing by some automatic circuitry. The program counter would then be reactivated, and the program would be resumed at a new program address.

4-2.3.2 The JUMP Instruction This instruction controls the address of the next instruction in the program counter. The instruction itself contains the address of the next instruction; consequently, the CPU fetches the next instruction from this nonsequential location in the program memory. According to the convention established for this book, JUMPs refer to nonsequential memory addresses within the main program only. BRANCHes, on the other hand, refer to nonsequential memory addresses outside the addresses in the main program. BRANCHes always refer to subroutines. We will consistently use this convention to distinguish JUMPs from BRANCHes in the rest of this book.

JUMPs can be either conditional or unconditional. There can also be forward JUMPs or backward JUMPs. Table 4-1 shows two forward JUMPs, one of them conditional and the other unconditional.

Table 4-1   EXAMPLE OF FORWARD JUMPS

Memory Address	Instructions	
0200	—	
0201	—	
0202	—	
0203	JUMP 0215	
•	•	
•	•	Unconditional
		JUMP
•	•	
0215	—	
0216	—	
0217	—	
0218	JUMP 0254 if C = 1	
•	•	
•	•	
•	•	
0254	—	
0255	—	
0256	—	

Conditional JUMP (label to the left bracketing 0218 → 0254)

Table 4-2 shows both forward and backward JUMPs in the same program.

Table 4-2   EXAMPLE OF FORWARD AND BACKWARD JUMPS

Memory Address	Instructions	
0300	—	
0301	—	
0302	—	
0303	JUMP 0322	
•	•	
•	•	Unconditional
•	•	JUMP forward
0322	—	
0323	—	
0324	—	
0325	—	
•	•	
•	•	
•	•	
0386	—	
0387	—	
0388	JUMP 0301 if S = ve	
0389	—	
0390	—	

Conditional JUMP backward (label to the left bracketing 0388 → 0301)

4-2.3.3 The BRANCH Operation The BRANCH instruction is very similar to the JUMP instruction, and it can be either a conditional or an unconditional BRANCH. Table 4-3 shows unconditional BRANCHes to the same routine, and Table 4-4 is an example of conditional BRANCHes.

4-2.3.4 The SKIP Instruction The SKIP instruction is usually a conditional instruction. If a certain specified condition is met (or not met, as the case may be), the program counter is incremented not just once, as usual, but twice before the address is sent out to the program memory. Consequently, the next sequential instruction in the program is skipped and the one following it is addressed by the program counter and fetched from the memory. The SKIP instruction could be either a conditional or unconditional instruction. A conditional SKIP is dependent on the state of one of the status flip-flops. In most μPs the usual conditions for SKIPS are:

1. SKIP if accumulator is cleared to 0.
2. SKIP if accumulator contains a positive operand.

Table 4-3 EXAMPLE OF UNCONDITIONAL BRANCHES TO SUBROUTINE

Main Program		Subroutines	
Memory Address	Instructions	Memory Address	Instructions
0000	—	1010	—
0001	—	1011	—
0002	—	•	•
0003	BRANCH 1010	•	•
0004	—	•	•
0005	—	1089	—
•	•	1090	RETURN TO MAIN PROGRAM
•	•		
•	•		
0345	—		
0346	—		
0347	BRANCH 1010		
0348	—		
•	•		
•	•		
•	•		
1454	—		
1455	BRANCH 1010		
1456	—		
1457	—		
1458	END OF PROGRAM		

Table 4-4 EXAMPLE OF CONDITIONAL BRANCHES TO SUBROUTINES

Main Program		Subroutines	
Memory Address	Instructions	Memory Address	Instructions
4172	—	8000	—
4128	—	8001	—
4129	BRANCH 8000	8002	—
4130	if S = −ve	•	•
4131	—	•	•
4132	—	8044	RETURN TO MAIN
•	—		PROGRAM
•	•		
4217	•		
4218	—		
4219	—	8120	
4220	—	8121	—
4221	BRANCH 8120	8122	—
4222	if Z = 0	•	—
•	—	•	•
•	—	8180	•
•	•		RETURN TO MAIN
4314	•		PROGRAM
4315	•	9710	
4316	—	9711	
4317	BRANCH 9710 if	•	—
•	C = 1	•	—
•	—	9814	•
•	—		•
4398	•		RETURN TO MAIN
	•		PROGRAM
	•		
	END OF PROGRAM		

3. SKIP if accumulator contains a negative operand.

Table 4-5 shows a simple example of a conditional skip if the carry flip-flop contains a 1. If the instruction following the SKIP instruction is a 2-byte or 2-word instruction, the program counter will be incremented three times (Table 4-6). Likewise, if the instruction following the SKIP is a 3-word instruction, the program counter will be incremented four times (Table 4-7).

4-2.3.5 The INCREMENT and SKIP IF ZERO (ISZ) Instruction ISZ is a special instruction used primarily for looping around a group of instructions a desired number of times. It is quite simple to keep on repeating a group of

Table 4-5 CONDITIONAL SKIP FOR SINGLE-WORD INSTRUCTION FOLLOWING THE SKIP INSTRUCTION

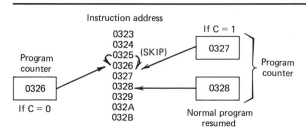

instructions in any program. An unconditional backward JUMP will bring the program back to the desired loop starting point. The problem with this approach is that the program can never get out of such a loop. In other words, the looping-around process continues indefinitely until the power to the computer is turned OFF. Obviously this is undesirable and therefore is not used. A conditional JUMP backward could accomplish what we want if we can keep track of the number of times the program loops back and if the JUMP can be made conditional on this number. It would be a simple matter to load the number representing the desired number of loops into a down counter. This counter would be decremented every time a looping operation was completed. When the counter reaches 0, the looping operation could be terminated and the normal operation resumed. This last step is done by using a SKIP IF ZERO instruction just before the JUMP back instruction. This would be a conditional skip instruction that would sample the status of the down counter. The problem with this approach is that you would require a special down counter for this purpose. The same goal can be achieved by an even simpler method without using a down counter by utilizing any available memory location. μPs use this method with the ISZ instruction. Execution of this instruction involves several separate operations.

Table 4-6 CONDITIONAL SKIP OPERATION FOR 2-WORD INSTRUCTION FOLLOWING THE SKIP INSTRUCTION

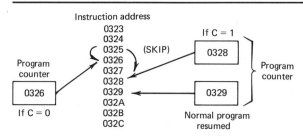

Table 4-7 CONDITIONAL SKIP OPERATION FOR 3-WORD INSTRUCTION FOLLOWING THE SKIP INSTRUCTION

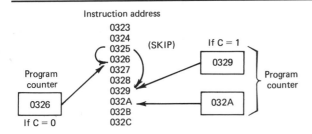

1. In the desired memory location we must first load a loop count word so that when the quantity n, which represents the number of desired loops, is added to it the count in this memory location will reach 0. This word can be readily determined by the formula,

$$LCW = N_{max} - n + 1$$

where

LCW = the desired loop count word

N_{max} = the maximum number in the memory word obtained when all the bits are 1s

n = the number of desired program loops

For example, if the memory location can accommodate a maximum of 8 bits in it and we wish to loop the program 10 times, the binary number to be loaded in this location is determined as follows.

$N_{max} = 255$ (i.e., 11111111)

$n = 10$

Thus:

LCW = 255 − 10 + 1

= 246

$246_{10} = (11110110)_2$

When $10_{10} = (00001010)_2$ is added to this, the memory location's contents will be as follows.

```
  1 1 1 1 0 1 1 0
+ 0 0 0 0 1 0 1 0
  0 0 0 0 0 0 0 0
```

2. The ISZ instruction adds a 1 to the LCW in the memory location.
3. The result of the addition process is then automatically examined or sampled.

4. If the result of the addition is not 0, the program proceeds to the next instruction as usual. In this case this next instruction will be an unconditional JUMP back to the starting address of the loop.

5. If the result of the addition is 0, the next instruction (i.e., the unconditional SKIP backward) is skipped.

The following example demonstrates how the ISZ instruction is used.

Example 4-1

Write a simple program to show how the multiplication 8×4 can be accomplished by program looping.

Solution

Simple multiplication can be done by successive additions. We can clear the accumulator and load it with 8 and then add 8 to it three more times to give us the desired result of 32. To simplify the process of loading the operand 8 into the accumulator four times, we will first preload 8 into memory location 0300 and then load it into the accumulator four times. Each time the accumulator will automatically add the incoming operand to the previous total.

To use the ISZ instruction and an 8-bit word memory, we calculate the LCW first.

$$\begin{aligned} \text{LCW} &= N_{max} - n + 1 \\ &= 255 - 4 + 1 \\ &= 252 \end{aligned}$$

Load the LCW in memory location 0310.

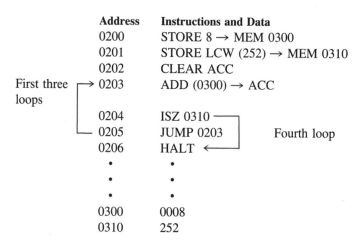

	Address	Instructions and Data
	0200	STORE 8 → MEM 0300
	0201	STORE LCW (252) → MEM 0310
	0202	CLEAR ACC
First three	0203	ADD (0300) → ACC
loops		
	0204	ISZ 0310
	0205	JUMP 0203 Fourth loop
	0206	HALT
	•	•
	•	•
	•	•
	0300	0008
	0310	252

4-2.4 Subroutine Linking Instructions

In many large programs certain groups of instructions are repeated several times during the execution of the main program. For instance, if the main program is involved with the solution of a mathematical problem that frequently requires a square root operation, the same group of instructions for square root computations would have to be inserted at many appropriate locations in the main program. This is unnecessary and expensive because it uses up storage space in the program memory. A more efficient method is to write a subroutine, consisting of this group of instructions, and locate it somewhere in the memory outside the main program. The main program then refers to the subroutine whenever needed and branches to it for execution. After completion of this subroutine, control is returned to the main program. A library of several such subroutines is often maintained in ROMs, and these could be utilized by several different main programs. The use of such subroutines does require two additional instructions, which we have already discussed. The CALL subroutine instruction provides a linkage between the main program and the subroutine. This is a BRANCH instruction that could be either a conditional or an unconditional BRANCH. This instruction also contains the starting address of the subroutine. Control of the program operation is returned to the main program by the RETURN or BRANCH BACK instruction, which is the last instruction in the subroutine. The role of the program counter and the stack in these operations has been adequately covered and so is not repeated here.

There is another instruction that also performs the subroutine CALL function. It is a special-purpose instruction called RESTART. If the computer system operation is disrupted by some unexpected external event, such as power failure, it is usually necessary to call out some initialization subroutine before the full operation can be resumed. The RESTART instruction does this. The callout of the starting address of the initialization subroutine is not required in this instruction. The proper starting address for the appropriate subroutine is automatically called out by means of the hard-wired logic in the μP.

4-2.5 Operation Instructions

This group of instructions performs operations on a register, counter, or flip-flop. No data are transferred from one part of the computer to another. The operations referred to here generally involve situations where the source of the operand is the same as the destination. In most μPs the following instructions are available in this category.

1. *CLEAR Instruction*. This instruction clears the prior binary data in a register, counter, or (more likely) an accumulator and stores 0s in all the bit positions.
2. *INCREMENT Instruction*. The numerical value stored in a counter or a register, usually the accumulator in many μPs, is increased by 1 when this instruction is executed.
3. *DECREMENT Instruction*. This instruction reduces by 1 the numerical value stored in a counter or a register that in most μPs will be the accumulator.
4. *COMPLEMENT Instruction*. When this instruction is executed, each binary bit in the specified register, usually the accumulator, is complemented; that is, all the 1s are changed to 0s and all the 0s changed to 1s.
5. *CLEAR LINK Instruction*. The link flip-flop is cleared to the 0 side. In most μPs the link flip-flop referred to here is the CARRY flip-flop.
6. *ROTATE LEFT Instruction*. This instruction may or may not include the link or CARRY flip-flop in the execution of the operation. a ROTATE LEFT for the accumulator without the link is shown in Fig. 4-4a. The same 8 bits in the same accumulator are then rotated left with the inclusion of the CARRY flip-flop (Fig. 4-4b). The CARRY flip-flop in this case contains a 1 prior to rotation. Of course, it could have contained a 0 instead. Notice that each execution of this instruction, with or without including the link flip-flop, will rotate the contents of the accumulator left only 1 bit position at a time. If we wish to perform more than one

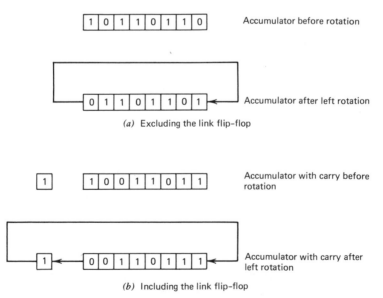

(a) Excluding the link flip–flop

(b) Including the link flip–flop

Figure 4-4 ROTATE LEFT instruction.

rotation left, this instruction would have to be repeated the corresponding number of times.

7. *ROTATE RIGHT Instruction.* This is very similar to the just described ROTATE LEFT instruction except that the bits in the register are rotated right instead of left, 1 bit at a time for every such instruction. Like the previous instruction, the link or the CARRY flip-flop may or may not be included. The accumulator with the same 8 bits is rotated right one place in Fig. 4-5a; in Fig. 4-5b the CARRY flip-flop, containing a 1, is included in the operation.

4-2.6 I/O Instructions

In this category there are only two basic instructions.

1. *INPUT Instruction.* The peripheral device, or some chip external to the CPU, places the appropriate data word on the I/O bus. By executing this instruction, these data bits are input into the CPU through the appropriate input port, which very likely will be the accumulator in most μPs.
2. *OUTPUT Instruction.* When this instruction is executed, the contents of the CPU are outputed and placed on the I/O bus from the appropriate output port, usually

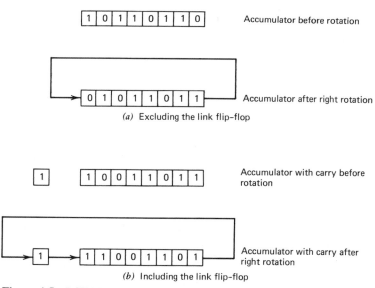

Figure 4-5   ROTATE RIGHT instruction.

the accumulator. From the I/O bus these bits are then sent to and accepted by the peripheral device, or the external chip.

Note that the execution of I/O instructions requires the proper peripheral device (or external chip) to be addressed by its own address or unique code, very similar to the memory addresses. In fact, in most μPs, memory and I/O devices are treated in exactly the same way by the CPU.

4-3 INSTRUCTION ENCODING

4-3.1 Machine Language or Machine Codes

In all digital computers instructions are stored in the program memory in binary form, that is, by means of electrical signals representing 1 and 0 bits. Since data words are also coded in binary form, the CPU would not be able to distinguish between a data word and an instruction word (if it were not for the fact that they are stored in different locations in the mainframe memory and that they have their respective, uniquely identifiable addresses).

Instructions encoded in binary form are said to be in machine code or machine language. When called out from the program memory and presented to the CPU, machine language instructions are then decoded and the appropriate signal paths are established within the computer system to execute each specific instruction.

4-3.2 Mnemonic Codes (Assembly Language)

The human programmer has to define the various instructions that comprise a program and store them in the program memory using only language that the μP can understand: machine language. However, remembering and working with the machine language is a cumbersome and monotonous task and tends to introduce numerous errors in coding and storing the instructions. To alleviate this, the computer manufacturer provides a set of symbols for the entire instruction set. These symbols, called mnemonics, are given alphabetical or, in some cases, alphanumeric forms. Each mnemonic can be readily related to a basic computer operation by the programmer without having to go through the painful task of identifying each instruction in machine language. The mnemonics usually consist of two or three letters or numbers. They are selected such that they immediately identify or suggest to the programmer the definition of that particular instruction. A few basic commands and their commonly used mnemonics are:

Instruction	Mnemonics
Add	AD or ADD
Subtract	SU or SUB
Multiply	MU or MPL
Divide	DI or DIV or DVD
Load scratch pad 3	LD3 or LS3
Store	ST or STR
Move or transfer	MOV or TFR
Increment counter 1	IC1
AND	AN or AND
OR	OR
Exclusive-or	XO or XOR
Decrement counter 2	DC2

The programmer writes the program using the mnemonics, and this program is called the *source program*. Each instruction in this program must be translated into its corresponding machine code. The resulting machine language program is called the *object program*.

4-3.3 Assemblers and Interpreters

Mnemonic codes are very convenient and useful to programmers and simplify their task considerably. However, by themselves they are meaningless to the CPU because it can only understand machine language. The program, written in mnemonics, must therefore be translated into machine language and stored in the program memory before the CPU can execute it. It is possible to do this translation by hand. The machine language code, supplied by the manufacturer with the instruction set. can be written down by hand for each instruction in the program and then stored in the program memory, bit by bit.

Replacing each mnemonic instruction (with its binary equivalent) by hand is a long, and tedious task subject to many errors. The translation process is clearly defined and is very orderly and therefore quite suitable for automatic operation if efficiently implemented by a computer program. In actual practice, the mnemonic-to-machine code translation is performed by a special computer program called the *assembler*. The assembler has a translation dictionary stored in the memory. It compares the mnemonic code of each instruction in the source program with the dictionary and retrieves its corresponding binary equivalent. Thus the object program is assembled by this translation program on an instruction-by-instruction basis.

In addition to the fundamental translation process, assemblers can be designed to include and store the basic programming rules for a particular machine. If the programmer inadvertently violates any of these rules, the assembler will not accept them and, in some cases, will even point them out. It is possible to design even greater sophistication into the assembler by making it suggest possible solutions for the error or, taking it even a step further, automatically implementing the suggested solution.

The net result of the assembly effort is a program called the object module, which is loaded into the program memory of the computer for execution. The translation of the source code to the object code is also accomplished through another program called the *interpreter*. Unlike the assembler, the interpreter translates the instruction in the source program into machine code and them immediately executes that particular instruction before proceeding to the next instruction. The interpreter does not prepare an object module the way an assembler does, so the program cannot be run or executed completely by itself. The human operator or the programmer must interact with it. The principal advantage of the interpreter is that it permits the programmer to write the source program in a higher-level, interactive language such as BASIC, FO-CAL, or FORTRAN, verify the statement, debug and modify it if it is incorrect, and obtain the result immediately before proceeding further. Assemblers and interpreters are discussed in detail in the software section of this book.

4-4 BASIC INSTRUCTION FORMATS

All computer instructions may be divided into the following two broad categories.

1. Nonmemory reference instructions (NMRI).
2. Memory reference instructions (MRI).

In both these instructions there is a group or a field of bits that defines the particular operation to be performed. This field is known as the operations code or, more commonly, the OP code. The number of bits contained in the OP code are different in each μP, depending on the design and performance capabilities of that particular machine. The placement of the OP field within the instruction word may also be different in different μPs. Generally, they occupy the leftmost or the highest-order bits within the instruction word.

4-4.1 Nonmemory Reference Instructions (NMRI)

In this group of instructions the CPU does not make any references to the data memory, which means that words are neither read from nor written into the data memory during the execution of these instructions. Such instructions involve manipulation of data internally within the CPU itself. This group of instructions can be further divided into two subgroups, each of which will generally involve slightly different instruction formats, as explained next.

4-4.1.1 Register-to-Register Transfers In this type of instruction data bits are moved from one internal register/counter to another in the CPU. The format for such an instruction must include and identify the following three items.

1. An OP code that specifies it as an internal, register-to-register transfer.
2. An address or a code identifying the source register.
3. An address or a code identifying the destination register.

Based on this, we can show a generalized format of a register-to-register transfer instruction (Fig. 4-6).

In some μPs an instruction such as that in Fig. 4-6 may include some operation in addition to the movement of data between registers and/or counters. For example, an instruction could be indicated as follows.

MOV (A) → B,   (B) + 1 → B

This instruction says that the contents of register A will be transferred to register B, the contents of register B will then be incremented and the final result stored in register B.

Another example of such an instruction is:

MOV (B) → C,   O → B

This instruction will transfer the contents of register B to register C and then clear register B.

A third example of such an instruction is:

MOV (ACC) → X,   (X) RTL

This instruction transfers the contents of the accumulator to register X, and then the contents of X will be rotated left once. In all three examples the group of bits in the OP code field indicates both the transfer and the respective operation after the transfer.

Fiugre 4-6   Generalized instruction format for register-to-register transfers.

4-4.1.2 Nontransfer Instructions These instructions do not involve any internal transfers within the CPU. They indicate some operation that is to be performed on the contents of a register or a counter or, in some cases, even a single flip-flop. Some typical examples of such instructions are shown next together with their explanations.

1. CLR ACC—clear accumulator to 0.
2. RTR (B)—right rotate contents of register B.
3. COM (ACC)—complement the contents of the accumulator.
4. SET CTR X—set all bits of counter X to the 1 side.
5. CLR OV—clear the overflow status flip-flop to the 0 side.
6. SET C—set the carry status flip-flop to the 1 side.

The format for these instructions basically includes only one field, the OP code. It is possible that other fields, if they exist in that particular machine's format, may be ignored by these OP codes.

4-4.1.3 Multiword NMRI Instructions The instructions just described may be multiword or multibyte instructions. This would more likely be applicable to register-to-register transfer instructions where addresses or codes of source and destination locations must be included in the instruction. In most μPs this situation would likely result in a 2-word or 2-byte instruction. The format of Fig. 4-6 would still be the same, but the three fields (a field is an assigned group of bits) would have to be distributed between 2 words or bytes. One possible scheme for this is shown in Fig. 4-7.

4-4.1.4 Multiword Instruction Identification Since instructions are sequentially stored in the program memory and called out or fetched by the CPU in an ascending order of addresses, a unique problem arises with multiword instruction.

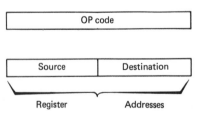

Figure 4-7 Generalized 2-word per byte instruction format for register-to-register transfers.

1. The very first word or byte of the multiword instruction must identify itself as the first word of such an instruction.
2. The first word must also include a code that clearly indicates the total number of words making up that particular instruction. In most μPs the maximum number will be 3 although, in some cases, it may be 4.
3. The program counter must be incremented the appropriate number of times so that the entire multiword instruction is presented to the CPU before execution of the instruction begins. In other words, even though the very first word will contain the OP code, execution must be deferred for another one, two, or three machine cycles.
4. In the CPU it is necessary that some provision be made for accommodating 1, 2, or 3 more words in the instruction register in addition to the normal first word, which contains the OP code. It is possible to design an instruction register long enough to accommodate all the words of the instruction, but the common practice in most μPs is to design the instruction register to hold only the first word and to provide either one or two additional registers, called the temporary or auxiliary registers, to hold the additional words of the instruction.

A 2-bit code can be used to indicate the number of words in the instruction.

Code	Instructions
0 0	1-word instruction
0 1	2-word instruction
1 0	3-word instruction
1 1	Either a 4-word instruction or an ignore code if μP has only maximum of 3-word instructions

Up to this point we have presented only the nonmemory reference instructions (NMRI). We will discuss memory reference instruction (MRI) in Section 4-4.2. This means that the CPU must also be informed as to which type of instruction, NMRI or MRI, is loaded into the instruction register. This is necessary because the instruction format of the MRI will be different from that of the NMRI, and the CPU must interpret each type of instruction properly for correct execution. Since there are only two possibilities, a single bit in the instruction (the first word in the case of multiword instructions) would be required. For example, we would assign this code as:

0—nonmemory reference instructions (NMRI).
1—memory reference instructions (MRI).

Using the just cited code conventions, Fig. 4-8*a* shows the generalized format for a single-word, nontransfer NMRI; Fig. 4-8*b* shows the generalized format for a 2-word, register-to-register transfer NMRI.

4-4.2 Memory Reference Instructions (MRI)

Memory reference instructions are used to access some location in the memory from which an operand is fetched or into which an operand will be written. Like all other computer instructions, these instructions must contain an OP code. Additionally, the instruction must include some indication of the location in the memory to be accessed (i.e., the location address).

Addressing the memory locations can be accomplished in several different ways. All of today's popular μPs contain more than one addressing mode. Some of the μPs currently on the market contain almost all of the addressing modes.

Only one addressing mode can be used by the μP at any one time. Thus it becomes obvious that, in addition to the address, the MRI must also contain some code to indicate which particular mode of addressing is utilized in that particular instruction. Bits representing the addressing mode are often called tag bits; the operand address field is also called the displacement field. A generalized version of the MRI is shown in Fig. 4-9. In future discussions we will refer to the OP code field as the **O** bits, the addressing mode or tag bits field as the **M** bits, and the displacement or operand address field as the **A** bits.

Most of today's μPs are 8-bit machines. From Fig. 4-9 it is apparent that an 8-bit instruction word would be most inadequate for all three codes required for a MRI. Multiword or multibyte instructions are therefore widely used. With an 8-bit address we would be able to access only 256 locations, while

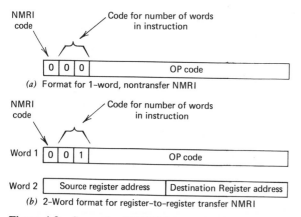

(a) Format for 1-word, nontransfer NMRI

(b) 2-Word format for register-to-register transfer NMRI

Figure 4-8   Generalized NMRI formats for 1- and 2-word instructions.

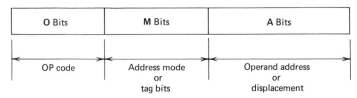

Figure 4-9 Generalized format for the memory refrence instruction (MRI).

with a 16-bit address we are able to access up to 65,536 locations; this is usually referred to as a 64K memory. We therefore conclude that for a μC with a very modest memory requirement, a 2-byte MRI may be adequate. For applications requiring a larger memory, 3-byte (or, in some cases, even a 4-byte) MRI will probably be necessary, depending on the addressing modes used. In most multibyte MRIs the first byte will generally contain the **O** and **M** bits. The subsequent byte (or bytes) will contain the **A** bits. This is shown in Fig. 4-10 for the 2- and 3-byte MRIs.

4-5 SUMMARY

In this chapter the functions and formats of the basic instructions were introduced. Typical instructions in a μP and their respective functions were presented without reference to any particular product. They included:

1. Transfer data instructions,
   (a) Register-to-register transfers.
   (b) Store, CPU-to-memory transfers.
   (c) Load, memory-to-CPU transfers.
   (d) Exchange, register-to-register, register-to-memory, memory-to-memory transfers.

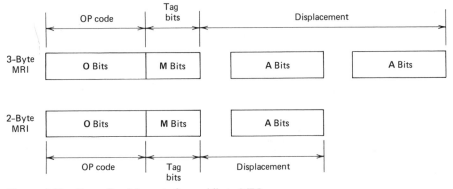

Figure 4-10 Generalized formats for multibyte MRIs.

2. Arithmetic instructions.
  (a) Transfer contents of memory location to accumulator and add to the previous contents of the accumulator.
  (b) Transfer contents of memory location to accumulator and subtract from the previous contents of the accumulator.

3. Logic instructions.
  (a) AND.
  (b) OR.
  (c) EXCLUSIVE-OR.

4. Transfer of control instructions.
  (a) JUMP, BRANCH, SKIP.
  (b) They could be conditional or unconditional and determined by the state of a status or flag flip-flop if conditional.
  (c) Externally initiated control instructions such as HALT.

5. Operation instructions.
  (a) CLEAR.
  (b) INCREMENT/DECREMENT.
  (c) COMPLEMENT.
  (d) CLEAR LINK.
  (e) ROTATE RIGHT/LEFT.

6. I/O instructions.

Also included were common mnemonic codes that aid human programmers in writing the program. A brief discussion was also given on assemblers and interpreters.

Instruction sets of all computers include both memory reference (MRI) and nonmemory reference (NMRI) instructions; the basic formats of both were shown (see Figs. 4-8 and 4-9). Multiword or multibyte instructions are widely used in μCs. Typical examples of both the MRI and NMRI instructions were included. Typical 2- and 3-word instruction formats were shown in Fig. 4-10 for memory reference instructions.

4-6 REVIEW QUESTIONS

4-1 Identify and explain two phenomena associated with computer instructions that determine the computing power or capabilities of the machine.

4-2 Explain in your own words how the instructions are stored in the program memory and how the CPU sequences through them.

4-3 Describe how the CPU handles 2- and 3-word instructions.

4-4 Briefly state the various operations that take place in the μC system when the instructions categorized as transfer data instructions are executed.

4-5 Briefly describe in your own words what each of the following instructions, which are symbolically shown, accomplish within the μC system.
(a) (IR) $\longleftrightarrow$ (AAAA).
(b) (AAAA) $\longleftrightarrow$ (MMMM).
(c) $(M_1M_1M_1M_1) \longleftrightarrow (M_2M_2M_2M_2)$.

4-6 Explain what the following symbolically expressed logical instruction means.
(A) $\oplus$ (MMMM) $\rightarrow$ A,   O $\rightarrow$ L

4-7 Describe in your own words the two things that the HALT instruction performs. Is the HALT an internally, program-initiated operation? Explain.

4-8 Refer to Table 4-1 and explain what the following instruction means.
JUMP 0254 if C = 1

4-9 Is it possible to branch unconditionally to the same subroutine from the main program more than once? If so, what is the advantage in doing so?

4-10 The following questions relate to the program looping operation. Answer them and explain as appropriate.
(a) Is it possible to perform a looping operation without using a dedicated down counter?
(b) Is a conditional or an unconditional JUMP required for this operation? Why?
(c) How would this conditional JUMP process be deactivated? Why?

4-11 Name at least five of the operation instructions most often available in μPs.

4-12 Name some advantages and disadvantages of using mnemonic codes.

4-13 Explain what the following instruction means and what it will do.
MOV (ACC) $\rightarrow$ X,   (X) RTL

4-14 Briefly state what the following instructions mean.
(a) SET CTR X.
(b) CLR OV.
(c) COM (ACC).
(d) SET C.
(e) RTR (B).

4-15 How does the CPU know whether an instruction, which is fetched from the program memory, is a single-word or multiword instruction? Explain.

4-16 How does the CPU know whether the instruction fetched from the program memory is a memory reference instruction (MRI) or a nonmemory reference instruction (NMRI)?

4-7 PROBLEMS AND EXERCISES

4-1 Accumulator A contains BCD quantity 22 and memory location MM contains BCD quantity 33. Determine the contents of the register RR when the following instructions are executed.

(a) $(A) + 1 \rightarrow A$.

(b) (MM) ADD $A \rightarrow A$.

(c) $(A) - 1 \rightarrow A$.

(d) MOV $(A) \rightarrow RR$.

4-2 The following HEX numbers are preloaded in CPU registers and memory locations as shown here.

ACC AA1 contains A342

ACC AA2 contains 7800

MEM M_1M_1 contains 0019

MEM M_2M_2 contains 0033

Establish what will be in the two accumulators after completion of the following program.

(a) (M_1M_1) ADD $(AA2) \rightarrow AA2$.

(b) (M_2M_2) ADD $(AA1) \rightarrow AA2$.

(c) $(AA1) \leftrightarrow (AA2)$.

4-3 The following HEX operands are preloaded into memory and CPU registers.

1 1 0 1   into ACC A1.

0 0 1 0   into ACC A2

1 0 0 0   into MEM location M1

1 0 1 0   into MEM location M2

Determine the contents of accumulator A1 when the following instructions are executed.

(a) $(A1) \cdot (M2) \rightarrow A1$.

(b) $(M1) \oplus (A2) \rightarrow A2$.

(c) A1 rotate right.

(d) $(A1)$ ADD $(A2) \rightarrow A2$.

4-4 Memory location M3 contains 0011 and location M4 contains 1100. The program of Problem 4-3 is continued with the following additional instructions. Determine the contents of A1 and A2 after completion of these additional instructions.

(a) $(A1)$ SUB $1 \rightarrow A1$.   (d) $(M4)$ AND $(A1) \rightarrow A1$.

(b) $(A2)$ ADD $1 \rightarrow A2$.   (e) Rotate A2 Left.

(c) $(M3)$ OR $A2 \rightarrow A2$.

4-5 Memory locations MM1 and MM2 contain HEX code operands AA04 and 93B5, respectively. The μP has only one accumulator, ACC, which can be used for incrementation and decrementation. Write down the group of instructions that will be needed to increment MM1 and decrement MM2. (*Note.* The accumulator in this μP *does not* automatically clear the previous quantity when a new operand is loaded into it.)

4-6 Memory locations MM4 and MM5 contain binary operands 10101010 and 11000111, respectively. Write the instructions that will perform a logical AND on these operands in the accumulator and load the result into memory location MM3. Also determine what will be contained in MM3.

4-7 The following binary operands are preloaded into the memory locations as shown.
11001101 in MM6
00110010 in MM7
00000001 in MM8
Write a program that will do the following.
  (a) Add the three operands in the memory locations in the accumulator.
  (b) If the cumulative sum in the accumulator is greater than 0, branch the program to the subroutine starting at memory address 7865.
  (c) If the accumulator contains 0, complement the contents of memory location MM6.

4-8 Refer to Problem 4-7. Determine the contents of the accumulator and the three memory locations after the program in Problem 4-7 has been executed.

4-9 Memory locations MM10 and MM11 contain operands 10011011 and 11100001, respectively. The overflow flip-flop is used as a link with the accumulator. Write the instructions that will add the contents of MM10 and MM11 and rotate the contents of the accumulator left twice. If an overflow is indicated (by a 1 in the overflow flip-flop), complement the accumulator and increment it. If not, JUMP to memory location 3333.

4-10 Refer to Problem 4-9. Determine the contents of the accumulator after completion of the program and establish whether the program will or will not JUMP.

4-11 Write a simple program for multiplying 6 × 5 by the program looping method using the ISZ instruction. An 8-bit per word memory is available. The program must be stored between addresses 0610 and 0660 of the program memory. Any of the required constants can be stored in addresses 0950 to 0975 of the data memory. At the end of the multiplication process, terminate the program.

4-12 Using the ISZ instruction and program looping, write a program to perform two multiplications, 6 × 3 and 7 × 3, and then add their products. Use memory addresses 0200 to 0250 for storing data and constants and store the program starting with address 0100. Write the program using the least possible number of instructions. An 8-bit per word memory is used.

4-13 Using the ISZ instruction and program looping, write a program to perform the following algebraic operation.
$R = 8 \times (A + B + C + D)$
Store data and constants in locations 0200 to 0225 and start the program at location 0025. The memory word is 8 bits long.

5

ADDRESSING MODES
IN MICROCOMPUTERS

5-1 INTRODUCTORY REMARKS

Memory locations may be accessed either consecutively in a preestablished orderly manner, as in the *program* memory, or in a *random* manner, as in the *data* memory. In either case, two distinctly separate processes are involved in the addresses required for accessing memory locations.

1. The *generation* of the address.
2. The *utilization* of the address.

In Section 4-1, we discussed how *consecutive* addresses for the program memory are generated by the program counter and how *nonconsecutive* addresses are handled when a JUMP or a BRANCH instruction is executed (Sections 4-2.3.2 and 4-2.3.3). The address so generated in the program counter is used for fetching the instruction from the program memory. The address is transferred from the program counter to a dedicated register called the memory address register (MAR), or simply the address register. The address is latched into the MAR; from there it is transferred to the memory through the address bus. The MAR is generally located in the CPU, but there are instances where it could be located external to the CPU.

Generation of the address for accessing the data memory, as described in this chapter, is either more complex or fairly simple. In Section 4-4.2 it was pointed out that **A** bits of the instruction (Figs. 4-7 and 4-8) contain the *operand* address. Initially, this address in the **A** bits field could be inserted by the programmer, but that does not necessarily mean that it is the ultimate data memory address that will be accessed for either reading or writing of the operand. There are many ways in which the address in the **A** field could be modified or altered to give the final address, which is generally called the effective address. In the rest of this chapter we will describe the various modes or methods used in μCs to access data memory.

5-2 DIRECT ADDRESSING

The direct addressing mode is considered the most primitive method of addressing the data memory and is the simplest and easiest to use. The **M** bits in the instruction word specify this *mode* of addressing and the **A** bits specify the *absolute* address. The **A** bits represent the *true* address of the location that is required to be accessed. The OP code, or the **O** bits, indicate whether the data bits are to be *written into* or *read from* the memory and what specific register or accumulator in the CPU is involved in the word transfer.

Because of its simplicity, the direct mode of memory addressing is used extensively in μCs, but it has its shortcomings. In a typical 8-bit μP it is impossible to use direct memory addressing with a single-word instruction. Even with a 2-word instruction, if the second word is used for the **A** bits, we may only access 256 locations in the memory. Because of this limitation, in several μC systems direct memory addressing is often limited to Page 0 of the RAM, where the addresses may range from 0000 to 00FF. This limited address range is inadequate for most applications. We must provide either a larger number of bits in the **A** field of the instruction (using extra words) or invent other schemes to access larger memories. Some of these schemes are described next.

5-3 INDIRECT ADDRESSING

The principal shortcoming of the direct addressing mode (i.e., the limitation in the number of directly accessible memory locations) may be overcome by the *indirect addressing mode,* which is available in most μPs. Two major techniques for indirect addressing are used in μPs. Additionally, modifications of these two schemes are also available, and those most often used in μCs are discussed here. Indirect addressing significantly increases the range of accessible memory locations, but there are also practical limitations to this range.

5-3.1 Using Internal CPU Pointers

In the direct addressing mode the **A** bits of the instruction are transferred into the MAR, regardless of the number of words comprising the instruction. The **M** (or mode) bits in the instruction identify it as the direct addressing mode. The control and timing circuitry in the CPU recognizes this and sets up the appropriate internal logic to accomplish the transfer (see Fig. 5-1).

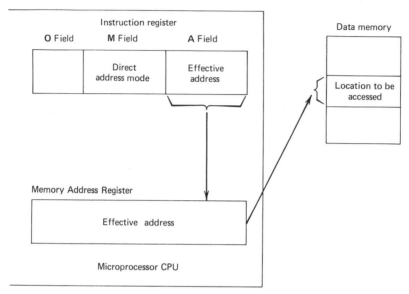

Figure 5-1   The direct memory addressing mode.

In direct addressing the *displacement* (i.e., the **A** field in the instruction) provides the true or effective *address* of the *memory location*. This is not so in indirect addressing. Here the **A** field contains the address or a unique code of an *intermediate pointer* register (located in the CPU) containing the effective memory address of the location to be accessed. The contents of this intermediate pointer are transferred to the MAR and, from there, the appropriate memory location is accessed (Fig. 5-2).

The intermediate pointer register in Fig. 5-2 could be one of the registers of the scratch-pad memory directly addressed by the **A** bits of the instruction. Since the typical μP will have only 8 to 16 scratch-pad memory locations, any of them could be readily accessed with only 4 bits in the **A** field of the instruction. Usually μPs have scratch-pad registers that are 8 to 16 bits long. In some cases it is also possible to use two 8-bit registers to make a single 16-bit scratch-pad register. If the effective address of the data memory location to be accessed is stored in such a 16-bit scratch-pad memory, we can reach any address in a 64K RAM by means of a single instruction word containing only 4 bits in the **A** field. To do this, the effective address of the desired location in the RAM must be stored in the appropriate scratch-pad register prior to executing a memory reference instruction containing an indirect addressing mode code.

One advantage of using the scratch-pad memory register as an intermediate pointer register is that scratch-pad registers are already available as part of the

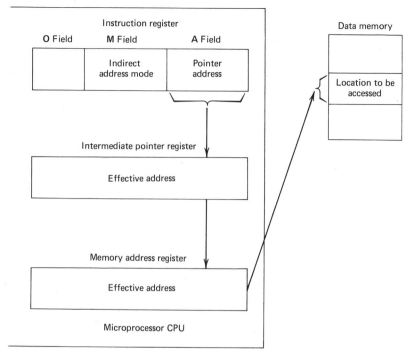

Figure 5-2 Indirect memory addressing using single-level internal CPU pointer.

CPU with their own respective addresses. A separate register or external registers for this purpose are not needed.

A second advantage is that *all* of the available scratch-pad registers in a μP could be used as intermediate pointer registers. This enables us to prestore several effective addresses in the scratch-pad memory, as needed for a certain part of the program, and then access these RAM locations by means of a single-word instruction using the indirect addressing mode.

A final and important scratch-pad advantage is that it makes it very easy to access the *same* memory location more than once. For instance, say we wish to call out an operand from the RAM, add it to the contents of the accumulator, and write the resulting sum back into the *same* location in the RAM. The effective address in the RAM can be stored in the scratch-pad and used twice, once for the *read* operation and then again for the *write* operation. The following examples illustrate these advantages.

Example 5-1

The GEMINI-A computer uses an 8-bit μP with a 16-bit instruction word, as shown in Fig. 5-3, for the **O, M,** and **A** fields. A 16-bit MAR and a 16-bit address bus

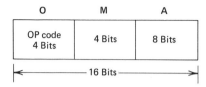

Figure 5-3   Sixteen-bit instruction word.

are provided. The **O**- and **M**-bit codes are also shown. When the direct memory addressing mode is used, the uppermost 8 bits of the address register are automatically all 0s. Using Fig. 5-1 as an example, show by means of a sketch the contents of the various blocks when the instruction register contains 0001000000001101.

M-*Bit Codes*

0000—direct addressing.
0001—indirect addressing by scratch-pad memory.
0010—indirect addressing by base page (Page 0).

O-*Bit Codes*

0001—Store, (ACC) → MEM
0010—Load, (MEM) → ACC and add
                     (ACC) + (MEM) → ACC

Solution

We will first fill in the 16 bits of the instruction word in the proper format, as shown in Fig. 5-4. The **M**-field code indicates that it is a direct addressing mode. The 8-bit contents of the **A** field are transferred into the lower 8 bits of the MAR. The upper 8 bits of the MAR are all 0s when the **M**-field code is executed. The contents of the accumulator are then transferred into the accessed location of the data memory.   ■

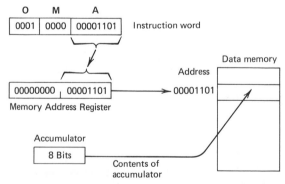

Figure 5-4   Solution for Example 5-1 using the direct memory addressing mode.

Since all the fields of the instruction word of the GEMINI-A μP are multiples of 4 bits, each field can be readily written using the hexadecimal coding system. Likewise, the memory addresses can also be coded in the hexadecimal system. In examples 5-2 and 5-3 we will use the hexadecimal codes and also the following additional OP codes and the **M** codes.

M-Bit Codes

1111—nonmemory reference instruction (field **A** will then be 00$_H$).

O-Bit Codes

0011—Load, (MEM) → ACC and subtract
                    (ACC) − (MEM) → ACC
0100—clear ACC

Example 5-2

A 64K memory is used with the GEMINI-A μP system. We wish to add the contents of memory location EE1A to the contents of memory locations 312B and leave the result in the accumulator. The effective addresses can be prestored in any locations in the 16-bit, 8-register scratch-pad memory whose HEX addresses run from 00 to 07. Write the program for this problem using HEX codes and indirect addressing modes and sketch the various components of this problem similarly to Fig. 5-2.

Solution

This problem uses the indirect addressing mode. Arbitrarily, the effective addresses are prestored in the scratch-pad locations 03$_H$ and 04$_H$ respectively. Since there are two transfers from the data memory into the accumulator, we will show two sketches for these two operations plus a third for the fact that we first have to clear the accumulator. We first write the program using the HEX codes as shown.

Instruction	Operation
4F00	Clear ACC
2103	Load ACC and add indirect from MEM location EE1A
2104	Load ACC and add indirect from MEM location 312B

In this program note how the instruction is composed. The leftmost digit represents the **O** bits of the instruction, that is, the 4 bits in the HEX code. The next alphanumeric character represents the 4-bit **M** code. The remaining two alphanumeric characters represent the 8-bit **A** field of the instruction. The three figures, one for each of the three program instructions, are shown here. Figure 5-5 shows the clear accumulator instruction.

Figure 5-6 shows the instruction to load the accumulator with the first operand from the memory.

Instruction word

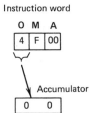

Figure 5-5 Clear accumulator instruction.

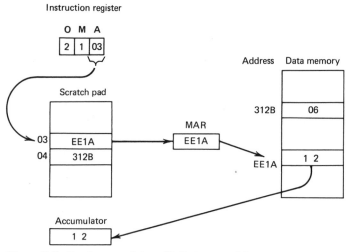

Figure 5-6 Load accumulator with first operand from memory.

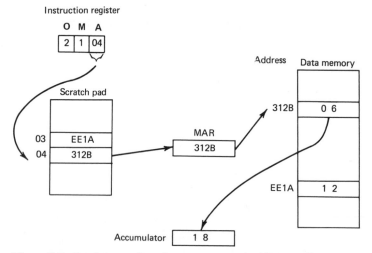

Figure 5-7 Load accumulator from memory and add to previous contents.

Figure 5-7 shows the instruction to load the accumulator from memory and add to the previous contents.   ■

Example 5-3

Operands *P*, *Q*, and *R* are stored in the 64K data memory of the GEMINI-A µC system in the following locations: *P* in location 102B; *Q* in location 22CC; and *R* in location 4148.

The effective addresses are prestored in the following scratch-pad locations: 102B in 02; 22CC in 04; and 4148 in 05.

Using the accumulator and the previously given instructions, write a program that will accomplish the following operations.

1. *Q* + *P* = *Y*.
2. *Y* → MEM location 0018.
3. *R* − *P* = *Z*.
4. *Z* → MEM location 00A9.

Solution

There are two distinctly separate operations (involving summations *Y* and *Z*). This means we will have to clear the accumulator *twice*, once before and once after the first operation (because different operations are involved). This is shown in steps 1 and 5. The program is as follows.

Step	Instruction	Operation
1	4F00	Clear ACC
2	2104	Load ACC with operand *Q*
		(22CC) → (ACC + 0) → ACC
3	2102	Load ACC with operand *P* and add
		(102B) → (ACC + Q) → ACC
4	1004	Store, transfer contents of ACC to MEM
		(ACC) → (MEM) 0018
5	4F00	Clear ACC
6	2105	Load ACC with operand *R*
		(4148) → (ACC + 0) → ACC
7	3102	Load ACC with operand *P* and subtract
		(102B) → (ACC − P) → ACC
8	10A9	Store, transfer contents of ACC to MEM
		(ACC) → MEM 00A9 ■

5-3.2 Using Base Page Pointers

This second method of indirect addressing is very similar to the method described in Section 5-3.1 (which uses the internal CPU registers as pointers for storing the effective addresses of the memory locations to be accessed). If the scratch pad is used for this purpose, as in Examples 5-2 and 5-3, there are two distinct *disadvantages*. First, there are only a few scratch-pad registers available in a μP. This severely limits the number of indirect memory accesses that can be performed at any time. If a large number of indirect memory accesses are needed in a program (not unusual in many programs), it becomes necessary first to load additional effective addresses in the scratch pad before more locations can be accessed. This is cumbersome and slow. Second, in normal program execution, the CPU uses the scratch pad for many other operations than storing effective addresses for indirect memory accessing. This means that if indirect memory accesses are interspersed among other instructions in the program, as is usually the case, it is possible that the same address or addresses may have to be reloaded into the scratch pad several times during the program. The disadvantages of such procedures are obvious.

These disadvantages are remedied using a certain preestablished portion of the data memory (i.e., RAM chips in μCs) to store the effective addresses of locations that are to be accessed indirectly. To the student this might seem to be a real puzzle at first sight. Why use the indirect addressing mode if we can access the locations where the effective addresses are stored directly from the CPU in the first place? The answer is that the effective addresses are stored in the locations in the memory that can be readily accessed by a single-word instruction. To understand how this is done, let us review what a memory page is.

A memory page is a natural grouping of consecutive memory locations by higher-order address bits. Thus pages can be identified by holding the high-order bits of the address constant while varying the lower-order bits over all possible combinations of 1s and 0s. This means the memory is divided into equal-length segments called pages. These (memory) pages are numbered, and the first page is Page 0. In μCs the memory page numbers are sometimes assigned to individual chips. In other words, if the μC uses memory chips, each containing 256 words, the memory can be conveniently divided into several pages of 256 words per page.

The instruction format of the GEMINI-A μP contains 8 bits in the **A** field. This makes it possible for us to reach the first 256 ($2^8 = 256$) addresses of the memory, or all the locations on Page 0, directly using only 1 instruction word. Thus Page 0 is used for storing the effective addresses of other memory locations. Example 5-4 shows how the base page (i.e., Page 0) is used in indirect addressing. Notice how we are able to reach a much larger data memory using only one instruction word. This is the real advantage of the indirect addressing scheme.

Example 5-4

The GEMINI-A μC system uses a 64K RAM memory. Page 0, which contains 256 words, can be used for storing effective addresses that can be used for indirectly addressing other locations in the RAM. Operands are not stored in Page 0. Operands A, B, C, . . . I are stored in the locations shown here. Using the previously given instructions, write a program that will give the sum of operands A to I and store the sum S in address $106F_H$ of the memory. Effective addresses of all operands and S are prestored in locations 00_H to 09_H.

Operands	RAM Addresses
A	D010
B	D011
C	A018
D	A019
E	A01A
F	A01B
G	A01C
H	A01D
I	A01E
S	106F

Solution

Assume that the effective addresses for all 10 operands A . . . I and S are prestored in Page 0 addresses 00_H to 09_H in the same sequence as that given in the problem statement.

Step	Instructions	Operations
1	4F00	Clear ACC
2	2200	Load ACC with operand A
		$(D010) + (ACC + 0) \rightarrow ACC$
3	2201	Load ACC with B and add
		$(D011) + (ACC) \rightarrow ACC$
4	2202	Load ACC with C and add
		$(A018) + (ACC) \rightarrow ACC$
5	2203	Load ACC with D and add
		$(A019) + (ACC) \rightarrow ACC$
6	2204	Load ACC with E and add
		$(A01A) + (ACC) \rightarrow ACC$
7	2205	Load ACC with F and add
		$(A01B) + (ACC) \rightarrow ACC$
8	2206	Load ACC with G and add
		$(A01C) + (ACC) \rightarrow ACC$
9	2207	Load ACC with H and add
		$(A01D) + (ACC) \rightarrow ACC$
10	2208	Load ACC with I and add
		$(A01E) + (ACC) \rightarrow ACC$
11	1209	Store contents of ACC in MEM
		$(ACC) \rightarrow MEM\ 106F$

■

5-4 PAGE RELATIVE ADDRESSING MODES

5-4.1 Current Page Relative Addressing

Indirect addressing allows us to access a much larger memory without resorting to multiword instruction words. In previous examples we were able to access a 64K memory in the GEMINI-A system with a displacement of 8 bits (the **A** field) in the instruction. Since μC memories can be segmented into blocks or pages, we now have the opportunity to use several other schemes of addressing the data memory in addition to the previously described direct and indirect addressing modes.

Segmenting the data memory into pages allows us to use the less significant bits of the address to access *locations within* each page and the *upper* (more significant) bits to identify the page *number*. For example, let us put together a 4096-word data memory using 16 chips, each having 256 words per chip, and see how we can use a paging scheme ($256 \times 16 = 4096$). A single-word instruction in GEMINI-A could not possibly access *all* locations of this memory because 4096 words require a 12-bit address ($2^{12} = 4096$), and the **A** field is only 8 bits wide. We would have to use a 2-word instruction or resort to indirect addressing. A unique scheme called *current page relative addressing,* or just page relative addressing, allows us to access all 4096 locations of the memory with only 8 bits in the **A** field. Here is how it works.

In the page relative addressing mode the address of the operand in the **A** field of the instruction is interpreted as the address on the same memory page as that addressed by the high-order bits of the program counter. Thus the effective address of the operand in the data memory is obtained by joining (*concatenating*) the **A** bits of the instruction with the high-order bits of the program counter. Effectively, this then means that the operand address is located in the data memory in relation to where that particular instruction is inserted in the program. Examples 5-5 and 5-6 show how this is done.

Example 5-5

The **M**-bit code for page relative addressing in the GEMINI-A μP is 0011. Assume that the program counter is 12 bits wide. The data memory is composed of 16 256-word chips that are to be used in a paged configuration, numbered 00 to 15 decimal. The program counter contains $30B_H$. The operand DC_H is stored in location $8F_H$ of Page 3 of the data memory. Graphically show the contents of the program counter, the instruction register, and the accumulator for the accumulator load operation from the preceding location of the data memory. Include a rough sketch of the data memory.

Solution

The program counter contains 30B; therefore Page 3 of the data memory is to be accessed. However, MAR consists of 16 bits, so the high-order digits will be 03_H.

The **A** field of the instruction contains the local address of the location. Upon concatenation of these four digits, the MAR should contain 038F.

The OP code for memory-to-accumulator transfer is 0010 (i.e., 2_H), so the **O** field in the instruction must be 2.

The **M** field will contain the code for the page relative addressing mode, and this is 0011, or 3. The graphical representation for this operation is shown in Fig. 5-8.   ■

Example 5-6

The accumulator of the GEMINI-A μP contains the operand EO_H, which is to be stored in the 4K memory whose location address is 3864_{10}. The data memory consists of 16 chips of 256 words per chip. Graphically show the contents of the program counter, the accumulator, the instruction register, the MAR, and the memory page for this operation using the page relative addressing mode.

Solution

The desired address of the location in the data memory is expressed in decimal notation: 3864. Since the memory in the computer is paged and is expressed in the HEX notation, we must first convert this address into its page number and the local address in the HEX system as follows.

1. Determine the page number on which the desired address is located. Page 15 of the memory ends with address 4096_{10} and starts with 3840_{10} (4096 − 256 = 3840), so obviously the desired address is on Page 15.
2. Convert the local address from decimal to HEX. Since the starting address of Page 15 is 3840_{10}, the local address of the desired location is 3864 − 3840 = 24_{10}. The binary equivalent and the HEX equivalent of this is:

$$24_{10} = (0001\ 1000)_2 = 18_H$$

The graphical representation is shown in Fig. 5-9.   ■

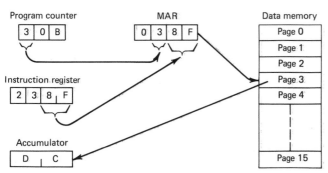

Figure 5-8   Solution for Example 5-5.

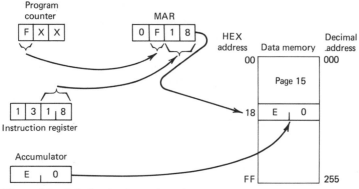

Figure 5-9 Solution for Example 5-6.

5-4.2 Page 0 Relative Addressing

In the current page relative addressing mode the effective address of the desired memory location obtained depended on the location of that instruction in the program memory. This location was determined and indicated by the high-order bits in the program counter. The principal shortcoming of this addressing mode is the artificial limitation it places on the point in the program from which the memory location can be accessed. (Refer to Example 5-6.) Address 18_H on Page F_H (i.e., Page 15) can only be reached by an instruction located on Page F of the program memory (dictated by the highest-order 4 bits in the program counter). If an instruction located on, say, Page 8 wanted to access the *same* operand on Page 15, it could not do so. This means that the same operand would have to be repeated on Page 8. Obviously this is wasteful of memory space and not very desirable. How can this be remedied?

The Page 0 relative addressing mode, usually called the base page addressing mode, overcomes this situation to some extent. In this mode, the displacement bits in the **A** field of the instruction word are interpreted as the absolute address of the operand in Page 0 of the data memory, regardless of the contents of the program counter. This makes the address mode independent of the program memory page where the particular instruction is located. Using this mode of addressing makes it possible to access a particular location from any part of the program. This is shown in Examples 5-7 and 5-8.

Students could justifiably say that we could do the same thing by using the previously discussed direct mode of addressing but do it with only a single-word instruction if the operand is stored in Page 0. This is certainly true but, by using the direct addressing mode in multiword instructions, we are able to reach memory locations beyond Page 0. Not so with the base page addressing mode. Thus we could reserve Page 0 for special items, such as a list of the effective addresses to be used by the indirect addressing mode. We could store a variety of frequently used mathematical constants, such as π and ϵ. We could reserve a portion of Page 0 for operation as the stack, if the computer uses a pointer-type stack.

Example 5-7

The **M**-bits code for the base page addressing mode in the GEMINI-A μP is 0100. The accumulator has been previously cleared and the operand $4A_H$ has been previously loaded in address 06_H of Page 0 of the data memory. Two instructions, located in addresses $3FF_H$ and 400_H, command the CPU to load this operand into the accumulator and add it to the previous contents each time. Graphically show the contents of the program counter, the instruction register, the accumulator, the MAR, and the data memory Page 0 for each instruction.

Solution

For the first instruction, see Fig. 5-10.
For the second instruction, see Fig. 5-11.
Note that both instructions are identical but are located on Pages 3 and 4 of the program memory. The same location in the data memory is accessed by instructions located on different pages of the program memory.   ■

5-4.3 Limitations of the page relative addressing modes

Both the page relative addressing schemes have certain advantages, but they also have limitations that make them undesirable in some applications. The limitations of the base page addressing mode are obvious. The base page or Page 0 has only a finite number of memory locations available, and this number cannot be exceeded by this mode of addressing. Remember that Page 0 is also shared with other μP features, such as the pointer-type stack.

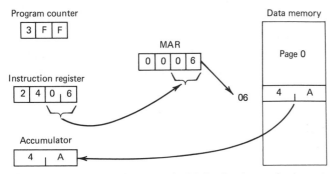

Figure 5-10   Solution for Example 5-7 for first instruction.

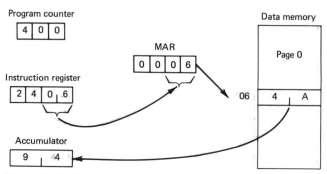

Figure 5-11 Solution for Example 5-7 for the second instruction.

The current page relative addressing mode has two severe drawbacks. Recall that in this mode the instruction in the program can access only the operands stored in the data memory page with the same page number as that in the program memory from which the instruction was fetched. This means that *many* locations in a certain page of the data memory would be wasted and not used at all unless all the instructions on the corresponding program memory page were all current page relative addressing mode instructions. Since this last situation is impossible, at least some locations on each data memory page would be wasted.

A second disadvantage is known as the *page boundary error*. Remember that the program counter is incremented after an instruction is fetched from the program memory. In the current page addressing mode, this creates an unusual problem if this instruction is the very last instruction on that particular page of the program memory. After fetching this instruction, the program counter increments and contains the first, or the starting, address of the next page. Upon concatenation with the **A** field of the instruction word, the memory location that is accessed occurs on the *next* page of the data memory and not on the current page. This is shown clearly in Fig. 5-12. What this really means is that a program such as a subroutine cannot reside *across the boundary* of a page or span two pages. The programmer must make sure that the last instruction on a program memory page is not a current page relative addressed instruction. Therefore memory mapping becomes quite difficult, and the programmer is required to manipulate the sizes of subroutines or memory modules in order to accommodate these limitation of the page relative addressing modes.

5-5 PROGRAM COUNTER RELATIVE ADDRESSING MODE

The page boundary error is remedied (to a large extent) by the program counter relative addressing mode, usually called the relative addressing mode. In this

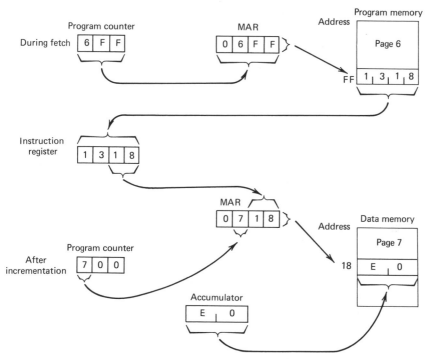

Figure 5-12 Page boundary error in current page relative addressing mode.

mode the address bits in the **A** field of the instruction word are treated as a signed, twos complement displacement that is added to the contents of the program counter. The sum of the two then provides the effective address of the target memory location, taking into consideration the sign bit of the **A** field. Using this mode, we are able to generate effective addresses one-half page ahead and one-page backward of the current instruction's address in the program counter. For example, in the GEMINI-A μP, the **A** field of the instruction contains 8 bits but, since the highest-order bit would be used for the sign bit, only 7 bits are left for calculating the effective addresses, and 2^7 = 128. So we can either add or subtract 128 from the contents of the program counter. Notice that this mode of addressing now allows us to access memory locations *across* the normal page boundaries, since the effective address is derived only in relation to the contents of the program counter. This is shown by Examples 5-8 and 5-9.

Example 5-8

The **M**-bits code for the program counter relative addressing mode in the GEMINI-A μP is 0101. The instruction using this addressing mode is stored in the program memory address $02F8_H$. The instruction is 1578_H. The accumulator contains 73_H.

What is the effective address in the data memory where the contents of the accumulator are to be stored? Show this operation graphically.

Solution

The instruction is fetched from address $02F8_H$ of the program memory and loaded into the instruction register. After fetching the instruction, the program counter will be incremented to $2F9_H$. This address will be added to the signed displacement in the **A** field of the instruction. Let us convert these quantities to pure binary numbers and perform the additions as shown.

Notice that the seventh bit of the **A** field is a 0, so the 7-bit displacement will be added to the contents of the program counter.

Program counter: $2F9_H \rightarrow$ 0010 1111 1001
A-field displacement: $78_H \rightarrow$ 0000 0111 1000
                                        $\overline{(0011 \quad 0111 \quad 0001)_2}$

The sum expressed in the HEX code is 371_H. Note that we are using the adder for doing this job, since we do not want to destroy or disturb the contents of the accumulator.
The operation is graphically shown in Fig. 5-13.   ■

A subtle point is brought out by Example 5-8. It was previously stated that this mode of addressing enables us to access 128 addresses ahead and 128 addresses backward of the address in which that particular instruction is located. This is not exactly correct, since the program counter increments im-

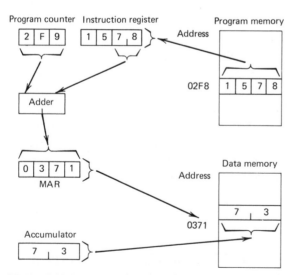

Figure 5-13   Solution for Example 5-8.

mediately after fetching the instruction and the displacement is added to this new address in the program counter. In reality, we are able to access $+129$ and -127 addresses relative to the original address of the instruction (instead of ± 128). Also observe in Example 5-8 that the instruction was located in Page 2 of the program memory, but the contents of the accumulator were stored in Page 3 of the data memory. Crossing the page boundaries did not create any problems (as expected).

Example 5-9

The accumulator of the GEMINI-A contains 12_H and the location to be accessed in the data memory by the effective address in the MAR contains 34_H. The A field of the instruction that is fetched from address 0535_H of the program memory is 93_H. This instruction uses the program counter relative addressing mode and calls for the contents of the location in the data memory, as accessed by the effective address in the MAR, to be loaded in the accumulator and added to its previous contents.

1. What is contained in the instruction register?
2. What is contained in the program counter after the instruction is fetched?
3. Will the displacement in the A field of the instruction be added or subtracted from the contents of the program counter? Why?
4. What is the effective address in the MAR?
5. Is the accessed location in the data memory on the same page as the instruction, a page ahead of it, or a page behind it?
6. What is the final quantity in the accumulator?
7. Show this operation graphically.

Solution

1. Since the operation involves a transfer from the data memory to the accumulator, the **O** field of the instruction word is 2. The **M** field has to be a 5 because it is the program counter relative addressing mode and the **A** field is already given in the problem statement. Therefore the instruction register will contain 2593_H.
2. Since the instruction is fetched from address 0535_H in the program memory for execution of the instruction, the incremented contents will be used. Therefore the program counter will contain 536_H.
3. The displacement in the **A** field of the instruction is $93_H = (10010011)_2$. Since the highest-order binary bit is a 1, it indicates a negative quantity that will be subtracted from the address in the program counter.
4. The effective address in the MAR is obtained by treating the **A** field in the instruction as a signed two complement number.

$93_H = (0000\ 1001\ 0011)_2$

Since the program counter contains 3 digits in the HEX notation, we must also have 3 HEX digits for the quantity we are subtracting from it. Therefore, using the twos complement rules from Chapter Two, we perform the subtraction as follows. The twos complement of the **A** field is:

1111 1110 1101   (complement of 93_H)

Recall that the sign bit, bit 7, is not complemented. Therefore the final result is:

536_H $\rightarrow$ 0101   0011   0110
Complement of $93_H \rightarrow$ 1111   1110   1101
                                    0100   0010   0011
                                     ↓   ↓
                                    (1)   (1)

Discard

$(0100\ 0010\ 0011)_2 = 423_H$

5. The effective address in the MAR is 0423_H. The instruction concerned is on Page 5 of the program memory. The accessed location in the data memory is a page behind it, on Page 4.

6. The final quantity in the accumulator is the sum of the original quantity 12_H and 34_H. This is given as:

$12_H \rightarrow$ 0001   0010
$34_H \rightarrow$ 0011   0100
             0100   0110

$(0100\ 0110)_2 = 46_H$

7. The graphical representation of this operation is shown in Fig. 5-14.   ■

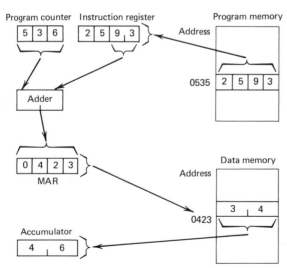

Figure 5-14   Solution for Example 5-9.

Up to now we have seen how we can access data memory locations that are within one-half page, either way, of the address of the instruction itself (incremented by 1, of course) by means of the program counter relative addressing mode. This mode is very useful for performing JUMPs to addresses within the program memory that are located relatively close to the instruction address. It is always possible to use the direct addressing mode for JUMPs, but the program counter relative addressing mode offers an advantage. The direct addressing mode may require the use of a 2- or 3-word instruction. With program counter relative addressing we may be able to get by with either a one- or a 2-word instruction. It is possible to perform forward or backward JUMPs, which could be either conditional or unconditional. Example 5-10 shows this.

Example 5-10

The **O** field code for an unconditional JUMP in the GEMINI-A μP is 0111. The instruction containing an unconditional JUMP forward and utilizing the program counter relative addressing mode is located in address 0328_H of the data memory. The **A** field of this instruction contains 53_H. Graphically show the contents of the:

1. Instruction register.
2. Program counter before execution of the instruction.
3. MAR as necessary.
4. Program counter after execution of the instruction.

Solution

We determine from the problem statement that the instruction involved must be 7553_H. The contents of the **A** field of this instruction are added to the incremented address in the program counter.

Program counter: $329_H \rightarrow$ 0011 0010 1001
A field: $53_H \rightarrow$ 0000 0101 0011
0011 0111 1100

$(0011\ 0111\ 1100)_2 = 37C_H$

This new address is loaded into the program counter and from there into the MAR; then the instruction at this address in the program memory will be fetched. Figure 5-15 shows the solution to Example 5-10 graphically. ■

5-6 IMMEDIATE ADDRESSING

This is the simplest of all addressing modes where the operand is included as part of the instruction itself instead of including in the instruction the address

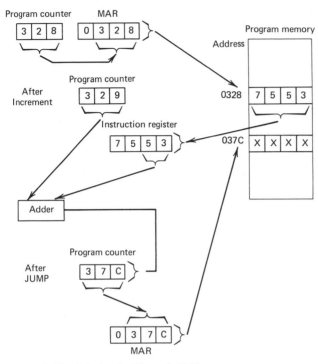

Figure 5-15   Solution for Example 5-10.

of the memory location where the operand is stored. The operand is located in the **A** segment of the instruction in most μPs, although it is possible to have it in some other location within the instruction. Immediate addressing instructions are either 2 or 3 bytes long; this enables us to load either an 8- or 16-bit internal register with an operand. Immediate addressing is generally used to initialize counters and registers, indirect addresses and, many times, to store mathematical or other constants required in subsequent calculations. For instance, a very common use of immediate addressing is to load the scratch pad with 16-bit pointers for indirect memory addressing schemes.

5-7 INDEXED ADDRESSING

5-7.1 Direct Indexed Addressing

This is another mode of addressing similar to the program counter relative addressing mode, but it is different in some respects. The indexed addressing mode uses the contents of a special register called the index register instead of the contents of the program counter. The index register is often called the B register; sometimes it is called a B-box. In this mode of addressing the index register is preloaded with a certain operand or number. During execution of this instruction, the displacement in the **A** field of the instruction word is automatically added to the contents of the index register to give the effective or true address of the memory location to be accessed (see Fig. 5-16). This modified address is then loaded into the MAR and is directly used to access the desired memory location.

The direct indexed addressing mode is very useful in applications requiring frequent use of look-up tables. In many applications, particularly those involving mathematical and scientific computations, it is necessary to look up the values of certain functions, such as the trigonometric ratio of a given angle. Tables of such functions, or sometimes portions of such tables covering the parameter range of interest, are often prestored in the memory. Each such table would have a starting address that is often called the base address. The process of accessing any location in such a table is greatly simplified by the direct indexed addressing mode. The base address of the table would be given in the displacement bits of the **A** field in the instruction. The parameter whose value is to be looked up in the table is preloaded in the index register. The addition of these two quantities gives the effective address of the proper location in the appropriate look-up table. This process is shown in Examples 5-11 and 5-12. The following common tables are used in these examples.

In these tables only the 4-digit mantissas are shown. A decimal point to the left of the most significant digit exists. Students can ignore this. The μP will take care of it.

In addition to Table 5-1, the following **M**- and **O**-bit codes are needed for the remaining examples of this chapter for the GEMINI-A μP.

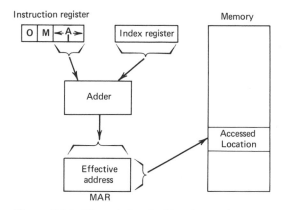

Figure 5-16   Direct indexed addressing mode.

Table 5-1   TRIGONOMETRIC FUNCTIONS OF ANGLES
OF INTEREST

(a) Natural Sines (50 - 59°)		(b) Natural Tangents (30 - 39°)	
Addresses		Addresses	
0100	Base Address	0200	Base Address
0150	7660	0230	5774
0151	7771	0231	6009
0152	7880	0232	6249
0153	7986	0233	6494
0154	8090	0234	6745
0155	8192	0235	7002
0156	8290	0236	7265
0157	8387	0237	7536
0158	8480	0238	7813
0159	8572	0239	8089

O-Bit Codes

Binary	Hex	
0101	5	Load index register (if the **M** code is immediate addressing mode, the second word of that instruction will be loaded into the index register)
0110	6	Load scratch pad immediately. The address of the scratch pad will be given in the **A** field of the instruction, and the operand will be in the second word of the instruction.

M-Bit Codes

Binary	Hex	
0110	6	Immediate addressing (2-word instruction)
0111	7	Direct indexed addressing (2-word instruction)
1000	8	Indirect indexed addressing (postindexing)
1001	9	Indexed indirect addressing (preindexing)

Example 5-11

Using the GEMINI-A μC we are required to look up the natural sine of 54° and load it into the previously cleared accumulator. Use the direct indexed addressing mode and graphically show and explain how:

1. The index register is loaded.
2. The effective address is generated.
3. The desired value is called out and loaded into the accumulator.

Use the values given in Table 5-1.

Solution

1. The first thing to do is to load the 16-bit index register with the target address in the particular look-up table. This address in this particular case is 0154_H because we are required to obtain the natural sine of 54°. The first instruction will therefore consist of two words. The low-order 8 bits of the first word (**A** field) will be ignored, and 54_H will be in the second word. The **M**-code for this instruction will be the immediate addressing code, 6_H. The **O**-code will be to load index register code 5_H. This is graphically shown in Fig. 5-17.

2. To generate the effective address, the second instruction will be used. This will also be a 2-word instruction. Once again the low-order 8 bits of the first word of this instruction will be ignored. The second word will contain the starting, or base, address of the natural sine look-up table, which in this case is 0100_H. The **M**-bits code for this instruction will be the direct indexed addressing code: 7_H. The **O**-bits code will be load from memory into the accumulator and ADD: 2_H. The adder will perform the addition process of the contents in the index register and the displacement in the second word of the **A** field and give:

Index register $\rightarrow$ 0054
A-field displacement $\rightarrow$ $\underline{+0100}$
0154

3. The effective address, generated by the adder, is transferred into the MAR, and the contents of location 0154 in the memory will be loaded into the previously cleared accumulator. The execution of the second instruction is shown in Fig. 5-18. ∎

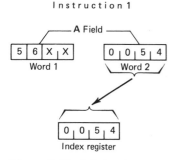

Figure 5-17 Solution for Example 5-11, first instruction.

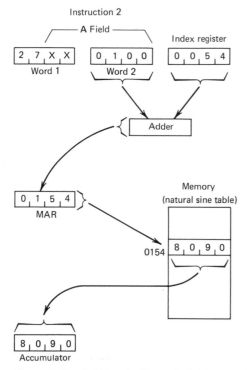

Figure 5-18   Solution for Example 5-11, second instruction.

Example 5-12

Graphically show how the natural tangent of 37° is obtained from Table 5-1*b*, stored in the memory, and loaded into the accumulator using the direct indexed addressing mode of the GEMINI-A μP. Detailed explanations are not required.

Solution

1. For loading the index register first, see Fig. 5-19.
2. For effective address generation and accumulator loading, see Fig. 5-20. ■

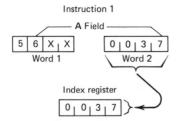

Figure 5-19   Solution for Example 5-12, first instruction.

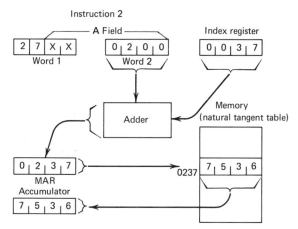

Figure 5-20   Solution for Example 5-12, second instruction.

5-7.2 Indexed Indirect Addressing (Preindexing)

This mode of addressing combines the indirect mode and the indexed mode. There are two possible ways in which this can be done. The first method is the indexed indirect method, which is often called the preindexing mode. In this case the displacement or **A** field in the instruction word is added to the prestored quantity in the index register. The resulting sum is the address where the indirect pointer is stored. This indirect memory location contains the complete effective address of the target location in the memory (see Fig. 5-21). In this case the scratch pad is used for storing the indirect pointer. It is also possible to use Page 0 of the memory to store these indirect pointers. For

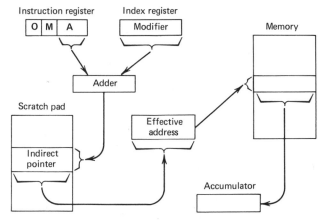

Figure 5-21   Indexed indirect addressing mode (preindexing).

instructional purposes and the examples that follow in this chapter, we will assume that the GEMINI-A μP uses only the former method, the scratch pad, for storing the pointers. In this method the displacement in the instruction (i.e., the contents of the index register) is first modified *before* the indirect pointer is called out from the scratch pad. This is why this mode is often called the preindexing mode.

5-7.3 Indirect Indexed Addressing (Postindexing)

This mode of addressing also combines the indirect mode and the indexed mode but in a manner different from the preindexing method. In this mode, also called the postindexing method, the displacement in the instruction contains the address of the indirect pointer that is stored in the scratch pad. The pointer could also be stored in the base page of the memory. The contents of the prestored index register are added to the indirect pointer to give the effective address that is then used, through the MAR, to access the desired location in the memory. This is shown in Fig. 5-22, where the contents of the accessed memory location are then loaded into the accumulator. Since the process of modification by the contents of the index register takes place *after* the indirect pointer is called out, this method is often called the postindexing mode of addressing. Examples 5-13 and 5-14 show both processes.

Example 5-13

The accumulator of the GEMINI-A μP is previously cleared and the index register is preloaded with 0002. The displacement field in the instruction word contains 01.

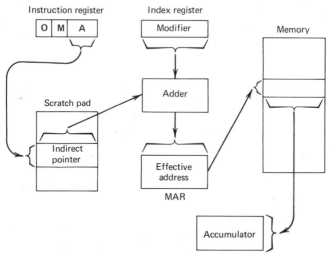

Figure 5-22   Indirect indexed addressing mode (postindexing).

The addresses and their respective contents in the scratch pad and the data memory (natural sine table) are as shown in the table.

Scratch pad		Memory (Sine Table)	
Address	Contents	Address	Contents
00	0153	0153	7986
01	0154	0154	8090
02	0155	0155	8192
03	0156	0156	8290
04	0157		

Using the indexed indirect addressing mode (preindexing), determine the contents of the adder, the MAR, the instruction register, and the accumulator when loaded with the contents of the accessed memory location; graphically illustrate the operation.

Solution

1. The **A** field of the instruction register contains 01 as given by the problem statement. The **M**-bit field contains the preindexing mode code, which is 9. The **O** field will contain the (MEM) $\rightarrow$ ACC and add code, which is 2. Therefore the instruction will be 2901.

2. The adder contains the sum of the index register contents (0002) and the **A**-field contents (01). Therefore the adder will contain 0003.

3. The contents of the adder address the scratch-pad location 03, and the contents of this location are loaded into the MAR. Therefore the MAR will contain the effective address 0156.

4. At address 0156, the sine table in the memory contains 8290, so the accumulator will contain 8290.

Figure 5-23 shows the process graphically. ∎

Example 5-14

We wish to load the natural tangent of 37° in the previously cleared accumulator of the GEMINI-A μP using the look-up table (Table 5-1b). The scratch pad is previously stored with indirect pointers, as given here.

Scratch pad	
Address	Contents
04	0100
05	0200
06	0300
07	0400

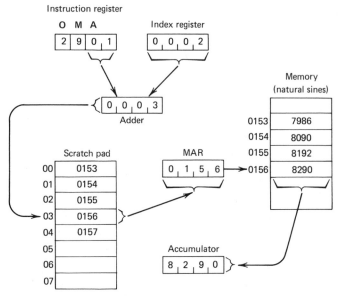

Figure 5-23   Solution for Example 5-13.

Using the indirect indexed addressing mode (postindexing), show how this can be accomplished. Explain each step and graphically illustrate the process.

Solution

1. Working the problem backward, we see that the tangent of 37° is stored in address 0237 of the natural tangent look-up table. Therefore both the MAR and the adder must contain 0237.

2. The effective address generated by the adder is the sum of the contents of the indirect pointer, stored in the scratch pad, and the contents of the index register. From the problem statement we see that address 05 of the scratch pad contains 0200. Since the required effective address is 0237, the contents of the index register must be 0037 (0200 + 0037 = 0237).

3. The indirect address of the pointer in the scratch pad is given by the displacement in the instruction. So the **A** field is 05. Since the postindexing mode is used, the **M** field must contain the code 8. Because this operation involves the transfer of memory contents into the accumulator, the **O**-field code must be 2. The instruction word therefore is 2805.

The graphical representation of this operation is shown in Fig. 5-24.   ■

5-8 OTHER TERMS USED IN ADDRESSING MODES

The types and number of addressing modes available within the CPU are key factors in determining the computing capabilities of the system. Some of the

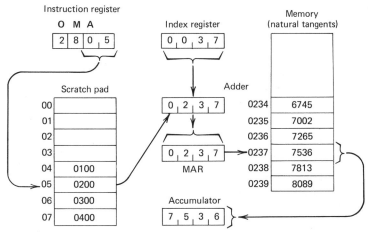

Figure 5-24 Solution for Example 5-14.

addressing modes, discussed in this chapter, are often referred to by other names. Here is a very brief description of some of them.

1. *Immediate Addressing—Zero-Level or Literal Addressing.* The actual operands in the instruction itself are called literals.
2. *Direct Addressing.* Often called first-level addressing.
3. *Indirect Addressing.* Often called second-level addressing.

5-9 SUMMARY

In this chapter various addressing modes used in μPs were presented with examples worked out for each mode. Experience indicates that students often have trouble with the indirect addressing mode. Special attention was given to this particular mode; a detailed explanation of each step in several examples that are included was provided.

To illustrate the fundamental principles involved in the various addressing modes, a hypothetical μP, the GEMINI-A, was used. This μP was oversimplified for instructional work but was sufficiently realistic for the intended purpose. The same μP will be used for the review problems that follow. To facilitate solving these problems, the **O**- and **M**-field codes are presented in Tables 5-2 and 5-3.

5-10 REVIEW QUESTIONS

5-1 The following questions relate to the direct addressing mode. Answer them and explain as necessary.

Table 5-2   THE O-FIELD CODES FOR THE GEMINI-A INSTRUCTIONS

Binary	HEX	Instruction
0001	1	Store, (ACC) → MEM
0010	2	Load, (MEM) → ACC and add (MEM) + (ACC) → ACC
0011	3	Load, (MEM) → ACC and subtract (ACC) − (MEM) → ACC
0100	4	Clear ACC
0101	5	Load index register (if the **M** code is the immediate address mode, the second word of that instruction will be loaded into the index register).
0110	6	Load scratch pad immediately. The address of the scratch-pad register will be given in the **A** field of the instruction, and the operand to be loaded will be in the second word of the instruction.
0111	7	JUMP, unconditional

(a) From where is the effective address for the memory location to be accessed obtained?

(b) To what part of the CPU are the contents of the address field in the instruction transferred?

(c) Is it possible to use the direct addressing mode by means of a single-word instruction? If so, explain its shortcomings.

5-2 The following questions relate to the indirect addressing mode.

(a) What does the **A** field of the instruction word contain?

(b) If an internal CPU register is used for storing the effective address of the memory, what is the most likely register to be used for this purpose?

(c) If the indirect mode of addressing is used, is it possible to get by with a single-word instruction? Explain.

Table 5-3   THE M-FIELD CODES FOR THE GEMINI-A INSTRUCTIONS

Binary	HEX	Instructions
0000	0	Direct addressing
0001	1	Indirect addressing through scratch pad
0010	2	Indirect addressing through base page (Page 0)
0011	3	Page relative addressing (current page)
0100	4	Base page relative addressing
0101	5	Program counter relative addressing
0110	6	Immediate addressing (2-word instruction)
0111	7	Direct index addressing (2-word instruction)
1000	8	Indirect indexed addressing
1001	9	Indexed indirect addressing
1111	F	Nonmemory reference instruction—**A** field of the instruction is ignored

5-3 The data memory of a certain μC system contains 16 pages; each page is capable of storing 4096 words. The first 256 words of the base page (addresses 000 to 255) are reserved for storing look-up tables. If the **A** field of the instruction contains only 4 bits and we wish to be able to access any of the 65,536 words of the memory by means of a *single-word instruction only,* should we use the scratch-pad register or the base page for storing the effective address? Explain.

5-4 Briefly explain how the effective address of the memory location (to be accessed) is generated using the current page relative addressing mode.

5-5 The data memory of a μC system contains 16 pages, each page containing 1024 words. The **A** field in the instruction contains the address 986_{10}. What page in the data memory will the CPU access when the Page 0 relative addressing mode is used?

5-6 Identify the shortcomings of the base page and the current page relative addressing modes.

5-7 Is it true that by using the program counter relative mode of addressing we are able to generate effective addresses a full page ahead and a full page backward of the current instruction's address in the program counter? If this is not true, explain why.

5-8 From what memory location is the operand fetched in the immediate addressing mode?

5-9 Explain how the effective address is derived in the direct indexed addressing mode.

5-10 Describe how the direct indexed addressing mode would be utilized in a table look-up operation.

5-11 For the indexed indirect addressing mode, explain how the address of the indirect pointer is obtained.

5-12 Explain how the effective address is obtained in the indirect indexed addressing mode.

5-11 PROBLEMS AND EXERCISES

5-1 The 16-bit instruction register of the GEMINI-A μC contains 0001000001100111 and the 8-bit accumulator contains 11010011. Answer the following questions and graphically show the execution of the instruction involved.
(a) What will the upper half of the MAR contain and why?
(b) What will be the contents of the accessed memory location? Explain why.
(c) In what page of the data memory is the accessed address located and why?

5-2 The operation graphically shown in Fig. 5-25 takes place in the GEMINI-A

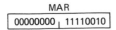

MAR

| 00000000 | 11110010 |

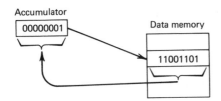

Figure 5-25   Figure for problem 5-2.

μC system. Determine the contents of the instruction register that will cause the execution of this operation, and complete the sketch. (Assume an addition process in the accumulator upon completion of the instruction.)

5-3   The GEMINI-A μC system uses a 64K data memory. Location $AA34_H$ contains the operand 34_H and location $372B_H$ contains the operand 45_H. The effective addresses are prestored in the 16-bit, 8-register scratch pad, as shown. Using HEX codes, write a program that adds the two operands and leaves the sum in the accumulator.

Scratch pad Address	Effective Address Stored
05_H	$AA34_H$
07_H	$372B_H$

5-4   Refer to Problem 5-3 and graphically show all the operations involved in the solution of that problem by a sketch or sketches, as appropriate.

5-5   Operands K, L, and M are stored in the 64K data memory of the GEMINI-A μC in the following locations.
K in location 51CD
L in location 4270
M in location A771
The effective addresses are in the following scratch-pad locations.
51CD in 01
4270 in 02
A771 in 03
Using the accumulator, write a program that will accomplish the following operations.
(a) $K + L = N$
(b) $N - M = P$
(c) $P \rightarrow$ MEM location 0044

5-6   Operands A, B, C, and D are stored in the RAM addresses of the GEMINI-A μC, as shown in the following table. The base page indirect addressing mode is used, and the locations that are used for storing the effective addresses are

also given. Write a program to solve the problem:
$E = A + B - C + D$

Operands and Results	Stored in RAM Addresses	Effective Addresses stored in
A	2123	00A0
B	718C	00A1
C	B8BB	00A2
D	9180	00A3
E	56DA	00A4

5-7 Operands *A, B, C,* and *D* are stored in the RAM addresses of the GEMINI-A μC, as shown in the following table. Both the scratch pad and the base page are used for storing the effective addresses, and the indirect addressing mode is used. Write a program to solve the problem:
$R = B - D + A - C$

Operands and Result	Stored in RAM Addresses	Effective Addresses in	
		Scratch pad	Base Page
A	1001	03	—
B	2002	—	001D
C	3003	07	—
D	4004	05	—
R	5005	—	OOBB

5-8 Assume that the data memory of the GEMINI-A μC consists of 16 RAM chips, numbered 00 to 15 decimal, and each chip contains 256 words of 8 bits per word. Also assume that the 12-bit program counter contains 201_H. The operand $6D_H$ is stored in location 73_H of Page 2 in the data memory. Graphically show the contents of the instruction register, the MAR, the program counter, and the accumulator for the operation that transfers the contents in the data memory location to the accumulator, using the page relative addressing mode.

5-9 Assume that the data memory of the GEMINI-A μC contains 12 pages, numbered 00 to 11, and that operand 88 is stored in location 1234 decimal. Determine what the contents of the program counter, the instruction register, and the MAR will be for the operation where the contents of this data memory location are transferred into the accumulator. There are 256 words per page in the memory. Express all quantities in HEX notation.

5-10 Operand BB_H is preloaded in address 9A of Page 0 in the data memory of the GEMINI-A μC. Instructions located in addresses $2E1_H$ and $62B_H$ of the program memory both transfer the contents of this data memory location into the previously cleared accumulator. Using the base page addressing mode, determine the contents of the program counter, the instruction register, and the MAR for each of the two instructions, and the contents of the accumulator after both instructions have been executed.

5-11 The instruction in the GEMINI-A µC, using the program counter relative addressing mode, is stored in the program memory address 0462_H. The instruction itself is 1536_H, and the accumulator contains FD_H, which is to be transferred into the data memory. Calculate the effective address in the data memory where the accumulator contents will be stored. Show this operation graphically.

5-12 The accumulator of the GEMINI-A µC contains 24_H. The location to be accessed in the data memory contains 36_H. The instruction, which uses the program counter relative addressing mode, is fetched from address 0666_H of the program memory. The **A** field of the instruction contains 81_H. The **O** field of the instruction commands the µP to transfer the contents of the accessed data memory location into the accumulator and add it to the previous contents. Determine the contents of:

(a) The instruction register.
(b) The program counter after the instruction is fetched.
(c) The MAR.
(d) The accumulator after the instruction is executed.

5-13 Refer to Problem 5-12. Accidentally, the programmer inserted 71_H in the **A** field of the instruction instead of the intended 81_H. Calculate the effect of this error on Problem 5-12.

5-14 The instruction fetched from address 0619_H of the program memory of the GEMINI-A µC contains an unconditional JUMP forward and utilizes the program counter relative mode of addressing. The **A** field of the instruction contains 46_H. Determine the contents of:

(a) The instruction register.
(b) The program counter before execution of the instruction.
(c) The program counter after execution of the instruction.
(d) The MAR with the new program memory address.

5-15 The accumulator of the GEMINI-A µP is first cleared and the sine of 58° is to be loaded into it by referring to the sine look-up table (Table 5-1*a*). The direct indexed addressing mode is used. Graphically show how:

(a) The index register is preloaded.
(b) The effective address is derived.
(c) The sine of 58° is called out and loaded into the accumulator.

5-16 The index register of the GEMINI-A µC is preloaded with 0003. The **A** field in the instruction word contains 02. The addresses and their respective contents in the scratch pad are shown in the table. Using the indexed indirect addressing mode (preindexing), determine the contents of the instruction register, the adder, the MAR, and the accumulator after the instruction is executed. Assume that the accumulator is precleared, and use the look-up data in Table 5-1.

Scratch pad	
Address	*Contents*
00	0230
01	0231
02	0232
03	0233
04	0234
05	0235
06	0236
07	0237

5-17 The natural tangent of 33° is to be loaded in the previously cleared contents of the accumulator of the GEMINI-A µP using the look-up data of Table 5-1*b*. The scratch pad is preloaded with indirect pointers as shown. Using the indirect indexed addressing mode (postindexing), show how this is done.

Scratch pad	
Address	*Contents*
03	0100
04	0200
05	0300
06	0400
07	0500

6

INSTRUCTION EXECUTION AND MICROSEQUENCES

6-1 INTRODUCTORY REMARKS

In Chapter One we briefly described the major functional blocks of a digital computer (Fig. 1-1). To review these functions, we stated that the memory section stores the instructions and the data (both fixed and variable) required in the execution of a program. The input unit brings into the system the data to be processed. The output unit provides the means for presenting the processed data to the outside world. The processing operations are performed by the arithmetic and logic unit (ALU) section (of the CPU), which is the heart of the computer. The control and timing unit, which is the principal topic of this chapter, provides the control and coordination of the rest of the units in the computer. As such, it can be described as the brain or the *nerve center* of the system.

The major functions performed by the control and timing unit are as follows.

1. It *fetches the instruction* from the program memory. It does this by:
   (a) Updating the address in the program counter.
   (b) Transferring the contents of the program counter to the address register.
   (c) Sending the address from the address register to the program memory, either on a dedicated address bus or on a time-shared data bus.
   (d) Loading the fetched instruction into the instruction register located in the CPU.
2. It *decodes* the *fetched instruction* into its appropriate *electrical* signals.
3. It *executes* the decoded instruction, taking into consideration various *control signals* presented to it. These may be external signals such as INTERRUPT, STOP, WAIT, and HALT or internally generated signals such as those provided by the various *status flags*.
4. It provides the proper *timing* and *control signals* to the various memory chips and to the I/O chips if transfer of data is involved.

148

6-2 HOW THE CPU EXECUTES INSTRUCTIONS

6-2.1 The Macroinstructions

In Chapter Four we presented, in general terms, the basic instructions common to all digital computers (including µPs) without reference to any one or more specific computer products. Each instruction, very fundamental to the operation of the computer, is really comprised of a series of rudimentary computer operations performed in a set sequence. The machine language code of the instruction (consisting of 1s and 0s) essentially establishes and controls the various data paths within the hardware of the CPU and directs each subsystem to perform certain specific functions. These machine language instructions are called *macroinstructions*. The prefix *macro* means *large* or *long*. Generally, the macroinstructions, supplied by the computer manufacturer, consists of a fixed set of instructions that are *hard-wired* into the timing and control unit of the CPU. They cannot be altered or modified.

6-2.2 The Microinstructions

The execution of each macroinstruction consists of a series of subcommands to the various hardware blocks of the computer. These subcommands are called *microinstructions*. These *microinstructions* are hard-wired into the *control unit* of the machine. Microinstructions are often abbreviated as µinstructions. The µinstructions are controlled by the timing and control unit of the CPU, and they are executed in the proper sequence as dictated by that particular µinstruction. The concept of the differences between the macro- and the microinstruction can be best understood by means of some simple examples.

6-2.3 The Internal Data Bus

In any computer system the hardware architecture of the CPU contains at least one *data bus* over which data words can be transferred from one subsystem to another. All µPs have such an internal data bus. Some have two or more.

In some computers the internal data bus is nothing more than an extension of the external data bus, shared by the memory and the I/O devices for the transfer of data between the CPU and the other devices. For the examples in this chapter, we will consider only the *internal* data bus for *internal* data transfers within the CPU.

6-3 SIMPLE GENERALIZED EXAMPLES OF MICROINSTRUCTIONS

We will now show some simple examples of how the microsequences resulting from the execution of a macroinstruction are handled by the control unit of the μP. For simplicity in instruction and learning, we will show only the portions of the μP CPU that are pertinent to each example involved in each of the diagrams. How each functional subsystem block is connected to, or disconnected from, the internal data bus (and how the *direction* of data flow is controlled) will be shown later in the chapter. For now, let us assume that the way they will be handled exists.

Example 6-1

We wish to perform an unconditional relative JUMP using the CANCER μP, which is an 8-bit machine. This operation involves the following steps.

1. Add the contents of the address portion in the instruction register to the address of the current instruction in the program counter.
2. Transfer the result of the addition to the program counter.
3. Send the contents of the program counter to the address register and from there to the program memory.

For these steps, graphically show all the microsequences involved by means of appropriate control signals from the control and timing unit. Use the adder for the addition process.

Solution

The microsequences involved in this example are shown in Fig. 6-1 in graphical form. The numbers shown in circles indicate the microsequence or μinstruction involved. These correspond to the numbers of the μinstructions shown here. If more than one transfer involves the same block and the same subbus, the direction of transfer is shown by an appropriate arrow on the circle.

   Note that the current instruction, contained in the instruction register, must first be transferred to the instruction decoder before the appropriate control signals can be generated by the control and timing unit of the μP. Also note that the program memory is shown external to the CPU along with the clocking system. Although two clock phases are shown, it could be either a single-phase system or could have more than two phases. The μinstructions involved are shown in their proper sequence. Remember that the data bits must be first put on the internal data bus before they can be transferred to another subsystem.

1. Contents of instruction register (OP code and the address mode) → instruction decoder.
2. Instruction is decoded, and the control and timing unit generates the appropriate control signals in the proper sequence.
3. Contents of instruction register (address portion) → internal data bus.
4. Internal data bus → adder.
5. Contents of program counter → internal data bus.
6. Internal data bus → adder.

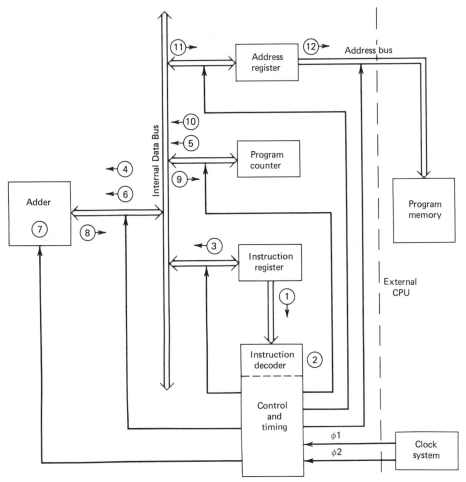

Figure 6-1 Microsequences involved in unconditional JUMP (program counter relative addressing mode).

7. The add operation in the adder.
8. Contents of adder → internal data bus.
9. Internal data bus → program counter.
10. Program counter → internal data bus.
11. Internal data bus → address register.
12. Address register → program memory (through the address bus). ■

In Example 6-1 we used the program counter relative mode of addressing; that is, we jumped unconditionally, but to an effective address that was obtained by adding the **A** field of the instruction to the contents of the program counter. Such a macroinstruction involves 12 μinstructions. If the effective address had been given in the **A** field of the instruction and the direct addressing mode used, the macroinstruction would have been executed with fewer μinstructions. This is shown in Example 6-2. In the microsequences for Fig. 6-1, observe that the first two μinstructions are required regardless of the macroinstruction given the CPU. Therefore, for simplification, we may omit these two steps in the rest of the examples in this chapter with the understanding that they are automatically executed by the CPU.

Example 6-2

In the CANCER μP, the current instruction calls for an unconditional JUMP. The direct addressing mode is specified in the **M** field of this instruction. Write down the microsequences involved in the execution of this instruction and graphically show the operation of each step.

Solution

The execution of this macroinstruction is graphically shown in Fig. 6-2. The following μinstructions are involved in execution of this macroinstruction.

1. Contents of instruction register (**A** field) → internal data bus.
2. Internal data bus → program counter.
3. Program counter → internal data bus.
4. Internal data bus → address register.
5. Address register → program memory (through the address bus).   ■

In Examples 6-1 and 6-2 it seems that two microsequences are not necessary for the execution of the unconditional JUMP macroinstruction, regardless of the addressing mode used. They are the two steps that transfer information between the internal data bus and the program counter. Students may wonder why the transfer from the adder to the program counter in Example 6-1 and the transfer from the instruction register to the program counter in Example 6-2 are necessary. They may also ask why the contents of the two sources could not be transferred directly into the address register, bypassing the program counter completely. It is possible to do this but, for the program to continue the operation, the updated address of the subsequent instructions must be generated by the program counter and transferred to the address register. Therefore loading the program counter with the nonsequential, jumped address is unavoidable. A more complex set of microsequences is shown in Example 6-3.

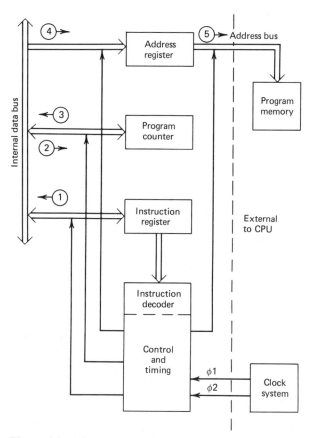

Figure 6-2   Microsequences involved in unconditional JUMP (direct addressing mode).

Example 6-3

A macroinstruction for the CANCER μP calls out for a conditional BRANCH to a subroutine. The following steps will result from this macroinstruction.

1. Compare the contents of the data register with the contents of the accumulator.
2. If the comparison results in equality, increment the program counter and continue with the program normally.
3. If the comparison indicates inequality, transfer the contents of the program counter into the stack.
4. Transfer the contents of the instruction register (**A** field) to the program counter and proceed normally.

List the μinstructions required to execute these steps and show them pictorially.

Solution

The microsequences involved in the execution of this macroinstruction are shown in Fig. 6-3. The following μinstructions will be executed in the shown sequences.

1. Contents of data register → internal data bus.
2. Internal data bus → comparator in the ALU.
3. Contents of accumulator → internal data bus.
4. Internal data bus → comparator.
5. The compare operation.
6. Comparator → status register (signal indicating equality/inequality).
7. Status register → program counter (signal commanding either program counter incrementation or transfer from program counter).
8. Increment program counter (if comparison indicates equality).
9. Contents of program counter → internal data bus (if comparison indicates inequality).
10. Internal data bus → cascade stack.
11. Contents of instruction register (**A** field) → internal data bus.
12. Internal data bus → program counter.   ■

In Example 6-3 the number of μinstructions involved will depend on the outcome of the comparison process. If equality is indicated, the execution of the macroinstruction will be completed in only 8 microsteps or μinstructions. Otherwise, a total of 10 μinstructions will be required. How is the decision to continue with the 4 additional steps made? Observe that a control line goes from the status register to the program counter. This line, which indicates equality, signals the program counter to increment. In case of inequality, the status register sends a signal to the control and timing unit. As a result, microsequences 9, 10, 11, and 12 will be initiated by the control and timing unit. Because of inequality, microsequences 7 and 8 will not be initiated. Thus, in this case, the total number of microsequences required will be 10, although in the solution of the problem all 12 microsequences are shown.

Example 6-4

The CANCER μP uses the twos complement method for subtraction and the previously described sign convention for the most significant bit (MSB) position. It also has an 8-bit increment/decrement register that, on receipt of the proper signal from the control and timing unit, will either increment or decrement the contents of this register. An 8-bit minuend is preloaded into the data register, and an 8-bit subtrahend is preloaded into the accumulator. The minuend is positive and larger than the subtrahend, which is smaller and negative. Write down the μinstructions necessary for performing the subtraction operation called out by the SUBTRACT

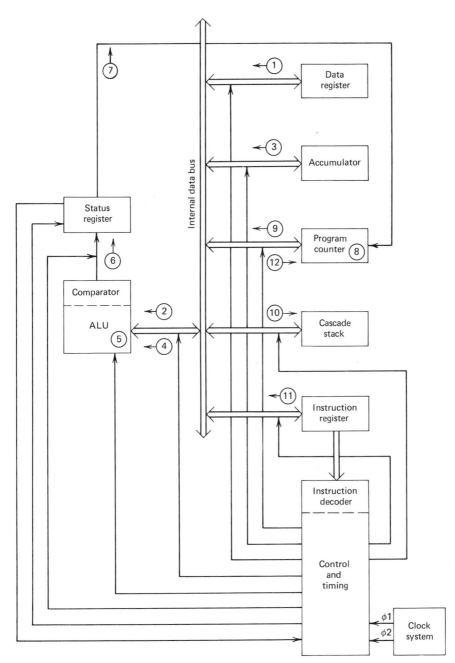

Figure 6-3 Microsequences involved in conditional BRANCH (direct addressing mode).

macroinstruction and pictorially show the microsequences involved in this operation. Load the final result into the accumulator.

Solution

Since the minuend is positive and larger than the subtrahend, which is negative and smaller, Rule 1 for binary subtraction in twos complement, (see Section 2-2.3) will apply. Also note that the complementer will not complement the MSB of the operand loaded into it, since it is the sign bit. The microsequences are shown next; Fig. 6-4 gives a graphical representation of them.

1.   Data register (+ minuend) → internal data bus.
2.   Internal data bus → adder.
3.   Accumulator (subtrahend) → internal data bus.
4.   Internal data bus → complementer.
5.   The complement operation (except MSB).
6.   Complementer → internal data bus.
7.   Internal data bus → Increment/Decrement register.
8.   The increment operation.
9.   Increment/decrement register → internal data bus.
10.   Internal data bus → adder.
11.   The add operation (this is really the subtraction process).
12.   Adder → internal data bus.
13.   Internal data bus → accumulator.   ∎

The MSB bits of both the data register and the accumulator are fed into the control and timing unit. These two signals, in conjunction with the operation code (O field) in the instruction, initiate and execute the microsequences in accordance with the previously mentioned Rule 1 for binary subtraction in twos complement.

6-4 GENERALIZED REALISTIC μP CPU

Up to now, for simplicity, we have only considered certain portions of the μP that were pertinent to the solutions of particular problems. Other portions were temporarily ignored. We will now cover some of them.

6-4.1 The Scratch-pad Memory

Although it is possible to provide an external RAM chip that could be used as a scratch pad, most μPs have some built-in registers right on the CPU chip

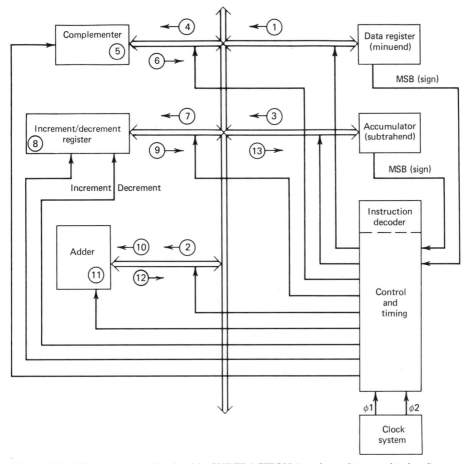

Figure 6-4 Microsequences involved in SUBTRACTION (+ minuend > − subtrahend).

that are used for this purpose. Such an approach has both advantages and disadvantages.

1. Advantages
   (a) Scratch-pad registers' access speeds are compatible with the rest of the CPU speeds.
   (b) Direct addressing by the **A** field of the instruction can be used with the appropriate code in the **M** field.
   (c) Being located on the CPU chip reduces the need for additional package pins for external connections.
   (d) Saves on cost, since additional memory chips are not needed for scratch pad use.

2. Disadvantages
    (a) Only a limited number of scratch pad registers are available (4 to 8 in most cases).
    (b) Programmer must keep track of which registers are used and make sure that subsequent instructions do not accidentally destroy information in them.
    (c) More frequent loading and unloading of information into the limited number of registers will require additional instructions and thereby lengthen the program.

6-4.2 The Index Register

In Chapter Five we described the indexed mode of addressing. Not all μPs have this mode of addressing, but many do. A more realistic μP CPU should include this register.

6-4.3 The Cascade Stack

Although several μCs use the *pointer-type* stack for saving return addresses from BRANCH operations, the *cascade* stack is often used in μPs. In previous diagrams the cascade stack was shown communicating directly with the internal data bus (Fig. 6-5a). If used in this manner there is a definite disadvantage. For both the *push* and the *pop* operations, the internal data bus is tied up and thus not available for any other use. Recall that the only functional block in the CPU with which the cascade stack communicates is the program counter. Consequently, it would be very desirable to have a special, dedicated, bidirectional bus connecting the cascade stack to the program counter directly (fig. 6-5b). Such a procedure would allow the internal data bus to be used for other CPU operations, while the program counter and the cascade stack are involved in push-pop operations. This would increase the speed of the CPU. Many 8-bit μPs use either a 12- or 16-bit address for accessing the program memory. Transfers between the stack and the program counter would have to be performed in two steps through the 8-bit internal data bus, if that scheme is used. The CPU time is doubled for push and pop operations. This could be avoided using the scheme shown in Fig. 6-5b by making the dedicated bus either 12 or 16 bits wide, as appropriate.

6-4.4 Communicating with the Shared Address Bus

The CPU generates and transfers three types of addresses to the external parts of the system.

1. The address of the instruction to be fetched from the program memory (usually the ROM chips).

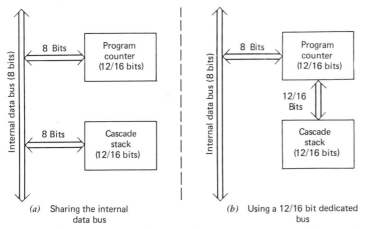

Figure 6-5 Communication between the program counter and the cascade stack.

2. The address of the data memory location to be accessed for read/write operations (the RAM chips).
3. The address of the I/O devices to be accessed for read/write operations (the I/O chips).

In μCs the memories and the I/O devices are treated alike by the CPU. A common address bus is shared for all three types of addresses. Two functional blocks within the CPU must communicate with the shared address bus: the *program counter* and the *address register*. This requires some means of *multiplexing* information bits from either of these two blocks on to the address bus. We previously stated that addresses always originate *in* the CPU as the source and that they are always sent out *from* the CPU. This makes the shared address bus a *unidirectional* bus. This is true in normal operations, but in some instances addresses could be transferred to the CPU for further processing or modification. Thus the shared addresss bus may also be considered *bidirectional* in some cases. Figure 6-6 shows how this is handled with a *multiplexer/demultiplexer* in the μP CPU.

6-4.5 Communicating with the Shared Data Bus

The CPU receives the instruction word and transfers data to or from the various I/O devices and RAM chips through a bidirectional *shared data* bus. The point of entry into or exit from the CPU for these data can be either an accumulator or a special register, called the *data register*. Let us assume that the μP under discussion has a data register. In many μPs this register will communicate with the *internal data bus* as well as with the adder. In this case another dedicated bus is required (Fig. 6-7) because the ALU often receives one or

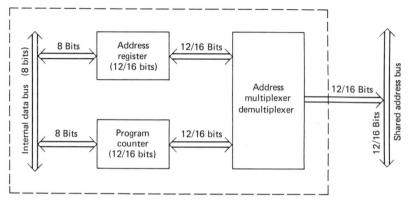

Figure 6-6 Communication between the CPU and the shared address bus.

more operands from I/O devices that may be slower than the CPU. The ALU could, likewise, transmit processed data to slower memory or I/O chips. Providing a dedicated bus between the ALU and the data register frees the internal data bus for other internal CPU transfers during this time, thereby speeding up the overall µP operation. Such operation of the data register, therefore, requires the use of another multiplexer/demultiplexer (Fig. 6-7). By this means the logic blocks in the rest of the CPU can communicate with the *shared data*

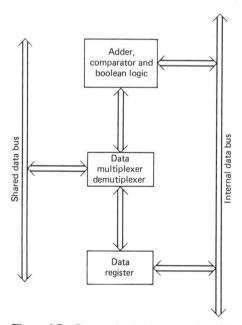

Figure 6-7 Communication between the CPU and the shared data bus.

bus (through the data register and the data multiplexer/demultiplexer), completely bypassing the adder/Comparator/Boolean logic block. Likewise, the adder block can also communicate directly with the internal data bus.

6-4.6 Realistic, Typical μP CPU Block Diagram

We can now discuss a realistic μP CPU, as shown in Fig. 6-8. It is typical of several μPs on the market today. In Fig. 6-8 note that:

1. The five functional blocks shown in dotted lines are generally considered as the ALU. Most of the arithmetic and the logical or Boolean operations are performed in these blocks.
2. Although the clock system is shown as being external to the CPU, advances in semiconductor technology have made it possible to put this on the same chip as the CPU (with the exception of the crystal that regulates the primary frequency source). Future μPs may have the entire clock system on the CPU chip.
3. The *accumulator* is *not* included in the ALU group. Very often it is considered as part of the ALU. For the time being we will consider the accumulator separately, as shown in Fig. 6-8.
4. The same comments in point 3 are also applicable to the *index register*.

6-4.7 The Control Unit and Control Signals

6-4.7.1 Control Signals Functions The CPU of Fig. 6-8 must be controlled by the control and timing unit so that it may perform the function(s) commanded by each instruction in the instruction register and subsequently decoded by the instruction decoder in the control unit. Three types of controlling signals, emanating from the control unit, are:

1. *ALU Initiate (AL) Signals*. These signals initiate activity in the appropriately selected functional blocks within the CPU. Some of these are to complement the contents of the complementer or right/left shift the contents in the shifter.
2. *Data Transfer (DT) Signals*. These signals control the access of each of the functional blocks in the CPU to the internal data bus and to the shared data and the shared address busses. For operations involving double-length data/address/instruction words, separate DT signals are used to indicate transfers of the upper or lower half of the word.
3. *Mode Control (MC) Signals*. These signals signify to the CPU whether an ALU operation or a data transfer operation is involved. In the case of data transfer, they indicate whether the transfer is *into* a certain functional block or *out of* it.

For each microsequence resulting from a decoded macroinstruction, all three signals must be issued by the control unit. These clearly specify the functional

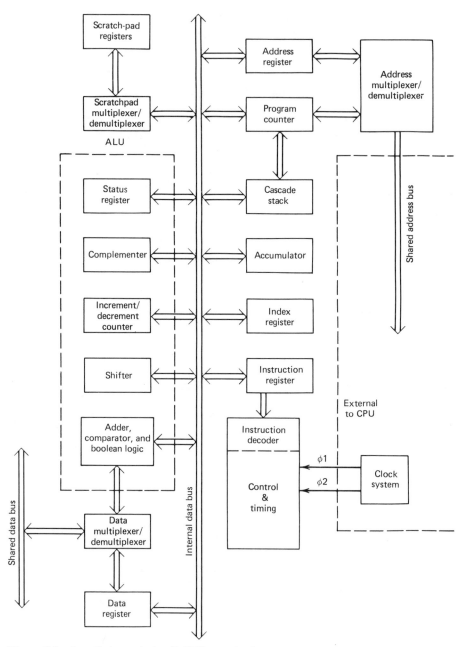

Figure 6-8   A realistic, typical, μP CPU organization.

block involved, the transfer and its direction, and the ALU function initiated (if applicable). During data transfers, all ALU operations are *inhibited*. Conversely, during ALU operations, all *data transfers* are inhibited.

6-4.7.2 Data Transfer Control Logic

6-4.7.2 Data Transfer Control Logic It is assumed that readers know how such ALU functions (shift, complement, add, etc.) are initiated in binary from previous digital logic courses. These are not covered in this chapter. But students should know how the data transfer signals and the mode control signals operate. Most students also wonder how the bidirectional and unidirectional busses operate. These are now described.

Let us assume that we have two registers, A and B, in the CPU; both are 8 bits long and both are bidirectional. They are connected to an 8-bit internal data bus (Fig. 6-9).

The ALU initiate (AL), the mode control (MC), and the data transfer (DT) signals are shown in Table 6-1 for simple transfers between these two registers.

The mode code (MC) signals are composed of two binary signals that are generated by the control unit. These two signals are called control signals (CS). How they affect the mode codes is shown in Table 6-2.

The logic involved in the data transfers is shown in Fig. 6-10. For simplicity we will consider only 1 flip-flop, flip-flop 0, from each of the registers, connected to only 1 line, line 0, of the internal data bus. Every flip-flop of every register will have 2, 4-input AND gates; each of these will be connected to the respective line in the internal data bus in an exactly similar manner as for flip-flop 0.

One input of each AND gate is inverted and therefore is active *low*. The CS1 and CS2 signals from the control unit are fed into these inputs of all

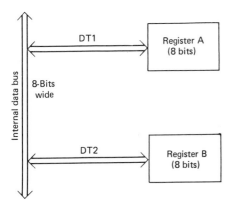

Figure 6-9 Bidirectional data transfers between registers A and B.

Table 6-1   CONTROL SIGNAL DEFINITIONS

Signals	Definitions
ALO	Inhibit all ALU operations
DT0	Inhibit all data transfers
DT1	Register A $\leftrightarrow$ internal data bus transfers
DT2	Register B $\leftrightarrow$ internal data bus transfers
MC0	No data transfers involved, ALU operations only
MC1	Transfer direction, register $\rightarrow$ internal data bus
MC2	Transfer direction, internal data bus $\rightarrow$ register

ANDs associated with each flip-flop. They control the direction of bit flow to and from the internal data bus. Also note that D-type flip-flops are generally used and so only 1 data input line is required. Also, the output signal need only be taken from one side of each flip-flop. (For simplicity, the clock signal lines are not shown.)

The DT1 and DT2 signals from the control unit activate one of the two registers, A and B. They are gated through 2 AND gates, C and D, respectively, and these two gates are controlled by the DT0 signal. When the control unit sends a logical 1 on the DT0 line (to indicate that no data transfers are involved), gates C and D are disabled because of the inverter.

Two μinstructions are required for transfer of data from A to B or from B to A. Each μinstruction must include all three codes: AL, DT and MC. These μinstructions are shown next.

Transfer, register A $\rightarrow$ register B

1. AL0, DT1, MC1—register A $\rightarrow$ internal data bus
2. AL0, DT2, MC2—internal data bus $\rightarrow$ register B

Transfer, register B $\rightarrow$ register A

1. AL0, DT2, MC1—register B $\rightarrow$ internal data bus
2. AL0, DT1, MC2—internal data bus $\rightarrow$ register A

Table 6-2   MODE CONTROL SIGNALS AND CODES

Mode Code	Control Signals CS2	CS1	Functions
M0	0	0	No data transfers (only ALU operations)
M1	0	1	Register $\rightarrow$ internal data bus
M2	1	0	Internal data bus $\rightarrow$ register
—	1	1	Invalid code; ignore; control unit will not issue this code

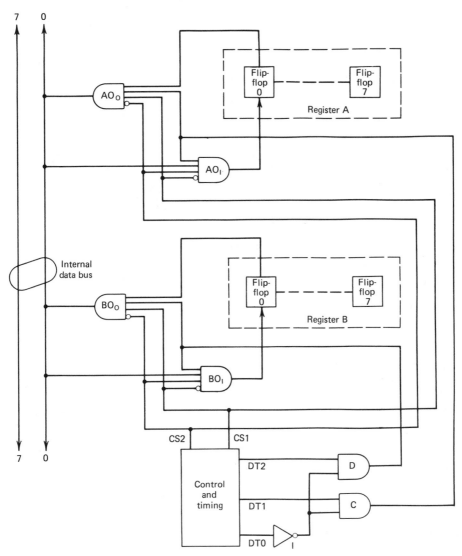

Figure 6-10   Example of data transfer control logic.

6-5 MICROPROGRAMMING A μP CPU

6-5.1 The CPU Features and the Block Diagram

The realistic, typical μP CPU of Fig. 6-8 is now expanded with some more features, as shown in Fig. 6-11. Note the following features of this μP, which is called LEO.

1. All functional blocks are 8 bits long with the following exceptions.
   (a) The address register (16 bits).

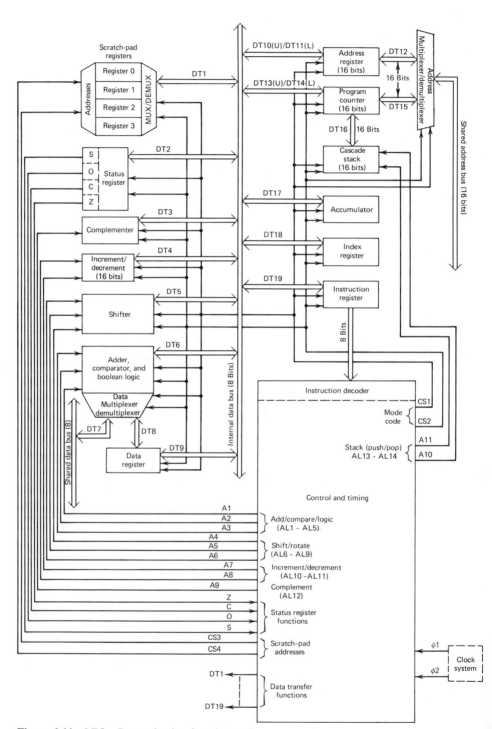

Figure 6-11 LEO μP organization for μinstructions.

(b) The program counter (16 bits).

(c) The cascade stack (LIFO type) (16 bits).

(d) The increment/decrement counter (16 bits).

2. The shared data bus is 8 bits wide.

3. The shared address bus is 16 bits wide.

4. All internal data busses are 8 bits wide with the exception of the three dedicated busses identified as DT12, DT15, and DT16, which are 16 bits wide.

5. Data transfers between the 8-bit internal data bus and the 16-bit address register/ program counter are accomplished in two steps; the upper byte is always transferred and accepted first, followed by the lower byte.

6. A 2-phase clock system is used.

7. The mode control signals are identified as CS1 and CS2, as issued by the control unit.

8. Addresses for the 4-register scratch-pad memory are identified by the two signals CS3 and CS4.

9. All data transfer control signals are identified as DT1 to DT19 and correspond to the respective internal busses.

10. The control signals that initiate and operate the various CPU functional blocks are identified as AL1 to AL14. For convenience, these lines are shown as A1 to A11 coming out of the control unit.

11. The following 4 status flags are used, and the outputs of these are fed into the control unit. For simplicity, inputs to the status register from several functional blocks are not shown.

(a) Sign flag (S).

(b) Overflow flag (O).

(c) Carry flag (C).

(d) Zero flag (Z).

6-5.2 The Mode Control Signals

The mode control signals for the LEO μP are given in Table 6-3.

6-5.3 The ALU Function Initiate Signals

We have seen that the mode code and the scratch-pad addresses are made up of control signals identified as the CS signals. These signals are generated by the instruction decoder in the control unit and result from a combination of the macroinstruction (from the instruction register) and inputs from the status register, if any. In the LEO μP there is a total of 13 such CS signals that are generated by the instruction decoder (see Fig. 6-12). CS3 and CS4 are used for addressing the scratch-pad registers as shown in Table 6-4.

Four of the CS signals, CS5 to CS9, are further decoded into 14 more code

Table 6-3 MODE CONTROL SIGNALS FOR THE LEO μP

| Mode Code | Control Signals | | Functions |
	CS2	CS1	
M0	0	0	No data transfers (only ALU and functions operations)
M1	0	1	Register → internal data bus Address MUX/DEMUX → address register/program counter Data MUX/DEMUX → data register/shared data bus
M2	1	0	Internal data bus → registers Address register/program counter → address MUX/DEMUX Data register/shared data bus → data MUX/DEMUX
—	1	1	Invalid code (ignore; control unit will not issue this code)

combinations by the ALU function decoder and logic (Fig. 6-12) and are available on a total of 11 output lines, A1 to A11, from the control unit, as shown in Fig. 6-11. The output line functions and their respective codes are shown in Table 6-5.

6-5.4 The Data Transfer Signals

From Fig. 6-12 it is seen that five control signals, generated by the instruction decoder, CS9 to CS13, are further decoded into 19 data transfer signals identified as DT1 to DT19. As previously explained, each of these signals will connect the functional block in Fig. 6-11 to the corresponding busses or multiplexers/demultiplexers. Table 6-6 shows the control codes involved in each of the data transfer functions.

Table 6-4 SCRATCH-PAD REGISTER ADDRESSES

| Address Signals | | Scratch-pad Registers |
CS4	CS3	
0	0	Register 0
0	1	Register 1
1	0	Register 2
1	1	Register 3

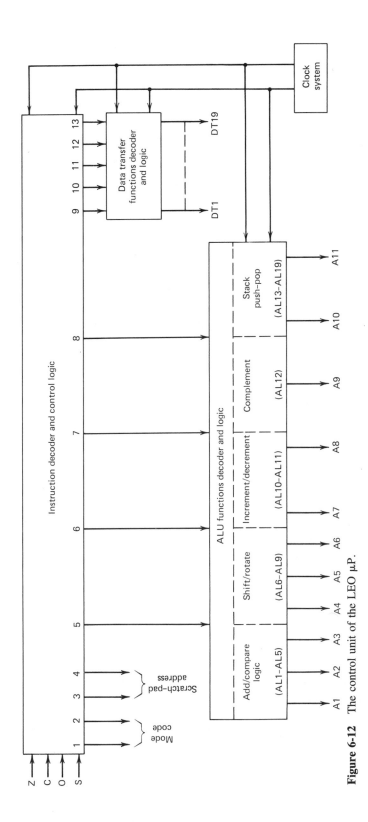

Figure 6-12 The control unit of the LEO μP.

169

Table 6-5 ALU FUNCTION INITIATE CODES

Function Mnemonic	Control Signal Codes				ALU Functions
	CS8	CS7	CS6	CS5	
AL 0	0	0	0	0	Inhibit all ALU operations (data transfers)
AL 1	0	0	0	1	Initiate ADD operation
AL 2	0	0	1	0	Initiate COMPARE function
AL 3	0	0	1	1	Initiate AND function
AL 4	0	1	0	0	Initiate OR function
AL 5	0	1	0	1	Initiate exclusive-OR function (X-OR)
AL 6	0	1	1	0	Right shift logical
AL 7	0	1	1	1	Left shift logical
AL 8	1	0	0	0	Right rotate
AL 9	1	0	0	1	Left rotate
AL10	1	0	1	0	INCREMENT counter
AL11	1	0	1	1	DECREMENT counter
AL12	1	1	0	0	Initiate COMPLEMENT function
AL13	1	1	0	1	Initiate stack PUSH operation
AL14	1	1	1	0	Initiate stack POP operation
AL15	1	1	1	1	Invalid code

6-6 EXAMPLES OF MICROPROGRAMMING THE LEO μP

The following examples will show how the LEO CPU executes macroinstructions. Before attempting to code each microsequence, it is important to make a clear, concise and unambiguous statement of the problem involved. This could be done symbolically. Each macroinstruction will, very likely, involve several substeps. Each substep will require one or more μinstructions. Remember that every μinstruction *must* include all of the CS signals discussed previously. For uniformity and conformity to the formats used in Tables 6-3 to 6-6, we will write the μinstruction codes in descending order, (i.e., from CS13 to CS1). Remember that each μinstruction must contain binary bits for all 13 CS signals. In some cases we will show XX for CS1 and CS2. This means that the binary bits here could be any combination of 1s and 0s, and they will not affect the execution of the μinstruction involved. For scratch-pad addresses we will use the designation SCAD. Thus the order of mnemonic writing for the μinstruction will be:

- DT code.
- AL code.
- SCAD code.
- M code.

Table 6-6   DATA TRANSFER-INITIATE CODES

Function Mnemonic	Control Signal Code					Data Transfer Functions
	CS13	CS12	CS11	CS10	CS9	
DT0	0	0	0	0	0	Inhibit all data transfers (ALU operations only)
DT1	0	0	0	0	1	Scratch-pad registers ↔ internal data bus
DT2	0	0	0	1	0	Status register ↔ internal data bus
DT3	0	0	0	1	1	Complementer ↔ internal data bus
DT4	0	0	1	0	0	INCREMENT/DECREMENT counter ↔ internal data bus
DT5	0	0	1	0	1	Shifter ↔ internal data bus
DT6	0	0	1	1	0	Adder/comparator/logic ↔ internal data bus
DT7	0	0	1	1	1	Data MUX/DEMUX ↔ shared address bus
DT8	0	1	0	0	0	Data MUX/DEMUX ↔ data register
DT9	0	1	0	0	1	Data register ↔ internal data bus
DT10(U)	0	1	0	1	0	Address register (upper byte) ↔ internal data bus
DT11(L)	0	1	0	1	1	Address register (lower byte) ↔ internal data bus
DT12	0	1	1	0	0	Address register ↔ address MUX/DEMUX
DT13(U)	0	1	1	0	1	Program counter (upper byte) ↔ internal data bus
DT14(L)	0	1	1	1	0	Program counter (lower byte) ↔ internal data bus
DT15	0	1	1	1	1	Program counter ↔ address MUX/DEMUX
DT16	1	0	0	0	0	Program counter ↔ cascade stack
DT17	1	0	0	0	1	Accumulator ↔ internal data bus
DT18	1	0	0	1	0	Index register ↔ internal data bus
DT19	1	0	0	1	1	Instruction register ↔ internal data bus
DT20	1	0	1	0	0	Invalid Codes
DT31	1	1	1	1	1	

Example 6-5

The macroinstruction in the instruction register of the LEO μP is a transfer instruction symbolically stated as:

(Register 2) → index register

Write down the microsequences involved in the execution of this instruction. Show both the mnemonic codes and the CS signal codes.

Solution

This problem calls for transferring the contents of the scratch-pad register 2 into the index register. In this operation, two separate microsequences are involved. The first step will transfer the contents of register 2 to the internal data bus, and the second one will transfer the data on the internal data bus into the index register. The μinstructions are shown in the table. Note that the internal data bus is abbreviated as IDB. We will use abbreviations wherever we can.

		Microinstructions									
		CS Signals									
		DT Codes				AL Codes				Scad		M Codes
Functions	*Mnemonics*	*13 12 11 10 9*	*8 7 6 5*	*4 3*	*2 1*
1. Register 2 → IDB	DT1, AL0, 10, M1	0 0 0 0 1	0 0 0 0	1 0	0 1
2. IDB → index register	DT18, AL0, XX, M2	1 0 0 1 0	0 0 0 0	X X	1 0

To simplify the process of writing the μinstructions, students should follow the given procedure in the given sequence.

1. Fill in all the microsequence steps involved in each macroinstruction in the Functions column.
2. Then refer to Fig. 6-11 and Table 6-6 and write down the DT mnemonic and the corresponding CS binary code for each microsequence step.
3. Next fill out the AL mnemonic and its equivalent CS code for each microsequence by referring to Table 6-5.
4. Follow the same procedure for both the SCAD and the M codes by referring to Tables 6-4 and 6-3.

Example 6-6

The macroinstruction in the instruction register of the LEO μP is an ALU type instruction which is symbolically stated as:

(Address register + 1) → address register

Write down the microsequence involved in the execution of this instruction. Show both mnemonic codes and the μinstructions codes.

Solution

This example calls for incrementing the contents of the address register. To do this we must first transfer the contents of the address register in 2 bytes to the INCREMENT/DECREMENT counter, increment this counter, and then transfer the contents from the counter back into the address register, also 1 byte at a time. The μinstructions are shown here. The INCREMENT/DECREMENT counter is abbreviated as I/D for this example.

		Microinstructions										
		CS Signals										
		DT Codes				AL Codes				Scad	M Codes	
Functions	Mnemonic	13 12 11 10 9				8 7 6 5				4 3	2	1
1. Address register (U) → IDB	DT10, AL0, XX, M1	0 1 0 1 0				0 0 0 0				X X	0	1
2. IDB → I/D counter	DT4, AL0, XX, M2	0 0 1 0 0				0 0 0 0				X X	1	0
3. Address register (L) → IDB	DT11, AL0, XX, M1	0 1 0 1 1				0 0 0 0				X X	0	1
4. IDB → I/D counter	DT14, AL0, XX, M2	0 0 1 0 0				0 0 0 0				X X	1	0
5. INCREMENT I/D counter	DT0, AL10, XX, M0	0 0 0 0 0				1 0 1 0				X X	0	0
6. I/D counter → IDB	DT4, AL0, XX, M1	0 0 1 0 0				0 0 0 0				X X	0	1
7. IDB → Address register (U)	DT10, AL0, XX, M2	0 1 0 1 0				0 0 0 0				X X	1	0
8. I/D counter → IDB	DT4, AL0, XX, M1	0 0 1 0 0				0 0 0 0				X X	0	1
9. IDB → Address register (L)	DT11, AL0, XX, M2	0 1 0 1 1				0 0 0 0				X X	1	0

■

In Examples 6-5 and 6-6 we have shown the μinstructions for each of the microsequences. These examples will show students how simple microprograms are constructed. The rest of the examples in this chapter are more complex but are readily handled by following the same procedures as those used for Examples 6-5 and 6-6. For simplifying the procedures for these examples, we will not require the detailed binary CS codes for each microstep. We will work only with the *mnemonic* codes.

Example 6-7

The macroinstruction in the instruction register of the LEO μP calls out for an unconditional JUMP that can be symbolically stated as:

1. (Instruction register) + (program counter) → program counter
2. Program counter → address MUX/DEMUX

Write down the microsequences involved in the execution of this macroinstruction using only the mnemonic codes. Assume the following points.

1. The macroinstruction consists of 2 bytes: byte 1 is the OP code and byte 2 is the JUMP address.
2. Byte 2 is now sitting in the instruction register, and only this byte will be used in this operation.
3. Both bytes from the program counter must be used in this particular operation. But the logic of the LEO CPU is designed such that the byte from the instruction register will be treated only as the lower byte when adding it to the 2 bytes of the program counter.

Solution

This operation requires the use of the 16-bit adder. We will first transfer both bytes of the program counter into the adder and then the contents of the instruction register. The instruction register now contains byte 2, which is the modifier and is to be added to the program counter contents. Note that this macroinstruction uses the program counter relative mode of addressing.

	Functions	*Mnemonics*			
1.	Program counter (U) → IDB	DT13(U)	AL0	XX	M1
2.	IDB → adder	DT6	AL0	XX	M2
3.	Program counter (L) → IDB	DT14(L)	AL0	XX	M1
4.	IDB → adder	DT6	AL0	XX	M2
5.	Instrument register → IDB	DT19	AL0	XX	M1
6.	IDB → adder	DT6	AL0	XX	M2
7.	Initiate ADD operation	DT0	AL1	XX	M0
8.	Adder (U) → IDB	DT6	AL0	XX	M1
9.	IDB → program counter (U)	DT13(U)	AL0	XX	M2
10.	Adder (L) → IDB	DT6	AL0	XX	M1
11.	IDB → program counter (L)	DT14(L)	AL0	XX	M2
12.	Program counter (U and L) → MUX/ DEMUX	DT15	AL0	XX	M2

Example 6-8

A fairly complex macroinstruction in the instruction register of the LEO μP calls for an incoming data word (from a peripheral unit) to be subtracted from the contents of scratch-pad register 0; the result is to be added to the previous contents of the accumulator. First, symbolically show the major steps involved. Then write down the microsequences involved in this operation using only the mnemonics.

Solution

The symbolic representations of the major steps are as follows.

(Register 0) → adder
(Shared data bus) → data MUX/DEMUX
(Data MUX/DEMUX) → data register
(Data register) → complementer
Initiate COMPLEMENT function
(Complementer) → adder
Initiate adder function
(Adder) → ACC

	Functions	Mnemonics			
1.	Register 0 → IDB	DT1	AL0	XX	M1
2.	IDB → adder	DT6	AL0	XX	M2
3.	Shared data bus → data MUX/DEMUX	DT7	AL0	XX	M2
4.	Data MUX/DEMUX → data register	DT8	AL0	XX	M1
5.	Data register → IDB	DT9	AL0	XX	M1
6.	IDB → complementer	DT3	AL0	XX	M2
7.	Initiate COMPLEMENT function	DT0	AL12	XX	M0
8.	Complementer → IDB	DT3	AL0	XX	M1
9.	IDB → adder	DT6	AL0	XX	M2
10.	Initiate ADD function	DT0	AL1	XX	M0
11.	Adder → IDB	DT6	AL0	XX	M1
12.	IDB → ACC	DT17	AL0	XX	M2

■

6-7 THE MICROPROGRAMMABLE MACHINE

6-7.1 The Control Memory

From the preceding discussions and the examples, it is apparent that each macroinstruction is a composite of several μinstructions that the control unit then executes. These microsequences are hard-wired into the logic of the control unit, and they are not accessible to users externally. Therefore the user or the programmer must work with the set of macroinstructions provided by the μC manufacturer. Such a machine is said to be *nonmicroprogrammable*.

From Fig. 6-12 it is seen that the inputs to the instruction decoder and control logic, from the instruction register, are in *binary* form. Each such macroinstruction input results in a series of μinstructions that are also in binary form and are identified as CS signals. These μinstructions could be stored in a ROM chip in the desired sequence instead of in hard-wired logic. The macroinstruction would then specify the starting address of its respective group of μinstructions and a special counter, called the microprogram sequencer, would automatically increment the starting address, similar to the familiar program counter when executing either the main program or a subroutine. Such a computer is called a *microprogrammable computer*.

The ROM chip(s) of a microprogrammable CPU is called a control ROM or a CROM. The CROM essentially replaces most of the hard-wired hardware in the conventional control unit. In a microprogrammable machine the μinstructions can be arranged in the desired sequence by the programmer. In other words, the programmer can create a personal set of macroinstructions by sequencing several groups of μinstructions. This capability gives the programmer a high degree of flexibility, and microprograms can be created to perform specific tasks much more efficiently than with a set of fixed macroinstructions available in a nonmicroprogrammable computer. The general scheme of a microprogrammable computer is shown in Fig. 6-13.

6-7.2 Advantages and Disadvantages

6-7.2.1 Advantages
1. A microprogrammable computer is very flexible. Within reasonable limits, the programmer can create a personal set of macroinstructions that can be tailored to perform a specific task.
2. Hard-wired logic is generally more expensive and eats up a lot of real estate on the silicon chip. Costs of memory chips are continuously going down. Replacing higher-cost hard-wired logic with lower-cost CROMS can be cost effective. Also, the area on the chip that would be released by the CROM could be gainfully used to include more computing capabilities in the machine.
3. By replacing CROM(s) with other CROM(s) that contain different groups of μinstructions, the machine can be virtually reconfigured for each specific task, thus making it more efficient.
4. With microprogramming, it is possible for the machine to emulate other existing computers. This means that with a microprogrammable machine A, the programmer will be able to create a set of macroinstructions that will be exactly like that of another machine B.

6-7.2.2 Disadvantages
1. The initial programming costs are higher, since the programmer has to write down and debug a separate subroutine for each macroinstruction instead of dealing with just one macroinstruction at a time.

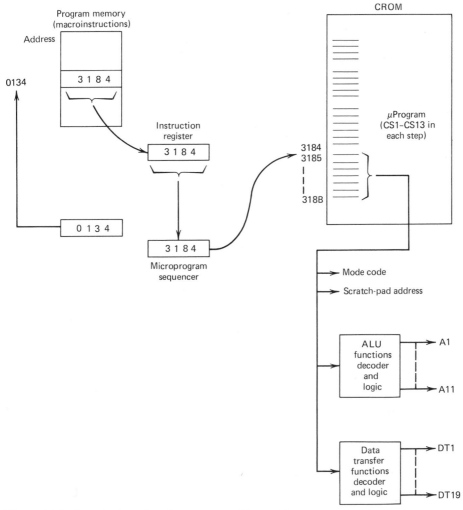

Figure 6-13   Organization of a microprogrammable machine.

2. The programmer must have a reasonable degree of familiarity and proficiency with the hardware (in addition to the software) involved.

3. Many programmers are not familiar with microprogramming techniques and therefore tend to avoid it.

6-8 SUMMARY

The CTU of any computer is complex. Because of this, most texts avoid a detailed discussion of it. This chapter (1) took away some of the mystery surrounding the CTU, and (2) at the same time, presented a realistic and reasonably typical model of the hardware architecture of a μP CPU. Advances in semiconductor technology will undoubtedly add more features to the CPU in the future. Nevertheless, the LEO μP incorporates most of the basic hardware features of today's μP CPU. The microsequence examples gave students a basic understanding of how macroinstructions are broken down into a series of substeps or μinstructions, how they are executed, and what is accomplished at each step.

6-9 REVIEW QUESTIONS

6-1   State the four major functions performed by the CTU of a computer.

6-2   Enumerate the four steps involved in fetching the instruction from the program memory.

6-3   What function is performed by the machine language code of the macroinstruction, consisting of 1s and 0s, in the CPU?

6-4   In the CANCER μP (Fig. 6-2) the current instruction calls for an unconditional BRANCH to a subroutine. As compared to the unconditional JUMP instruction of Example 6-2, how many more μinstructions will be required if the direct addressing mode is used?

6-5   Refer to the CANCER μP (Fig. 6-2) and explain why it is necessary to transfer the contents of the **A** field in the instruction to the program counter first instead of directly to the address register only.

6-6   Is it desirable to have scratch-pad memory registers right on the CPU chip? If so, what are the advantages?

6-7   List some of the shortcomings of having scratch-pad memory registers on the same chip as the CPU.

6-8   Explain why a dedicated bus is provided for connecting the cascade stack to the program counter.

6-9   What chips in the μC system are addressed by the addresses generated and transferred by the CPU?

6-10   Refer to Fig. 6-7 of the CANCER μP. It is observed that the shared data bus is able to communicate with the internal data bus through two different routes. Explain why. State the advantages, if there are any.

6-11   Refer to the realistic, typical μP CPU organization of Fig. 6-8 and briefly describe the three categories of signals required to control it.

6-12   The data transfer control logic is shown in Fig. 6-10. The CTU puts out the following control signals: CS1 = 1; CS2 = 0; DT0 = 0; DT1 = 0; and DT2 = 1. Answer the following questions with these signal conditions present.
(a) Is this an ALU operation or a data transfer operation?

(b) Is register A or register B involved in this operation?

(c) Is the transfer in or out of the register involved?

6-13 Refer to Question 6-12 and the control signals given there and indicate the logical outputs of the following logical blocks.

(a) $I = ?$

(b) $C = ?$

(c) $BO_I = ?$

(d) $BO_O = ?$

(e) $AO_I = ?$

(f) $AO_O = ?$

6-14 Again refer to the data transfer control logic in Fig. 6-11. If the instruction calls for a transfer of data from the internal data bus into register A, what would be required for the following control signals and outputs of logical blocks?

(a) $CS1 = ?$

(b) $CS2 = ?$

(c) $DT1 = ?$

(d) $DT2 = ?$

(e) $BO_I = ?$

(f) $BO_O = ?$

(g) $AO_I = ?$

(h) $AO_O = ?$

6-10 PROBLEMS AND EXERCISES

6-1 The macroinstruction in the instruction register of the LEO μP is a transfer instruction symbolically stated as:

(ACC) → shifter

Write down the microsequences involved in the execution of this instruction. Show both the mnemonic codes and the CS signal codes.

6-2 The macroinstruction in the instruction register of the LEO μP is an unconditional SKIP that can be symbolically stated as:

(a) (Program counter) + 2 → program counter

(b) (Program counter) → address MUX/DEMUX

Write down the microsequences for the execution of this instruction, showing both the mnemonic and the CS signal codes. (Note. The + sign in the symbolic statement represents arithmetic addition and not a logical OR function.)

6-3 The CPU of the LEO μP is initialized by a subroutine that clears all CPU register/counter/adder, and so on except the scratch-pad registers, to the 0. The instructions in the main program, following this subroutine, call for the sum of the contents of the scratch-pad registers 1, 2, and 3 to be loaded into the index register.

(a) Show the steps involved in this operation symbolically.

(b) Write the microsequences using only the mnemonics.

6-4   The LEO μP is executing a subroutine, and the very last macroinstruction is now inserted in the instruction register.
(a) Symbolically show the steps involved in the execution of this instruction.
(b) Write the μinstructions involved using only the mnemonics.

6-5   The current instruction (0391) calls for complementing the contents of the accumulator. The next instruction (0392) is a conditional SKIP, SKIP if (ACC) = −ve. Instruction 0393 calls for transferring the contents of the accumulator to scratch-pad register 2. Instruction 0394 calls for transferring the contents of the accumulator to an external peripheral I/O device. Symbolically show the steps involved in this operation if the original 8-bit contents of the accumulator were 10011101.

6-6   Refer to Problem 6-5 and the conditions present in it. Write down the μinstructions involved in this operation using only the mnemonics.

6-7   Refer to the instruction in Problem 6-5. Assume that the original contents of the accumulator are 01010101 and do the following.
(a) Symbolically show the various steps involved.
(b) Indicate what bits the peripheral I/O device will receive, if any.
(c) Write down the μinstructions for this operation using only the mnemonics.

6-8   The accumulator of the LEO μP contains 01011001. The scratch-pad registers contain the following operands.
REG 0 = 11011110
REG 1 = 11000001
REG 2 = 01001010
REG 3 = 01011101
The following instructions are executed:
No.
3814   REG 2 ⟶ ACC
3815   REG 3 ⟶ ACC
3816   JUMP (4190) if ACC = 0
Indicate whether the following control lines into the CTU will be 0 or 1 when instructions 3816, 3817, and 3818 are executed.
(a) Z = ?
(b) C = ?
(c) O = ?
(d) S = ?

7
MICROCOMPUTER MEMORIES

7-1 INTRODUCTION

7-1.1 Microcomputer Memory Philosophy

In addition to low cost, μPs have the inherent advantages of low weight, small size or volume, and low power consumption. Therefore the use of large, bulky, power-consuming memories is physically incompatible for use with μCs. Most applications, where μCs can be effectively used, are such that they require memories of modest size, usually 4 to 8 bytes. If larger storage capacities are needed, auxiliary memories such as disks or tapes can be used. As technology advances, μCs will undoubtedly use and require larger memories. At the present time, 64K memories are available. Even larger memories, 128K and over, are planned for the future.

7-1.2 Chip Memories

Semiconductor memories are almost exclusively used in μCs. Their weight, volume, and low power consumption make them compatible with μPs and suitable in μC systems. Semiconductor memories, often called chip memories, utilize both bipolar and MOS/CMOS technologies and perform different functions. Before we consider memories, we will define some terms associated with them.

7-2 DEFINITIONS OF MEMORY TYPES

1. *Volatile Memory*. A memory in which the original binary information is *destroyed* if the power is turned OFF or even momentarily interrupted. When power is **181**

restored, all bit locations in the memory will have either a 1 or a 0, but this pattern will not be the same as the original, preinterruption pattern.

2. *Nonvolatile Memory*. A memory in which the original bit pattern is retained even when the power is temporarily interrupted or OFF. When power is restored, the original bit pattern remains.

3. *Destructive Readout (DRO)*. The process of reading out the binary information destroys the original information in some memories, which are called destructive read-out (DRO) memories. In order to retain the original binary information for future use, immediately after completion of the readout, the information is re-written in the same memory location. Magnetic core memories are typical examples of DRO memories. In core memories the read-out process consists of forcing all bit positions of the addressed word or byte to either the 1 or the 0 state and sensing the change in electrical signals, if any, in the output or sense circuits. The information is retained by following the *read* cycle with a *write* cycle.

4. *Nondestructive Readout (NDRO)*. In some memories the process of reading out does not destroy the original information. Such memories are called nondestructive read-out (NDRO) memories. Magnetic tapes and disks are examples of NDRO memories. NDRO memories could be nonvolatile, such as disks and tapes, or they could be volatile, such as semiconductor *read/write* memories.

5. *Sequentially Addressed Memories*. These memories in which it is necessary to go through all prior addresses on a fixed sequence before the desired location can be addressed. Magnetic tapes are examples. In such memories the access time for each location has to be different. A minimum time is required for the very first address and a maximum time for the last location. This group of memories usually are the NDRO, nonvolatile memories.

6. *Random Access Memories (RAMs)*. This class of memories is designed so that any word or byte (or even just a single bit in some cases) can be randomly accessed without going through the prior addresses. The principal feature of this class of memories is that the access time for all addresses in the memory is the *same*, regardless of the location. RAMS can be NDROs and nonvolatile, such as magnetic cores, or they could be NDROs and volatile, such as some semiconductor memories.

7. *Read/Write (R/W) Memories*. These are memories in which binary information can be written into or read from during the normal operation of the computer and under control of the computer. R/W memories can be RAMs or sequentially addressable memories, DRO or NDRO, and volatile or nonvolatile.

8. *Read-Only Memories (ROMs)*. These memories are designed so that information can only be read out of the addressed location during normal operation of the computer system. Information is written into ROMs either during the manufacturing process or written in by the user off-line by means of special equipment prior to inserting the chip in the computer system (see Section 7-3). ROMs are nonvolatile, NDRO, random access memories.

7-3 ROMS IN MICROCOMPUTERS

ROMs, fabricated in chip form by using semiconductor processes, are widely used in μC systems. These memory chips are available in slightly different forms, but their ultimate uses may be the same or similar. The differences stem from how the binary information is written into the chip.

7-3.1 ROMs

For ROM chips, the information to be written into each location is first determined by the user and supplied to the semiconductor manufacturer, either as a program listing (Fig. 7-1) or a truth table (Fig. 7-2). Hexadecimal notation is used for both the addresses and the 16-bit memory contents in each case. The manufacturer then fabricates a mask (or several masks, in many cases) which is used in the manufacturing process of the chips. Therefore such chips are often called mask-programmed ROMs. The main shortcoming of this approach is that mask fabrication is an expensive process, and they cannot be altered once they are fabricated. Consequently, any errors in the original program listing or subsequent additions or alterations would require completely new masks. The main advantage is that once an acceptable mask (and program) is produced, the process lends itself to the production of a large number of programmed chips at reasonable cost.

Address	Contents
0 6 0 4	3 7 8 A
0 6 0 5	1 1 9 4
0 6 0 6	F F 5 6
0 6 0 7	7 9 1 C
0 6 0 8	8 8 8 0
0 6 0 9	1 1 7 B
0 6 0 A	D D 3 2
0 6 0 B	E 4 D 6
⋮	⋮

Figure 7-1 Example of user-supplied program listing for mask-programmable ROM chips.

3 B 1 C	1 1 0 1	1 1 1 1	0 0 1 0	0 0 0 1
3 B 1 D	1 0 1 0	1 0 1 0	0 0 0 1	1 1 1 0
3 B 1 E	1 0 1 0	1 0 1 1	0 1 0 1	1 1 0 0
3 B 1 F	1 0 1 1	1 1 0 1	1 0 1 1	1 0 0 1
3 B 2 0	0 0 0 1	1 1 1 1	1 1 1 0	0 0 0 0
3 B 2 1	0 0 1 0	1 1 0 1	1 1 1 1	0 1 0 1
3 B 2 2	1 0 1 1	1 0 0 0	0 1 1 0	1 0 1 1
3 B 2 3	0 1 0 0	1 1 1 0	1 1 1 1	0 1 0 0
•	•	•	•	•
•	•	•	•	•
•	•	•	•	•
•	•	•	•	•

Figure 7-2   Example of user-supplied truth table for mask-programmable ROM chip.

7-3.2 PROMS

PROMS are programmable ROMS that can be programmed by the user in the field using special equipment. The manufacturer supplies the chip with all positions preset at either a 1 or a 0. Using special PROM programming equipment, the user applies pulses to the inputs to reflect the desired program, depending on the requirements. Standard PROMS usually have all 1s written into all locations. The standard PROM chips can be programmed only once. PROMS are more expensive than ROMS, but they provide the user with some flexibility that ROMS do not have.

7-3.3 EPROMS

EPROMS are erasable PROMS that are more expensive than PROMS but allow the user to erase the previous bit pattern on the chip and rewrite a different pattern. To erase the original information, the chip is removed from the circuit board and exposed to high-intensity, ultraviolet (UV) light for a period of time (15 to 20 minutes), as recommended by the manufacturer. The EPROM can be reprogrammed and reused an indefinite number of times if the chip is *not* overexposed to UV for extensive periods of time. To permit exposure of the chip to the UV rays, the chip is mounted in a package with a glass window on top. EPROMS *cannot* be *selectively* erased. When exposed to the UV rays, *all* bits on the chip are erased. EPROMS are particularly useful during the program development stages of a system.

7-3.4 EAROMS

EAROMs are electrically alterable ROMs. They do not require UV for erasure but are *directly* reprogrammed without having to be removed from the circuit board. Unlike EPROMs, which may require minutes for erasure and rewriting, EAROMs can be reprogrammed in milliseconds. Although the reprogramming speeds are not compatible with computer speeds, they are nonetheless faster and more convenient than other schemes. EAROMs are more expensive than EPROMs; since the technology is relatively new, their use is somewhat limited. In the future we expect that advances in technology will bring their cost down, improve their reliability and production yields, and thereby result in wider use.

The principal features of the four semiconductor read-only memories (ROMS) are summarized in Table 7-1.

7-3.5 The Use of ROMS

Today every μC uses at least one ROM chip. Most systems have *several* such chips. ROMS are used to store fixed programs, subroutines, microprograms, and even main programs in many cases. ROMS are particularly useful for storing mathematical tables such as trigonometric tables (sine, cosine, etc.), multiplication and division tables, logarithm and square root tables, and several systems programs (to be discussed later) such as assemblers, compilers, editors, monitors, and bootstrap loaders.

Table 7-1 PRINCIPAL FEATURES OF SEMICONDUCTOR ROMS

Features	*ROM*	*PROM*	*EPROM*	*EAROM*
1. Special mask required for programming?	Yes	No	No	No
2. Special equipment for programming by user?	No	Yes	Yes	Yes
3. Reprogramming capability available?	No	Only once	Yes	Yes
4. Chip removal required for reprogramming?	n/a	Yes	Yes	No
5. Selective reprogramming possible?	n/a	No	No	No
6. NDRO capability?	Yes	Yes	Yes	Yes
7. Nonvolatile capability?	Yes	Yes	Yes	Yes

Although RAMS can also be used for storing these items, in μCs ROMS are especially well suited for this purpose. Unlike large computing systems, which are installed in environmentally controlled locations with operating and maintenance personnel readily available at all times, most μC applications are such that proper facilities and maintenance personnel may not be readily available in the immediate vicinity. Thus, in a μC, if something goes wrong with the system, the information in an R/W memory could be erroneously altered or even totally erased. Such a catastrophic failure might be intolerable in many applications.

The ROM chip requires special equipment and set procedures for alteration or erasure. Information in it *cannot* be modified during normal operation of the system. Furthermore, semiconductor RAMs are generally volatile and, unless some power back-up system is provided, the information in it will be lost if power is interrupted. All ROMs are nonvolatile.

7-4 ORGANIZATION OF THE PROGRAM MEMORY

7-4.1 Introductory Comments

Generally, semiconductor memories (both ROMs and RAMs) can be organized in the same manner as other memories, such as magnetic cores or films, regardless of whether they are used either as *program* memories or *data* memories. However, certain characteristics of semiconductor memories make them more attractive for some applications than others. A R/W memory generally requires more logic hardware, external to the memory elements themselves, than read-only (ROM) memories. The reason is apparent. In ROMs the only logic circuitry required is for addressing and read-out purposes. In R/W memories logic circuitry is required for addressing and reading purposes and also for writing operations.

7-4.2 Word-Organized ROMs

In μCs the program memory usually consists of one or more ROM chips. Such chips are usually *word-organized* or two-dimensional (2D) memories. This means that a complete word of information (i.e., a complete instruction word in the case of the program memory) is available on each X-axis of the memory matrix. This is shown in Fig. 7-3 for a program memory of 1024 words by 8 bits per word. Each location is sequentially addressed on the Y-axis of the memory matrix. The circles on this matrix represent a single memory cell in which a binary 1 or 0 is stored. Such a memory is called a $1024 \times 8 = 8192$ memory, or simply an 8 memory. ROM chips with larger than 8 storage capabilities are available at reasonable prices.

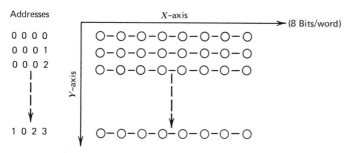

Figure 7-3 A 1024 × 8, word-organized, 2-dimensional, ROM array.

What happens if the instruction word length is greater than 8 bits, say 16 bits? Would it be possible to store such a word in word-organized, 8 ROM chips having 8 bits per word? Yes. Two 8 ROM chips could be used (Fig. 7-4). Notice that the memory is still word organized. This is possible because the addressing process involves activating only one of the possible 1024 word lines, or only 1 line along the X-axis. In such a situation, although two separate chips are used, as far as the organization of the memory is concerned, they act like a single chip with 1024 words that are 16 bits long each. Appropriate electrical connections between the chips would be necessary. Information for these would be supplied by the chip manufacturer.

The selected word line is activated by an address decoder (Fig. 7-5). In addition to the X-axis, or word select lines, the memory array also contains 8 Y-axis, or bit read-out, lines. After selecting a particular word, the CPU sends out a READ signal to the ROM chip. This enables the stored information in each memory cell of that particular word to be read out on each of their respective bit lines. These bits are then sensed and sent out to the CPU by the sensing logic, as shown in Fig. 7-5. Although only one 1024 × 8 array is shown in Fig. 7-5, the same setup would be applicable to the two-chip scheme in Fig. 7-4.

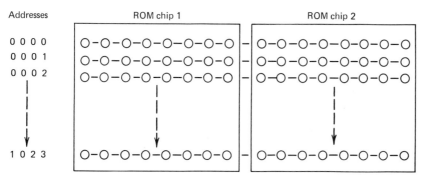

Figure 7-4 A 1024 × 16, 2D, ROM memory formed by using two 1024 × 8 ROM chips.

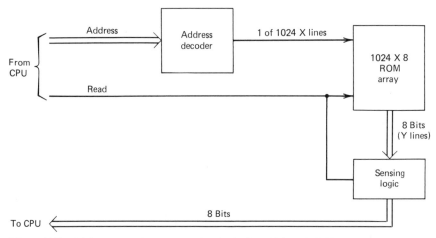

Figure 7-5   Address decoding and sensing logic for 1024 × 8 ROM array.

7-4.3 The Address Word

To access a 1024-word ROM, we would require a word that must be capable of uniquely addressing 1024 locations. A 10-bit address word would give us this capability, since $2^{10} = 1024$. However, if an 8-bit μP is assumed, it is apparent that only one word would not have the adequate number of bits. By concatenating 2, 8-bit words we can obtain the desired number of bits. Since $2^{16} = 65,536$, this would give us the capability to address a 64 ROM directly. This is far in excess of what we need. We can utilize the extra 6 bits of the address word for other purposes, as explained next.

7-4.4 The Chip Select Scheme

As shown in Section 7-4.3, 2-byte address words use only 10 bits. In the case of a 1024-word ROM, this leaves 6 bits for other uses. A fairly complex program, consisting of several subroutines, may require more than a single 1024-word ROM chip. The remaining 6 bits of the address word can be used for selecting one of 64 possible such ROM chips in the program memory. Such an address word scheme is shown in Fig. 7-6a, where the 6-bit code will select the appropriate chip and the remaining 10 bits (called the local address) will select one of the 1024 locations on the selected chip. This scheme is shown in Fig. 7-6b.

Most μC applications are such that 64 ROM chips may not be required very often. A much smaller number of ROM chips, say 6 or 8, would be adequate for most applications. If the μC system consists of say, 7 ROM chips, 3 chip select bits in the address would be adequate, leaving 3 bits available for other

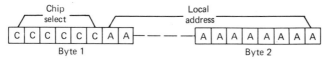

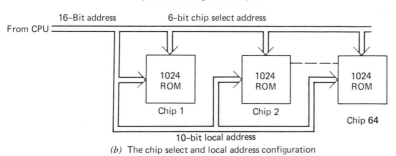

(a) 16-bit chip select and local address word obtained
by concatenating 2 8-bit bytes

(b) The chip select and local address configuration

Figure 7-6   Program memory addressing scheme.

uses. In such a situation, the remaining 3 bits could be used for selecting RAM modules (Fig. 7-7).

The scheme shown in Fig. 7-7 may lead students to believe that 8 ROM chips and 8 RAM modules can be addressed, since $2^3 = 8$. This is not true. The system will be confused and will not operate properly if legitimate 3-bit addresses are provided in both the B and C fields of the word in Fig. 7-7. If the ROM select bits are used, the RAM select bits must somehow be deactivated. This can be easily done by designing the system such that code 000, in either the B or C field, can be used to indicate valid bits in the other field. In other words, for a valid address, either the B or C field *must* contain 000. Thus, only 7 legitimate codes, 001 to 111, are available for chip or module selection. This setup, therefore, limits the number of chips/modules that we can use in a system to no more than 7 each.

A much better scheme is to use only 1 bit to indicate the selection of either the program memory (ROM chips) or the data memory (RAM modules) and use the remaining 5 bits to select the chips or the modules. This is shown in Fig. 7-8. Since $2^5 = 32$, we are able to use 32 ROM chips and 32 RAM modules with this arrangement. The S bit, shown in Fig. 7-8, is used to

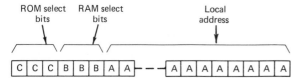

Figure 7-7   A 6-bit ROM/RAM address selection scheme.

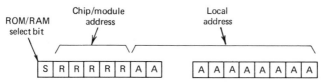

Figure 7-8   Addressing scheme using a single bit for ROM/RAM selection.

ENABLE/DISABLE the desired group of ROM chips or the RAM modules. The *R* bits will then select the appropriate chip or module.

The address word format in Fig. 7-8 often requires additional logic and circuitry for its implementation. A separate chip usually provides these functions, as shown in Fig. 7-9. Such a chip is often called the memory select chip. Notice the function of the inverter on this chip. If the ROM chips are designed so that they are activated by a 1 on the ROM/RAM select bit line, the RAM modules must be deactivated, and vice versa. The inverter does this. This assumes that both the ROM and the RAM are active HIGH. If one of them is active HIGH and the other is active LOW, the inverter would not be required.

7-5 ORGANIZATION OF THE DATA MEMORY

7-5.1 General Comments

The data memory, as the name indicates, stores the data or the operands on which various operations are performed, as dictated by the instructions. Very often even mathematical constants, which are utilized in certain specific program, are stored in the data memory. Data memory is always an R/W memory, thereby making it possible to update the data stored in it during normal computer operation. Likewise, programs can also be stored in the data memory; this is often done during the initial testing and debugging stages of program design.

In μCs semiconductor RAM chips are used for the data memory. Both the bipolar transistor and the MOS/CMOS technologies are used in RAM chips. *Bipolar* RAMS are used in applications where speed is the primary requirement. However, they are expensive in terms of power device density on the chip and, therefore, in dollars.

In MOS RAMS both the static and the dynamic modes of operation are used. Dynamic RAMS are generally less expensive but hold the data in them (i.e., 1s and 0s) for only a few microseconds or, at best, a few milliseconds. They have to be refreshed by periodically rewriting the information. External logic circuitry is required to accomplish this. Thus the initial cost advantage

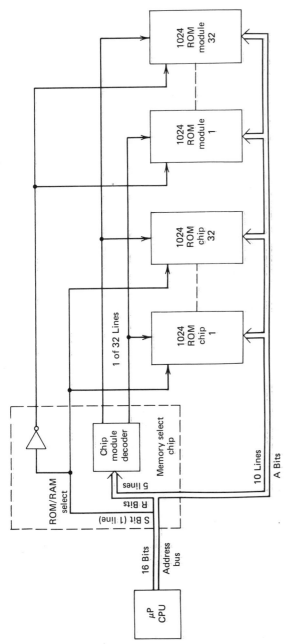

Figure 7-9 Memory selection and addressing system.

of the dynamic MOS RAM could be partially, or even completely, offset by the need for refreshing the memory cells.

On the other hand, static MOS RAMS initially cost more than the dynamic MOS RAMS. The main advantage is that they hold the bit information in them indefinitely as long as power is applied to the chip and do not require periodical refreshing. However, they are both volatile. The data in them will be altered or destroyed if power is interrupted or turned OFF.

7-5.2 Bit-Organized RAMS

In R/W memories the cost, in terms of cents per bit stored, depends on how the memory is organized. Of course, semiconductor RAMS can be word organized in a two-dimensional configuration the same as the previously described ROMS. However, their cost per bit of storage could be considerably higher. This higher cost is due to the external electronics and not the memory elements themselves. In ROMs external electronics is required to handle only the addressing and read-out functions. In R/W memories additional electronics must be provided for the *write* function.

The cost per bit of semiconductor R/W memories can be significantly lowered by a three-dimensional, bit-organized configuration, as shown in Fig. 7-10. In this scheme, assuming the memory word length is 8 bits, 8 RAM chips are used, and they comprise the RAM *module*. In this case each chip contains just 1 bit of each word in the *module*. For instance, if there were 1024 bits on the chip, all the bits on chip 1 will contain bit 0 of the 1024 word *module*. Chip 2 will contain bit 1 of the 1024 words, and so on.

The previously described addressing and chip/module select schemes will apply to this three-dimensional organization.

7-6 STANDBY POWER FOR VOLATILE RAMS

7-6.1 Power Failure/Return Operation

Since semiconductor RAMS are volatile, they present a problem if the primary power fails or is momentarily interrupted. Depending on the application involved, we may want the entire μC system to shut down in an orderly manner and then restart in an orderly manner when power is restored. In some applications it may be desirable to save only the contents of the RAM so that the human operator may restart the system when the power is available again.

In most cases an impending power failure is preceded by a gradual drop in voltage over a period of time (Fig. 7-11a). A power-fail sensing circuit can be designed to sense this condition before the minimum operating voltage level is reached. The signal output of this circuit is used to trigger an orderly

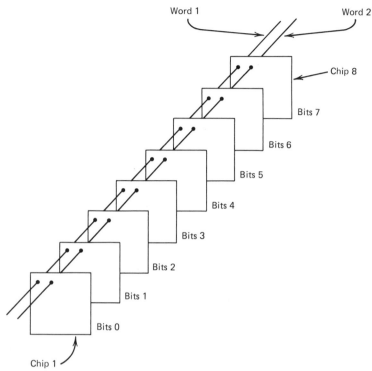

Figure 7-10 Eight bits-per-word, 3-dimensional, bit-organized semiconductor RAM module.

shutdown sequence or to disconnect the μP/RAM from the main power supply and switch it to standby battery power. The same circuit is also used to sense the return of the main power and then trigger the turn-on sequence that disconnects the standby batteries and reconnects the system to the main power supply. The power-on condition is shown in Fig. 7-11b.

7-6.2 Typical Power-Fail Sensing Circuit

A typical power-fail sensing circuit is shown in Fig. 7-12. Basically, it consists of a voltage comparator-amplifier unit (generally a single- or two-stage differential amplifier). One input to the comparator is tied to the positive side of the power supply through an R-C network, and the other input is held to some less positive reference voltage by a zener diode. From Fig. 7-11 it is seen that $V_d > V_f$. This voltage difference is mainly the result of the feedback resistor R_f, which provides a kind of hysteresis. If the power supply voltage dips slightly, but not enough to constitute a complete failure, and then begins to rise again, this hysteresis will provide sufficient time ($t_c - t_a$) for the standby

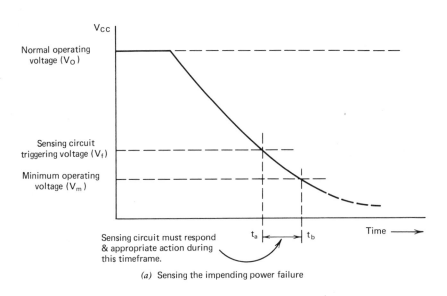

(a) Sensing the impending power failure

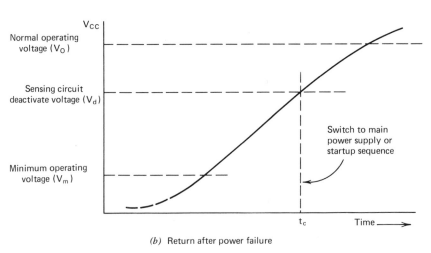

(b) Return after power failure

Figure 7-11   Operation of the power-fail-return sequence.

circuitry to go through a shutdown sequence completely and not be prematurely interrupted by the power restore/restart sequence.

The output of the comparator/amplifier is fed into the D input of a D-type flip-flop by an inverter. During normal operation, the output of the comparator is high that is at logic 1 level. This provides a logic 0 at the D input to the flip-flop with the result that the output Q is a 0. When the supply voltage, V_{CC}, begins to drop, the comparator detects this change and amplifies the voltage difference. When the voltage drops to V_f (Fig. 7-11a), V_0 begins to drop and R_f accentuates this drop. At the threshold where V_0 drops sufficiently,

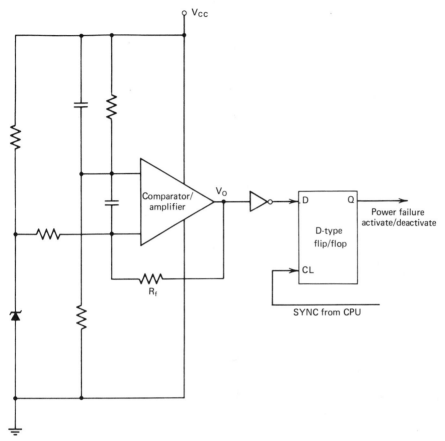

Figure 7-12 Typical power-fail-sensing circuit and the associated activate/deactivate logic.

the inverter recognizes it as a 0 input and applies a logical 1 to the D input of the flip-flop. Notice that a SYNC pulse from the CPU is applied to the clock input, CL, of the flip-flop. In the clocking system of the CPU the SYNC signal indicates the start of a new machine cycle. Thus the POWER FAIL output signal at Q is synchronized with the end of the machine cycle. This signal then activates the logic that switches the system from the main power supply to the standby battery system. When V_{CC} begins to rise, a reverse action takes place, the output at Q will go to a 0, the standby batteries will be disconnected, and the system will be returned to the main power supply.

7-7 SUMMARY

Chip memories that are widely used in μCs were discussed in this chapter. Definitions of various types of memories were first presented. They included volatile and nonvolatile memories, DRO and NDRO memories, sequentially addressed and random access memories (RAMS), and read/write (R/W) and read-only memories (ROMS).

ROMS are extensively used in μCs, so various types of ROMs were described. Included were mask-programmed ROMS, and how the users convery their requirements to the manufacturers (program listings and truth tables), field programmable ROMs (called PROMs), which can generally be programmed only once in the field, erasable PROMs (called EPROMS), which allow the user to erase the previous bit pattern by UV light and rewrite a new bit pattern, and electrically alterable ROMS (called EAROMS), which can be erased and rewritten electrically.

Program memories are usually word-organized memories. Such memories, also called two-dimensional (2D) memories, generally use ROMS. Their organization was described, and a block diagram of the address decoding and sensing logic for a 1024 × 8 ROM array was shown in Fig. 7-5. An addressing scheme for such a memory using several ROM chips was discussed and shown in Fig. 7-6. Addressing schemes for both ROM/RAM selection were shown in Figs. 7-7 and 7-8. A configuration that selects either ROM chips or RAM modules in a system was shown in Fig. 7-9.

A bit-organized (3D) scheme is generally used for the R/W data memory. The arrangement for such a module was shown in Fig. 7-10. Such a scheme reduces the cost (cents per bit) of an R/W memory.

If primary power fails or is momentarily interrupted, the data in R/W memories are lost. Standby power for volatile RAMs was discussed in Section 7-6. A typical power-fail sensing circuit was shown in Fig. 7-12.

7-8 REVIEW QUESTIONS

7-1   Briefly describe the difference between a volatile and a nonvolatile memory.

7-2   Explain why the original information is lost during the readout process in a DRO memory.

7-3   A random access memory has 1024 words, each 12 bits long. It takes 1 μs to access the word at address 0124. How long will it take to access the word at address 1020 and why?

7-4   Are R/W memories DRO or NDRO memories? Are they volatile or nonvolatile memories?

7-5   Answer the following questions about the read-only memories.
   (a) When is the information written into a ROM?
   (b) Are they volatile or nonvolatile?
   (c) Are they DRO or NDRO memories?

7-6   In mask-programmable ROM chips, what determines whether a particular cell should contain a 1 or a 0?

7-7 Is the desired binary bit pattern written into a PROM by the manufacturer or the user? How many times can this pattern be modified or rewritten?

7-8 The following questions apply to erasable PROMS or EPROMS.
(a) How is the previous information erased?
(b) Is it possible to erase only one word and save the rest?
(c) Can the chip be erased while still inserted in the circuit board?
(d) Is it possible to erase and reuse the chip several times?

7-9 Name a few advantages (and some disadvantages) that electrically alterable ROMS (EAROMS) have over erasable PROMS (EPROMS).

7-10 Briefly explain why ROMS are most desirable for many of the applications that are ideal candidates for utilization of μCs.

7-11 Which type of memory, ROM or R/W, requires more external logic circuitry for operation? Why?

7-12 We have a ROM chip, 1024 × 8, that is word organized. However, the instruction word in this machine is 12 bits long. How could this situation be handled (1024 × 4 ROM chips are not available)?

7-13 Refer to the address decoding and sensing logic for the 1024 × 8 ROM array of Fig. 7-5. Which signal(s), the address bits or the READ, are sent out by the CPU first? Why?

7-14 If the program memory consists of four 1024 × 8 ROM chips, is it possible for two (or more) chips to have the same addresses? If so, explain why.

7-15 The program memory of a μC system consists of four 8192 × 16 ROM chips, and the data memory also consists of four 8192 × 8 RAM modules. It is an 8-bit machine. Is it possible to access any part of these two memories with only a 2-byte address, or would 3 bytes be necessary? Explain.

7-16 Refer to the memory selection and addressing system of Fig. 7-9. What is the function of the inverter in the memory select chip?

7-17 The data memory of a μC is bit organized and contains 8 RAM modules. The total data memory size is 32,768 words, and there are 10 bits per word.
(a) How many words are there in each module?
(b) How many chips are there in each module?
(c) How many bits are there on each chip?

7-18 Refer to the power failure curve of Fig. 7-11a. Explain why the sensing circuit must respond and the appropriate action taken in the timeframe between t_a and t_b.

7-19 Refer to Fig. 7-12. What function does the feedback resistor, R_f, serve?

7-20 In the power-fail sensing circuit of Fig. 7-12, why is the SYNC pulse from the CPU used and what function does it perform?

8

PARALLEL I/O TRANSFERS— PROGRAMMED I/O

8-1 DATA TRANSFERS

No computer, regardless of its size, speed, computing capabilities, or other sophisticated features, is very useful unless it can communicate with the outside world (i.e., with other equipments in the system that are called *peripherals*). This communication involves raw data coming into the computer from the peripherals and the transfer of processed data (or control signals) from the computer to the peripherals.

The computer and the peripherals seldom operate at the same speed. The peripherals, which could be electromechanical devices, usually operate at much slower speeds than the all-electronic CPU. These speed and/or timing differences somehow must be reconciled. Furthermore, the data formats of the peripherals may be different from the format used by the computer. Some means of format conversion is needed. Some of the commonly used peripherals in μCs are:

1. CRT displays.
2. Input keyboards.
3. Floppy disk memories.
4. Paper-tape readers/punches.
5. Teletypewriters (TTYs).
6. D/A and A/D converters.
7. Magnetic tape cassettes.

8-2 INTERFACE NETWORK CHIPS

If more than one peripheral is used in a μC system (usually the case), one or more interface networks are required to provide data and signal compatibility between the CPU and the logic within the various peripherals. Thus buffer registers, format-conversion logic, multiplexers, demultiplexers, and logic for various other logic signals are involved in such interface networks. In μCs these networks are provided on one or more chips that are separate from the μP chips.

8-2.1 The I/O Ports

In interfacing the μC with peripheral devices, the following functions are involved.

1. *Data Buffering. Buffer registers* are required to hold the data for some time during the I/O transfers. This reconciles the timing differences between the faster μP and the slower peripheral. Buffers generally consist of *latches* (i.e., D-type flip-flops).
2. *Address Decoding for I/O Peripheral Selection.* It is possible to access several peripherals by using an external memory data bus and connecting the I/O device chips to it. Since data transfers take place through the data buffers, it is necessary that we first select the right buffer for the desired peripheral. This means that the μP must provide the buffer address, which must be decoded.
3. *Command Decoding.* After selecting the desired peripheral (through its address or unique code), the CPU must inform the peripheral what it wants it to do. The μP does this by sending out *command signals* on the control bus. These signals include commands to output or input data as well as other functions such as REWIND or STOP in the case of a magnetic tape peripheral.
4. *Status Decoding.* When the μP issues a command, the peripheral may or may not be in a position to comply with the command. For example, the μP may command a magnetic tape cassette to input data to the μP. But it is quite possible that the cassette might be rewinding (in response to a prior command) when this command comes in. Obviously, the peripheral cannot comply at that time. The cassette unit will inform the CPU, through a *status signal,* that it cannot input data at this time. Signals from the peripherals to the μP to inform the CPU of the current condition of the peripheral are called *status signals.* In μCs, because of the external pin limitations on the packages, status signals are generally limited to a signal that informs the CPU whether the peripheral is available or not. Such signals are usually called READY or BUSY status signals.
5. *Control and Timing.* It is important to synchronize all communications between the CPU and the peripherals and coordinate them with the rest of the system.

8-2.2 The I/O Device Chips and Port Expansion

In μCs I/O ports are generally available on one or more chips. In the rest of this book, when we refer to an I/O port, we are talking about *all* five functions described in Section 8-2.1 and not just the data transfers. A single-port I/O chip for an output device such as a display is shown in Fig. 8-1*a* in block diagram form. A similar setup for an *input* peripheral, such as a *keyboard,* is shown in Fig. 8-1*b*. The setup for a peripheral that has both input and output capabilities, such as a *cassette* unit, is shown in Fig. 8-1*c*. If the peripheral involved is a *serial* device, such as a cassette, the interface requires *serial-to-parallel* and *parallel-to-serial* conversion. Such a converter could be either on a separate chip or could be included in the I/O device chip.

The I/O interface situation shown in Fig. 8-1 requires the use of a separate I/O device chip to provide an I/O port for each peripheral device used in the system. When configuring a system, a separate chip for each peripheral could result in a fairly complex and cumbersome setup. Some μC manufacturers supply additional interface chips known as *port expansion* chips. The I/O device chips shown in Fig. 8-1 are basically single-port chips. Figure 8-2 shows the CPU communicating with the basic I/O device chip, which, in turn, communicates with the port expansion chip. This enables the CPU to communicate with two 8-bit peripherals through a single I/O device chip. It is possible that the logic and the interface networks for both the I/O device chip and the port expansion chip could be physically located on the same silicon chip. Advances in semiconductor technology have made this possible, although the number of pins available on a package is a limitation that must be considered.

A different configuration is shown in Fig. 8-3, where four peripherals are connected to a single port expansion chip. Notice that peripherals A and B have 8-bit data words, whereas peripherals C and D each have 4-bit data words. Such port expansion chips are available with some μPs. Also, I/O interfaces, similar to those in Figs. 8-2 and 8-3, are usually *programmable* interface chips. This means that within certain limits the port configuration of the expansion chip can be modified or altered under program control. We will discuss programmable interfaces in Chapter Twelve.

8-3 WHAT IS PROGRAMMED I/O?

Programmed I/O is a mode of transferring data between the CPU and the logic within the peripherals; the transfers are initiated and controlled entirely by the μP. Such data transfers usually are executed by an instruction, a series of program steps, or a subroutine.

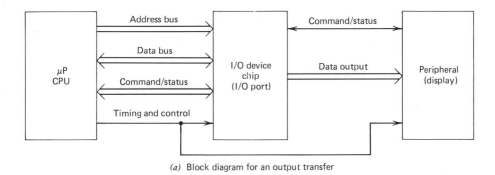

(a) Block diagram for an output transfer

(b) Block diagram for an input transfer

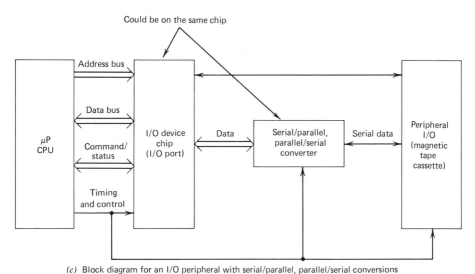

(c) Block diagram for an I/O peripheral with serial/parallel, parallel/serial conversions

Figure 8-1   I/O interface chip between μP and peripherals.

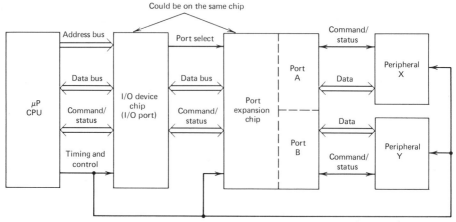

Figure 8-2   I/O interface with port expansion for two peripherals.

During data transfers, the system always follows a preestablished sequence of events called a protocol. For example, if the transfer involves outputting data from the CPU to the peripheral, the protocol tells the CPU to inform the addressed peripheral that the data word has been placed in a certain location (usually the output buffer register) from which the peripheral can access it. On the other hand, if the transfer involves inputting the data word into the CPU, the CPU will first inform the peripheral that it is waiting for it to output the word and place it in a predefined location such as the input buffer (in some cases it could be the accumulator). In some systems, after the peripheral has output the data word and placed it in the indicated location, the peripheral signals the CPU that it has completed the protocol step.

The principal feature of programmed I/O is that the logic in the external peripheral follows the CPU commands exactly. In other words, the peripherals are under control of the μC at all times.

8-4 THE DATA TRANSFER SCHEME

8-4.1 The Transfer Instruction

Programmed I/O is included in virtually all modern μCs. The transfer is executed by an I/O transfer (IOT) instruction. This instruction performs one or all of the following tasks.

1. Receive input data from the peripheral into the CPU.
2. Send output data from the CPU to the peripheral.
3. Send commands to the peripheral to tell it what to do, for example, a REWIND command to a magnetic tape cassette.

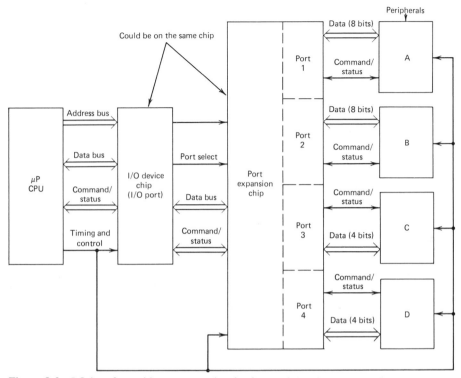

Figure 8-3   I/O interface with port expansion for four peripherals.

4. Inquire about the *status* of the peripheral and check it; for example, check if the cassette is still rewinding or if it is ready for recording new data. (*Note.* Status checking may not be available in some systems, depending on the application involved and the mode of programmed I/O transfer used.)

8-4.1.1 The IOT Instruction Format   The IOT instruction format is similar to the memory reference instruction (MRI) format discussed in Section 4-4.2 (see Fig. 4-9). However, there are some differences. The typical format of an IOT instruction is shown in Fig. 8-4.

1. *The Operation Code.* This field of the IOT instruction will generally contain bits to identify the following.
   (a) Bit (or bits) identifying the instruction as an IOT instruction separate from the various other instructions, as discussed in Chapter Four.
   (b) Bit (or bits) indicating whether it is a single-word or multiword instruction and the number of words involved if it is a multiword instruction.
   (c) Bit (or bits) to indicate the type of operation, whether it is an input or output

OP code	Command code	Address code

Figure 8-4   Format of the typical IOT instruction.

operation or one that involves neither of these but is an auxiliary operation such as a rewind for a tape peripheral.

2. *The Command Code*. This field contains the code commanding the I/O interface chip to perform an input or output operation. The bits in this code are decoded by the interface chip. The various commands are sent to the selected peripherals or single command lines in addition to the two previously mentioned operations on the interface chip itself.

3. *The Address Code*. This field is very similar to the address field in a MRI. When decoded by the peripheral address decoder on the interface chip, it will select and activate one of the several peripherals in the system.

8-4.1.2 Typical IOT Instruction

We now show how a typical IOT instruction could be designed to include the bit fields described in Section 8-4.1.1. An IOT instruction could be a single-word or multiword instruction. The instruction shown in Fig. 8-5 is a 2-word IOT instruction for an 8-bit word μP. The OP code field consists of 6 bits, the command code consists of 5 bits, and the address code consists of 5 bits. Within each field, a bit (or bits) must be assigned to indicate specific conditions and/or specific operations. The bit assignments for IOT instructions follow.

1. *OP Code*. We must identify the IOT instruction from the MRI and the NMRI instruction described in Chapter Four. It is also necessary to inform the CPU whether the instruction is a single-word or multiword instruction. Finally, the CPU must be informed about the type of operation to be performed. Bit assignments to handle these situations are as follows.

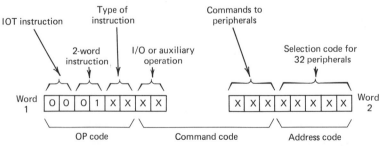

Figure 8-5   Typical IOT instruction. (*Note.* Here X denotes either a 0 or a 1.)

(a) Two bits—IOT instruction.

  Code: 00

(b) Two bits—number of words in the instruction.

  Codes: 0 0 — single-word instruction.

  0 1 — 2-word instruction.

  1 0 — 3-word instruction.

  1 1 — invalid code.

(c) Two bits—type of operation.

  Codes: 0 0 — input to CPU.

  0 1 — output from CPU.

  1 0 — auxiliary operation.

  1 1 — invalid code.

2. *Command Code.* The command code must initiate and activate the multiplexer or the demultiplexer (described later in Sections 8-5 and 8-6) on the interface chip. It must also issue the various commands to the peripherals via the interface chip. Bit assignments to handle these functions are:

(a) Two bits—I/O or auxiliary operation.

  Codes: 0 0 — input to CPU (activates the multiplexer on the interface chip).

  0 1 — output from CPU (activates the demultiplexer on the interface chip).

  1 0 — auxiliary operation of the peripheral (neither input nor output).

  1 1 — invalid code.

(b) Three bits—eight commands to various peripherals (codes will be determined by the actual peripherals used in the system; commands are decided on the interface chip).

3. *Address Code.* The appropriate multiplexer/demultiplexer channel must be selected for the addressed peripheral. The address is decoded on the interface chip (see Fig. 8-6). Five bits will allow selection of up to 32 peripherals.

8-4.2 The Block Diagram of the Programmed I/O Chip

In a μC system that uses programmed I/O, one (or more) interface chip is used between the μP and the peripherals. The interface chip is fairly complex and is often programmable (we will describe programmable I/O interfaces in Chapter Twelve).

The interface chip generally performs the following functions.

1. Decodes the address, supplied by the μP, to select and activate the proper peripheral.

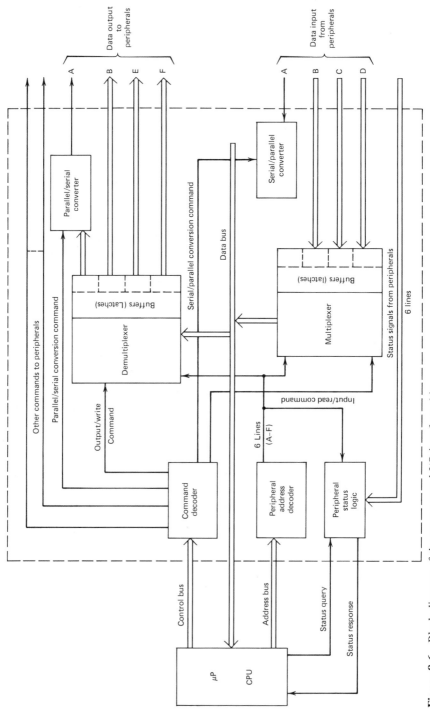

Figure 8-6 Block diagram of the programmed I/O interface chip.

2. Checks the status of the selected peripheral and channels the appropriate status information from the peripheral to the CPU.
3. Channels the proper commands from the μP to the peripherals.
4. Converts the data output from the CPU in the proper format for use by the peripheral involved. This may require conversion of a parallel-data word into a serial bit.
5. Converts the data output by the peripheral into the proper format for acceptance by the CPU. This may require conversion of a serial bit into a parallel-word format.

Figure 8-6 shows the block diagram of a typical programmed I/O interface chip. Six I/O channels are included. This means that this chip is capable of servicing six different peripherals. In this case the peripherals are not all alike.

1. Channel A is a *bidirectional* serial I/O channel. Hence the data come in and go out, 1 bit at a time, on a single line. Since the μP operates only on parallel words, this channel requires parallel-to-serial and serial-to-parallel converters. As shown in Fig. 8-6, these converters are included on the same chip as the rest of the interface.
2. Channel B is a *bidirectional,* parallel-word channel.
3. Channels C and D are both parallel-word, *unidirectional* channels. This means that the peripherals on these channels can only *input* to the CPU. Typical of such channels are input keyboard channels.
4. Channels E and F are also parallel-word, *unidirectional* channels, but they *output* data from the CPU to the peripherals. Typical peripherals in this case could be display units.

The block diagram of Fig. 8-6 is simplified for instructional purposes, and only the logic blocks pertinent to programmed I/O transfers are included. For example, the various lines involved in timing and control are not shown. In some cases even the transfer of parallel words between the CPU and the peripherals may require additional formatting logic not shown in Fig. 8-6.

The logic and operation of this chip is best understood by examining the output and input transfer operations separately. We do this in Sections 8-4.3 and 8-4.4, respectively.

8-4.3 The Output Transfer

In order to output data from the CPU to a peripheral, the programmer inserts an IOT instruction (calling for an output transfer) at the appropriate point in the program. The IOT instruction initiates the action in the interface chip. The events that are established by the protocol (Section 8-3) take place. This sequence is briefly described here.

1. The CPU transmits the address of the peripheral to the peripheral address decoder in the interface chip through the address bus, as shown in Fig. 8-6. This address, of course, originates in the address field of the IOT instruction, as shown in Figs. 8-4 and 8-5.
2. The peripheral address decoder decodes this address and a logical 1 is output on one of the output lines. Figure 8-6 shows 6 lines of this sort; they are labeled A to F, corresponding to the 6 peripherals labeled A to F. Each line goes to three different functional blocks on the chip. During an output transfer, the applicable channel in the demultiplexer is selected.
3. The CPU then checks the status of the peripheral (i.e., checks if it is ready to accept a data word outputted by the μP. It does this by sending a logical 1 on the STATUS QUERY line to the peripheral status logic block in the interface chip. (*Note*. In some μPs and/or some interface chips the status-checking feature may not be available.)
4. If the addressed peripheral is ready, it will respond by sending a logical 1 on one of the 6 status signal lines to the peripheral status logic block which, in turn, will send a logical 1 to the μP on the STATUS RESPONSE line.
5. The CPU will then put the data word on the data bus, thus making it available to the demultiplexer.
6. A command word, which originates in the command field of the IOT instruction (see Figs. 8-4 and 8-5), is sent by the computer to the command decoder in the interface chip on the control bus. The OUTPUT/WRITE command then latches the data word in the buffer latches and makes it available to the peripheral on its own output channel. Only the previously addressed buffer latches will be activated. This completes the output transfer operation.

8-4.4 The Input Transfer

The protocol for the input transfer is very similar to that for the output transfer described in Section 8-4.4. It is briefly described here. Remember that the input transfer program is also initiated by the IOT instruction that is inserted in the program by the programmer.

1. The CPU sends the address to the peripheral address decoder; this activates 1 of its 6 output lines, A to F. This line then selects the appropriate channel in the multiplexer.
2. The CPU then sends out the STATUS QUERY signal to the peripheral status logic block. If the peripheral is ready, it responds with a 1 signal to the peripheral status logic which, in turn, sends it to the CPU on the STATUS RESPONSE line.
3. The CPU then sends the command word to the command decoder, which sends a signal to the peripheral to transfer the data word, on its appropriate channel, to the buffer latches in the multiplexer.
4. At the same time, the INPUT/READ command will latch in the input word and make it available to the CPU through the data bus.

Since the multiplexer and the demultiplexer make it possible to transfer data between the CPU and various peripherals through a single data bus, this method of I/O transfers is often called party-line I/O.

8-5 UNCONDITIONAL PROGRAMMED I/O TRANSFER

8-5.1 General Comments

Programmed I/O transfers are of two types, the *unconditional* (often called the *synchronous* transfer) and the *conditional* (also called the *asynchronous* transfer) type.

The unconditional transfer is the simplest and most straightforward transfer. The transfer takes place whenever the CPU so directs it. It is initiated by the IOT instruction in the program. In the unconditional transfer no check is made by the CPU to determine the READY or BUSY status of the peripheral concerned. In other words, the peripheral must be ready to accept an output word or to input a word to the CPU whenever the CPU initiates such a transfer.

This type of a transfer has two major shortcomings that limit its use in μC applications.

1. The *unconditional* transfer requires the peripheral to be ready for a transfer at all times, whenever the CPU initiates it. This means that such a transfer can only be used with peripherals whose timing is known and fixed (i.e., does not vary during operations). In other words, the peripheral must be able to accomplish the required transfer within the specified instruction time of the μP.
2. Since peripherals are generally much slower than the μPs, the preceding requirement imposes some restrictions on the programmer. Adequate time must be allowed for each transfer to be completed by a slower peripheral. This means that the programmer cannot insert a series of IOT instructions in the program in a consecutive sequence. If such a requirement is needed, the programmer is forced to slow down the CPU artificially by inserting several NO OP (no operation) instructions, which could also be called software delay, between successive IOT instructions. This is wasteful of CPU time.

In spite of these limitations, unconditional programmed I/O is used in many applications.

8-5.2 Input Operation

In Section 8-4.5 we briefly described the input transfer and the protocol involved by using the generalized block diagram of the programmed I/O interface chip (Fig. 8-6). In unconditional input transfers the status of the peripheral is not checked; therefore the peripheral status logic block and its various input and output signals are not included on the chip. If they are included on the chip, they are disconnected or not used.

The various events and sequence involved in the protocol are presented in Fig. 8-7.

To describe the input operation, the pertinent logic blocks are redrawn in greater detail in Fig. 8-8. The following assumptions are made.

1. The same six peripherals as those in Fig. 8-6 are used.
2. The data bus is 8 bits wide.
3. The peripheral address word is 4 bits wide, but only the first 3 bits are used in this application.

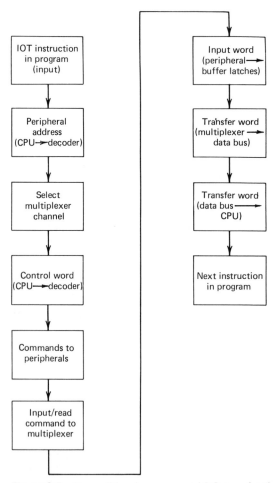

Figure 8-7   Unconditional programmed I/O transfer (input operation).

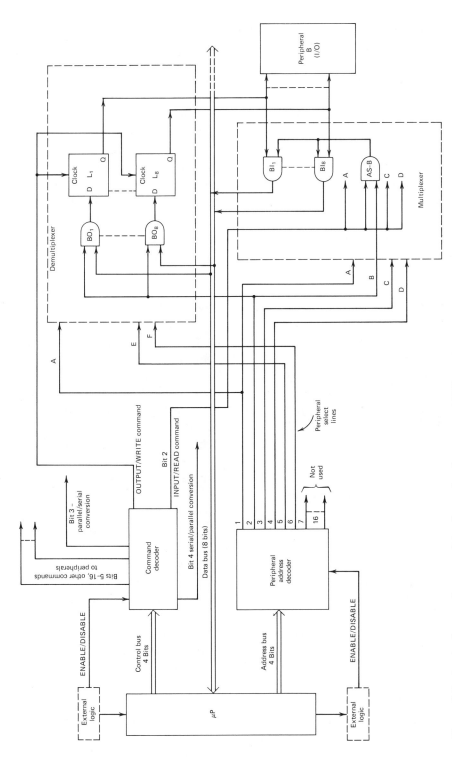

Figure 8-8 Logic diagram for unconditional transfers (programmed I/O).

4. The command word is 4 bits wide and the bits are assigned as follows.
   (a) Bit 1—OUTPUT/WRITE command.
   (b) Bit 2—INPUT/READ command.
   (c) Bit 3—PARALLEL/SERIAL conversion command.
   (d) Bit 4—SERIAL/PARALLEL conversion command.
   (e) Bits 5 to 16—other commands to peripherals.
5. The ENABLE/DISABLE signals to the two decoders come from the timing and control in the μP. They control the timing of the decoder's outputs. (*Note.* Depending on the architecture of the μP involved, external logic may be required for generation, timing, and control of these two signals.)
6. For simplicity, other clock and timing signals to the various logic blocks are not shown.
7. It is assumed that students are familiar with the functions and operations of decoders from prior digital logic courses.

In both the multiplexer and the demultiplexer, only the logic associated with peripheral B is shown in Fig. 8-8. Similar logical configurations are also present for the other five peripherals in addition to the two converters for serial peripherals. In the multiplexer, only 2 input AND gates (BI_1 and BI_8) are shown. Actually, there are 8 gates. Also, only 1 controlling AND gate (AS-B) is shown. Each peripheral has 1 such gate. Likewise, in the demultiplexer, only AND gates (BO_1 and BO_8) and 2 D-type flip-flops (L_1 and L_8) are shown. (There are 8 each.) Finally, although flip-flop latches are not shown in the multiplexer, some interface chips may have them.

The following sequence of events takes place during an input operation.

1. The input operation is initiated by an IOT instruction in the program that puts a 4-bit address word on the address bus.
2. The peripheral address decoder decodes this address and selects one of its 16 output lines; that is, it puts a 1 on this line while the rest are 0s. (In this case peripheral B is selected, so line 2 will have a 1 on it.)
3. Line 2 enables AND gates (BO_1 to BO_8) in the demultiplexer and the AS-B AND gate in the multiplexer. (The decoded output is only issued when the timing and control in the μP issue the proper ENABLE/DISABLE signal described in paragraph 5 above.
4. A 4-bit control word is put on the control bus by the CPU. In response, the command decoder outputs a 1 on the bit 2 INPUT/READ command line when it receives the ENABLE/DISABLE signal from the μP.
5. AND gate AS-B is fully enabled and outputs a 1, which enables input AND gates BI_1 to BI_8.
6. The command decoder issues a command to peripheral B through one or more of the bit lines 5 to 16. Peripheral B responds by outputting the 8-bit data word.

7. Since AND gates BI_1 to BI_8 were previously enabled, the data word from peripheral B is transmitted by these gates to the 8-bit data bus and from there to the μP.

8-5.3 Output Operation

The output transfer is similar to the input transfer in many ways (see Fig. 8-9).

The following sequence of events takes place during an output operation.

1. The output operation is initiated by an IOT instruction in the program that puts a 4-bit address word on the address bus.

2. The peripheral address decoder decodes this address and selects one of its 16

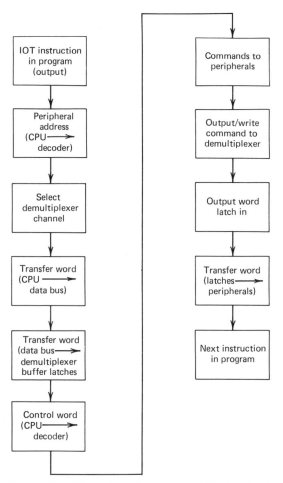

Figure 8-9   Unconditional programmed I/O transfer (output operation).

output lines; that is, it puts a 1 on this line while the rest are 0s. (In this case peripheral B is selected, so line 2 will have a 1 on it.)

3. Line 2 enables AND gates BO_1 to BO_8 in the demultiplexer. (The decoded output is only issued when the timing and control in the μP issue the proper ENABLE/ DISABLE signal.)

4. The CPU outputs the data word on the 8-bit data bus and makes these bits available to the other input lines of gates BO_1 to BO_8 which are now fully enabled.

5. AND gates BO_1 to BO_8 output either a 1 or a 0, depending on the word output by the CPU, and these appear at the D input of the 8 D-type flip-flops L_1 to L_8.

6. The CPU outputs a 4-bit control word to the command decoder, which responds with a 1 on the bit 1 OUTPUT/WRITE command line.

7. Since the bit 1 line from the command decoder is connected to the clock inputs of L_1 to L_8 flip-flops, the bits presented at the D inputs are latched into these 8 flip-flops.

8. The data bits are now available at I/O port of peripheral B for acceptance.

9. The command decoder sends the appropriate signal(s) through bit 5 to 16 lines to peripheral B, which accepts the bits output by the latches, L_1 to L_8, and the transfer is completed.

The data bits remain latched in L_1 to L_8 until another CPU signal on the CLEAR terminal, not shown in Fig. 8-8 for simplicity, clears the flip-flops in preparation for another write or output operation.

8-6 CONDITIONAL PROGRAMMED I/O TRANSFER

8-6.1 General Remarks

The *conditional* programmed I/O transfer, also called the *asynchronous* transfer, is more extensively used in μCs. Sometimes it is also called hand-shaking I/O. The conditional transfer first queries the peripheral status to see if it is ready to perform the transfer. The actual transfer takes place only if the peripheral shows the READY status. If the peripheral responds with a NOT READY or BUSY signal, the program goes into a loop and keeps repeating the query until the peripheral is READY.

The conditional transfer requires two IOT instructions, as follows.

1. *IOT Instruction 1.* Acquires the status of the addressed peripheral and informs the μP of the current status. The CPU makes the decision whether to repeat the query by looping around or to proceed to the next instruction, depending on the status of the peripheral.

2. *IOT Instruction 2.* When the peripheral indicates to the CPU that it is ready for the transfer, the program advances to the next instruction, which executes the transfer, either an input or an output.

The principal shortcoming of the conditional transfer is that repeated queries on the current status of the peripheral waste CPU time. The main advantage is that it accomplishes synchronization between the µP and slower peripherals whose timing may not be fixed or known.

8-6.2 The Protocol in Conditional Transfers

The logic involved in conditional transfers is basically the same as that shown for the unconditional transfers (Fig. 8-8) as far as addressing, data paths, and control signals are concerned. Additional logic and signals are required for the hand-shaking process. This logic and its operation are described in Section 8-6.3.

In all conditional transfers the following general sequence of events occurs.

1. The desired peripheral is selected by addressing it.
2. The status of the peripheral is checked to see if it is ready to perform the transfer.
3. If the peripheral is busy, probably still executing a prior instruction, it responds with either a BUSY or NOT READY signal to the CPU.
4. The program loops back to query again and keeps on querying until it receives a READY response from the peripheral.
5. The CPU issues the appropriate transfer command (READ or WRITE), and the data transfer takes place.
6. After completion of the transfer, the CPU essentially deactivates the peripheral by removing its address and thereby makes the data bus available for future use.

In the preceding protocol, a conditional JUMP (backward) is performed every time the CPU query results in a NOT READY response from the peripheral. Figures 8-10 and 8-11 show the input and output operations, respectively, for conditional programmed I/O transfer.

8-6.3 The Status Check Logic

In the interface chip block diagram (Fig. 8-6) we showed the peripheral status logic block but did not explain how it works. The logic involved in status checking is simple and straightforward and is shown in Fig. 8-12. For convenience, only the logic of the interface, pertinent to status checking, is shown.

The following sequence of events occurs, assuming that peripheral B is addressed by the CPU.

1. The µP sends a 4-bit address word to the peripheral address decoder, which outputs a 1 on line 2.
2. One of the three inputs to AND gate S2 is now enabled.
3. Each peripheral has a status flip-flop in its logic that is set to the Q side when it

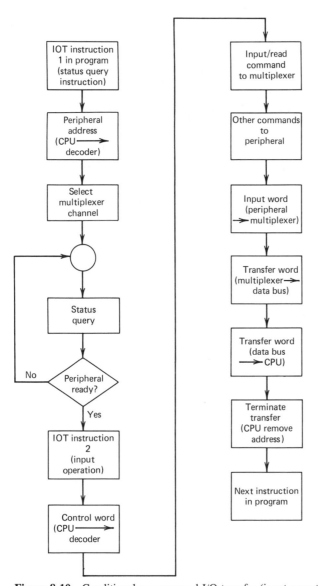

Figure 8-10 Conditional programmed I/O transfer (input operation).

is ready for a transfer. Otherwise, the flip-flop is set to the $\overline{Q}$ side. The Q output of this flip-flop of peripheral B is fed into the second input to the S2 AND gate.

4. IOT instruction 1 in the program sends out a STATUS QUERY signal from the CPU to the peripheral status logic on the chip.

5. If the status flip-flop of B is on the $\overline{Q}$ side (showing that B is BUSY), the output of S2 is a 0.

6. Since none of the other AND gates S1, S3, S4, S5, and S6 are fully enabled, all

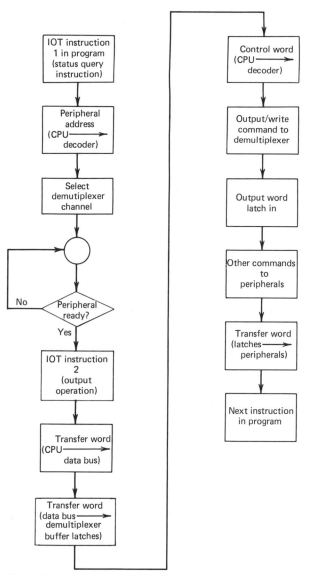

Figure 8-11   Conditional programmed I/O transfer (output operation).

inputs to S0 gate are disabled and a 0 output is sent to the CPU, indicating that B is not ready for a transfer.

7. The CPU sends out another 1 on the STATUS QUERY line and repeats this process until B is ready for a transfer.

8. When B is ready for a transfer, the status flip-flop is set on the Q side; this enables all three inputs to S2.

9. A 1 output from S2 is transmitted to the μP by S0.

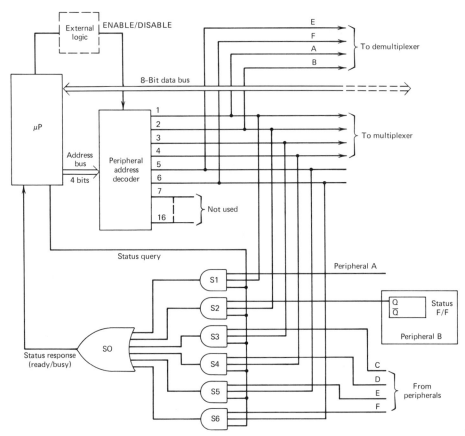

Figure 8-12 Logic diagram for peripheral status checking (conditional programmed I/O transfer).

10. The CPU stops sending out 1s on the STATUS QUERY line, and the program advances to IOT instruction 2.
11. The word transfer, either an input or an output, is then completed as shown in Figs. 8-10 and 8-11, respectively.
12. When the transfer is completed, peripheral B returns the status flip-flop to the $\overline{Q}$ side.
13. The μP now disables the command decoder and the peripheral address decoder through the lines labeled ENABLE/DISABLE. This releases the DATA BUS for the next operation.

As shown in Fig. 8-12, the STATUS QUERY and the STATUS RE-SPONSE signals use two separate lines. In many μCs there are schemes available in which these signals can be transmitted on either one or two lines: the data bus or the control bus. In this situation the lines operate in a *time-shared* mode.

8-7 SUMMARY

Programmed I/O is the most widely used form of parallel I/O transfers in μCs. The concept of parallel data transfers between the CPU and various peripherals was first introduced by means of block diagrams for both output and input transfers. In Fig. 8-2 a scheme for including an additional peripheral unit was shown by using a port expansion chip. A scheme for expanding the system capability to 4 peripherals was shown in Fig. 8-3.

The typical IOT instruction format was presented in Fig. 8-5. Regardless of the number of bytes used, the IOT instruction must have OP code, command code, and address code fields. Typical IOT instruction format codes were discussed in Section 8-4.1.2. A block diagram of the programmed I/O interface chip was shown in Fig. 8-6. If unconditional programmed I/O transfers are used, the peripheral status logic in this block diagram is not used. Figure 8-8 showed the logic diagram for the unconditional transfers, and the operation of the multiplexer and the demultiplexer were given in Sections 8-5.2 and 8-5.3, respectively.

In conditional programmed I/O transfers the CPU queries the selected peripheral to determine its availability for a transfer. The actual transfer does not take place until the peripheral signals that it is ready. This operation was shown in Fig. 8-11 in flowchart form. The logic involved in status checking was shown in Fig. 8-12.

8-8 REVIEW QUESTIONS

8-1 What role do the I/O interfaces play in a μC system? What functions do they perform?

8-2 Explain why there are speed differences between the μP and external peripheral devices, even though most of these external devices contain some digital electronic circuitry and logic.

8-3 Name the five basic functions that the interface chip(s) must perform when interfacing peripheral devices with μC systems.

8-4 Suppose the external peripheral, to be interfaced with a μC, is a serial device that accepts and outputs digital bits in a serial stream. In addition to the normal interfacing functions (mentioned in Question 8-3), would any additional logic or circuitry be required for such a setup? If so, where would it be located?

8-5 Is it always necessary to have a separate I/O chip for each peripheral in the system? If not, how would this be handled? Where would any additional circuitry be located?

8-6 Is it possible to use peripherals with different word lengths in the same μC system? If so, what additional circuitry would be required to accomplish this? Explain.

8-7   Briefly explain how a programmed I/O transfer is controlled and executed.

8-8   Briefly state the four major functions that an IOT instruction can perform in a programmed I/O transfer.

8-9   List the three code fields that every IOT instruction must have.

8-10   Give the three items that the bits in the OP code field of the IOT instruction must identify.

8-11   Using the typical IOT instruction format and codes shown in Section 8-4.1.2 and Fig. 8-5, explain what the following 2-word instruction means.

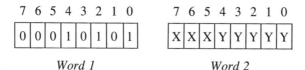

7 6 5 4 3 2 1 0		7 6 5 4 3 2 1 0
0 0 0 1 0 1 0 1	X X X Y Y Y Y Y
Word 1	*Word 2*

8-12   List the five major functions performed by the typical programmed I/O interface chip whose block diagram is shown in Fig. 8-6.

8-13   For the programmed I/O interface chip of fig. 8-6, briefly list the sequence of events (protocol) that takes place for an output transfer.

8-14   For the programmed I/O interface chip of Fig. 8-6, briefly list the sequence of events (protocol) that takes place for an input transfer.

8-15   In an unconditional programmed I/O transfer, which logical function in the interface chip (Fig. 8-6) is not activated or used? Why?

8-16   What are the primary requirements of a peripheral unit if it is to be used in a μC system using the unconditional programmed I/O transfer mode?

8-17   What are the functions of the two ENABLE/DISABLE signals to the command decoder and the peripheral address decoder in Fig. 8-8?

8-18   Refer to the logic diagram of Fig. 8-8. Identify the output line(s) from the decoder(s) that will make it possible for peripheral D to input a data word to the μP.

8-19   In the multiplexer of the logic diagram for unconditional transfer (Fig. 8-8), explain the function of the AND gate AS-B.

8-20   Briefly describe the function of the D-type flip-flops in the demultiplexer of Fig. 8-8.

8-21   Does the conditional programmed I/O transfer require one or more IOT instructions? If more than one is required, explain why.

8-22   Explain the function of the status flip-flop in peripheral B (see Fig. 8-12).

8-23   Referring to Fig. 8-12, describe the role of the peripheral address decoder in the status-checking operation.

9

PARALLEL I/O TRANSFERS— INTERRUPT I/O

9-1 WHY INTERRUPT I/O?

The programmed I/O transfers (both unconditional and the conditional) discussed in Chapter Eight, have certain shortcomings that make them undesirable in some μP applications. The main disadvantage of the unconditional transfer is that the peripheral or I/O device must be compatible in speed with the speed of the CPU. Few peripherals are that fast. Consequently, if the peripheral is not ready (i.e., if it is still performing a previously commanded operation), when the CPU initiates a transfer, chaos will result. In some systems the CPU can be programmed to *suspend* the program when this situation arises. Operation is resumed only when restarted by the operator.

The conditional transfer also has one major drawback. The CPU checks for the status of the peripheral before the actual transfer of data takes place. If the peripheral is not ready the CPU goes into a loop, as shown previously in Figs. 8-10 and 8-11. During the querying and looping process, no productive work is done by the μP.

In both types of programmed I/O transfer, the μP, not the peripheral or the external device, initiates the transfer. A much more efficient and time-saving system has the peripheral interrupt the main program and request service only when it is ready for a transfer. Interrupt I/O interfaces provide this capability. In an interrupt I/O system, even though the transfer is initiated and requested by the external device, the computer executes the actual transfer under program control. Furthermore, in several μCs it is possible to ignore or override the interrupt request by disabling this capability, also under program control.

9-2 SEQUENCE OF EVENTS

In a μC with interrupt I/O capability, IOT instruction(s) cannot be inserted in the main program, as in programmed I/O. The programmer cannot predict at what point in the execution of the program any one of the several peripherals or I/O devices will interrupt and request service. The μP must be programmed to service any external device at all times. This is accomplished by branching the program to an appropriate *service subroutine,* stored in the memory, after an interrupt is received and the interrupting device is properly identified.

A service subroutine may require the use of several functional blocks within the CPU, such as the accumulator, the program counter, and the scratch-pad registers. Obviously, the original contents of such registers/counters will be destroyed during service subroutine execution. After completion of this subroutine, the main program must be resumed, and all data must be in their respective preinterrupt functional blocks. This is done by storing the contents of the critical registers/counters in preassigned memory locations prior to executing the subroutine (called status saving) and then loading them back into the same registers/counters after completion of the subroutine (called restoring CPU status).

Figure 9-1 shows a generalized sequence of events that takes place in an interrupt I/O. The circled numbers next to each block correspond to the following paragraphs, which briefly explain each event in the sequence.

1. *Interrupt Request.* The peripheral or the I/O device must first signal the μP that it is ready for an I/O operation and request service from the CPU. This signal, usually designated INT or INT REQ, comes to the μP on a single line, which is the output of an OR gate. The interrupt or ready signal from each peripheral is fed into each input line of this OR gate.

2. *Interrupt Acknowledge.* The μP completes the current instruction and sends out an acknowledgment signal to the peripheral. This signal is generally referred to as INT ACK or ACK. In the absence of this signal, the external device would keep on sending the request or the INT signal to the μP.

3. *Status Saving.* Before servicing the interrupt request, it is necessary to assure that after completion of the subroutine the CPU will be able to return to the main program to resume its normal operation. This is done by temporarily storing the contents of the program counter and other registers/counters in some preassigned memory locations. In some computers it is possible to use several specially reserved scratch-pad locations for this purpose instead of using locations in the data memory.

4. *Peripheral Identification.* Since the INT REQ comes to the μP on a single input line, the CPU must first identify the requesting peripheral or I/O device so that it can call out the appropriate service subroutine from the memory. Identification of

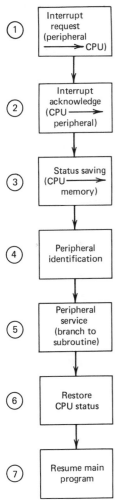

Figure 9-1   General sequence of events in interrupt I/O.

the requesting peripheral can be done in one of several ways to be discussed later in this chapter.

5. *Service Peripheral.* Having identified the particular requesting device, the program branches out to the starting address of the specific subroutine in the memory and services the peripheral.

6. *Restore CPU Status.* After completion of the service subroutine, the data from the CPU registers/counters, temporarily stored in the data memory, are reloaded back into their respective locations, and the CPU is restored to its preinterrupt status.

7. *Resume Main Program.* When all the CPU registers/counters, including the pro-

gram counter, are restored to their preinterrupt status, the main program resumes its operation.

9-3 CPU RESPONSE TO INTERRUPTS

9-3.1 Sequence of Events

What happens to the µP when an interrupt request is received from an external source? Before servicing the interrupt, the CPU goes through several events (see Fig. 9-2). Since instructions for servicing the peripherals are *not* included in the main program, the CPU, after completion of each instruction, must query and check for an interrupt before proceeding to the next instruction. This is done in hardware and is explained in Section 9-3.2

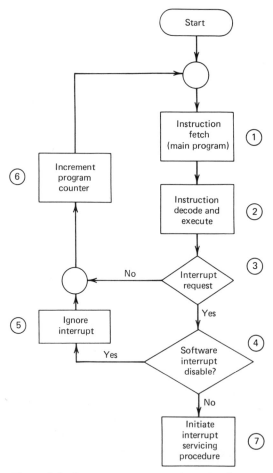

Figure 9-2   Interrupt request querying procedure.

As shown in Fig. 9-2, when each instruction execution is completed, the CPU queries the INT REQ line to see if an interrupt request has been received. In the absence of this signal the program counter is incremented, and the next instruction is fetched and executed. This process repeats itself, and the main program continues its execution until an INT REQ signal is received.

In some applications certain portions of the program may be critical, and servicing interrupts during this group of instructions may not be desirable. Such groups of critical instructions can be protected from interrupts by means of a software disable feature. A special instruction in the program, just ahead of this critical group, disables the INT REQ signal and the program proceeds, as shown in Fig. 9-2. Another special instruction in the program, placed immediately after the last instruction in the critical group of instructions, restores the INT REQ circuitry back to its normal operating state.

9-3.2 INT REQ Querying Logic

The logic for performing the querying function, shown in Fig. 9-2 and described in Section 9-3.1, is shown in Fig. 9-3. Operation is as follows.

1. The INT REQ signal is fed into one of the inputs to the 2-input AND gate 2. The second input to A2 comes from the output of flip-flop 1, which is normally set to the Q side.

2. If a group of critical instructions in the main program is to be protected from interrupts, the special *interrupt disable* instruction (just prior to this group) results in a software interrupt disable output from the instruction decoder.

3. Flip-flop 1 is now set to the $\overline{Q}$ side, thereby disabling A2 and blocking the INT REQ signal from going any further.

4. When execution of the protected group of instructions is completed, flip-flop 1 is set to the Q side by the special interrupt enable instruction in the program that is decoded by the decoder. The resulting signal, software interrupt enable, is fed into the S input of flip-flop 1.

5. Normally, the M signal is a 0 and this, when inverted, enables AND gate A4. Thus, when an INT REQ signal comes in, the output from A4 puts flip-flop 2 to the $\overline{Q}$ side.

6. AND gate A1 is now disabled and prevents the INCREMENT SIGNAL (from control and timing) from reaching the program counter and from incrementing.

7. The $\overline{Q}$ output of flip-flop enables AND gate A3, which sends out a properly timed INT ACK signal to the interrupting peripheral.

8. The $\overline{Q}$ side of flip-flop also goes to the logic, which initiates the interrupt service procedure.

9. A 1 output on the M line output disables A4. This provides a hardware lockout so that INT REQ signals from other peripherals will not interfere with the processing of the first interrupt.

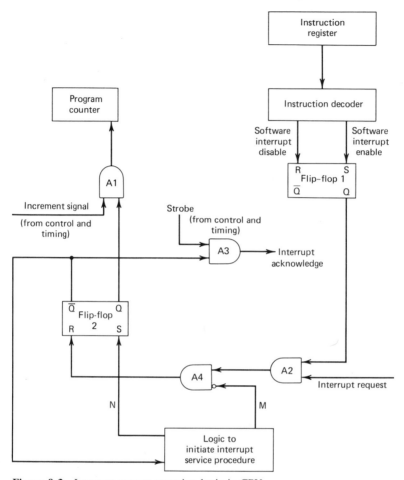

Figure 9-3   Interrupt request querying logic in CPU.

10. A pulse on the N output line sets flip-flop to the Q side and enables A1, so that subsequent increment signals will be able to increment the program counter when the service subroutine is executed.

9-4 INTERRUPT SERVICE INITIATION

9-4.1 Sequence of Events

Up to this point we have discussed the events that take place as depicted by block 1 in Fig. 9-1. After the INT REQ is honored by the CPU, the procedure for servicing the interrupt must be initiated (see block 7 of Fig. 9-2). This involves calling up a subroutine that must handle a number of events in proper sequence (Fig. 9-4). This sequence is generally triggered by the INT ACK signal, which is generated by the CPU, as shown in Fig. 9-3.

Servicing an INT REQ involves branching to a subroutine. After completing this subroutine control must be returned to the main program in an orderly manner. This means that the main program return address must be saved in a stack. The usual cascade stack could be used for this purpose, but it has a serious shortcoming. It is possible that, when the INT REQ signal arrives, the stack may already be full from other operations. As explained in Section 3-5.2.1, this will create problems. Consequently, for saving the program counter contents in an interrupt operation, a special pointer-type stack in the data memory is more convenient and is frequently used in several μCs. Since the arrival time of the INT REQ signal is unpredictable, it is necessary that the in-process data in the CPU be saved for later return to the original, preinterrupt

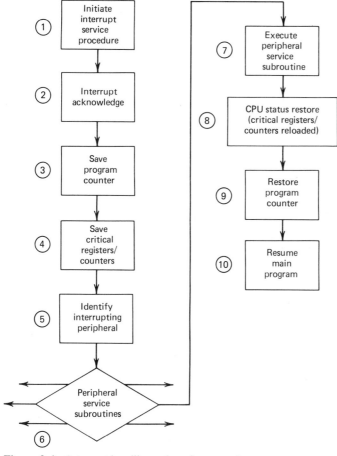

Figure 9-4   Interrupt handling subroutine procedure.

point in the program. This means that the contents of some of the critical registers/counters must be temporarily stored somewhere else. A pointer-type stack in the data memory provides a convenient system for status saving (see Fig. 9-4). Some of the critical registers/counters that are commonly saved during interrupt processing are:

- The accumulator(s).
- The address register/counter.
- The status register.
- The index register.

The next step in the process is to identify the interrupting peripheral so that the appropriate service subroutine can be called out. There are three methods by which the interrupting peripheral can be identified. They are described later in this chapter. The last instruction in the service subroutine returns control to the interrupt handling subroutine. The critical registers/counters are first reloaded with their preinterrupt contents; finally, the program counter is reloaded with the updated return address, which resumes operation at the preinterrupt, original point in the program.

9-4.2 Interrupt Handling Subroutine

The sequence of events described in Section 9-4.1 raises the question of how the main program branches to the interrupt handling subroutine when it receives the INT REQ signal. Four techniques are used; they are described later in this section. However, let us first look at some interrupt situations in a program that are graphically shown in Fig. 9-5.

In Fig. 9-5 three interrupts are shown coming from peripherals Q, P, and W, in that order. The INT REQ signals arrive during execution of the instructions whose addresses are 0074, 0323, and 039B, respectively. When the first INT REQ arrives, the current instruction at 0074 is completed, INT ACK is sent out, and the main program branches to the starting address of the interrupt handling subroutine whose first instruction is located at address 5000. This subroutine does the following.

1. *5000, SAVE (PC + 1)*. This instruction pushes the incremented program counter contents (0075 in this case) into the special pointer-type stack in the data memory.
2. *5001 to 5004, SAVE A-D*. These four instructions will push the contents of the four critical registers/counters (such as those mentioned in Section 9-4.1) into the stack and temporarily store them there during interrupt processing.
3. *5005, IDT PER*. This instruction identifies the interrupting peripheral (peripheral Q in this case). Only one instruction is shown here for simplicity, but it is possible

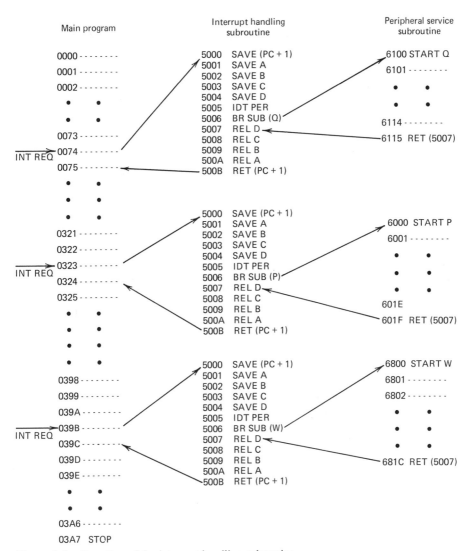

| | Main program | | Interrupt handling subroutine | | Peripheral service subroutine |

Figure 9-5 Operation of the interrupt handling subroutine.

to have more than one instruction for this function, depending on the technique used for identifying the peripheral.

4. *5006, BR SUB (Q)*. This is a BRANCH instruction that inserts the starting address of the service subroutine for the peripheral, identified by the previous instruction, into the program counter. In this example it is 6100, which is the starting address for peripheral Q service subroutine. Addresses 6100 to 6114 will service peripheral Q. Address 6115 contains the RETURN instruction, which returns control back to the interrupt handling subroutine. In this system the last instruction in service subroutines for all the peripherals will contain the RET (5007) instruction.

5. *5007 to 500A, REL D-A*. These four instructions pop the contents of the special stack in the data memory and reload or restore the four critical registers/counters to their preinterrupt status.

6. *500B, RET (PC + 1)*. This is a RETURN instruction that pops the stack in the data memory and reloads the program counter with the incremented address, thereby returning control to the main program.

Subsequent interrupts for peripherals P and W are processed similarly by the interrupt handling subroutine except that the BRANCH instruction in address 5006 will contain the starting addresses 6000 and 6800 for P and W, respectively.

9-4.3 Branching to Subroutine

In Section 9-4.2 we discussed the interrupt handling subroutine, which processes the INT REQ from a peripheral. How does the main program branch from its normal operation to this subroutine when there is no specific BRANCH instruction inserted in the main program at this point? There are several techniques by which this is accomplished.

9-4.3.1 Using a BRANCH Instruction This technique involves the use of the CPU-generated INT ACK signal to do the following.

1. Disable the memory and the I/O ports so that effectively they are disconnected from the main system data bus (Fig. 9-6).
2. Enable the special interrupt instruction register in the I/O interrupt chip.

The I/O interrupt chip of Fig. 9-6 receives the interrupt requests from the external peripherals and transfers them to the μP as the INT REQ signal. The CPU then sends out the INT ACK signal, which disconects the various ports from the data bus. The same signal enables the interrupt instruction register in the I/O interrupt chip. The contents of the register are sent to the μP through the system data bus. This is a BRANCH instruction that is loaded into the instruction register in the μP. This instruction contains the starting address of the interrupt handling subroutine, which is then loaded into the program counter. In the example used in Fig. 9-5 this address would be 5000. It is possible that this BRANCH instruction could be a multibyte or multiword instruction. The branching process is then executed as any other normal BRANCH instruction. The sequence of events in this operation is graphically shown in Fig. 9-7.

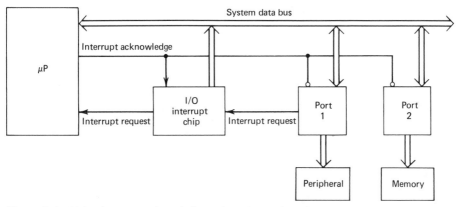

Figure 9-6   Using interrupt acknowledge to branch to subroutine.

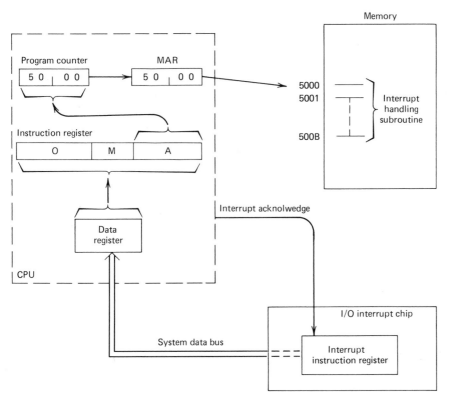

Figure 9-7   Operation of the BRANCH instruction.

The BRANCH instruction, including the starting address of the interrupt handling subroutine, can be hard-wired into the interrupt instruction register of the chip during the manufacturing process, or a chip can be designed in which this register could be loaded with a different address under program control. Such an address could be loaded into the register during the initialization process. If this is so, the unidirectional bus from the I/O interrupt chip to the system data bus (in Fig. 9-6) must be replaced by a bidirectional bus. The Intel 8080 μP uses a scheme similar to that just described.

9-4.3.2 Using an Address Pointer Another simple technique is to store the starting address of the interrupt handling subroutine as a pointer in either a dedicated register in the CPU or a dedicated location in the data memory. When an INT REQ signal is received (and honored) by the CPU, the logic in the CPU will automatically call out this pointer from the dedicated location, and jam it into the program counter. This process is executed independent of the INT ACK signal.

The scheme using internal CPU registers is shown in Fig. 9-8. In this particular scheme two registers in the scratch pad are dedicated for storing the address pointer. A 16-bit program counter and a 16-bit memory address require two registers in the 8-bit-wide scratch pad for this function. Notice that unlike the BRANCH instruction (discussed in Section 9-4.3.1), this technique bypasses the instruction register, which only comes into action when the first instruction of the interrupt handling subroutine (address 5000) is called out and loaded into it. The RCA 1802 COSMAC μP uses this technique.

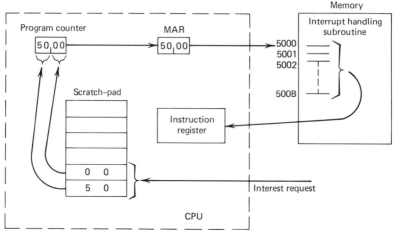

Figure 9-8   Pointer technique using internal CPU registers (scratch pad).

The technique using a dedicated location in data memory is shown in Fig. 9-9. In this case the pointer is stored in location 7000 in the RAM. Of course, it could also be stored in ROM. The Motorola 6800 μP uses a similar technique.

9-4.3.3 *Using an Externally Supplied Address*

9-4.3.3 Using an Externally Supplied Address This technique is a simple method where the interrupting peripheral itself supplies the starting address of its own subroutine to the CPU. When the INT REQ is received, the current instruction will be completed and the INT ACK sent out. The incremented contents of the program counter will be pushed into the stack and saved for the return to the main program. The interrupting peripheral then sends the starting address of its own service subroutine to the CPU through the system data bus. This address is jammed into the program counter, and the service subroutine execution starts. The last instruction in this subroutine returns control to the main program by popping the stack.

Notice that the interrupt handling subroutine, which is a separate routine and is used in the two methods described in Sections 9-4.3.1 and 9-4.3.2, is not used here as a separate program. The instructions for CPU status saving and status restoring are included as part of each service subroutine. This makes the service subroutine longer but allows each subroutine to save only the CPU registers/counters required for that particular operation instead of saving all of

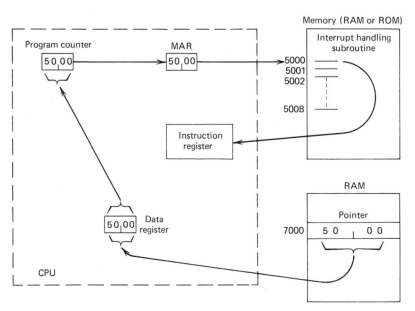

Figure 9-9 Pointer technique using dedicated RAM location.

them. A technique very similar to this is used in the SIGNETICS 2650 μP. Graphically, the operation is shown in Fig. 9-10 for peripheral B. The starting address of its service subroutine is 2C0D.

Note. The starting instruction of the service subroutine is often called the TRAP instruction and the address, the TRAP address. The locations in the memory where the subroutine is stored is called the TRAP CELL.

9-4.4 Status Saving and Restoring

In most μCs it is necessary that some critical registers/counters besides the program counter be saved during interrupt processing. Generally, three approaches are commonly used, as described here.

1. *Using a Memory Stack.* A certain portion of the R/W memory is designated as the stack for saving the status of the critical registers/counters. Such a stack must, of course, use a pointer for its operation. The starting address of the stack is inserted into the pointer register by the interrupt handling subroutine. This approach is simple and straightforward and is very convenient if all the predetermined registers/ counters are to be saved every time an interrupt is processed. The Motorola 6800 μP does exactly that. The contents of all the registers/counters are saved in the

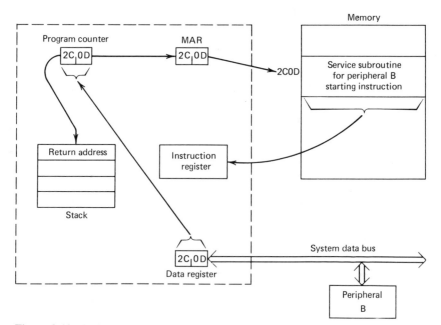

Figure 9-10   Peripheral-supplied starting address.

stack. However, this procedure would waste unnecessary time if the interrupt by a particular peripheral does not require the use of all the saved registers/counters in its service subroutine. Also, care must be taken that the stack does not overflow or that some other data are not accidentally inserted in the memory locations reserved for the stack. When the service subroutine is completed, the registers/counters will be restored in the CPU in LIFO order from the stack.

2. *Using Duplicate Registers/Counters.* In some μPs a completely different approach is used. A duplicate set of the critical registers/counters is provided. During normal program operation set 1 of these registers/counters is used. When an INT REQ is received and honored, set 1 is disconnected from the rest of the system, so the contents of these registers/counters are automatically saved and not disturbed during the execution of the service subroutine. The duplicate set 2 is switched into the system, and these will be used by the service subroutine. When interrupt processing is completed, set 2 is disconnected from the system and set 1 is reconnected. This system has a speed advantage, since no transfers of data, either during the saving or during the restoring phases of the operation, are involved. Its major shortcoming is that only a few registers/counters can be duplicated because real estate on a silicon chip is always at a premium. The SIGNETICS 2650 μP uses this approach.

3. *Using Available RAM Locations.* In this approach the programmer must identify which registers/counters (as allowed by the design of the μP and the instructions available in the instruction set) are to be saved during the execution of a particular service subroutine. During the status-saving phase of the operation, a memory store instruction (with the available memory location address) must be inserted in the interrupt handling subroutine for each register and counter to be saved. After the service subroutine is completed, the contents of each register and/or counter must be reloaded from the memory. Each requires a separate load instruction. This is the approach shown in the interrupt handling subroutine operation of Fig. 9-5. Any available location in the RAM can be used for status saving using this approach. Another advantage is that the programmer controls which registers/counters are saved. All registers/counters need not be saved for each service subroutine.

9-4.5 Identifying the Interrupting Peripheral

Before the service subroutine can be called out and executed, the peripheral that is sending the INT REQ signal must be properly identified since this signal comes to the CPU on a single line. Three methods, described in Sections 9-5, 9-6, and 9-7, are used for identifying the interrupting peripheral. Two of these approaches use software techniques, and one uses a hardware technique. Each is unique and has its advantages and disadvantages.

9-5 THE VECTORED INTERRUPT

9-5.1 Introductory Remarks

This is a simple, straightforward, software technique in which the interrupting peripheral branches the main program directly to its own particular service subroutine. This is accomplished by the peripheral identifying itself to the CPU as soon as it receives the INT ACK from the μP in response to its INT REQ signal. The identification process includes a unique address or code that the peripheral sends to the CPU through the external or system data bus. In the system using the vectored interrupt, this code or address is the starting address of its own subroutine, which is jammed into the program counter of the CPU. Prior to accepting this starting address, the program counter is incremented, and this return address is pushed into the stack. This process is shown in Fig. 9-10.

9-5.2 The Sequence of Events

Before initiating the interrupt service procedure, the μP goes through a querying sequence (see Fig. 9-2 and Section 9-3.1). The subsequent sequence of events is shown in flowchart form in Fig. 9-11. The circled numbers next to each block correspond to the following numbered explanations.

1. After determining that the software interrupt disable is not activated (Figs. 9-2 and 9-3), the interrupt service procedure is initiated, since the INT REQ is honored.
2. The program counter is incremented, and this address is pushed into the stack for return to the main program after servicing the interrupt.
3. To insure that a second INT REQ signal does not come in and interfere with the execution of the first signal, the disable hardware interrupt system is activated. This is done by setting flip-flop 2 of Fig. 9-3 to the $\overline{Q}$ side, which in turn disables AND gate A4 through the logic block shown as "Logic to Initiate Interrupt Service Procedure."
4. Regardless of when the INT REQ arrives, the CPU always completes its current instruction.
5. The INT ACK signal is sent out to the interrupting peripheral through AND gate A3 of Fig. 9-3.
6. The interrupting peripheral responds to the INT ACK signal by placing its own unique code or address on the system data bus. How this is done will be explained in Section 9-5.3. This is usually the starting address of that particular peripheral's own service subroutine, which is stored in the memory.
7. The service subroutine starting address is jammed into the program counter of the CPU.

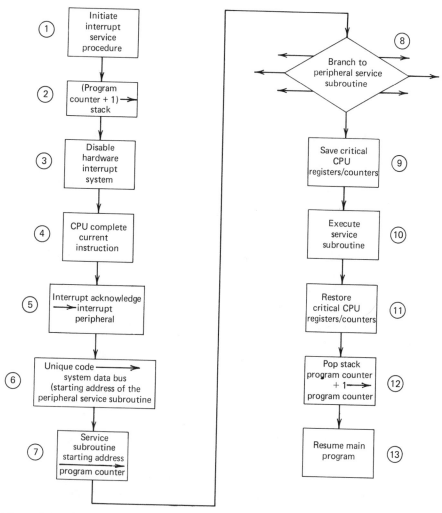

Figure 9-11 Sequence of events for vectored interrupt system.

8. Now the program automatically branches to the appropriate service subroutine. Note that a separate BRANCH instruction for this purpose is not required.

9. The service subroutine starts out by saving the critical registers/counters in the CPU using one of the three approaches presented in Section 9-4.4.

10. The service subroutine of the interrupting peripheral is executed.

11. The last few instructions in the service subroutine are used to reload or restore the original contents back into the critical registers/counters in the CPU.

12. The final instruction in the service subroutine is a RETURN instruction that pops the stack and loads the updated address into the program counter.

13. The main program is resumed. Note that in Fig. 9-3, flip-flop 2 is now set to the Q side by signal N and the AND gate A4 is enabled by a 0 on line M. This makes it possible for the system to accept future INT REQ signals.

9-5.3 Interface Chip Logic

Figure 9-12 shows a simplified logic diagram of an I/O interface chip for vectored interrupts as used in μCs. The operation of this chip will be described by explaining these four main operations: (1) the interrupt request and peripheral identification; (2) the peripheral selection and activation; (3) the data input operation; and (4) the data output operation.

The following assumptions are made.

1. An 8-bit μP is used.
2. N number of peripherals are used in this system, but only two are shown in Fig. 9-12. For simplicity, only the logic gates, associated with peripheral 1 and peripheral N, are shown.
3. Peripheral 1 is an input-only device such as an entry keyboard.
4. Peripheral N is an output-only device such as a display.
5. The address or unique identifying code of each peripheral is 8 bits long. In the following discussion we refer to this as "the vector," which is generally the starting address of that particular peripheral's service subroutine.

9-5.3.1 INT REQ and Peripheral Identification Operation is as follows.

1. Any one of the N peripherals can send an interrupt request to the CPU when it is ready for data transfer. By setting its internal INT flip-flop to the Q side, a 1 is sent to the μP as the INT REQ signal through the OR gate 02. INT REQ also partially enables the AND gate AA.
2. At the same time, the interrupting peripheral (e.g., the keyboard) sends out its unique code or the vector to the *device vector register* through the 8-bit *vector transfer bus*.
3. After completing its current instruction, the μP sends out the INT ACK signal, which now fully enables AND gate AA. A 1 output from AA enables the 8 address input AND gates AI_1 to AI_8, which transmit the vector out of the device vector register to the CPU through the system data bus.
4. The vector is loaded into the program counter in the CPU, and the interrupt, processing operation begins.
5. Note that, in this case, the same 8-bit bidirectional system data bus lines are time-shared to transmit the peripheral vector to the CPU.

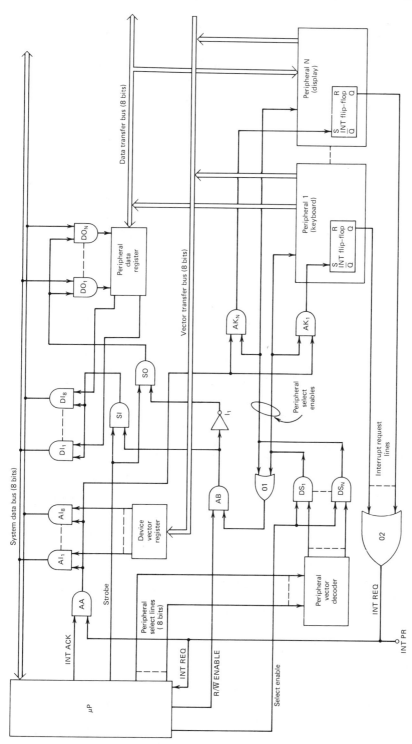

Figure 9-12 Logic diagram of vectored interrupt on the I/O interface chip.

9-5.3.2 Peripheral Selection and Activation Operation is as follows.

1. The CPU sends the appropriate PERIPHERAL SELECT code or signals to the PERIPHERAL VECTOR DECODER in the interface chip. Depending on the design of the μP and the system, this could be the code or the vector sent by the peripheral itself. These 8 bits are then decoded, and a 1 is put on only one of its N output lines.
2. One of the AND gates labeled DS_1 to DS_N is partially enabled.
3. Following this, the CPU sends a 1 signal on the SELECT ENABLE line. If the interrupting peripheral were the keyboard (i.e., 1), DS_1 was previously partially enabled (step 2 preceding). DS_1 is now fully enabled and outputs a 1.
4. The 1 output from DS_1 signals the peripheral 1 to output its data and transfer them to the PERIPHERAL DATA REGISTER through the 8-bit data transfer bus.
5. The 1 output from DS_1 also partially enables AND gate AB through the OR gate 01.

9-5.3.3 Data Input Operation Operation is as follows.

1. The μP puts out a signal on the R/$\overline{W}$ ENABLE line. This is the R/W select line. As shown in Fig. 9-12, the symbol R/$\overline{W}$ means that for reading into the μP, the line is active high (i.e., has a 1 on it), and for writing into the peripheral (output from the CPU), the line is active low (i.e., has a 0 on it).
2. For data input into the CPU, a 1 on the R/$\overline{W}$ ENABLE line fully enables AND gate AB, whose 1 output partially enables AND gate SI. Note that the 1 output of AB disables the AND gate S0 because of the inverter I_1.
3. The CPU issues a 1 on the STROBE line, which fully enables SI.
4. The 1 output of SI partially enables the 8 data input AND gates labeled DI_1 to DI_8. The previously loaded data are thus gated out from the PERIPHERAL DATA REGISTER to the CPU through these AND gates and the 8-bit system data bus.
5. In this sequence, during the input operation, the output of AND gate S0 is 0 because of I_1. This disables the 8 data output AND gates DO_1 to DO_8. If these gates were not disabled, 8 feedback loops would be established, and the data output by the PERIPHERAL DATA REGISTER would be reloaded into it, thus creating an erroneous situation.

9-5.3.4 Data Output Operation Operation is as follows.

1. An output operation, say to the display (peripheral N), follows the same procedures described in Sections 9-5.3.1 and 9-5.3.2.
2. The only difference is that now the CPU puts out a 0 on the R/$\overline{W}$ ENABLE line. A 0 output from AB disables the input AND gates DI_1 to DI_8.

3. Because of inverter I_1, AND gate S0 is partially enabled.
4. When the CPU puts a 1 on the STROBE line, the 1 output from S0 partially enables the 8 data output AND gates DO_1 to DO_8. The data output by the μP are then loaded into the PERIPHERAL DATA REGISTER through the system data bus and, from there, into peripheral N.
5. In this sequence, during the output operation, the output of gate SI is a 0. this disables gate DI_1 to DI_8. If these gates were not disabled, 8 feedback loops would be established, and the data output by the CPU would return back to it through the DI_1 to DI_8 gates and the system data bus.

9-6 THE SOFTWARE-POLLED INTERRUPT

9-6.1 Introductory Remarks

The vectored interrupt system, described in Section 9-5, services the interrupts from the peripherals strictly on a first-come first-served basis. As shown in Fig. 9-12, the interrupt requests from all the peripherals are ORed and input to the CPU on a single INT REQ line. Whenever one interrupt is serviced, others are locked out (see AND gate A4 in Fig. 9-3). If two peripherals send in their INT REQ signals almost at the same time, only one will be honored (i.e., the one arriving slightly ahead of the other). But it is possible that for some reason it may be more important to service the second interrupting peripheral first in a particular system. In other words, some sort of interrupt *priority* system might be desirable.

The software-polled interrupt establishes a priority system for servicing peripherals. If two (or more) peripherals send in their INT REQ signals simultaneously, the one with the higher priority will be serviced first. The priority of each peripheral is established by its relative position in the polling sequence. The priority of each peripheral is established by the designer during the design phase of the system.

9-6.2 The Sequence of Events

Before initiating the interrupt service procedure, the μP goes through a querying sequence (see Fig. 9-2 and Section 9-3.1). The subsequent sequence of events is shown in flowchart form in Fig. 9-13. The circled numbers next to each block correspond to the following numbered explanations.

1. After determining that the software interrupt disable is not activated (Figs. 9-2 and 9-3), the interrupt service procedure is initiated, since the INT REQ is honored.
2. The program counter is incremented, and this address is pushed into the stack for return to the main program after servicing the interrupt.

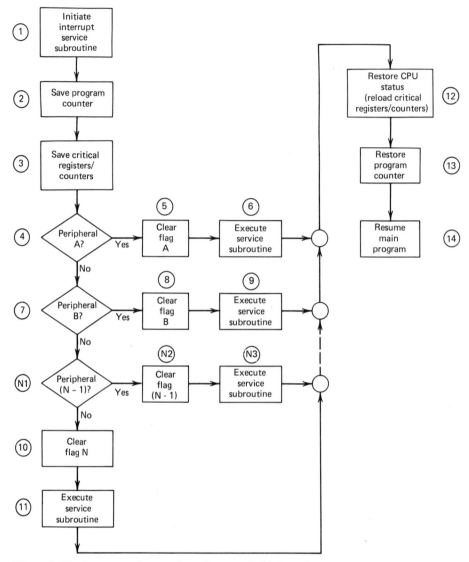

Figure 9-13 Sequence of events for software-polled interrupt.

3. The contents of the critical registers/counters are saved using one of the techniques described in Section 9-4.4.
4. The interrupt handling subroutine now starts the polling sequence. A special instruction, which we will call the TEST I/O instruction, sends out a STROBE signal to the first peripheral (the one with the highest priority in the system) to determine if it is the interrupting unit. If peripheral A is the one that sent out an

INT REQ signal, it will respond to the TEST I/O instruction by sending a return signal that will set a flag in the CPU. The next instruction is a conditional BRANCH instruction that will test the status of the flag.

5. If the flag is set, the CPU logic will clear this flag so that it will not interfere with the rest of the operation that follows.

6. The program now branches to the service subroutine of peripheral A and executes it.

7. If the flag in the CPU is not set the interrupt handling subroutine proceeds to the next instruction, which is a TEST I/O instruction that tests the internal INT flip-flop of peripheral B.

8. If peripheral B were the interrupting unit, the flag in the CPU is cleared.

9. The service subroutine for peripheral B is then executed. The preceding procedure is followed for all the remaining peripherals up to peripheral $N - 1$. If none of the peripherals to this point are identified as the interrupting peripheral, it must be peripheral N.

10. For the reason just explained, no check is made to determine if the INT REQ came from peripheral N. The CPU flag is cleared.

11. The service subroutine for peripheral N is executed.

12. After completing the service subroutine for any of the peripherals, control is returned to the interrupt handling subroutine and the critical registers/counters are reloaded with their preinterrupt contents.

13. The contents of the stack are popped and loaded into the program counter.

14. Control is returned to the main program, and the normal preinterrupt operation is resumed.

Note. Honoring higher-priority interrupts during the servicing of lower-priority interrupts is covered in Section 9-8).

9-6.3 Interrupt Handling Subroutine

The sequence of events described in Section 9-6.2 and shown in Fig. 9-13 requires some modifications in the interrupt handling subroutine from that previously described in Section 9-4.2 and shown in Fig. 9-5. These differences are described in a program in Fig. 9-14. The following assumptions are made.

1. Four peripherals are used in this system. They are labeled A, B, C, and D. They are arranged in sequence of their priorities; A has the highest priority and D the lowest.

2. In addition to the program counter, three critical registers, X, Y, and Z, must be saved during interrupt processing.

3. After completing the interrupt process, Z, Y, and X are restored, in that order.

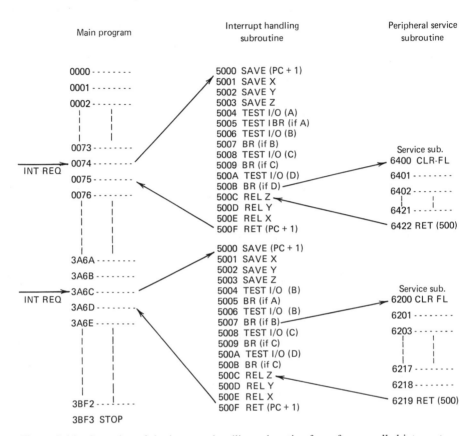

Figure 9-14   Operation of the interrupt handling subroutine for software-polled interrupt.

In Fig. 9-14 two interrupts are shown coming from peripherals D and B, in that order. The INT REQ signals arrive during execution of the instructions whose addresses are 0074 and 3A6C, respectively, in the main program. When the first INT REQ arrives, the current instruction is completed, and the program branches to address 5000. This is the starting address of the interrupt handling subroutine. The subroutine does the following.

1. *5000, SAVE (PC + 1).* This instruction pushes the incremented program counter contents (0075 in this case) into the pointer-type stack in the data memory.
2. *5001 − 5003, SAVE X − Z.* These three instructions will push the contents of the three critical registers into the stack and temporarily store them there during interrupt processing.
3. *5004 − 500B, TEST I/O, BRANCH.* These eight instructions are paired as TEST I/O and BRANCH for each of the four peripherals in the system (i.e., A, B, C, and D). The first instruction in the pair tests the internal INT flip-flop of each

respective peripheral and sets a flag in the CPU if that particular unit is the peripheral requesting the interrupt processing. The second instruction, BRANCH, samples this CPU flip-flop and conditionally branches to the starting address of the service subroutine (address 6400 in this case).

4. *500C − 500E, REL Z − X.* These three instructions pop the contents of the stack in the data memory and restore the three critical registers to their preinterrupt status.

5. *500F, RET (PC + 1).* This is a RETURN instruction that pops the stack in the data memory and reloads the program counter with the incremented address, thereby returning control to the main program.

Notice what happens when peripheral B sends an INT REQ during execution of the instruction at address 3A6C. The interrupt handling subroutine branches to the service subroutine from address 5007. In the previous interrupt it branched from address 500C. In either case they return to address 500C when the service subroutine is completed. This means that the time required for polling is *shorter* for peripheral B than for peripheral D. In this case a saving of four instruction time in the interrupt handling subroutine results. Thus considerable polling time is saved by assigning *higher* priorities to the peripherals that are likely to demand interrupt service *more frequently* and lower priorities to those that are likely to interrupt less frequently.

9-6.4 Polling Operation in the CPU

Figure 9-15 shows the logic in the CPU associated with identifying the interrupting peripheral and branching to the corresponding subroutine. Refer to Fig. 9-14 for the first INT REQ from peripheral D. Before considering the instructions relating to peripheral D, let us back up two instructions and see how peripheral C was polled.

When the program counter contained 5008, TEST I/O C, the **A** field in the instruction register sent out a STROBE to peripheral C through the AND gate AA. Prior to this, the **A** field of the instruction sent out the proper address of peripheral C to the interface chip. If peripheral C were the interrupting unit, it would have responded with a 1 on the STATUS RETURN line and the FLAG flip-flop to the Q side. Since C was not the interrupting unit, the FLAG was set on the $\overline{Q}$ side. The program counter now advances to 500B, and the conditional BRANCH is inserted in the instruction register. The FLAG flip-flop disables the AND gate AB, and so the program counter increments and contains address 500A.

Address 500A in the program counter loads the TEST I/O (D) instruction in the instruction register. The **A** field sends out the address of peripheral D on the ADDRESS BUS. This is followed by the timed STROBE to D. Since

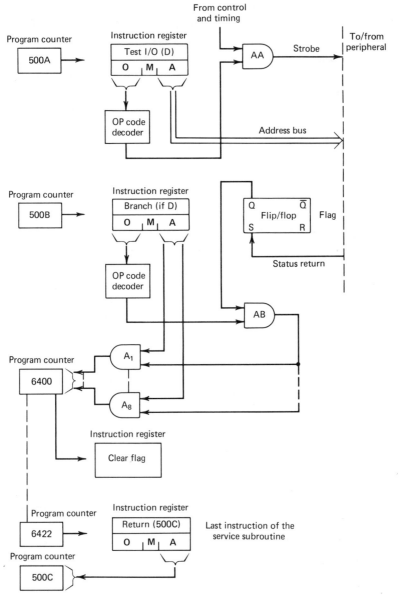

Figure 9-15   CPU operation for software-polled interrupt.

D is the interrupting peripheral, it puts a 1 on the STATUS RETURN line, which sets the FLAG to the Q side, and partially enables AND gate AB.

The program counter now increments and contains 500B, which loads the BRANCH (if D) instruction in the instruction register. The **O** field of the instruction is decoded, and the single-line output fully enables AND gate AB whose 1 output partially enables the 8 gates labeled A_1 to A_8. The **A** field of this instruction contains the starting address of the service subroutine for peripheral D (i.e., 6400), which is now loaded into the program counter. The last instruction in the service subroutine is RET (500C), which returns control to the interrupt handling subroutine.

9-6.5 Interface Chip Logic

Figure 9-16 shows a simplified logic diagram of the software-polled interrupt on the I/O interface chip commonly used in μCs. The operation of this chip is described in conjunction with the first INT REQ sent by peripheral D, as shown in Fig. 9-14. Also, reference is made to the CPU operation as explained in Section 9-6.4 and shown in Fig. 9-15. Operation is as follows.

1. Instruction TEST I/O (A) at address 5004 in the interrupt handling subroutine is decoded by the peripheral address decoder in Fig. 9-16. A 1 is output on line 1.
2. When the STROBE signal is sent by the CPU, 2 inputs to the 3-input AND gate AA are enabled.
3. Gate AA, however, is not fully enabled because the INT flip-flop of peripheral A is set to the $\overline{Q}$ side. Therefore the STATUS RETURN line to the CPU has a 0 on it.
4. As shown in Fig. 9-14, the program counter now contains 5005. The BR (if A) instruction does not perform the conditional branch, and the program proceeds on to address 5006 in the program counter.
5. Since the INT flip-flop of peripherals B and C are also set to the $\overline{Q}$ side, the next four instructions (addresses 5006 to 5009) will be executed, but no branching to service subroutine takes place in either case.
6. As a result of the instruction at 500A, line 4 in Fig. 9-16 has a 1 on it. The INT flip-flop of peripheral D is set on the Q side.
7. When the CPU issues the STROBE signal, AND gate AD is fully enabled and sends a 1 to the CPU as a STATUS RETURN signal through the OR gate OS.
8. The FLAG flip-flop in the CPU is set to the Q side (Fig. 9-15) and, as explained in Section 9-6.4, the program branches to the service subroutine for peripheral D.

9-7 THE HARDWARE-POLLED INTERRUPT (DAISY-CHAIN)

9-7.1 The Basic Principle

Hardware polling is a relatively simple method of determining the identity of the interrupting peripheral; it is frequently used in μCs. It combines some of the techniques of the vectored interrupt (Section 9-5) and software-polling

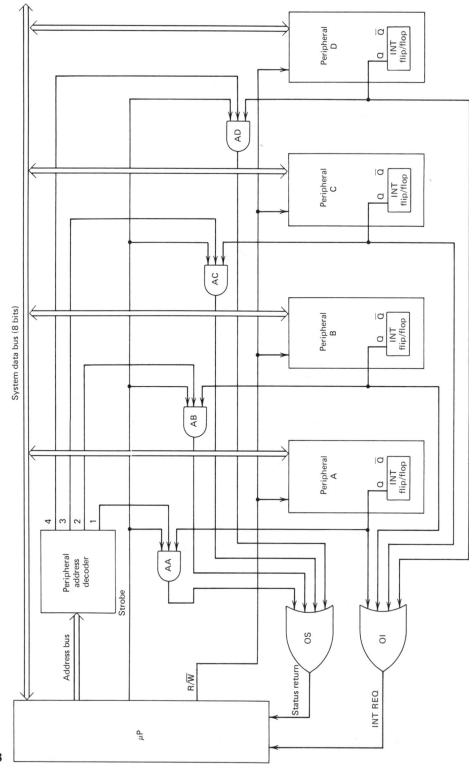

Figure 9-16 Logic diagram of software-polled interrupt on the I/O interface chip.

248

(Section 9-6) approaches. It is similar to the vectored interrupt because each interrupting peripheral sends its vector or unique code to the CPU through the system data bus. This vector is the starting address of its corresponding service subroutine and is jammed into the program counter in exactly the same manner as shown in Fig. 9-10. It is similar to the software-polled interrupt because the peripherals are polled in a preestablished sequence by querying the status of the interrupt flip-flop. The difference is that the querying is not done by the interrupt handling subroutine but by the hardware on the I/O interface chip.

9-7.2 The Logic Diagram

A simplified logic diagram of the I/O interface chip is shown in Fig. 9-17. The Q outputs of each of the INT flip-flops in each of the four peripherals are ORed into the OR gate OI. A 1 on any one of the 4 input lines sends the INT REQ signal to the μP. After receiving this signal, the CPU commences the polling operation by sending the INT ACK signal to the two AND gates A1 and A2. We will describe the sequence of events that follow by assuming that the interrupting unit is peripheral C.

Since the INT flip-flop of peripheral A is not set, the Q output of this flip-flop has a 0 and so disables A1. The 0 output of A1 now fully enables A2, whose 1 output partially enables A3. the INT flip-flop of peripheral B is not set, so A3 is disabled and its 0 output now fully enables A4, which has a 1 output. Since peripheral C is the interrupting unit, its INT flip-flop is set to the Q side. Note that now both the inputs to A5 are 1, so its output is a 1. When a peripheral sets its INT flip-flop to the Q side, it simultaneously puts its vector (i.e., the starting address of its service subroutine) on the vector transfer bus and loads it into the peripheral vector register.

The 1 output of A5 does the following.

1. It disables A6, so the INT ACK signal does not propagate any further.
2. It enables the 8 address output gates AA_1 to AA_8 through the OR gate OB.
3. The contents of the peripheral vector register (i.e., the vector of peripheral C) are input to the CPU through the system data bus.
4. It puts a 1 on the SELECT C line. This does one of the following.
   (a) If the following operation is an input into the CPU, peripheral C loads the peripheral data register through the peripheral data bus.
   (b) If the following operation is an output from the CPU, peripheral C will be ready to accept a transfer of data from the peripheral data register.

The main program in the CPU now branches to the service subroutine of peripheral C. Assume that an input into the CPU (i.e., a read operation) is called out. A 1 is put on the R/$\overline{\text{W}}$ line. This enables AND gate SI but disables

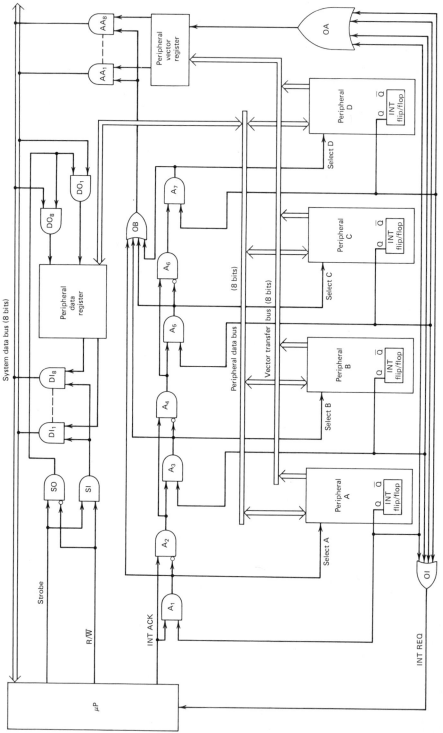

Figure 9-17 Logic diagram of hardware-polling (daisy-chain) interrupt on the I/O interface chip.

AND gate SO. A little later the CPU sends out a 1 signal on the STROBE line, fully enabling SI. The 1 output of SI enables the data input AND gates DI_1 to DI_8. The previously loaded data from the peripheral data register are thus input into the CPU through the system data bus.

On the other hand, if the operation involved a write or an output from CPU operation, the same sequence for peripheral identification takes place. The data word is then output on the system data bus by the CPU. A 0 on the $R/\overline{W}$ line disables SI and partially enables SO. A 1 output from SO enables data output gates DO_1 to DO_8, and the data on the system data bus are loaded into the peripheral data register. From there, these data bits are available to peripheral C through the vector transfer bus.

9-8 MULTILEVEL PRIORITY INTERRUPTS

9-8.1 The Operation

What happens if an interrupt is received by the CPU while servicing a prior INT REQ from another peripheral? If the μC uses any of the three interrupt schemes discussed in this chapter, the answer is that during the processing of the first peripheral, interrupt requests from other peripherals will be ignored. The CPU will complete the service subroutine of the first interrupting peripheral, return to the main program, and then service the next interrupt, either immediately if the system uses vectored interrupt or by determining its priority if a polling scheme is used.

In some applications it is desirable to provide multilevel or cascaded interrupts. In such a system a peripheral with a higher assigned priority will interrupt the service subroutine in progress of another peripheral with a lower assigned priority. Figure 9-18 shows how such an interrupt system operates. Let us assume that four peripherals, A, B, C, and D, are used. Also, let us assume that they are assigned interrupt priorities as shown here, with the first peripheral having the highest priority: (1) peripheral B; (2) peripheral D; (3) peripheral A; (4) peripheral C.

Now suppose that interrupt requests from these four peripherals come up in the following time sequence: (1) peripheral A; (2) peripheral C; (3) peripheral D; and (4) peripheral B.

Figure 9-18 shows the sequence in which these interrupts will be serviced. An explanation of each step follows.

1. As soon as peripheral A interrupts the main program, it will be serviced with its own service subroutine.
2. While A is being serviced, C will attempt to interrupt but will be ignored because of its lowest priority.

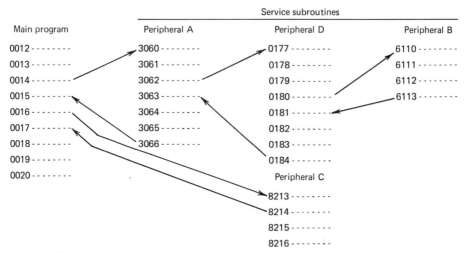

Figure 9-18   Example of multilevel interrupts.

3. Before servicing of A is completed, peripheral D interrupts. Since D has a higher priority than A, the service subroutine for A will be suspended until D is fully serviced.

4. However, before the subroutine for D is completed, peripheral B interrupts and, since B has the highest priority in the system, the processing of D is suspended.

5. After peripheral B is completely serviced, the subroutine for D is resumed and completed. Subroutine for A is then resumed and completed, and control is returned to the main program.

6. During this time, C has been interrupting but has been ignored. Finally, it gets serviced when all other peripherals with higher priorities have been fully serviced.

It is apparent from Fig. 9-18 that this process is similar to that of the normal subroutine branching, with several levels of nesting, but with the following two exceptions.

1. Subroutine branching is not initiated by an instruction either in the main program or in a subroutine but by an INT REQ from an external source.

2. If an interrupt from a peripheral interrupts the subroutine in progress for another peripheral, the logic in the system must determine the previously established priority of the second peripheral in relation to the first peripheral and decide whether or not the second interrupt should be honored.

Since subroutines are called out, the incremented return addresses in the program counter must be saved in the stack. Figure 9-19*a* shows what the

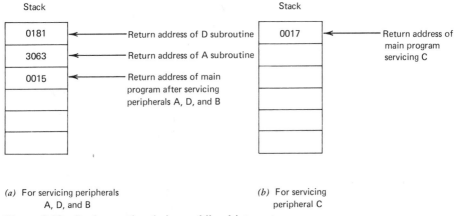

(a) For servicing peripherals
   A, D, and B

(b) For servicing
   peripheral C

Figure 9-19   Stack operation during multilevel interrupts.

stack will contain during the servicing of interrupts from peripherals A, D, and B; Fig. 9-19*b* shows what will be in the stack for servicing peripheral C.

9-8.2 Interrupt System Block Diagram

It is apparent from Fig. 9-18 that the vectored interrupt system, which was previously described in Section 9-5, would be appropriate and convenient to use in a multilevel priority interrupt system, since each peripheral would supply its own vector to the CPU. In multilevel priority interrupts it is necessary to save the contents of the critical registers/counters every time the INT REQ is honored for a higher-priority peripheral. This means that additional facilities for storing these data must be provided for each level of interrupts. This can be done by providing dedicated register stacks either in the CPU or in RAM chips using pointer-type stacks for dedicated locations (see Section 4-4.4).

For multilevel priority interrupt systems, the service subroutine for each peripheral must be self-contained and must first save the contents of the critical registers/counters before proceeding with the I/O operation. Also, after completing the I/O operation, the critical registers/counters must be restored before returning to a previous subroutine or the main program.

The logic for the I/O interface chip using the vectored interrupt (Fig. 9-12) can be used in this system but with the following modification. The INT REQ lines from the peripherals are not fed into the inputs to the OR gate 02 of Fig. 9-12. Instead, they are fed into the inputs of the interrupt priority chip, and a single INT REQ output from this chip is connected to the input terminal marked INT PR on Fig. 9-12. The resulting system configuration, for four peripherals, is shown in block diagram form in Fig. 9-20.

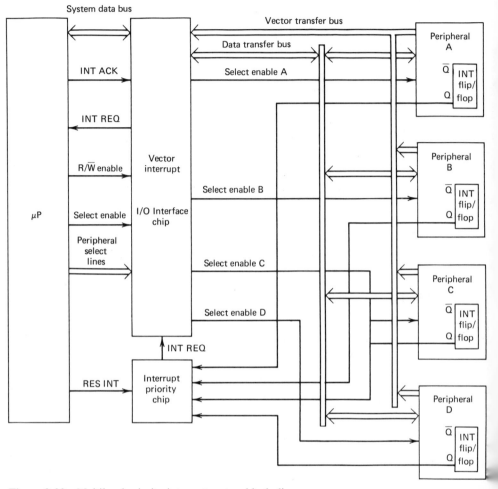

Figure 9-20   Multilevel priority interrupt system block diagram.

9-8.3 Multilevel Priority Interrupt Chip

The logic required for the multilevel priority interrupts is implemented by several different schemes in different μC systems. The simplest possible scheme is the one shown in Fig. 9-21. Although it is shown for only four peripherals, the scheme is so simple that it can be readily extended beyond four peripherals. The main drawback of this scheme is that it requires an additional control signal from the μP, which we will call RES INT (reset interrupt) and whose function is explained below.

The basis of this logic scheme is simply that the interrupt request from the highest-priority peripheral should be input unimpeded into the OR gate OI while at the same time disabling the interrupt requests from all lower-priority

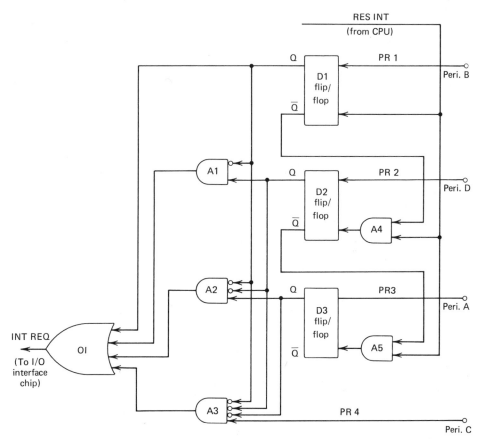

Figure 9-21   Logic diagram for four-peripheral, multilevel interrupts.

peripherals. The same logic applies to each of the descending priority-level peripherals. In Fig. 9-21 this concept is implemented by the three AND gates A1, A2, and A3. The INT PR lines to this logic are labeled PR1 to PR4; PR1 has the highest priority and PR4 has the lowest. In our previous example in Section 9-8.1 we established the BDAC priorities for the four peripherals; they are connected as shown in Fig. 9-21.

Let us see how the previously designated order of interrupts (ACDB) is handled by this chip.

1. The three latches (D-type flip-flops) are previously cleared to the $\overline{Q}$ side.
2. When the interrupt request from A comes in, it sets flip-flop D3 to the Q side.
3. Because of the two inverted inputs into AND gate A2, D3 now fully enables A2, whose 1 output goes through the 4-input OR gate OI as an INT REQ to the vector interrupt I/O chip (Fig. 9-20).
4. This starts the process previously described in Section 9-5.

5. While peripheral A is being serviced, peripheral C sends an interrupt request on PR4 line to A3. However, this signal is blocked from going any further because D3 is still set to the Q side, and this signal is input as a 0 on one of the inputs to A3.

6. Before the service subroutine for peripheral A is completed, an interrupt request from D comes in on line PR2 (see Fig. 9-18).

7. This signal passes through gate A1, since the D1 flip-flop is cleared to the $\overline{Q}$ side. The program will branch to the service subroutine of D and start executing it.

8. Before the subroutine for D is completed, peripheral B sends an interrupt signal on line PR1 (Fig. 9-18). this sets D1 to the Q side and sends an INT REQ signal to the CPU through the OI gate. The service subroutine for A is called out and executed.

9. The last instruction in every subroutine is a return (RET) instruction that pops the stack and returns control to the preinterrupt program.

10. Additionally, the OP code of the RET instruction also sends out a RES INT signal that comes and clears D1 to the $\overline{Q}$ side in Fig. 9-21 and partially enables A4.

11. The subroutine for peripheral D is resumed and completed, and the last RET instruction sends out the RES INT signal, which goes through A4. This clears D2 to the $\overline{Q}$ side which, in turn, partially enables A5.

12. Now the subroutine for peripheral A is resumed and completed (Fig. 9-18). The last RET instruction sends out the RES INT signal, which goes through A5 and clears D3 to the $\overline{Q}$ side.

13. Since D1, D2, and D3 are all cleared to the $\overline{Q}$ side, all three inverted inputs to A3 are now active.

14. Now the interrupt request of peripheral C fully enables A3, which sends an INT REQ to the CPU. This signal is now honored, and peripheral C is serviced.

   In this configuration the role of the three flip-flops is to disable the interrupt signals from all other lower-priority peripherals when higher priorities are being serviced. While gates A1 to A3 provide the actual blocking mechanism, the flip-flops help to maintain this condition for the time duration when the higher-priority subroutine is being executed. Gates A4 and A5 clear flip-flops D2 and D3. If they are not cleared, the lowest-priority peripheral C would never get serviced.

9-9 SUMMARY

The interrupt I/O is not initiated by the μP but by the peripheral, so the CPU does not waste time querying if the peripheral is ready for a transfer as in programmed I/O (conditional transfers). Consequently, interrupt I/O is more efficient and time saving. Since the arrival time of interrupt requests cannot be anticipated by the programmer, it is necessary that certain registers/ counters, containing critical, in-process data, be saved during interrupt servicing and that the CPU be restored to its preinterrupt status when the interrupting peripheral is fully serviced.

Before proceeding to the next instruction in the main program, the CPU must inquire if an interrupt request has arrived. The querying logic is shown in Fig. 9-3. An interrupt handling subroutine is used to handle incoming interrupt requests; the procedure involved in this subroutine was flowcharted in Fig. 9-4. How this subroutine actually operates was shown by a sample program in Fig. 9-5.

The CPU responds to an interrupt request with an INT ACK signal that initiates a number of events. Figure 9-6 showed how the INT ACK is used to branch to subroutine, and Fig. 9-10 showed the operation of the BRANCH instruction in the CPU. Some μPs store the starting address of the interrupt handling subroutine as a pointer in either a dedicated register in the CPU or a dedicated location in the data memory. The first approach was shown in Fig. 9-8 and the second in Fig. 9-9. Still another approach uses a technique where the interrupting peripheral itself supplies the starting address to the CPU. This was shown in Fig. 9-10.

CPU status saving is accomplished by using a memory stack, using duplicate registers/counters, or using any available RAM locations.

The three commonly used methods of identifying the interrupting peripheral were described. In the vectored-interrupt system, the interrupting peripheral identifies itself to the CPU by means of an address or a unique code, called the vector, which could be the starting address of its service subroutine. See Fig. 9-11 for the sequence of events and Fig. 9-12 for the logic diagram.

The second method uses a polling technique. A polling subroutine, which checks the status of the INT flip-flop in each peripheral, is used to identify the interrupting peripheral. The sequence of events was flowcharted in Fig. 9-13, and a sample program was shown in Fig. 9-14. The operation of the CPU for the software-polled interrupt was shown in Fig. 9-15. The logic diagram was shown in Fig. 9-16. The priority of each peripheral is established by its relative position in the polling sequence.

The third method uses a hardware polling system called the daisy-chain, which was shown in Fig. 9-17. The polling is done by a series of AND gates, using the INT ACK signal; when the interrupting unit is found, it identifies itself by sending its own address or vector to the CPU. Here, also, the priority of each peripheral is established by its relative position in the polling sequence.

Figure 9-18 showed an example of multilevel-priority interrupts. In such a system a peripheral with a higher preestablished priority can interrupt the interrupt processing of a lower-priority peripheral. A block diagram of such a system was shown in Fig. 9-20. The logic diagram for a four-peripheral multilevel interrupt was shown in Fig. 9-21.

9-10 REVIEW QUESTIONS

9-1   What is the principal disadvantage of the unconditional programmed I/O transfer?

9-2   What is the major drawback of the conditional programmed I/O transfer?

9-3   Briefly explain how the interrupt I/O overcomes the disadvantages of programmed I/O (both unconditional and conditional) stated in answers to Questions 9-1 and 9-2.

9-4   Explain briefly what is meant by "status saving" and "CPU status restoring."

9-5   Why are the INT REQ signals from all the peripherals in the system ORed and presented to the CPU on one input pin instead of on a separate input pin for each individual peripheral's INT REQ?

9-6   Refer to the interrupt request querying procedure of Fig. 9-2.
(a) Is the querying procedure implemented with hardware or with software?
(b) What is the function of software interrupt disable (block 4)?

9-7   The following questions relate to the interrupt request querying logic of Fig. 9-3.
(a) What is the function of A2?
(b) What is the function of the signal M and what is its normal logic state?
(c) What is the function of the AND gate A1?
(d) What is the function of the AND gate A3?

9-8   Which type of stack (cascade or pointer-type) is more frequently used in μCs to save the contents of the program counter when the interrupt handling subroutine procedure (Fig. 9-4, block 3) is initiated? Why?

9-9   Name some of the critical μP registers/counters commonly saved during interrupt processing.

9-10   Refer to the interrupt handling subroutine shown in Fig. 9-5.
(a) Why is the last instruction—RET (5007)—the same in all three peripheral service subroutines?
(b) What two functions are performed by the CPU after the RET (5507) instruction is executed?
(c) If the third INT REQ would have arrived during execution of the instruction at address 0399 instead of at 039B, what would be the last instruction in the service subroutine of peripheral W?

9-11   Refer to Fig. 9-6 and explain the function(s) performed by the INT ACK signal from the μP.

9-12   Are the contents of the interrupt instruction register in Fig. 9-7 hard-wired during the manufacturing process? If not, how is this register loaded?

9-13   Figure 9-8 shows the pointer technique for branching to the interrupt handling subroutine. From where does the starting address of this subroutine originate? Explain how it calls out this subroutine.

9-14 Figure 9-9 shows the pointer technique using dedicated RAM locations. Explain why the pointer (located in address 7000) is loaded into the data register.

9-15 The peripheral-supplied starting address technique is shown in Fig. 9-10. According to this diagram the pointer, 2C0D, is transferred and saved in the stack. Is this correct? If not, why not?

9-16 What is a TRAP CELL? Explain.

9-17 Identify the three techniques used for status saving and status restoring. (The techniques in this case refer to the locations where the contents of the critical registers/counters are stored.)

9-18 Refer to Fig. 9-12, the logic diagram of the vectored interrupt. What is the ultimate destination and use of the contents of the device vector register?

9-19 List the four main operations performed by the vector interrupt logic of Fig. 9-12.

9-20 What are the two functions performed by peripheral 1 of Fig. 9-12 when it requests service from the CPU?

9-21 Refer to Fig. 9-12. What function(s) does the INT ACK signal perform?

9-22 Explain why the R/$\overline{\text{W}}$ ENABLE signal from the CPU is sent out to the logic in fig. 9-12 on a single line instead of using a separate line for READ and WRITE signals.

9-23 What is the function of the inverter I_1 in Fig. 9-12?

9-24 In the software-polled interrupt system, how is the priority of a given peripheral established?

9-25 The following questions relate to the operation of the interrupt handling subroutine for the software-polled interrupt shown in Fig. 9-14.
(a) What does the instruction at address 5006 do?
(b) Why does the program branch to address 6400 when the INT REQ comes in during execution of the instruction at address 0074?

9-26 Refer to Fig. 9-15, the logic diagram of the software-polled interrupt operation in the CPU.
(a) The program counter contains 500A. What do the bits in the **A** field of this instruction accomplish?
(b) The program counter still contains 500A. What does the OP code decoder do in this instruction?
(c) The program counter contains 500B. What does the OP code decoder do now?

9-27 Refer to the logic diagram of the daisy-chained interrupt (Fig. 9-17).
(a) Which signal from the CPU identifies the interrupting peripheral?
(b) If peripheral B were interrupting, what prevents the INT ACK signal from querying the status of peripheral C?
(c) What function does the SELECT B signal perform?

9-28 Assume that the μC system uses the simple vectored interrupt described in Sec. 9-5. What happens if an interrupt is received by the CPU while servicing a prior INT REQ from another peripheral?

9-29 In a multilevel-priority interrupt system, in addition to its normal instructions, what must be included in the service subroutine for each peripheral?

9-30 Refer to Fig. 9-21, the logic diagram of the multilevel interrupt chip. Peripheral D is currently being serviced. Explain how an interrupt from peripheral B will override this and interrupt D's service subroutine.

10

PARALLEL I/O TRANSFERS—DIRECT MEMORY ACCESS

10-1 DATA TRANSFERS AND THE TIME ELEMENT

In many applications, large quantities of data are transferred between the *data memory* and various I/O devices (usually auxiliary memory devices such as disks, drums, tape units, cassettes, etc.). In several data-processing applications, *raw data* are first transferred to the data memory of the computer. The CPU then processes raw data, and the finished data are also first stored in the data memory. Finally, the finished data are transferred to some units such as *printers,* or they could be stored in *auxiliary* memories.

Using the previously described programmed I/O (Chapter 8) and interrupt I/O (Chapter 9) for such transfers (which often involve several groups of data) is cumbersome, time consuming, and wasteful of computer time. The CPU using such transfers would be tied up mostly for such transfer operations. Figure 10-1 shows such an operation in block diagram form. It is apparent that the CPU would *not* be able to perform any other tasks during such transfers.

Direct memory access (DMA) provides an attractive way to transfer large blocks of data between the computer's data memory and the auxiliary memory by effectively *bypassing* the CPU. A block of data is a group of data words that are stored in successive memory locations. However, such a system requires additional interface circuitry, called the DMA controller, which is available on a chip. Ideally, the DMA operation should bypass the CPU completely, as shown in Fig. 10-2, thereby leaving the CPU to perform its programmed tasks. Such a configuration permits the system to perform two jobs in parallel (i.e., simultaneously).

In most μCs systems, however, an idealized setup (such as the one in Fig. **261**

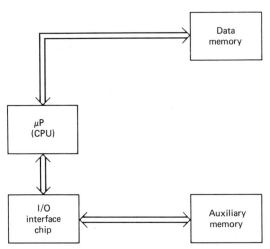

Figure 10-1   Data transfers between data memory and auxiliary memory using programmed or interrupt I/O.

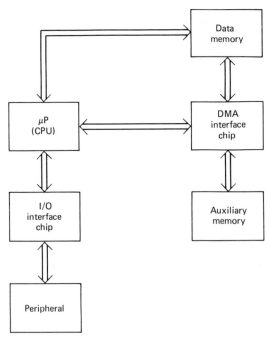

Figure 10-2   Data transfers between data memory and auxiliary memory using idealized DMA transfers.

10-2) is rarely feasible. Separate channels into the data memory (which are RAM chips) would involve either extensive modifications in the RAM chip logic or additional external logic on separate chips. It is much more expedient to use the *same* channel (as the one used for data transfers between the CPU and the data memory), which includes the *address bus*, the *data bus*, and the *control bus*. This results in a configuration such as the one shown in Fig. 10-3. In this case either the CPU or the DMA is able to access the data memory at any one time, requiring the other to be electrically disconnected from the system bus (or channel). If the DMA channel is communicating with the data memory, the CPU is free to perform its own programmed tasks as long as it does not access the data memory or use the busses.

10-2 DMA INITIATION

DMA operation has many similarities to the interrupt I/O (Section 9-5). The auxiliary memory (or the peripheral device) initiates the DMA transfer by sending a DMA REQ signal to the CPU when it is ready to perform a transfer. On most μPs the terminal on which this signal is received is labeled PAUSE,

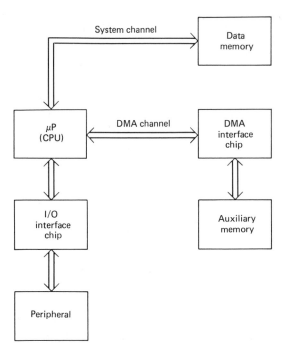

Figure 10-3   Realistic configuration of DMA transfers in a typical μC system.

WAIT, HOLD (or designated by some other such nomenclature). There are two methods or modes by which the DMA transfer is initiated: the memory status indication mode and the cycle stealing mode.

10-2.1 Memory Status Indication Mode

This is a simple method of DMA operation in which the actual transfer takes place without informing the CPU. There are *many* machine cycles in which the CPU does not access the memory but, instead, performs some process on a word, or words, already within its internal registers/counters/accumulators. A typical example is an ADD operation or a ROTATE operation. In such a situation the CPU informs the rest of the system of this fact using a special signal indicating that the system channel (or bus) to the memory is available. During this time, a DMA transfer can take place. For example, the Motorola 6800 μP has a terminal labeled VMA (valid memory address). A *high* signal on this pin indicates that the CPU has placed a valid memory address on the address bus, thereby signifying a memory access operation. A *low* signal on this pin indicates that a DMA transfer could take place during this time.

The main advantage of this mode is that it does not impede or slow down the programmed operations of the CPU. The principal disadvantage is that it slows down the DMA operations. The DMA transfers can only take place when the CPU is *not* accessing the memory. In other words, the data transfer rates tend to be irregular and erratic.

10-2.2 Cycle Stealing Mode

In this method the CPU is forced to relinquish control of its operations to the DMA operation for one time slice. After receiving the DMA REQ, the CPU completes its current instruction and suspends operation or idles for the next time slice (machine cycle). The programmed job, as dictated by the main program, is thus delayed. During the next time slice, the DMA transfer takes place and one datum (usually one word) is transferred between the auxiliary memory and the data memory.

Note that the CPU queries or examines the DMA request input during the execution of every instruction of the main program. This is done during the EXECUTE portion of the instruction cycle. Thus DMA transfer takes place by stealing one cycle of time slice from the main program. This is graphically shown in Fig. 10-4a.

During the time slice when the data transfer takes place, the various counters/registers/accumulators in the CPU are not disturbed. Hence the status of these does not have to be saved and stored in memory and then restored. The CPU can resume its normal programmed operation after each DMA oper-

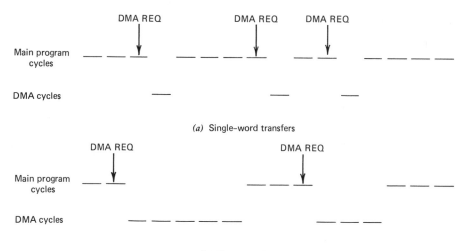

(a) Single-word transfers

(b) Block transfers

Figure 10-4 Cycle-stealing DMA transfers. Reprinted, with minor modifications, from Branko Soucek, "Microprocessors and Microcomputers", © 1976, with permission from John Wiley & Sons, New York.

ation. From Fig. 10-4*a*, it is seen that operations of DMA transfers are really interleaved with cycles of the CPU programmed operations. Thus DMA transfers are essentially time-shared with operations of the main program.

Transfer of one word of data does not justify the use of DMA operations. For DMA to be cost-effective, large numbers of words, or blocks of words, have to be transferred. This means that after receiving a DMA REQ, the CPU will idle for more than one time slice. In fact, whole blocks of data are interleaved with the main program, as shown in Fig. 10-4*b*.

10-3 SINGLE-WORD DMA TRANSFER

10-3.1 Using Single Auxiliary Memory

A μC system could have one or more auxiliary memories. Figure 10-5 shows (in flowchart form) the sequence of events involved in a DMA system with only a single auxiliary memory. The word transfer could be in *either* direction. The entire operation consists of the following six steps. Note that the paragraph numbers correspond to the functional steps of Fig. 10-5 as indicated in circles.

1. The entire sequence of DMA transfer is initiated by a DMA REQ signal from the auxiliary memory to the CPU.
2. The CPU immediately responds with a DMA ACK signal to the auxiliary memory, although it continues with the execution of the programmed instruction currently

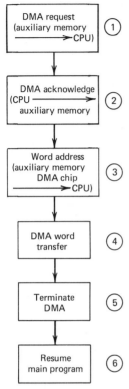

Figure 10-5   Flowchart for DMA transfer of only one word. (single auxiliary memory).

in progress. After completing the current instruction, the CPU goes into an idling mode and relinquishes control to the hardware (i.e., to the DMA interface chip).

3. Before the actual DMA word transfer can take place, the location in the data memory must be identified so that it can be accessed. The auxiliary memory does this by sending the desired address to the data memory through the DMA chip.

4. The actual word transfer then takes place. The auxiliary memory specifies the direction of the word transfer by an appropriate READ/WRITE signal to the data memory through the DMA chip.

5. After completing the word transfer, the auxiliary memory indicates this condition to the CPU by resetting the DMA request flip-flop on the DMA chip, which then removes the DMA REQ signal from the CPU. This terminates the DMA operation.

6. The main program resumes its normal operation until another DMA is made.

10-3.2 Using Several Auxiliary Memories

If more than one auxiliary memory is used in the μC system, an additional function must be performed in the sequence of events shown in Fig. 10-5. For the system to function properly, only one auxiliary memory may communicate

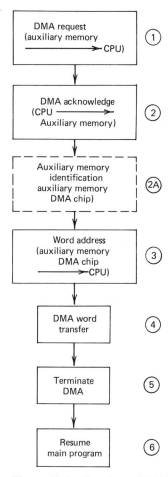

Figure 10-6 Flowchart of DMA transfer of only one word (several auxiliary memory units).

with the data memory. This means that the auxiliary memory must identify itself to the DMA chip which, in turn, must connect this unit into the system and lock out the rest of the auxiliary memory units. This function is added to the flowchart of Fig. 10-5, which is redrawn in Fig. 10-6. The additional block is shown in broken lines and is numbered 2A. The rest of the blocks are the same as those in Fig. 10-5.

10-4 DMA TRANSFER OF SINGLE DATA BLOCK

10-4.1 Basic Requirements for Block Transfer Execution

From the discussion in Section 10-3, it is clear that a DMA transfer for a single word requires either six or seven basic steps (as shown in Figs. 10-5 and 10-6), depending on whether one or more auxiliary memory units are involved in the system. However, a simple single-word transfer hardly justifies the additional hardware and system complexity required by the DMA capability. More realistically, DMA transfers involve a *block* of data that are stored, or required to be stored, in a *series* of *consecutive* memory locations.

Thus a block transfer requires that the auxiliary memory first provide the starting address of the data block to the memory and, second, that the system keep track of the subsequent, sequential address of each of the following word transfers. This is usually done by loading a special counter with the initial address of the first word in the block and incrementing the counter after each word is transferred. This process is continued until the entire block of data is transferred and the main program is resumed.

In the previous situation in Section 10-3, where only one word was transferred, the time slices for the DMA operation were "stolen" from the main program one cycle at a time. Remember that the DMA cycles were interleaved with the main program cycles. In block transfers the main program is not resumed until all the words in that particular block are transferred. In other words, whole blocks are *interleaved* with the main program cycles, as shown in Fig. 10-4b.

10-4.2 Flowchart of DMA Block Transfers

A flowchart for the DMA transfer of one block of data is shown in Fig. 10-7. The following paragraphs correspond to the circled numbers next to each block in this diagram.

1. The auxiliary memory sends the DMA REQ to the CPU through the DMA interface chip.
2. The CPU responds with a DMA ACK signal to the auxiliary memory (through the DMA interface chip), completes the current instruction, and suspends the operation of the main program.
3. The auxiliary memory sends the first address of the data memory location of the block to be transferred. This address is loaded in the special address counter in the DMA interface chip.
4. The first word of the data block is transferred, either from the auxiliary memory to the data memory or vice versa.
5. When the transfer of the first word is completed, the auxiliary memory is queried to see if the block transfer is completed. If the response is negative, the DMA sequence performs a loop.
6. The memory address in the special counter is incremented, and the new address is sent to the data memory. DMA transfer of the next word in the block takes place. When this transfer is completed, the auxiliary memory is queried again to determine if the block transfer is completed. If the response is again negative, the

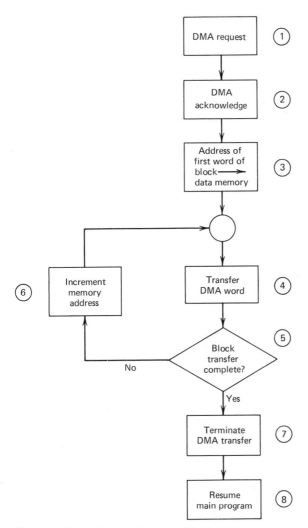

Figure 10-7   DMA transfer of one block of data.

memory address is incremented and the process is repeated until the auxiliary memory sends a positive response to the query.

7. The DMA operation is terminated and control is returned to the main program.

8. Execution of the main program is resumed.

Notice that the operation of the main program is *not* resumed until the entire block transfer is completed. Also, during the time that the block transfer takes place, the CPU is not executing any main program instructions. But, since none of the internal CPU registers/counters/accumulators are disturbed, the

CPU can continue to operate on its own to complete the pre-DMA operations, such as arithmetic or logical processes, during the block transfer time. However, these CPU operations cannot include any memory reference or I/O reference operations.

10-5 DMA TRANSFER OF SEVERAL DATA BLOCKS

10-5.1 The Situation

In many applications, a DMA transfer may involve not just one block of data but *several different* blocks. These blocks may or may not be placed in adjacent locations in the data memory, and each block may or may not contain the same number of words. In any case, the DMA transfers of each of these blocks can be accomplished in a continuous fashion.

For example, let us assume that each block to be loaded into the data memory is 150 words long. Within each block, the words are located in adjacent, sequential addresses. It is possible to have a transfer requirement of six blocks that may be located as shown below:

Block	Starting Address	Last Address
1	0 0 0 1	0 1 5 0
2	0 1 5 1	0 3 0 0
3	3 1 2 0	3 2 6 9
4	3 2 7 0	3 4 1 9
5	3 4 2 0	3 5 6 9
6	6 2 3 0	6 3 7 9

It is apparent that in addition to the starting data memory address of each block, the auxiliary memory will also have to inform the DMA interface chip as to how many blocks must be transferred at each DMA request. This will insure that execution of the main program will be resumed only after all the blocks of data are properly transferred.

10-5.2 The Flowchart

A flowchart for DMA transfer of several blocks of data, each block containing a different number of words and not necessarily located contiguously in the data memory, is shown in Fig. 10-8. The circled numbers next to each block correspond to the following paragraphs.

1. The auxiliary memory initiates the DMA transfer with a DMA REQ signal.

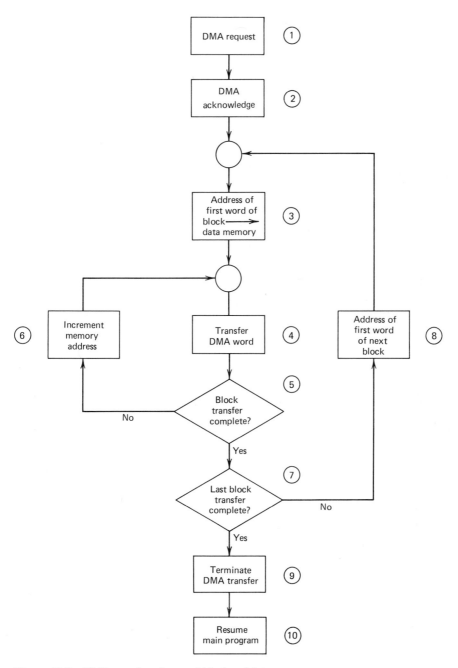

Figure 10-8   DMA transfer of several blocks of data.

2. The CPU completes its current instruction and initiates the DMA sequence by sending a DMA ACK to the DMA interface chip.
3. The auxiliary memory sends the address of the first word of the first block to the data memory. At the same time, the auxiliary memory indicates to the interface chip how many words are involved in the current block and how many blocks are to be transferred at that particular DMA request.
4. The first DMA word is transferred.
5. A query is made to see if the transfer of the entire block is completed. If the response is negative, the DMA sequence performs a loop.
6. The address in the special counter is incremented, and the sequence indicated by blocks 4, 5, and 6 in Fig. 10-8 is repeated until a positive response to the query is received.
7. Another query asks if all the blocks have been transferred.
8. If a negative response is received, the address of the first word of the next block is sent to the data memory through the DMA interface chip. The process represented by blocks 3 to 8 is repeated until a positive response to the query is received.
9. When the transfer of the last word of the last block is completed, the DMA operation is terminated.
10. Control is returned to the CPU, and the main program is resumed.

10-6 DMA LOGIC ACTIVATION IN CPU

10-6.1 Using CPU Registers

The realistic configuration of DMA transfers in a typical μC system (see Fig. 10-3 and Section 10-1) shows that it is advantageous to use the existing hardware in the system for special features such as DMA. This is especially true of the facilities already existing in the CPU, where real estate on the silicon chip is always at a premium.

The data memory in the μC system is, of course, involved in DMA transfers, but it is connected to the rest of the system for its normal non-DMA operations. Recall that the data memory is treated like any other I/O device in the system (see Fig. 3-7 and Section 3-1.4). The data memory communicates with two registers in the CPU: (1) the data register, through the shared data bus; and (2) the address register, through the shared address bus (see Figs. 6-8 and 6-11).

Since the normal functions performed by these registers are also performed during the DMA operations, the registers can be used by sending the data memory DMA address and the DMA data words (in either direction) to them. However, from Figs. 6-8 and 6-11, we see that these two registers also communicate with the internal data bus of the μP. During the DMA operations, it is necessary that both the data and the address registers in the CPU are dedicated to DMA transfers only. Thus it is obvious that before DMA transfers actually take place, the communication paths between the internal data bus and these registers are first disabled or disconnected, and then the DMA address bus and the DMA data bus are both connected to the respective registers. How this is done is explained in Section 10-6.2.

10-6.2 CPU Response to DMA REQ Signal

When the CPU receives the DMA REQ signal from the auxiliary memory through the DMA interface chip, it first completes the current instruction and then performs the following five tasks before the actual DMA transfer takes place.

1. Disables the communication path between the internal data bus and the data register.
2. Disables the communication path between the data register and the ALU (Figs. 6-8, 6-11, and 10-9).
3. Disables the communication path between the internal data bus and the address register.
4. Enables the communication path between the address register and the DMA address bus.
5. Enables the communication path between the data register and the DMA data bus.

Figure 10-9 shows a conceptual block diagram of how these functions are performed. The blocks labeled T_1 to T_5 can be either a group of AND gates, if bipolar transistor technology is used in the μP, or they could be bidirectional, tristate, transmission gates if MOS/CMOS technology is used in the μP. For explanation purposes, we will just refer to them as AND gates in the rest of this section.

When the control and timing section of the μP receives the DMA ACK signal (from the auxiliary memory through the DMA interface chip), the current instruction is first completed and the DMA ACK signal is then issued. The DMA ACK signal is sent to the DMA interface chip, where it performs several functions that are described in Section 10-7. In the CPU the DMA ACK signal performs the following functions.

1. It disables AND gates labeled T_1. This disconnects the data register from the internal data bus.
2. It disables AND gates T_2. This disconnects the data register from the ALU.
3. It disables AND gates T_3. This disconnects the address register from the internal data bus.

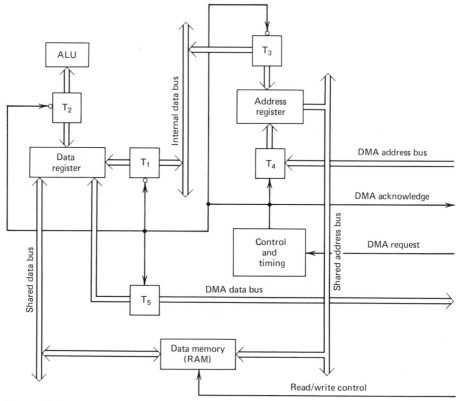

Figure 10-9   DMA logic activation in the μP CPU.

4. It enables AND gates T_4. This connects the address register to the DMA address bus.

5. It enables AND gates T_5. This connects the data register to the DMA data bus.

With these tasks completed, the data memory, the data register, and the address register are completely isolated from the rest of the CPU; they are connected only to the DMA interface chip. The functions of this chip are described in Section 10-7.

10-7 OPERATION OF THE INTERFACE CHIP

10-7.1 DMA REQ and Response

The DMA interface chip is a fairly complex chip and normally contains logic that, at times, operates in a manner similar to the CPU logic. Figure 10-10 is a simplified conceptual diagram of such a chip. It is intended only to explain

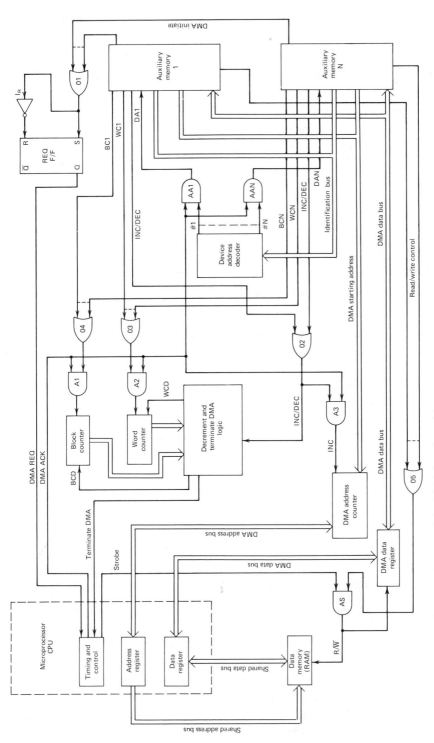

Figure 10-10 Simplified logic diagram of the DMA interface chip.

the concepts involved in DMA transfers; therefore some assumptions are made for explanation purposes. Also, the auxiliary memories, shown as 1 to N in Fig. 10-10, contain a significant amount of logic circuitry. The entire operation of the chip can be explained much better if we assume that one auxiliary memory unit, say 1, initiates the DMA transfer operation and follow the various steps involved.

Auxiliary memory 1 initiates the operation by putting a digital 1 on the DMA INIT (initiate) line, which is one of N inputs to OR gate 01. The 1 output of this gate sets the REQ flip-flop to the Q side, which sends a DMA REQ signal to the timing and control section in the μP. In this particular design it is assumed that the DMA INIT output signal from the auxiliary memory stays at a 1 level until the DMA operation is completed.

The μP completes its current instruction, goes into an idling mode, and sends out a DMA ACK signal to the DMA interface chip.

10-7.2 Auxiliary Memory Lockin

Before the DMA request can be processed, the requesting auxiliary memory must be locked into the system while other auxiliary memory units are locked out. This is accomplished as follows.

1. Simultaneously with the DMA INIT signal output, auxiliary memory 1 (referred to simply as unit 1 in the following explanations) sends out its own unique address or vector on the identification bus. We will assume that the vector is 8 bits long. It is sent to and loaded into the device address decoder.
2. The device address decoder decodes this vector, and a 1 is output on line 1 of the decoder and sent to AND gate AA1.
3. When the DMA ACK signal from the CPU arrives, AA1 is fully enabled and outputs a 1 on the DA1 line that is sent to unit 1.
4. This signal triggers off a number of events in unit 1 that start the DMA operations. These are described in Section 10-7.3.

10-7.3 Word and Block Count

When unit 1 receives the DA1 signal, the following operations take place.

1. Unit 1 issues a series of serial binary bits on the BC1 line. These bits represent the number of blocks to be transferred during the current DMA operation. Assume that this number is represented by 8 bits.
2. The block count bits pass through OR gate 04, through AND gate A1 (which is enabled by the DMA ACK signal), and are serially loaded in the block counter.
3. Unit 1 issues a series of serial binary bits on the WC1 line. These bits represent

the number of words to be transferred in the first block. Assume that this number is also represented by 8 bits.

4. The word count bits pass through OR gate 03, the AND gate A2 (which is enabled by the DMA ACK signal), and are serially loaded in the word counter.
5. Notice that both the block counter and the word counter can only be loaded when the DMA ACK signal is present.
6. The block counter is loaded once (i.e. only at the beginning of the DMA operation). The word counter is loaded several times (i.e., on completion of the transfer of the previous block if more than one block is to be transferred).

10-7.4 Data Memory Access Address

In parallel with the events described in Section 10-7.3, the following operations occur.

1. Unit 1 sends out the starting address in the data memory that has to be accessed for the transfer of the first word of the first block.
2. This address is loaded into the DMA address counter through the DMA starting address bus.

Let us take the example discussed in Section 10-5.1 and summarize what has happened up to this point in the DMA operation. Assume that the transfer involves a READ operation (i.e., data are read out from unit 1 and loaded into the data memory).

The following operations are performed up to this point.

1. Since 6 blocks (each containing 150 words) are to be transferred, 006 is loaded into the block counter.
2. Next, 150 is loaded into the word counter.
3. Address 0001, which is the starting address of the first word of block 1, is loaded into the DMA address counter.

10-7.5 The Transfer Operation of the First Word

The following operations transfer the first word of the first block.

1. The contents of the DMA address counter are loaded into the address register, located in the CPU, through the DMA address bus. This accesses location 0001 in the data memory.
2. Unit 1 loads the first word of block 1 into the DMA data register through the DMA data bus.
3. Unit 1 now sends out a READ signal on the READ/WRITE control line to the OR gate 05. Assume that 1 indicates a read operation and 0 a write operation.

4. The 1 output of 05 gate is fed into one of the inputs to the AND gate AS.
5. The timing and control section of the CPU sends out a 1 on the STROBE line. AND gate AS is now fully enabled and sends a 1 on the $R/\overline{W}$ line to the data memory.
6. The 1 signal on the $R/\overline{W}$ results in the transfer of the word, which was previously loaded in the DMA data register, into the addressed location of the data memory through the DMA address bus, the data register, and the shared data bus.

10-7.6 Data Memory Address Update

After completing the transfer of the first word of the first block, the following operations take place.

1. Unit 1 sends out a 1 on the INC/DEC line to OR gate 02.
2. The 1 output of 02 now fully enables AND gate A3, which was previously partially enabled by the DMA ACK signal.
3. A 1 output from A3 increments the address in the DMA address counter, which now contains 0002.

10-7.7 Word Counter Update

The 1 output from gate 02, which is labeled INC/DEC, goes to the decrement and terminate DMA logic. (The logic and functioning of this block is explained in Section 10-7.10.) The same signal emerges from this block as WCD and decrements the word counter, which now contains 149. After completing each word transfer, the word counter is decremented until all the words in that block are transferred. The word counter will then contain 000.

10-7.8 Block Counter Update

After completing the transfer of the first block, a 1 signal is issued by the decrement and terminate DMA logic block on the BCD line. This decrements the contents of the block counter, which now contains 005. How this is accomplished is explained in Section 10-7.10. This process is repeated after each block of data is transferred.

10-7.9 Termination of DMA Operation

When the transfer of the last word of the last block is completed, both the word counter and the block counter contain 000. These counts are both sent to the decrement and terminate DMA logic through their respective 8-bit busses. The logic in the block senses these conditions and sends a 1 on the terminate DMA line that goes to the timing and control section of the CPU and terminates the DMA operation.

10-7.10 Decrement and Terminate DMA Logic

The logic involved in decrementing the word counter and the block counter as well as the generation of the terminate DMA signal is shown in Fig.10-11.

Recall that both counters consist of flip-flops. When they both contain 000, a 1 is available from the $\overline{Q}$ side of each flip-flop in each counter. The INC/DEC signal from OR gate 02 (Fig. 10-10) goes to the word counter as the WCD signal (Fig. 10-11) after the transfer of each word. When the count reaches 000, the $\overline{Q}$ side of each flip-flop is on the 1 side, so the four inputs to each of the two AND gates are all 1s. A 1 output from W_1 and W_2 enables AND gate W_0, which enables one of the gates of B_0 and also goes to the block counter as the BCD signal. This decrements the block counter. This process continues until the block counter contains 000. At this time, AND gates B_1 and B_2 both output a 1. Since W_0 also outputs a 1, when the last word of the

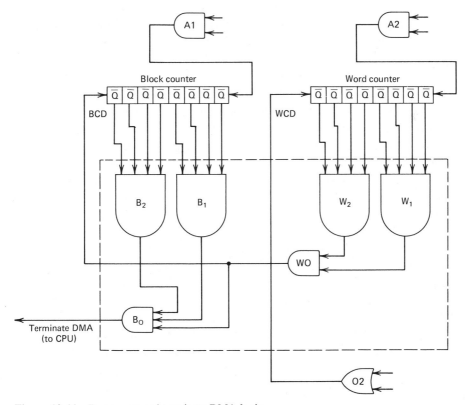

Figure 10-11   Decrement and terminate DMA logic.

last block is transferred all three inputs to the AND gate B_0 are 1. A 1 output from B_0 is sent to the CPU on the terminate DMA line. This terminates the DMA operation, and operation of the main program is resumed.

10-8 SUMMARY

Direct memory access (DMA) is an attractive alternative to programmed I/O and interrupt I/O, particularly when blocks of data are to be transferred. Both programmed and interrupt I/O are wasteful of CPU time if large amounts of data are to be transferred between the data memory and auxiliary memory units, such as magnetic tapes; during the transfer times, the CPU cannot do any productive processing as required by the main program. Additionally, when interrupt I/O is used, even more CPU time is wasted in saving and restoring CPU register status.

Although DMA requires the use of additional hardware (i.e., the DMA chip), data transfers can take place without disturbing the contents of the CPU registers. DMA operations steal cycles from the CPU; this slows down the CPU's programmed tasks, but this is partially offset by saving the time required that would otherwise be lost in CPU registers' status saving and restoring. The CPU can perform internal, programmed tasks in parallel with the DMA operations, thereby saving even more time.

DMA operations are under control of the hardware, so it simplifies the programming tasks to some extent. In this chapter we have described the basic concepts involved in DMA operations. It is possible to include additional features in a DMA system. For example, it is possible to provide several DMA channels on the same DMA chip. This was shown in Fig. 10-10. A multiple-level priority DMA system, similar to the interrupt I/O priority system discussed in Section 9-8.3, can be used. In such a system a DMA system with a higher priority could interrupt the operation of another DMA system with a lower priority.

DMA transfers can be done by one of two modes. In the memory status indication mode, a transfer takes place when the DMA logic determines that no CPU/data memory transfer operations are taking place. In fact, the DMA transfer takes place without the CPU being informed about it. In the cycle stealing mode the CPU is forced to relinquish a time slice for DMA transfer. In either case, the DMA address bus and the DMA data bus are switched into the CPU, while the shared address bus, the shared data bus, and the internal data bus are disconnected during the DMA operation, as shown in Fig. 10-9 and explained in Section 10-6.

10-9 REVIEW QUESTIONS

10-1 Explain the shortcomings of the programmed I/O and the interrupt I/O when several blocks of data are to be transferred between the μC's data memory and an auxiliary memory such as a magnetic tape unit.

10-2 Briefly state why DMA is more efficient in transferring blocks of data than either the programmed or the interrupt I/O and why it saves CPU time.

10-3 Explain why the DMA transfer scheme in Fig. 10-2 is not feasible in real μC systems.

10-4 Refer to the realistic DMA transfer configuration of Fig. 10-3.
  (a) Can the auxiliary memory send data to the data memory at the same time that the CPU is reading data out of the data memory?
  (b) Can the CPU receive data from the I/O interface chip at the same time that the auxiliary memory is receiving data from the data memory?
  (c) Is it possible for the I/O interface chip to send data to the data memory while the CPU is performing an add operation?

10-5 Which of the following three items initiates a DMA operation?
  (a) The data memory.
  (b) The CPU.
  (c) The auxiliary memory.

10-6 What is the principal advantage and disadvantage of the memory status indiction mode of DMA transfers?

10-7 Briefly state the major steps involved in the DMA transfer of one datum or word in a single auxiliary memory system and indicate where the signal(s), address, and data words originate and their destinations.

10-8 Refer to Question 10-7. State the additional functions that must be included in the steps involved in the DMA transfer when the system contains more than one auxiliary memory.

10-9 Figure 10-7 is a flowchart showing the DMA transfer of one block of data. Refer to the decision block 5, block transfer complete? Explain how the system determines if the transfer of the whole block is completed.

10-10 If more than one block of data is to be transferred in a DMA operation, what additional information must be supplied by the auxiliary memory? How does the system determine if the transfer of all the blocks is completed?

10-11 Refer to Fig. 10-9, DMA logic activation in the μP CPU, and list:
  (a) The gates that isolate the CPU from the system.
  (b) The gates that connect the DMA interface chip into the system.

10-12 Explain the function(s) and operation(s) of the device address decoder in the DMA interface chip of Fig. 10-10.

10-13 What happens in the μP when it receives the DMA REQ signal from the DMA interface chip?

10-14 Explain the function of the DMA address counter in the DMA interface chip of Fig. 10-10.

10-15 What purpose does the inverter I_R serve (Fig. 10-10)? Explain its function and how it performs this function.

10-16 In the DMA transfer of one block of data that consists of 100 words, is it possible to store them in nonsequential locations of the data memory? If not, why not?

10-17 What is the function of the AND gate AS in Fig. 10-10? Is it really necessary?

10-18 Refer to the decrement and terminate logic in Fig. 10-11. Explain the function(s) of AND gate WO.

11

SERIAL I/O TRANSFERS

11-1 INTRODUCTION

Today's computers, including μCs, operate on digital data in a parallel fashion. The computer handles and processes single-word data or multiword data and operates on *all* bits simultaneously, rather than on one bit at a time. In μCs handling or processing 8-bit bytes is common. This means that data must be presented to the processor in a *parallel* manner from the various peripherals in the system, and the peripherals, in turn, must be able to accept the data output by the processor in *parallel* form, regardless of how it uses these data.

Many peripherals handle data in a *serial* fashion (i.e., 1 bit at a time). An example of such a device, frequently used in μC systems, is a magnetic tape cassette. Also, digital data are often transmitted over single lines. Transmission of digital data over common carrier lines, such as leased telephone lines, is now common.

Serial transmission of digital data presents some unique problems and therefore requires some different concepts and circuitry. *Digital communications* is a highly complex and specialized subject, beyond the scope of this book. In this chapter we will, however, present some basic concepts as they affect μC systems. Discussions will be confined to the application where digital data are transferred to and from the μC on single telephone lines.

11-2 CONVERSION AND SYNCHRONIZATION LOGIC

11-2.1 Block Diagram of Serial I/O

Systems, using computers with serial I/O, generally involve two other system blocks (Fig. 11-1).

Since μCs accept as well as output data only in parallel form, the data coming in on the telephone line (in a *serial* stream of voltage levels) must be converted into an appropriate format for the μC to accept. The *modem* (mod-

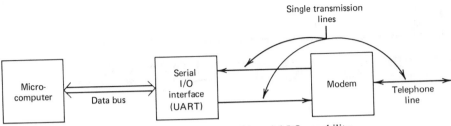

Figure 11-1   Block diagram of microcomputer with serial I/O capability.

ulator-demodulator), shown in Fig. 11-1, converts the incoming signals on the telephone line, which are in *analog* form, into a *digital* format. This process of analog-to-digital conversion (A/D) is called *demodulation*. Likewise, the digital data output by the µC must be converted into the appropriate *analog* form. The modem also does this. The process of digital-to-analog conversion (D/A) is called *modulation*. Note that the modem only performs A/D and D/A conversions. On the digital end, the modem inputs and outputs the data only in serial form. These data are independent of the µC and are not synchronized with the timing of the µC.

The serial I/O interface is usually a programmable unit that performs serial-to-parallel and parallel-to-serial conversion of digital data. It is often called the *universal asynchronous receiver-transmitter* (UART). A programmable interface is an interface whose operating features and characteristics can be modified by the µC under program control. Programmable interfaces are discussed in Chapter 12.

The UART, which is generally one chip in most µC systems, performs the following functions in addition to serial/parallel conversions. The UART:

- Establishes the proper voltage levels.
- Synchronizes or times the signals.
- Properly spaces the signals.

In the UART the transmitter and the receiver are separate and independent sections, but both are under control of the µC. The UART can operate either in the *half-duplex* mode (i.e., alternate reception and transmission of data) or in the *full-duplex* mode (i.e., simultaneous reception and transmission of data).

11-2.2 Serial/Parallel Conversion

One of the basic functions of the UART is to convert the serial-bit stream into a parallel form and vice versa. If the incoming serial data are already converted into the appropriate binary bits, the serial-to-parallel conversion can be readily performed by a single *serial-in/parallel-out* shift register. This is shown in Fig. 11-2a, where an 8-bit byte is assumed. Likewise, to convert a computer-output 8-bit parallel byte into a serial stream of bits, only a single *parallel-in/ serial-out* shift register, shown in Fig. 11-2b, is needed.

11-2.3 Level Normalization

Refer to Fig. 11-1. Notice that the modem converts the incoming analog signals into digital signals that are then sent to the UART on a single line. The voltage levels of such signals, which could come from either the modem or some other peripheral such as a magnetic tape cassette, are not always the same as or compatible with the levels required by the digital circuitry. Before such signals can be processed by the computer, their voltage levels must be normalized to those used by the digital equipment. Another problem is that the incoming signals may come at random times not in synchronism with the timing of the digital system. Both problems can be solved with simple logical configurations.

The simplest level normalization logic consists of a D-type flip-flop, (Fig. 11-3).

Such a flip-flop is designed so that its output voltage is at levels fully compatible with the levels required by the digital circuitry. The data input levels, at D_I, are different from the computer system levels but compatible with the digital levels of the peripheral or the modem outputs. We will explain the operation of this flip-flop with some examples but, first, we briefly review this flip-flop. A D-type flip-flop has the following basic characteristics:

1. It has only one data input terminal, identified as D.

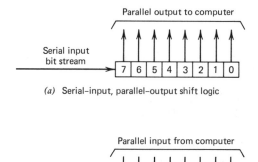

(a) Serial-input, parallel-output shift logic

(b) Parallel-input, serial-output shift logic

Figure 11-2   Serial I/O conversion logic.

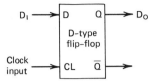

Figure 11-3 Simple level normalizer using a D-type flip-flop.

2. It is a clocked flip-flop. The logical state at output Q changes only when a clock pulse is present at the CL terminal.
3. The output condition at Q (i.e., a 1 or a 0) will be determined by the condition at D (a 1 or a 0) before and during part of the clock pulse at CL.
4. If a 1 is present at D before arrival of the clock pulse, Q will jump to a 1 at the *leading edge* of the clock pulse (assuming that it was previously at 0).
5. Q then stays at 1 for 1 full clock period, regardless of what condition may be present at D. A clock period is defined as the time between the leading edges of 2 successive clock pulses.
6. If a 0 is present at D before arrival of the clock pulse, Q will jump to a 0 at the *leading edge* of the clock pulse (assuming that it was previously at 1).
7. The $\overline{Q}$ output will always be the complement of Q. For most of our discussions, $\overline{Q}$ is *not* used (and so is ignored).

Example 11-1

A D-type flip-flop is used as a level normalizer. The clock input and the data input waveforms are shown in Fig. 11-4. Sketch the output waveform at D_0 (see Fig. 11-3) in relation to the input waveform, showing the proper timing relationships. Explain in your own words how the output waveform represents the input signal levels.

Solution

The output waveform at D_0 is shown in Fig. 11-5. The following sequence explains the output waveform.

1. Input pulse A comes up ahead of the leading edge of CL1. Therefore, output at D_0 goes up at the leading edge of CL1 and stays up for 1 full clock period, T1. Thus A′ represents input level A.
2. Input level B comes up after the leading edge of CL3 but stays up until after the leading edge of CL4. Therefore, at the leading edge of CL4, D_0 goes high and stays up for the clock period T4.
3. Input level C goes high ahead of the leading edge of CL5 and does not come down until after the leading edge of CL6. Therefore D_0 stays high for 2 clock periods, T5 and T6. Therefore C′ and C″ at D_0 represent level C at D_I. ∎

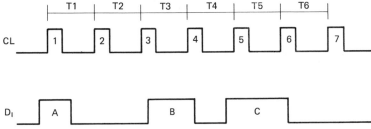

Figure 11-4 Clock pulses and input waveform for Example 11-1.

In Fig. 11-5, even though level C at D_I seems to be a *single* pulse, in reality it could represent 2 digital pulses. At D_0, it is properly represented by a high level for the duration of 2 clock periods, T5 and T6. An unusual situation that could happen with this logical approach is shown in Example 11-2.

Example 11-2

A D-type flip-flop is used as a level normalizer. The clock input and the data input waveforms are shown in Fig. 11-6. Sketch the output waveform at D_0 (see Fig. 11-3) and show the proper timing relationships. Are all the input signal levels properly represented at D_0? If not, explain why.

Solution

The output waveform at D_0 is shown in Fig. 11-7.
In this example, input level B is not represented at output D_0. The levels at D_I are low at the leading edges of CL3 and CL4. Hence the output level is low during T3 and T4. Since level B is high only between the trailing edge of CL3 and the leading

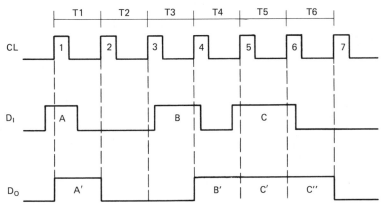

Figure 11-5 I/O waveforms for Example 11-1.

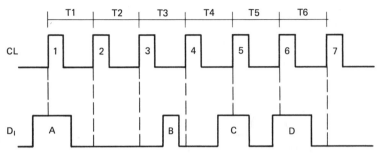

Figure 11-6 Clock pulses and input waveform for Example 11-2.

edge of CL4, it has no effect on the D-type flip-flop as previously explained in this section regarding the basic characteristics of the D-type flip-flop.

A', C', and D' during T1, T5, and T6 represent levels A, C, and D, respectively. Level B is lost in this configuration.　■

Example 11-2 demonstrates the principal shortcoming of the simple level normalizer. Level B in Fig. 11-7 is not taken into consideration in the output D_0. Since level B carries information or intelligence, its omission is intolerable and must be remedied. A buffered level normalizer is shown in Fig. 11-8. This configuration uses an AND gate and a set/reset (R/S) flip-flop in addition to the D-type flip-flop. Operation of this logical configuration is explained by using the same input waveform as the one in Example 11-2. This is shown in Example 11-3. A brief review of the R/S flip-flop and its characteristics as used in this application, is presented next.

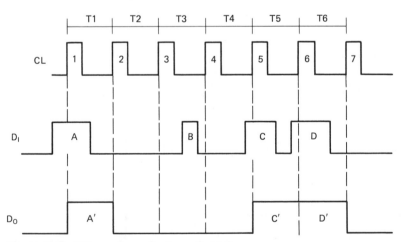

Figure 11-7 I/O waveforms for Example 11-2.

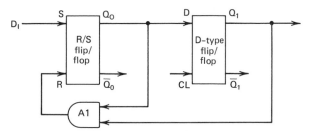

Figure 11-8 Buffered level normalizer. John L. Hilburn, Paul M. Julich, MICROCOMPU-TERS/MICROPROCESSORS: HARDWARE, SOFTWARE AND APPLICATIONS, © 1976, pp. 171, 173. Reprinted by permission of Prentice-Hall, Inc., Englewood Cliffs, New Jersey. A few minor modifications have been made to conform to the material in this text.

1. When a 1 is present at D_I (i.e., at the S input of the R/S flip-flop), Q_0 goes to a 1 if it were previously at 0 and if the input at R is a 0.
2. A 1 at the R input will flip it over and $\overline{Q}_0$ will be a 1 if the 1 at S is no longer there.
3. If the 1 input at S is still present, a 1 input at R will have no effect on the flip-flop and Q_0 will continue to be a 1.

Example 11-3

The input waveform for the buffered level normalizer of Fig. 11-8 is the same as that shown in Fig. 11-6. Sketch the waveforms at Q_0, Q_1, and R showing the proper relations with respect to the input at D_I; explain the entire sequence of operations.

Solution

The waveforms are shown in Fig. 11-9 and the sequence of operations is explained as follows.

1. As soon as the signal at D_I goes high, Q_0 jumps to a 1, since the R/S flip-flop is independent of the clock pulses.
2. The high level at Q_0 applies a high level to the D input of the D-type flip-flop. At the leading edge of CL1, Q_1 jumps to a 1 and stays high for the clock period T1.
3. Both Q_0 and Q_1 are now high, and these signals are fed into the AND gate A1. The output of A1 goes high and applies a 1 to the R input of the R/S flip-flop.
4. The high input at R has no effect on the flip-flop as long as the S input is high, but as soon as D_I goes low, the Q_0 output also goes low. This removes the 1 input from one of the inputs to A1, and R goes low.
5. Level B at D_I goes high after the trailing edge of CL3, so Q_0 goes high and stays high until the leading edge of CL4.
6. At the leading edge of CL4, Q_1 goes high; this fully enables A1, resulting in

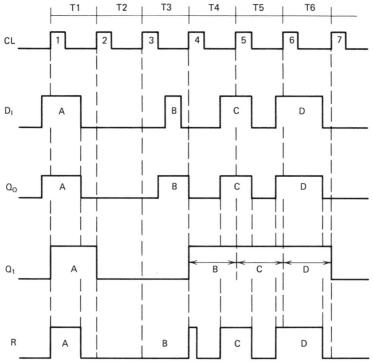

Figure 11-9 I/O waveforms for Example 11-3.

a short pulse at R. As soon as R is high and D_I is low, Q_0 goes low. This explains why the B pulse at R is so short. It may seem to be a noise spike, but it is really a legitimate pulse.

7.   Since both levels C and D at D_I come up ahead of the CL5 and CL6 pulses, respectively, Q_1 stays high during T5 and T6. However, the C and D levels at R are high only during the time that the high levels of Q_0 and Q_1 overlap.

8.   Therefore *all* four high levels at D_I are accounted for during T1, T4, T5, and T6 for A, B, C, and D respectively. ■

11-2.4 Level-to-Bit Conversion and Synchronization

The outputs of the configurations used in Examples 11-2 and 11-3 show that the outputs are still levels that are normalized to the digital voltage levels. However, they are still only levels (and *not* binary signals) on which the computer can operate, as seen in Figs. 11-7 and 11-9. The proper binary bits can be easily obtained by superimposing a series of clock pulses in these signal levels. This can be done by feeding the signal levels into 1 input of a 2-input AND gate and the clock pulses into the other input (see Fig. 11-10). This arrangement not only produces the binary signals, usable by the computer,

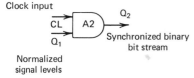

Figure 11-10   Level-to-bit conversion and synchronization logic.

but also *synchronizes* them with the *system clock*. This is shown in Example 11-4.

Example 11-4

Use the Q_1 output shown in Fig. 11-9 and the AND gate of Fig. 11-10 and sketch the output of the AND gate. Use 8 clock input pulses and identify the 8-bit byte.

Solution

The 8-bit byte in this example is 1 0 0 1 1 1 0 0 (Fig. 11-11).

11-2.5 Synchronization of Random Input Pulses

In many applications the data coming into the computer from peripherals may be in digital form, but the serial binary bits may be coming in randomly and not in synchronism with the computer's clocking system. Many peripherals operate from their own separate clocking systems that are independent of the computer's clock. An example is a DMA transfer to or from a magnetic tape unit. In such situations it is necessary that incoming binary bits are properly synchronized with the computer's clocking system before they are used by the computer. Figure 11-12 shows a simple *pulse synchronizer* that uses two J/K flip-flops and an AND gate. The working of this configuration is explained in Example 11-5.

The basic properties of the J/K flip-flops follow.

1. If neither the J or the K input is enabled (i.e., has a digital 1), when the clock pulse comes, the flip-flop outputs will not change states.
2. If *both* the J and the K inputs are enabled, when the clock pulse comes, the flip-flop complements or the outputs change states, regardless of what state the outputs were in originally.
3. If only *one* of the 2 inputs (either J or K) is enabled, the flip-flop acts like a simple clocked R/S flip-flop [i.e., either it will or will not change states, depending on which state the flip-flop was in initially and which input (J or K) is enabled].
4. The output changes states only at the trailing edge of the next clock pulse.
5. J/K flip flops usually have 2 asynchronous inputs labeled PRESET and CLEAR.

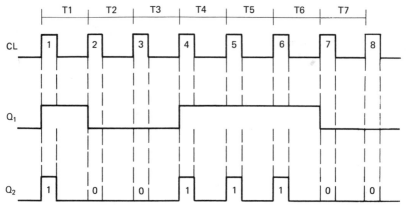

Figure 11-11   I/O waveforms for Example 11-4.

When PRESET is enabled, the flip-flop is set to Q_1 (i.e., the Q_1 output immediately goes to a 1, independent of the clock input). Likewise, when CLEAR is enabled, the $\overline{Q_1}$ output goes to a 1, independent of the clock input.

Example 11-5

The unsynchronized input data pulses of Fig. 11-13 are fed into the PRESET terminal, labelled D_I, of the random input pulse synchronizer of Fig. 11-12. Sketch the output waveforms at Q_1, Q_2, and Q_3 and explain the sequence of events that take place.

Solution

In Fig. 11-12 the unsynchronized input data serial pulses are fed into the PRESET input of flip-flop A, which is labeled D_I. The rest of the PRESET and CLEAR

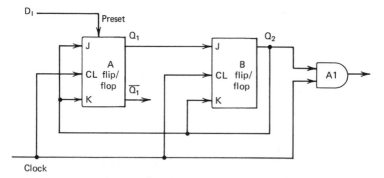

Figure 11-12   Random input pulse synchronizer. John L. Hilburn, Paul M. Julich, MICRO-COMPUTERS/MICROPROCESSORS; HARDWARE, SOFTWARE AND APPLICATIONS, © 1976, pp. 171, 173. Reprinted by permission of Prentice-Hall, Inc., Englewood Cliffs, New Jersey. A few minor modifications have been made to conform to the material in this book.

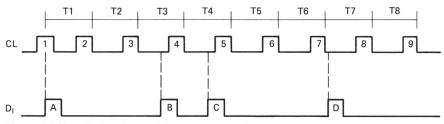

Figure 11-13 Clock pulses and input waveform for Example 11-5.

inputs to both the flip-flops are not used in this particular application. Figure 11-14 shows the various waveforms.

The following sequence of events take place:

1. As soon as pulse A comes in at D_I, output Q_1 jumps high or to a 1 regardless of the clock pulses because the signal is input into the asynchronous input of flip-flop A. This enables the J input of flip-flop B.

2. At the trailing edge of the next clock input pulse (i.e., CL2), Q_2 goes high. Since the output at Q_2 is fed back into the K inputs of both flip-flops, at the trailing edge of CL3 both Q_1 and Q_2 drop low or to a 0.

3. Since the output at Q_2 also enables 1 input to the AND gate A1, the output at Q_3 goes to a 1 during the time that CL3 enables the other input.

4. Prior to the coming of CL4, signal B comes up at D_I, so Q_1 immediately goes high. At the trailing edge of CL4, Q_2 also goes high and then comes down at the trailing edge of CL5. Thus, at CL5, Q_3 goes up for 1 clock pulse duration.

5. Note that before Q_1 comes down at the trailing edge of CL5, another input signal, C, comes up at D_I. However, since Q_1 is already up at this time, signal C does not make its presence felt in the system.

6. Likewise, input signal D at D_I, which comes up between CL7 and CL8, is synchronized with CL9 at output Q_3.

7. Notice that inputs A, B, and D are now fully synchronized with the computer clock pulses CL3, CL5, and CL9.

8. Since input C comes up before completion of the clock period T4, it is missed in the configuration. ■

For the logic of Fig. 11-12 to work in a consistently accurate and predictable manner, the input signals must be separated (in time) between their leading edges by an equivalent of at least 2 clock periods. What if 1 or more inputs do not meet this time separation requirement? In that case some binary bits will be lost. However, in most real applications, such a situation is most unlikely, since the pulse repetition rate of the computer clock is considerably higher than that of the peripheral unit's internal clock. This is understandable; most peripherals are electromechanical devices that are considerably slower than the all-electronic CPU.

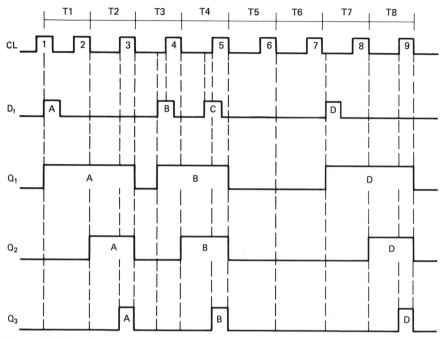

Figure 11-14   I/O waveforms for Example 11-5.

11-3 DATA IDENTIFICATION IN SERIAL BIT STREAM

11-3.1 The Problem

When binary bits are transferred in a parallel manner, they are transferred as either a complete word or a complete byte (or sometimes as a complete nibble). All the bits in a word or a byte are transmitted simultaneously. An individual wire or lead is provided for each word to be transferred. There is no question about where the word or the byte starts and where it ends. In other words, no special effort is needed to identify the first or the last bit in the word or the byte.

The situation is very different when the word or the byte comes in, 1 bit at a time, on a single wire. When a serial string of continuous words or bytes come in, the receiving logic has no way of knowing where one word ends and the next one starts. To make matters worse, there may be periods of time when, in serial transmission, no legitimate data may be transmitted. During such periods, a low-level signal is usually present on the line, and the receiving equipment often interprets this as digital 0s. Obviously, it is not sufficient just to be able to synchronize the 1 and 0 levels with the system clock pulses. Some method must be provided for properly bracketing each word or byte.

11-3.2 Byte Start Identification Method

A fairly straightforward method of bracketing or framing is shown in Fig. 11-15, where an 8-bit byte is used for explanation purposes. By means of a simple up counter, a byte start signal is generated for every 8 clock pulses. This signal can be used to separate the serial incoming words.

However, such an arrangement has one serious shortcoming. What happens if the serial bit stream, representing a legitimate byte, starts coming in between byte start pulses A and B, as in Fig. 11-15? In such a situation several of the first or leading bits of the byte would be lost. Since there seems to be no way to synchronize the incoming data directly, some other means must be provided. Before discussing the solution to this problem, we should be familiar with synchronous and asynchronous data transmissions.

11-3.3 Synchronous and Asynchronous Serial Transmissions

The synchronous mode of transmission sends the serial bit streams in a continuous fashion. If the transmitting device does not have legitimate data to send, it inserts dummy characters called SYNC characters in the blank slots; however, they really do not perform any synchronization functions.

In asynchronous data transmission, if the transmitting device does not have any legitimate data to send, it stops transmitting. In this case no SYNC characters are inserted, so the serial bit stream will have blank spaces or breaks in the data stream.

In asynchronous transmissions the word or the byte is framed by start bit

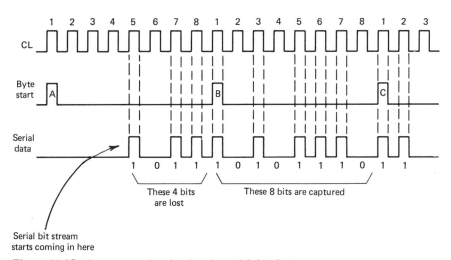

Figure 11-15 Byte start pulses bracket the serial data byte.

and stop bit(s). Figure 11-16 shows how this is done. A parity bit could also be included. The system shown in Fig. 11-16 includes the following.

- Start bit—0.
- Stop bits—1 1.
- Parity bit—1 or 0, depending on selected odd or even parity scheme.
- Data bits—8-bit byte.

In synchronous transmissions each data stream is always preceded by a predetermined identification word that always has a set pattern of 1s and 0s. The ASCII code is widely used in μC systems. In ASCII the identification pattern (called the SYNC pattern) is 0 1 1 0 1 0 0 1.

To safeguard against any freak data pattern of 1s and 0s that may be identical to this SYNC pattern, *two* such SYNC patterns are sent consecutively ahead of the data word. The logic in the receiving equipment detects and decodes these patterns and sets up the logic to capture the next 8 bits that come in *serially*. The data bits are then converted into a *parallel* format, and the 8-bit byte is gated out to its ultimate destination in the μC system in a parallel fashion. A logical configuration that does this is shown and explained in Section 11-3.4.

11-3.4 Byte Capture Logic for Serial Bit Stream

Figure 11-17 shows a simple logic scheme that identifies the two SYNC patterns and captures the next 8-bit byte. The following events take place.

1. The incoming serial bit stream is fed into two places, the SYNC pattern shift register 2 and the AND gate A5. Note that A5 is disabled because the RS flip-flop A is outputting a 1 on the $\overline{Q}$ side. Therefore the incoming bits are not loaded into the 8-bit serial/parallel converter.
2. From the SYNC pattern register 2, the bits are serially shifted into the SYNC pattern register 1 and, from there, the bits are lost.
3. From both the SYNC pattern registers, the data are continuously fed in a parallel manner in SYNC pattern decoders 2 and 1, respectively. These decoders each

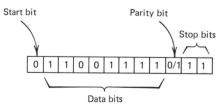

Start bit   Parity bit

| 0 | 1 | 1 | 0 | 0 | 1 | 1 | 1 | 1 | 0/1 | 1 | 1 |

Data bits

Figure 11-16 Asynchronous transmission of data byte.

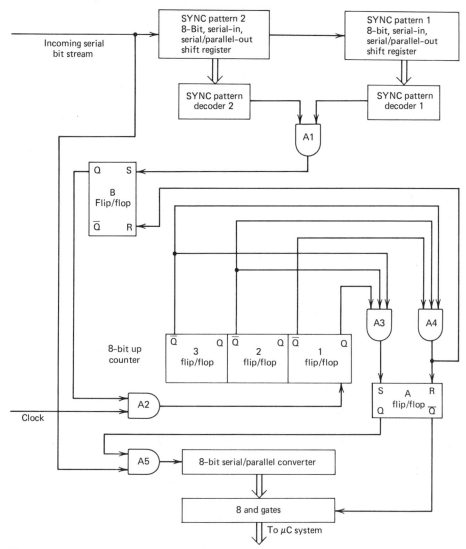

Figure 11-17   Logic for capturing the data byte in serial bit stream.

output a 1 when they are loaded with the ASCII SYNC pattern, that is, 0 1 1 0 1 0 0 1.

4. When two consecutive ASCII patterns are simultaneously decoded, AND gate A1 is fully enabled and puts out a 1, which sets the B flip-flop to the Q side. A 1 output on the Q side enables AND gate A2.

5. When the next clock pulse arrives, A2 is fully enabled and so outputs a 1, which is fed into the flip-flop 1 of the 8-bit up counter.

6. Note that the next 7 clock pulses will step the counter and increment it by 1 each

time. Also note that this is possible because the B flip-flop keeps A2 enabled for 8 clock pulses.

7. When the up counter receives the first clock pulse, AND gate A3 is fully enabled because of the way the outputs of flip-flops 1, 2, and 3 are connected. A 1 output from A3 sets the A flip-flop to the S side. Note that the A flip-flop will be reset to the R side only when the up counter reaches a count of 0 0 0 and fully enables AND gate A4.

8. Thus, for the next 8 pulses, the 1 output from the Q side of the A flip-flop will enable AND gate A5. Also, after 8 clock pulses, the outputs of A4 resets the B flip-flop which disables A2 and prevents any further clock pulses from restarting the counter.

9. During the 8 clock pulses when flip-flop A is sitting on the Q side, A5 is enabled, and the 8 serial data bits are loaded into the 8-bit serial/parallel converter.

10. After all 8 data bits are fully loaded, flip-flop A flips back to the Q side. This enables the 8 AND gates, and the 8-bit data byte is output to the μC system in a parallel fashion.

11. The whole sequence is repeated when the next two ASCII SYNC patterns arrive and indicate the legitimate start of another 8 bits of data.

11-4 SUMMARY

While computer systems operate on data words or bytes in a parallel manner, many *peripherals* output and accept words/bytes in a *serial* fashion. This is particularly true of μC systems, which use existing telephone lines for communication of data. Since the communication lines use analog signals and the appropriate equipment to handle them, A/D and D/A conversions are necessary. Additionally, problems are created by timing differences between the CPU and the external serial devices and in recognizing and framing the data words/bytes in serial bit streams.

Both serial-to-parallel and parallel-to-serial conversions of digital data can be easily performed by simple *shift registers,* but signal levels of digital bits usually need to be normalized to those that can be used by the μC system. Simple and buffered level *normalizers* are available and were explained through examples. After the signal levels are properly normalized, the levels must be converted to binary bits usable by the μC. A simple 2-input AND gate accomplishes that. Many peripherals output serial bit streams that have the proper signal levels but are random with respect to the μC timing. A logical configuration, using two JK flip-flops, can be used to synchronize such random input pulses. Some input pulses in such a configuration could be missed if they come in at a rate such that the time separation requirement of at least two clock periods between the leading edges of 2 input pulses is violated.

In a *serial* bit stream, identifying the start and the end of a legitimate word/ byte of data is a problem. In asynchronous transmission no data are sent if the transmitting equipment does not have any legitimate data to send. In synchronous transmissions dummy characters are inserted in such blank spots. For asynchronous transmissions the word/byte is framed by start and stop bits. A parity bit may or may not be used. In synchronous transmissions the data word/byte is preceded by two ASCII 8-bit SYNC patterns. A logical configuration for recognizing these patterns and capturing the data bits was also shown and discussed.

11-5 REVIEW QUESTIONS

11-1 Refer to the block diagram of a microcomputer with serial I/O capability (Fig. 11-1) and briefly explain the functions of the modem and the serial I/O interface (UART).

11-2 Refer again to Fig. 11-1. In addition to serial-to-parallel and parallel-to-serial conversions, what other functions are performed by the serial I/O interface unit?

11-3 What are the two modes in which the serial I/O interface unit can possibly operate? Briefly explain each mode.

11-4 Refer to the simple level normalizer in Fig. 11-3 and the I/O waveforms in Fig. 11-5. Explain why inputs A and B are each represented at D_0 by one clock period (T1 and T4) when input C is represented at D_0 by two clock periods (T5 and T6).

11-5 The C input at D_I in Fig. 11-5 is of a long time duration. Explain what the implication of this is and how it might affect the output waveforms at D_0.

11-6 The I/O waveforms for a simple level normalizer, using a D-type flip-flop, are shown in Fig. 11-7. Explain why the output waveform does not include the input level B.

11-7 Refer to the buffered level normalizer of Fig. 11-8 and the I/O waveforms for Example 11-3, shown in Fig. 11-9. Explain why the B pulse at the R input to the RS flip-flop is so short while the other three (A, C, and D) are not.

11-8 Again refer to Figs. 11-8 and 11-9. Explain why level B at R, in spite of the fact that it is so much shorter in time (as compared to A, C, or D), still gives a normal B level at output Q_1.

11-9 The Q_1 outputs of the buffered level normalizer of Fig. 11-8 are levels as shown in Fig. 11-9. Is it possible to convert these levels into binary pulses that are synchronized with the μC's system clock? If so, explain how.

11-10 Is it possible that serial data coming into the μC system from peripherals are in digital format but their timing is different from that of the μC system clock? If so, explain why.

11-11 The following questions relate to the JK flip-flop. (Refer to Fig. 11-12.)

(a) The outputs are $Q_1 = 0$ and $\overline{Q}_1 = 1$, and the inputs are $J = 0$ and $K = 0$. What will be the outputs immediately after the leading edge of the next clock pulse and immediately after the trailing edge of the same clock pulse?

(b) The outputs are $Q_1 = 1$ and $\overline{Q}_1 = 0$ and the inputs are $J = 1$ and $K = 0$. What will be the outputs after the trailing edge of the next clock pulse?

(c) The outputs are $Q_1 = 1$ and $\overline{Q}_1 = 0$ and the inputs are $J = 0$ and $K = 1$. What will be the outputs after the trailing edge of the next clock pulse?

(d) The outputs are $Q_1 = 0$ and $\overline{Q}_1 = 1$ and the inputs are $J = 1$ and $K = 1$. What will be the outputs after the trailing edge of the next clock pulse?

(e) The outputs are $Q_1 = 1$ and $\overline{Q}_1 = 0$ and the inputs are $J = 1$ and $K = 1$. What will be the outputs after the trailing edge of the next clock pulse?

11-12 Refer to the JK flip-flop in Fig. 11-12. The outputs are $Q_1 = 0$ and $\overline{Q}_1 = 1$. What will the outputs be when $D_I = 1$ and, if they change states, what will it be after the trailing edge of the next clock pulse? Explain.

11-13 Refer to Fig. 11-14, which shows the I/O waveforms for the random input pulse synchronizer, Fig. 11-12 (Example 11-4). The A input pulse at D_I is a short pulse, less than one clock period wide. Why then is the A level at Q_1 two clock periods wide?

11-14 From the I/O waveforms (Fig. 11-14) for Example 11-4 it is seen that the output at Q_3 does not contain the C input pulse that is present at D_I. Explain what happened to it.

11-15 Refer to the loss of input pulse C in Question 11-14. Is it possible to avoid such a situation? If so, explain how. Is such a situation likely to happen in real applications?

11-16 Briefly describe the problem of identifying the start and end of the data word or byte when it is transferred in a serial manner.

11-17 Refer to Fig. 11-15, which is used to describe the byte start approach using a simple up counter for indicating a byte start. The first byte transmitted is 10111010, as shown in Fig. 11-15. Will all the 8 bits of this byte be captured by this approach? If not, which will be captured? Explain.

11-18 Which of the serial transmission modes, the synchronous or the asynchronous, inserts dummy characters in blank spots if it has no legitimate data to send?

11-19 What happens in an asynchronous serial transmission if the transmitting device has no legitimate data to send?

11-20 An 8-bit byte (i.e., 00101101) is to be transmitted serially by asynchronous transmission. A 1 even parity scheme is used, and it is framed by conventional start and stop bits. Show what the complete word will be and its direction of serial transmission; identify each bit.

11-21 What is the ASCII SYNC pattern used in synchronous transmission of serial data? What happens if a word accidentally consists of bits that have the same bit configuration as the SYNC pattern? Is it possible to avoid the resulting confusion? If so, how?

11-22 The following questions relate to the logic for capturing the serial data byte in synchronous transmission as shown in Fig. 11-17.
(a) Why are two SYNC pattern decoders used in this configuration?
(b) What is the function of the B flip-flop?
(c) What function(s) does the A flip-flop serve?

11-23 Is it possible to modify the byte capturing logic of Fig. 11-17 so that a 16-bit serially transmitted word can be captured using the same two ASCII SYNC patterns? If so, explain what changes would have to be made in Fig. 11-17.

12

PROGRAMMABLE I/O INTERFACES

12-1 WHAT ARE PROGRAMMABLE INTERFACES?

The I/O transfer schemes discussed in previous chapters (i.e., Chapters 8, 9, 10, and 11) are basically schemes that are fixed, or *nonprogrammable*. While it is true that the actual I/O transfers take place under program control, the primary functions performed by these systems are fixed and unalterable. In μC systems these I/O interfaces are usually available on 1 or more chips. The various features, available in these chips, and their operating characteristics are fixed during their fabrication, and the user must employ them as specified by the chip manufacturer. On the other hand, programmable I/O interface chips are available and widely used. Within certain preestablished limitations, the functional characteristics of such interfaces can be modified or altered by means of certain instructions from the computer. Such interfaces obviously offer the user a high degree of flexibility. Some of the typical tasks performed by programmable interfaces include:

1. Controlling the bidirectional flow of parallel data between the CPU and the peripheral.
2. Controlling the bidirectional transmission of serial data between the CPU and the modem.
3. Handling interrupts from peripherals to the CPU.
4. Implementing DMA (direct memory access) transfers between the CPU and auxiliary memories.

In μC systems programmable I/O interfaces for both serial and parallel transfers of data are available. Such interfaces are generally provided on a single chip, although it is possible that more than one chip may be involved. We will discuss programmable I/O interfaces for both serial and parallel transfer of data in this chapter.

12-2 PROGRAMMABLE INTERFACES FOR SERIAL TRANSFERS

12-2.1 The UART

12-2.1.1 Basic Functions and Features The problems involved in identifying data words in the transmission of a serial bit stream have been discussed in Sections 11-3.1, 11-3.2, and 11-3.3. Asynchronous transmission is used in systems that utilize serial peripherals at low data rates. Such systems require interfaces that generate and check parity bits, recognize or add start and stop bits so that data bits can be properly identified, recognize and add parity bits as appropriate, and accept the appropriate control and status signals. Additional complications arise because data rates and data formats vary with different peripherals. For example, data words can range from 5 to 8 bits. Asynchronous serial transmissions are used with low data transmission rate equipments whose speeds generally range up to 30 characters per second. Obviously, electromechanical peripherals are usually in this speed range. The asynchronous transmission is also used for medium speed applications in which data rates range from 30 to 500 characters per second.

To accommodate the requirements just cited, semiconductor manufacturers have come up with a variety of *universal asynchronous receiver transmitter* (UART) chips. Each UART chip has its own unique features, but all of them perform the following basic functions.

1. They convert incoming serial digital data into parallel formats acceptable for use by the µC system.
2. They convert outgoing parallel data from the µC system into serial formats acceptable for use by modems or other serial peripherals.
3. During parallel-to-serial conversions (i.e., when performing the transmitting function), they generate the appropriate parity bit.
4. During the transmitting operations, they frame the data words (including the parity bit, if any) with the proper start and stop bits.
5. During serial-to-parallel conversions (i.e., when performing the receiving functions), they recognize the start and stop bits and eliminate them from further processing.
6. During the receiving operations, they check the parity of the word and flag out a parity error if there is one.
7. They receive and act on the status signals from the peripherals and also send signals indicating the UART's status to the peripherals (e.g., it has output data or received data and is ready for the next transmission). Status signals are also sent to the CPU. The UART sends specific commands to the peripherals, too.
8. Finally, during receiving operations, the UART clocks and synchronizes serial data at a rate compatible with the µC's clocking system.

12-2.1.2 Timing and Synchronization In asynchronous serial transmissions, the digital 1s are represented by a high level signal and the digital 0s by a low level. In Section 11-3.3 it was stated that a legitimate data word (including the parity bit, if any) is preceded by a start bit, which is a 0, and followed by 1 or 2 stop bits (digital 1s). Between legitimate word transmissions, wide gaps of indeterminate time durations could occur. When the line goes high for the stop bits (because of the 1s), it stays high for an arbitrary number of 1 bits. Thus the beginning of the next character is indicated by the negative-going edge between the high bits and the low start bit.

In serial asynchronous transmissions there is no common system clock that provides synchronization of incoming and outgoing data streams. Each peripheral has its own clock, and the μC system has its own clocking system. These clocks are calibrated but not synchronized. The *high-to-low* transition on the signal line starts the clock in the receiver portion of the UART or the peripheral.

UARTs generally use a clock rate that is either 16 or 64 times the frequency of the bit rate or *bit time;* 16 times the bit time is most commonly used. The bit time (t_b) of the data is defined as the time duration of any of the bits of a character, which includes the start bit, the data bits, the parity bit (if any) and the stop bit(s). An asynchronous serial data character is shown in Fig. 12-1. A parity bit, 2 stop bits, and an 8-bit data word is assumed.

If t_{cp} is the clock period of the receiver clock, for a typical system, the bit time is given by the following relationship.

$$t_b = K \times t_{cp} \quad (\text{constant } K = 16 \text{ typically}) \tag{12-1}$$

Thus it is seen that each bit time is divided into 16 subslots. How these subslots are utilized for synchronizing the incoming serial bit stream with the receiver is explained next.

Notice that the *high-to-low* transition on the signal line indicates the start

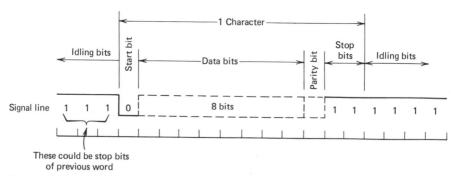

Figure 12-1 Typical asynchronous serial transmission character.

bit to the receiver. This means that a spurious noise spike, when the idle bits are transmitted, on the signal line would be erroneously interpreted as a start bit by the receiver. To eliminate the possibility of a false start, the high-to-low transition starts a counter in the receiver. The counter counts up to 9 clock pulses and then samples the line to determine if it is high or low. Figure 12-2 shows the situation where a noise spike triggers the counter. However, the line goes high after the noise pulse, so after the 9 clock pulses it is still high. The logic in the receiver assumes that the condition was caused by a noise pulse and not a legitimate start bit. Consequently, no data bits are recognized by the receiver.

What happens in the event of a legitimate start bit is shown in Fig. 12-3. In this case note that during the 9-bit time delay, the data line has nine consecutive 0s (i.e., a low-level signal). The logic in the receiver recognizes this as a proper start bit. At this point, the counter recycles (is reset to zero) and starts a count of a full bit time, (i.e., 16 full clock periods).

The scheme, described in Fig. 12-3, starts the counter approximately in the middle of the bit time. The counter recycling will be repeated automatically 12 times since, in this situation, we have assumed 12 bits per character, as shown in Fig. 12-1. The receiver logic will then start looking for another legitimate start bit and synchronize on it (see Fig. 12-3) while ignoring any noise pulses (see Fig. 12-2).

In Fig. 12-3 the counter recycling starts in the *middle* of the start bit; however, the actual capturing of the remaining 11 bits of the character is done in synchronism with the clock and by the logic in the receiver, essentially independent of the counter recycling. Starting the counter recycling in the middle of the start bit eliminates the possibility of *false starts* by noise pulses and assures that the next character will be recognized only if it is preceded by a proper start bit. Thus character time (i.e., the time required to transmit a character) is given by

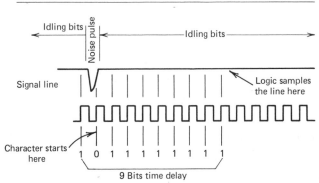

Figure 12-2   Noise pulse on the data line.

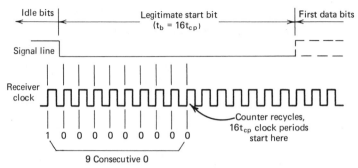

Figure 12-3 Legitimate start bit detection and synchronization. Reprinted from John B. Peatman, "Microcomputer-Based Design." Copyright 1977, by permission of McGraw-Hill Book Company. Minor modifications have been made to conform to the material in this book.

$$T_C = N_0 t_{cp} + N_C \times t_b$$
$$= N_0 t_{cp} + N_C \times (K t_{cp}) \tag{12-2}$$

where

T_C = the time required to transmit the complete character

N_0 = the number of consecutive 0s in the start bit

t_{cp} = the clock period

N_C = the number of bits in the character

K = a constant representing clock periods per bit time, usually 16 or 64

t_b = the bit time

12-2.1.3 Baud Rate and Data Rate

The baud rate is defined as the bit rate at which serial transmission of data takes place. The baud rate establishes the number of bits transmitted per second and includes the data bits, the start bit, the parity bit, and the stop bit(s). Thus the baud rate is given by

$$B = N_C \times C \tag{12-3}$$

where

B = the baud rate

N_C = the number of bits in the character

C = the number of characters transmitted per second

The bit time, t_b, is the reciprocal of the baud rate and is given by

$$t_b = \frac{1}{B} = \frac{1}{N_C \times C} \tag{12-4}$$

The baud rate is a figure of merit of the bandwidth required for a serial transmission channel. Basically, it is an indication of the maximum rate of code modulation expressed in bits per second.

The data rate is *not* the same as the baud rate. In determining the baud rate all the bits in a character are included. However, not all bits in the character represent useful data. The data rate, therefore is given by

$$D_r = D_b \times C \tag{12-5}$$

where

D_r = the data rate expressed as bits per second
D_b = the data bits per character, ranging from 5 to 8
C = the number of characters transmitted per second

Example 12-1

A serial data transmission system uses 8 data bits, an even parity bit, and 1 stop bit per character. The baud rate is 110 bauds. (1) What is the bit time (t_b)? (2) What is the receiver clock frequency if 16 clock pulses per character are transmitted?

Solution

1. The bit time is the reciprocal of the baud rate. Therefore

    $$t_b = \frac{1}{B}$$

    $$\frac{1}{110} = 0.0090909 \text{ s} = 9.09 \cong 9.1 \text{ ms} \tag{12-4}$$

2. Also, $t_b = K \times t_{cp}$ (12-1)
    Since there are 16 clock pulses per bit, the bit time is

    $$t_b = 16 \times t_{cp}$$

    Therefore

    $$t_{cp} = \frac{t_b}{16} = \frac{9.1 \times 10^{-3}}{16}$$
    $$= 0.568 \times 10^{-3} \text{ s} = 0.568 \text{ ms}$$

The clock frequency is

$$f = \frac{1}{t_{cp}} = \frac{1}{0.568} = 1.76 \times 10^3 = 1.76 \text{ kHz}$$

■

Example 12-2

Ten characters are serially transmitted per second. Each character consists of 1 start bit, 8 data bits, 1 parity bit, and 2 stop bits. Sixteen clock periods per bit time are used. Calculate:

1. The baud rate (B).
2. The bit time (t_b).
3. The clock period (t_{cp}).

Solution

1. The number of bits in the character is

$$N_C = 1 \text{ (start)} + 8 \text{ (data)} + 1 \text{ (parity)} + 2 \text{ (stop)}$$
$$= 12$$

Since 10 characters are transmitted per second, the baud rate is

$$B = N_C \times C = 12 \times 10 = 120 \text{ bauds} \tag{12-3}$$

2. The bit time is the reciprocal of the baud rate.

$$t_b = \frac{1}{B} = \frac{1}{120} = 8.33 \text{ ms} \tag{12-4}$$

3. The clock period is

$$t_b = K \times t_{cp} \tag{12-1}$$

and

$$t_{cp} = \frac{t_b}{K}$$
$$= \frac{8.33 \times 10^{-3}}{16}$$
$$= 0.52 \text{ ms}$$

■

Example 12-3

Refer to Example 12-2. The start bit uses 9 consecutive 0s. Calculate:

1. The receiver clock frequency.
2. The time required to transmit a character.
3. The data rate.

Solution

1. The receiver clock frequency is,

$$f = \frac{1}{t_{cp}} = \frac{1}{0.52 \times 10^{-3}} = 1.92 \text{ kHz}$$

2. The time required to transmit a complete character is given by

$$
\begin{aligned}
T_C &= N_0 \, t_{cp} + N_C \times K \times t_{cp} && \text{(12-2)} \\
&= (9 \times 0.52 \times 10^{-3}) + (12 \times 16 \times 0.52 \times 10^{-3}) \\
&= (4.68 \times 10^{-3}) + (99.84 \times 10^{-3}) \\
&= 104.52 \text{ ms}
\end{aligned}
$$

3. The data rate is

$$
\begin{aligned}
D_r &= D_b \times C && \text{(12-5)} \\
&= 8 \times 10 \\
&= 80 \text{ bits per second} \quad \blacksquare
\end{aligned}
$$

12-2.1.4 Data Buffering Buffers are small memories that have special characteristics. For example, the stack, which is used to save return addresses in BRANCH operations, is a buffer memory in which the last inserted word is read out first. We call this the LIFO (last-in, first-out) stack. Queues, on the other hand, are FIFO (first-in, first-out) memories. Both stacks and queues are *buffer* memories that hold some word(s) until either the CPU or some other device calls them out and uses them. They are often used to reconcile speed differences between various devices.

The UART uses buffer registers in both its receiver and transmitter sections. A process called *double buffering* is used in both sections. This process speeds up operations by allowing the faster CPU to operate with slower peripherals, such as the teletypewriter. Figure 12-4 shows a typical *double buffer* in the transmitter section of the UART. In this case an 8-bit data word, 1 start bit, 1 parity bit, and 2 stop bits are assumed.

The 8-bit data word from the CPU is loaded into the 8-bit transmitter buffer register in a parallel manner. At the appropriate time, these 8 bits are shifted out in parallel to the parity bit generator and simultaneously to the transmitter shift register. The parity bit generator determines the appropriate parity bit for the particular data word and inserts it in the flip-flop marked P in the transmitter shift register, as shown in Fig. 12-4. The start-stop bit generator generates and inserts a 0 in the rightmost position of the transmitter shift register. Likewise, it generates two digital 1s and inserts them in the two leftmost positions of the transmitter shift register. The completed 12-bit character is then *serially* shifted out on the single data output line, starting with the start bit.

It is possible to load the 8-bit data word directly into the parity bit generator

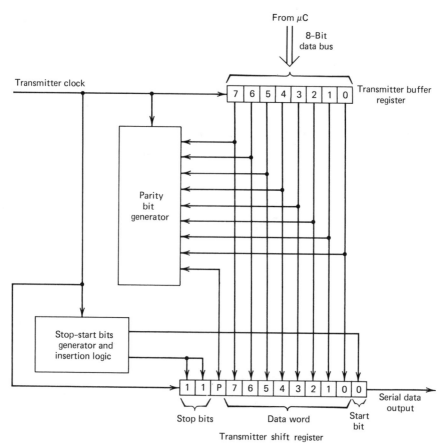

Figure 12-4 Double buffering in UART transmitter section. Reprinted from John B. Peatman, "Microcomputer-Based Design." Copyright 1977, by permission of McGraw-Hill Book Company. Minor modifications have been made to conform to the material in this book.

and the transmitter shift register, completely bypassing the transmitter buffer register. Such a scheme is called *single buffering*. However, double buffering has one distinct advantage. Since serial shifting on a single output line is done 1 bit at a time, the CPU could load the next word into the transmitter buffer register at any time while the 12 bits are shifted out. The CPU does not have to wait to load the next word until the first word is completely shifted out. This speeds up the entire process.

Figure 12-5 shows how double buffering is used in the receiver section of the UART. A check for a legitimate start bit is first made on the incoming serial signals. When a proper start bit is recognized, as explained in Section 12-2.1.2 (also see Fig. 12-3), the following 11 bits, comprised of 8 data bits, 1 parity bit, and 2 stop bits, are shifted into the receiver shift register, as shown in Fig. 12-5. At the appropriate time, these 11 bits are shifted out in

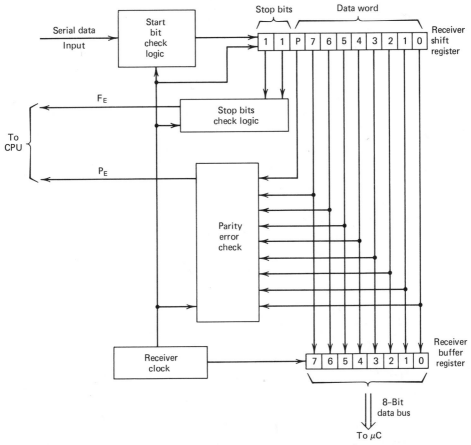

Figure 12-5 Double buffering in UART receiver section. Reprinted from John B. Peatman, "Microcomputer-Based Design." Copyright 1977, by permission of McGraw-Hill Book Company. Minor modifications have been made to conform to the material in this book.

parallel. The 2 stop bits are sent to the stop bits check logic to determine that the incoming character was properly framed. The 8 data bits are loaded into the receiver buffer register and simultaneously fed into the parity error check logic. The parity bit is, likewise, sent to the parity error check logic. If the parity is not correct, a signal is sent to the CPU. Notice that the 8-bit data word is held in the receiver buffer register and can be transferred to the μC any time during the period while another character is being loaded into the receiver shift register.

12-2.1.5 *UART Error Indications* UARTs generally contain circuitry to detect certain errors that occur either in the character transmission process or the serial/parallel conversion processes. Such error signals are transmitted to the μC, where certain flags are set. The μP then takes the appropriate action(s). Three error conditions are widely used in UARTs; they are briefly described here.

1. *Parity Error (P_E).* Most systems and equipments that receive/transmit data serially use some parity checking system. A 1 parity bit is used to indicate either odd or even parity. The receiver section of the UART checks the incoming data word for the proper number of odd or even 1s as indicated by the parity bit. If a parity error is detected, a P_E signal is sent to the CPU, as shown in Fig. 12-5. The computer then takes the necessary preplanned action. Usually, in case of a parity error indication, the data word in the receiver buffer register is inhibited from being put on the 8-bit data bus (Fig. 12-5).

2. *Overrun Error (O_E).* Refer to the double buffering scheme in the UART receiver section shown in Fig. 12-5. In serial transmissions, it is possible that a whole string of characters is received by the UART without any idling bits between consecutive characters. In such a situation it is mandatory that the first character, loaded into the receiver buffer register, is called out by the CPU and transferred out before the next character's data bits are loaded into it. The time window available to the CPU to transfer the first data word out of the receiver buffer register is the time it takes for the next serial character to be loaded into the receiver shift register. If the CPU fails to meet this time constraint or deadline, an overrun error occurs and an O_E signal (not shown in Fig. 12-5) is sent to the CPU for the appropriate action. Notice that without double buffering, the CPU would have to transfer the data word out of the receiver shift register directly, and almost immediately, as soon as the entire character is loaded into the receiver shift register.

3. *Framing Error (F_E).* It is necessary that the data word (including the parity bit, if any) is properly framed by both the start bit and the stop bit or bits. The receiver section checks for the proper synchronization by looking at the leftmost bit position (or the leftmost two bit positions if 2 stop bits are used), which should contain a 1 (or two 1s). If a 0 (or two 0s) is detected a framing error occurs and an F_E signal (not shown in Fig. 12-5) is sent to the CPU for the appropriate action.

12-2.1.6 UART Initialization The UART is a programmable I/O interface, which means that, under program control, its operating characteristics can be modified within certain predesigned limits. The programmable features of the UART make it flexible and therefore adaptable to a wide variety of applications using different peripheral equipments. The available features of the UART have to be selected and programmed into the chip prior to its actual use. In other words, the chip must be first initialized.

Both the receiver and the transmitter sections of the UART are under control of a common control section. The initialization process consists of loading a special register into the control section, called the *control register*. The CPU sends a special control word (or words) that is loaded into the control register. This word is then decoded much like the instruction word in the CPU, and the resulting signals are set up and initialize the various features of the chip. A control register and an 8-bit control word format are shown in Fig. 12-6. The various bits and their explanations, which are also given in Fig. 12-6, are typical of an 8-bit control word but do not refer to any specific UART chip.

12-2.1.7 Commands and Flags Both the receiver and the transmitter sections of the UART contain several flags and commands. Flags are signals that are generated by the UART to indicate certain conditions that exist within the

SF	BR	SB	PS	PI	D W L	MC	Control register
7	6	5	4	3	2 1	0	

Bit 0	MC	—	1 Master clear
Bits 1 and 2	DWL	—	Data word length
	00	—	5 bits
	01	—	6 bits
	10	—	7 bits
	11	—	8 bits
Bit 3	PI	—	Parity check inhibit
	O	—	No parity
	1	—	Parity used
Bit 4	PS	—	Parity select
	0	—	Odd parity
	1	—	Even parity
Bit 5	SB	—	Stop bit select
	0	—	1 stop bit
	1	—	2 stop bits
Bit 6	BR	—	Baud rate select
	0	—	Baud rate = clock rate/16
	1	—	Baud rate = clock rate/64
Bit 7	SF	—	Status flag enable/disable
	0	—	Status bits deactivated
	1	—	Status bits activated

Figure 12-6   Typical UART control word format.

UART with regard to the data or the movement of data. Flag signals are sent out to external devices that could be the CPU or the peripheral(s) involved. On the other hand, commands are generated externally (either by the CPU or the peripherals) and sent to the UART chip. They may indicate the status of the data words or characters sent or received, or they could be signals that command the UART to do other things. Some of the common flags and commands are briefly described here.

Transmitter Flags The transmitter section usually has the following two flag signals.

1. *Transmitter Buffer Register Ready (TBR$_R$).* This flag indicates that the first word, loaded into the transmitter buffer register, has been shifted out to the transmitter shift register and the parity bit generator (see Fig. 12-4). In other words, it indicates that the transmitter buffer register is ready to accept the next word. This signal is sent to the μP.
2. *Transmitter Shift Register Complete (TSR$_C$).* This flag signal is issued by the transmitter shift register and indicates that all the bits of the first word have been serially shifted out of this register. This signal is sent to the peripheral, which is to receive the serial data output by the UART.

Transmitter Commands In most UARTs the transmitter section receives the following two commands.

1. *Transmitter Shift Register Clock (TSR$_{CL}$).* This is the clock input from the μP system to the transmitter shift register. It establishes the baud rate at which the serial output data are transmitted from the UART to the receiving peripheral.
2. *Transmitter Buffer Register Data (TBR$_D$).* This command also comes from the μP. It informs the transmitter buffer register in the UART that the CPU has output a legitimate word on the 8-bit data bus (Fig. 12-4) and that the transmitter buffer register should accept it.

Receiver Flags The three most commonly used flags in the receiver section have been described in Section 12-2.1.5. They are P$_E$, O$_E$, and F$_E$. In some UARTs, in addition to the overrun error flag, a signal is sent to the transmitting peripheral when the first character is transmitted in parallel from the receiver shift register to the receiver buffer register (see Fig. 12-5). This flag, which could be called the receiver shift register ready signal (RSR$_R$), generally sets a flip-flop in the status register, which in turn sends it to the peripheral concerned. Notice that the O$_E$ flag signal is sent to the CPU, as explained in Section 12-2.1.5, whereas the RSR$_R$ is sent to the peripheral.

Receiver Commands Most UART receiver sections receive three command signals, two from the CPU and one from the peripheral. They are briefly described next.

1. *Receiver Shift Register Clock (RSR$_C$).* These are clock pulses from the μC system that synchronize the parallel transfer out of the data word (including the parity bit but excluding the stop bits) into the receiver buffer register and the parity error check logic, as shown in Fig. 12-5.
2. *Receiver Buffer Register Open (RBR$_O$).* The receiver buffer register is a tristate buffer. The RBR$_O$ command from the CPU puts the outputs of this buffer in the high-impedance state, thereby making the 8-bit external data available for transfer of data between the CPU and other chips in the μC system.
3. *Status Flag Reset (SF$_R$).* Refer to the description of the receiver shift register ready (RSR$_R$) signal that set a flip-flop in the status register. When the peripheral transmits a serial character to the UART, it sends the status flag reset (SF$_R$) signal, which resets this flip-flop in the status register. Fundamentally, this command indicates to the UART that a serial character has been transmitted and that it should be accepted as a legitimate character.

12-2.1.8 UART Block Diagram A conceptual block diagram of a typical UART chip used in μC systems is shown in Fig. 12-7. Double buffering is used in both the receiver and the transmitter sections of the UART. The common control section uses the control register and the 8-bit control word. Notice that a 6-bit status register in the control section is used to transmit 4 flags to the μP (3 from the receiver section and 1 from the transmitter section) and 2 to the peripheral involved (1 each from the receiver and the transmitter sections). The transmitter section receives two commands from the μP, while the receiver section receives two commands from the CPU and one from the peripheral.

In this particular UART chip the status flag signal from the *control register* is capable of disabling both flags to the peripheral. While this is commonly done in some UARTs, it is also possible to inhibit other status signal outputs from the status register simply by inserting AND gates in the output lines, similar to those used for TSR$_C$ and RSR$_R$ status flags, and controlling them from bit 7 of the control register.

Remember that Fig. 12-7 is only a conceptual block diagram and not a detailed logic diagram. Consequently, some of the logical functions, such as adjustments to data word length, are shown only as logical functions performing these tasks.

In the receiver section the receiver clock controls the baud rate at which the

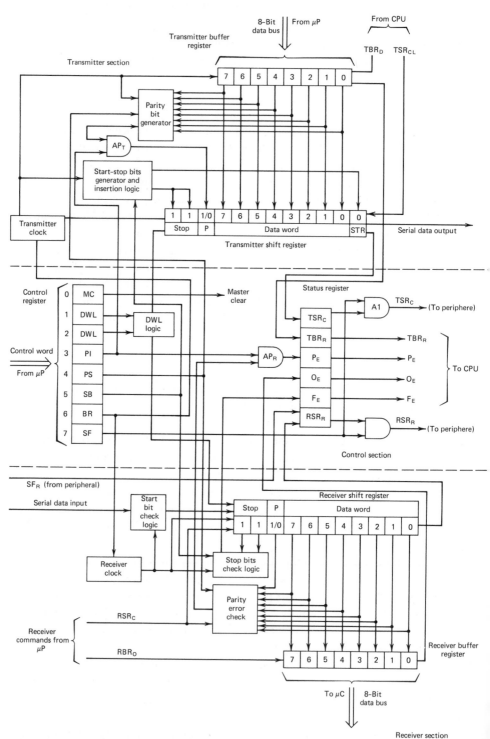

316 **Figure 12-7** Block diagram of typical UART chip.

incoming serial data character is loaded into the receiver shift register. The RSR_C command from the CPU, on the other hand, synchronizes and controls the parallel transfer of the parity and the data bits out of the receiver shift register.

The UART, shown in Fig. 12-7, can operate in a full-duplex mode; that is, transmission and receiving of serial data can proceed simultaneously because the transmitter and the receiver sections are totally independent of each other although controlled by the same control register.

As shown in Fig. 12-7, both the receiver and the transmitter sections operate at the same baud rate; however, this rate can be altered during initialization of the chip. It is also possible to receive and transmit simultaneously at different baud rates. In this case bit 6 of the control register (identified as BR in Fig. 12-7) is replaced by 2 bits, 1 each for the transmitter and the receiver clocks. In this situation, a 0 could be used to indicate clock rate/16 and a 1 for clock rate/64, individually for each clock. More bits in the control word are required if baud rates other than the two standard rates are used.

12-2.2 The USART

Much equipment used in μC systems receives and transmits serial data in a synchronous mode, as explained in Sections 11-3.3 and 11-3.4. To accommodate such systems, an interface chip called the *universal synchronous/asynchronous receiver/transmitter* (USART) is available with several μC systems. The USART is similar to the UART (see Fig. 12-7) in many respects. The principal difference is that UARTs use start and stop bits to frame the data word and also the parity bit, if it is used. In the USART these bits are not used. Instead, the data word is preceded by two 8-bit ASCI SYNC patterns (01101001). The word capture logic in the receiver section (see Section 11-3.4) then captures the data word.

The main difference in the transmitter section also involves the logic concerned with the start and stop bits. Unlike the UART, these bits are not involved in the USART. Two consecutive ASCII SYNC patterns are inserted ahead of the data word (and parity bit, if used) before it is serially shifted out. The rest of the logic and the concepts are very similar to those of the UART (Fig. 12-7).

It is possible that a *separate* chip may be designed and built only for synchronous serial transmissions. Such a chip is called the *universal synchronous receiver/transmitter* (USRT). If the features of both the asynchronous and synchronous transmissions are combined and available on the same chip (i.e., a USART), an additional mode bit is included in the control word. During the initialization process, this bit will set up the chip for operation in either the synchronous or asynchronous mode.

12-3 PROGRAMMABLE INTERFACES FOR PARALLEL TRANSFERS

12-3.1 Basic Functions and Features

Many peripherals used in μC systems transfer data to and from the μP in parallel formats. Unfortunately, there is no universal data format that is used for parallel transfers. They vary in word lengths, timing, and handshaking requirements. This means that it is difficult to design interfaces that can be used universally in all applications. However, programmable I/O interface chips for parallel transfers are available and, under program control, they provide flexibility that makes them suitable for many different situations.

In Section 12-2.1.6 we showed how the UART chip is initialized (i.e., customized for a specific task) by loading a control word in the control register (see Fig. 12-6 for typical UART control word format). The parallel transfer interface chip is similarly initialized by a control word from the CPU that is loaded in a control register.

Programmable interfaces for parallel transfers provide the following four standard features.

1. *CPU Interfaces.* The interface chip is compatible with the CPU and is directly interfaced with the system's data, address, and control/status busses.
2. *Buffers and Latches.* To deal with the timing differences between the CPU and the peripherals and the asynchronous nature of most peripherals, latches and buffers are provided in the interface chip for both incoming and outgoing data.
3. *Control and Status.* The interface chip provides a means of communicating control and status signals between the CPU and various peripherals. In addition to the standard signals for handshaking, such as BUSY and READY, some parallel interface chips also provide for other control and status signals such as interrupt request (INT REQ) and interrupt acknowledge (INT ACK).
4. *Commands and Timing.* Timing signals from the CPU are also transmitted to the peripherals by the interface chips. Additionally, certain commands from the CPU to the peripherals (such as START, STOP and REWIND commands to magnetic tape units) are also sent through the interface chips.

12-3.2 Additional Features and Capabilities

In addition to the standard features, most programmable parallel interface chips have several unique features and capabilities that are described next.

1. *Port Expansion Capabilities.* Each programmable parallel interface (PPI) chip can be designed so that they provide standard address, data, and control/status ports on the CPU side and provide more than one data port on the peripheral side of the

chip. This makes it possible for the CPU to transfer parallel data words to more than one peripheral through a single PPI chip. Each I/O port (and, consequently, each peripheral connected to it) is separately addressable. Two and four I/O ports are usually available on PPI chips.

2. *Multiple Word-Length Capabilities*. Not all peripherals used in μC systems use the same number of bits in their data words. Furthermore, it is possible that the number of bits in the data word, handled by the CPU, may be different from those handled by the peripherals. The I/O ports on the peripherals side of the PPI are designed to accommodate these differences in word lengths. Generally, facilities for 8-bit and 4-bit data words are provided on PPI chips. While it is possible to provide for other combinations of word lengths, they are limited by the number of available pins on the package. Figure 12-8 shows the interfaces of a typical PPI chip. On the peripherals side of the interface, four I/O ports are available, two for 8-bit words and two for 4-bit words. Although only one PPI chip is shown in Fig. 12-8, it is possible to have more than one such chip in a μC system.

3. *Bit Set/Reset Capabilities*. In some PPI chips it is possible to use 1 or more of the

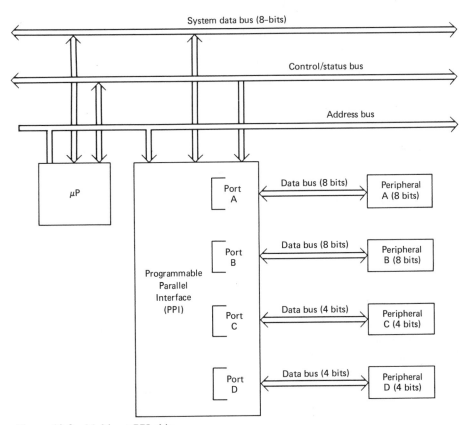

Figure 12-8   Multiport PPI chip.

I/O port lines as control/status lines. For instance, in Fig. 12-8, the 4 lines of port C could be used as control/status lines for port A and the 4 lines of port D as the control/status lines for port B. Each of these 8 lines can be either set or reset to 1 or 0, respectively. Recall that a programmable interface chip must be first initialized by a control word or words from the CPU. By means of a bit set/reset bit in the control word, any line in port C or port D could be set or reset. In fact, we can set or reset all 8 lines individually. This requires an initialization subroutine consisting of 8 separate control words, 1 for each line. This feature is particularly useful in several control-type applications where it significantly reduces software requirements.

4. *Data Direction Capabilities*. In Fig. 12-8 the data busses between the PPI and the 4 peripherals are shown as bidirectional busses. In some PPI chips it is possible to identify and use these lines as input or output lines under program control. For example, it is possible to use all the lines of an addressed port as input lines, all the lines as output lines, or any combination of any specified lines as input lines and the rest as output lines. This feature, if included in the PPI chip, has a data direction register associated with each I/O port. These registers are preloaded with binary bits, each bit identifying the data direction of each selected I/O port line. A 0 in the data direction register indicates an input function for that particular line, and a 1 indicates an output capability.

12-3.3 The INTEL 8255 Programmable Peripheral Interface (PPI)

To understand the features and capabilities of programmable interfaces for parallel transfers, described in Sections 12-3.1 and 12-3.2, we will describe a chip that is widely used in μC systems and embodies many of the features discussed. The INTEL 8255 programmable peripheral interface (PPI) is a silicon gate MOS chip for use with the popular 8080 μP family. The chip is available in a 40-pin, dual, in-line package (DIP) and has some unique features that can be utilized under program control.

12-3.3.1 The Block Diagram A conceptual block diagram of the INTEL 8255 PPI is shown in Fig. 12-9. The PPI communicates with the CPU through an 8-bit, bidirectional data bus. The control signals from the CPU are sent to the PPI on 6 unidirectional control lines.

On the peripheral side, the PPI has 24 I/O lines that can be individually programmed in two groups of 12 lines each. These groups are used in three different modes of operations that are explained in Section 12-3.3.2. The PPI has the bit set/reset capability that gives the system a high degree of flexibility

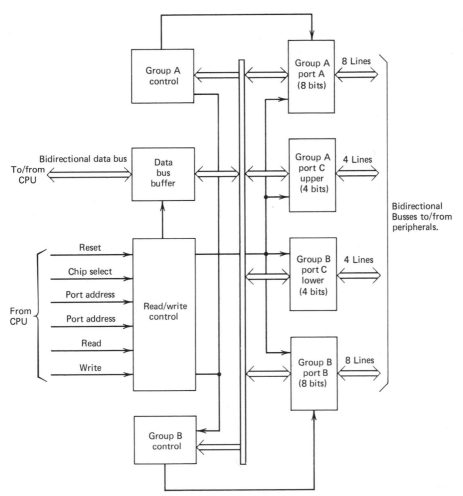

Figure 12-9 The INTEL 8255 PPI—block diagram. Reprinted by permission of Intel Corporation, Copyright 1976. Minor modifications have been made to conform to the material in this text.

(see Section 12-3.2). Also, the PPI is capable of providing 1 ma of current at 1.5 V, which makes it possible to drive bipolar transistor Darlington configurations for applications such as printers.

12-3.3.2 Modes of Operation The 8255 has three major modes of operation. In mode 0, which is the basic mode, each group is programmable as either input or output set of lines. Basically, mode 0 gives three 8-bit I/O ports A, B, and C. Mode 1 has two 8-bit ports that can be defined as either an input or output port. Each of the two ports has associated with it a 4-bit control port. In mode 2, an 8-bit, bidirectional data bus is provided with an associated 5-bit control port. The additional control line is borrowed from one of the other groups. Each mode is now described in detail.

Mode 0 Configuration The 24 I/O lines to the peripherals are connected to package pins and numbered as follows (see Fig. 12-9).

Port A—8 lines—pins 0 to 7.
Port B—8 lines—pins 8 to 15.
Port C (lower)—4 lines—pins 16 to 19.
Port C (upper)—4 lines—pins 20 to 23.

In Fig. 12-9, the 4 ports are grouped as group A and group B for control purposes. Mode 0 configures the 24 I/O lines into ports that are used for simple I/O operations. No handshaking operations are provided in this mode. The data words are simply read from or written into the port that is addressed. Since 2 port address bits are provided by the CPU to the read/write control block (see Fig. 12-9), it is possible to address 4 ports individually.

The mode 0 operation and capabilities are summarized here.

1. Sixteen different I/O configuration combinations are possible.
2. Two 8-bit I/O ports are available.
3. Two 4-bit I/O ports are available.
4. Each port must be identified as either an input or an output port.
5. Outputs are latched.
6. Inputs are not latched.

Mode 1 Configuration In this mode the 24 I/O lines are divided into two equal groups, group A and group B. Within each group, the 8 lines can be used in either direction for data transfers. The 4 lines are used as a 4-bit control port. The pin configurations appear as follows.

Group A
Port A—8 data lines—pins 0 to 7.
Port C (upper)—4 control lines—pins 20 to 23.

Group B
Port B—8 data lines—pins 8 to 15.
Port C (lower)—4 control lines—pins 16 to 19.

Basically, mode 1 provides for operation of the chip as strobed I/O with peripherals in the handshaking mode. Ports A and B use the lines in port C for generating or accepting these handshaking signals.

In both groups A and B, the 4 control lines perform the following basic tasks.

1. Report buffer full status.
2. Strobe data from the buffers to the latches.
3. Handle interrupt requests from the peripherals.
4. Acknowledge receipt of the data.

The mode 1 operation and its capabilities are summarized next.

1. Two groups of I/O ports are available.
2. Each group contains an 8-bit data port.
3. Each 8-bit data port can be either an input or an output port.
4. Both inputs and outputs in each data port are latched.
5. Each group contains its own 4-bit control port for handshaking signals (control and status signals for the associated 8-bit data port).

Mode 2 Configuration In modes 0 and 1, the data ports were essentially unidirectional ports. Although the port(s) could be used either to input or output data, the direction of data flow for each port was preestablished during the chip initialization process. After it is initialized, data can only be input into or output from that particular port. The direction of data flow in any port can only be changed by reinitializing the chip.

The mode 2 configuration provides for strobed, bidirectional I/O bus operation. Only one data port can be used in mode 2. All 24 I/O lines are not used; only 13 lines are used, as follows.

Eight bits—bidirectional data port (port A).
Five bits—control/status port (port C).

The 8-bit data port is not specifically defined as either an input or output port. Any line in this port can be used to input or output a data bit. The control port is used to perform the same basic tasks as those for mode 1 operation.

Note. The remaining free lines can be used at this same time in another mode, such as the bit set/reset mode.

The mode 2 operation and its capabilities are summarized as follows.

1. Basically, only group A of the PPI is used.
2. One 8-bit, bidirectional data port is available, and that port is port A.
3. One 5-bit control port is available; 4 lines from port C (upper) and 1 line from port C (lower) are used.
4. Both incoming and outgoing data are latched.

12-3.3.3 Control Word—Mode Definition In order to define the mode of the
I/O configuration to be used during data transfers, the CPU sends out an 8-bit
control word to initialize the PPI chip. The control word is input to the data
bus buffer (Fig. 12-9) on the 8-bit bidirectional data bus. This control word
then sets up the appropriate logic in the two blocks labeled group A control
and group B control. The bit position in this word and the functions performed
by them are outlined next.

> Bit 0—port C (lower)
>> 1—input
>> 0—output
> Bit 1—port B
>> 1—input
>> 0—output
> Bit 2—group B mode selection
>> 0—mode 0 select
>> 1—mode 1 select
> Bit 3—port C (upper)
>> 1—input
>> 0—output
> Bit 4—port A
>> 1—input
>> 0—output
> Bits 5 and 6—group A mode selection

6	5	
0	0	—mode 0 select
0	1	—mode 1 select
1	X	—mode 2 select

> Bit 7—Always a 1 (identifies mode definition control word)

Note. X in bit 5 means "don't care."

12-3.3.4 Control Word—Control Port (Bit-Set/Reset) We have seen that in
modes 1 and 2 we have control ports in addition to the data ports. The 8255
PPI can set or reset each individual bit of the control port, under program
control. The bit set/reset functions are also performed by an 8-bit control word
from the CPU sent exactly like the mode definition control word described in
Section 12-3.3.3. The functions performed by this control word are as follows:

> Bit 0—bit set/reset operation
>> 1—set
>> 0—reset

7	6	5	4	3	2	1	0
Control word identifier	Group A mode selection		Port A	Port C upper	Group B mode selection	Port B	Port C lower
1 (always)	0 0 1	0 - mode 0 1 - mode 1 X - mode	1 - input 0 - output	1 - input 0 - output	0 - mode 0 1 - mode 1	1 - input 0 - output	1 - input 0 - output

(a) Mode definition control word

7	6	5	4	3	2	1	0
Control word identifier	Not used			Control line select (port C)			Bit - set/reset function
0 (always)	X	X	X	1/0	1/0	1/0	1 - set 0 - reset

(b) Bit-set/reset control word

Figure 12-10 Control word formats for the INTEL 8255 PPI. Reprinted by permission of Intel Corporation, Copyright 1976. Minor modifications have been made to conform to the material in this text.

Bits 1, 2, and 3—select control line in the control port

Bits 4, 5, and 6—not used (don't care)

Bit 7—Always a 0 (identifies control port, bit set/reset control word)

Figure 12-10 graphically shows the formats of the two control words. Notice that only bit 7 distinguishes the two control words.

12-4 SUMMARY

Interfacing the CPU with peripherals is a complicated task. The large variety of peripherals presently available on the market introduces another dimension of complexity. Different peripherals have different operating speeds, data formats, signal requirements, and control/status structures. In μC systems the I/O interface chips must reconcile these differences and make these peripherals compatible with the characteristics of the μP. Fixed or nonprogrammable interfaces have their limitations and, consequently, restrict system designers in their choice of equipment. Programmable I/O interfaces, both serial and parallel types, provide a certain degree of flexibility that can (and does) enhance system utilization.

Programmable I/O interfaces for both serial and parallel data transfers are available on single chips. The principal function of the UART is to convert asynchronous serial data into parallel data acceptable to the μP after checking the parity and stripping the start, stop, and parity bits from the incoming character. Going in the other direction, the parallel word output by the μP is serialized, the parity is checked, the appropriate parity bit is inserted, and the word is framed by the start and stop bits before serially transmitting the character to the peripheral. A variety of optional features are available in UART chips that are chosen by the user under program control. They include inhibition of the parity bit, selection of the parity bit, selection of data word length (usually from 5 to 8 bit lengths), selection of baud rate, choice of 1 or 2 stop bits, and enabling and disabling of certain status flags. UARTs can be operated in either half- or full-duplex modes. The chip can be initialized by loading a control word in the control register. Although not done very often, it can be reconfigured dynamically during normal program operation. Synchronous serial transmissions use SYNC characters to indicate the start of a legitimate data word. Two ASCII SYNC characters are used to avoid the possibility of erroneous identification in case the data word bits happen to have the same bit pattern as the ASCII SYNC patterns. USRTs and USARTs can also operate in the half- or the full-duplex modes.

A wide variety of programmable I/O chips is available for parallel transfers of data. Such chips generally include I/O port expansion capabilities (usually 2 to 4 ports), multiple word-length capabilities (generally 8 bits or 4 bits), capabilities to set each line of the I/O port as an input line or an output line, and bit set/reset capabilities for each line of the control port. These capabilities were explained by describing the popular INTEL 8255 PPI chip.

12-5 REVIEW QUESTIONS

12-1   List some of the typical tasks performed by programmable I/O interfaces.

12-2   Briefly explain the differences between nonprogrammable and programmable I/O interfaces.

12-3   List the items that the typical UART chip performs before it transmits the serial character to the peripheral.

12-4   List the items that the typical UART chip performs when it receives the serial character from the peripheral.

12-5   In a typical UART chip, is it possible for it to transmit serial data out at the same time that it receives serial data input from another peripheral? If yes, explain why it is possible.

12-6   Explain what is meant by the "bit time of the data."

12-7   The bit time of the data, t_b, is given by the Eq. 12-1, where t_{cp} is the receiver clock period and K is a constant. What are the typical values of this constant?

12-8   Refer to Fig. 12-2. Explain why the high-to-low transition of the signal line, caused by the noise spike, is not interpreted as a legitimate start bit by the receiver.

12-9   Refer to Question 12-8. What would have happened if the original high-to-low transition had been caused by a legitimate start bit instead of by a false noise spike? Explain.

12-10   Define character time.

12-11   Define the following terms that are commonly used in the transmission of serial binary data.
(a) Baud rate.
(b) Bit time.
(c) Data rate.

12-12   What are buffer memories? Explain the difference between the LIFO and FIFO memories. What is the principal reason for using buffer memories?

12-13   What is double buffering? Explain why and how it is used in a typical UART.

12-14   Refer to the UART transmitter section of Fig. 12-4. Briefly explain how the parity bit generator works.

12-15   Refer to the UART transmitter section of Fig. 12-4. Briefly explain how the stop-start bits generator and insertion logic works.

12-16   Refer to the UART receiver section of Fig. 12-5. Explain the purpose of the F_E signal and how it works.

12-17   Refer to the UART receiver section of Fig. 12-5. Explain the purpose of the P_E signal and how it works.

12-18   Refer to the UART receiver section of Fig. 12-5. What is the time window available to the CPU to transfer the first word out of the UART before an O_E signal is generated?

12-19   Explain the functions of the following transmitter flags with reference to the UART block diagram of Fig. 12-7.
(a) TSR_C.
(b) TBR_R.

12-20   Refer to the transmitter section of the typical UART chip in Fig. 12-7 and explain what the two commands from the μP accomplish.

12-21   What is the function of the SF_R command from the peripheral to the receiver section of the UART in Fig. 12-7?

12-22   What are the principal operating differences between an UART and an USART chip?

12-23   With respect to the (PPI) chips, what limits the number of ports that can be designed on the peripheral side of the chip?

12-24 What are the most commonly used word lengths that are available in the ports on the peripheral side of the PPI chips?

12-25 Explain what the bit set/reset capability in a PPI chip does. In Fig. 12-8 which port(s) would normally have this capability?

12-26 In a PPI chip, is it possible to designate some lines in a given port as input lines and the rest as output lines? If so, how?

12-6 PROBLEMS AND EXERCISES

12-1 In an asynchronous serial data transmission system the bit time is 9.1 ms; 64 clock pulses per bit are used. Calculate:
(a) Baud rate
(b) Clock period of the receiver clock.
(c) Clock frequency.

12-2 In a serial data transmission system the receiver clock operates at a frequency of 15 kHz, and 16 clock pulses per bit are used. Calculate the baud rate of this system.

12-3 Each character in a serial transmission system consists of 12 data bits, 1 start bit, 1 stop bit, and 1 parity bit. Sixteen clock periods per bit time are used, and 6 characters are transmitted per second. Calculate the following.
(a) Baud rate.
(b) Bit time.
(c) Clock period.

12-4 Refer to Problem 12-3. Calculate the clock period for the same system if 2 stop bits but no parity bit are used.

12-5 Refer to Problem 12-3. The start bit uses nine consecutive 0s. Calculate:
(a) Receiver clock frequency.
(b) Time required to transmit a character.
(c) Data rate.

12-6 In a serial transmission system the character that is transmitted contains 6 data bits, and the data rate is 1440 bits per second. The character contains 9 bits. Calculate:
(a) Baud rate.
(b) Bit time.

12-7 Refer to Problem 12-6. Calculate the receiver clock frequencies for the situations when:
(a) Sixteen clock pulses per bit time are transmitted.
(b) Sixty-four clock pulses per bit time are transmitted.

12-8 Refer to Problem 12-6. Calculate:
(a) Baud rate.

(b) Bit time for the same data rate when the character contains 2 stop bits instead of 1.

12-9   Refer to Problem 12-8. Calculate the receiver clock frequencies for the situations when:
(a) One hundred twenty clock pulses per bit time are transmitted.
(b) Two hundred forty clock pulses per bit time are transmitted.

12-10   Refer to Problems 12-6 and 12-7. Calculate the time required to transmit a character when the start bit uses nine consecutive 0s.

12-11   A serial transmission system has the following parameters.
(a) Time to transmit one character = 1.558 ms.
(b) Clock period = 2 μs.
(c) Number of bits per character = 12.
(d) Clock periods per bit time = 64.
Calculate the number of consecutive 0s in the start bit.

13

DIGITAL-TO-ANALOG AND ANALOG-TO-DIGITAL CONVERTERS

13-1 INTRODUCTION

Prior to this chapter we have considered input and output signals coming in and going out of the μC system in *binary* forms only. These could be either in *parallel* or *serial* formats. In most data-processing applications this is the case. However, in another category of applications this is not true. Microcomputers (and also other specialized digital controllers) are used in process-control applications and equipment. Here both the input and output signals are in *analog* (instead of digital) form.

The primary sources of analog signals are generally mechanical components whose outputs are *transduced* to an electrical signal. For example, thermocouples are often used to measure temperatures, which are then converted into electrical signal outputs. Gas pressures can be measured by pressure transducers whose outputs are electrical analog signals. Potentiometers are electrical devices whose electrical output signals vary with angular mechanical rotation of a shaft. For control equipment the binary signals, output by the μC, must first be changed to analog signals, which may then be used for control purposes.

As previously shown, digital signals used in computers have *discrete* states (high or low voltage levels). Analog signals, however, are *continuously variable* signals that *do not* have *discrete levels* or *states*. Obviously, circuits that convert one kind of signal to another are required. A system that changes a physical measurement (such as pressure or temperature), which is represented by a voltage or current level, is called an *analog-to-digital (A/D) converter.* Such a device is often called an *encoder,* or simply a *coder.* Circuitry that

330

performs *digital-to-analog (D/A)* conversion is often called a DAC or a *decoder*.

13-2 DIGITAL-TO-ANALOG CONVERTERS (DACs)

13-2.1 Voltage Output DACs

In this type of DAC the circuit output voltage is determined by the combination of digital 1s and 0s at the input. The digital inputs are converted to analog signals by means of a *resistor network* and the output voltage is fed into an *operational amplifier*. Figure 13-1 shows a conceptual diagram of such a configuration with 4 digital inputs. The resistor network is designed so that with all digital inputs at 0s, the network output, V_R, will be at ground. With all inputs at digital 1s, the output will be a maximum, for example, $15 \times V$ volts, where V is defined as the unit incremental voltage provided by each binary input bit.

Figure 13-2*a* shows the expected analog output voltage in truth table form for all possible digital input combinations. In Fig. 13-2*b*, the truth table of Fig. 13-2*a* is shown in pictorial form; each step of the analog voltage corresponds to a particular input digital combination. We will now consider two methods of implementing the resistive network of Fig. 13-1, their advantages, and their shortcomings.

13-2.1.1 The Resistor Summing Network One simple way to implement the resistor network of Fig. 13-1 is by means of *binary-weighted summing resistors*. In such a network several resistors are connected in parallel with the output voltage available at a common node. The other end of each resistor is connected to a reference voltage through a switch, as shown in Fig. 13-3, or to ground. The reference voltage then represents a digital 1 and ground by a digital 0.

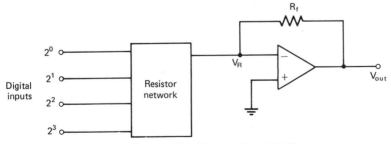

Figure 13-1   Conceptual diagram of a 4-input voltage DAC.

Step Num-ber	Digital Input Combinations				Analog Output Voltage V_R (volts)
	2^3	2^2	2^1	2^0	
1	0	0	0	0	0XV
2	0	0	0	1	1XV
3	0	0	1	0	2XV
4	0	0	1	1	3XV
5	0	1	0	0	4XV
6	0	1	0	1	5XV
7	0	1	1	0	6XV
8	0	1	1	1	7XV
9	1	0	0	0	8XV
10	1	0	0	1	9XV
11	1	0	1	0	10XV
12	1	0	1	1	11XV
13	1	1	0	0	12XV
14	1	1	0	1	13XV
15	1	1	1	0	14XV
16	1	1	1	1	15XV

(a)   Truth table for DAC of Fig. 13-1

Figure 13-2   Analog output voltages for 4-bit digital inputs.

The resistors in this configuration are weighted according to their respective positions in the binary input scheme. Notice that the highest resistance R is in the leg representing the *least-significant bit* (LSB) of the digital input. The value of the resistor in each succeeding leg is reduced by half. The 2^3 leg, representing the *most-significant bit* (MSB) of the digital input, has the lowest resistance in the network. Thus the current through each resistor leg doubles as the digital rank of the leg doubles. This is clearly shown in Fig. 13-2b.

Although simple, single-pole, double-throw (SPDT) switches are shown in Fig. 13-3 for explanation purposes, in real DACs *electronic switches* are used. It is even possible to use only SPST switches (or their electronic equivalents) but, in that case, the gain of the amplifier varies with the digital input. This adversely affects some of the characteristics of the amplifier, such as band-width. For this reason, the configuration of Fig. 13-4 is used more often.

The *resistor summing* DAC is relatively simple, but it has the following disadvantages.

1. For good stability and accuracy of the DAC, a high degree of absolute accuracy

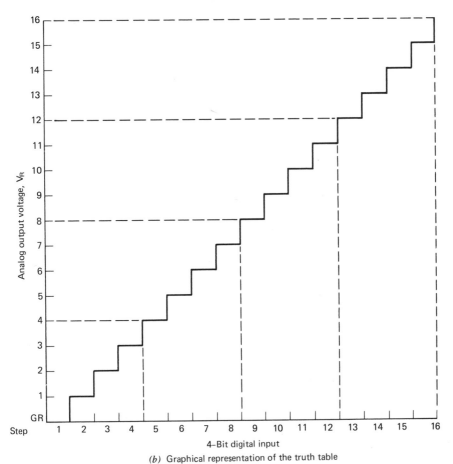

(b) Graphical representation of the truth table

Figure 13-2 (*Continued*)

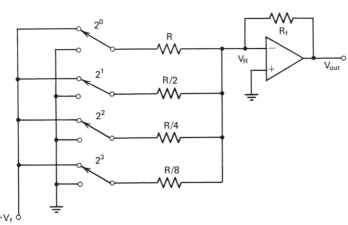

Figure 13-3 DAC using binary-weighted resistor summing network.

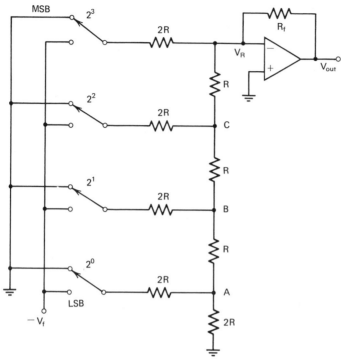

Figure 13-4 DAC using resistor ladder network.

of the resistors is necessary. This is hard to achieve, particularly in DACs that utilize the IC technology.

2. The resistors in the network must have good temperature tracking capabilities, relative to each other.

3. Since all the resistors in the network have different absolute values, identical tracking with respect to other parameters, such as aging (besides temperature), is very difficult to obtain. This further aggravates the accuracy and stability problems of the DAC.

4. Since the resistor value of each digital input leg is half the preceding one (from LSB to MSB), the range of absolute values becomes large as the number of digital input bits increases. This increases the stability problems of the resistors.

13-2.1.2 The Resistor Ladder Network Many of the shortcomings of the resistor summing network can be remedied by the *resistor ladder* network, shown in Fig. 13-4. Unlike the resistor summing network of Fig. 13-3, here only *two* resistor values are used (R and 2R). For this reason this configuration is often called the *R-2R ladder* DAC. Also notice that while the MSB (i.e., the 2^3) switch is closest to the ground input in Fig. 13-3, in the R-2R ladder network, the LSB (i.e., the 2^0) switch is closest to the ground input in Fig. 13-4.

The operation of this ladder network depends on the principle of the voltage-divider network. The analog output of this circuit must have an impedance of 2R to ground. If the digital inputs are all 0s, the four input switches are at ground, as shown in Fig. 13-4. With all 2R resistors returned to ground, all nodes A, B, and C and the output node V_R are at ground. This represents the step 1 condition in Fig. 13-2.

When the digital input is different, say 0010, a different action takes place. Now the 2^1 switch is returned to the reference voltage, V_f. Current will flow through this leg and get divided at node B. Because of the resistor values and the circuit configuration, this current gets divided by a factor of 2 at each circuit node. Therefore the current available at the output node V_R is binary weighted and is determined by the number of nodes through which it has passed.

In comparing it with the resistor summing network of Fig. 13-3, the R-2R ladder network has the following advantages.

1. Regardless of the combination of digital 1s and 0s at the input, the impedance that the input side of the operational amplifier sees is always constant. Therefore the characteristics of the amplifier, such as bandwidth, remain constant.
2. Since all the resistors used in the ladder are of only two values (R and 2R), the accuracy of the DAC does not depend on the absolute values of the resistors but only on the value differences between them.
3. With only two values of resistors, the problem of tracking (particularly temperature tracking) is greatly reduced. It is now necessary to have good tracking capabilities between only two resistors, Rs and 2Rs, instead of four resistors as in the resistor summing network of Fig. 13-3.

These advantages are not obtained without a price. The price is that this configuration uses *twice* the number of resistors as the resistor summing network. This could be a significant disadvantage if the DAC is manufactured on a single silicon chip using IC technology (since resistors use up a lot of space on the silicon chip).

13-2.1.3 The BCD-Weighted DAC Both the resistor summing and the resistor ladder networks lend themselves nicely to *binary-coded-decimal* (BCD) applications with slight modifications. (Review Sections 2-4.1 and 2-4.2 to recall the BCD system and the notation used in it.) Each BCD digit requires 4 binary bits to represent it. Also, each BCD digit is a decimal digit, so each digit's position in a number is decimal weighted (i.e., weighted by the base 10). A

BCD-weighted resistor summing network DAC for a 4-digit BCD input is shown in Fig. 13-5.

In Fig. 13-5 we note two items. First, the 4 binary bits in each BCD digit are weighted in the same manner as in Fig. 13-3 (i.e., the relative weights of the resistors are 1-2-4-8). Second, the resistors in each BCD group are also weighted in terms of the diminishing relative rank of the BCD digit by a factor of 10. From Fig. 13-5 we are able to write a general expression for determining

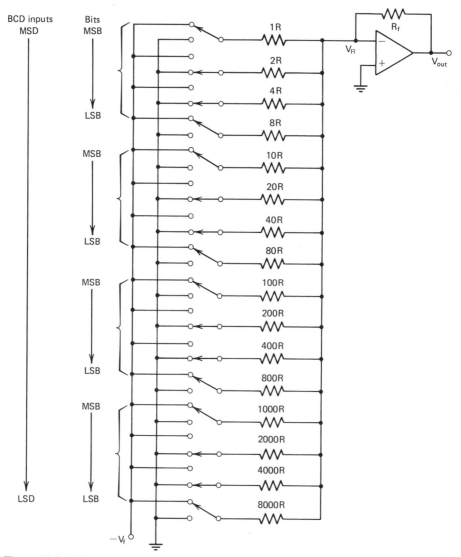

Figure 13-5   BCD-weighted resistor summing network.

the value of any resistor in the BCD-weighted, resistor summing network, as shown here.

$$R_0 = 10^{n-1} \times mR \qquad\qquad (13\text{-}1)$$

where

R_0 = the value of the desired resistor
n = the rank of the BCD digit, with the most significant digit (MSD) having rank 1, the next lower digit to MSD having the rank 2, and so on
m = the rank of the binary bit in the BCD digit (i.e., 1, 2, 4 or 8), with the MSB having the rank 1 and the LSB having the rank 8

The R-2R ladder network can also be used to construct a BCD-weighted DAC. Figure 13-6 shows how this is done. Four BCD digits are represented here. Each BCD decade uses 4-input, R-2R ladder sections and switches, as shown in Fig. 13-4. For simplicity, these four sections are shown in block diagram form in Fig. 13-6. The output of each R-2R ladder network in parallel is summed through decade-weighted resistors labelled R_D in Fig. 13-6.

Note that in Figs. 13-3 to 13-6, we have shown mechanical switches to indicate binary inputs. In reality, these are electronic switches.

13-2.2 Current Output DAC

The current output (or the current mode) DAC is implemented by generating binary-weighted currents from active sources, usually transistors, and summing them on a common output node. Figure 13-7 shows a simplified circuit of a 4-bit, current mode DAC using bipolar NPN transistors. Mechanical switches are shown for simplicity; they are really electronic switches. While only 4 bits are shown in Fig. 13-7, the circuit configuration can be extended to any desired number of bits. The four transistors have their bases tied to a common node whose potential is controlled when the circuit is in operation. This voltage effectively turns ON all four transistors, Q_1 to Q_4.

The value of the resistors and the number of emitters of the transistors are *different* in each leg of the circuit. The transistors, together with their respective binary-weighted resistors, constitute the active current sources. The four switches, S1 to S4, perform the logic steering functions, and their positions are controlled by the 4 digital inputs to the circuit. The operation of the circuit is as follows.

1. The switch positions, shown in Fig. 13-7, are for the condition when all 4 digital inputs are 0, in other words, for the 0000 input condition.

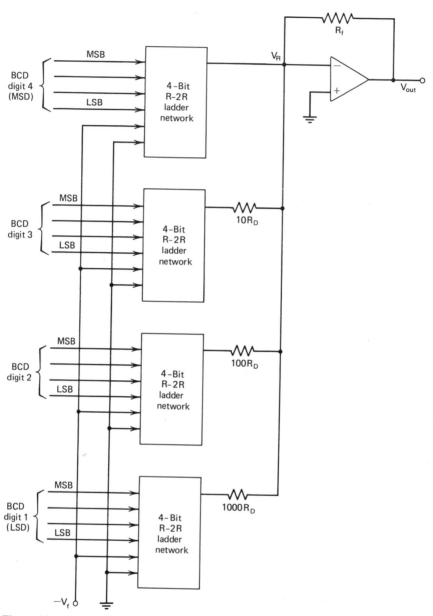

Figure 13-6   BCD-weighted R-2R ladder network DAC.

2. The current flow through each transistor is different in each case and is determined by the respective resistor values. The multiple emitters in Q_1, Q_2, and Q_3 effectively support these higher current values and hold the V_{be} drop across each transistor's base-emitter junction constant.

3. The circuit is designed so that the same value of current flows through the transistor, say Q_1, regardless of the position of S1. Effectively, S1 simply switches

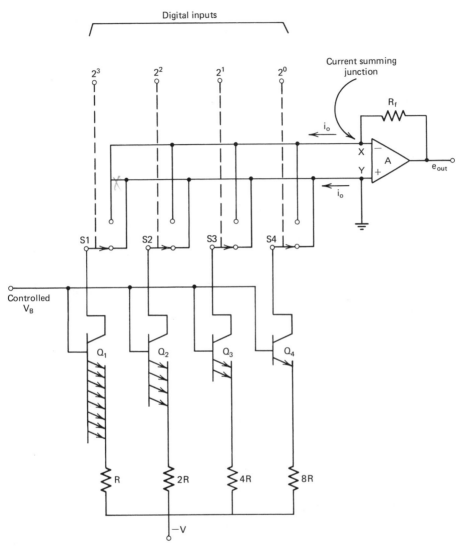

Figure 13-7   Current mode DAC.

the source for this current. For the 0000 input condition shown in Fig. 13-7, the total current for all four transistors is supplied by ground (terminal Y).

4. Now if S1 is in the UP position, the required current for Q_1 is supplied through terminal X by the output of the operational amplifier A through the feedback resistor R_f.

5. Since the current input to the amplifier of A through terminals X and Y must be the same, the current output of A is automatically adjusted to accommodate this input requirement.

6. Thus the current at the summing junction or node reflects the various combinations of the switches S1 to S4, which are controlled by the digital inputs.

7. The output voltage of the operational amplifier, e_{out}, is the drop across the resistor R_f and represents the digital input combination of 1s and 0s.
8. The current through each leg is binary weighted and is dependent on the value of the emitter resistors, which in turn are a function of the bit position for that leg in the incoming binary number.
9. The MSB (the Q_1 and R combination) contributes the largest current to the summing node and the LSB contributes the least current. The total current at the summing node therefore depends on the binary inputs into the circuit. Since the OP amp is configured as current-to-voltage converter, the output is still that of a voltage DAC.

13-2.3 DAC Operating Parameters

Students should be familiar with the most commonly used parameters of DACs. They are *resolution, linearity, accuracy,* and *settling time*.

1. *Resolution* refers to the number of bits input to the DAC. Resolution can be expressed as a percentage or as parts per million (PPM). The following equation expresses *resolution* as a percentage, R_{PC}.

$$R_{PC} = \frac{100}{2^n} \%$$
(13-2)

where n is the number of input binary bits.
If $n = 0$ in equation 13-2,

$$R_{PC} = \frac{100}{2^0} = \frac{100}{1} = 100\%$$

This shows that 100% resolution would be equivalent to 1 million PPM. Therefore resolution can be expressed in PPM as follows.

$$RPPM = R_{PC} \times 10^4 \text{ PPM}$$
13-3)

2. *Linearity* is defined as the *maximum* deviation (in the output of a DAC) from the linear. This is found as the *best straight line* that can be drawn on the output steps as the DAC is sequenced through all of its successively increasing stages, usually by means of a counter. Refer to Fig. 13-2. It shows an idealized analog output waveform for 4-bit digital inputs. Its linearity is *perfect,* as shown by the straight line in Fig. 13-8a. However, in real situations such ideal linearity is seldom obtained, as shown in Fig. 13-8b. The difference between the best straight line and the actual voltage levels at each step, shown as Δ in Fig. 13-8b, is the parameter required to ensure good linearity. In engineering linearity requires that the maximum allowable deviation, Δ_{max}, be equal to or less than one-half the magnitude of the theoretically perfect step voltage, V_{PF}. The theoretical perfect step is ob-

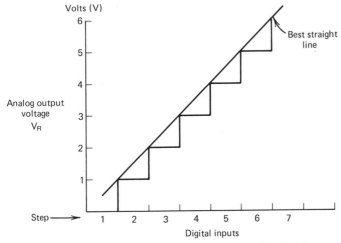

(a) DAC output with theoretically perfect linearity

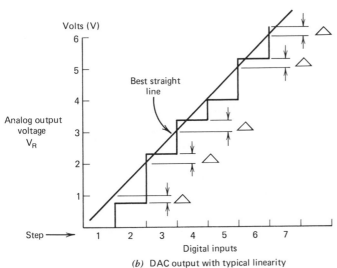

(b) DAC output with typical linearity

Figure 13-8 DAC output linearity. Based upon a figure in "Digital-to-Analog Converter Handbook" by the Applications Engineering Department of Hybrid Systems Corporation, Copyright 1970.

tained by dividing the full scale output of the DAC by the number of steps involved. Thus,

$$\Delta_{max} \leq \frac{V_{PF}}{2}\ V \tag{13-4}$$

3. *Accuracy* is a measurement of the deviation of the actual output of a DAC from the theoretically calculated output for any specific combination of digital inputs.

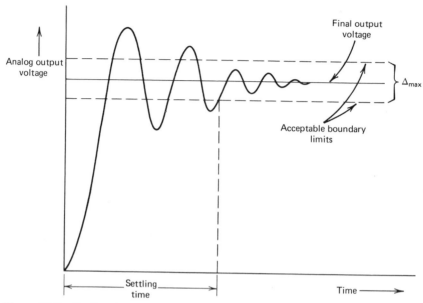

Figure 13-9 Settling time of DAC. Based upon a figure in "Digital-to-Analog Converter Handbook" by the Applications Engineering Department of Hybrid Systems Corporation, Copyright 1970.

Accuracy is often used interchangeably with resolution and linearity. This is not correct. Accuracy involves scale factor. A slight change in the internal reference of a DAC, such as the controlled V_B in Fig. 13-7, will not affect resolution or linearity. This is because, in many applications, the absolute magnitude of the output for various combinations of digital inputs is desired.

4. The *settling time* of a DAC is the time (or duration) required for output transients to reduce to a value well within the specified limits of the final desired value for a given combination of digital inputs. The acceptable boundary limits of the final output is generally the maximum linearity, defined here and shown in Fig. 13-8b. Settling time is basically shown in Fig. 13-9. Observe that the settling time is fundamentally a function of the operational amplifier used in the DAC as well as the resistors and the switches.

Example 13-1

A 4-input DAC has a maximum output voltage range of 0 to $+16$ V. How many volts does each analog step represent?

Solution

Since there are 4 digital inputs, the DAC output will be divided into $2^4 = 16$ levels. The output range is 16 V, so each analog step will represent

$$\frac{16 \text{ V}}{16 \text{ levels}} = 1 \text{ V/level}$$

■

Example 13-2

The output voltage range of a DAC is 10 V and it has 8 digital inputs. What is the resolution of this unit expressed in (1) percentage, (2) PPM, and (3) actual voltage?

Solution

1. From Equation 13-2,

$$R_{PC} = \frac{100}{2^n} = \frac{100}{256} = 0.3906\%$$

2. From equation 13-3,

$$R_{PPM} = R_{PC} \times 10^4 = 0.3906 \times 10^4 = 3906 \text{ PPM}$$

3. The resolution in actual volts is

$$\frac{\text{Voltage range}}{2^n} = \frac{10}{256} = 0.039 \text{ V}$$

■

Example 13-3

Refer to Example 13-1. Calculate (1) the theoretical perfect step voltage for this DAC, and (2) its linearity.

Solution

1. The theoretical perfect step voltage is

$$\frac{16 \text{ V}}{16 \text{ steps}} = 1 \text{ V}$$

2. The linearity is given by Equation 13-4 and is

$$\Delta_{max} = \frac{V_{PF}}{2} = \frac{1}{2} = 0.5 \text{ V}$$

■

Example 13-4

Refer to the BCD-weighted resistor summing network DAC of Fig. 13-5. Assume there are 6 BCD digits in this DAC and $R = 1 \text{ k}\Omega$. Calculate the desired resistor value for the bit having the rank of 4 in the BCD digit with the rank of 5.

Solution

In this case, $n = 5$ and $m = 4$. Then the desired resistor value is given by Equation 13-1.

$$R_0 = 10^{n-1} \times mR$$
$$= 10^{5-1} \times 4 \times 10^3$$
$$= 10^4 \times 4 \times 10^3$$
$$= 4 \times 10^7 \, \Omega$$
$$= 40 \, M\Omega$$

■

13-3 ANALOG-TO-DIGITAL CONVERTERS

13-3.1 The Comparator

Analog-to-digital (A/D) conversion can be performed in many different ways. In this chapter we describe the two most common techniques, the *ramp-voltage* method and the *successive-approximation* method. Before we do this we will briefly discuss the *comparator,* which plays an important role in A/D conversion.

As used in A/D converters, the comparator is simply a differential amplifier whose output is a function of the difference in voltage between two signals applied at its inputs. One of the two inputs is a *reference signal*. The other is the input analog signal that is being digitized. The comparator is designed to accept either voltage or current analog signals. As shown in Fig. 13-10*b,* the output voltage signal sharply transitions from a digital 0 to a digital 1 when the input analog signal exceeds the reference signal.

13-3.2 The Ramp-Voltage Method

This method of A/D conversion is often used in measuring instruments such as *digital voltmeters*. The analog voltage to be digitized is fed into 1 input of a *comparator*. The reference voltage, which is applied to the other input, is a *ramp voltage* that linearly increases with respect to time, as shown in Fig. 13-11*a*. The time it takes for the ramp voltage to reach and slightly exceed the analog input voltage is a measure of the magnitude of the analog input. The comparator triggers whenever this happens. This time measurement is performed by a counter that is incremented by a fixed-frequency clock. The quantity in the counter is the digital representation of the analog input voltage.

The logic configuration that performs this conversion is shown in Fig. 13-11*b;* its operation is as follows.

1. The analog input signal to be digitized is applied to 1 input of the comparator.
2. A digital 1 at the *start* terminal initiates the conversion process by performing the following three functions.
   (a) It clears the counter, thereby removing any information contained in it from the prior operation.

Analog signal

+

Output voltage

−

Reference signal

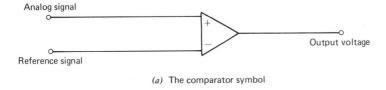

(a) The comparator symbol

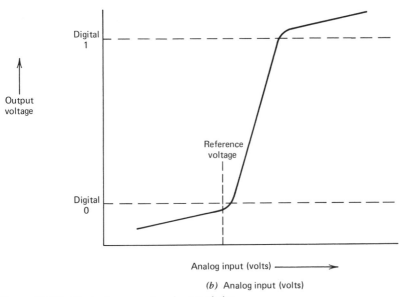

(b) Analog input (volts)

Figure 13-10   Typical comparator characteristics.

    (b) It sets the R-S flip-flop to the Q side, thus enabling the AND gate A1.

    (c) It starts the ramp-voltage generator through AND gate A2.

3. The reference voltage from the ramp generator is fed into the second input of the comparator and this voltage linearly increases as shown in Fig. 13-11a.

4. In the meantime, the pulses from the fixed clock are gated into the counter through the AND gate A1 and start incrementing it.

5. When the ramp voltage reaches and slightly exceeds the analog input voltage (Fig. 13-11a), the output of the comparator changes from a 0 to a 1.

6. This resets the flip-flop to the $\overline{Q}$ side, thus disabling AND gate A1 and preventing the clock pulses from further incrementing the counter.

7. The 1 output from the comparator also disables AND gate A2, which in turn turns OFF the *ramp-voltage generator*, thus returning the *comparator* output to a 0 in preparation for the next A/D conversion operation.

8. The counter contains the digital equivalent of the analog input signal.

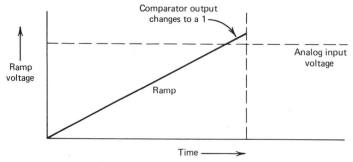

(a) Comparator output versus ramp voltage input

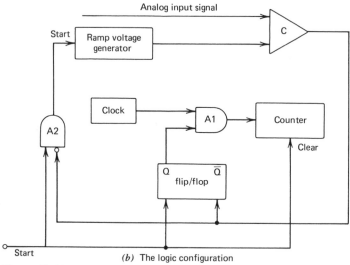

(b) The logic configuration

Figure 13-11 The ramp voltage technique for A/D conversion.

Example 13-5

Refer to the ramp-voltage technique of A/D conversion in Fig. 13-11. The slope of the ramp is 0.5 V/2μs, and the analog input signal is 6.5 V. How long will it take for the comparator to output a digital 1? (Neglect the response time of the comparator to transition from a 0 to a 1.)

Solution

The time for the comparator to change from a 0 to a 1 is

$$\frac{6.5 \text{ V} \times 2 \text{ μs}}{0.5 \text{ V}} = 26 \text{ μs}$$

Example 13-6

A ramp-voltage A/D converter has a ramp slope of 1 V/5 ms (or 0.2 V/ms). An 8-bit counter is used with a clock frequency of 1 kHz. The analog input signal is 10 V. Calculate the digital count in the counter representing the analog input signal. (Neglect the comparator response time.)

Solution

The time for the comparator output to change states is

$$\frac{10 \text{ V} \times 5 \text{ ms}}{1 \text{ V}} = 50 \text{ ms}$$

The clock period is

$$\frac{1}{f} = \frac{1}{1 \text{ kHz}} = 1 \text{ ms}$$

Thus, during the time interval of 50 ms, 50 clock pulses are issued by the clock and the counter will be incremented 50 times. Therefore the counter will contain the binary number 00110010, which is equivalent of the analog input signal. ■

Example 13-7

Refer to Example 13-6. What will the counter contain if it takes 10 ms for the comparator to change from 0 to 1?

Solution

The response time of the comparator is added to the time required by the ramp voltage to reach the analog input voltage. Therefore 10 additional clock pulses will be fed into the counter.
The counter contains a count of

$$50 + 10 = 60$$

The binary contents of the counter is

0 0 1 1 1 1 0 0

13-3.3 Successive-Approximation Method

Another technique that is widely used for A/D conversion is *successive approximation*. In this case a series of digital signals is generated, and each signal is successively converted into analog equivalents. Each signal is fed into one of the inputs of the *comparator* as a reference signal. The analog input signal to be digitized is fed into the other input to the comparator. The process is repeated several times with a different reference signal, which we will call the *trial signal*. The output of the comparator is either a digital 1 or a 0, depending on whether the analog input is greater or less than the trial signal. In this manner successive trial signals are used to approximate the input analog signals. The successive digital outputs of the comparator are utilized in two ways, which are described in Sections 13-3.3.1 and 13-3.3.2. Although successive approximation is used in both methods, the techniques are different. Both techniques use counters and DACs.

13-3.3.1 Simple-Counter Method This method of A/D conversion (which is an example of the direct comparison method alluded to in Section 13-3.1) is very similar to the ramp-voltage method except that instead of using a voltage ramp (Fig. 13-11*a*) as the reference input to the comparator, a step voltage output of a DAC (as shown in Fig. 13-2) is used. The logic configuration for this method is shown in Fig. 13-12. A brief description of its operation is:

1. The analog input signal, to be digitized, is applied to 1 input of the comparator.
2. A digital 1 at the start terminal initiates the conversion process by clearing the 4-bit counter, and setting the R-S flip-flop to the Q side.
3. The pulses from the fixed-frequency clock are passed through the AND gate A1

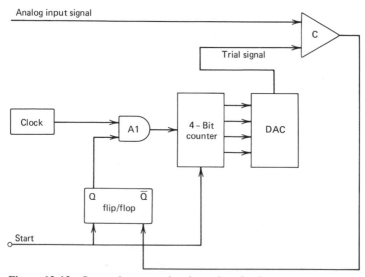

Figure 13-12 Successive approximation using simple counter.

(which is enabled from the Q side of the flip-flop) and start incrementing the 4-bit counter.

4. The 4-bit output of the counter is fed into the DAC, whose output is fed into the other input to the comparator.
5. When the output of the DAC exceeds the analog input signal, the comparator triggers and outputs a 1, which resets the flip-flop to the $\overline{Q}$ side.
6. AND gate A1 is now disabled and the counter stops incrementing. The counter contains the digital equivalent of the analog input signal.

Example 13-8

An A/D converter uses the simple counter method for successive approximation. A 4-bit DAC is used with its output characteristics, as shown in Fig. 13-2b. Calculate:

1. The counter contents if the analog signal is 8 V and a 50-kHz clock is used. Neglect the response time of the comparator.
2. How long it takes to complete this operation.

Solution

1. The output of the DAC must exceed the analog input signal of 8 V for the comparator to trigger a 1 output. From Fig. 13-2b we see that the DAC output must be 9 V, which will require 9 input steps or a count of 9 in the counter. Thus the 4-bit counter will contain 1001.
2. The clock period is

$$\frac{1}{f} = \frac{1}{50 \text{ kHz}} = 0.02 \times 10^{-3} = 20 \text{ }\mu\text{s}$$

Since the counter must be incremented 9 times, the total time required for this operation is
$9 \times 20 \text{ }\mu\text{s} = 180 \text{ }\mu\text{s}$ ■

13-3.3.2 The Sequencing Method This is a more sophisticated but more complex method of A/D conversion. Notice that the simple counter method is really not much different from the ramp-voltage method except that a digital reference voltage instead of an analog ramp voltage is applied to the comparator. The sequencing method provides a *higher* degree of accuracy, which can be further improved by increasing the number of bits.

In this method the MSB is first applied to the DAC; a *trial signal* establishes if it is larger or smaller than the analog input voltage to be digitized. If the analog input is larger, the comparator outputs a 1. Otherwise, a 0 is output. The trial signal is one-half the full-scale value of the analog input value for the MSB. This establishes whether the analog input signal is within the upper or lower half of the full scale. If it is within the upper half, the lower half is ignored for the rest of the operation. If it is in the lower half, the upper half is ignored for the rest of the operation. The output of the comparator, either a 1 or a 0, is stored in a *special register*. Another digital signal is now applied to the DAC for the next lower bit. The value of the trial signal output is one-half the value of the scale (i.e., either the upper or lower half as established by the previous bit). The resulting output from the comparator is stored in the next lower bit position of the register. This process is repeated with the trial signal value halved at each step to represent the midpoint of the appropriate half of the scale. Students will be able to understand this process much better by means of Examples 13-9 and 13-10.

Example 13-9

Graphically show how A/D conversion by successive approximation is performed for an analog input signal of $+13.9$ V for a full-scale range of 0 to $+16$ V using the sequencing method and a register of 6 bits for storing the digitized value.

Solution

The graphical representation is shown in Fig. 13-13. The following sequence of events occur.

1. A trial signal of $+8$ V results in a 1 output from the comparator for the MSB, and it is stored in the sequencing register (SR).
2. Since the MSB is a 1, one-half the value of the trial signal will be added to the previous trial signal for the next bit, which will be $+12$ V ($+8 +8/2 = 12$ V).
3. Since the analog input is $+13.9$ V, the output of the comparator is again a 1. Therefore one-half of the increment [i.e., $(16 - 12)/2 = 2$ V] is added to the previous trial signal making it $+14$ V ($12 + 2 = 14$ V).
4. Since the analog input is now less than the trial signal, the output of the comparator is now a 0 and, therefore, one-half of the scale difference is subtracted from the previous trial signal voltage, which is now 13 V [$14 - (14 - 12)/2$]. A trial signal of 13 V gives us a 1 output from the comparator.
5. The new trial signal is $13 + (14 - 13)/2 = 13.5$ V. Once again the comparator output is 1.
6. The trial signal for the sixth bit, or LSB, is now $13.5 + (14 - 13.5)/2 = 13.75$ V. Since the analog signal is larger than the trial signal, the comparator output for the LSB is a 1, giving us 110111 for the 6-bit equivalent of analog input of $+13.9$ V.

In this example note that a much greater digital accuracy is possible if more bits are used in the *successive approximation* process.   ■

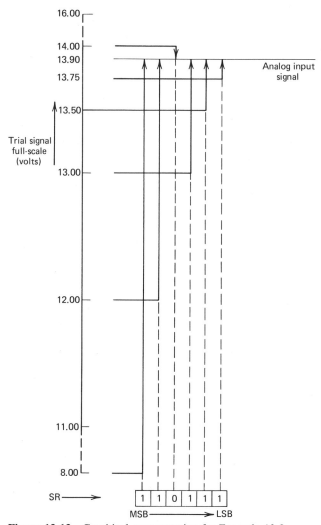

Figure 13-13   Graphical representation for Example 13-9.

Example 13-10

Graphically show how A/D conversion by successive approximation is performed for an analog input signal of $+3.4$ V for a full-scale range of 0 to $+8$ V using the sequencing method and a register of 8 bits for storing the digitized value.

Solution

The graphical representation is shown in Fig. 13-14. The successive-approximation process is exactly the same as explained in Example 13-9 and so is not repeated here. Note the major difference between the two examples. In Example 13-9 the upper half of the full scale was used. In Example 13-10 the lower half is used

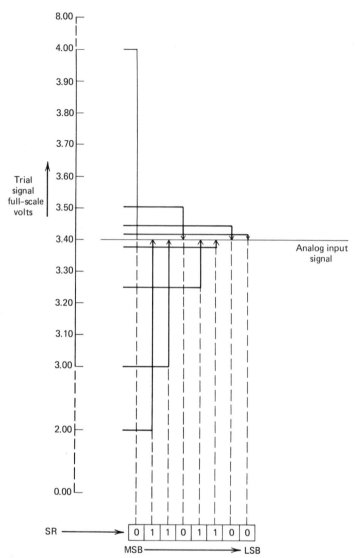

Figure 13-14 Graphical representation for Example 13-10.

because of the location of the analog input signal on the full scale in each case. The digital representation of $+3.4$ V is 01101100. ■

The logic configuration that performs successive-approximation by the sequencing method is shown in Fig. 13-15. An 8-bit DAC and an 8-bit sequencing register (SR) are used in this particular case. The digital sequencer (DS) is controlled by the clock and sends out a digital 1 on 8 output lines, on 1 line

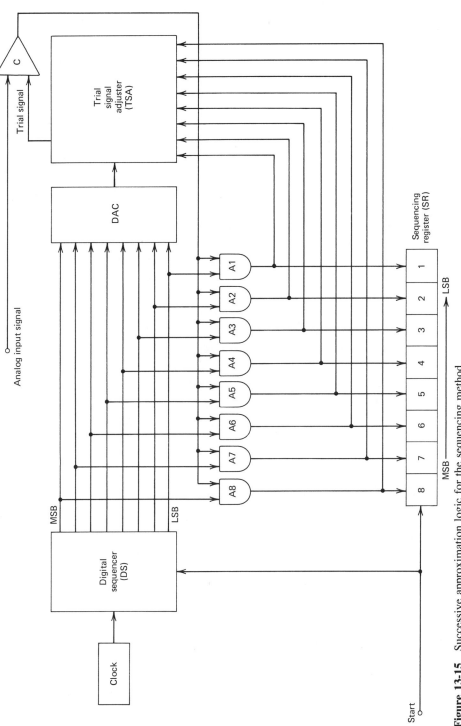

Figure 13-15   Successive approximation logic for the sequencing method.

at a time, starting with the MSB. At the start of the operation, both the SR and the DS are cleared.

The following sequence of events occurs.

1. The DS sends a 1 on the MSB line. This also enables gate A8. The input to the DAC is 10000000.
2. The output of the DAC is input into the *trial signal adjuster* (TSA). The TSA outputs a trial signal that is one-half the full scale. (Referring to Example 13-10, this would be 3 V.)
3. If the analog input signal is smaller than this trial signal, the comparator outputs a 0; this is fed into the second input of A8. The output of A8 is 0, so bit 8 (the MSB) of the SR stays a 0.
4. If the analog input signal is larger than this trial signal, the comparator outputs a 1 that fully enables A8. In this case a 1 will be loaded in bit 8 position of the SR.
5. The 1 output of A8 is also fed into the TSA. This tells the TSA to add one-half the value, as explained in Examples 13-9 and 13-10. (The value will be subtracted when the output of A8 is 0.)
6. Now the DS issues a 1 on the next lower output line. The input to the DAC is 01000000, and the output of the DAC is one-half the previous output value.
7. The TSA will adjust the output higher or lower, depending on whether the output from the prior operation was a 1 or a 0.
8. This process is repeated with the DS outputting a digital 1 on each subsequent output line at each successive step. Thus, at each successive step, the process results in an approximation that gets closer to the analog input signal.
9. After 8 process steps, the SR contains the digital approximation of the analog input signal.

13-3.4 A/D Converter Operating Parameters

The following are some of the operating parameters usually associated with A/D converters.

1. *Resolution* refers to the number of bits output by the A/D converter.
2. *Input range* refers to the range of analog signal input voltages that can be digitized by the A/D converter.
3. Commercially-available A/D converters have *output codes* available in either pure binary or binary-coded-decimal (BCD) form.
4. *Conversion time* is generally expressed as the *maximum worst-case* time required for A/D conversion.
5. Since the input to an A/D converter is an analog signal, the *input impedence* to the converter is an important parameter that ensures impedance matching with the

analog signal source and thereby prevents signal deterioration. High input impedance is desirable to avoid loading the analog source.

13-4 SUMMARY

Microcomputers (μCs) are used in many applications, such as instrumentation
and process control, where they are required to interface with equipment that
operate on continuously variable signals instead of with signals that have
discrete levels or states. In such applications the μC system must be provided
with interface circuitry that must be capable of analog-to-digital (A/D) and
digital-to-analog conversion (DAC).

DACs are either voltage output or current output types. Both use operational
amplifiers as the output devices. Resistor networks are used in the voltage
output DACs. There are two types of resistor networks. The simple resistor
summing network uses binary-weighted summing resistors in the input end of
the DAC where they are connected in parallel, with the output voltage available at a common node. The other end of each resistor is connected to either
ground (0) or a reference voltage (1) through a switching arrangement. The
second type is the resistor ladder network. Only two values of resistors are
used, and they are often called R-2R ladder DACs. Such a network operates
on the principle of a voltage divider network. Both types of voltage DACs
can be designed for pure binary inputs or BCD-weighted inputs.

The current output DAC operates by generating binary-weighted currents
from active sources and summing them on a common output node. Resolution,
linearity, accuracy, and settling time are the most important operating parameters of DACs.

The two most commonly used methods for A/D conversion are the ramp-
voltage and successive-approximation methods. The first method uses a linearly increasing voltage ramp as a reference to compare it with the analog
input signal to be digitized. The output of the comparator is used to determine
the digital bit. Two techniques are used in successive approximation. The first
one uses a simple counter to generate a step voltage that is used as a digital
reference voltage similar to the ramp-voltage method. The second technique
is the sequencing method, where a digital 1 is applied to each input to a DAC
successively. Additional logic in the A/D converter then sends out a trial signal
that is compared with the analog input signal, and a digital 1 or a 0 is established based on the result of this comparison. Each successive trial signal
halves the range of voltage scale and thereby approximates the input analog
signal. The most important operating parameters of A/D converters are resolution, input range, output range, conversion time, and input impedance.

13-5 REVIEW QUESTIONS

13-1 The microcomputer is a digital system. Explain why it is necessary to have analog interfaces and what they are used for.

13-2 Explain how analog electrical signals are different from digital electrical signals.

13-3 Refer to Fig. 13-1, the conceptual diagram of a 4-input voltage DAC, and briefly explain how it works.

13-4 In the DAC, using the resistor summing network (Fig. 13-3), it is observed that the smallest resistor (R/8) is in the leg representing the MSB of the digital input. Explain why.

13-5 Name the four principal shortcomings of the resistor summing network of the DAC in Fig. 13-3.

13-6 State the basic principle on which the DAC using the resistor ladder network (Fig. 13-4) works.

13-7 Briefly state the three major advantages of the DAC using the R-2R ladder network as compared to the DAC using the resistor summing network.

13-8 Refer to the BCD-weighted resistor summing network DAC of Fig. 13-5. Explain why the resistor in the LSB leg of the MSD input is 8R and the resistor in the LSB leg of the LSD input is 8000R.

13-9 Refer to the BCD-weighted R-2R ladder network DAC in Fig. 13-6. Are the resistor values (R and 2R) the same in all four ladder networks? If so, what differentiates the BCD rank of the 4 BCD input digits in this configuration?

13-10 The following questions relate to the current mode DAC of Fig. 13-7.
  (a) Is the current flow in all four transistors, Q_1 to Q_4, the same or different?
  (b) The current through Q_2 is I amperes when switch S2 is in the low position (i.e., connected to ground). What is the current flow through Q_2 when S2 is in the UP position?
  (c) What is the function of the four switches S1 to S4 in the operation of this circuit?
  (d) If all four switches S1 to S4 are in the UP position, how are the four currents for the transistors supplied?

13-11 Briefly define the following operating parameters of a DAC.
  (a) Linearity.
  (b) Settling time.
  (c) Resolution.
  (d) Accuracy.

13-12 Define the response time of a comparator.

13-13 What is the function of the flip-flop in the logic configuration of the ramp-voltage technique for A/D conversion (Fig. 13-11*b*)?

13-14 In the successive-approximation technique using a simple counter, is a ramp voltage used for the trial signal? If not, why not?

13-15 Refer to Fig. 13-15, successive approximation logic for the sequencing method, and explain the function of the DS.

13-16 Refer to Fig. 13-15 and explain the function and operation of the TSA.

13-17 Briefly define the following operating parameters of an A/D converter.
(a) Input range.
(b) Conversion time.
(c) Resolution.

13-6 PROBLEMS AND EXERCISES

13-1 In the BCD-weighted resistor summing network DAC of Fig. 13-5, R = 512 Ω. There are 3 BCD digits in the DAC. Calculate the value of the register for the bit having the rank of 2 in the BCD digit with the rank of 3.

13-2 A 4-input DAC has a maximum output voltage range of 0 to 8 V. How many volts does each analog step represent?

13-3 Each analog step of the output of a DAC represents 2 V and the total output range is 64 V. How many digital inputs are there in this DAC?

13-4 A DAC has 6 digital inputs and an output range of 12 V. Calculate the resolution of this DAC in percentage and in PPM.

13-5 Refer to Problem 13-4. Calculate the resolution of this DAC in actual volts.

13-6 Refer to Problem 13-3. What is the theoretically perfect step voltage? Determine its linearity.

13-7 A BCD-weighted DAC uses a resistor summing network (see Fig. 13-5). The value of the resistor in the third leg (i.e., rank 4) of BCD rank 4 is 4 MΩ. Calculate the value of the resistor in bit rank 1 of BCD rank 1.

13-8 An A/D converter uses the ramp-voltage technique with a ramp slope of 1.2 V/4 ms. The analog input signal is 12 V. Neglecting the response time of the *comparator,* calculate the time it takes for the comparator to output a 1.

13-9 Refer to Problem 13-8. Calculate the actual total time if the response time of the comparator (i.e., 200 μs) is taken into consideration.

13-10 The comparator response time of an A/D converter using the ramp-voltage technique is 100 μs. The actual input signal is 8.75 V, and the total time for the unit to output a 1 is 400 μs. Calculate the slope of the ramp voltage.

13-11 An A/D converter has a ramp-voltage slope of 1 V/7.5 ms. An 8-bit counter is used with a clock frequency of 2.5 kHz, and the analog input signal is 8.0 V. Neglecting the response time of the comparator, what will be the digital count in the counter representing the analog input signal?

13-12 Refer to Problem 13-11. What will the counter contain if it takes 9 ms for the comparator to change from a 0 to a 1?

13-13 An A/D converter uses the simple counter method for successive approximation. A 5-bit DAC is used with its output characteristics as shown in Fig. 13-2*b*.
   (a) What will the counter contain if the analog input signal is 10 V and a 100-kHz clock is used, neglecting the response time of the comparator?
   (b) How long will it take to complete this operation?

13-14 Refer to Problem 13-13. The response time of the comparator is 60 μs. What will the counter contain and how long will it take to complete this operation if this additional time is taken into consideration?

13-15 Successive approximation is performed by an A/D converter using the sequencing method. The full-scale range is 0 to +16 V, and a 6-bit sequencing register is used. The analog signal is 10.7 V. Fill in the following table to show how successive approximation is performed using whatever number of steps are necessary for this particular operation.

Step	Trial Signal (Voltage)	Comparator Output (1/0)
1		
2		
3		
4		
5		
6		
7		
8		
9		
10		

13-16 Refer to Problem 13-15. Fill in the following table to show how *successive approximation* is performed when the analog input signal is 4.8 V. Use however many steps are necessary.

Step	Trial Signal (Voltage)	Comparator Output (1/0)
1		
2		
3		
4		
5		
6		
7		
8		
9		
10		

TWO

MICROCOMPUTER SOFTWARE

14

INTRODUCTION TO MICROCOMPUTER SOFTWARE

14-1 INTRODUCTION

14-1.1 What is Software?

This question often confuses the students, particularly if they have little or no previous knowledge of or contacts with computers and computing systems. A common misconception is that *software* is programming or, more commonly, that activity in programming referred to as *coding*. This is not true. Coding is the writing of a program used by the computer and stored in its program memory. Coding is only one activity involved in software development. As a rule the average programmer writes no more than 10 or 12 fully corrected lines of program each working day. In other words, studies indicate that actual coding takes up less than 20% of the programmer's time.

14-1.2 Software versus Hardware

We have just stressed what software is not. We can best define software as all the activities associated with the successful development and operation of a computing system other than the hardware pieces themselves. Even more simply, hardware does the actual computing, and the software is anything that drives the computer. Of course, in the development of software, much hardware equipment is used.

Integration of hardware and software into a harmoniously operating system is an important aspect of *systems* engineering. Also, it is often possible to perform several hardware functions by software. So hardware-software trade-offs become a very important consideration in systems design. In the μC field an understanding of both hardware and software is essential.

14-1.3 Areas of Software Activities

Basically, software for all computers (including μCs) covers three major areas: *application programs, system programs,* and *documentation.*

1. *Application programs* are created, written, and loaded into the computer memory to perform a specific, well-defined task for a particular application in a particular field.
2. *Systems programs* aid in the creation of application programs. Generally, they consist of all programs associated with a computing system other than application programs. Systems programs are usually available from the computer manufacturer as part of the overall system.
3. *Documentation* plays an important role in software even though it is not a part of programming in the strict sense. It includes everything put down on paper, such as a statement of the problems, flowcharting and coding, instruction sets, procedures, and the like.

14-1.4 Software Development Cycle

The development of software for a computer system involves a prescribed number of specific procedures, activities, and tasks. They are shown as a flowchart in Fig. 14-1. The numbers next to each block in Fig. 14-1 correspond to the following list. Each stage requires refinements and corrections before final, acceptable software is developed.

1. *Problem Statement and Specification.* This step is perhaps the most important in the software development cycle and is the starting point of all succeeding activities. The problem to be solved is defined, the various tasks to be performed are clearly outlined, and specifications are written. The specifications should be clear, concise, and written so that the ultimate user of the software can readily understand them. The various inputs and expected outputs are specified along with any other constraints or limitations that may be recognized and known. Procedures for handling errors are also included.
2. *Program Designing.* This phase starts out with a plan of attack for solving the problem defined in the previous stage. Several techniques are available for this (e.g., *modular* programming, *top down* design, *structured* programming). For students with limited backgrounds, *flowcharting* provides a convenient starting point. After the overall plan is established, the designer can select the individual *algorithms* for doing the job. (An algorithm is a precise, well-defined set of procedures or methods used to solve a given problem in a finite number of steps.) During this stage, the designer often considers adapting some existing available programs to the particular problem at hand.

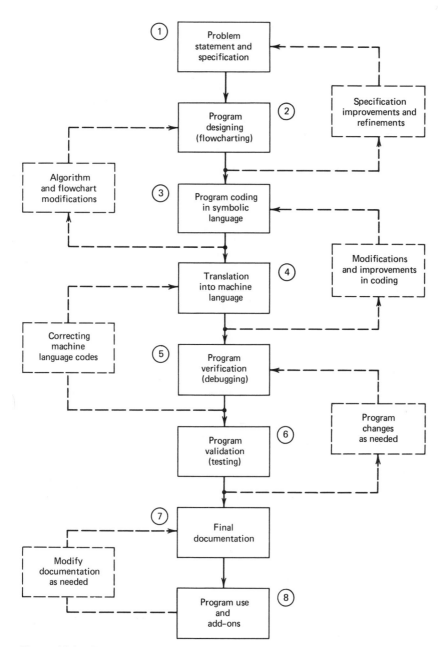

Figure 14-1 Computer software development cycle.

3. *Program Coding in Symbolic Language.* This stage consists of transcribing the previously designed program into a *symbolic language* (BASIC, FORTRAN, etc.) that can be translated into the *machine language* for the particular computer involved. The program that is produced in symbolic language codes is called the *source* program. The program that is then produced in machine language is called the *object* program. The source program may be in either assembly language or in a higher-level symbolic language such as FORTRAN, COBOL, or BASIC.

The machine language, in terms of 1s and 0s, is the only language the computer can use. The same is not true of the human programmer to whom the language of 1s and 0s is unreal and cumbersome and subject to many errors. Since the programmer is more comfortable with alphabetical and numerical symbols used in everyday life, symbolic languages are developed and extensively used in programming computers.

All computer manufacturers include alphanumeric symbols with each instruction in the *instruction set.* These symbols are called *mnemonics.* Memory locations and addresses of various logic blocks in the computer, such as registers and counters, are also identified or addressed by mnemonics. Usually, mnemonics are designed to resemble the instructions and aid the programmer in memorizing them. Thus the programmer can write the entire program in symbolic language *without* using 1s and 0s.

4. *Translation into Machine Language.* Mnemonic codes, used in the source program, are very convenient and useful to the programmer but meaningless to the CPU, which only understands machine language. Therefore the source program written with mnemonics must be translated into an object program in machine language and stored in the program memory before the computer can execute it. It is possible to do this step by hand. The machine language code, supplied with the instruction set, can be written down by hand for each instruction in the source program and stored in the memory bit by bit. This is a long, tedious task, however, and is subject to many errors. In practice the mnemonic-to-machine code translation is performed by a special program called the *assembler,* which effectively stores the binary equivalent of the mnemonic instructions in the computer memory. The assembler produces the object program.

If the source program is written in a higher-level language, another program, called a *compiler,* is used to perform the translation task.

5. *Program Verification (Debugging).* Every program, no matter how carefully designed, contains at least a few errors. Such errors must be found and corrected. This phase of software development is time consuming and, at times, very frustrating. Isolating the particular fault is called *debugging.* Fortunately, several tools are available to simplify the debugging process. There are hardware debugging tools such as logic analyzers, and software tools such as debugging programs and *editors.*

6. *Program Validation (Testing)*. The *debugging* state generally involves finding errors introduced during the coding and/or translation process. After the program is debugged, the next step is program *validation*. Validation involves testing the program to see if it meets the original requirements and specifications of block 1 (Fig. 14-1). The process involves running the program with various inputs and checking the outputs against the expected outputs.

7. *Final Documentation*. Usually some *documentation* is required for each step of the previous six steps in the program development cycle. After the program is debugged and validated, final documentation is prepared for the ultimate user as well as the maintenance people. Such final documentation is also used by designers if the programs are to be modified or extended at some future date. Software documentation usually includes, in addition to program listings, specifications, requirements, flowcharts, and memory maps.

8. *Program Usage and Add-Ons*. As successful programs are used, the user tends to change the ways in which they are used in a particular application. This requires changes in the programs. Most of the time, such changes improve the programs and tend to make them more sophisticated. Also, the user often wants to extend the programs beyond the tasks for which the programs were originally designed. Such extension is possible if adequate (original) documentation is available.

Figure 14-1 shows that each of the six blocks provide feedback to previous blocks. The functions provided by these feedback blocks are self-evident. Feedback is important and generally results in cost savings if properly used.

14-2 SYSTEMS SOFTWARE

Systems software refers to programs that are tools to assist the computer user to generate *application programs,* debug and test them, modify them and, finally, execute them. These programs are generally written by the computer manufacturer for one specific computer or system. The same systems programs can be used by many different users and many different application programs. In the rest of this chapter we will discuss these systems programs further but, first, let us take another close look at programming in machine language and its shortcomings.

14-2.1 The Machine Language

Computers execute commands or instructions fed into their program memories in machine language, (i.e., words comprising of binary 1s and 0s). Machine language is accomplished simply by means of switches located on the front panel or the operator console. These switches are manually set to correspond to the binary code of each instruction; they are then stored in the program memory. After loading the entire program, the address of the first instruction is manually loaded into the program counter from the front panel. The program is then executed by pushing the START button.

The manual process of loading an application program into the computer memory is straightforward and does not require any systems programs. However, it has the following disadvantages.

1. The program must be first written entirely in machine language (i.e., with 1s and 0s). Any additions, alterations, or corrections must also be made in machine language. This is very time consuming and subject to many errors, particularly if it is a fairly lengthy program.
2. Manually setting the individual switches on the front panel, corresponding to each instruction in the program, is a very tedious and cumbersome process and leads to many errors.
3. If errors are detected *after* the program is stored in the memory, it is quite possible that the programmer may have to correct and reload several instructions in the memory. This consumes even more time.
4. Programs written in machine language for a specific machine cannot be used for another machine which has its own unique machine language. Thus, rewriting the same program for another machine is a laborious and time-consuming proposition.

14-2.2 The Assembler

Most of the shortcomings of programming in machine language are overcome by programming in *assembly language*. Each instruction in the instruction set of a computer has mnemonics associated with it. The entire program can be written using these mnemonics and such a program is said to be written in *assembly language*. All commercially available computers, including μCs, have *assemblers* which are programs designed to translate assembly level codes into their equivalent machine language codes for that particular machine. Programming in assembly language, therefore, makes it unnecessary to write programs in either *pure* or *absolute binary, octal* codes or in *hexadecimal* notation. The steps involved in writing and executing a program in assembly language are briefly described.

1. *Source Program.* This program is written using *OP codes* and labels in the assembly language of the particular computer. Both are *alphanumeric* codes. No machine language codes (1s and 0s) are used. OP codes refer to various *operations* in the computer such as *shift, add,* and *subtract.* The labels refer to memory locations. The *assembler,* which is a special program, is loaded in the memory. This program

essentially checks each instruction written by the programmer for accuracy and acceptability. The assembler converts each OP code into its machine language code in binary. Likewise, it assigns *absolute* or *relative* addresses to the labels. At this stage, the program is still a *source program*.

2. *Program Listing*. The *assembler* is also capable of producing a hard-copy listing. Such a listing usually consists of the following items.

   (a) *The label*. This is usually a name assigned to the address of either the instruction or an operand. Most assemblers allow labels that consist of letters, numbers, or some special characters.

   (b) *The OP Code*. This is the mnemonic for the operation code in the instruction. Each line in an assembler listing *must* have some OP code. This field may also contain other codes called *pseudo-instructions* or *pseudo-codes*. These codes do not result in the generation of OP codes for the μC. Instead, they direct the assembler to perform certain functions.

   (c) *The Operand Field*. This field contains the addresses of the operands involved in a particular operation. In case *immediate addressing* is involved, this field contains the immediate or actual data. If the instruction involves a nonmemory reference operation, this field could contain additional information for execution of the instruction.

   (d) *Comments*. This field consists of the programmer's comments, which are generally related to the program logic.

   Figure 14-2 shows the headings of a typical assembler statement.

3. *The Object Program*. The principal function of the assembler is to convert the source program into a machine language program that can be loaded into the program memory of the computer. The assembler performs a one-to-one translation, (i.e., for each input statement from the source program, it outputs 1 line of machine language instruction). During this conversion or translation process, the assembler assigns an absolute or relative address to the label. A list of machine language instructions is thus generated and output. Such a program is called an *object program* or *object module*. The object program is usually produced and saved on magnetic tapes, paper tapes, or other nonvolatile storage medium. Object programs can also be loaded directly into the computer memory.

4. *Types of Assemblers*. In software systems for μCs and other small computing systems three types of assemblers are generally available.

   (a) *The One-Pass Assembler*. In this type of assembler, the entire source program is scanned only once and, from this, both the program listing and the object program (usually on a tape) are produced. Since the source program is scanned

Label	OP code (mnemonics)	Operand (pseudo–codes)	Comments

Figure 14-2   Assembler statement.

only once, the one-pass assembler is usually fast, but it has its shortcomings. One-pass assemblers are limited in their capabilities and do not offer the programmer the features and flexibility that two- and three-pass assemblers can offer. Generally, one-pass assemblers have more rigid rules for generating addresses and allocating memory locations.

(b) *The Two-Pass Assembler.* In this case the source program is scanned twice. During the first pass or scan, the program translates the OP codes into machine language codes. It then prepares a list called the *symbol table* and collects all the definitions. The symbol table shows the variable names and relative addresses of the memory locations that these names represent. During the second scan, the assembler prepares the listing and the object program, which will probably be available on tape.

(c) *The Three-Pass Assembler.* In this type of assembler the source codes are scanned three times. The symbol table is prepared during the first scan. The listing is printed out in the second scan, and the object codes are generated during the third pass, when the object tape (paper tape or cassette) is produced.

Most assemblers offer several options to the programmer, such as stop and wait after each scan, prepare a listing but not the object module, and produce an object module without a listing.

14-2.3 The Compiler

Programming in assembly language is much easier than programming in machine language. However, the programmer is required to write a source code for each instruction in the program, and the assembler performs translation strictly on a one-to-one basis only. This means that the programmer must understand, allocate, and utilize all of the resources of the computer, including the instruction set of the particular μC, the various registers in the CPU, and allocation of memory locations. This increases the probability of errors, particularly in large programs. The principal advantage is that the user maintains total control of the computer operation, since each instruction originates with the programmer. Programming in assembly language offers the greatest degree of efficiency in operation and execution.

Higher-level languages, beyond the assembly-level languages, have been designed and are widely used. These languages are procedure-oriented languages that have been developed primarily to enable the *nonexpert* programmer to program the machine in a language similar to (or, in some cases, identical to) the language or professional jargon of the user. For example, FORTRAN and BASIC are replete with scientific jargon and use scientific notations and subroutines in programming formats that are similar to mathematical formulas and equations. On the other hand, COBOL contains business jargon and emphasizes items such as interest rates and other terms widely used by the business community.

Compilers are programs that translate programs written in higher-level languages into machine language. Unlike the assembler, the compiler generates several machine language instructions for each source statement. The compiler can be readily modified and made to interface with several different computers. The program is not written for any specific computer. The nonexpert user can thus write fairly sophisticated programs that can be adapted to several computing systems. Thus, by means of a compiler, the user is capable of formulating problems efficiently without precise knowledge of the computer architecture. The main shortcoming of compilers is that they are complex, long programs compared to assemblers. Consequently, they require more storage space in the memory than assemblers, and are not always available on small computers.

14-2.4 The Interpreter

The assembler and the compiler perform an intermediate function in the translation from the source program to executing the object program. Generally, the source program is first produced on some other medium such as magnetic tape or paper tape. The assembler or the compiler produces the object program, which is loaded into the computer memory and executed by the computer.

The interpreter is another programming tool that differs from the assembler or the compiler on several significant points. The interpreter does not prepare an object module or an object program. It translates and immediately executes each instruction, one at a time, as it is input into it. Thus the interpretive language is an *interactive language* because it enables the user to load one instruction into the computer at a time and have it translated and executed. This process allows the programmer to check the processed information or datum immediately, so the interpreter is an important debugging tool that is particularly useful during the program development stage. In the interpretive mode the total execution time of the program is deteriorated badly, but the program developmental effort and the program development time are reduced.

Since considerable time is wasted between the translation/execution of one instruction and the following instruction, it is possible for interpreters to process more than one program simultaneously. For instance, programs can be input into the computer through several I/O devices, such as teletype terminals, with one interpreter serving all the programs. The first statement from the first program is accepted, translated, and executed. The interpreter goes to the first statement of the next program and serves that one. It proceeds in that manner until the first statements of all programs are serviced; then it returns to the second statement of the first program. The process is repeated until all programs are serviced. Since the human being reacts more slowly than the computer, each programmer is serviced independently for all practical purposes.

14-2.5 The Text Editor

When developing a new program, it is often necessary to edit it. Editing generally involves making corrections or modifications to instructions, deletions, and additions of instructions and resequencing instructions. When the source program is input to the assembler or the compiler from input media such as paper tape, magnetic tape, or punched cards, editing becomes an awkward and cumbersome process. Additionally, it is often necessary to re-arrange source data and properly format the output data. This is often referred to as *input edit* and *output edit,* respectively. A special software system (or program) called the *editor* greatly simplifies such tasks.

The editor (or the text editor, as it is often called), makes it possible for the user to retain the program (or data files) in the computer memory and modify them as required by specifying the changes to be made. For editing purposes, a portion of the memory, called a *buffer,* is reserved. Lines of instructions or text material are entered from an external I/O device and stored in the buffer by the editor. To aid in the identification of each instruction or data line, the editor assigns a number to each such line and to each correction or modification. The editor automatically corrects line numbers if instructions or data lines are added or deleted. Finally, the edited program or text can be listed on a printer, recorded on magnetic tape, or punched into perforated tape or punched cards.

14-2.6 Loaders

The application program that is assembled or compiled must be stored in the program memory of the computer before it can be executed. The program memory could be either a ROM (more likely a PROM) or a RAM (mainly during the program developmental stage).

To assist the programmer in loading the program, special software tools, called *loaders,* have been developed. The loader is usually a small program that allows the user to enter directly the instructions as well as variable data words with absolute addresses for data storage by means of an external tape unit or a keyboard. The loader consists of a set of instructions that allows the input device (keyboard or tape unit) to assign a starting address in the memory and read in 1 word or byte of either instruction or datum at a time.

1. *Bootstrap Loaders.* the loader program, once it is in the computer memory, will load the application program and the related data, but first the loader must be loaded into the memory. This can be done by one of the following methods.

(a) *Manual Entry*. By means of the keyboard, the user keys into the machine a program called the bootstrap loader. This program is usually on a tape, and the operator must manually key in a few instructions that initialize the reading of the loader. After that, the bootstrap program loads itself into a computer memory. From then on the loader is used to load the application program into the program memory.

(b) *Entry Using ROM*. It is possible to store the initialization instructions permanently in some portion of the ROM instead of manually entering them by a keyboard or the front panel. When the bootstrap program is required, the operator simply directs the machine by means of panel switches to execute these permanently stored instructions in the ROM. Entering a bootstrap by ROM is advantageous because the operator does not have to enter the initialization instructions manually, so the chance of errors is eliminated by storing these instructions in the ROM; the possibility of accidental erasures is also eliminated.

2. *Absolute Loaders*. This is a program that loads each instruction of the object program in a fixed, preestablished memory location. Thus each instruction is given an *absolute address*. The *absolute loader* simply reads the object code line containing the starting address of the instructions/data and loads successive words (or bytes) in successive memory locations. The absolute loader has one serious shortcoming when used in large computing systems. In such systems the combination or mix of the jobs to be performed changes from day to day. This requires that the program/data be stored in different memory locations at different times. If absolute loaders are used, the object program would have to be modified and retranslated to reflect the different desired memory location prior to each instruction. This is a time-consuming activity that is subject to errors. In such situations relocatable loaders (see Section 14-2.6) are used. Absolute loaders are generally designed to check and test each instruction as it is read in for accuracy. If an illegal instruction is detected the loading process is terminated. In μC systems the absolute loader is often included as part of the *monitor*.

3. *Relocatable Loaders*. This loader overcomes the principal disadvantage of the absolute loader. The *relocatable loader* is a more sophisticated program. It usually incorporates most of the features and characteristics of the absolute loader but additionally allows the user to select and specify the memory locations in which the instruction/data words are to be stored. Thus the same program can be loaded in different parts of the memory without having to reassemble or recompile them. During the assembling or compiling of the object program, the program starts with the address 0. The succeeding instructions are assigned successive locations. However, the addresses are not absolute addresses; that is, they do not represent the true locations in the memory where the program is to be stored. Instead, they are

relative addresses. The programmer inserts the true starting address at the beginning of the relocatable loader. This address is an offset that is added to each of the assigned memory locations in the program, thus giving the true address for each instruction/data in the program. The relocatable loader offers some significant advantages.

(a) It allows the programmer to make room for additional instructions or data words by repositioning the block instructions or data in the memory.

(b) Two or more pieces of programs or software modules can be loaded into contiguous locations in the memory. This makes it possible to delete erroneous or undesirable instructions and still maintain a single composite program.

The advantages of the relocatable loader are available, but at a price. The usual price is that this program is much longer than the simple absolute loader.

14-2.7 Linkage Editors and Library Loaders

Many computer manufacturers supply subroutines that are used in several different application programs; examples include subroutines for trigonometric functions and square and square root computations. Some of the available assemblers incorporate special capabilities that facilitate the use of such subroutines. Some assemblers are capable of assembling the subroutine along with the main program as an integral part of that program. To do this, the assembler makes references to such subroutines in the main program. The same information is also provided to a special program called a *linkage editor,* which supplies the actual address of the desired subroutines. If a linkage editor is available, it relieves the programmer of the burden of having to assemble the subroutine(s) along with the main program.

Application programs written by some users often are useful in other applications and are maintained in a *library*. Such libraries are usually stored in mass storage devices such as *disks* or *tapes*. A *library loader* is a program that performs one or more of the following functions.

1. It can search the library for the desired user program and load it into the mainframe memory of the computer.

2. It can transfer the desired user program from one library to another.

3. It can add or delete any programs from the library under control of the programmer.

4. It can prepare a list of all the programs stored in a particular library file.

14-2.8 Testing, Debugging, and Diagnostic Programs

Programs created and written by human beings are prone to error. To expect a newly created program to run correctly the first time is unrealistic. Before a program can be put into productive use it must be *debugged*. What is a *bug?* The dictionary defines a bug as a *defect* or *imperfection*. In the context of programming it is an error introduced by the human programmer that results in the production of undesirable results by the program.

Testing a newly developed program involves validation of program design. It is aimed at a satisfactory answer to the question, "Will the program perform its intended function?" Thus testing involves data that are intentionally made to reflect the worst-case situations.

To assist the programmer in locating and rectifying programming errors or bugs, several aids or tools are available. These aids could be either hardware aids such as *logic analyzers* or software aids such as *debug* programs. The debug program is loaded into the memory with the object program that is to be debugged. If errors occur during this run, the debug program is activated to identify, locate, and correct this error. The debug program includes several features that aid the programmer in the debugging task. Some of the common features are described here.

1. *Display Register Contents.* This feature allows the programmer to inspect the contents of certain key registers in the CPU during the execution of the object program. The contents of the desired register can be printed out or displayed on a CRT terminal. Furthermore, the programmer is able to modify the contents of a certain register or replace them completely if so desired.

2. *Display/Replace Memory Contents.* With this feature the programmer can access the contents of any desired memory location and display it. The contents can then be modified or replaced as required.

3. *Memory Dump.* This feature makes it possible for the programmer to command the computer to print out the contents of a specified group of memory locations. This enables the programmer to review and study the contents of each desired memory location individually and determine the accuracy of the data/results. A line printer or CRT display would be required for this feature.

4. *Output Memory Contents.* This feature is very similar to a memory dump except that instead of printing out the contents of the selected memory locations, the contents are transferred and stored in some other mass storage devices such as disks or magnetic tapes.

5. *Breakpoints. Breakpoints* are interrupt points placed in the object program by the debug program to examine the current status of certain critical CPU registers, memory locations, or I/O ports. When the object program reaches a breakpoint, its execution is interrupted and temporarily halted. The debug program assumes control and allows the programmer to examine and alter the contents of the selected register, memory location, or I/O port to pinpoint and correct the problem.

6. *Disassembly.* This feature performs the reverse of the assembly process. The operation consists of reading out the contents of the program memory, which are in

machine language, and converting them into assembly language mnemonics or op codes, which are then printed out.

14-2.9 Executive Programs

There are special programs, alternatively referred to as *monitors, supervisors, executive programs,* and *operating systems,* that are used to monitor and control the overall operation of the entire computing system. These programs generally aid the running of the system. They are used in handling interrupts and error conditions. Monitors and supervisors are the simplest of these programs. More sophisticated executive programs perform other additional functions such as assigning computer resources to certain tasks.

14-3 SUMMARY

In this chapter students were introduced to another major topic μC software. The differences between software and coding, which are often misconstrued to be the same thing, were emphasized. The various activities involved in software were discussed. They included application programs, system programs, and documentation. The steps involved in the developmental cycle of computer software were presented in pictorial form (see Fig. 14-1). Specific terms connected with software development were defined, and the relationships of the different processes to each other in this activity were pointed out.

The rest of the chapter dealt with systems software; this was defined first, and then it was explained how it differs from application programs. Application programs can be written in machine language and manually loaded into the computer memory; the many disadvantages to such a procedure were explained. The differences between the source program and the object program were pointed out and the role of the assembler in translating from the former to the latter program was explained. The one-pass, two-pass, and the three-pass assemblers were described along with the advantages and disadvantages of each. Both compilers and interpreters were introduced and their functions briefly described. The use of the text editor during the program development phase was pointed out, and some of its functions were explained.

The application program that is developed must be loaded into the program memory of the μC. The loader programs were discussed, including bootstrap loader, the absolute loader, and the relocatable loader. Since some subroutines can be used in several different application programs, many μC manufacturers supply linkage editors and library loaders, which were briefly discussed. Programs available for testing and debugging were introduced; the chapter concluded with a brief mention of executive programs.

14-4 REVIEW QUESTIONS

14-1 What is computer software? Briefly define it and state how it differs from computer hardware.

14-2 State the three major areas of activities included in computer software. Describe each area without going into detail.

14-3 During the development of computer software, the statement(s) of the problem(s) is written down. State the reasons for this and what is included in such statements.

14-4 Briefly define an algorithm.

14-5 Name some of the techniques usually available to the programmer for the task in block 2 in the flowchart for the software development cycle of Fig. 14-1.

14-6 Explain the difference between machine language and symbolic language. Why were symbolic languages developed?

14-7 Define mnemonics and explain what it includes.

14-8 What are the commonly used names for the program written in symbolic language and the one written in machine language (1s and 0s)?

14-9 What is an assembler? What is a compiler? Briefly state the difference between the two.

14-10 What are some of the tools available to perform the program verification phase identified as block 5 in the flowchart of Fig. 14-1?

14-11 What is the difference between program verification (block 5 in Fig. 14-1) and program validation (block 6 in Fig. 14-1)?

14-12 Briefly state what systems software (or programs) is and what it does.

14-13 If the same computer hardware is used for several different applications, is it possible to use the same systems software for all the application programs? Explain.

14-14 Is it possible to load an application program directly into the program memory of a computer without using systems software? If so, explain how.

14-15 Briefly explain the shortcomings of the program loading method described in the answer to Question 14-14.

14-16 Explain what OP codes and labels refer to when programming in assembly-level language.

14-17 Name and briefly explain the four major tasks performed by an assembler.

14-18 In the listing produced by an assembler the field for the OP code contains other codes. What are these codes and what do they do?

14-19 Briefly describe the one-pass assembler and point out its principal shortcomings.

14-20 Briefly describe the operation of the two-pass assembler.

14-21 Briefly describe the operation of the three-pass assembler.

14-22 Name some of the assembler options available to the programmer.

14-23 Which offers a higher degree of efficiency in operation and execution, programming in assembly language or programming in higher-level language? Why?

14-24 Briefly describe how a compiler differs from an assembler.

14-25 Explain the difference between an interpreter and an assembler or a compiler.

14-26 In your own words explain the function(s) of a text editor.

14-27 Name and briefly explain the two methods by which a bootstrap loader can be loaded into the computer memory.

14-28 Define an absolute loader.

14-29 What is a relocatable loader? How does it differ from an absolute loader?

14-30 What are some of the functions performed by a library loader?

14-31 List the five most commonly available features in a debug program.

15

PROBLEM DEFINITION AND FLOWCHARTING

15-1 PROBLEM STATEMENT

15-1.1 The Need

The very first block in Fig. 14-1 is problem statement and specification. Section 14-1.4 stated that this is perhaps the most important stage in the software development cycle. In this chapter we will examine this phase in more detail prior to explaining flowcharting.

Before the programming effort starts, the problem to be solved and the various tasks to be performed must be clearly understood and the specifications properly written. The software designer must understand the problem and what results are required by the end user before the start of the design effort.

In most applications μCs are used as one element in a complete system. By their very nature, μCs are most suitable for process control applications. Thus, in such a situation, the requirements of the entire system must be defined before individual tasks for the μC are delineated. A well-defined problem statement, at the system level, must include the following minimum items.

1. *The Objective.* A statement of the system requirements and the functions of the μC should be made.
2. *Input Signals.* The electrical signals that are input to the μC system must be properly identified. If signals are output by analog devices, circuitry for analog-to-digital conversion will be required.
3. *Output Signals.* The output signals from the μC, required for control purposes, must be identified. If analog devices are being controlled, circuitry for digital-to-analog conversion will be required.
4. *Processing Requirements of the μC.* Some statement about what the μC is expected to do is required. The processing to be performed by the μC may involve mathematical computations, logical operations, or a combination of the two.

5. *Timing Considerations and Restrictions*. Although the processor is usually fast enough for the job, other elements may impose several time constraints. For instance, the reaction times of mechanical or electromechanical components in the system cannot be ignored. Likewise, A/D and D/A conversions also require additional time. These limitations and response times must be identified and considered when designing the program.

6. *Accuracy Requirements*. The accuracy of the input signals must be clearly defined. This is particularly significant if the inputs are in analog form. Also, the accuracy of the outputs (D/A converters) must be stated.

7. *Malfunctions and Safety Handling*. System malfunctions, which can be caused by equipment failure or human error, must be identified and appropriate steps taken to insure safety requirements.

15-1.2 An Example

The seven points just outlined can be better understood by means of a simple example. Note that Example 15-1 is intended to illustrate some of these items very generally so no numerical data are included.

Example 15-1

In a laboratory environment the experiment involves monitoring and controlling the temperature and pressure of a certain liquid flowing through the equipment in predefined ranges. The pressure is regulated by a pump and the temperature by a heating element. A μC is used to perform the monitoring and controlling functions. The speed of the pump motor is varied by means of a rheostat, and the temperature of the heating element is controlled by varying the applied voltage. The μC continuously monitors the pressure and temperature and keeps them within the desired range. If the temperature/pressure product exceeds a predefined limit the μC must shut the entire equipment off immediately. Draw a simple sketch of the system and prepare a *problem statement,* in general terms, using as many of the previous seven points as applicable without using any specific quantitative units.

Solution

Figure 15-1 shows the major elements of the computer system as applicable to this problem. Let us define the safe operating temperature range by t_1 and t_2, the safe operating pressure range by p_1 and p_2, and the critical temperature/pressure product as CP.

Problem Statement

1. *Objective*. Both the temperature of the liquid and its pressure are monitored on a continuous basis. If the temperature falls below t_1 the control potentiometer

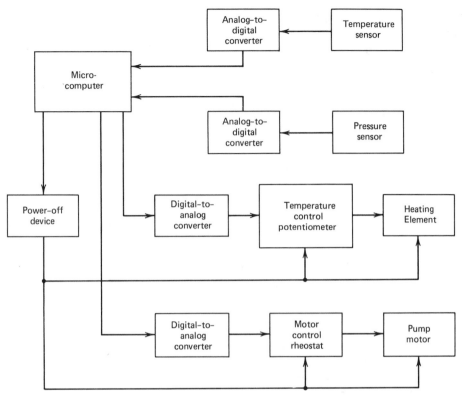

Figure 15-1   Block diagram for Example 15-1 system.

must be adjusted to apply a larger voltage to the heating element. If it exceeds t_2, the voltage to the heating element must be reduced to bring back the temperature to or below t_2. The speed of the pump motor must be increased if the pressure drops below p_1 and decreased if it exceeds p_2. The μC will continuously calculate the product of the temperature and the pressure after each reading, and immediately turn the power off to the system if $t_x p_y$ product exceeds CP.

2. *Input Signals.* One input to the system is from an A/D converter connected to the temperature sensor. The μP will check this input, as fed to it by the A/D converter, to determine if the reading falls between t_1 and t_2, as determined by the program. The second input is also from an A/D converter that is connected to the pressure sensor. The μP checks this input, as presented by its A/D converter, to establish if this reading is between p_1 and p_2.

3. *Output Signals.* The μC outputs three digital signals. A D/A unit converts the first digital output into an analog signal that controls the setting of the temperature control potentiometer, which in turn applies the appropriate voltage to the heating element. The second digital output is fed into another DAC unit whose output is fed into a rheostat that controls the speed of the pump motor

and, therefore, the liquid pressure in the system. The third digital output of the μC is a single digital signal that is normally a 0. This signal is fed into a power-off device (such as a relay) that applies voltages to the control potentiometer, the heating element, the control rheostat, and the pump motor. A 1-signal output from the μC cuts off the power to all the units.

4. *Processing Requirements.* The two temperature range readings, t_1 and t_2, are prestored in two scratch-pad locations in the μC. Likewise, the two pressure limit readings, p_1 and p_2, are also prestored in the scratch pad. The value of the critical product, CP, is also prestored in the scratch pad. The program is designed to sample the two inputs. The temperature reading, t_x, is first compared to t_1 and t_2. If $t_x < t_1$, the μP will determine this condition and calculate the required correction. The digital output is sent to the D/A converter, and the appropriate analog signal resets the potentiometer accordingly. If $t_x \geq t_1$, a comparison is made with t_2. If $t_x \leq t_2$, nothing will happen. If $t_x > t_2$, the μP will compute the required correction and send it to the D/A converter, and the potentiometer will be adjusted accordingly. A similar process will take place with the pressure input reading p_y, which will be compared with p_1 and p_2. Appropriate signals to the rheostat will adjust the speed of the pump motor. The μP takes the two input readings, t_x and p_y, computes their product, and compares it with the prestored value, CP, in the scratch pad. If $CP < t_x p_y$, a 1 signal is sent to the power-off device, which turns off the power to the system. If $CP \geq t_x p_y$, a 0 output from the μC leaves the power on, the program proceeds to acquire two new temperature and pressure readings, and the entire cycle is repeated.

Note. Since no timing or accuracy figures are given in the original problem, the problem statement does not include these. ∎

15-2 FLOWCHARTS

15-2.1 What is a Flowchart?

A flowchart is basically a systems analysis tool or technique that provides a graphic or pictorial representation of a set of procedures or major steps of work in process. The primary function of flowcharts in the computer field is to provide a blueprint of the logical steps involved in the solution of a problem. It is a tool used by the programmer in preparing the program that enables the programmer to proceed from point A (the problem statement) to point B (the final coded program) logically and systematically.

The symbols used in a flowchart may represent machines, documents, or actions taken during a certain process, or they may simply represent certain logical steps in the process. In computer work a flowchart can be used to represent graphically the flow of information through the various components of a data-processing system. A flowchart does *not* depict or illustrate *how* a certain process is performed or accomplished. Instead, it shows *who* (or what *equipment*) does *what* and *when* in the data-processing operation.

15-2.2 When is a Flowchart Prepared?

A flowchart is usually drawn during the program development effort. Flowcharts become an integral and important item in the previously mentioned documentation phase of the software development cycle. There is some controversy regarding when flowcharts should be drawn (i.e., at what point in the development cycle). Without debating the advantages or disadvantages of the issue, we will follow the procedure of drawing flowcharts *before* any program is written. Such a procedure is particularly beneficial to students because a flowchart is a convenient pictorial breakdown of the problem as well as a graphical representation of the major steps involved in the logical solution of that problem.

15-2.3 Program Flowchart Symbols

In this book we use conventional flowchart symbols that are widely used in the United States. Occasionally, some users and some computer manufacturers use different symbols. The commonly used program flowchart symbols are shown in Fig. 15-2, and a brief explanation of each follows. Program flowchart symbols are generally used to represent procedures or process steps. They do not represent any specific hardware or equipment.

The following are brief explanations of the symbols shown in Fig. 15-2. They are explained in the same order as in the diagram.

1. *Process or Processing.* This is a single program instruction or a group of instructions used to perform a specific, major task or function in the program.
2. *Input/Output.* This refers to any function of an I/O device such as a tape unit, printer, or keyboard that makes information available for processing or accepts the processed information from the computer.
3. *Decision.* This symbol denotes certain points within the program where either a JUMP or a BRANCH (or a SKIP operation in some cases) decision is made to an alternate path, depending on certain conditions or variables.
4. *Predefined Process.* Either of these two symbols is used to indicate a group of operations (or instructions) that are not specifically included in the flowchart in any detail. They usually depict subroutines.
5. *Terminal or Termination.* This indicates either the beginning, the end, or a point of interruption (usually temporary) within a program.
6. *Connector.* This usually denotes an entry to or exit from some part of the program. (*Note.* Occasionally it is used as a symbol for offpage connector.)

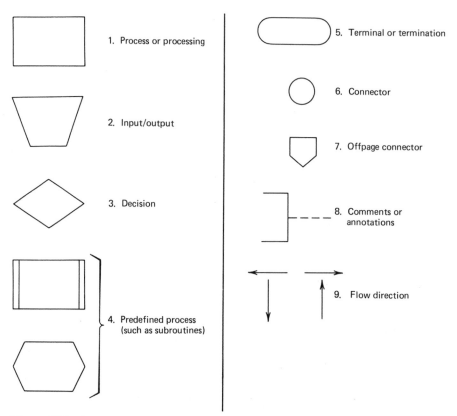

Figure 15-2 Program flowchart symbols.

7. *Offpage Connector.* This is commonly used to indicate exit from or entry into a page. (*Note.* Sometimes it is used as a connector to other parts of the program. The symbols in points 6 and 7 are occasionally used interchangeably.)
8. *Annotations.* This is used for additional notes or descriptive comments.
9. *Flow Direction.* Arrows are used to indicate the direction of either data flow or processing flow.

15-2.4 Systems Flowchart Symbols

In addition to the program flowchart symbols shown in Fig. 15-2, other symbols are also used in systems flowcharts. A systems flowchart indicates system operation and/or hardware equipments used in a specific system. Figure 15-3 shows the symbols used in systems flowcharts.

The following are brief explanations of the symbols shown in Fig. 15-3. They are explained in the same order as in the diagram.

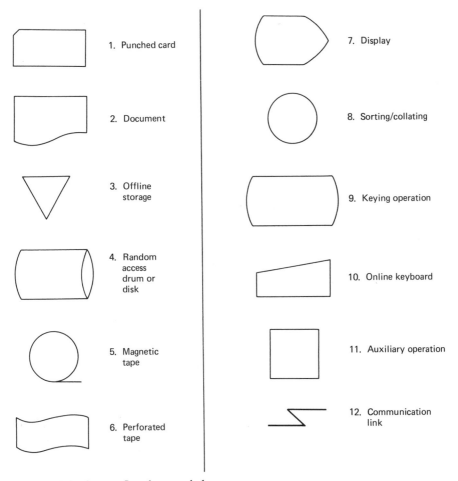

Figure 15-3 System flowchart symbols.

1. *Punched Card*. This symbol indicates all kinds of punched cards including tearoff stubs.
2. *Document*. This indicates documents of all kinds. Generally, it is used to indicate source documents, finished listings, or reports.
3. *Offline Storage*. This depicts offline storage of magnetic tapes, punched cards, or documents.
4. *Random Access Drums or Disks*. This symbol is used for random access bulk storage devices such as drums or disks. They may be operating either online or offline.
5. *Magnetic Tape*. This is a common symbol for all kinds of magnetic tapes including reel-to-reel types, cartridges, and cassettes.

6. *Perforated Tape*. This indicates perforated tapes of all kinds, including paper and plastic tapes.
7. *Display*. This symbol usually denotes information displayed on CRT-type units. However, it is also used for information displayed by plotters.
8. *Sorting/Collating*. This indicates any operation on sorting or collating equipment.
9. *Keying Operation*. This symbol is used to indicate any operation that uses key-driven equipment.
10. *Online Keyboard*. This indicates any information supplied to the computer by an online device or information supplied by the computer to an online device.
11. *Auxiliary Operation*. This signifies any machine operation that supplements the main data-processing functions.
12. *Communication Link*. This symbol indicates transmission of data or information, automatically, from one location to another by communication lines or links.

Note. Occasionally, flowcharts are drawn using symbols from both lists of program and systems flowchart symbols.

15-3 LEVELS OF FLOWCHARTING

15-3.1 Concept-Level Flowchart

Generally, there are three levels of flowcharts involved in software development. They are:

- Concept-level flowcharts.
- Algorithm-level flowcharts.
- Instruction-level flowcharts.

The *concept*-level flowchart is a broadly stated flowchart using simple rectangular boxes with arrows or flow lines. Only the major steps involved in the solution of a problem are shown. No details or decision points are included. A concept-level flowchart is shown in Example 15-2.

Example 15-2

Draw a simple concept-level flowchart for a payroll application that involves a given number of employees in a production department who are paid a fixed salary for a 40-hour week plus time-and-a-half for each hour of overtime. All deductions, such as FICA, and income taxes, are precalculated for each employee and are fixed for each weekly pay period. These deductions are lumped together and must be deducted as a single quantity from the gross earnings. A payroll listing and the checks are to be printed out.

Solution

Before we draw the concept-level flowchart, let us identify the various quantities or operands as follows.

N = the number of employees in the production department
A = the fixed weekly salary of each employee
B = the number of overtime hours worked by any of the N employees
C = the overtime rate (time-and-a-half)
D = the lumped deductions for each employee
E = each employee's net pay for the period

Figure 15-4 shows the concept-level flowchart for this problem. ■

Note the following points about concept-level flowcharts from example 15-2.

1. Only rectangular boxes are used for symbols.
2. Only major steps involved in the entire process are shown.
3. Decision points are not involved.
4. The statement in each box indicates only *what* the process is and *when* it is performed, not *how* it is accomplished.
5. No computing system is identified, so this flowchart is applicable to any computing system.

15-3-2. Algorith-Level Flowchart

An *algorithm* is a set of well-defined steps or processes that are established to provide a solution to a specified problem in a finite number of steps. Thus an *algorithm* can be thought of as a logical process that transforms the given data or operands into the desired outputs that are the solution to the problem.

Recall from Section 15-3.1 that the concept-level flowchart is a broadly stated flowchart that does not include any details of the procedures involved in the logic of solving the given problem. An algorithm-level flowchart, on the other hand, is more specific and gives a clear picture of the logic involved in arriving at the desired solution. It is possible to arrive at the same solution to a given problem by using a different sequence of procedures or steps. Consequently, different algorithms are possible for the same solution. An algorithm-level flowchart can use any of the flowchart symbols shown in Figs. 15-2 and 15-3. The algorithm-level flowchart depicts only the logic involved in the solution of the problem. It does not describe the specific steps or processes that a particular μC goes through to solve the problem. Example 15-3 illustrates a simple algorithm-level flowchart.

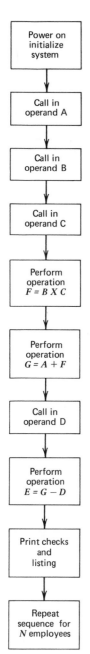

Figure 15-4   Concept-level flowchart for Example 15-2.

Example 15-3

Draw an algorithm-level flowchart for the problem in Example 15-2. Use any symbols shown in Figs. 15-2 or 15-3 as appropriate. The N number of employees in the department are each identified by a clock number that starts with number M and ends with number $(M + N)$. The clock numbers run consecutively. The identifying data for each employee, which include the clock number, the employee's name, the employee's fixed salary rate for a 40-hour week, and the lumped deductions total, are all prestored on magnetic tape. The number of hours worked by each employee is also prestored on a different magnetic tape. A payroll listing and employee paychecks are to be printed out.

Solution

It is assumed that the fixed salary rate for each employee is or could be different for each employee for a 40-hour week. Thus, the overtime pay rate, C, is given by,

$$C = K_1 \left(\frac{A}{K_2} \right)$$

where $K_1 = 1.5$ (the overtime factor) and $K_2 = 40$.
The overtime pay, H, is given by

$$H = B \times C$$

The gross salary for each employee, L, is given by

$$L = A + H$$

Assume that:

1. The constant K_1 is prestored in scratch-pad register P.
2. The starting clock number for the department, M, is prestored in counter C1.
3. The constant K_2 (i.e., 40 hours) is prestored in scratch-pad register R.

Figure 15-5 shows the algorithm-level flowchart for this problem.   ■

Example 15-3 points out some interesting facts about the use of the connector symbol. Notice the GO TO AA and the GO TO BB designations as shown in Fig. 15-6a. The connector symbol with the arrow pointing away from it, either downward or to the side, indicates either a BRANCH or a JUMP operation. We could say that such symbols represent points of exit from the program. On the other hand, the symbols shown in Fig. 15-6b indicate points of entry into the program. Each point of exit *must* have a corresponding point of entry.

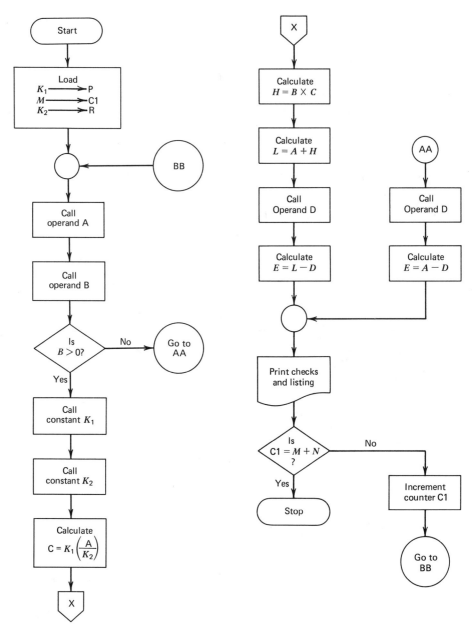

Figure 15-5   Algorithm-level flowchart for Example 15-3.

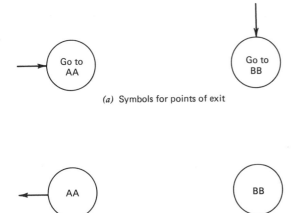

(a) Symbols for points of exit

(b) Symbols for points of entry

Figure 15-6   Symbols for connectors with points of program exit and entry.

15-3.3 Instruction-Level Flowchart

In the *instruction*-level flowchart more detailed information is given. These flowcharts are constructed with a particular μP in mind. This means that the selected machine's architecture and the instruction set must be known before the instruction-level flowchart can be drawn. The primary reason for this flowchart is to provide the programmer with a detailed set of procedures from which the program can be coded.

Since the architecture and the instruction set of the μP are taken into consideration in drawing these flowcharts, the instruction-level flowcharts for the same problem will be different when drawn for two (or more) different μPs. Examples 15-4 and 15-5 demonstrate this point.

Example 15-4

The VIRGO-A μC system has 8 programmable scratch-pad registers whose addresses are F00 to F07. The CPU includes one adder, one accumulator (ACC1) and five programmable up/down counters, respectively called C1 to C5. The following three sets of operands are prestored in the data memory.

1. A_1 to A_5 in locations 000 to 005.
2. B_1 to B_5 in locations 010 to 015.
3. C_1 to C_5 in locations 020 to 025.

All addresses and data are expressed in hexadecimal notations. For each corresponding set of these three operands, the following operations are to be performed.

1. $A + B = D$.
2. $D - C = E$.
3. Total all Ds (i.e., ΣD) and store ΣD in location 050.
4. Total all Es (i.e., ΣE) and store ΣE in location 051.

Draw an instruction-level flowchart for this problem.

Solution

The flowchart is shown in Fig. 15-7. We will store E in successive scratch-pad locations, starting with address F00.

Comments

1. Notice that there are two sets of loops involved in this program. The first loop, identified by exit and entry points AA, is concerned with the following.
    * $A + B = D$.
    * $D - C = E$.
    * Calculation of ΣE.
2. The second loop, identified by exit and entry points BB, deals with the calculation of ΣD.
3. Since this µP contains only one accumulator, we are able to obtain the cumulative total of only E at first. This is why the result D of each operation is first stored in the scratch-pad locations and then transferred into the accumulator.
4. Notice that the accumulator is first cleared to 0 before the ΣD process starts.   ■

Example 15-5

Refer to Example 15-4 and the VIRGO-A µC system. The updated version of this µP, VIRGO-B, has all the capabilities of its predecessor but additionally includes a second accumulator (ACC2). Draw an instruction-level flowchart for the same problem outlined in Example 15-4 using the VIRGO-B µP.

Solution

The normal addition and subtraction processes in this example (i.e., $A + B = D$ and $D - C = E$) are performed in the adder. Since two accumulators are now available, we do not have to store the D for each operation in the scratch pad as we did in Example 15-4. Both ΣD and ΣE can be directly loaded into a separate accumulator. The flowchart for this problem is shown in Fig. 15-8.

Comments

1. The availability of a second accumulator greatly facilitates the solution to this problem, as is evident from the flowchart.

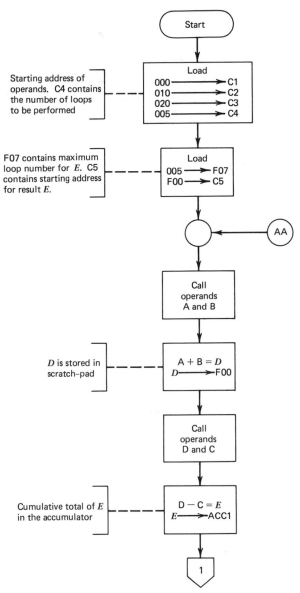

Figure 15-7 Instruction-level flowchart for example 15-4.

2. Notice that only one loop is involved as compared to the two loops required in Fig. 15-7.

3. Only four counters are used as opposed to five counters in the previous example.

4. Unlike Example 15-4 where we were compelled to use the scratch-pad locations, no scratch-pad registers are used in example 15-5.

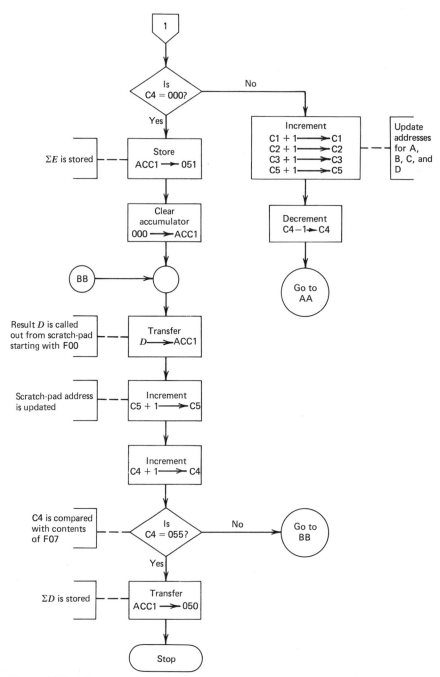

Figure 15-7 (*Continued*)

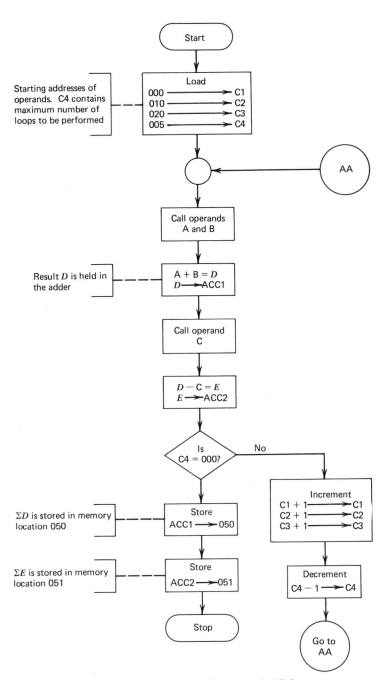

Figure 15-8 Instruction-level flowchart for Example 15-5.

5. It is obvious from a comparison of the two flowcharts that the number of instructions required for Example 15-5 will be much smaller than the number required for Example 15-4.

6. The availability of one additional accumulator greatly reduces the programming effort and points to the advantages of software/hardware tradeoffs.   ■

15-4 PROGRAM LOOPING

15-4.1 What are Iterative Loops?

In many applications it is necessary to repeat a certain portion of the program several times. It is possible to repeat that particular group of instructions over and over again in the main program as many times as desired. Such a procedure is obviously not very efficient because it eats up a lot of storage space in the program memory. Also, adding more instructions tends to make the program more prone to error. A much better procedure would be to write the program, or portion of the program, only once and then loop it around as often as required. Iteration of instructions is performed on either a portion of the program or, if so desired, on the entire program. Except in a few cases, iterative loops generally involve updating of some or all of the data that are being processed and/or some or all of the data locations (i.e., addresses) involved in the operation. Iterative loops can be conditional or unconditional. In Sections 15-4.2 and 15-4.3 we briefly discuss both of them.

15-4.2 Unconditional Iterative Loops

Unconditional iterative loops involve either a portion of the instructions or all the instructions in the program. The number of loops that are executed is predetermined and does not depend on the data being processed. In other words, regardless of the values of the operands involved, the program (or portion thereof) will loop around a fixed number of times. Such loops were clearly involved in Examples 15-4 and 15-5. Notice that in each case five sets of operands were involved, so the same set of instructions were executed with updated addresses. This updating was accomplished by using appropriately preloaded counters. Neither the values of A, B, C, D, E or the values of ΣD and ΣE had anything to do with the number of loops. Students could legitimately argue that the number of iterations were conditional on the contents of counter C4 in both examples, so it was conditional looping. This is true, but in neither of the two examples did the contents of C4 represent any of the processed data.

15-4.3 Conditional Iterative Loops

Conditional iterative loops involve the whole program or a portion of it. The number of loops that are executed is not predetermined. Instead, the number of loops will be determined by some of the data that are being processed by the program. If different data are used, the number of iterations will be different. Students will understand this better by considering the following two examples.

Example 15-6

The VIRGO-B µC system is used to calculate the area of squares of different dimensions. Starting with the dimension of 1 cm, the length of the sides must be increased in increments of 0.5 cm for each successive calculation. The program will terminate when the area is greater than 30 cm². The dimensions and the area of the square are to be listed and printed out for each dimension used. Draw an instruction-level flowchart for this problem.

Solution

In this problem, two constants are involved: the maximum permissible area (i.e., 30 cm²) and the dimension incrementing quantity (i.e., 0.5 cm). We will store them in scratch-pad locations F00 and F01, respectively. Since the problem statement does not call out for storing the dimensions or the areas in the memory, we will print these out for each calculation individually after confirming that the area does not exceed 30 cm². The flowchart is shown in Fig. 15-9.

Comments

1. Notice that, except for the load/store/clear portions, the entire operational part of the program is looped around several times.
2. From the flowchart itself it is not readily apparent how many iterations will be performed, although this can be easily calculated for this very simple problem.
3. The listing is printed out after completing each legitimate multiplication step.
4. The number of loops is not predetermined. The decision to loop or not to loop is made upon the magnitude of one of the operands: the result of the multiplication process. ■

Example 15-7

The VIRGO-B µC is used to make simple calculations for an electric circuit using Ohm's law. The applied voltage is varied from 110 V to 220 V in steps of 1 V. For each voltage step the current value is to be determined for resistance values ranging from 52 Ω to 72 Ω in increments of 1 Ω each. For each step the power consumed by the circuit is calculated from the equation $P = E \times I$. If the calculated

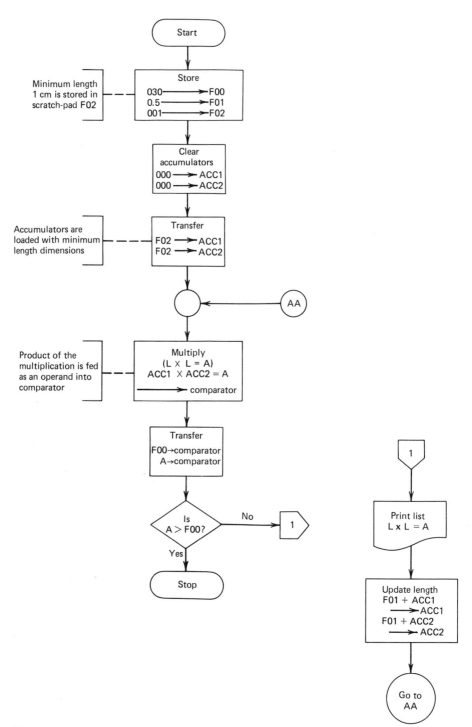

Figure 15-9 Instruction-level flowchart for Example 15-6.

power exceeds 500 W, no further current values are calculated for that particular voltage. The values of the current, voltage, resistance, and power are to be printed for each legitimate step. Draw an instruction-level flowchart for this problem.

Solution

Since the voltage is increased in steps of 1 V, we can load the lowest value (i.e., 110 V) directly into ACC1 and increment it from then on. However, we are unable to do the same with the lowest resistance value because, for each voltage value, the computations must start from 52 Ω. This value will, therefore, be stored in scratch-pad location F00. The upper limiting values of voltage, resistance, and power will be stored in scratch-pad locations F01, F02, and F03, respectively. The flowchart is shown in Fig. 15-10.

Comments

1. This example shows many of the points covered in this chapter.
2. Notice that basically there are two loops involved in this flowchart, as identified by entry and exit points AA and BB.
3. The loop represented by points AA loops the entire program except for the scratch-pad and ACC1 loading operations. This is unconditional iterative looping because it is not dependent on any of the calculated data. It will loop around a total of 110 times (220 − 110 = 110).
4. Also notice that we accomplished this looping without the use of any counters, using only accumulator ACC1, the scratch pad and the comparator.
5. There are two loops represented by entry and exit points BB. Both these loops are considered to be conditional iterative loops. The first one checks the resistance values and could be mistakenly taken for unconditional loops. They are conditional loops because, for each voltage value, the number of iterations depends also on the power values and could be different in each case.
6. The second BB loop depends only on the calculated power value and so is obviously conditional. ∎

15-5 SUMMARY

This chapter introduced two major items in computer software. The first concerned the statement of the problem. Seven minimum items involved in a well-defined problem statement were presented, followed by a sample problem statement that exemplified several of these items. Flowcharts are very useful tools for the development of software, and these were introduced. Conventional flowchart symbols, which are widely used in the United States, were presented with a brief explanation of each. Both program flowchart and system flowchart symbols were included. The three levels of flowcharts were presented, starting with the simplest concept-level flowchart. An example showed

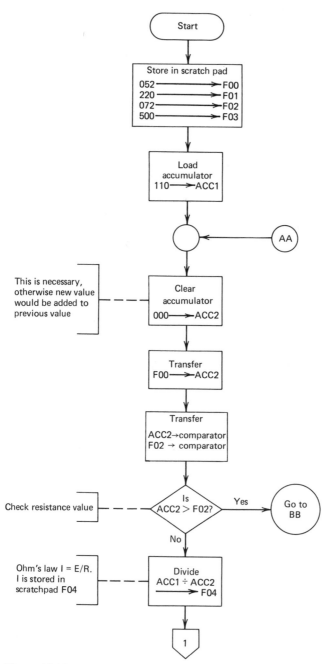

Figure 15-10 Instruction-level flowchart for Example 5-7.

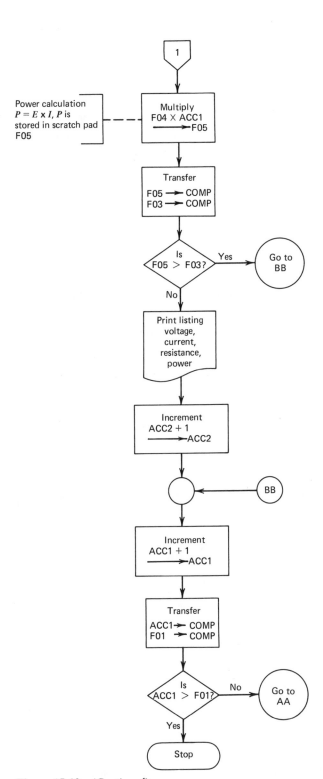

Power calculation
$P = E \times I$, P is
stored in scratch pad
F05

Multiply
F04 × ACC1
⟶ F05

Transfer
F05 ⟶ COMP
F03 ⟶ COMP

Is
F05 > F03?   Yes   Go to
BB

No

Print listing
voltage,
current,
resistance,
power

Increment
ACC2 + 1
⟶ ACC2

BB

Increment
ACC1 + 1
⟶ ACC1

Transfer
ACC1 ⟶ COMP
F01 ⟶ COMP

Is
ACC1 > F01?   No   Go to
AA

Yes

Stop

Figure 15-10   (*Continued*)

how a concept-level flowchart was constructed. The same example was used to explain the algorithm-level flowchart. The instruction-level flowchart was presented and explained with the help of two examples. The principles involved in flowcharting program loops were then presented. Both unconditional and conditional iterative loops were discussed, and an example for each was presented.

15-6 REVIEW QUESTIONS

15-1 Explain why it is necessary to define the requirements of the entire system instead of only the μC system.

15-2 Briefly state the minimum items that should be included in a well-defined problem statement.

15-3 Briefly explain what input signal requirements should be included in the problem statement.

15-4 What processing requirements of the μC should be included in the problem statement?

15-5 What are some of the common accuracy requirements that are included in problem statements for systems involving μCs?

15-6 State what output signal requirements should be included in the problem statement.

15-7 Briefly explain why timing restrictions are so important in a well-defined problem statement.

15-8 What is a flowchart?

15-9 In the μC field who uses flowcharts and for what purpose?

15-10 What do the symbols in the flowchart represent?

15-11 State what a flowchart does and does not show.

15-12 Should a flowchart be prepared before, during, or after coding a program? Why?

15-13 Explain the difference between program flowchart symbols and system flowchart symbols.

15-14 Identify the flowchart symbols shown in Fig. 15-11 and state whether they are program flowchart or system flowchart symbols.

15-15 What are the various levels of flowcharts?

15-16 Explain what a concept-level flowchart is and what it includes.

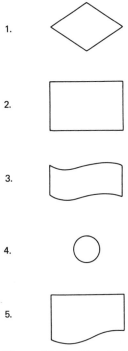

1.

2.

3.

4.

5.

Figure 15-11   Flowchart symbols for question 15-14.

15-17 What is included in the symbol blocks of a concept-level flowchart?

15-18 What is an algorithm? What does it do?

15-19 Briefly describe an algorithm-level flowchart. How does it differ from the concept-level flowchart?

15-20 Does the algorithm-level flowchart use program flowchart symbols or system flowchart symbols?

15-21 Is it possible to have two or more different flowcharts for obtaining a solution to the same problem? If so, what type of flowchart would be used?

15-22 Briefly describe an instruction-level flowchart.

15-23 Can the same instruction-level flowchart designed for machine A for a certain problem be used on machine B for the same problem? Explain.

15-24 What is the principal advantage of using iterative loops in a program?

15-25 Briefly describe unconditional iterative loops.

15-26 Briefly describe conditional iterative loops.

15-7 PROBLEMS AND EXERCISES

15-1   Draw a simple concept-level flowchart for the equation $C = \pi d$ for values of d starting with 5 cm and increasing to 15 cm in increments of 1 cm. (*Note.* This equation is for calculating the circumference of a circle.)

15-2   Draw a simple concept-level flowchart for determining the areas of a circle from the equation $a = \pi r^2$, where the radius r varies from 50 cm to 60 cm in increments of 1 cm.

15-3   Refer to Problem 15-1. Draw an algorithm-level flowchart for this problem.

15-4   Refer to Problem 15-2. Draw an algorithm-level flowchart for this problem.

15-5   Refer to Problem 15-1. Draw an instruction-level flowchart for this problem using the VIRGO-A μC system described in Example 15-4. Assume that the instruction set for this μP contains an instruction that increments accumulator ACC1. Also assume that the results will be automatically displayed and retained on a CRT display as they are calculated.

15-6   Refer to Problem 15-2. The VIRGO-A μC has a software subroutine that is capable of performing the square operation. It is stored in data memory starting at hexadecimal address OD91. Draw an instruction-level flowchart for the problem assuming that ACC1 can be incremented under program control and the result is automatically displayed on the CRT as it is calculated.

15-7   Using the VIRGO-A μC and the equation for determining the circumference of a circle, draw an instruction-level flowchart for diameter values starting with $d = 5$ cm and increasing in increments of 2 cm each time. The program must be terminated if the diameter exceeds 35 cm or the circumference exceeds 90 cm. The circumference value for each legitimate calculation is displayed on the CRT.

15-8   Refer to Problem 15-2. The radius of the circle is now increased in increments of 4 cm up to a maximum of 84 cm, at which point the program must be terminated. Also, the program is terminated if the area exceeds 16,000 cm^2. Draw an instruction-level flowchart for the VIRGO-A μC that has a squaring subroutine stored in the memory starting at address OD91. The results are displayed on the CRT.

15-9   Refer to Problem 15-8. Instead of running the solution on the VIRGO-A, it is run on the VIRGO-B, which has two accumulators ACC1 and ACC2, four incrementing/decrementing counters, and a squaring subroutine starting at address OD91. Instead of displaying the area a on the CRT, the values of both r and a for each legitimate calculation are to be stored in memory locations starting with 80A and 9DD, respectively. Draw an instruction-level flowchart.

15-10 The VIRGO-B μC is used for solving the following algebraic equation.

$$R = ay^4 + by^3 + cy^2 + dy$$

The values of the four coefficients are:

$$a = 12, \quad b = 15, \quad c = 18, \quad d = 21$$

The values of y range from 30 to 45 in increments of 1. Draw an instruction-level flowchart to determine the values of R. The only subroutine available for raising a number to any power is the squaring subroutine.

15-11 The volume of a cylinder is given by the equation $v = 1 \times \pi r^2$, where 1 is the length of the cylinder and r is the radius. Use the VIRGO-B μC system, which has a square operation subroutine. It is stored in the memory starting at address 08AA. The radius, r, starts from 7 cm and can go up to 17 cm and the length, l, starts from 12 cm and can go up to 22 cm in increments of 1 cm (for both of them). Draw an instruction-level flowchart for calculating the volumes of these cylinders, assuming that ACC1 and ACC2 can be incremented under program control and the result is automatically displayed on the CRT as it is calculated. (*Hint.* See Problem 15-6; the same scheme can be modified and used here.)

15-12 The quadratic equation $ax^2 + bx + c = 0$, where x is the unknown quantity whose value is to be determined by the standard formula

$$x = \frac{-b \pm \sqrt{b^2 - 4ac}}{2a}$$

and coefficients a, b, and c are known quantities. The VIRGO-B μC system has a square operation subroutine in the memory starting at address 08AA and a square root subroutine starting at address 11AA. The coefficients are stored in data memory as follows and are periodically updated by the CPU.

a in address B01
b in address B02
c in address B03

Design an instruction-level flowchart for calculating both the positive and the negative values of x and displaying them on the CRT as they are calculated. Each coefficient will have its appropriate positive or negative sign bit.

16

ORGANIZING THE DATA

16-1 DATA AND INFORMATION

16-1.1 Difference between Data and Information

Digital computers are designed to work with binary bits. Regardless of how the programmer or the user interprets these bits, the machine interprets them as only 1s and 0s and operates on them accordingly. The human being can only assign any suitable meaning to a bit or a group of bits to suit the individual requirements of the particular problem at hand. For example, in the octal system we included 3 bits in each group and assigned a numerical value to each group, depending on the combination of 1s and 0s in the group (see Section 2-3). In binary-coded-decimal (BCD) and the hexadecimal systems (Sections 2-4 and 2-5) we included 4 bits in each group. In the BCD case we assigned numerical values to such groups and in the hexadecimal system we assigned both numerical values and alphabetical designations to the various combinations of 1s and 0s.

It is apparent that the same word of binary bits takes on different meanings when grouped, and subsequently interpreted, by different systems of coding. This is clearly shown in Fig. 16-1, where the same 12-bit word is interpreted differently in three different coding systems. In Fig. 16-1a the 12 bits are interpreted as a pure binary number, which is 339. When arranged in groups of 3 bits, as in Fig. 16-1b, they represent 0523 in the octal system. In Fig. 16-1c they are arranged in groups of 4 bits, so they represent 153 in the BCD system.

From Fig. 16-1 we see that the coding system gives some meaning to the binary bits. Thus we can define *data* as groups or words consisting of binary bits that are devoid of any specific meaning or interpretation. We can say that digital computers process data. On the other hand, *information* is data that have meaning or interpretation. Internally, the CPU processes data, but the computer system operates on information. Input sections and I/O devices take

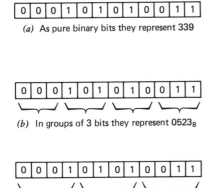

(a) As pure binary bits they represent 339

| 0 | 0 | 0 | 1 | 0 | 1 | 0 | 1 | 0 | 0 | 1 | 1 |

(b) In groups of 3 bits they represent 0523_8

| 0 | 0 | 0 | 1 | 0 | 1 | 0 | 1 | 0 | 0 | 1 | 1 |

(c) In groups of 4 bits they represent 153 BCD or hexadecimal

Figure 16-1 Twelve-bit word representing quantities in different coding system.

external information, strip it of its interpretation, and present data to the computer, which processes these data. The computer presents the processed data to the output unit or device, which adds or attaches meaning to them and converts them back into information. This process is shown in Fig. 16-2 for a keyboard, a display unit, and a computer.

16-1.2 The ASCII Code

From Fig. 16-1 it is seen that the coding system used provides a means of transforming data into information, and vice versa. One well-known coding system is the ASCII (American Standard Code for Information Interchange) code. This system, which is widely used in the data-processing industry, uses 7 bits to denote a total of 128 ($2^7 = 128$) numericals, alphabetical letters (both uppercase and lowercase), symbols, and control characters. The ASCII system and character set are shown in tabular form in Appendix A.

Since 8 bits are a convenient grouping of bits for computer operations, the 7-bit ASCII code becomes awkward to handle. Two solutions are generally used. A simple method is to insert a digital 0 in the eighth or the most-

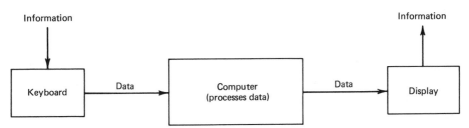

Figure 16-2 Data/information relationships.

significant-bit (MSB) position of an 8-bit register holding an ASCII code or character. This is shown in Fig. 16-3*a*. If serial transmissions of data are involved, the MSB position of the register can be used to insert a parity bit, as shown in Fig. 16-3*b*. (Refer to Chapter 11 for explanation regarding the parity in serial transmissions.)

16-1.3 Packing and Unpacking Data

In Fig. 16-1 we had a 12-bit register. The same 12-bit combination represented three different pieces of information, depending on which coding system was applied to those 12 bits (i.e., pure binary, octal, or BCD). Now consider this situation. Could this register be used to hold 2 words instead of 1, each word representing a different coding system? Of course it could. For instance, the lower 8 bits of the register could represent bits in the ASCII code, while the upper 4 bits could be in the BCD code. This is shown in Fig. 16-4*a*. Notice that when these interpretations are applied, the register contains 1S. If, on the other hand, the upper 8 bits were to represent the ASCII code of the same bit combination and the lower 4 bits the BCD code, the register would contain NAK 4, as shown in Fig. 16-4*b*.

We have previously seen that the 8-bit byte is commonly used in today's μPs and that multibyte words are extensively used. This is accomplished by concatenating two or more 8-bit registers, but the resulting group of bits is essentially treated as a single word. Such multibyte words often contain bits that represent information in two or more coded forms. *Packing* is the process of including two or more short items of information into 1 computer word by utilizing different groups of bits to specify each brief item using different coding systems.

The packing process is a matter of convenience. A word packed with bits in different coding systems cannot be intelligently processed by the CPU to give meaningful results. Before actual processing, the word must be unpacked. Thus *unpacking* is defined as the process of separating the various elements of a packed word into groups of bits that can be used for processing or storing purposes. The process of packing and unpacking is shown in Examples 16-1 and 16-2.

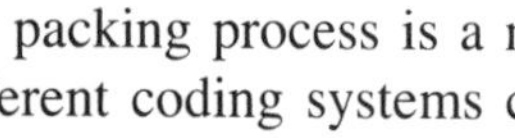

```
 0 |   7-Bit ASCII code   |
 7  6  5  4  3  2  1  0
```
(*a*) A 0 inserted in the MSB position of the register

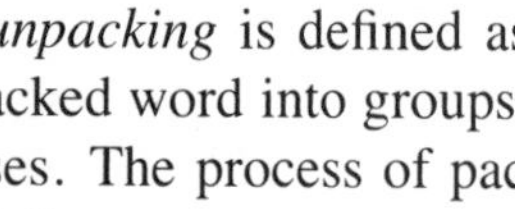

```
 P |   7-Bit ASCII code   |
 7  6  5  4  3  2  1  0
```
(*b*) Parity bit inserted in MSB position of the register

Figure 16-3   Seven-bit ASCII code in an 8-bit register.

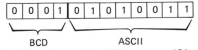

(a) Upper 4 bits BCD and lower 8 bits ASCII represent 1S in the register

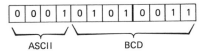

(b) Upper 8 bits ASCII and lower 4 bits BC represent NAK 4 in the register

Figure 16-4   BCD and ASCII code bits packed in 12-bit register.

Example 16-1

In a certain 8-bit μC the memory addresses are coded in 2-digit hexadecimal codes. The 8-bit RAM contains the following information.

In address 3E—22 in BCD.
In address A9—NAK in ASCII.
In address B2—33 in BCD.

The two BCD codes are called out and added in the adder with BCD capabilities. The result and the ASCII code called out from the memory are packed into a 16-bit word in two concatenated auxiliary registers R1 and R2. Graphically show this process in machine language.

Solution

The solution to this problem is graphically shown in Fig. 16-5. Notice that the adder in the CPU must be able to handle BCD operations. The two operands to be added are 22 and 33, respectively. The result (i.e., 55) is converted into BCD form. In Fig. 16-5 the resulting sum is shown in BCD in the adder. Steps 1 and 2 consist of transferring the two BCD operands into the adder. Step 3 transfers the BCD result into register R1, which is concatenated with R2. Step 4 transfers the ASCII code (NAK) into R2. The concatenated combination of R1 and R2 contains the packed word 55NAK. ■

Example 16-2

Refer to the packed word in Example 16-1. Graphically show how we could send the ASCII code to the printer and store the BCD sum in RAM address DF.

Solution

The solution to this problem is graphically shown in Fig. 16-6. Notice that although registers R1 and R2 are concatenated and contain a packed word, in this example

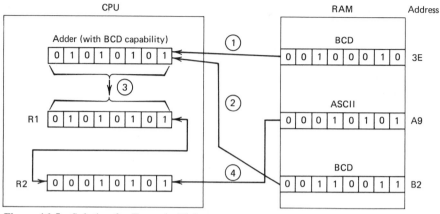

Figure 16-5 Solution for Example 16-1.

the word is unpacked and transferred to RAM and the printer as 2 separate words in two steps, each word in a different coding system. ■

16-1.4 Multiple Precision Capability

Section 16-1.3 shows that it is possible to combine two or more groups of bits (representing different coding systems) into a single register. In many cases we may concatenate two or more registers to give us the necessary word-length capability. Nonetheless, such concatenated registers still contain a single word.

On the other hand, there are many situations where a single word-length capability is not enough for a specific job. For example, in an 8-bit machine with an 8-bit address we can directly access a memory of 256 words ($2^8 =$

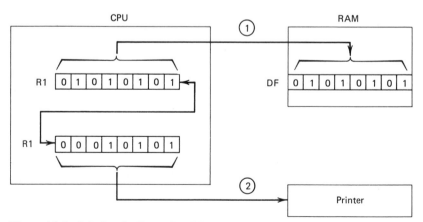

Figure 16-6 Solution for Example 16-2.

256). What if our application calls for directly addressing an 8k memory? Obviously, we would require an address word capability of 13-bit words (2^{13} = 8192). We would require two 8-bit words to satisfy such a situation. It is possible that we may need more than 2 words to satisfy the requirements. For example, suppose we have an 8-bit μC used in an inventory control application where we may need to store numbers representing quantities of items in stock up to as much as 500,000. To represent this number in pure binary code would require 19 bits (2^{19} = 524,288). Such a number cannot be stored in an 8-bit memory. But, if an 8-bit memory is all we have, we can still store such large numbers by using adjacent memory registers. In this situation we would use three adjacent 8-bit registers in the memory. If we do so we must decide how we will use the multiple-word storage capability, since only 19 out of the possible 24 bits are used. The decisions to be made will involve considerations such as using the lower-order or the higher-order 19 bits for storing the numbers and what to do with the remaining 5 bit positions (whether to store 0s or 1s or ignore them).

There are other situations where multiple-word capabilities are required in the CPU. Multiplication and division algorithms using the accumulator method are common examples that require a double-word capability, regardless of the basic word length of the computer. In such situations extra or auxiliary registers are provided in the CPU. In the case of multiplication and division an extra accumulator is used. Computers that have such capabilities are often referred to as machines with *double-length* or *double-precision* words or capabilities. If the word then can be increased beyond two, the machine is said to have *multiple-word* or *multiple-precision* capabilities.

16-2 NUMERICAL QUANTITIES IN SCIENTIFIC NOTATION

16-2.1 Exponential Notation

In many applications, particularly scientific and engineering applications, we work with numbers that are very large or very small. For example, in dealing with circuit parameters we often use large resistance values and small current values. We use convenient terms such as megohms to indicate millions of ohms or kilohms to indicate thousands of ohms. Similarly, we use milliamperes to indicate current values in thousandths of an ampere or microamperes to indicate millionths of an ampere. Prefixes such as *mega-, kilo-, milli-,* and *micro-* are convenient in human language and communications, they are hardly suitable for use in mathematical formulas or computations using digital computers. We resort to the scientific method for expressing very large and very small quantities using a system of exponential notation. In our everyday decimal system we use the radix 10 raised to the desired exponential power. Thus we express 3000 Ω or 3 kΩ as 3×10^3 and 3 million Ω or 3 MΩ as 3×10^6 Ω. In such a system the basic quantity need not necessarily be an integer. It could be a fraction. For example, 300,000 Ω can be expressed as 0.3×10^6 Ω.

Since the digital computer uses the binary number system, expressing large or small quantities as exponents of the radix 10 becomes awkward. The radix 2 is a more natural quantity to use.

Notice that in the preceding situations the effect of the exponent is to shift the decimal point to the right of the integer an equivalent number of places. For 3×10^3, we take the integer 3 and move the decimal point three places, as indicated by the exponent, giving us 3000. A similar situation exists in the binary system, using the radix 2, as shown in Examples 16-3 and 16-4.

Example 16-3

Using a 3-bit integer, show how the number 28 can be expressed by scientific notation in the binary system.

Solution

Since only 3 bits are to be used in the integer, we can only have a maximum of 111 representing decimal 7. However, $7 \times 4 = 28$, so we can obtain 7×2^2 by writing 111×2^2. To multiply a binary number by 4, all we need to do is shift the binary point two places to the right. Thus $28 = 7 \times 4 = 7 \times 2^2$, which gives us

$$111 \times 2^2 = 11100 = 28$$

Example 16-4

Using a 3-bit integer, show how the number 56 can be expressed by scientific notation in the binary system.

Solution

Once again 3 bits will give us a maximum integer of $111 = 7$. We can obtain 56 by multiplying it by 8, which is 2^3. Thus all we have to do is shift the binary point 3 places to the right, giving us

$$111 \times 2^3 = 111000 = 56$$

16-2.2 Sign Convention

In Section 16-2.1 we considered only large numbers and how they could be expressed by scientific notation in both the decimal and the binary number systems. In this case a positive exponent was assumed. A negative exponent is used for expressing fractions or quantities less than one. For example 5 MA of current (meaning 5 thousandths of an ampere) would be shown as 0.005 A. In the scientific notation system this would be expressed as 5×10^{-3}. It is not so easy to express an exponent of 3 in the binary system; the exponents have to be multiples of 2, since a shift either right or left of the binary point would multiply or divide the quantity by 2. We can make the exponent either -4 or -2 and adjust the binary point on the integer accordingly to accommodate this situation. Thus

$$5 \times 10^{-3} = 50 \times 10^{-4} = 0.5 \times 10^{-2}$$

The fractional approach works out very nicely in this situation. We see that $5_{10} = 101_2$. If we place the decimal point in the leftmost position

$$0.5 \times 10^{-2} = 0.101 \times 2^{-2} = 0.00101$$

To express binary quantities in the scientific notation we must somehow specify whether the exponent is a positive or a negative quantity. The conventional sign bit, a 0 for positive and a 1 for negative exponents, is used.

Using this method, we can use the binary system to express large and small numbers by scientific notation. Such a number could be inserted in a single register by packing three different groups of bits signifying three pieces of information: the number (either the integer or the fraction), the exponent, and the sign of the exponent. Figure 16-7 shows one way in which these three pieces of information can be packed in a single register.

The system represented in Fig. 16-7 must have one other convention established before it can be used (i.e., the location of the binary point). In many situations it is convenient to place the binary point in the leftmost position. This means that the numerical quantity is expressed as a fraction.

The scientific notation is only a way of expressing very large and very small numbers. It is possible that the large or the small number itself could be a negative quantity. To express this polarity, we will use the same sign convention. This means that the register would be packed with four pieces of information, as shown in Fig. 16-8.

In Fig. 16-8 the placement of the fraction bits and exponent bits is arbitrary.

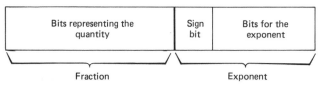

Figure 16-7   Register packed with information for scientific notation.

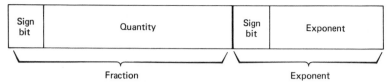

Figure 16-8   Four pieces of information packed in a register.

It is, of course, possible to have the exponent bits in the higher-order position of the register and the fraction bits in the lower-order position. The numerical quantity, regardless of the placement of the binary point, is often called the *mantissa* and the exponent bits the *exponent*. The most often used form of packing the information in a single register (or two or more concatenated registers) is shown in Fig. 16-9. The mantissa is sometimes also referred to as the *precision* part of the number.

16-2.3 Floating-Point Operations

In Sections 16-2.1 and 16-2.2 we have seen how very large and very small numbers can be conveniently expressed by scientific notation in the decimal or the binary system. The placement of the radix point (i.e., the decimal point or the binary point) is determined by the exponent in each case. This means that the radix point is not fixed but is floating. It is possible to perform arithmetic operations by the fixed-point method, but it is difficult and cumbersome to keep track of the radix point. By expressing the numbers involved in scientific notation, we can perform a floating-point operation, which offers a way to keep track of the radix point automatically while at the same time extending the range of the numbers that can be represented and used for arithmetic operations. For performing the four basic arithmetic operations—add, subtract, multiply, and divide—in floating-point operation four basic rules apply that are stated next.

   Rule 1   To perform floating-point addition, the exponent values of the two quantities to be added must be made the same. To accomplish this, either the mantissa of the addend or the augend, or both, may have to be shifted right or left one or more places. The mantissas are then added, and the exponent is the common exponent obtained by the previous shifting of the mantissa.

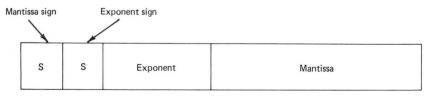

Figure 16-9   Commonly used format for packing information in scientific notation.

Rule 2 To perform floating-point subtraction, the mantissa of either the subtrahend or the minuend, or both, must be shifted right or left so that the same exponent is obtained for both quantities. The mantissa representing the subtrahend is then subtracted from the mantissa representing the minuend. The exponent of the resulting difference is the common exponent obtained by the previous shifting of the mantissa.

Rule 3 To perform floating-point multiplication, the exponents of the multiplicand and the multiplier are not changed. The two mantissas are multiplied, and the product is the resulting mantissa. The exponent of the product is obtained by adding the exponent of the multiplicand to the exponent of the mutiplier, taking into consideration the sign of each exponent.

Rule 4 To perform floating-point division, the exponents of the dividend and the divisor are not changed. The mantissa representing the dividend is divided by the mantissa representing the divisor. The result represents the mantissa of the quotient. The exponent of the quotient is obtained by subtracting the exponent of the divisor from the exponent of the dividend, taking into consideration the sign of each exponent.

Examples 16-5 and 16-12 show how these four rules are applied to floating-point operations. For simplicity we first apply them to decimal numbers only.

Example 16-5

Add the following two decimal numbers using scientific notation.

$A = 3.56 \times 10^4$
$B = 73.89 \times 10^3$

Solution

Since the two exponents are not the same, we must adjust one or the other of the two quantities to make both exponents equal. We will arbitrarily adjust A to make the exponent 3. The decimal point in the mantissa is therefore moved one place to the right so that the absolute value of A remains unchanged. Thus

$A = 35.6 \times 10^3$
We now perform the addition.

$$\begin{array}{rl} A = & 35.6 \times 10^3 \\ + B = & 73.89 \times 10^3 \\ \hline C = & 109.49 \times 10^3 \end{array}$$ ■

Example 16-6

Add the following two decimal numbers using scientific notation.

$A = 834.2 \times 10^{-5}$
$B = 1564.39 \times 10^{-7}$

Solution

This time we will make the two exponents equal by shifting the decimal point of the mantissa for B two places to the left, giving us

$$B = 15.6439 \times 10^{-5}$$

The addition is performed.

$$
\begin{array}{rl}
A = 834.2 & \times\ 10^{-5} \\
+\ B = 15.6439 & \times\ 10^{-5} \\
\hline
C = 849.8439 & \times\ 10^{-5}
\end{array}
$$

Notice that the signs of both exponents were negative, so the resulting exponent is negative, too. Also, the negative exponent of B determines the shift of the decimal point to the left instead of to the right. ■

Example 16-7

The following numbers are expressed in the decimal system. Subtract B from A using scientific notation.

$$A = 6.3446 \times 10^{3}$$
$$B = 48.179 \times 10^{2}$$

Solution

We will shift the decimal point of A one place to the right, giving us

$$A = 63.446 \times 10^{2}$$

The subtraction is performed as follows.

$$
\begin{array}{rl}
A = 63.446 & \times\ 10^{2} \\
-\ B = 48.179 & \times\ 10^{2} \\
\hline
C = 15.276 & \times\ 10^{2}
\end{array}
$$

■

Example 16-8

The following numbers are expressed in the decimal system. Subtract B from A using scientific notation.

$$A = 78491.2 \times 10^{-4}$$
$$B = 0.00038269 \times 10^{+7}$$

Solution

This is a more complex situation that requires an adjustment of the decimal point in both A and B in order to obtain a common exponent. We first determine the absolute placement of the decimal point for A and B for the given exponents as shown here where the arrows represent the decimal points.

$A = 78418.2 \times 10^{-3} = 78{\blacktriangle}49182$
$B = 0.00038269 \times 10^{+7} = 0003826{\blacktriangle}9$

To obtain a common exponent for both numbers, we can now adjust the true decimal points right or left the same number of places. Let us say that arbitrarily we shift it right two places; then we can write them as follows and perform the subtraction.

$$
\begin{array}{rl}
A = & 7849.182 \quad\ \times 10^{-2} \\
- B = & 000382690.0 \times 10^{-2} \\
\hline
C = & -374840.82 \times 10^{-2}
\end{array}
$$

The result is negative because the larger number is subtracted from the smaller number.   ■

Example 16-9

The following numbers are expressed in the decimal system. Multiply them using scientific notation.

$A = 3.78 \times 10^4$
$B = 14.5 \times 10^2$

Solution

Now the exponents do not have to be equal. Multiplying the mantissa gives us

$3.78 \times 14.5 = 54.81$

The exponent for the product is obtained by adding the two exponents. Thus

$4 + 2 = 6$

The correct answer is therefore

54.81×10^6 ■

Example 16-10

The following numbers are expressed in the decimal system. Multiply them using scientific notation.

$$A = 48.381 \times 10^{-4}$$
$$B = -39.165 \times 10^{+3}$$

Solution

We multiply the mantissa to give the product

$$+48.381 \times (-39.165) = -1894.841$$

Notice the negative product. The exponent of the product is given by

$$(-4) + (+3) = -1$$

Therefore the correct answer is

$$-1894.841 \times 10^{-1}$$

■

Example 16-11

The following numbers are expressed in the decimal system. Divide A by B using scientific notation.

$$A = 69.31 \times 10^{+12}$$
$$B = 31.82 \times 10^{+9}$$

Solution

The mantissa of dividend A is divided by the mantissa of divisor B, giving us

$$+68.31 \div +31.82 = +2.178$$

The exponent of the quotient is obtained by subtracting the exponent of the divisor from the exponent of the dividend, giving us

$$(+12) - (+9) = +3$$

Therefore the correct answer is

$$2.178 \times 10^{+3}$$

■

Example 16-12

The following numbers are given in the decimal system. Divide B by A using scientific notation.

$A = -3.812 \times 10^{-2}$
$B = -6.79 \ \times 10^{+3}$

Solution

The mantissa of dividend B is divided by the mantissa of divisor A as follows.

$-6.79 \div -3.812 = +1.781$

The exponent of the quotient is given by

$(+3) - (-2) = +5$

Therefore the correct answer is

$+1.781 \times 10^{+5}$ ■

These examples show how the four basic rules of floating-point operations apply to a large range of decimal numbers. The same rules also apply to numbers in the binary system numbers. As of this writing all µCs on the market have decimal, fixed-point arithmetic capabilities that are incorporated into the hardware of the µP. To the best of my knowledge no hardware floating-point capabilities are available in µCs. Floating-point arithmetic can be accomplished only by means of software subroutines. Since many µCs use the hexadecimal or BCD systems of notation, we will confine our discussions and the following examples to the BCD system.

Since 4 binary bits are required to represent decimal digits from 0 to 9, four 8-bit bytes are used for floating-point operations. This means that four 8-bit registers are concatenated for these operations. Of course, the four registers can be packed using either of the two formats shown in Figs. 16-8 and 16-9. For simplicity in explanation and for the examples that follow, we will use a slightly modified version of the format of Fig. 16-9, as shown in Fig. 16-10.

In the previously mentioned 4-byte system, 1 byte is used for the exponent and its sign and 3 bytes for the mantissa and its associated sign. Such a configuration is shown in Fig. 16-11, where the Y bits represent the exponent and S_E represents its sign bit and the X bits represent the mantissa and S_M its sign bit.

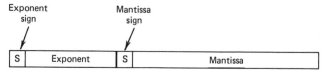

Figure 16-10 Modified format for packing information.

The following observations are made regarding the capabilities of the 4-byte format of Fig. 16-11.

1. In byte 4 only 7 bits are available for expressing the BCD values of the exponent, since the MSB represents the sign. Thus the exponent range is $\pm 111\ 1111$, which in BCD notation represents ± 79.
2. Likewise, only 7 bits of byte 3 are available for BCD while all 8 bits of bytes 2 and 1 can be used. Therefore the BCD range of the mantissa is ± 0.799999.

The floating-point subroutines are designed so that in this case BCD numbers beyond cited ranges would be meaningless and could be rejected by the computer. Examples 16-13 to 16-16 show how the previously discussed rules of floating-point operations are used in the BCD system.

Example 16-13

Three 4-bit registers are concatenated and used for BCD floating-point operations. Normal sign conventions apply to both the exponent and the mantissa. Sketch the bit format of this register and indicate the range of numbers represented by it when the most significant 4 bits are used for the exponent and its sign.

Solution

The format of the 12-bit register is shown in Fig. 16-12.
The range of the exponent is ± 7 and the range of the mantissa is ± 79. Therefore the BCD number possible with this configuration is

$$\pm 0.79 \times 10^{\pm 7}$$

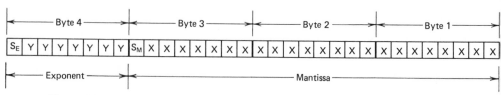

Figure 16-11 Format of information packed in four 8-bit registers (BCD) operation.

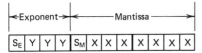

Figure 16-12   Solution for Example 16-13.

Example 16-14

Refer to the three 4-bit registers of Example 16-13 and show how BCD quantity $+5.8 \times 10^{-3}$ will be represented in binary system.

Solution

First, we will move the radix point one place to the left to conform to our convention of making the mantissa less than 1. This gives us $+0.58 \times 10^{-2}$. The resulting binary bits in the 12-bit registers are shown in Fig. 16-13.   ∎

Example 16-15

Four 4-bit registers are concatenated for BCD operations. Nibble 4 is used for the exponent. The following quantities are added.

$A = +0.58 \times 10^5$
$B = +12.0 \times 10^3$

Show the resulting bits in this 12-bit register.

Solution

We first make the exponents of both quantities equal by shifting the decimal point of B two places to the left. This gives us $B = 0.12 \times 10^5$. Then the sum is given by

$$\begin{array}{r} A = 0.58 \times 10^5 \\ + \; B = 0.12 \times 10^5 \\ \hline C = 0.70 \times 10^5 \end{array}$$

The resulting bit configuration is shown in Fig. 16-14.   ∎

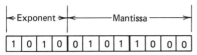

Figure 16-13   Solution for Example 16-14.

Figure 16-14 Solution for Example 16-15.

Example 16-16

Four 8-bit registers are concatenated for BCD operations. $A = 14.381 \times 10^{+12}$ and $B = 46.25 \times 10^{-4}$. Byte 4 is used for the exponent and its sign. Multiply these two quantities and show their product in this 32-bit register.

Solution

The decimal points of both quantities are shifted left two places to make the mantissa less than one. Thus

$$A = 0.14381 \times 10^{+14}$$
$$B = 0.4625 \; \times 10^{-2}$$

The product is obtained by multiplying the two mantissas and adding the two exponents.

$$C = A \times B = 0.0665121 \times 10^{+12}$$

Since the mantissa of the product is a positive quantity, the product will appear in the 32-bit register, as shown in Fig. 16-15.   ∎

16-3 SUMMARY

Two important points regarding data representation were covered in this chapter. The first introduced the concept of packing and unpacking data in a single register which, in most cases, is composed of two or more smaller concatenated registers. The difference between data and information was pointed out, and examples showed how the same configuration of bits convey different information when considered in different groupings such as the octal coding system (3 bits) and the BCD coding system (4 bits). It was stated that the CPU processes data while the computing system processes information. The popular

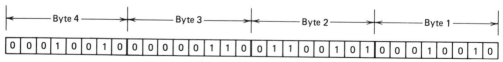

Figure 16-15 Solution for Example 16-16.

7-bit ASCII coding system and how multibyte words are used to represent information in two or more coded forms was also discussed. The concept of multiple-precision word lengths was then presented.

The second important point covered in this chapter was related to the problem of representing very large or very small numbers. The system of exponential notation, usually called scientific notation, was described. Four rules on how addition, subtraction, multiplication, and division are handled with exponential notation were presented, and each rule was further explained with examples, first with the familiar decimal system. The exponential notation system, which is often referred to as floating-point arithmetic, was described as applied in digital computers using the binary system. The sign convention was explained, and various arithmetic operations were described by means of several examples.

16-4 REVIEW QUESTIONS

16-1   Is it possible to interpret the same group of bits in different manners? If so, explain why.

16-2   Explain the difference between data and information.

16-3   Does the CPU process data or information? What does the computing system, which includes the CPU, process?

16-4   How many bits are used in the ASCII coding system and what do these codes represent?

16-5   Since 8 bits are a convenient grouping of bits for a computer and the ASCII code uses only 7 bits, explain how vacant bit position is handled in an 8-bit register in which an ASCII code word is inserted.

16-6   Briefly define packing.

16-7   Can the CPU directly process a word packed with information in different coding systems and come up with meaningful results?

16-8   What is the multiple-word or multiple-precision capability in a CPU? Explain.

16-9   In the decimal system, using exponential notation, what is the net effect of increasing the value of a positive exponent by 2?

16-10   What is the net effect of decreasing the value of a positive exponent by 1 in the binary system?

16-11   If exponential notation is used in the binary system, where is the radix point located?

16-12   Briefly explain how floating-point addition is performed.

16-13 How is the exponent of the product obtained when two quantities are multiplied in floating-point arithmetic?

16-14 When floating-point subtraction is performed, is the exponent of the result obtained by subtracting the smaller exponent from the larger exponent?

16-15 How is the exponent of the quotient obtained in floating-point division?

16-5 PROBLEMS AND EXERCISES

16-1 The memory addresses in a μC are coded in 3-digit hexadecimal codes. The 12-bit RAM contains the following information.
In address 4A6—632 in BCD.
In address BB7—317 in BCD.
Register RR (8-bit register) in the CPU contains ENQ in ASCII code. The two BCD codes are called out from the RAM and added in the 12-bit adder, which has BCD capabilities. The result of the addition and the ASCII code are packed in a 24-bit register that is concatenated by using two 12-bit registers R1 and R2. Graphically show the preceding process in binary bits.

16-2 Using a 4-bit integer, show how the number 144 can be expressed by scientific notation in the binary system.

16-3 Using a 2-bit integer, show how the number 384 can be expressed by scientific notation in the binary system.

16-4 Add the following two decimal numbers using scientific notation.
$A = 6.93 \times 10^6$
$B = 43.81 \times 10^5$

16-5 Add the following two decimal numbers using scientific notation.
$A = +73.461 \times 10^{+4}$
$B = +0.00132 \times 10^{-2}$

16-6 Add the following two decimal numbers using scientific notation.
$A = +378.2195 \times 10^{-3}$
$B = -23922.82 \times 10^{-5}$

16-7 Add the following two decimal numbers using scientific notation.
$A = -3992.125 \times 10^2$
$B = -864.169 \times 10^3$

16-8 Multiply the following two decimal numbers using scientific notation.
$A = 38.76 \times 10^4$
$B = 154.8 \times 10^2$

16-9 Multiply the following two decimal numbers using scientific notation.
$A = -0.61134 \times 10^{+5}$
$B = -431.68 \times 10^{-3}$

16-10 The following numbers are expressed in the decimal system. Divide B by A using scientific notation.
$A = 367.12 \times 10^9$
$B = 724.89 \times 10^{12}$

16-11 The following numbers are given in the decimal system. Divide A by B using scientific notation.
$A = +93.12 \times 10^{-4}$
$B = -23.8 \times 10^{+2}$

16-12 Four 6-bit registers are concatenated and used for BCD floating-point operations. Normal sign conventions are used for both the exponent and the mantissa. Sketch the bit format of this register and indicate the range of numbers represented by it when the MSB are used for the exponent and its sign.

16-13 Refer to the four 6-bit registers of Problem 16-12 and show how BCD quantity $+17.882 \times 10^{+12}$ will appear in this register.

16-14 Again refer to the four 6-bit registers of Problem 16-12 and show how the BCD quantity $-53.78 \times 10^{+8}$ will appear in this register.

16-15 Four 4-bit registers are concatenated for BCD operations. Nibble 4 is used for the exponent and normal sign conventions are used. The following quantities are added.
$A = +0.53 \times 10^{+6}$
$B = +6.38 \times 10^{+4}$
Show the resulting bits in this 12-bit register.

16-16 Refer to the registers of Problem 16-15. Add the following numbers and show the resulting bits in this 16-bit register.
$A = +0.53 \times 10^{+6}$
$B = -6.38 \times 10^{+4}$

16-17 Four 4-bit registers are concatenated for BCD operations. $A = 1.37 \times 10^2$ and $B = 38.2 \ 10^1$. Nibble 4 is used for the exponent, and normal sign conventions are used. Multiply these two quantities and show the resulting product in this 16-bit register.

16-18 Four 6-bit registers are concatenated for BCD operations. $A = +4.381 \times 10^{-11}$ and $B = -73.29 \times 10^{-9}$. Divide A by B using the most significant 6-bit register for the exponent and normal sign conventions. Show the quotient in this 24-bit register.

17

ORGANIZING THE DATA TRANSFORMATION PROCESS

17-1 ORGANIZATION OF DATA STRUCTURES

17-1.1 Graphical Representation of Data Structures

In Chapter 16 we saw that the *processor* processes *data* while the *computing system* processes *information*. Generally, information does *not* exist in formats suitable for processing by the computer system. We must, therefore, *format the information* so that it can be converted into data structures that the computing system can process. Unfortunately, in the field of data processing, no universally accepted standard exists to describe and structure data. In any computing system the program operates on a body of data and transforms them into some different and usable form.

Data can be described and structured in several different ways. The simplest way is by *graphical* representation. Here the various elements comprising a record are broken down into several *items*. Each item is assigned a certain number of characters. Formatting in this manner provides a coherent method of expressing the data. The computer program is designed to operate uniformly on the variables in each record. The graphical approach of representing data structures is shown more clearly by Example 17-1.

Example 17-1

Graphically show how a typical payroll record can be structured for a group of factory employees who are paid on an hourly basis with time-and-a-half for overtime. The fixed elements in the employee's record include employee name, clock number, social security number, department identification code, hourly rate, and number of exemptions claimed.

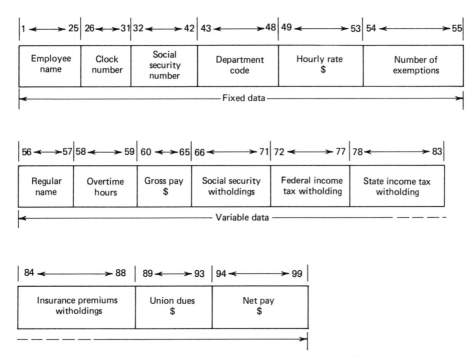

Figure 17-1   Graphical representation of data structure for Example 17-1.

The *elements* in each employee's record (which can vary from one pay period to another) include number of regular hours, number of overtime hours, gross pay, social security withholding, federal income tax withholding, state income tax withholding, retirement fund withholding, insurance premiums withholding, union dues, and net pay. Assign any reasonable number of characters to each item and indicate them on the pictorial representation.

Solution

The data structure of this problem and the number of characters assigned to each field are graphically shown in Fig. 17-1. Notice that we can use ASCII characters, simple numerical characters, or dollar figures, as appropriate.   ∎

17-1.2 Systematic Organization of Data

17-1.2.1 Types and Items   The graphical representation of data, as shown in Example 17-1, is a good way to lay out the various items involved in a typical record. In the initial stages of software design it is a very useful tool, but it has its shortcomings. It is impossible to generate a program from such a pictorial representation. Another way to describe a record is in *tabular* form, as shown in Example 17-2.

Example 17-2

Refer to Example 17-1. Show how the same record could be expressed in tabular form. Indicate the number of characters that would be required for each specific item in the record and what system or codes are used to represent them.

Solution

A look at the various segments of the record in Example 17-1 shows that we can conveniently categorize them in three groups and assign codes as follows where applicable.

1. ASCII codes for descriptive items such as names,
2. Decimal numerics for numerical quantities such as hours,
3. Decimal numerics for dollars and cents.

The record is shown below in a convenient tabular form.

Item Field	Character Numbers	Code Type	Number Required
Fixed data			
Employee Name	1-25	ASCII	25
Clock number	26-31	Numerics	6
Social security number	32-42	Numerics	11
Department code	43-48	ASCII	6
Hourly rate	49-53	$ & ¢	5
Number of exemptions	54-55	Numerics	2
Variable data			
Regular hours	56-57	Numerics	2
Overtime hours	58-59	Numerics	2
Gross pay	60-65	$ & ¢	6
Social security	66-71	$ & ¢	6
Federal income tax	72-77	$ & ¢	6
State income tax	78-83	$ & ¢	6
Insurance premiums	84-88	$ & ¢	5
Union dues	89-93	$ & ¢	5
Net pay	94-99	$ & ¢	6

Examples 17-1 and 17-2 illustrate two concepts that are very important in programming computers, principally in higher-level programming languages. Notice in Example 17-2 that the variable data can be grouped into two distinct *subcategories*. The first subcategory is the *number of hours* (both regular and overtime) that are coded in simple digital numerics. The second subcategory includes *monetary* quantities expressed in dollars and cents. These subcategories introduce us to the concept of *type*. In programming languages type is defined as the various kinds of data any variable quantity may assume. In the preceding examples, the two types of variable data are *hours* and *dollars* and *cents*. Before such variables can be used in higher-level programming languages, some explicit statements declaring the types used are necessary. The type information is necessary when programming in higher-level languages because this information determines:

1. How the values of these variables are represented and coded
2. How the various operations are to be interpreted
3. How much memory needs to be allocated to them.

Again looking at Example 17-2, notice that the two previously mentioned types (hours and dollars and cents) each contain several similar but *separate* pieces of information. These pieces of information that comprise a certain type are called *items*. For instance, in the type previously referred to as the number of hours, we have two items: regular hours and overtime hours. The computing system operates on items and not types. Likewise, only items occupy space in the memory, not types. These types are really abstract concepts, whereas items are real or actual implementations of these abstractions in a computing system and are stored in the memory.

17-1.2.2 Arrays In Sections 17-1.1 and 17-1.2 we discussed and showed two different types of data structures. There is still another form of data structure called an *array*. An array is a block of data in which each element is an item. All items are identical in form and are stored in consecutive locations in the memory. The range of memory addresses occupied by each data word in the array is called the *length* of the array. Each individual item in an array is addressed by a pointer during program operation. The pointer, which is usually preloaded into the index register, provides the starting address of the array. Each item in the array is successively accessed by adding the contents of the index register to the contents of a counter, which is initially cleared to zero and then incremented (or decremented in some cases) through the entire length of the array. (*Note*. In μP literature the term *table* is often used to indicate an array.)

In real-world applications many arrays are used to process a certain given task. Even though the items in each array will have different values, the length of each array and the general formats will be identical. The program in such an application is required to perform the same operations on each corresponding item of each array, so the common program is designed for all the arrays of that application. Such a program involves *looping*. Declaration statements at the beginning of the program give several items such as the value of the pointer, the length of the array, and the number of loops or iterations to be performed. A generalized flowchart of the operation is shown in Fig. 17-2. In this case two counters are used—one for updating the pointer and the other for keeping track of the number of loops.

The flowchart of Fig. 17-2 shows only the steps involved in processing a single array of data. For most applications we would be processing more than

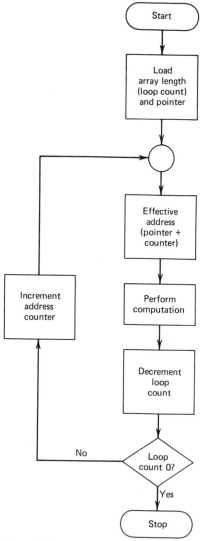

Figure 17-2   Flowchart for processing a single-array data structure.

one array. In that case we would have to store the array count in another counter and decrement this counter after each array is processed. The flowchart of Fig. 17-2 is, therefore, modified and shown in Fig. 17-3, which is a generalized flowchart for processing several arrays of data.

In the case of multiple arrays the starting address (i.e., the pointer) will be *different* for each array. A new pointer would have to be loaded in the index register after the processing of each array is completed. In the algorithm-level flowchart of Fig. 17-3 we have solved this problem by means of the following technique.

All arrays are of equal length. The pointer, which is the starting address of each succeeding array, is separated by the length of the array. If we add the array length to the pointer after processing each array, we can obtain the starting address (i.e., the pointer) for the *next* array. The *updated* pointer is then loaded into the index register. The principles involved here are shown in Examples 17-3 and 17-4.

Example 17-3

An array consists of five items. The items are loaded in memory locations D4 to D8. (The addresses are given in hexadecimal notation.) These five items are to be added and the resulting sum stored in D9. The declaration statements can be stored in locations just prior to the data items. Draw an algorithm-level flowchart for processing this array and explain the steps involved.

Solution

In this example two declaration statements will have to be stored in locations D2 and D3 as follows.

1. Pointer D4 → location D2.
2. Loop count 5 → location D3.

The flowchart for this problem is shown in Fig. 17-4. A previously cleared accumulator is used for generating a progressive total of the five data items. ■

Example 17-4

The array of Example 17-3 is repeated six times (a total of seven times). The initial starting address of the first array is again D4, and the sum is stored in location D9. The declaration statements may be stored in D0 to D3. Draw an algorithm-level flowchart for processing these arrays and explain the steps involved.

Solution

We will now have to load the array count 7 in another counter and decrement it after processing each array. We will use counter C1 for incrementing the address, counter C2 for decrementing the loop count, and counter C3 for decrementing the

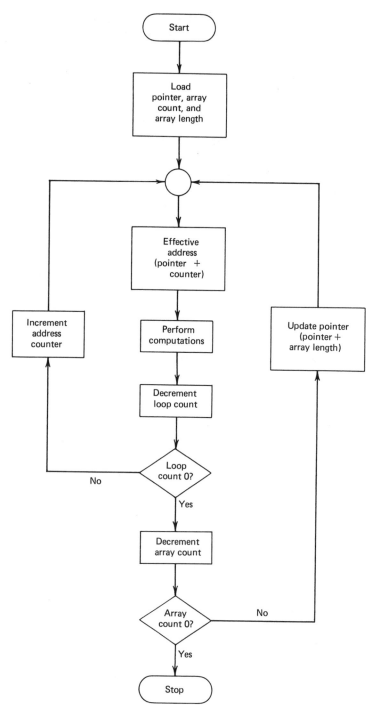

Figure 17-3 Flowchart for processing a multiple-array data structure.

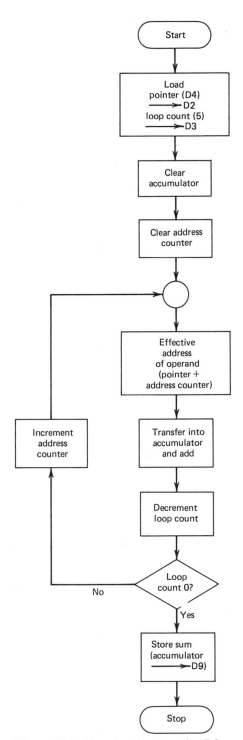

Figure 17-4   Flowchart for Example 17-3.

array count. We will also use two accumulators, ACC1 for progressive totals of the items in the arrays, and ACC2 for generating updated pointers for each successive array. The flowchart is shown in Fig. 17-5. ∎

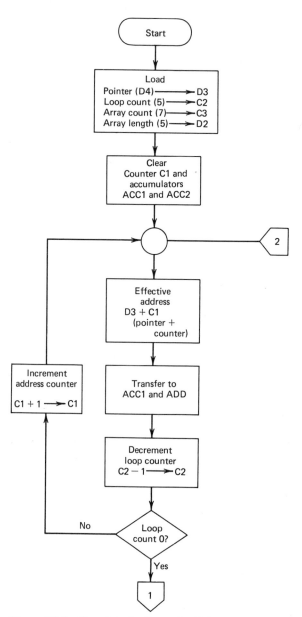

Figure 17-5   Flowchart for Example 17-4.

17-1.2.3 Lists Structuring the data in arrays is simple because each item in the array is stored in contiguous memory locations. Similarly, multiple arrays involved in the same application are also stored in consecutive memory locations. This was shown in Example 17-4. However, in arrays the number of data items involved is the same in each array, so it is easy to estimate the number of required memory locations and, consequently, the memory size in the computing system. For certain applications, such as the payroll application in Examples 17-1 and 17-2, this works well because the number of items (including the fixed and variable data items) is the same in each array. In certain other applications the number of data items in a record could be dif-

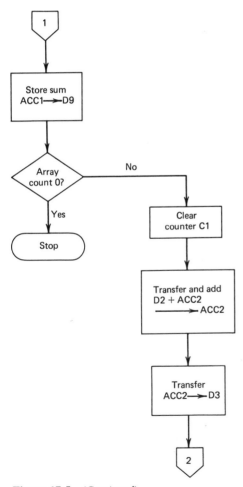

Figure 17-5 *(Continued)*

ferent from one computer run to another. In such a situation structuring the data in arrays would be impossible, since the length of the array may vary each time. This can be better understood by means of the following typical application.

Consider a typical bank credit card billing application. The fixed data include the following items.

1. The cardholder's name.
2. The cardholder's address.
3. The cardholder's account number.
4. The periodic rate of interest on the unpaid balance.

The variable data items include:

1. The previous month's balance.
2. The amount of the last payment by the cardholder.
3. The beginning balance for the current month.
4. Current month's purchases.
5. The total of the beginning balance and current charges.
6. The interest applied to this total.
7. The total outstanding for the current month.
8. The minimum payment due this month.

If these items are structured in an array all the data items would fit nicely except item 4 in the variable data list. A peculiar problem arises with current month's purchases or charges. The number of times that the cardholder uses the credit card for purchases varies from month to month. It is possible that the cardholder may not make any purchases one month and then use the credit card for several purchases the very next month.

Furthermore, the total number of purchases made by all cardholders varies each month. How many different memory locations should be allocated for item 4? The *simplistic* answer to this question is to allocate the *maximum* number of memory locations for each cardholder. But that presents another problem. The maximum number of monthly purchases also varies from one cardholder to another. Besides, even if the maximum number were known and, therefore, the desired number of locations allocated, the total memory size would be very large. The memory would not be utilized in the most effective or economical manner. Clearly, structuring the data in arrays is *not* desirable in such applications. A *list structure* provides a much better solution.

A *list*, or a *chain*, as it is sometimes called, is a group of items where each item consists of two parts: the *data* part and the *pointer*. The data portion of the item contains the actual data on which the computer performs some operation. The pointer portion contains the address of the memory location where the next item in the list is stored. This means that all the items in a record need not be stored in consecutive memory addresses as in an array. It is therefore possible to store items in the list in many different parts of the memory. Each pointer can address a location either ahead or back from its position in the memory. This is shown in Fig. 17-6. The first item in the list is called the *head* of the list. The list is called out by some variable in the memory that points to the head. The last item in the list is called the *tail* of the list. A variable in the memory also points to the tail of the list.

Figure 17-6 shows some interesting points. The head points to memory address 204, which contains the pointer 209. The chart shown in Fig. 17-7 helps to understand the sequence of memory addresses and pointers of the *list* shown in Fig. 17-6.

In Fig. 17-6 note that memory addresses 205 to 208 are not used at all. Also, several items, such as those in addresses 203, 204, 20C, 20D, and so

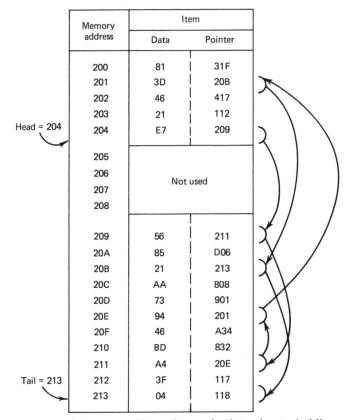

Figure 17-6   Memory address, data, and pointers in a typical list.

Pointer in Address	Points to	Item in Address
204 (Head	⟶	209
209	⟶	211
211	⟶	20E
20E	⟶	201
201	⟶	20B
20B	⟶	213 (Tail)

Figure 17-7   Memory address/pointer chart for Figure 17-6 list.

on, contain data words and pointers but are not used in this list. The items in these locations are parts of lists other than the one in Fig. 17-6.

Each item in the list in Fig. 17-6 contains a pointer that points to the address of the next item in the list. In other words, the processing of the data in the list proceeds in one direction only (i.e., starting with the head and ending with the tail). Such a list is called a *single-ended list* or a *one-way list*. The pointer used in each item in such a list is called a *forward pointer* (sometimes also called a *right pointer*).

There are certain applications where it is desirable to process the items in the list in *reverse* order. This would not be possible with a single-ended list such as the one in Fig. 17-6. To process this list in reverse order, we would require a *backward pointer* (or a *left pointer*), which points to the address of the preceding item in the list. Such a list is called a *double-ended* or *two-way list*. The list of Fig. 17-6 can be converted into a double-ended list by including both forward and backward pointers in each item, as shown in Fig. 17-8.

To simplify the list in Fig. 17-8, several entries for backward pointers not related to this particular list are omitted. Also, note that the roles of the head and the tail are reversed when the list is processed in the reverse order. The chart in Fig. 17-9 helps students to understand the sequence of memory addresses and backward pointers for the double-ended list of Fig. 17-8.

17-1.2.4 Data Structures and Memory Requirements Regardless of how they are structured, data are stored in the data memory. How data are structured determines how much memory is required to process certain tasks. Memory costs money, so it is always desirable to utilize the available storage space in the most efficient and cost-effective manner. If the number of items in each record is preestablished and does not vary, as in the payroll application in Examples 17-1 and 17-2, an array structure would be most effective and would use the *least* number of memory locations. On the other hand, if the number

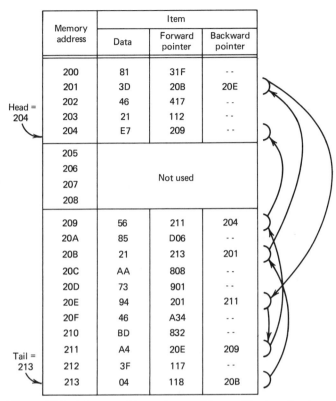

Memory address	Item		
	Data	Forward pointer	Backward pointer
200	81	31F	- -
201	3D	20B	20E
202	46	417	- -
203	21	112	- -
204	E7	209	- -
205			
206		Not used	
207			
208			
209	56	211	204
20A	85	D06	- -
20B	21	213	201
20C	AA	808	- -
20D	73	901	- -
20E	94	201	211
20F	46	A34	- -
210	BD	832	- -
211	A4	20E	209
212	3F	117	- -
213	04	118	20B

Head = 204

Tail = 213

Figure 17-8   Memory address, data, and forward/backward pointers in a typical double-ended list.

of items cannot be precisely pinpointed and varies, as in the previously discussed billing application, the array structure would not be used. The list structure, such as the one in Fig. 17-6, would be most effective.

When using the list structure, we are still faced with the question of how much memory space should be allocated to each list. Referring to Fig. 17-6, we see that memory locations 205 to 208 are not used. In the billing application it is possible that, during the next month's billing cycle, even less location may be required and therefore more memory space available. In the following month the situation may be reversed for this particular cardholder, and more memory locations may be required. This raises the question of how we could allocate the empty memory locations that are made available.

The problem of keeping track of the available memory space is solved by means of a device or approach called a *free-space* list. This list is a continuous record of all the free or empty locations available in the memory. The items in the free-space list contain only the addresses of the other locations that are empty (in other words, only pointers). The free-space list is a bank of available

Backward Pointer in Address	Points to	Item in Address
213 (Tail)	⟶	20B
20B	⟶	201
201	⟶	20E
20E	⟶	211
211	⟶	209
209	⟶	204 (Head)

Figure 17-9   Memory address/backward pointer chart for Figure 17-8 double-ended list.

memory resources and is a flexible list. It keeps expanding and shrinking. When a certain record, such as that of the cardholder in the billing application, is updated with new items, an item can be removed from the free-space list and appended to the main list that is being processed. Likewise, items from the main list can be deleted and the available space added to the free-space list. Figure 17-10 shows such a list.

The list approach to structuring data is very flexible. Data items can be inserted in and deleted from existing lists quite conveniently. In an array, however, if an item must be *inserted*, all the succeeding items *below* the insertion point must be moved *down*. Similarly, if an item has to be *deleted*, a gap is created and the items succeeding such a deletion must be moved *up*. For applications having lengthy arrays and also a large number of arrays,

Memory	Item	
Address	Data	Pointer
385	—	6A2
6A2	—	700
700	—	34D
34D	—	21E
21E	—	AAA
AAA	—	245
245	—	910
910	—	638
638	—	—

Figure 17-10   Memory address, data, and pointers in a typical free-space list.

additions and deletions of numerous items could be very expensive in terms of processing time and, ultimately, in dollars. List structures are more desirable in these cases. There are also other advantages. If data are arranged in list structures, sorting and merging operations can be accomplished with relative ease.

17-2 FUNDAMENTAL FUNCTIONAL STATEMENTS

Computer software may be designed and developed using one of several different languages, ranging from the simplest machine language, consisting of 1s and 0s, to high-level languages such as FORTRAN, COBOL, and BASIC. Regardless of which language is used, the program incorporates one or more of six basic fundamental groups of statements that are covered in this section. In Section 17-1 we discussed the various ways in which data may be structured. The role of the computer is to operate on these data and transform them into desired results. This transformation is accomplished by software. Transformation of data involves certain processes and procedures. These processes and procedures can be expressed in many different ways. Unfortunately, there is no standardized system of expressing them. In this chapter we show a very simple system where statements are similar to everyday English-language statements. This will help students to get started without being embroiled in a maze of complex codes and terminology. Before we show the procedures and processes, let us look at the six categories of statements.

1. *Descriptional and Data Transfer Statements*. This group of statements deals primarily with the movement of data within the computing system under *program control*. They assign the sources and destinations of data movements such as various registers/counters in the CPU, the memory, and the different I/O devices. As a matter of convenience, a single statement is often used to indicate a transfer (or transfers) of entire groups of items.
2. *Data Operation and Manipulation Statements*. These statements perform certain specific, but limited, functions on data that are moved or transferred within the computing system by means of the descriptional and data transfer statements. The statements in this group perform some computation or logical operation. They comprise the majority of statements in the program.
3. *Decision or Conditional Statements*. These statements, generally referred to as IF statements, make it possible for the program to perform (or not perform) certain specific functions only if certain conditions are prevalent. The decision to perform (or not to perform) these functions is made automatically by the computer as the actual data are being processed. Decisions will vary depending on the input data and the prescribed conditions.

4. *Transfer of Control Statements*. This group of statements effectively INTERRUPT and HALT the statements currently being processed. The control of the program is transferred to some other statement located some other place in the program. In some transfer statements, control is automatically returned to the original statement that was previously interrupted or halted. In other words, return of control is not necessarily automatic.

5. *Iterative or Looping Statements*. The purpose of these statements is to loop or cycle through a given set of statements in a *repetitious* manner. The number of loops or iterations could be *predetermined* and so indicated in the program. In this case the program automatically loops through these statements for a fixed number of times, regardless of the data being processed or any other conditions. In many cases the number of loops can be made dependent on some criterion in the data being processed. Such a criterion is usually automatically monitored after completing each loop, and the decision is made whether to loop once more or break out of the loop.

6. *Miscellaneous Statements*. Occasionally, there are statements that do not fall neatly into any of the five preceding categories. Nonetheless, they may be needed for a particular application. Such statements are usually grouped into a miscellaneous category.

17-3 THE PROBLEM DEFINITION PROCESS

The six categories of statements in Section 17-2 would not be useful unless we can organize them into a format that will enable us to construct a useful program. Of course, the primary reason for designing a *generalized* program is that the *same* program can be used to obtain the results from different sets of data that are input into the system. For instance, if we are able to calculate the area of a circle having a given radius, a computer program would not be worthwhile if the areas of only one or two circles had to be calculated. A simple hand-held calculator would do the job nicely. On the other hand, if we were required to calculate the areas of circles having 300 different values of radii, the calculator is inadequate. Now a computer program is justified.

17-3.1 Generalized Statements

17-3.1.1 Single-Pass Structure Before we put down a statement structure, we must decide the *order of magnitude* for the input data and the calculated results to have. This is necessary because the data will be stored in the data memory of the computer, and we must allocate required space in that memory. In the case of the area of the circle we must know whether the radii are expressed in inches, feet, yards, or miles, in centimeters, meters, or kilometers, or in some other units. It is also necessary to know *what* I/O devices will be involved in the program. The following statement structure is generalized and so is applicable to any problem. As shown, this structure will execute only a single pass through the program.

ALLOCATE MEMORY AREAS FOR INPUTS
INPUT THE DATA
PROCESS
OUTPUT RESULTS

This statement structure does not specify what the process is or what the data inputs are. This will be clarified later in this chapter by means of examples.

17-3.1.2 Iterative Loops Structure The statement structure in Section 17-3.1.1 will not be adequate if more than one pass through the program is to be executed. If a preestablished number of passes are desired, the structure would be modified to include an additional statement, as shown.

ALLOCATE MEMORY AREAS FOR INPUTS
INPUT THE DATA
PROCESS
OUTPUT RESULTS
"IF" LESS THAN PREESTABLISHED LOOPS, "THEN" RETURN TO THE STATEMENT INPUT THE DATA. "ELSE" TERMINATE PROGRAM.

Examples 17-5 to 17-7 show how these generalized statement structures can be used in specific applications.

Example 17-5

Construct a statement structure in simple English for a program to calculate the area of a circle of a given radius. Only one pass is made through the program. Explain each statement.

Solution

The area of a circle is given by the formula $A = \pi r^2$ where A = the area of the circle, r = the radius of the circle, and $\pi = 3.14159. . .$, which is a constant.
    The structure consists of the following five statements:

1. ALLOCATE MEMORY LOCATIONS FOR A, r AND π.

2. INPUT r AND π.
3. $A = \pi r^2$.
4. OUTPUT A.
5. END OF PROGRAM.

Statement 1 stores r and π into the memory and assigns a location for A. Statement 2 calls out the two input quantities, and statement 3 processes them by the appropriate formula. Statement 4 stores the computed result in the memory, and statement 5 terminates the program. ∎

Example 17-6

Refer to Example 17-5. Construct a statement structure in simple English to repeat or loop this program 15 times for 15 different values of radii.

Solution

This time the structure will contain one more statement.

1. ALLOCATE MEMORY LOCATIONS FOR A, r, AND π.
2. INPUT r AND π.
3. $A = \pi r^2$.
4. OUTPUT A.
5. IF CALCULATED LESS THAN 15 TIMES, THEN RETURN TO THE STATEMENT INPUT r AND π. ELSE PROCEED.
6. END OF PROGRAM.

Statement 5 performs the monitoring and looping around a preestablished number of times (15). ∎

Example 17-7

Construct a statement structure in simple English to calculate the circumference of circles whose radii increase from 5 cm upward in increments of 1 cm. The calculated circumference must not exceed 96 cm. If it does, the program must be terminated.

Solution

The solution in this problem is more complicated. After completing each circumference calculation, which is given by the formula $C = 2\pi r$, the radius will have to be updated for the next computation. Also, after completing each computation, the result must be checked against the maximum of 96 cm before looping around again. Let

$$I = 1$$

r_0 = 5 cm
r_1 = the updated value of radius (r_1 = r_0 + I)
C_{max} = 96 cm
C = the calculated value of the circumference
π = 3.14159. . .

The statement structure follows.

1. ALLOCATE LOCATIONS FOR I, r_0, r_1, C_{max}, C, 2, AND π.
2. INPUT r_1 and π.
3. $C = 2\pi r_1$.
4. OUTPUT C.
5. IF C IS LESS THAN C_{max} THEN PROCEED. ELSE TERMINATE PRO-GRAM.
6. UPDATE r_1 (i.e., r_1 + 1) AND RETURN TO STATEMENT INPUT r, π.
7. END OF PROGRAM.

Notice that at first pass, r_1 = r_0. At subsequent passes, I is added to r_1. ∎

17-3.2 Using Subroutines

Examples 17-6 and 17-7 use transfer-of-control statements that effectively return control to some location other than its original location that was the point of exit from the main program. This is always the case with program looping and is graphically shown in Fig. 17-11a. In this section we will discuss transfer-of-control statements that return control back to the same point in the main program. Obviously, such statements involve subroutines. This is shown in Fig. 17-11b.

The situation in Fig. 17-11b, which could call out more than one subroutine or the same subroutine several times, can be shown by the following generalized statement structure. In this case two different subroutines are called out from different parts of the main program.

ALLOCATE AREAS FOR INPUTS
INPUT THE DATA
PROCESS
CALL SUBROUTINE X
RETURN TO THE MAIN PROGRAM
PROCESS
CALL SUBROUTINE Y
RETURN TO THE MAIN PROGRAM
PROCESS
OUTPUT RESULT

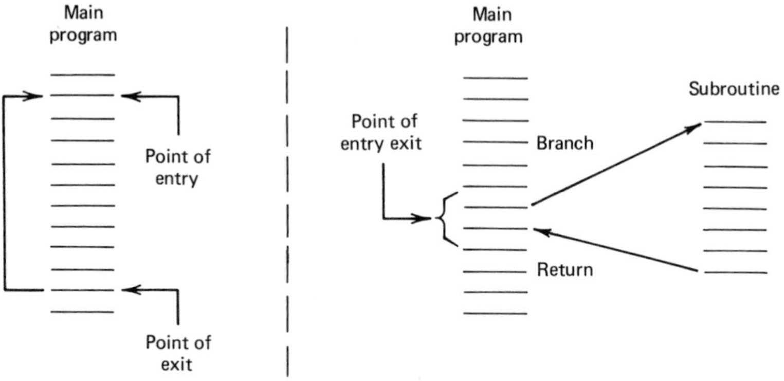

(a) Control returned to different location (looping)

(b) Control returned to the same location (branch to subroutine)

Figure 17-11   Two cases of transfer-of-control statements.

Figure 17-12 shows this statement structure graphically. Example 17-8 shows the situation involved in Fig. 17-12.

Example 17-8

A quadratic equation is of the form $ax^2 + bx + c = 0$, where x is the unknown quantity, a, b, and c represent known numbers, and $a \neq 0$. The value of x can be determined by the following general quadratic equation formula.

$$x = \frac{-b + \sqrt{b^2 - 4ac}}{2a}$$

Construct a statement structure to process the quadratic equation formula for six different sets of values for a, b, and c.

Solution

In this case we will use *two* subroutines. The first one will perform a square root operation on the result of the operation $(b^2 - 4ac)$, and the second one will be a *division* subroutine that divides the numerator by the denominator. The statement structure follows.

1.   ALLOCATE LOCATIONS FOR INPUTS a, b, c AND CONSTANTS 2 AND 4.
2.   INPUT THE DATA.
3. $b^2 - 4ac = y_1$.
4.   CALL SUBROUTINE, $\sqrt{y_1} = y_2$.
5.   RETURN TO THE MAIN PROGRAM.
6. $-b + y_2 = y_3$.

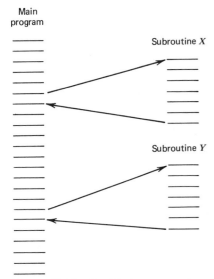

Figure 17-12   Main program Subroutine X Subroutine Y

Figure 17-12   Graphical representation of the statement structure of Figure 17-11.

7. $2a = y_4$.
8.   CALL SUBROUTINE, $y_3/y_4 = x$.
9.   RETURN TO THE MAIN PROGRAM.
10. IF CALCULATED LESS THAN 6 TIMES, THEN RETURN TO THE STATEMENT INPUT THE DATA. ELSE PROCEED.
11. END OF PROGRAM.   ■

Example 17-8 uses all the categories of functional statements discussed in Section 17-2 except one—miscellaneous statements. The various categories involved and the step numbers of Example 17-8 are now summarized.

1. *Descriptional and Data Transfer Statements*
   Step 2   INPUT THE DATA
2. *Data Operation and Manipulation Statements*
   Step 3 $b^2 - 4ac = y_1$
   Step 6 $-b + y_2 = y_3$
   Step 7 $2a = y_4$
3. *Decision or Conditional Statements*
   Step 10   IF CALCULATED LESS THAN 6 TIMES, etc.
4. *Transfer of Control Statements*
   Step 4   CALL SUBROUTINE, $\sqrt{y_1} = y_2$
   Step 5   RETURN TO MAIN PROGRAM
   Step 6   CALL SUBROUTINE, $y_3/y_4 = x$
   Step 7   RETURN TO MAIN PROGRAM

5. *Iterative or Looping Statements*
   Step #10   IF CALCULATED LESS THAN 6 TIMES, etc.

17-3.3 Miscellaneous Statements

Until now we have not used any miscellaneous statements. They are nonetheless very important. Miscellaneous statements consist of comments, explanations, and remarks relating to the main program, the various subroutines, and other pertinent facts concerning the *software* effort. These statements are of historical importance and are written in plain, understandable English. Reference to the program at a later date, either by another person or the same programmer (for purposes of explanation or modifications) may result in much wasted time, to say nothing of personal embarassment and anguish if such comments are *not* included. What are these comments and explanations? Refer back to Example 17-8. Some of the typical comments on this program follow.

Comments on the Main Program. The program calculates the value of the unknown quantity in a quadratic equation for six sets of values of the known quantities. Quantity a is not zero. The program allocates memory locations for all six sets of known quantities a, b, and c as well as the two constants 2 and 4.

The general quadratic formula is used for the solution. The formula is broken down into four segments identified as y_1, y_2, y_3, and y_4, and each segment is processed separately. A looping statement executes six passes through the program, one for each set of known quantities a, b, and c. Two standard subroutines are used, as explained next.

Comments on Subroutines. A standard subroutine for performing square roots (available in the library of subroutines) is used. The result of the algebraic operation $b^2 - 4ac$ is called y_1 and is processed first. Then the square root of y_1 (called y_2) is obtained by executing this square-root subroutine. A standard subroutine for performing division (also available in the library of subroutines) is used. The value of the number referred to as y_3 is calculated first by performing $-b + y_2$. The value of the denominator, referred to as y_4, is obtained by performing the operation 2a. The final solution to the problem (i.e., the value of x) is obtained by dividing y_3 by y_4 using the division subroutine.

17-4 SUMMARY

The first part of this chapter dealt with various forms of data structures and their organization. A graphical representation of data structures was shown by means of an example using a typical payroll record. The same example was used to show the record in tabular form. The number of characters required and the system or codes used were also included in this tabular form. The concepts of types of data and the various items that make up the types were introduced. It was pointed out that types were abstractions whereas items were real entities that could be stored in the memory and operated on by the computer.

The concept of arrays was presented. The processing of data, structured as arrays, was explained by means of flowcharts for both single-array and multiple-array data structures. The shortcoming of the array were pointed out using a credit card record application where the number of data items periodically varied. The concept of a list or chain and how it could overcome some of the disadvantages of the array was introduced. Definitions of the head and tail of a list were included, and the use of the pointer was explained. One-way lists and two-way lists were discussed along with the use of two pointers. The impact of data structures on memory space requirements was discussed, and the concept of free-space list was explained.

The second part of the chapter included discussions on the concept of functional statements in computer software. The six principal categories of functional statements were presented and discussed. For simplicity, statements were presented in simple English, not in any specific computer language. Both single-pass and iterative loop structures were discussed with several simple examples. The use of subroutines was demonstrated by an example for the solution of a mathematical formula.

17-5 REVIEW QUESTIONS

17-1   Does *information* generally exist in formats suitable for computer processing? If not, how is it handled?

17-2   If data are presented in a graphical or pictorial format, what information is generally included in such a presentation? How is it handled?

17-3   Briefly describe how data in a record can be presented in tabular form and what is contained in such a table.

17-4   Define *type* as used in programming languages. Give some examples.

17-5   Define *items* as used in programming languages. Give some examples.

17-6   In a computing system, which are stored in the memory, *types, items,* or both? Which is (are) processed by the computer? Why?

17-7   Define an *array*.

17-8   What is meant by the *length* of an *array?*

17-9   For processing data structured as an *array,* a pointer is used. Where is this pointer located? What is its function and how does it operate?

17-10   If data are structured as arrays, does the program involve any looping? If so, why?

17-11 In a program several arrays are to be processed. Each array has a different starting address. Assuming that all arrays are of equal length, how is the starting address pointer updated?

17-12 Define the *list* method of structuring data for processing. What are the parts in an *item* in a normal *list?*

17-13 What do the terms *head* and *tail* mean as applied to data *lists?*

17-14 What is the difference, if any, between the pointer used in an array and the pointer used in a list?

17-15 What is the difference between *single-ended* and *double-ended* lists?

17-16 Which of the two data structures, the *array* or the *list,* provides greater flexibility? Why?

17-17 Would the array structure or the list structure require more memory space? Why?

17-18 What is the *free-space list?* What does it do?

17-19 What do the *items* in the *free-space list* contain?

17-20 Name the six fundamental functional statements that are used in different computer languages.

17-21 In simple English write a structure of statements that will execute a single pass through a program.

17-22 Refer to Question 17-20. Into which category does a statement that contains ''IF . . ., THEN . . ., ELSE . . .'' fall?

17-23 In simple English write a structure of statements that will execute a series of loops through a program.

17-24 Into which categories of fundamental functional statements do each of the following statements fall?
(a) CALL SUBROUTINE ($a = \frac{1}{2}bh$)
(b) RETURN TO MAIN PROGRAM.
(c) CALL SUBROUTINE ($v = \pi d^2/4 \times 1$).
(d) RETURN TO MAIN PROGRAM.

17-6 PROBLEMS AND EXERCISES

17-1 A mail-order house maintains a mailing list of all its customers in the memory banks of its computing system. For periodic mailings of its catalogs and other literature, address labels and a mailing list are prepared on the computer. Graphically show how a typical record can be structured for each customer who is also assigned a 6-digit account number. First two initials, last name, and complete address are used for each customer.

17-2 Refer to Problem 17-1. Show the same record in tabular form. Indicate the number of characters required for each item in the record and what system of codes is used to represent them.

17-3 An array consists of seven items that are loaded into memory locations 122 to 128. The addresses are in hexadecimal notations. These items are to be added and the resulting sum stored in address 121. The declaration statements are stored in locations just prior to the data items. Draw an algorithm-level flowchart for processing this array and explain the steps involved.

17-4 An array consists of 15 items that are loaded into memory locations C11 to C1F. The addresses are in hexadecimal notations. The first 9 items are to be added and the remaining 6 subtracted from this sum. The result is stored in location C10. The declaration statements are stored in locations just prior to the result location. Draw an algorithm-level flowchart for processing this array and explain the steps involved. Only one accumulator is available, but scratch-pad locations E00 to E07 can be used for storing partial results.

17-5 Refer to the array of Problem 17-3. Draw an algorithm-level flowchart for processing this array 24 times. In the CPU of this system four counters and four accumulators are available. Explain the steps involved.

17-6 The following table relates to a typical single-ended list. Compute entries for the column marked "Item in Address."

Pointer in Address	Points to	Item in Address
6801 (Head)	⟶	----
071D	⟶	----
1BB8	⟶	----
3C19	⟶	----
2807	⟶	----
9F12	⟶	----
1144	⟶	----
382A	⟶	2811 (Tail)

17-7 The following table relates to a typical double-ended list. Fill in the blanks in the appropriate columns.

Pointer in Address	Points to	Item in Address
732 (Head)	⟶	---
DA8	⟶	271
---	⟶	138
138	⟶	---
9E4	⟶	172
---	⟶	384
---	⟶	1BB (Tail)

17-8   Construct a statement structure in simple English for a program to calculate the circumference of a circle of a given radius. Explain each statement involved for only one pass through the program.

17-9   Refer to Problem 17-8. Construct a statement structure to repeat or loop this program 12 times for different values of radii.

17-10 Construct a statement structure for a program to calculate the volume of a cylinder whose length, l, in centimeters remains constant but whose diameter, d_{5-15}, varies from 5 to 15 cm in increments of 1 cm.

17-11 A, B, and C represent the three angles of any oblique triangle, such as those shown here, and a, b, and c represent the lengths of the sides opposite to those angles, respectively.

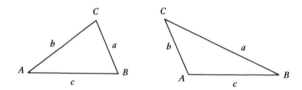

Construct a statement for calculating the area of any oblique triangle given the lengths of the three sides a, b, and c. Any standard subroutine in the library may be used.

18

INTRODUCTION TO BASIC

18-1 INTRODUCTORY REMARKS

We can always program a computer in machine language, the language of 1s and 0s that the computer understands and uses.

For the human being such a language is inconvenient, difficult to work with, and prone to errors. It is more desirable to program in a language that both the computer and the programmer can understand. From the programmer's point of view, the most desirable language is a *procedure-oriented* language that is oriented more toward the problem at hand and is essentially independent of the computer. There are several such procedure-oriented or higher-level languages available. For example, COBOL (Common Business-Oriented Language) is widely used for business type applications. FORTRAN (Formula Translation) is more suited for scientific and engineering problems.

One of the most popular higher-level languages used in microcomputers is BASIC, which is an acronym for Beginner's All-Purpose Symbolic Instruction Code. BASIC was developed by John Kemeny and Thomas Kurtz at Dartmouth College between 1963 and 1964. Because FORTRAN has certain complexities, it is somewhat difficult for the average student to understand and use. BASIC was developed to overcome this situation. Although it lacks some of the sophistication of FORTRAN, it is nevertheless a full-fledged, *higher-level* language that is widely used in the microcomputer field and is relatively easy to learn.

BASIC is fundamentally an interactive, interpretive language. It is popular in the microcomputer field because of several advantages, some of which are briefly described below.

1. Although it was developed primarily for scientific and engineering applications, BASIC has a certain degree of flexibility and can be readily used for many other types of applications or algorithms.
2. BASIC is an interactive language. It was specifically developed for conversational

453

use, thereby allowing the user to communicate and interact directly with the computing system. This allows the user to test, change, or replace an instruction or a group of instructions easily and as required. Consequently, the process of program development is significantly speeded up. The interactive nature of BASIC makes it particularly attractive for applications that require immediate responses from the computer.

3. BASIC was developed for use with I/O that are commonly available in several computing systems, such as teletype units and typewriters. The language was developed to use the characters available on the teletype unit.

4. The rules for structuring the BASIC statements (called the *syntax*) are simple and well defined. They are unambiguous and, therefore, are not subject to misinterpretations by different programmers and users. This feature makes it easy to document programs written in BASIC for future reference.

5. BASIC is used extensively in time-sharing applications, which allows several users to use interactively the resources of a central computer from remotely located terminals. Communication is generally over existing telephone lines. In such cases the main computer's time is shared to process several different tasks.

Since BASIC is so widely used in the field, many improvements, modifications, and additions have been made over the years. In this chapter we introduce "basic" BASIC (i.e., the simplest form of the BASIC language) as well as an advanced form often called *extended* BASIC.

18-2 THE STRUCTURE OF BASIC

18-2.1 Statements and Line Numbers

A program written in BASIC consists of a group of instructions called *statements*. Each statement is constructed with numbers, alphanumeric characters, and other symbols that are arranged according to the specific rules of grammar (or syntax) of the BASIC language. Generally, each BASIC statement corresponds roughly to one box in the previously designed flowchart.

Each BASIC statement can be input into the computer memory by typing it on a terminal, such as a teletype unit or a typewriter, or some other input media such as punched cards or paper tapes. A BASIC program stored in a computer memory still has to be translated into the machine language of the computer on which it has to be executed. A compiler is a program that scans each BASIC statement character by character, analyzes it for its precise meaning, and translates or converts each statement into a set or sequence of equivalent machine language instructions for that specific computing system. To facilitate this process, each statement is assigned a line number and each succeeding statement is given a number in numerically ascending order. One of the rules of BASIC is that the line numbers consist of 1 to 5 contiguous decimal digits with no spaces appearing in the line numbers. Also, the first statement in a BASIC program, or sequence, must have the lowest line number and the last statement the highest line number.

A program written in BASIC and consisting of numerous lines of statements is called the *source program*. The machine language program that results from the conversion process is called the *object program* (sometimes also called the *target program*).

18-2.2 The Reserved or Key Words

In BASIC each statement starts with a *key* word that directs the computer to perform a specific function such as input data, loop around, or branch. A group of such words is reserved for BASIC statements, and each word has a very *clear, precise,* and *unambiguous* meaning. A list of these words follows.

1. DATA.
2. DEF.
3. GOSUB.
4. GOTO.
5. END.
6. DIM.
7. INPUT.
8. MAT.
9. IF/THEN.
10. FOR/NEXT.
11. PRINT.
12. READ.
13. RESTORE.
14. LET.
15. RETURN.
16. STOP.
17. REM.
18. EXP.
19. LOG.
20. SQR.
21. SGN.
22. COS.
23. TAN.
24. SIN.
25. ATN.
26. ABS.
27. INT.
28. RND.

18-2.3 The BASIC Operators

The key words listed in Section 18-2.2 direct the computer system to perform certain functions. A BASIC statement may contain symbolic names that denote values. In some cases these values may be constants but, in many instances, they are variables. Since BASIC was primarily developed for scientific and engineering applications, many statements use arithmetic or algebraic expressions. Such expressions consist of operands (which may be either constants or variables) that are linked together by some operator such as a plus sign (+). Other operands or variables may also be linked by other operators that are not arithmetic operators but that express other relationships such as numerical comparison operators.

18-2.3.1 Arithmetic Operators These operators involve symbols that are involved in the four fundamental arithmetic operations: addition, subtraction, multiplication, and division, and exponentiation. The symbols are shown in the following table.

Symbols	Arithmetic Functions
+	*Addition.* Shown by the conventional plus sign
−	*Subtraction.* Shown by the conventional minus sign
*	*Multiplication.* Shown by an asterisk
/	*Division.* Shown by a stroke
↑	*Exponentiation.* Shown by an upward pointing arrow; sometimes ** (two asterisks) are substituted

18-2.3.2 Comparison Operators These operators allow the programmer to establish relationships between two quantities based on their relative numerical magnitudes. The following six operators are used in BASIC.

Symbols	Magnitude Relationships
=	Denotes "equal to" (e.g., $A = B$ means A equals B)
>	Denotes "greater than" (e.g., $A > B$ means A is greater than B)
<	Denotes "less than" (e.g., $A < B$ means A is less than B)
><	Denotes "not equal to" (e.g., $A >< B$ means A is not equal to B)
> =	Denotes "equal to or greater than" (e.g., $A > = B$ means A is equal to or greater than B)
< =	Denotes "equal to or less than" (e.g., $A < = B$ means A is equal to or less than B)

18-2.3.3 Other Operators In addition to the symbols given in Sections 18-2.3.1 and 18-2.3.2, several other symbols are used in BASIC. They are described next.

Symbols	Functions
,	A comma is used for separating elements of a list or subscripts
:	A colon is used for separating elements of a list (sometimes also used for separating multiple instructions on a single statement line)
( )	Parentheses are used to enclose literals or other groupings
) (	Inverted parentheses are used to enclose list or group expressions
.	Decimal point

18-2.4 Assigned Names

The main reason for designing a general-purpose program is that the same program can be used to process several runs with different sets or combinations of input data. The programmer assigns names to the various data items that are to be processed or manipulated by the computer. Such a procedure enables us to use different data for each run of the program. It also allows the numerical value of a certain quantity to be altered during program execution. Generally, the names assigned to the data items refer to a location in the mainframe memory (usually the data memory, although it is possible to refer to the program memory, too). Thus the data stored in that specific memory location or operated on by the processor during program execution can be referenced by using the name assigned to that particular memory location.

18-2.4.1 Numeric Variable Names Names assigned to quantities that vary or change in value(s) during program execution are called *variable names*. In BASIC a *numeric variable* is indicated by a single alphabetical letter (the capitals A to Z are used) or a single alphabetical letter followed by a single-digit numeral. Shown here are some typical examples of legitimate numeric variables in BASIC.

B,   D,   E7,   Z4,   D8,   H

Variable names such as those shown here are illegitimate and not acceptable in BASIC.

7E,   4Z,   8D,   M½,   S¼

18-2.4.2 Alphabetical Character Strings In many data-processing applications groups of related alphabetical characters (called *alphabetical character strings*) are processed or manipulated on just like variable data. Names can also be assigned to such character strings. In BASIC names assigned to character strings consist of a single alphabetical letter (capitals) followed immediately by a dollar sign ($). Note that each name represents a specific number of characters, and this number depends on the particular version of BASIC that is used. In most computers the maximum length of a character string is 18 characters, but it could be shorter. Here are some typical examples of names assigned to character strings.

G$,   A$,   D$,   P$,   V$

18-2.4.3 Literal Constants A string of alphanumeric characters that is treated as a single unit by the computer is called a *literal constant*. Such a character string is normally stored in the memory and printed out in its entirety as a group. The values of these character strings are not altered during program execution. Such strings are used for printing out names, addresses, account numbers, and the like. In BASIC literal constants are indicated by enclosing them in quotation marks. Some typical examples are:

"CHARLIE BROWN JR"
"123 MAIN STREET"
"CAPITAL CITY USA"
"ACCOUNT NO 268-34D"

18-2.5 Storage of Arrays

In Section 17-1.2.2 we described the structure of an array, where all items (or elements) in the array are identical in form and are stored in consecutive memory locations. BASIC provides a means of storing arrays in memory. It is possible to assign a separate name for each element or item in an array, but this is cumbersome. It is much easier to assign a name to the array and name each item by its respective position in the array by means of a subscript. An example follows in which the array is named F and each of the eight locations in it is identified by a subscript. The contents of a location can then be called out by its assigned name.

Assigned Name	Memory Contents
F(1)	37
F(2)	21
F(3)	88
F(4)	91
F(5)	10
F(6)	16
F(7)	43
F(8)	51

18-3 CATEGORIES OF BASIC STATEMENTS

All the functional statements in BASIC fall into one of the six fundamental categories. They are listed here with a short explanation of each category.

1. *Assignment Statements*. These statements assign the desired numerical value(s) to different quantities. The quantities may be constants or variables.
2. *Control Statements*. These statements direct the computing system to perform several different operations. Typical operations in this group include program decisions to JUMP, LOOP, or BRANCH.
3. *Arithmetic Statements*. These statements direct the computer to perform arithmetic operations such as addition, subtraction, and so forth.
4. *I/O Statements*. These statements direct the computer to perform one of the following three operations.
   (a) Read and input data from within the program
   (b) Input data from the typewriter or the teletype unit
   (c) Output data and print out on either the typewriter or the teletype unit.
5. *Matrix Statements*. These statements direct the computer to perform operations on numerical quantities according to the rules governing matrix algebra.
6. *Specific Statements*. These are miscellaneous statements that perform a variety of functions. Typically, they assign memory locations for arrays, define mathematical formulas, and so on.

The functions performed by these categories of statements will be better understood by several examples that are given later in this chapter. First, we will describe the fundamental BASIC statements and how they are used.

18-4 FUNDAMENTAL STATEMENTS OF BASIC

In this section we examine and describe the fundamental statements of BASIC, their forms, what they mean, and how they are used. Students should pay particular attention to these statements because they are the foundation of all programming in BASIC.

18-4.1 The REM Statement

This is the REMARKS statement, which is inserted in the body of the program. These statements simply provide a mechanism for documenting annotations and comments concerning the program right in the program itself. Of course, programs can be written without REMARKS but, if the need arises to revise or modify the program at a later date (regardless of who wrote the original program), these annotations can simplify your task very much.

The use of this statement assumes that the text of the REMARKS is in printable characters. The standard format of this statement is shown here. Notice that it must start with the line number, followed by the letters REM, which are followed by a line of the text.

Line number REM text

In the program listing the REM statement is printed out exactly as entered by the programmer without any changes in order or spacing. If the text of the statement is too long to be accommodated on one line, it is divided into two separate statements.

When the letters REM are placed after the line number, the compiler recognizes the following text as remarks or annotations and not a procedural statement. Consequently, the remarks are saved in the memory and retained in the source program but are ignored when the object program is produced. Some examples of the REM statement follow.

Example 18-1

A program for inventory control is written in BASIC using 2 digits for the line number. Write down a typical REM statement for this program.

Solution

A typical statement in BASIC is

34   REM PROGRAM I09 INVENTORY CONTROL

In this statement 34 is arbitrarily assigned as the line number. The particular program for inventory control is identified by Program I09.   ■

Example 18-2

In a program written in BASIC an annotation is desirable when the program reaches a certain point where the progressive total of several variables is computed and checked against a constant, that is, 8050. A decision must be made to continue with the main program if the sum is less than 8050. If it is equal to or greater than 8050, the program must branch to subroutine 345. Write down the REM statement(s) for this situation. You are limited to 42 alphanumeric characters (including blanks) in the text portion of each line of the statement.

Solution

Since we are limited to 42 alphanumeric characters (including blanks) in the text portion of each line, we will have to break up the statement into two lines.

```
104   REM   IF   SUM   <   8050   CONTINUE MAIN PROGRAM
105   REM   IF   SUM   > = 8050   BRANCH TO SUBROUTINE 345
```

18-4.2 The LET Statement

The LET statement is an assignment statement that assigns a new value to a variable. This statement consists of:

1. The line number.
2. The letters LET.
3. The name of the variable.
4. The equal sign (=).
5. The expression or formula that determines the value of the variable.

The general format of this statement is
Line number   LET   variable name = the expression

The LET statement is used to assign a numerical or an alphanumeric value to a name or to perform an arithmetical calculation. It performs two functions; first, it evaluates the formula or expression to the right of the = sign and determines its value; second, it assigns this new value to the variable name to the left of the = sign.

The LET statement can be used in seveal different ways. It can also contain more than one variable that may appear on both sides of the = sign. Examples 18-3 to 18-7 clarify these points.

Example 18-3

Show how the values 18, 3, 7 and 24 can be assigned to variables D, S, G, and M, respectively, using BASIC statements.

Solution

These are simple assignment statements with respective line numbers. As shown, it is assumed that the variables are stored in consecutive memory locations.

```
633  LET  D = 18
634  LET  S =  3
635  LET  G =  7
636  LET  M = 24
```
■

Example 18-4

Variables K, L, M, and N are to be incremented. Write down statements in BASIC that will accomplish this. Line 301 is assigned to variable K, and the rest are stored in consecutive memory locations.

Solution

Again the LET statements are used, as shown.

```
301  LET  K = K + 1
302  LET  L = L + 1
303  LET  M = M + 1
304  LET  N = N + 1
```
■

Example 18-5

Write down a BASIC statement that can be used to calculate the area of a rectangle whose two sides are the variables B and C.

Solution

The area of a rectangle, A, is given by the product of its two sides. The following LET statement assigns the value of the area in BASIC.

```
881  LET  A = B * C
```

Note that we have used the proper arithmetic operator, the *, to indicate multiplication. Note that in this statement, B and C are also variables. In other words, variables appear on both sides of the = sign.

Example 18-6

Write down BASIC statement(s) that can be used to calculate the area of a circle.

Solution

We know that the area of a circle is given by the formula $A = \pi r^2$, where A is the area, r is the radius of the circle, and the constant $\pi = 3.1416$.

As shown below, two LET statements are used to express this formula in BASIC.

```
317  LET  P = 3.1416
318  LET  A = P * R * R
```

In this statement R is the variable used for the radius, since there is no r in BASIC. Instead of these two statements, we can also write

```
317  LET  A = 3.1416 * R * R
```

■

Example 18-7

Variables P, Q, and R are assigned the value of 48.27 and variables S, T, U, and V are assigned the value 4567. Show how these are expressed in BASIC statements.

Solution

Since each set of variables has the same value, we can express them with only two statements, as shown here.

```
111  LET  P = Q = R = 48.27
112  LET  S = T = U = V = 4567
```

■

18-4.3 The PRINT Statement

The PRINT statement is an output command to the terminal, usually the typewriter or the teletype unit. It results in the printout of one of the following three data outputs.

1. *Constants*. These could be numerical or literal constants.
2. *Variables*. These could also be alphabetic or numerical variables.
3. *Arithmetic Expressions*. These are generally the results of calculations executed by the program.

The standard format of the PRINT statement is
Line number   PRINT   list
Here the word list indicates a list of expressions that are separated by commas or semicolons. To avoid the confusion caused by the numeral 0 and the alphabetical character O, the letter is written and printed out as an alphabetical O with a superimposed stroke (i.e., as Ø).

The standard teletype carriage has spaces for 72 characters per line of printing. At the end of each PRINT statement, the carriage-return and line-feed functions are automatically performed unless the output is ended with either a coma or a semicolon. A list in the PRINT statement can be terminated with either a comma, a semicolon, or a blank. The printed line on the terminal device is divided into zones; each zone contains 15 spaces. The following rules apply for spacings between various elements of the list and terminating the list in a PRINT statement.

Rule 1 Elements in the list separated by *semicolons* result in printouts separated by 3 spaces on the same line for each element.

Rule 2 Elements in the list separated by *commas* result in printouts with each element starting with the next zone (or field, as it is also called). Since 15 spaces are allocated to each zone, the printout for each element will start at positions 1, 16, 31, 46, and 61 if the elements in the list are separated by commas.

Rule 3 If a PRINT list is terminated by a *blank,* the next PRINT statement will output to a new line on the printout.

Rule 4 If a PRINT list is terminated by a *comma,* the carriage-return function is inhibited, and the next PRINT statement starts its printout in the next zone of the same or current line.

Rule 5 When messages or elements in the list are separated by a *colon,* no spacing occurs in the printout.

Rule 6 If the PRINT statement does *not* contain the element list the printout contains blanks on the current line, and the system proceeds to the next PRINT statement for the following printout line. Effectively, a blank line results.

Rule 7 If letters or text material in the list section of the PRINT statement are enclosed in quotation marks, they are printed out as they appear but without the quotation marks.

Rule 8 If letters in the list are *not* enclosed in quotation marks they are treated as variables, and the assigned or calculated values are printed out.

We now apply these rules to the printouts shown in Examples 18-8 to 18-12.

Example 18-8

Show what the printout for the following program will look like. Also explain why the printout appears that way.

```
650   PRINT   "THE NAME IS"
651   PRINT
652   PRINT   "JOHN AND MARY SMITH"
```

Solution

Since the list elements in line 650 are enclosed in quotation marks, they will be printed out as they appear but without the quotation marks (Rule 7). Also, since the list in line 650 is terminated with a blank, the next PRINT statement will output to a new line (Rule 3). Line 651 will result in a blank line in the printout, since PRINT statement does not contain the element list (Rule 6). Again, the element list is enclosed in quotation marks in line 652. Therefore it will be printed out as is but without the quotation marks (Rule 7). The final printout will appear as:

THE NAME IS
JOHN AND MARY SMITH

    Note that the printout is left-justified and that the two lines are vertically separated by a blank line.   ■

Example 18-9

Show what the printout for the following BASIC program will look like and explain why the printout appears that way.

```
330  PRINT  "JOHN AND MARY SMITH"
331  PRINT
332  PRINT  "     1234 MAIN STREET"
333  PRINT
334  PRINT  "         CAPITAL CITY USA"
```

Solution

Lines 330, 332, nd 334 will be printed as is, since they are enclosed in quotation marks (Rule 7). Line 330 will be left-justified, but lines 332 and 334 will be indented because of the blanks preceding the text material. Lines 331 and 333 will result in two blank lines in the printout (Rule 6) that will appear as:

JOHN AND MARY SMITH
    1234 MAIN STREET
       CAPITAL CITY USA   ■

Example 18-10

In the following BASIC program the following values are assigned to the variables.
A = 2, B = 17, C = 9, D = 11, R = 10, S = 26, T = 18, P = 38
    Show the printout for this program.

```
124  PRINT  "A"; "B"; "C"
125  PRINT
126  PRINT  "P"; "D"; "T"; "R"; "S"
```

Solution

Since all the variables are enclosed in quotation marks, they will be treated as text material and printed out as is (Rule 7). Line 125 will be a blank (Rule 3). Since the variables on lines 124 and 126 are separated by semicolons, they will be separated by 3 spaces (Rule 1), and the printout will appear as:

```
A  B  C
P  D  T  R  S
```

Example 18-11

Refer to Example 18-10 and show the printout for the following program and explain.

```
871   PRINT   "A"; B; C
872   PRINT
873   PRINT   D, R, C
874   PRINT
875   PRINT   "A", B, C
```

Solution

In this program, A is treated as text material, since it is enclosed in quotation marks (Rule 7), but the rest are treated as variables and their assigned values will be printed out (Rule 8). List elements on line 871 separated by semicolons will be separated by 3 spaces in the printout (Rule 1), but elements in lines 873 and 875 are separated by commas and so, on the printout, each will be on a separate zone and will be spaced apart as per Rule 2. The printout is:

```
A  17  9
11           10           9
A            17           9
```

Example 18-12

Refer again to Example 18-10 and show the printout for the following program and explain.

```
444   PRINT   "A"; B,
445   PRINT   "D"; R, C
446   PRINT
447   PRINT   "T"; "P"; "C"
```

Solution

Since the element list in line 444 is terminated with a comma, line 445 will be printed out in the next zone of the current line in the printout (Rule 4). The rest of the printout will follow the rules as explained in the previous examples.

```
A   17          D   10   9
T   P   C
```

BASIC allows us to work with and print out both positive and negative and large and small numbers. The following rules apply to numbers used in BASIC.

Rule 9 Numbers can be expressed as whole integers or as fractions using the decimal system with a decimal point. If the number is an integer, the decimal point is *not* printed.

Rule 10 Numbers can be positive or negative and are always printed from the leftmost position of the zone. Negative numbers are preceded by a minus sign (−). Positive numbers are preceded by a space that implies a plus sign.

Rule 11 The maximum number of spaces allowed for printing numbers, including the sign and the decimal point (if any), is 10.

Rule 12 The number of significant digits in a decimal number (i.e., the digits to the left of the decimal point) is restricted to 6. The leading 0s to the left of the decimal point are not printed. Likewise, the trailing 0s to the right of the decimal point are also not printed.

Rule 13 The scientific notation system (discussed in Chapter 16) is used to express large numbers as well as numbers smaller than 1. The capital letter E is used to indicate the base 10, and the numeral(s) following it indicate the power to which E is raised. For negative exponents a minus sign follows the E but precedes the numeral(s) indicating the exponent.

The use of these rules is shown by Example 18-13.

Example 18-13

Show how the following numbers would appear in a BASIC printout:

1. $+17845.$
2. $-48,384,000.$
3. $+0.000684.$
4. $-183.42 \times 10^{4}.$
5. $-7726.3 \times 10^{-2}.$

Solution

The printouts for these will appear as:

1.   17845.
2. $-4.3884E7$.
3.   6.84E-4.
4. $-1.8342E6$.
5. $-7.7263E1$ ■

18-4.4 The INPUT Statement

Sometimes it is not practical to store all the data needed for a program in the computer memory. It is possible to use external data files and call out the data as needed from them, but this can only be accomplished if BASIC is used. Also, in many situations it is desirable to introduce data into the program interactively (i.e., data to be entered by the programmer or the operator during execution of the program). The INPUT statement allows us to do this. The general format of this statement is

Line number INPUT list

The variables in the list are separated by commas. When this statement is encountered in a program, the following events take place.

1. The computer stops executing the program.
2. A question mark (?) is displayed on the user's terminals.
3. The programmer/operator at the terminal types in the *numerical* value of each variable in the list. Each such value is separated by a comma during typing.
4. When all the values of the variables have been properly typed in, a RETURN is typed. This terminates the list, and the computer resumes execution of the program as indicated by the next statement.
5. If the operator types in values that are fewer than the number of variables in the list, the computer repeats, displaying the question mark (?).
6. If the operator types in more numbers than indicated by the variables in the list, the computer will ignore the extra ones and warn the operator of this fact.

18-4.5 The GØ TØ Statement

Normally, the BASIC program executes statements as indicated by the next line number in ascending order. This sequence can be interrupted and control transferred to another part of the program. The GØ TØ statement effectively performs an UNCONDITIONAL JUMP to the line number indicated in the statement. The standard format is

Line number GØ TØ line number

As explained in Section 4-2.3.2, a JUMP can be either a forward or a backward JUMP. Likewise, the line number indicated in the GØ TØ statement can be a number larger than (forward) or less than (backward) the statement line number. The GØ TØ statement does not make any provision for returning control to the line number following the GØ TØ statement. This is shown by Examples 18-14 and 18-15. Note that spaces are usually not allowed in BASIC statements. However, it is common to insert a space between the words GØ and TØ and also between the word TØ and the line number.

Example 18-14

Show the printout from the following BASIC program and explain why it is that way.

```
210   PRINT   "D"; "G"; "A"
214   PRINT
218   PRINT "MICROCOMPUTERS",
219   PRINT   "ARE"
226   GØ TØ 336
332   PRINT
336   PRINT "L"; "M"; "Q"
342   PRINT   "FASCINATING"
364   PRINT
372   PRINT
384   GØ TØ 342
```

Solution

The three alpha characters in line 210 will be printed as is, since each is enclosed by quotation marks. They will be separated by three spaces because of the semicolons. Line 214 will result in a blank line on the printout. Line 218 will be printed as is, and line 219 will also be printed on the current line, since line 218 is terminated with a comma. Since line 226 is a GØ TØ statement, lines 336 and 342 will be printed as they are. Lines 364 and 372 will be blanks, and line 384 will return control to line 342 and print it out. The program now goes into an *infinite loop,* and line 342 will be repeatedly printed out with two blank lines in between. The printout is shown next.

```
D   G   A
MICROCOMPUTERS ARE
```

L   M   Q
FASCINATING

FASCINATING

FASCINATING

FASCINATING

    .

    .

    .   ■

Example 18-15

Refer to Example 18-14. Using all of the same line numbers in exactly the same
order, show how this program can be modified (minimal changes) to print out only

MICROCOMPUTERS ARE
FASCINATING

Explain what you did and why.

Solution

The alpha characters in lines 210 and 336 would have to be eliminated. Since line
342 has to be printed only once, the GØ TØ statement on line 384 is replaced with
a blank PRINT statement. If the GØ TØ statement on line 226 is left unchanged,
the printout will have two blank lines between the two printed lines. To avoid this,
we change line number from 336 to 342 for this statement. The revised program
is:

```
210   PRINT
214   PRINT
218   PRINT "MICROCOMPUTERS",
219   PRINT   "ARE"
226   GØ TØ 342
332   PRINT
336   PRINT
342   PRINT "     FASCINATING"
364   PRINT
372   PRINT
384   PRINT
```
                                                                        ■

18-4.6 The FØR/NEXT Statement

One of the most attractive features of a digital computer is its ability to perform the same tasks repetitively, in other words, to loop around a given group of instructions. Such repetitive loops can be performed a fixed or predetermined number of times, or they could be made conditional, depending on some stated condition.

A pair of statements, the FØR statement and the NEXT statement, provide a simple method of looping in BASIC. The format of the FØR statement is

Line number FØR index variable = initial value TØ final value

The format of the NEXT statement is

Line number NEXT same index variable

The instructions to be repeated or looped around are always bracketed by the FØR statement at the beginning and the NEXT statement at the end. The *index variable* is generally indicated by the capital letter I. The index informs the computer how many loops are to be performed on the following group of instructions. For instance, if the FØR statement is

212   FØR   I = 1   TØ   6

the computer will repeat the succeeding group of instructions between the FØR and the NEXT statements six times. The NEXT statement must contain the same index as the FØR statement. In this case, the NEXT statement will be

217   NEXT   I

There are several fundamental rules for constructing valid FØR/NEXT statements in BASIC. These rules are given and clarified by examples.

Rule 1 The index of the loop can be indicated by I or any other alphanumeric combinatin that is valid in BASIC. Likewise, the initial and the final values of the index can also be expressed in valid BASIC alphanumeric combinations that can, therefore, range from A, B, C, D . . . Z6, Z7, Z8, Z9.

The following are typical examples of *valid* FØR/NEXT statement pairs.

1. 212 FØR I = 1 TØ 8

.

.

224 NEXT I

2. 120 FØR M = 1 TØ 13

.

.

.

216 NEXT M

3. 616 FØR T2 = S TØ 86

.

.

.

714 NEXT T2

The following are typical examples of *invalid* FØR/NEXT statement pairs.

1. 333 FØR I = 1 TØ 24

.

.

.

484 NEXT M

2. 737 FØR K = 22 TØØ 88

.

.

.

843 NEXT K

3. 186 FØR W = 11 TØ 18

.

.

.

172 NEXT W

Rule 2 The value of the index need not necessarily increase in increments of 1 only. It can be increased (or decreased) in any increments. If increments other than 1 are used, this fact is noted in the FØR statement by the word STEP, which follows the final value. The desired increment follows the word STEP. The standard format is then as follows.

Line number FØR index = initial value TØ final value STEP increment

The following are examples of index increments of values other than one.

1. 382 FØR I = 1 TØ 12 STEP 2

.

.

408 NEXT I
In this case the values of I would include 1, 3, 5, 7, 9, and 11.

2. 382 FØR I = 1 TØ 12 STEP 3

.

.

.

408 NEXT I
In this case the values of I would include 1, 4, 7, and 12.

3. 382 FØR I = 3 TØ 12 STEP 2

.

.

408 NEXT I
In this case the values of I would include 3, 5, 7, 9, and 11.

Rule 3 The index increments could be negative as well as positive. If they are negative, the index begins at the larger value and decreases to the smaller value in indicated decrements.

The following are examples of decrementing index values.

1. 382 FØR I = 6 TØ 1 STEP −1

.

.

394 NEXT I
In this case the values of I would include 5, 4, 3, and 2.

2. 382 FØR I = 12 TØ 1 STEP −2

.

.

408 NEXT I
In this case the values of I would include 10, 8, 6, and 4.

3. 382 FØR I = 12 TØ 1 STEP −3

.

.

408 NEXT I
In this case the values of I would include 9, 6, and 3.

Rule 4 The initial and the final values in the FØR statement can be positive, negative, or a combination of the two and can work with increments or decrements.

The following are typical examples of positive/negative initial and final values as well as positive/negative STEP values.

1. 380 FØR I = −5 TØ 9 STEP 3

.

.

.

412 NEXT I

In this case the values of I would include −2, 1, 4, and 7.

2. 380 FØR I = −4 TØ −17 STEP −4

.

.

.

412 NEXT I

In this case the values of I would include −8, −12, and −16.

3. 380 FØR I = 16 TØ −8 STEP −5

.

.

.

412 NEXT I

In this case the values of I would include 11, 6, 1, and −4.

Rule 5 Variables may be used to indicate the initial value, the final value, the increment/decrement value, and the index.

The following is a typical example.

100 LET A = 2
101 LET B = 6
102 LET C = 18
103 FØR J7 = A TØ C STEP B/A

.

.

.

112   NEXT J7

In this case the increment value is B/A = 6/2 = 3, so the values of the index J7 will include 5, 8, 11, 14, and 17. In this case the increment value was not given as a numeral but as a mathematical formula B/A.

18-4.7 The IF/THEN Statement

The previously described GØ TØ statement (Section 18-4) is used to perform an UNCONDITIONAL JUMP. But there are many situations where a JUMP (or a BRANCH) is performed only when a certain preestablished condition is asserted. In BASIC the IF/THEN statement permits us to perform CONDI-TIONAL JUMPS and also CONDITIONAL BRANCHES. Any of the BASIC comparator operators described in Section 18-2.3 can be used to establish the specific desired *condition*. The standard format for the IF/THEN statement is

Line number IF formula relationship formula THEN line number

In this statement the formula relationship formula, between IF and THEN could be a simple relationship such as $X = 25$. On the other hand, it could be a complex relationship such as $A + > = X/Y$. This explains why the word formula is present on either side of the word relationship in the standard format for this statement. Notice that the IF/THEN statement can be used to perform *conditional looping* based on results in the calculated results in the program meeting some preestablished criterion or condition. Recall that the FØR/NEXT statement performs a fixed number of iterations as dictated by the index in the statement, regardless of the results obtained by executing the program. By using the IF/THEN statement in conjunction with the GØ TØ statement, we can make the number of iterations dependent on the results of the program calculations meeting certain preestablished conditions. Example 18-16 shows how this is done.

Example 18-16

The initial values assigned to the three variables are:

$A = 2, B = 5, C = 7$

Write a program in BASIC that will:

1. Perform the operation $D = A + B + C$.
2. Print out the values of $A, B, C,$ and D.
3. If $D < = 789$, increment A by 4, B by 3, and C by 1 and repeat steps 1 and 2.
4. If $D > 789$, go to the next statement in the program.

Solution

```
201 LET A = 2
202 LET B = 5
203 LET C = 7
204 LET D = A + B + C
205 PRINT "A = "; A, "B = "; B, "C = "; C
206 PRINT "D ="; D
207 IF D > 789 THEN 212
208 LET A = A + 4
```

```
209 LET B = B + 3
210 LET C = C + 1
211 GØ TØ 204
212   .
213   .
214   .
```

Lines 201, 202, and 203 assign the initial values of A, B, and C. Line 204 performs the addition D. Line 205 prints out the three variables and their respective values with an equal (=) sign between them. Similarly, line 206 prints out D with the calculated value. Line 207 performs a decision based on a comparison of the value of D with the criterion 789. If D is larger than 789 it breaks out of the loop, and the program continues at line 212. Otherwise, lines 208, 209, and 210 update the values of A, B, and C. Line 211 loops the program back to line 204.

18-4.8 The GØSUB and RETURN Statements

You are aware of the need for subroutines in the field of computers. Unlike loops, which can be called out from only one point in the program, subroutines can be called out from any point within the program. In BASIC subroutines can be called out by the GØSUB statement whose standard format is:

Line number GØSUB line number

The line number following GØSUB is the line number of the starting statement in the subroutine. At first sight, the GØSUB statement seems to be the same as the GØ TØ statement, at least as far as standard format. The GØ TØ statement transfers control to the statement whose line number is shown, without any provision for returning back to the original point from which it exited in the program. Not so with the GØSUB statement. The line number of the statement following the GØSUB statement is saved in the LIFO stack by means of the push operation, which was explained in section 3-5.2. The very last statement in the subroutine is a RETURN statement whose standard format is:

Line number RETURN

When the RETURN statement is executed, the last statement number inserted in the stack is popped out, and control is returned to the statement following the GØSUB statement. Since a LIFO stack is used, it is possible to *nest* subroutines within subroutines. Once again remember that the number of nested subroutines will depend on the depth of the stack.

The GØSUB by itself executes an UNCONDITIONAL BRANCH. However, it is possible to provide the CONDITIONAL BRANCH capability by using the GØSUB statement in conjunction with the IF/THEN statement. This is shown in Example 18-17.

When nesting subroutines in BASIC, one precaution must be observed. Subroutines may be nested provided they are not *recursive*. This means that a subroutine may not call out itself as a nested subroutine either directly or indirectly by nesting another subroutine (2) which, in turn, nests the first subroutine (1). Also, subroutines in BASIC use the same variables as those used in the main program.

Example 18-17

The initial values assigned to the three variables are:

$A = 2, B = 5, C = 50$

Write the main program and the subroutine in BASIC to perform the following:

1. Execute the operation $D = A + B + C$.
2. Print out the values of A, B, C, and D.
3. If $D > 789$, branch to subroutine.
4. If $D < = 789$, go to the next statement in the program.

The subroutine is:

1. Print out IN GOD.
2. Print out WE TRUST.
3. Return to the main program.

Solution

The main program is:

```
201 LET A = 2
202 LET B = 5
203 LET C = 50
204 LET D = A + B + C
205 PRINT "A ="; A, "B ="; "C ="; C
206 PRINT "D ="; D
207 IF D > 789 THEN 209
208 END
209 GØSUB 300
```

The subroutine is:

```
300 PRINT "IN GOD"
```

301 PRINT "WE TRUST"
302 RETURN   ■

18-4.9 The READ/DATA Statements

These two statements are always used together. The READ statement is used to indicate variables to which different values can be assigned. The standard format of this statement is

Line number READ variable(s)

The actual numerical value(s) to be assigned to the variable(s) in the READ statement is (are) given in a subsequent DATA statement whose standard format is

Line number DATA numerical values

The numerical values in the DATA statement are always separated by commas. Likewise, if more than one variable is used in the READ statement, they are also separated by commas. The operation of the READ/DATA statements is as follows.

1. When the program comes to the READ statement, it assigns the first value from the DATA statement to the variable in the READ statement, assuming that the READ statement contains only one variable.
2. The statements between, or after, the READ and DATA statements are executed.
3. The second time the READ statement is processed, the second value from the DATA is assigned to the variable and the subsequent statements are processed. This procedure continues with each subsequent loop, assigning different values to the variables until all the values have been used up.
4. If the READ statement contains two variables, the first two values from the DATA statement are assigned. On the second loop, the next pair of values are assigned, and so on. As many values are assigned from the DATA statement on each loop as there are variables in the READ statement.

Examples 18-18 and 18-19 show how the READ/DATA statements operate.

Example 18-18

Write a BASIC program to calculate the circumference of circles whose diameters are 2, 4, 8, 9, 11, and 13 centimeters, respectively. The circumference for each respective diameter should also be printed out.

Solution

The circumference of a circle is given by the formula $C = \pi d$, where $C =$ the circumference, $d =$ the diameter, and $\pi = 3.14159 \ldots$ For the program we will assign C = circumference, D = diameter, and P = π = 3.14159 . . . The program is shown here.

```
201 READ D
202 DATA 2, 4, 8, 9, 11, 13
203 LET P = 3.1416
204 LET C = P * D
205 PRINT "D ="; D, "P ="; P
206 GØ TØ 201
    .
    .
    .
```

■

Example 18-19

Write a BASIC program to calculate the area of a rectangle with sides B and C. The respective values for B and C pairs are:

$$B = \quad 3, \quad 8, \; 17, \; 34, \quad 9, \; 14$$
$$C = \; 11, \; 18, \; 82, \; 48, \; 29, \; 13$$

The area of each rectangle with the respective B and C values are to be printed out.

Solution

The area of a rectangle is given by the product of its two sides, $A = B \times C$. The program for this is:

```
608 READ B, C
609 DATA 3, 11, 8, 18, 17, 82, 34, 48, 9, 29, 14, 13
610 LET A = B * C
611 PRINT "B ="; B, "C ="; C, "A ="; A
612 GØ TØ 608
    .
    .
    .
```

■

18-4.10 The STØP/END Statements

Every BASIC program must be *terminated*. The statement that terminates the program is the END statement whose standard format is

Line number END

Since the END statement is the very last statement in the program, it must have the highest line number in the program.

There are, however, many situations that require the program to be terminated prematurely, prior to reaching the END statement. This happens often in subroutines that, when executed, give results that make further execution of the main program unnecessary. In this case a GØ TØ statement that directs the computer to the line number of the END statement would do the job. This is shown in Fig. 18-1a. Notice that in each statement the GØ TØ statement is preceded by the IF/THEN statement and followed by the RETURN statement. The IF/THEN statement specifies the condition under which control

Main Program	Subroutine X	Subroutine Y
100 ------	205 ------	666 ------
101 ------	206 ------	667 ------
102 GØSUB 205	207 ------	668 ------
103 ------	208 IF . . . THEN 210	669 ------
104 ------	209 GØ TØ 110	670 IF . . .THEN 672
105 ------	210 RETURN	671 GØ TØ 110
106 GØSUB 666		672 RETURN
107 ------		
108 ------		
109 ------		
110 RETURN		

(a) Using the GØ TØ statements

Main Program	Subroutine X	Subroutine Y
100 ------	205 ------	666 ------
101 ------	206 ------	667 ------
102 GØSUB 205	207 ------	668 ------
103 ------	208 IF . . .THEN 210	669 ------
104 ------	209 STØP	670 IF . . .THEN 672
105 ------	210 RETURN	671 STØP
106 GØSUB 666		672 RETURN
107 ------		
108 ------		
109 ------		
110 END		

(b) Using the STØP statements

Figure 18-1   Prematurely halting the program.

may be returned to the main program or terminated by going to the END statement. The STØP statement accomplishes the same goal and terminates the program prematurely. In fact, it can replace the two GØ TØ statements of Fig. 18-1*a*. This is shown in Fig. 18-1*b*. The subroutines in both cases will perform in an identical manner. The standard format for this statement is

Line number STOP

18-5 HIERARCHY OF BASIC OPERATORS

In Section 18-2.3 we presented five arithmetic operators used in BASIC, which is a language well suited for solving mathematical problems. In solving mathematical expressions these operators are assigned an order of priority. This hierarchy is shown in Table 18-1. The highest priority is assigned priority 1 and the lowest is assigned priority 4.

The priorities in Table 18-1 simply mean that if a mathematical expression involves these operators, the system will first handle the variables and their operators within the parentheses. It will then handle any exponentiation that exists. Multiplication or division will be performed next and, finally, any addition or subtraction. When a mathematical expression involves operations having the same priority numbers, the system performs operations from left to right. Examples 18-20 to 18-22 show how this is done.

Example 18-20

The following mathematical equation is solved by a computer using BASIC for different values for variables A, B, C, and D. Show and explain the priority in which each operation will be handled by the system.

$$R = A - B + C - D$$

Table 18-1   HIERARCHY OF BASIC
ARITHMETIC OPERATORS

Priority Number	Symbol	Function
1	( )	Grouping
2	↑	Exponentiation
3	*	Multiplication
3	/	Division
4	+	Addition
4	−	Subtraction

Solution

The only operators involved here are addition and subtraction, which have the same priority number according to Table 18-1. Therefore the operations will be handled on a left-to-right basis, as explained next.

1. Variable B will be subtracted from variable A.
2. Variable C will be added to the result of the subtraction operation in step 1.
3. Variable D will be subtracted from the result obtained from step 2.   ■

Example 18-21

Briefly state the order in which a BASIC program will handle the following mathematical expression.

$$R = A + B - (E + F + G)/D$$

Solution

The variables and the operators in the parentheses will be handled first. The order in which BASIC will handle this expression is:

1. $E + F + G = H$.
2. $H/D = I$.
3. $A + B = J$.
4. $J - I = R$.   ■

Example 18-22

Show the order in which a BASIC program will handle the following mathematical expression.

$$R = A * B + C + E \uparrow F - D/G$$

Solution

In this case the highest-priority operator is exponentiation ($\uparrow$). This means that the variable E is raised to the power F. The order of operation, therefore, is:

1. $E \uparrow F = H$.
2. $A * B = J$.
3. $D/G = K$.
4. $J + C = L$.
5. $L + H = M$.
6. $M - K = R$.   ■

18-6 CONCLUDING REMARKS

This chapter is intended to introduce students to a higher-level computer language, BASIC. This particular language was chosen because it is widely used in the microcomputer field. No attempt is made to cover *all* aspects of BASIC or all the statements available either in BASIC or extended BASIC. It is neither intended nor expected that students will be able to write elegant programs in BASIC just by studying this chapter. Additional study is in order. Many excellent books on BASIC are available, and students are urged to refer to them. I have found the following books particularly useful and recommend them for further study. However, students should not limit reading to just these books. In Chapter 19 we will talk about BASIC again when we discuss interpreters and describe some interactive commands such as file manipulation and line editing commands.

The following books on BASIC are suggested.

1. Kemeny, John G., and Thomas E. Kurtz, *Basic Programming,* second edition, Wiley, New York, 1971.
2. Mullish, Henry, *A Basic Approach to BASIC,* Wiley, New York, 1976.
3. Forsyth, Richard, *The BASIC Idea, An Introduction to Computer Programming,* Chapman and Hall, London, 1978.
4. Forsythe, A. I., C. E. Hughes, R. M. Aiken, and E. I. Organick, *Computer Science, Programming in BASIC,* Wiley, New York, 1976.
5. Barnett, Eugene H., *Programming Time-Shared Computers in BASIC,* Wiley-Interscience, New York, 1972.

18-7 SUMMARY

A higher-level computer language, BASIC, was introduced in this chapter. Only the fundamental concepts and statements were presented. The advantages of BASIC, which is an interactive, interpretive language, were enumerated. The structure of BASIC (i.e., the statements and line numbers) was described. The reserved or key words were presented. The various operators used in BASIC, including the arithmetic and the comparison operators along with their respective symbols, were presented with a brief explanation of each. The concepts of numeric variable names and alphabetical character strings as used in BASIC were discussed. The six categories of BASIC statements were described.

The 10 fundamental statements of BASIC were presented, and a detailed explanation of each statement was given along with typical examples of how each of them is used. The 10 statements were: REM, LET, PRINT, INPUT, GØ TØ, FØR/NEXT, IF/THEN, GØSUB and RETURN, READ/DATA, and STØP/END. The rules governing the use of these statements were presented so that students should be able to use them easily. Finally, the hierarchy of BASIC operators was presented along with examples showing how it is used.

18-8 REVIEW QUESTIONS

18-1 What is a procedure-oriented computer language? For which specific computer is the procedure-oriented language best suited?

18-2 For what class or category of problems was BASIC developed? Is it possible to use BASIC for other classes of problems?

18-3 What is an interactive language? Is BASIC an interactive language? What is the principal advantage of such a language?

18-4 What are the most common types of I/O units used in computer systems that are programmed in BASIC?

18-5 What is timesharing? Is BASIC used in timesharing computer systems?

18-6 What does syntax mean as applied to the BASIC language?

18-7 Is there any correspondence between a program flowchart and statements in BASIC? If so, what is it?

18-8 How are BASIC statements, which are written on paper, input into a computer system?

18-9 What is a BASIC compiler? Explain.

18-10 What do the reserved or key words do in a BASIC statement? Where are they located?

18-11 What are the functions performed by arithmetic operators in BASIC?

18-12 What are comparison operators in BASIC? What do they do?

18-13 Is a comma an operator in BASIC? If so, what does it do?

18-14 In BASIC what are variable names? What symbols are used for variable names?

18-15 What are alphabetical character strings? Are they different from variable names? How are they identified in BASIC?

18-16 What are literal constants? How are they identified?

18-17 How are the various items of an array identified in BASIC?

18-18 What are assignment statements? Do they apply to variables or constants?

18-19 What are REM statements? Where are they written?

18-20 What is a LET statement? Of what does it consist?

18-21 Name the various things that the PRINT statement will handle. What do these statements contain?

18-22 Is it possible to use scientific notation in BASIC? If so, how?

18-23 What is the function of the INPUT statement? What does it contain?

18-24 What does the GØ TØ statement do? What does it contain?

18-25 What statement(s) in BASIC is (are) used to perform iterative loops in a program? Explain.

18-26 Is it possible to increment the index in the FØR/NEXT statements by increments other than 1? If so, how?

18-27 What statement(s) in BASIC is (are) used to perform CONDITIONAL JUMPS or BRANCHES?

18-28 Is it possible to BRANCH to subroutines in BASIC? If so, how?

18-29 Does the GØSUB statement perform a CONDITIONAL or UNCONDITIONAL BRANCH? How can it perform a CONDITIONAL BRANCH?

18-30 Explain what the READ/DATA statements do.

18-31 Is it possible to terminate the program prematurely without using the END statement? How?

18-9 PROBLEMS AND EXERCISES

18-1 The following four statements appear in a main program written in BASIC. The programmer forgot to put in some parts in the statements. Insert the missing parts so that each becomes a complete legitimate statement.
(a) 340   BRANCHES TO THE PERCENTAGE CALCULATION SUBROUTINE #A-38-1
(b) 782 LET A = 39
(c) 649 LET B = 413
(d) 112   THIS SUBROUTINE IS USED TO CALCULATE THE AREA OF A TRIANGLE.

18-2 Write BASIC program annotations for the following three decision points in the main program.
(a) If H is less than B continue main program (line 44).
(b) If B is greater than or equal to 1000 jump to statement on line 118 (line 340).
(c) Branch to subroutine G-84 if $X + Y$ is less than Z (line 08).

18-3   Show how the values 11, 14, 17, 20, 23, and 26 can be assigned to variables *F, E, D, C, B,* and *A,* respectively, and assign consecutive line numbers starting with 420. Write the appropriate BASIC statements.

18-4   Write BASIC statements to show how variables *M, N, P,* and *Q* can be incremented by 3, 1, 4, and 7, respectively, and variables *D, B,* and *E* decremented by 1, 13, and 8, respectively. Use consecutive line numbers starting with 300.

18-5   Using the multiplication operator, write a BASIC statement to calculate the area of a square whose side dimension is expressed by the variable *S.*

18-6   Refer to Problem 18-5. Is it possible to use some operator other than the multiplication operator to solve this problem? If so, write a BASIC statement using the other operator and explain.

18-7   Using the exponentiation operator, write BASIC statements to calculate the area of a circle.

18-8   Write BASIC statements to show that variables *A, F, G,* and *P* are assigned the value of 734.51 and variables *C, E,* and *H* are assigned the value of 31.4 $\times$ 10^{-6}.

18-9   Write a BASIC program to point out the following.
PROGRAMMING IN BASIC
IS FASCINATING,
CHALLENGING AND REWARDING

18-10   The following is a BASIC program.
89 PRINT "Q"; "S"; "T"
90 PRINT
91 PRINT
92 PRINT "J"; "K"; "J"
Show what the printout will look like.

18-11   The six variables in a BASIC program are assigned the following values.
$C = 4, D = 8, E = 7, F = 9, H = 17, K = 12$
Show the printout for the following program.
646 PRINT "D"; C; "F"
650 PRINT
651 PRINT "E"; H, K
652 PRINT F, D, C

18-12   What is the printout for the following BASIC program?
100 PRINT "BE GOOD"
101 PRINT
102 GØ TØ 100
103 PRINT
104 PRINT "TO YOUR NEIGHBOR"
105 PRINT

106 PRINT
107 GØ TØ 102
Will any statement be repeated in the printout? If so, how many times?

18-3   We wish to print out 300 return address labels, as shown, on a computer.
RETURN TO
KLUDGE KOMPUTER KORPORATION
ANY CITY USA
Write a BASIC program to print these out.

18-14   The initial values assigned to the two variables are $A = 14$ and $B = 23.84$.
Write a BASIC program to do the following.
(a) Perform $C = 10.82 \times A \times B$.
(b) If $C < 1084$, print out A, B, and C and increment A by 2 and B by 3.6.
(c) If $C > = 1084$, terminate the program.

18-15   What will be the printout for the following program and the subroutine?
Main Program
200 LET A = 4
201 LET B = 18
202 LET C = 114
203 LET D = A + (B * C)/272.38
204 GØSUB 308
205 LET E = B − C + D
206 LET F = A − B + C
207 END

Subroutine
308 PRINT "MICROCOMPUTERS ARE"
309 PRINT "ALL AMERICAN LIKE"
310 PRINT "HOT DOGS APPLE PIE"
311 PRINT "AND CHEVROLET"
312 RETURN

18-16   The area of a triangle is given by $A = \frac{1}{2}b \times h$, where $A =$ the area, $b =$ the base length, and $h =$ the height. Write a BASIC program to calculate the areas of triangles having the base and height pairs as follows:
$b = 15, 6, 8$
$h = 7, 9, 4.6$
Also print out the A, b, and h values.

18-17   Write a BASIC program to solve the following mathematical expression.

$$R = \frac{C \times (B + D)}{A \times E} \times H^6$$

19

INTRODUCTION TO ASSEMBLERS AND INTERPRETERS

19-1 INTRODUCTION TO ASSEMBLY LANGUAGE

19-1.1 Process of Program Assembling

Computers, including microcomputers, may be programmed at one of three language levels: *machine-level, assembler-level,* and *higher-level* languages. The machine-level language is the most *fundamental* level of communication between the programmer and the computer. It requires the programmer to think in terms of the machine functions and write each instruction of the program in the binary machine language code of the particular computer (i.e., in 1s and 0s). Machine-level programming is perhaps the most difficult and time consuming from the programmer's point of view. Although machine-level language codes use notations that are foreign to the programmer, they do enable the programmer to have complete control over each step that the computer performs in the execution of the program.

The assembler-level programming relieves the programmer of the burden of writing the program instructions in binary 1s and 0s. The *assembler,* which is a computer program, allows the programmer to write the program in *symbolic* language that is very much like everyday English. The assembler takes this source program and translates it equivalently into a machine-language program. The translation is performed on a one-to-one basis (i.e., one instruction in machine code is produced for one instruction in assembly language). Although assembly language greatly reduces the programmer's task, it is more expensive. First, the assembler must be designed and produced for the particular μC. An assembler written for one machine cannot be directly used on another machine. Second, the assembler must be stored in the computer memory, so additional memory must be provided for this.

488

Consequently, assembly-level programming can (and often does) result in inefficient use of the memory, thereby pushing the memory costs even higher.

The higher-level languages such as BASIC and FORTRAN further simplify the programmer's task. They employ symbols and jargon familiar to users in their usual professional work. Each higher-level language is customized to satisfy the usual user requirements in a specific field of activity. These languages further remove a programmer from the actual machine functions, so there is even less direct control over machine functions. Another major disadvantage is that memory is even more inefficiently used than in assembly-language programming. Like the assembly-language situation, a special program is needed to perform the translation from the higher-level language into machine language. Such a program is called a *compiler*. Unlike the assembler, which translates a program on a one-to-one basis, the compiler can and does translate each higher-level instruction into one or more machine language instructions. Note that the machine-level program produced by both the assembler and the compiler is called an object program, which is loaded into the computer's program memory.

In this chapter we will discuss assemblers and then, briefly, *interpreters,* which further help the programmer in the program-generation process.

19-1.2 Problems in Manual Assembly

It is always possible to assemble a computer program without using an assembler. The process of manually assembling a program includes the following tasks.

1. Converting mnemonic codes into their binary equivalents.
2. Converting decimal numbers (if any) into their binary equivalents.
3. Assigning addresses in the program memory for each instruction in the main program.
4. Assigning addresses in the program memory for each instruction in each subroutine.
5. Counting the number of data word locations required in the data memory for the main program and each subroutine.
6. Assigning addresses in the data memory for the data words.

These tasks are not particularly difficult to perform manually. However, they are tedious, time consuming, and certainly very error prone, making the whole process expensive. Machine language programs are much easier to write if the program is written in either octal or hexadecimal codes instead of in binary codes. However, instructions written in either hexadecimal or octal codes nevertheless must be translated into their binary equivalents. Most μC manufacturers supply a program (usually called the monitor) to perform this function.

The computer can do many more functions in addition to octal-to-binary or hexadecimal-to-binary conversion. In fact, it can perform all these tasks very effectively and accurately and in a fraction of the time without committing errors. Furthermore, the computer can point out programming errors that may be committed by the programmer. Of course, the assembler performs all these tasks.

19-2 THE ASSEMBLER PROGRAM

Unlike procedure-oriented programming languages such as BASIC, which was described in Chapter 18, assembly language is a *computer-oriented* language unique to the particular machine for which it is designed. A program designed in assembly language for one machine may not be run on a different machine. If assembly language is used the programmer must be thoroughly familiar with the computer architecture.

19-2.1 The Objectives

Briefly, the objectives of designing and using an assembler are:

1. To enable the programmer to write a program in assembly language using mnemonics and symbols that are provided by the manufacturer for the particular computer.
2. To provide a computer-operated method of translating instructions written in assembly-level codes (source program) into instructions available in machine language, that is, in binary codes (object program).
3. To assign an absolute memory address for each instruction that, in the source program, is identified by a label.
4. To assign an absolute memory address for each data word that, in the source program, is identified by a label.
5. To provide an error checking facility that minimally catches some obvious inconsistencies in the program.

19-2.2 The Translation Process

The assembler is a translator; this means that the machine language code for each instruction must be prestored in the memory of the computer on which the program is to be assembled. Figure 19-1 shows a simple diagram that explains the fundamental steps involved in assembling a program. Each step is now explained.

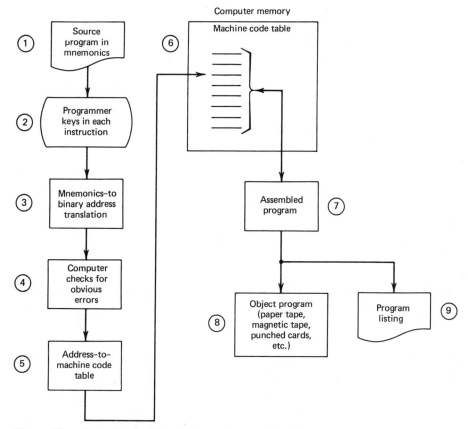

Figure 19-1   Steps involved in assembly program generation.

1. The source program is prepared by the programmer on coding sheets. This program is written with mnemonics and symbols supplied by the manufacturer with the computer's instruction set.

2. By means of a keyboard, the source program is entered into the computer system.

3. Each instruction, in mnemonic form, is decoded into an effective address in the computer memory (usually a ROM), where its machine language equivalent is prestored in a table.

4. Before calling out the contents of the addressed memory location, the computer checks the instruction for obvious errors. Most assemblers will only detect errors in syntax (violations of the grammatical rules of the language). Generally, errors in semantics (instructions that are syntactically correct but inappropriately used by the programmer) are not detected by the assembler.

5. The address is sent to the computer memory.

6. The contents of the particular addressed memory location, which is in the machine language code, is fetched.

7. The assembled program now consists of the source program instructions translated into their machine language equivalents.

8. The assembled program is then output as an object program on a storage medium such as perforated tape, punched cards, or magnetic tape.

9. A listing of the object program is usually also prepared on a printer or a typewriter.

19-2.3 Assembly Language Syntax

All languages, whether spoken by human beings or used for communication with computers, must follow certain rules of grammar. The term *syntax* refers to the rules governing structure of sentences in the spoken language. In computer languages syntax refers to the rules governing the statement in that particular language. As applied to the assembler, syntax is the structure of the assembler statement.

19-2.3.1 Statement Structure The assembler consists of a group of statements; each statement has four fields, as shown in Fig. 19-2.

19-2.3.2 Label Field Each machine language instruction must be assigned a specific address and stored in the program memory. Since the assembler translates the statement into machine code on a one-to-one basis, the desired address for storing each instruction in the memory must be indicated in the assembler statement. The *label* field allows us to do just that. However, instead of assigning a specific memory address, a name or a label can be assigned to each address and included in the label field. The label may consist of numbers, letters, or some other characters or symbols. Most assemblers accept labels one to six characters long. Most of them also require that the first character of a label be an alphabetical letter so that the assembler can distinguish between numbers and labels. In any program a unique label must be used only once. One advantage of using labels is that the programmer need not commit any instruction to a specific memory location when first writing a large program because the available memory location may not be known at that time. Another advantage is that the instruction may be called out from another part of the program by referring to its label instead of to its absolute address. This is particularly useful in JUMP and BRANCH situations.

Label (name)	Op code (mnemonic)	Argument (operand or address)	Comment

Figure 19-2   Assembler statement format.

19-2.3.3 Operation Code Field This is the most important field in the assembler statement, and it contains the mnemonic code of the particular instruction for the specific computer. This is the one field in the assembler statement that must never be left empty. The statement is meaningless without this field. The assembler simply uses this code as an address in the memory where a list of the instruction mnemonics, in machine code, is stored. Depending on how the mnemonic codes of a particular instruction set are structured, the operation code field in the assembler statement is designed to have the appropriate number of characters. Generally, this field contains from 3 to 10 characters.

19-2.3.4 Argument Field As used in mathematics, *argument* refers to an independent variable. In computer jargon argument refers to either an independent operand or an independent location address. In the assembler statement, the argument field contains either the actual operand required for the execution of the instruction (as specified by the operation field) or the address of the location where the operand is stored. The address in this case is either a memory address or a code identifying a register in the computer.

19-2.3.5 Comment Field This field contains brief comments or explanatory notes pertinent to that particular assembler statement. This field is optional, and the programmer may choose to leave it out of the statement. However, comments are helpful and, occasionally, are *very* helpful in tracing the steps in a program, particularly in a long program. Comments inserted in this field are not executed by the assembler, but they are included in the program listing with each instruction if they are included in the source program.

19-2.3.6 Field Identification The assembler must be informed where one field in the statement ends and another begins. Many assemblers use a *fixed format* for the fields in the statement. Certain areas in the input medium, such as punched cards or paper tapes, have assigned fields that are preestablished. The main advantage of the fixed format is that no special symbols or codes are required for separating the four fields of the statement.

Another method that is very widely used in μCs is the *free format* in which the boundaries for each field are not preestablished. A field may start anywhere on the statement line and *end anywhere*. In this case, special symbols or characters, called *delimiters,* are used to separate and identify each field. Symbols and characters, usually available on standard typewriter keyboards, are generally used as delimiters. They include comma, slash, question mark, colon, semicolon, asterisk, and so forth.

If the free format is used for field identification, certain rules are established so that the assembler may interpret each field properly. In many assemblers a space code is used as a delimiter. The following rules are applied for field identification.

1. The characters in the statement are left justified. The assembler interprets the field, which starts with the first character and ends with the delimiter as the label field.
2. If the label field is not used in the statement the very first character in the statement is a delimiter. The assembler assumes that the label field is empty.
3. The characters inserted between the first and second delimiter are interpreted by the assembler as the mnemonic (i.e., the operation code).
4. In some statements the operation code is such that it does not require an argument field. In that case the assembler treats the remaining characters in the statement as belonging to the comment field. If there are no comments, the assembler quits and proceeds to the next statement of the source program.
5. If the statement is such that it does include the argument field, the assembler interprets all the characters between the second and the third delimiters as belonging to either an address or an operand.
6. In some cases several space codes or symbols are used contiguously as delimiters. The assembler treats such spaces or codes as only one delimiter.

19-2.4 Assembly Language Directives (Pseudo-operations)

In many assemblers certain conveniences are provided. Sophisticated assemblers contain several codes, which are inserted in the operation code field of the assembler statement (see Fig. 19-2). This category of instructions is called *assembler directives*. Unlike the mnemonic codes, these codes do not have binary equivalents that are executed by the μC. Instead, they provide the assembler with certain information that it cannot deduce entirely on its own without outside assistance. For this reason they are referred to as pseudo-operations. Generally, the functions performed by pseudo-operations include:

- Generating fixed tables.
- Defining symbols and characters.
- Assigning programs and subroutines to specific areas in the memory.
- Assigning memory space for storing variables.
- Establishing the format of the program listing.

Some of the assembler directives used in μCs ae now briefly described.

1. *Origin Directive (ORG)*. The ORG directive, which is a pseudo-operation code, does not generate an object code. Computer programs usually contain several subroutines such as initialization subroutines and interrupt service subroutines.

This means that there are several starting or origin points within a main program. The ORG directive simply allows the programmer to start programs (i.e., subroutines, or segments of the main program if JUMP instructions are involved) at specific memory locations. The ORG directive can also be used to indicate specific locations for data. Since every program must start somewhere in the memory, pseudo-operations code ORG is always present in any program at least once.

2. *End Directive (END)*. Obviously, every program that starts at some place in the memory must also terminate at some other point in the memory. The pseudo-operations code END simply indicates the end to the assembler program. When END is inserted in the operations field of the statement, it informs the assembler that beyond that point, no additional executable instructions are present in the program. Some of the more sophisticated assemblers have an additional feature. The last statement contains END in the operations code field, and the word FIRST is in the argument field of the same statement. This feature tells the computer that if the program has been successfully assembled (i.e., without any errors), the computer should start executing the assembled program at the statement whose label field contains the word FIRST.

3. *Equate Directive (EQU)*. The EQU directive assigns a value to a label. The statement using this directive has the name put in the label field, EQU in the operations code field, and the value or number in the argument field. Thus, if we write an assembler statement,

COOL   EQU   609

it means that the value 609 is automatically assigned to the code word COOL whenever it is used in the program. EQU directives are used mostly to define commonly used values and are generally placed at the start of the program so that they can be easily located and used in program documentation.

4. *Define Constant Directive (DC)*. This directive allows a constant to be assigned to be stored in the memory. The pseudo-operations code DC is placed in the operations code field of the statement, and the constant is placed in the argument field. Thus

DC   22F

means that a constant 22F is stored in memory. This directive generally implies that a byte is placed in that memory location.

5. *Define Address Directive (DA)*. This directive specifies 2 bytes of actual data in consecutive memory locations. The pseudo-operations code most often used is DA. The use of this directive is explained by means of Example 19-1.

Example 19-1

The following seven statements are part of a source program for a table in the memory written in assembly language for translation into machine language. Draw a simple memory map showing the addresses and the contents that will result from the assembly process and briefly explain each step. All quantities are expressed in HEX notation.

Mnemonic	Argument
ORG	169E
DC	7B
DC	F4
DA	5D9B
DC	AC
DA	RB08
END	

Solution

The starting address of this subroutine is given as 169E by the ORG statement, and for each successive statement the address is incremented. The memory map is as follows.

Address	Contents in Memory
169E	7B
169F	F4
16A0	5D
16A1	9B
16A2	AC
16A3	RB
16A4	08

In address 169E the first constant, 7B (which is a single byte), is stored. The address is then updated, and the second constant, F4, is stored in that location. The next statement is a DA directive that stores 2 bytes of actual data in the next two memory locations. Notice that the lower-addressed location stores the first byte (5D) and the next higher-addressed location stores the next byte in the statement (9B). Another constant AC is stored in the next memory location. The next statement is also a DA directive, so the 2 bytes are stored in the succeeding two memory locations. The END statement is not included in the table, which is stored in the memory. It is simply a directive to the computer to terminate the program. ∎

19-2.5 Symbol Tables or Dictionaries

19-2.5.1 Fixed Tables From previous discussions in this chapter it is clear that the mnemonic, which is inserted in the operations code field of the statement, is merely a *symbol*. This symbol is first decoded into an equivalent memory address where the machine language code for that particular instruction is stored. This means that the entire instruction set of the subject computer must be first stored in the memory of the computer that is used to assemble the program. The table that stores the machine language equivalents of the mnemonics is a *static* table. The contents of this table are not destroyed or altered during the assembly process; such tables are therefore called *static tables* or *fixed dictionaries*. The mnemonic codes are always predefined. If the programmer accidentally spells this code incorrectly, most assemblers are designed to reject that statement. However, in some cases it is possible to misspell a mnemonic for the intended instruction that may still be accepted by the assembler as a legitimate, unintended instruction. For instance, the intended instruction may be a *compare function* whose legitimate mnemonic may be CMP. If the programmer accidentally puts down the mnemonic CML for the intended compare operation, it is possible that the assembler may not reject it but accept it as a legitimate mnemonic for the *complement function*. Such an error is an error in semantics, not an error in syntax, and the assembler is unable to catch it.

19-2.5.2 Dynamic Tables Recall from Section 19-2.3 that we can also assign symbols for instruction addresses and insert them in the label field of the assembly language statement. Similarly, we also assign symbols for addresses in memory where data words or bytes can be located. This feature of the assembler permits us to write a program without committing absolute addresses to each instruction or data word/byte. However, the object program requires that all addresses be in machine language code. During the assembly process, symbolic addresses are converted to absolute addresses by referring to another table that is prestored in the memory. This process is very similar to the mnemonic-to-machine code translation process. This symbolic table is not fixed. It is *dynamic* and is often called the *address dictionary*. Prior to the assembly process, the user establishes the symbolic code (usually limited to 6 digits or characters). The assembler then takes care of assigning memory addresses to the symbolic codes (with the exception of the EQU and the ORG statements).

Since the mnemonic table is fixed, it is usually stored in ROM chips. The symbolic address table, on the other hand, can be changed, so it is stored in RAM chips.

19-2.6 Macro Assembler

In many programs some groups of instructions are used many times during the execution of the program. The conventional approach to such a machine is to construct a subroutine of the sequence of these instructions. The main program branches to this subroutine, executes it, and returns to the main program. At times, certain sequences of instructions are required, depending on the design of the μP, which are not obvious to the user but are nonetheless necessary. Such sequences differ from conventional subroutines. These differences will become apparent after we consider a few simple examples.

Some of the sophisticated assemblers provide a feature called a *macro* ability, which allows the programmer to assign a name to the previously mentioned sequence of instructions. This name effectively defines the *macro,* so the programmer can call out the sequence of instructions simply by using this single name in the assembler statement.

Of course, before the macro can be used, we must first define it. Generally, the word MACRO is used at the start of the sequence of statements in the operations field. The assigned name, or code, of the sequence is included in the label field. The end of the sequence is indicated by a code, such as ENDM, in the operations field of the statement. Example 19-2 shows a simple macro consisting of a single-instruction sequence.

Example 19-2

A left shift logical is to be performed on the contents of an 8-bit accumulator and the result stored in the same accumulator. A 0 is to be inserted in the LSB position of the accumulator after completion of the shift. The original byte in the accumulator is 01011011. However, the accumulator *does not* have the conventional left shift capability. Explain how this can be accomplished and write down the statements that would be used in an assembler with a macro facility.

Solution

Since the accumulator does not have a left shift logical capability, it is possible to obtain the same result by adding the contents of the accumulator to itself and storing the result in the accumulator.

```
    0 1 0 1 1 0 1 1  ← Original accumulator contents
  + 0 1 0 1 1 0 1 1  ← Add the same contents
    1 0 1 1 0 1 1 0  ← Resulting sum is left shifted logical with a 0 in LSB
                       position
```

The macro for this operation is

```
LSL   MACRO
      ADD ACC
      ENDM
```

LSL is the mnemonic for the macro, which is inserted in the label field of the statement. The word MACRO, the pseudo-operations code in the operations code field, marks the beginning of the macro definition. The next statement, ADD ACC, is translated into the machine code, which adds the contents of the accumulator to itself, thereby performing a left shift logical. The final statement, ENDM, marks the end of the macro definition.   ∎

In Example 19-2 we performed only a simple add operation and used only one operand, which was added to itself. It is, of course, possible to use more than one operand and call them out from memory by means of symbolic addresses inserted in the argument field of the statement. This procedure is shown in Example 19-3.

Example 19-3

Two operands are stored in memory locations identified by ADR1 and ADR2, respectively. An exclusive-NOR operation is performed on them, and the result is stored in the accumulator. Write a macro definition for this operation to be used in an assembler.

Solution

The exclusive-NOR function is performed in two steps. First, the two operands are used to perform an exclusive-OR and the result is stored in the accumulator. Then the contents of the accumulator are complemented. The macro definition is

```
EXNOR    MACRO      ADR1
         EXOR       ADR2
         CML AC
         ENDM
```

In this definition the *macro* is identified by the label EXNOR. The first operand is fetched from address ADR1. The second statement fetches the second operand from address ADR2, performs the exclusive-OR operation, and stores the result in the accumulator. The third statement complements the contents of the accumulator, and the fourth statement marks the end of the definition.   ∎

In some macro definitions it may be necessary to repeat the same statement several times in order to perform the desired operation. This is shown in Example 19-4.

Example 19-4

The contents of two 4-bit registers, R1 and R2, are to be exchanged without using an auxiliary register or a memory location. Explain how this can be done where R1 = 1010 and R2 = 0001 and write a macro definition for this operation.

Solution

The contents of any two registers can be exchanged by concatenating them and then rotating them, either right or left, as many times as there are bits in the single word. Since both R1 and R2 have 4 bits, we will concatenate R1 and R2 and rotate them right four times, as shown in Fig. 19-3. After completing the fourth right rotate, the contents of R1 and R2 are exchanged. The macro definition is

```
EXR1R2   MACRO
         RTR      R1R2
         RTR      R1R2
         RTR      R1R2
         RTR      R1R2
         ENDM
```

In comparing macros with subroutines, we find many similarities that result in common advantages. In both cases the programmer writes the sequence of instructions only once. The sequence is then called out and executed with only one instruction in either case. Standard sequences, which have been tested and proven, can be used in either case. The programs can be readily understood and documented. The principal difference between the two is that macros can be executed faster than subroutines because they do not require BRANCH instructions or BRANCH BACK or RETURN to the main program instructions. No stack or push-pop operations are involved in the execution of macros.

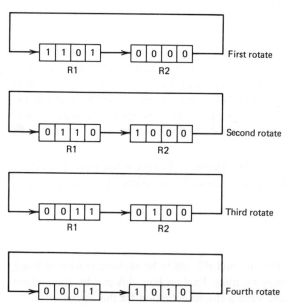

Figure 19-3   Four right rotates for Example 19-4.

The major shortcoming of macros is that they eat up more memory space. When a macro is referenced, it results in assembling of the entire sequence. In other words, every time the same macro is called out in the program, the entire sequence is assembled and included in the program. On the other hand, a subroutine is assembled and stored in the program memory only once. Generally, subroutines are preferred for larger sequences of instructions, and macros are preferred for shorter sequences.

19-3 MECHANICS OF ASSEMBLER OPERATION

19-3.1 Single-Pass Assembler

Previously in this chapter we presented the different features and the statement format for the assembler. Here we will discuss the operation of the *assembly* process. The source program can be translated into the object program in only one pass through the assembly operation. In most μCs, however, more than one pass is necessary.

The single-pass assembler performs all the assembly steps in one pass of the source program through the system. Usually, the completed object program is stored in the mainframe memory when it is fully assembled. After completing the assembly process, the object code is transferred to some auxiliary storage medium such as paper tape or a floppy disk. Generally, the single-pass assembler does not offer the features and advantages of a two-pass assembler. Also, it imposes stricter restrictions on the programmer regarding allocation of resources and assignment of addresses.

19-3.2 Two-Pass Assembler

Most assemblers designed for μCs are two-pass assemblers. This means that the source program must be read and processed through the system *twice* in order to obtain the final object program.

Pass 1. During the first pass of the source program, the assembler creates the symbol table. Each symbol used in the source program is placed in the memory together with its starting address. The symbol table consists of one entry for each address label of the source program and its actual address in the memory, either in the RAM or the ROM chips. The assembler assigns addresses to the symbols that have not been assigned by the pseudo-operations instructions.

Pass 2. During the second pass of the *source program,* the symbol definitions are effectively ignored. However, the operation codes and the pseudo codes are now translated into their respective binary equivalents by referring them to the fixed table in which the machine codes for the mnemonics and pseudo-operations have been previously stored. Also, during the second pass, both the source and object programs are printed out, and the object code is written into some storage medium such as a floppy disk, paper tape, or cassette, from which it can be loaded into the program memory of the μC that is used to execute the program.

19-3.3 Resident or Self-Assemblers

The assembly of a program must be done on some computer if it is not hand assembled. It is, of course, possible to load the assembler in the same computer's memory as the machine on which the ultimate object program will be run. In other words, the μC assembles its own object program. Such assemblers are called *resident* or *self*-assemblers, and they are usually loaded and available in ROM chips. Resident assemblers generate an object program for only the specific μC in which it resides. Of course, it can also reside in RAM chips, in which case the assembler would have to be loaded into the memory every time it is used. This is time consuming. If it is stored in ROM chips the assembler can be readily called into operation with the flip of a switch. Regardless of where it is stored, the resident assembler has to coexist with other programs and data in the μC's memory, so a larger memory is required.

Resident assemblers for μCs are usually simple. Typically, they require from 4 to 8k bytes of memory and can be operated with a minimum system configuration, including a μC with a teletypewriter with paper tape I/O capability. Since they are small in memory size and I/O capabilities, μC resident assemblers may require some programmer intervention during the assembly operation to read, review, and reread the source program as the need arises.

19-3.4 Nonresident Assemblers

Constraints on memory size often make it impossible to store the assembler in the computer's mainframe memory. In such situations the assembler can be permanently stored in some auxiliary memory such as a cassette or a disk. When required, the assembler would be read out from the external memory medium and loaded into the computer's mainframe memory. Such assemblers are referred to as nonresident assemblers and, as previously mentioned, the process is more time consuming because of the slow I/O devices involved.

19-3.5 Cross-Assemblers

Because of limitations in capabilities of μCs, some manufacturers provide assemblers that can be operated on larger computers other than the subject or target μC system. Such assemblers, called *cross-assemblers*, never reside in the μC memory. They are generally designed to operate on larger minicomputers or medium-scale computers that are called *host computers*.

Since they are not resident in μCs, cross-assemblers are portable (i.e., they are designed to operate on several different host computers). Minicomputer cross-assemblers are generally written in FORTRAN because they are easier to design and write. Also, FORTRAN is used by a large variety of minicomputers and larger machines, which enhances the portability of the μC cross-assembler. However, cross-assemblers written in FORTRAN do have certain disadvantages. They generally require larger memories and take longer to execute. The assembled program must still be communicated or transferred from the host computer to the target μC. This means that some other I/O medium such as punched paper tape or a cassette would still be required.

In some situations access to an in-house host computer may not be possible. An alternative solution is provided by nationwide time-sharing networks, such as TYMESHARE, which make cross-assemblers (written in FORTRAN) available to several subscribers through telephone line networks, including mass storage facilities together with extensive software that is time tested and proven. Access to these networks is by TTY (teletypewriter) terminals that are connected to a large, central host computer through telephone lines. The same TTY unit can be used for normal I/O operations with the μC system. Additionally, most time-sharing services offer sophisticated text editors that allow the user to modify or update programs rapidly and accurately. Time-sharing networks also offer other μC support software.

19-4 THE INTERPRETER

19-4.1 What is an Interpreter?

We have seen that the assembler is a powerful tool for developing application programs. However, recall that the program has to be completely assembled first and an object module prepared before it can be loaded into the program memory of the target computer for execution. Using an assembler, the programmer cannot test or run the program until the entire object program is first assembled.

Another very useful software development tool is the *interpreter,* which is a computer program that translates each instruction in a *source program* into machine language code and then immediately executes that particular instruction on the target machine itself. Unlike the assembler, the interpreter does not prepare an object module, so a host computer is not required.

19-4.2 Advantages of Interpreters

1. *Interactive.* Interpreters are interactive, which means that during the program development phase, the programmer is able to maintain a dialog with the computer through a keyboard for entering instructions and data and a CRT for displaying

the results of the executed instruction. The *interpreter* permits the programmer to write the source program in a higher-level, interactive language, have it translated into machine code, and executed, thereby giving an immediate response from the system. This enables the programmer to check and debug the instruction on the spot, correct it if an error is indicated, and recheck the modified instruction before proceeding with the rest of the program. BASIC and FORTAN are two of the most commonly used interactive languages. The interactive and conversational facilities offered by such languages (using an interpreter) are presented in Fig. 19-4, which shows a sample of a dialog that would occur between the programmer and the computer for calculating the cube root of a number.

2. *Entry from Multiple I/O Devices.* Another significant advantage of the interpreter is that it can respond to entries from more than one I/O terminal connected to the system. Because only one instruction is translated and executed at a time, the same interpreter can simultaneously process several programs input from different terminals. The system accepts one statement from the first program, translates it, and executes it. The interpreter proceeds to the next program, accepts a statement from it, translates it, and executes it. This process is repeated until *all* the programs are served. Then it comes back to the first program, starts with the next statement, and the whole process is repeated.

Since the computer operates at speeds much faster than the response and reaction times of the human programmer, the entire operation appears as if each terminal and programmer are serviced independently.

3. *Error Detection.* We have seen that the assembler will detect errors in syntax but not in semantics. The interpreter has a significant advantage in this respect. It will certainly catch syntax errors but, additionally, because the source program state-

---

Programmer: CALCULATE CUBE ROOT
Computer: ENTER VALUE OF NUMBER
Programmer: 64
Computer: ITS CUBE ROOT IS 4
WANT CALCULATION REPEATED?
Programmer: NO
Computer: NEXT INSTRUCTION PLEASE
Programmer: END OF PROGRAM
Computer: THANK YOU
GOOD DAY TO YOU

Figure 19-4 Interactive dialog on CRT display.

ment is translated and executed immediately and the result displayed on the CRT, the programmer can also detect errors in semantics and take steps to correct them.

19-4.3 Shortcomings of Interpreters

There are two principal shortcomings associated with interpreters. First, if an assembler is used, this program is required to be present in the host computer's memory (or the target computer's memory, if it is a resident assembler) only during the time that an object program is prepared. At other times, the assembler can be removed, and the same memory space can be used for storing other information. When an interpreter is used, it must be present in the memory at all times. This means that a larger memory is required.

The second shortcoming of the interpreter is that the program run time can be significantly degraded. The interactive nature of the interpreter introduces an element in the system that is inherently slow—the human programmer—and this adversely impacts the program run time. (*Note.* The interpretive process is inherently slow even if no human input is required during the program operation.)

19-5 THE "BASIC" INTERPRETER

In Chapter 18 we discussed BASIC, which is presently perhaps the most popular interactive language used with μCs. In this section we will briefly describe two sets of commands that are commonly used with the BASIC interpreter: file manipulation commands and line editing commands. These commands vary from one system to another; students are advised to consult and study the manuals for the specific system before using them. However, the following descriptions give a reasonable overview of these interactive commands.

19-5.1 File Manipulation Commands

1. *The Opening Command.* Every file must be opened with some command that tells the interpreter to allocate a certain number of locations in the memory for the file. The programmer will later store data words in these locations. The command used for this purpose is NEW. Each file is assigned a name or code, usually consisting of no more than six characters. Any entry in the file can be accessed by reference to this name for execution or for modifying or changing the data.
2. *The Execute Command.* This command, which is indicated by the code RUN, orders the interpreter to execute the program that was previously stored in the memory. The interpreter now starts with the lowest line number in the memory,

translates it, and executes it. The process is then repeated on all the statements until the END statement is reached or an error condition in the syntax is detected.

3. *The List Command.* After the program is entered into the memory, it is always desirable to have a printed version of it available before running it for actual use. A listing of the stored program can be initiated by the LIST command. Such a listing enables the programmer to check for errors and also documents the program. The LIST command can be used in three different ways.

(a) If the word LIST is used all by itself the interpreter will interpret this as a command to print out the entire program.

(b) If the word LIST is followed by a number, such as LIST 100, the computer will print out only the statement on line 100 of the program. (*Note.* Here 100 is used only as an example. It could be any line number assigned to any statement.)

(c) If the word LIST is followed by two numbers separated by a comma, such as LIST 10, 25, the computer will print out all statements from line 10 to line 25.

4. *The Tape and Key Commands.* The BASIC interpreter allows the data to be input from a paper tape reader and from the keyboard. The command TAPE transfers control to the tape reader. After the file has been entered into the memory, the programmer can return control to the keyboard by typing in the command KEY.

5. *The Punch Command.* The BASIC interpreter also allows the programmer to create a hard copy of the data words stored in the memory. By typing in the command PUNCH, the file in the memory can be punched out on the paper tape.

6. *Miscellaneous Commands.* In time-sharing systems, it is necessary for many subscribers to share the resources of a single, central computer. Such services use interpreters that provide additional commands as conveniences for their users. They include commands such as CLEAR, GOODBYE, SAVE, and THANK YOU. The functions of such commands are self-explanatory.

19-5.2 Line Editing Commands

During the developmental stages, programs written in higher-level interpretive languages must be edited before they can be used. A text editor is a tool that allows the programmer to do just that. A BASIC interpreter incorporates commands that enable the programmer to perform many of the same functions. These commands are briefly described here. Students should be aware that the exact words for these commands vary with different systems. There are no standardized commands available at this time that I am aware of, so only the functions performed by these commands are described.

1. *Enter Lines.* With this command the programmer starts entering the lines of the source program into the computer. The interpreter automatically assigns a number to each statement as it is keyed in by the programmer and stores it in the memory.

2. *Insert Lines.* This command enables the programmer to add or insert a line anywhere in the program except after the END statement. To insert an additional line in the program, the programmer must assign the proper line number to that statement indicating the exact point in the program where the additional statement is to be inserted. The interpreter places it at the right point and adjusts the line numbers of the subsequent statements accordingly.

3. *Replace Lines.* Many times the programmer wants to alter the contents of one or more lines in the program. This is usually done by replacing the original line with the altered line or a completely new line. The replace command allows the programmer to do this. This is accomplished by the programmer by entering the appropriate line number, followed by the corrected or new statement. The interpreter replaces the old line with the new statement. The rest of the statements in the program are not affected.

4. *Delete Lines.* Sometimes the programmer wants to delete a line from the program completely. To perform this operation, the programmer enters the number of the line to be deleted and depresses the carriage return key. No specific word for the command is entered. The interpreter deletes the line without disturbing any other lines in the program.

5. *Reassign Line Numbers.* This feature allows the programmer to reassign numbers to the lines of the program in accordance with specific instructions such as resequence the line numbers to even 10s. The command for this operation is RE-NUMBER. In addition to automatically resequencing the line numbers (as commanded by the programmer), the BASIC interpreter will also correct any references to the renumbered lines by subsequent statements in the program.

6. *Delete Characters From Partially Typed Lines.* This is a feature that allows the programmer to erase typing errors while entering the statement in the system. Parts of a partially typed line can be erased by depressing the backspace key, which is indicated by a left arrow (←) on a standard keyboard. Every time this key is depressed, one character to the left is deleted. No special command word is used for this function. Only a partially typed line can be deleted in this manner. Once the statement is entered into the system and is part of the text, the whole line must be deleted.

19-6 SUMMARY

Two widely used tools for software development were introduced in this chapter: the assembler and the interpreter. Although machine language programming gives the programmer complete control over the system, it does have some significant drawbacks. The assembler, which allows the user to write the program in symbolic language (the mnemonics), overcomes many of these shortcomings. The problems involved in manual assembly of programs have been enumerated.

The assembler program, which uses a computer-oriented instead of a procedure-oriented language such as FORTRAN, was described, starting with a statement of five objectives. The steps involved in translating the source program (written in assembly language) into an object program (written in machine code) were presented. The rules of syntax for the assembler statement were discussed with a fairly detailed description of each field in the statement. The problem of field identification was also presented with some of the currently used solutions. Next, the assembly language directives, also referred to as pseudo-operations codes, were presented. Some of the assembler directives used in μCs were briefly described; some examples were presented. This was followed by descriptions of symbol tables, both fixed and dynamic, and the macro assembler, together with some typical examples. The mechanics of assembler operation, which include the single-pass assembler as well as the more widely used two-pass assembler, were discussed, followed by brief descriptions of resident, nonresident, and cross-assemblers.

Interpreters were introduced, and some of their principal advantages were discussed. The interactive nature of interpreters was pointed out along with its advantages and shortcomings. The chapter concluded with a description of typical file manipulation commands and line editing commands that are generally available in BASIC *interpreters*.

19-7 REVIEW QUESTIONS

19-1   State the three levels at which microcomputers can be programmed. Which level gives the programmer maximum control over the operations and resources of the computer?

19-2   Give the principal function of the assembler program. What is the language used by the assembler? Is it possible to run an assembler designed for computer A on computer B? If not, why not?

19-3   Are the memory costs of a computer system higher or lower if an assembler is used instead of programming the μC in machine language? Why?

19-4   How many process steps are involved in manually assembling a program? What are the main disadvantages of hand assembling a program?

19-5   Explain which kinds of programming errors will be detected by an assembler and which kinds will not be detected and why.

19-6   Name the four fields used in an assembler statement.

19-7   What does the label field of an assembler statement contain? How is it used?

19-8   In what part or field of the assembler statement is the mnemonic code inserted? How many characters are assigned to this field?

19-9 What does the term "argument" mean? What does it refer to when used in an assembler statement?

19-10 What is the main advantage of using a fixed format for field identification in assembler statements?

19-11 Name some of the delimiters used for field identification in assembler statements.

19-12 If the free format is used for field identification in an assembler statement, how is the mnemonic field identified from the rest of the fields?

19-13 Explain what assembly language directives are and what they do.

19-14 Briefly explain what the ORG and END directives are and what they do.

19-15 Which assembler directive assigns a numerical value to a label?

19-16 What is a constant directive? What is the pseudo-operations code for it, and where is it placed in the assembler statement? Where is the address placed in the assembler statement?

19-17 What is the fixed table or dictionary as it is used in assembler operations? Briefly explain its function.

19-18 What is the dynamic table or dictionary as it is used in assembler operations? Briefly explain its function.

19-19 What is macro ability as used in assemblers? What does it do?

19-20 Do macros require push-pop operation of the LIFO stack just like subroutines? If not, why not?

19-21 Briefly explain what a single-pass assembler does.

19-22 What is accomplished during the first pass in a two-pass assembler? Explain.

19-23 What is accomplished during the second pass in a two-pass assembler? Briefly explain.

19-24 What kind of an assembler enables a μC to generate its own object program? Where is such an assembler generally stored?

19-25 What is a cross-assembler? Does it reside in the memory of a μC? If not, why not? Where does it reside?

19-26 Briefly describe what an interpreter is. How is it different from an assembler?

19-27 Explain why interpreters are considered to be interactive.

19-28 In what language must the source program be written if an interpreter is used? What are the most popular languages used with μCs for this purpose?

19-29 Will the interpreter catch both the syntax and the semantics errors in the source program? Explain.

19-30 What does the opening command do in an interpreter? What is the command word usually used for this purpose?

19-31 The RUN command in an interpreter tells it to execute the previously stored program. How is the program terminated?

19-32 If a programmer wishes to modify the contents of one of the lines in the program using an interpreter, what command(s) would the programmer have to use?

20

OPERATING SYSTEMS AND SYSTEMS SOFTWARE

20-1 OPERATING THE COMPUTING SYSTEM

Fundamentally, computers (including μCs) are designed to produce certain results. To do this, the computer must be properly scheduled, loaded, and controlled either by manual or computer-assisted methods. In this chapter we present and discuss the latter methods. First, however, we briefly discuss the manual method.

20-1.1 Manual or Stand-Alone System

In the manual system, often referred to as the *stand-alone system* or *operation,* the human operator schedules the resources of the computing system (including setting up the appropriate I/O devices), loads the various programs into the computer memory, and controls and directs the running and operation of the entire system. Furthermore, in case of errors or malfunctions, the burden of finding and correcting the problem(s) falls on the operator. This is time consuming.

In the early days of computers the manual method of operating the system was the only one available. As technology advanced and the speed and reliability of computers and other peripheral equipment significantly increased, it became apparent that the human operator was the weakest link in the processing chain and the principal impediment to enhancing the *throughput rate* of the system. The throughput rate of a computing system is the average of jobs or tasks that the system processes per unit of time. Clearly, the stand-alone system is inefficient for scheduling and processing jobs involving large amounts of data. Fortunately, computer-assisted systems have been developed and are currently in wide use. These systems greatly reduce the burden on the human operator and significantly improve the throughput rate.

511

20-1.2 Systems Software

Systems engineering is concerned with configuring a system consisting of several different pieces of hardware and intended to perform specific jobs or tasks. The main effort involves designing and incorporating several interfaces for diversified pieces of equipment so that the equipment operates harmoniously as a coherent, integrated system.

The stand-alone system is not adequate for today's computing systems. A number of programs are used to replace the tasks performed by the human operator. In the computer profession such programs are called *systems programs,* and the programs are collectively referred to as *systems software.*

Systems software includes assemblers and interpreters, as well as compilers. Text editors, utility programs, loaders, and operating systems are also part of systems software. We will discuss them in this chapter.

20-2 OPERATING SYSTEMS

20-2.1 What are Operating Systems?

An *operating system* (OS) is a master control program that controls and monitors (supervises) all the programs that run on the computer. The OS controls the operation of the overall system. It handles interrupts, schedules I/O devices, and monitors the loading of programs into the computer memory. Either the entire OS or part of it generally resides in the mainframe memory of the computer. It is common practice to have another copy of the OS stored on some other off-line device such as magnetic tape to avoid the loss of this important program through accidental erasure or modification. Since the OS controls the entire system, all other systems programs (loaders, utility programs, etc.) and application programs interact with the OS, not the computer.

20-2.2 Advantages and Shortcomings

Any computer system can operate in a *stand-alone* mode. However, most computers today operate with minimal OS. The advantages of OS over the stand-alone systems are:

1. The OS relieves the human operator of the burden of scheduling each task and allocating the resources of the computer to these tasks. This enhances the throughput rate significantly.
2. The OS handles the job of loading programs into the computer memory.
3. The OS handles the job of processing each task in well-defined and organized manner. Thus all jobs are presented to the system in a consistent way, and the system therefore handles them consistently.

4. The OS handles several details involved in data transfers. For example, it relieves the human operator of the burden of switching the I/O devices ON and checking to see if it is available for data transfer at a particular time. In short, the OS greatly simplifies the task of I/O programming.
5. I/O programs are often written as subroutines. Using operating systems, these subroutines need not be included in each application program. Thus the OS saves significant time and effort in writing application programs.
6. If OSs are not used each I/O device must be identified and called out by its *physical* or actual address. The OS allows the programmer to assign dummy addresses, often called *logical addresses,* to call out the I/O devices in the program. When the program is run, the OS assigns a specific I/O device address or number to each logical address. The real advantage in using this procedure is that several different I/O devices can be used with the same application program.

There are also disadvantages of OS. The main one is that either the entire system or a minimum part of it must reside in the mainframe memory when an application program is run. The minimum memory requirement for the less sophisticated OS is about 500 bytes. The more sophisticated OSs require a minimum of 5000 bytes of memory space. This disadvantage is minimal compared to the advantages.

20-3 PRINCIPAL TASKS PERFORMED BY OSs

OSs are designed to perform several functions, most of which fall in three broad categories.

20-3.1 The Program Development Task

Programs are developed and written in many different languages. Some are written in assembly-level languages of different computers. Many are written in higher-level languages such as BASIC, FORTRAN, and COBOL. Many subroutines for specific mathematical functions such as multiplication and division have already been written. In fact, they could be considered as standard programs. The same is true of many data-processing or data-handling subroutines. Unfortunately, such routines are often written in different languages. It would be a waste of time and effort to rewrite these programs in a language acceptable to a particular user's computer.

Many OSs are designed to solve this particular problem. They accept routines written in more than one source language and then call up the appropriate *translator* program, which translates each source statement and reduces it to a machine language format acceptable to that particular computer. Effectively, the translator produces a standard format module. Several such modules can be produced and used in the application program. The standard modules produced by the OS are assigned relocatable object codes. This allows the modules to be located anywhere in the application programs, since no absolute addresses are assigned to the machine language statements. This technique saves programming costs because each previously developed routine does not have to be rewritten each time it is needed in an application program.

20-3.2 The Job Control Task

20-3.2.1 Basic Batch Processing

One technique used for processing data is batch processing, defined as a means by which items to be processed are coded and collected into groups *prior* to processing. Batch processing is different from operating on-line to the system. If the user issues a series of commands to the computer, one at a time, and gets a response to each command before proceeding to the next command, the process is referred to as an on-line operation. On the other hand, in a batch-oriented system, all the commands and data relevant to the program are grouped together and input into the computer as a single unit. A typical batch-oriented input would be by means of a deck of punched cards. Programs can also be input to the batch system from remote terminals. In this case the system is said to have a *remote job entry* capability.

One of the tasks performed by an OS is controlling the jobs performed by a computer system using the batch-processing technique. In such a system the computer controls the sequential processing of one job at a time. Likewise, it automatically handles the transition from one job to another. An input file, often also referred to as the input stream, is composed of several job modules. Each job module consists of three basic types of information.

1. *Control Information.* This information identifies the job to be performed and the start of the job module.
2. *Program Information.* This includes the program, either in source code or object code, that is to be executed.
3. *Data Information.* This includes sets of data that are to be used during program execution.

If we used punched cards for batch processing the job module would consist of one (or more) job card(s) giving the control information, several cards giving the program information, and several cards giving the data information. This is shown in Fig. 20-1. Notice that the input file consists of several job modules.

Figure 20-2 shows that the input file is fed sequentially into the data memory of the computer. Only one job module is present in the data memory at any

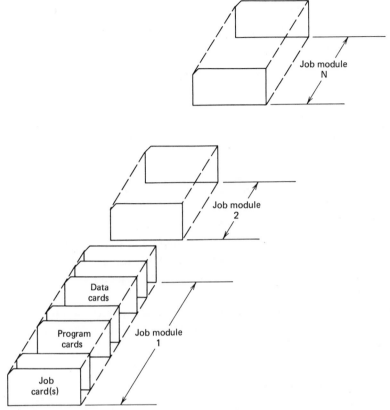

Figure 20-1   Input file for batch processing using punched cards.

one time. The OS is permanently stored in the program memory, which also contains the application or user program. The application program is usually stored in the program memory temporarily for the duration of processing that particular application only. The OS controls the entire operation.

20-3.2.2 Queued Sequential Batch Processing A more complex batch-processing system, called *queued sequential batch processing,* first loads the job modules into some mass storage device, such as a disk. The job modules are queued in this mass storage device sequentially, and a *sequence table* is constructed and stored in the data memory, as shown in Fig. 20-3. Each job module is assigned a starting address in the mass storage device; these addresses are maintained in the sequence table. Upon completion of each job, the computer searches the sequence table for the next job, which is then called out and executed.

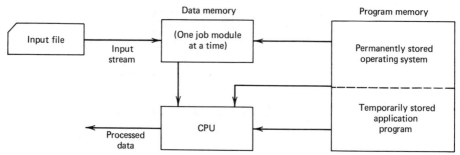

Figure 20-2   Basic batch processing operation.

20-3.2.3 Priority Queued Batch Processing A more sophisticated system is obtained by a slight modification to the queued sequential batch-processing system. The sequence numbers or addresses in the sequence table are replaced by priority numbers. When the processing of a particular job module is completed, the sequence table is searched for the next highest priority number. The module corresponding to this number, not the next sequential job module, is fetched from the job queue and processed.

In most batch-processing systems, paper punched tape devices are not used because they are slow. A card punch/reader unit is faster, more practical, and more often used.

20-3.3 The Data Control Task

One of the primary goals of OSs is to lessen the burden on the human operator. OSs are designed to facilitate the task of data management by reducing the

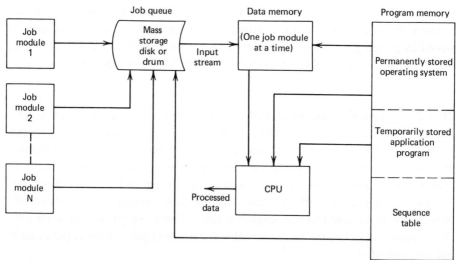

Figure 20-3   Queued sequential batch processing.

effort required by the programmer/operator to attend to the problems of data organization and storage. Several methods of data organization and access are provided by the software. Such facilities include:

- Error detection/correction in data transfers.
- Data buffering.
- Dynamically scheduling different I/O devices.
- Controlling data transfers between mainframe memories and auxiliary storage devices.
- Handling data uniformly to and from all I/O devices, regardless of the type of device used.

20-4 SYSTEMS SOFTWARE

20-4.1 What are Operating Systems?

As mentioned in Section 20-1.2, systems software consists of several programs that aid the user in operating the computer system. In this section we briefly describe some of the principal programs and capabilities of systems software.

20-4.1.1 Monitors and Supervisory Systems A *monitor* is a program generally used to oversee only one kind of activity of the computer system. In other words, it is a single-purpose program. For example, a simple monitor includes loading an application program, executing it, and terminating the job. Such simple monitors are generally used on very small computing systems.

More sophisticated monitors usually include I/O programs of a generalized nature. This means that the programmer is relieved of the burden of writing individual programs. When this capability is added to the monitor, the resulting system is called a *supervisory system*. With *supervisors,* it is often possible to store application programs in both source and object forms. When this capability is available, the supervisor accesses the assembler (and, in some cases, also the compiler). The source program is translated into an object program. After all the appropriate programs are translated, they are loaded into the computer memory by the supervisor and are then executed.

20-4.1.2 Resident Loader Once the source programs are translated into object programs, they must be loaded into the computer memory for execution. A *loader* is a program that performs the task of loading the object programs stored in auxiliary memory devices, such as disks or tapes, into the computer memory. Resident loaders are loader programs that are permanently stored in the computer memories. ROM chips are often used for storing resident loaders.

Besides performing the loading function, resident loaders are often designed to perform other related functions. For example, as the application program is loaded into the memory, the loader often checks each byte or word for parity to insure that bits are not lost during the loading process. The loader also checks the number of bytes in a record to insure that none have been lost during loading. Resident loaders are of two kinds (absolute and relocatable).

Absolute Loader Each instruction of an object program must be loaded into a specific memory location. An *absolute object program* is one in which a specific, *ultimate* memory location is assigned to each instruction. Each memory address is fixed and final. The loader reads an object code line and stores each successive instruction in successive addresses in the memory. Such a program is called an absolute loader, and it is the simplest loader program.

Relocatable Loader Absolute loaders are simple and work well in relatively simple systems. As computing systems get more sophisticated and complex, they are often required to run several programs *simultaneously*. Furthermore, the combinations of programs that are simultaneously executed often change from day to day as the mix of the jobs to be performed changes. If absolute object programs are used, they would have to be reassembled (or recompiled) every time they are executed. This is needed to accommodate the desired mix of programs in the computer memory, with different addresses for the same program during different runs. The shortcomings of such an approach are obvious.

Application programs can be assembled (or compiled) as *relocatable object programs*. In these programs the first location is always assigned as the zero address. Each subsequent instruction in the program is marked accordingly. The loader program is given the actual or absolute address in the memory where the programmer wishes to load the object program. This address is automatically added as an offset to each marked address in the object program by the loader. Thus the loader loads the program into the memory address specified by the programmer; this address could be different for different runs of the program. Such a loader is called a relocatable loader.

20-4.1.3 Servicing I/O Transfers Virtually all computing operations involve transfers of data between various I/O devices and the computer. Because of extensive usage and experience, standardized subroutines for I/O transfers have been developed. Such subroutines have two principal advantages. First, standardized subroutines result in a uniform or standard system for handling data and error conditions. Second, when more than one programmer designs programs for the same computing system, the use of standardized I/O subroutines insures compatibility between the various programs that are developed.

Most computing systems today operate under control of OS, and these systems are effectively used for the mechanics of handling I/O transfers. The actual I/O transfer instructions are not placed in each application program. Instead, they are included in the OS. When input or output data transfers are needed in the application programs, the programmer sends out a supervisor call by means of simple instructions such as READ or WRITE. The OS then takes over, calls out the appropriate I/O transfer subroutine, and supervises its execution. When the transfer is completed, the OS returns control to the application program.

The actual transfer of data between the CPU and each I/O device in the system takes place under control of the appropriate driver subroutine for that particular device. These subroutines are usually placed in the OS. The driver subroutines do more than just handle the transfers. Before transferring the data, the subroutine does the following.

- Checks if the power is turned ON for the appropriate I/O device.
- Checks the current status of the I/O device.
- In the case of tape units, checks if the tape is loaded.
- In the case of punched card units, checks if the cards are in the hopper.

Data transfers take place only after positive responses are received from the applicable I/O device. If not, an error message is generally displayed on the operator's console by the operating system.

20-4.1.4 Examining and Altering Memory Cells During the program development and debugging stages, it is often desirable to examine the contents of a certain memory location. The OS usually makes this possible. The programmer or operator can address the desired memory location and have the contents displayed on the CRT display or printed out by the console typewriter. If modifications are necessary, the programmer/operator is able to do so through the console and then re-store the modified contents in the same memory location.

20-4.1.5 Logical Addresses for I/O Devices Sometimes it is necessary to change I/O devices in the system. Since I/O devices are physically connected to the CPU, each I/O device has a physical address that refers to the actual lines connected to the device. If the physical or actual addresses are used in the applications programs, these addresses would have to be changed if the I/O devices are changed. This undesirable situation is usually avoided by incorporating into the OS the capability of handling *logical addresses*. A *logical name* is a dummy address that is assigned to an I/O device by the programmer and used in the application programs instead of the actual or physical address. Prior to running the application program on the system, the programmer/operator assigns the physical address to each logical address used in the application program. The OS then handles the appropriate I/O device when referred by its corresponding logical address in the application program. Thus I/O devices in the system can be easily changed without changing their physical addresses in the application programs.

20-4.1.6 Trap Subroutines Subroutines are widely employed in many application programs. Those frequently used subroutines are often made a part of the OS. By so doing, the programmer is able to call out and use these subroutines without physically writing them into each application program. When the application program needs any of these subroutines (also called *trap subroutines*), it branches to the OS. The OS in turn branches to the trap subroutine, which is then executed.

Trap subroutines are used for handling recurring functions such as multiplication, division, square root, and floating-point arithmetic. Sometimes trap subroutines are also used to simulate hardware features not actually present in the equipments used in the system. The trap subroutines are designed to perform the same functions that hardware would normally perform.

20-4.1.7 Program Status Word (PSW) Display If the program is prematurely terminated for any reason, the operator must determine the status of the system so that corrective action can be taken. The OS is often designed with a capability for displaying the *program status word* (PSW) on some output device such as a CRT display or the printer. The PSW is a computer-generated word giving the operator information about a specific point in the program that is being currently executed or the point at which the program is terminated. Generally, the PSW indicates to the operator the status or condition of the system at that particular time. If the program has failed or terminated too early, the PSW also gives the address of the instruction that was not executed properly so that appropriate corrective action can be taken.

20-4.1.8 Task Priority and Scheduling As mentioned in Section 20-1.1, the computer operator must load the various programs and schedule the different jobs in a stand-alone system. With an OS, the operator is relieved of many of these tasks. Scheduling the various jobs for the computer is handled by the OS. With an OS, the operator assigns priorities, as desired, to a group of jobs that are to be performed. These jobs are placed in the input stream of the computer. The OS automatically runs the jobs in accordance with their respective priorities, starting with the highest priority. If, for any reason, there is a gap in the job being processed, the OS will automatically switch to the next lower-priority job and start executing it. When the previous higher-priority job is ready, the OS switches back to the uncompleted higher-priority job, executes it, and resumes the lower-priority job.

20-4.1.9 Operator-Machine Communications

Two-way communications between the operator and the computer system is a very important aspect of successful system operations. The OS provides the principal means of achieving this objective. OS includes the capability of informing the operator of the computer status, indicating any actions the operator should take to maintain the system in an operating mode. Such instructions to the operator are usually printed out.

It is possible that the programmer inadvertently may have used an instruction not included in the instruction set. The OS detects such an illegal instruction and automatically branches to a subroutine for handling this instruction. This subroutine terminates the execution of the program and indicates this condition to the operator by printing out the appropriate error message. The OS also detects hardware malfunctions in the system and indicates this condition to the operator by means of a printed message.

20-4.1.10 Timekeeping Functions

In many computer installations different jobs are processed on a time-sharing basis for different customers. In such cases the computer system's operating time is charged to the respective customers' accounts. Many of these systems include a real-time clock, which enables the OS to log in jobs as they are started and log out jobs as they are completed. The time logging is done by the actual time of the day. The OS prints out the time a particular job was started and the time it was completed. Then the OS totals up the elapsed time and prints it out. This very desirable feature is widely used for billing purposes.

20-4.1.11 Memory Protection/Security

Many users using a single computer system on a time-sharing basis poses two critical problems. First, specific areas of the mainframe memory are allocated to different user programs. These areas of memory (user files) must be protected from accidental erasures and/or unintentional alterations of their contents. The OS includes features that provide protection against such erasures or alterations.

Second, since several users' personnel have access to user files stored in the memory, *security* is also a problem. Access to memory files by unauthorized personnel must be prevented. Again, the OS is called on to handle this problem. A list of authorized *ID numbers* or *passwords* is stored in the system, and this list is accessed by the OS. When anybody attempts to use the resources of the computer, the OS checks the ID number or password against the approved list before permitting access to the system and its memory files.

20-4.2 Utility Programs

In addition to the several software capabilities described in Section 20-4.1, systems software also includes several programs that are referred to as *utility programs,* or just *utilities.* These programs generally perform functions that are auxiliary to the execution of other application programs and support them. In this section we briefly describe four categories of utility programs.

20-4.2.1 Code Conversion Programs These programs are used to convert codes given in one system to their equivalents in other systems. Some of the commonly used programs convert pure binary numbers to numbers in the BCD system and vice versa, or they perform conversions from the binary to the hexadecimal system and vice versa. Similar conversion programs are used for computer systems that use the octal numbering system.

20-4.2.2 Sorting and Merging Programs *Sorting* is a process that arranges items of information (or records) according to certain specified rules. These rules are identified by a key (a field of digits) contained in the items or records to be sorted. For instance, in a digital sort, the key is first sorted on the *least-significant* digit. The process is repeated on each successive higher-order digit until the items or records are finally sorted on the *most-significant* digit.

The sorting process is generally followed by a *merging* process. The merging process produces a single sequence of items or records that is ordered according to some rule, from two or more previously ordered sequences. Note that in both the sort and merge operations neither the contents, size, structure, nor total number of items or records are changed. Usually, in computing systems, the sort program rearranges records on some auxiliary memory device such as disks or tapes. The end result of the sort/merge processes can be stored either in auxiliary devices or in the mainframe memory.

In using the sort/merge programs, the user supplies information on the file to be sorted and merged through some medium, such as punched cards, that also specifies the sorting criterion or key and the desired format of the output. The user specifies only the sorting process. The utility program takes care of implementing the details for execution. The sort/merge programs are generally required for computing systems that process large volumes of data.

20-4.2.3 Copy Programs In data processing systems data or information stored in one type of auxiliary storage device is often required to be copied into another type of auxiliary storage device. In this case the data are neither processed nor altered. For instance, we may want to copy the data stored in a tape unit onto a disk unit or take the data stored in a disk and transfer it to a printer for preparing a hard copy. Utility programs are written for such simple routine tasks, and these can be called out by the OS as needed.

20-4.2.4 Text Editors *Text editors* are programs that allow the programmer to specify and execute changes and modifications in source programs while they are stored in the computer. Although text editors are mainly used to prepare source programs, they are also used for editing other types of text material such as files, lists of names, addresses, numbers, and descriptors. Text editors are usually used to detect and analyze coding errors in source programs. The editor scans the source code and detects violations of programming rules as well as program format.

Three levels of editing commands are usually available in text editors. Some commands permit the programmer to manipulate whole programs or entire data files. They are usually capable of merging two or more separate programs. Sophisticated editors with such commands are generally available for larger computer systems.

At the next level, the commands allow manipulation on records or lines. Such programs enable the programmer to add, delete, or modify entire records or lines. Editors are designed to generate a listing that shows the existing text in the memory along with their respective assigned line numbers. Changes, insertions, and deletions are made by referencing the applicable line numbers. Most editors automatically resequence the modified lines and reassign the appropriate line numbers.

The third level of commands allows the programmer to edit and change only a single character in a line. Character editing is most useful in a complicated line in the program. Retyping an entire line introduces the possibility of other additional errors in that line. Character editing makes it possible to modify or change only a single character without disturbing the rest of the characters in the line.

20-5 RESIDENT OPERATING SYSTEMS

Previously in this chapter we discussed OSs and the various software programs and capabilities associated with them. In this section we discuss precisely where the OSs reside. This is important because it affects the time element required by the OS to respond to demands for its services and capabilities. This is particularly true in *real-time* systems.

Real-time systems respond to the occurrence of events before these events are concluded. The real-time system must respond rapidly so that real-time events can be serviced and/or controlled in the appropriate manner. On the other hand, an OS used in batch-processing applications takes and services one job at a time from a batch or stack of jobs. The following paragraphs describe the various places in the system that the OSs can reside together with their respective advantages and disadvantages.

20-5.1 Mainframe Memory-Resident OS

In this case the entire OS is stored in the mainframe memory. All the programs and/or subroutines and *utility programs* are resident in the mainframe memory at any time. The principal advantage of this approach is that it speeds up the overall system operations; since all the programs and subroutines comprising the OS are preloaded into the memory, no additional time is lost in loading them from auxiliary storage devices such as disks. The main disadvantage is that the OS programs occupy a significant portion of the mainframe memory, thereby making less memory space available for storing other programs and data. This approach is an inefficient use of the memory because many of the subroutines and utility programs available in the OS are not used very frequently.

20-5.2 Disk-Resident OS

In many computing systems the OS is not stored in the mainframe memory at all times. Instead, it is permanently stored on magnetic disks. The OS is copied into the mainframe memory from the disk only as and when needed. To do this, a much smaller disk drive program is permanently stored in the mainframe memory. This program calls out other subroutines as needed for functions such as error handling and scheduling.

Using a disk for permanent storage of the OS greatly reduces the demand for space in the mainframe memory, which can then be used for other purposes. Because of the time required to transfer the OS from the disk to the mainframe memory, this approach is slower than the approach just described. However, disk-to-mainframe memory transfers are done rapidly, so the time lost is minimal. One major advantage is that since the user is not restricted by the available space in the mainframe memory, a much more sophisticated OS with more subroutines can be used without tying up a significant portion of the available memory resources.

20-5.3 Tape-Resident OS

The magnetic disk storage device used for storing the OS can be replaced by magnetic tape units. All of the benefits and shortcomings of the disk unit approach also apply to the tape unit approach, with one additional disadvantage. Tape units are sequentially accessed storage devices, so *tape-resident OSs* will naturally take longer to operate than the *disk-resident OSs,* since disks are semirandom-access memory units.

20-6 SUMMARY

This chapter started with a description of the manual or stand-alone method of scheduling, loading, controlling, and operating a computer system. Since the human operator is an important part of this procedure, the system is inefficient and has several shortcomings, which were pointed out. The concept of a master program, called the operating system (OS), which resides in the mainframe memory of the computer and relieves the human operator of many of the routine tasks, was introduced. Systems programs, which generally make up the OS, were introduced and briefly described. The main tasks performed by the OS were discussed. This included the program development task, the job control task, queued sequential batch processing, priority queued batch processing, and data control tasks. Monitors and supervisory systems were presented along with the resident loader (including the absolute and relocatable loaders). Next, utility programs were described. These included code conversion programs, sort/merge, copy programs, and text editors. Finally, resident operating systems were discussed, including mainframe memory-resident OSs, disk-resident OSs, and tape-resident OSs.

20-7 REVIEW QUESTIONS

20-1 Briefly describe the role of the human operator in a stand-alone computer system.

20-2 How are programming errors and equipment malfunctions handled in a stand-alone computing system?

20-3 What is meant by the *throughput rate* of a computing system? Define it. How is it measured?

20-4 In a computing system, what is the principal obstacle to improving the throughput rate? Explain.

20-5 Briefly describe what should be done to stand-alone computer systems to improve the throughput rate.

20-6 What is systems software? Briefly state what it contains.

20-7 Briefly describe OSs.

20-8 Explain how I/O programs are written and handled in application programs when OSs are available for the intended computer system.

20-9 What is the difference between the physical address and the logical address as applied to I/O devices? Explain.

20-10 What is the principal disadvantage of OSs?

20-11 List the principal tasks performed by the OSs.

20-12 Describe the role of the OS in the program development effort.

20-13 Refer to Question 20-12 and the response to it. Is it possible to use the same standard format module, produced by the OS in more than one application program for the same computer? If so, explain how this is done.

20-14 Briefly describe batch processing.

20-15 Briefly describe the role played by the computer in a batch processing operation.

20-16 In a batch processing operation the input file consists of several job modules. State and briefly explain the three basic types of information contained in each module.

20-17 If queued sequential batch processing is used, how does the computer determine which job is to be executed after completion of the in-process job?

20-18 What does the sequence table contain if priority queued batch processing is used?

20-19 List five data management tasks that are handled by the *operating system* and not the human operator.

20-20 What is the principal difference between a monitor system and a supervisory system?

20-21 What is a resident loader? What does it do?

20-22 What is an absolute object program? What is an absolute loader?

20-23 Briefly describe a relocatable loader.

20-24 What are the two principal advantages of standardized subroutines for I/O transfers when used with OSs?

20-25 Explain how the OS handles I/O transfers when standardized I/O subroutines are used.

20-26 Is it possible to examine and alter the contents of memory cells if an OS is used? Explain why it is necessary.

20-27 What is a logical name or logical address as used in connection with I/O devices? Why is it used?

20-28 What are trap subroutines? Explain.

20-29 Briefly define the program status word.

20-30 Briefly state what operator-machine communications are possible by using an OS.

20-31 What is the function of a real-time clock in a computing system? Explain.

20-32 Explain why memory protection and security are necessary in time-sharing systems.

20-33 List the programs that are commonly categorized as utility programs.

20-34 State the three levels of program/data manipulations that are possible with text editors.

20-35 Define real-time systems and briefly state why they are used.

20-36 Is it possible to store the entire OS in the mainframe memory? If so, what are the principal advantages and disadvantages?

20-37 What are the principal advantages and disadvantages of disk-resident and tape-resident OSs?

A

THE ASCII CHARACTER SET AND CODES

The ASCII (American Standard Code for Information Interchange) code was mentioned and briefly discussed in connection with the transformation of data into information and vice versa (see Section 16-1.2). The ASCII code is a 7-bit code, with the least-significant bit labeled b_1 and the most-significant bit labeled b_7, as shown in Fig. A-1.

Table A-1 shows the ASCII character set, which contains numerals, uppercase and lowercase alphabetical characters, and various symbols, together with their respective bit codes. In columns numbered 0 and 1, various control codes are given. All of these codes plus the SP code in column 2 and the DEL code in column 7 are *nonprinting* codes. The rest of the characters in the table are all printable. An eighth bit, b_8, is usually added to the 7-bit ASCII code as the parity bit.

The following codes in column 0 are the *printer control characters:* BEL, BS, LF, CR.

The following codes in columns 0 and 1 are *auxiliary device control characters:* ENQ, DC1, DC2, DC3 and DC4.

b_7	b_6	b_5	b_4	b_3	b_2	b_1

Figure A-1 ASCII code bit format.

Table A-1   THE ASCII SYSTEM CHARACTER CODES

b₇ ⟶					0	0	0	0	1	1	1	1
	b₆ ⟶				0	0	1	1	0	0	1	1
		b₅ ⟶			0	1	0	1	0	1	0	1
b_4	b_3	b_2	b_1	Row Number	0	1	2	3	4	5	6	7
0	0	0	0	0	NUL	DLE	SP	0	@	P	'	p
0	0	0	1	1	OSH	DC1	!	1	A	Q	a	q
0	0	1	0	2	STX	DC2	'	2	B	R	b	r
0	0	1	1	3	ETX	DC3	#	3	C	S	c	s
0	1	0	0	4	EOT	DC4	$	4	D	T	d	t
0	1	0	1	5	ENQ	NAK	%	5	E	U	e	u
0	1	1	0	6	ACK	SYN	&	6	F	V	f	v
0	1	1	1	7	BEL	ETB	'	7	G	W	g	w
1	0	0	0	8	BS	CAN	(	8	H	X	h	x
1	0	0	1	9	HT	EM	)	9	I	Y	i	y
1	0	1	0	10	LF	SUB	*	:	J	Z	j	z
1	0	1	1	11	VT	ESC	+	;	K	[	k	{
1	1	0	0	12	FF	FS	'	<	L	\	l	:
1	1	0	1	13	CR	GS	-	=	M	]	m	}
1	1	1	0	14	SO	RS	.	>	N	∧	n	~
1	1	1	1	15	SI	US	/	?	O	—	o	DEL

Source. Carol Ann Ogdin, Software Design for Microcomputers, Copyright © 1978, p. 22. Reprinted by permission of Prentice-Hall, Inc., Englewood Cliffs, New Jersey. A few minor modifications have been made to conform to the material in this text.

B

SYSTEM TESTING, CHECKOUT, AND VALIDATION

B-1 PROBLEMS OF MICROCOMPUTER SYSTEM TESTING

Microcomputers represent a significant technological advance in the discipline of system design (provided everything works as it should). Getting the system to work in the desired manner is another matter. Furthermore, when it does not work as expected, troubleshooting the system may become a test engineer's nightmare. There are several reasons why testing microprocessor chips is more difficult and challenging than testing other digital semiconductor chips such as IC logic chips or semiconductor memory chips.

1. Many IC chips and memory chips are designed as regularly structured logic devices. In other words, the logical configurations are replicated many times on the same chip. Such chips may be tested easily with a series of repetitive bit patterns. On the other hand, microprocessors (and many of their support chips) are inherently more complex devices in which logical configurations are not replicated. They have many different logical blocks (registers, accumulators, counters, adders, etc.) and several internal data busses that transmit data to and from many different locations within the chip. Consequently, testing with simple, repetitive bit patterns is not very feasible.

2. In microprocessor chips it is impossible to isolate one solitary logic block such as a specific register or the adder and examine its contents with an oscilloscope or other similar test instrument. Such data can only be tested or examined in an indirect way (i.e., by monitoring the input data signals to the microprocessor and examining the output data signals). Furthermore, testing of both signals (input and output) must be done at the appropriate times. This means that synchronization of **531**

the test equipment with the timing of the microprocessor becomes a challenging task.

3. Another major problem with testing microprocessors is that the same processor has to work with several different programs. The fact that it works satisfactorily with one program does not necessarily mean that it will work satisfactorily with other programs. This might be due to more critical timing requirements in one program, say with I/O transfers, than in another.

4. Programs that have worked satisfactorily with the microprocessor are often changed or improved because of experience with it or because of changes in system requirements. The modified program may not work as well as the previous one when tested on the same microcomputer system. Therefore, if the program is modified or upgraded for any reason, it is also necessary to change the test program to reflect modifications and/or additions.

B-2 MICROCOMPUTER TESTING APPROACHES

There are several approaches to testing microcomputers. Most of them fall into one of four broad categories: computer simulation, signature testing, pattern recognition, and pattern generation.

B-2.1 Computer Simulation

B-2.1.1 Description This approach utilizes the services of a general-purpose (GP) computer, which is separate from and completely independent of the microcomputer under test. Often this GP computer is a minicomputer. Sometimes it is even a large-scale computer. A logic simulation program (often referred to as the *simulator*) is designed and run on this computer. The simulation program simulates the operation of the μC system including the CPU, the RAM, the ROM, and the operation of the I/O ports. The simulator also simulates the various interrupt inputs.

The simulation program, which is usually available from the manufacturer of the microcomputer, specifies the stimuli (i.e., various inputs) and their corresponding responses (i.e., the appropriate corresponding outputs). The simulator is designed so that each transistor in the chip is switched from the ON state to the OFF state and vice versa at least once during the testing operation and, in most programs, they are switched several times. Such a procedure enables the test engineer to detect and, hopefully, isolate any malfunctions that may result from a transistor being stuck in the 1 state or in the 0 state. The stimuli and their corresponding responses are generally stored in a buffer memory. During testing, they are burst out to the system under test.

B-2.1.2 Advantages There are two principal advantages to the simulation approach of testing.

1. The approach does not require any extensive programming effort once the *simulator* is designed and operating.
2. The approach is useful in detecting and, in most cases, isolating catastrophic failures that could result from some logic block like a flip-flop being stuck in one or the other logical state due to a faulty circuit element.

B-2.1.3 Disadvantages The disadvantages of this method of testing follow.

1. Since the stimuli and their corresponding responses must be stored, extra memory space must be provided, and this is expensive.
2. The simulation program is designed for a specific I/O pattern. It is not possible to modify or alter this I/O pattern without also changing the simulation program. This approach has built-in inflexibility.
3. When a failure occurs in a particular I/O pattern, the system does not give the user any specific information connecting the failure to the user's particular application program. In other words, the user learns hardly anything from the failure except that a failure did occur.
4. Successful completion of a simulation test merely proves that the chip is only free of *steady-state* faults such as a flip-flop being stuck in one or the other logical state. It does not prove that the system will be free of faults in a *dynamic operating* mode.

B-2.2 Signature Testing

B-2.2.1 Description This approach requires the use of two identical μC systems; one is the system being tested, and the other is a known good system that has been previously tested. Using one or more test programs that have been previously checked out and known to be error free, a set of test pattern inputs is applied to both μC systems. The output patterns from both systems are compared. If the system under test is operating as it should, the output patterns from both systems should be identical, since the same programs were used with identical inputs in both systems.

B-2.2.2 Advantages There are two main advantages to this approach to testing.

1. Unlike the simulation approach to testing, it is not necessary to provide a large storage capacity in either the system under test or the known good system for storing the stimuli and their responses. This results in considerable savings in memory size.

2. The test patterns that are used are usually designed by the CPU designer, who is very familiar with the logic of the CPU. Thus the test patterns can be designed to check out specific logic blocks in the CPU. Likewise, the test patterns can be designed to check out one or more specific sequence of instructions. Both situations can, and do, provide the test engineer with at least some information that could be used in diagnosing the fault(s) in the system.

B-2.2.3 Disadvantages There are three potential shortcomings to this method of testing.

1. This method of testing assumes that the known good system is in perfect operating condition when the testing is done. It is possible that this system itself might degrade and fail after running several tests. In that case the test engineer might be misled into believing that the system under test has failed.

2. Another problem (that may be particularly troublesome) is obtaining the proper synchronization between the system under test and the known good system.

3. Finally, if the test patterns are devised by the designer of the chip, these patterns tend to be rigid and less flexible to input changes. This diminishes the validity of the test(s) to some extent. Test patterns designed by persons other than the designer may (perhaps) be more exhaustive and would be considered more valid.

B-2.3 Pattern Recognition

B-2.3.1 Description The *pattern recognition* technique overcomes the basic shortcoming of the *signature testing* approach. Instead of using a complete known good system for generating the output pattern every time a new microprocessor system is tested, this approach captures and stores the output pattern only once. This pattern is used as a reference against which the output pattern of the unit under test is compared. Thus the known good system has to work in the fault-free mode only once to produce the reference output pattern.

Testing with this approach involves two separate steps or procedures. The first step deals with creating and storing the reference pattern. We refer to this step as the *fixed pattern generation* procedure. The second step involves using the *fixed pattern* for comparing it with the pattern created by the unit under test.

B-2.3.2 Fixed Pattern Generation Procedure The sequence of operations of any microprocessor (and its associated chips such as ROMS, RAMS, I/O chips, etc.) can be readily simulated. The predefined sequence of instructions and the various input data sets associated with each sequence can be stored in memories. The simulated outputs can be sampled at the appropriate sampling times. The steps involved in the fixed pattern generation procedure are shown in Fig. B-1; a brief explanation of each block is given.

1. *The Simulator.* This is the known good microcomputer system consisting of the CPU, the ROMS, the RAMS, and the I/O chips, whose operational sequences are simulated, usually by means of PROMS. The various inputs, which consist of input data patterns, the corresponding output patterns, I/O lines (which are identified as either drivers or receivers), and various control signals, are sampled at preestablished times and fed into the interface electronics.
2. *The Clock System.* This system performs two major functions. First, it provides the necessary clock pulses to both the *simulator* and the *interface electronics* as well as the rest of the system. Second, the interface electronics block provides the timing signals to the clock system that are then used to synchronize the two logic blocks, as shown in Fig. B-1.
3. *The Interface Electronics.* The principal function of this block is to provide the logic necessary for interfacing the outputs of the simulator to the *error detection* logic. This block contains various receiver and driver circuits for the corresponding drivers and receivers in the simulator.

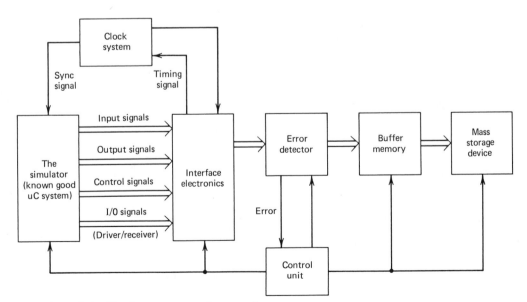

Figure B-1 Fixed pattern generation procedure.

4. *The Error Detector*. This block properly conditions all the I/O signals. Its principal function during the fixed pattern generation procedure is signal conditioning so that the outputs from the simulator could be properly stored in an auxiliary storage device. It plays a slightly different role during the subsequent test procedure.

5. *The Buffer Memory*. This is a high-speed semiconductor RAM that generally operates at transfer rates up to 10 MHz or, in some cases, even at higher rates. Its function is to reconcile the higher-speed electronics to the slower-speed, electromechanical mass storage device, which usually is some magnetic storage device.

6. *The Control Unit*. This unit provides control over the entire fixed pattern generation system. The signal flows in all the different electronic blocks are controlled by this unit.

7. *The Mass Storage Device*. The contents of the buffer memory are output to the mass storage device, which could be a drum, disk, or tape unit, in a burst mode. All the test patterns output by the simulator are stored in this device for the subsequent test.

B-2.3.3 The Test Procedure After the test patterns are stored in the mass storage device, the simulator is removed from the system and is replaced by the microcomputer system under test, as shown in Fig. B-2. Under control of the control unit, the test pattern is loaded into the buffer memory in a burst mode from the mass storage device.

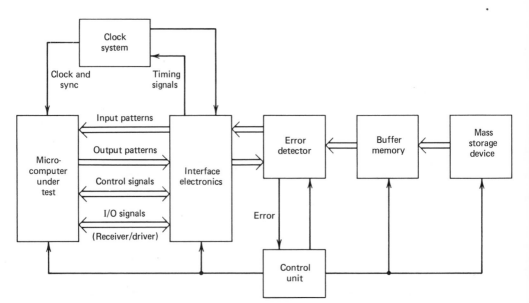

Figure B-2   The test procedure.

Notice that now the input signal patterns originating in the mass storage device, are fed into the microcomputer under test through the test system. This is also true of input signals to the μC on the I/O and the control lines. The output signals from the μC and the corresponding output signals from the test pattern that are stored in the mass storage device are compared in the error detector block. If an error is detected, a signal is sent to the control unit.

Depending on how the test system is designed, the testing can be stopped if an error is detected, or it can be programmed to branch to an error-processing routine, which could include a display or a printout of the error condition that was detected. In some cases more than one pass through the test procedure may be necessary, contingent on the complexity of the test patterns and the number of test patterns as well as the number of pins available on the μP.

B-2.3.4 Advantages The pattern recognition approach offers the following advantages.

1. Instead of using a complete, known good system for generating the output pattern every time a new μC system is tested, the desired output pattern is generated, captured, and stored only once.
2. The known good system has to work in the fault-free mode only once to produce the reference output pattern.
3. This approach allows the user to test simultaneously more than one microcomputer system located at several different test stations.
4. Minimal programming effort is required to program the test system.
5. This approach offers a fairly high degree of flexibility if changes or additions are made to the μC system under test. A new set of test patterns can be readily created with the modified or enhanced μC system as previously described.

B-2.3.5 Disadvantages The following are the disadvantages of this approach to testing μC systems.

1. The cost of hardware is a significant factor. In addition to the interface and the error-detection circuitry, a fairly large buffer memory must be provided. The cost of the mass storage device is in addition to this cost.
2. If modifications or enhancements are made to the μC system under test, additional PROMS are required for the simulation program. This increases the cost.
3. Further costs are added for support software needed to generate and maintain the pattern simulation function.

B-2.4 Pattern Generation

B-2.4.1 Description The *pattern generation* technique is widely used for testing μC systems. Every computer contains an instruction set. Each instruction in the set, when executed in association with its corresponding operand(s), produces an exact result. However, in practice it is not always possible to predetermine the exact result from the execution of every single instruction in a sequence of instructions or a program. Instead, the outputs are checked or monitored after execution of a group of instructions is completed. Each user of the μC is naturally interested in verifying the group of instructions that will be used in his/her particular application. The pattern generation approach, often referred to as the *algorithm pattern generation* technique, is a powerful tool because it permits testing of the system by means of *user-oriented* sequences of instructions or *algorithms*.

In this approach the entire instruction set is prestored in a high-speed buffer memory, usually in ROM chips. The desired pattern is generated by two processors, the *data generator* and the *address generator*. These generators are usually capable of both synchronous and asynchronous operations when used in conjunction with the μC system under test. The two generators operate under microprogram control. The microprogram is stored in a high-speed control memory (CROM).

When an instruction is executed by the system under test, a signal is sent to the pattern generator, which goes into a process routine. If the result output by the system under test is satisfactory, the next instruction in the sequence is processed. If not, an error condition is indicated.

B-2.4.2 Advantages This approach to testing has the following advantages.

1. The main advantage is that this testing approach reveals instruction sequences to which the system under test is particularly susceptible.
2. The approach is efficient because the delays involved in transferring the reference pattern from the mass storage device to the buffer memory are eliminated.
3. It is less expensive because a mass storage device is not required. Furthermore, a large buffer memory is not required, thereby resulting in additional cost savings.
4. The user can generate programs to verify instruction sequences. Changes and enhancements to existing programs can be readily made by the user.
5. This approach allows the user to diagnose any faulty instructions.

B-2.4.3 Disadvantages The following are the disadvantages to this approach.

1. The user has complete control over the test, so the user alone is totally responsible for it.
2. The user must be thoroughly familiar with the system under test as well as the applications in which the μC is used.
3. The user must understand the exact functioning of each instruction in the instruction set as well as the sequence of instructions or the program.
4. Finally, the user must be familiar with microprogramming and must be able to generate the microprograms that are required for controlling the pattern generator.

C

THE LOGIC ANALYZER

C-1 WHAT IS A LOGIC ANALYZER?

The triggered oscilloscope has long been the primary laboratory tool for ana-
lyzing real-time, recurring, electrical signals. It is not adequate for servicing
the requirements of today's complex digital equipment or microcomputers.
The *logic analyzer,* a form of digital oscilloscope, has evolved as the most
convenient troubleshooting tool for microcomputers. Despite its name, the
logic analyzer does not analyze the data. Instead, it displays digital data in a
convenient form, either as rectangular waveforms representing digital data or
in tabular forms as binary 1s and 0s that can be analyzed by the test engineer.

Before we describe how a logic analyzer works, we point out the principal
differences between this instrument and the conventional oscilloscope. Unlike
the time domain of real-time oscilloscopes or the frequency domain of spec-
trum analyzers, the logic analyzer acquires and displays information or data
from the digital domain. Information in the digital domain consists of binary
data that are simultaneously present in a bus (i.e., a group of parallel lines)
as well as the sequence in which these data change on these lines. The digital
domain also includes the clock and control signals, which control the flow and
processing of data and addresses in a digital computer. Unlike the continuous
range of values obtained in analog applications, a channel of digital information can only have two discrete values or states.

In traditional oscilloscopes the instrument captures and displays events that
occur after a trigger is applied. Furthermore, for a *stable* display, the event(s)
must be *repetitive.* In a logic analyzer the events preceding the application of
a trigger are captured and displayed. In other words, in an oscilloscope the
trigger initiates the capture and display of information. In a logic analyzer the
trigger terminates the capture of information and initiates a stable display.

Most logic analyzers have the following basic characteristics.

1. They have several parallel input channels. Sixteen channels (or even more) are
   quite common.

2. The incoming digital information is stored in semiconductor memory chips (i.e., in RAMS).

3. The incoming binary bits are stored on a single pass. Unlike the oscilloscope, the incoming information does not have to be recurring.

4. Logic analyzers capture and display information that has arrived prior to the application of the trigger.

5. For display purposes, either as waveforms or as truth tables on a CRT display, the repetition of data is performed internally within the instrument after capturing and storing the incoming bits.

6. The binary bits coming in all the input channels can be captured, stored, and displayed as requested by the operator.

7. Logic analyzers are not restricted to displaying only one variable as a function of time. Two variables can be displayed. A typical example of this is the situation where the test engineer wishes to examine the logic states on one or more channels whenever an interrupt occurs.

C-2 TYPICAL LOGIC ANALYZER BLOCK DIAGRAM

Figure C-1 shows a generalized block diagram of the functional elements of a typical logic analyzer. The four basic internal functions of this instrument are the data acquisition function, the trigger function, the data storage function, and the data display function.

C-2.1 Data Acquisition Function

Most logic analyzers are designed to acquire 4 to 32 channels of information simultaneously. To avoid confusion, several channels are combined in a single, multiple-lead probe head. A set of color-coded leads are provided from the head to the probe pods.

The incoming signal pulses are fed into a threshold detector that detects and converts the signals to the proper binary levels required by the analyzer. In many instruments the threshold voltage is selectable by the operator to match the threshold voltages applicable to the logic family used in the device under test. Some logic analyzers even have threshold select capability, which enables the test engineer to select and set the minimum high- and maximum low-level voltages suitable for the binary states of the logic family used in the device under test. Most instruments generally have one fixed threshold setting of 1.4 V to accommodate the standard TTL family of logic circuits. Additionally, they have a range selection that varies from ± 2.5 to ± 12.0 V. Other fixed threshold voltage settings are also used. A threshold setting of -1.3 V is often used for testing the ECL family of logic circuits.

542

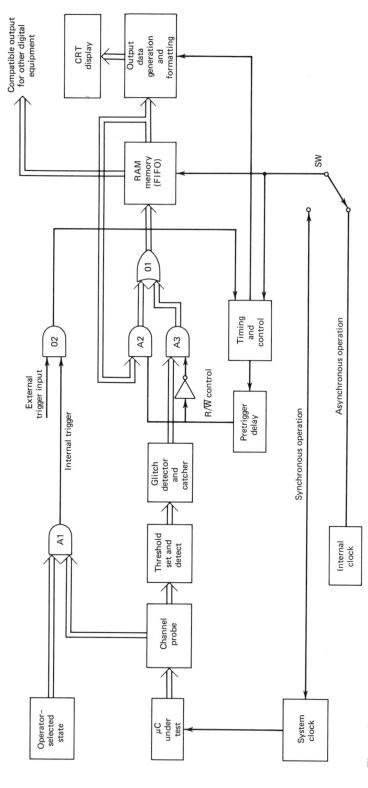

Figure C-1 Generalized block diagram of typical logic analyzer.

C-2.1.1 Sampling Modes Prior to storing the incoming binary bits in the RAM, the 1s and 0s must be sampled. Two sampling methods are available. In the first method, the pulses from the output of the clock in the system under test are used for sampling and storing the bits in the memory. This results in synchronous recording mode. As shown in Fig. C-1, the switch SW selects this mode. The clock pulses are also fed into the timing and control logic of the analyzer. In this mode a D-type flip-flop is used, so the incoming bits are defined at the leading edge of the clock pulses. This mode of sampling is widely used to detect, capture, and observe bugs in the µC under test that are the result of programming errors. The main shortcoming of this approach is that if an undesirable, narrow *glitch* occurs between two clock pulses, the analyzer will simply ignore it. This is clearly shown in the waveforms of two input channels and their respective synchronously sampled data in Fig. C-2. Such a situation may be acceptable in software debugging but may *not* be acceptable for hardware debugging.

The second method does not use the system clock of the µC under test. Instead, it uses an independent clock, provided internally within the logic analyzer, as shown in Fig. C-1. The internal clock runs at a speed considerably higher than the system clock. Thus, when the internal clock is used, the incoming bit streams are asynchronously sampled at a much higher rate. Consequently, much higher resolution of the incoming data is obtained and

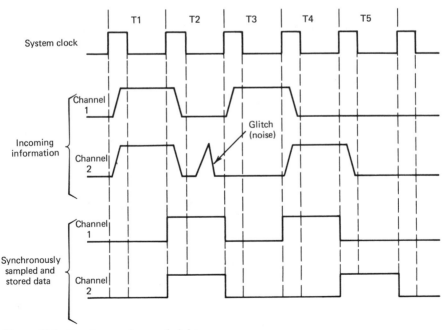

Figure C-2 Synchronously sampled data.

recorded. Also, events occurring between the bits of incoming data, such as the glitch in Fig. C-2, can be captured and recorded, as shown in Fig. C-3.

C-2.1.2 Latch Mode Figure C-3 shows that the glitch, which was ignored in the synchronous sampling mode, was captured and recorded in the asynchronous mode by using a much faster internal clock. Notice in Fig. C-3 that the internal clock rate was fast enough and the glitch was wider than one clock period and so was captured without any difficulty. However, if the glitch were an extremely narrow, high-speed transient that was present in the short time interval between two pulses of the internal clock, it would still be missed the same way as in the synchronous sampling mode of Fig. C-2. The *latch mode* handles this situation.

In the latch mode a logic configuration, sometimes called the *glitch detector* or the *glitch catcher,* is used. Figure C-4a shows that the narrow, high-speed glitch occurs between two clock pulses of the internal clock. In the normal sampled mode it is not captured. With a glitch catcher it is captured and displayed as shown.

The latch mode sets up a condition in which the glitch triggers a latch flip-flop as soon as it arrives. The output of this latch is then held until the arrival of the next internal clock pulse. The logic configuration of the glitch catcher is shown in Fig. C-4b. The channel data is input into the 2-input AND gate A1. The second input to the A1 gate is from the internal clock, and this is inverted. Thus the AND gate is enabled only during the time between two

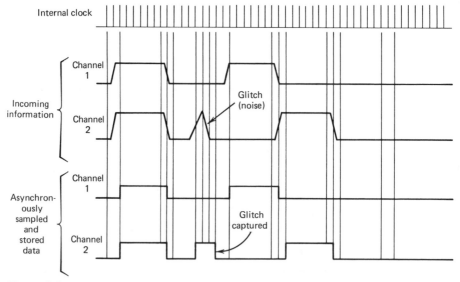

Figure C-3 Asynchronously sampled data. (Glitch in channel 2 is captured.)

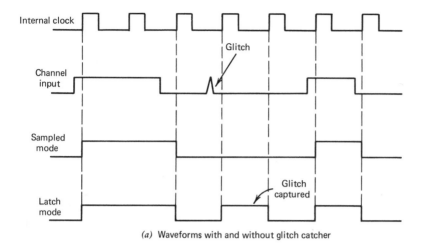

(a) Waveforms with and without glitch catcher

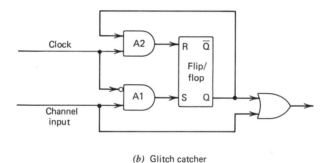

(b) Glitch catcher

Figure C-4   The latch mode.

normal clock pulses. Any high-speed transient on the channel input line between clock pulses results in a 1 output from the AND gate, which sets the
R/S flip-flop. The Q output of the flip-flop is a stable output that represents
the captured transient. It is then passed through the OR gate and available to
the rest of the circuitry as a legitimate input for subsequent storage in the
RAM. The next incoming clock pulse resets the flip-flop to the $\overline{Q}$ side through
the A2 AND gate, which is enabled by the Q side of the flip-flop. The glitch
is captured and retained for one full clock period, as shown in Fig. C-4a. The
normal inputs on the channel bypass the flip-flop and go through the OR gate,
as previously explained.

C-2.2 Triggering Function

A logic analyzer is an instrument that allows us to record and analyze data
that preceded the occurrence of some event that is indicated by the trigger. In
Fig C-1 notice that the information to be recorded in the RAM passes through

AND gates, represented by A3, and then through OR gates, represented by O1. The trigger, referred to as R/$\overline{\text{W}}$ control in Fig. C-1, is normally low and, since it is inverted, enables A3 and is loaded into the RAM through O1. After applying a trigger, A3 is disabled, so the bits on the channels are not written into the RAM.

Triggering can be accomplished in several different ways. All logic analyzers have a combinational triggering capability called *word recognition*. The operator preselects a binary word that is input into the big AND gate A1 of Fig. C-1. The logic state of each incoming channel is likewise input into A1. When the two words compare, the output of A1 generates an internal trigger that is fed into timing and control through OR gate O2. It is possible to use a trigger that is generated external to the logic analyzer. For each channel, the operator can select either a 1 state, a 0 state, or a "don't care" state.

Another triggering feature (often called a *qualifier*) available on some logic analyzers also triggers on a certain combination of bits, but the combination is not preselected by the operator. In this case the trigger is generated only when the bits on two preassigned channels are simultaneously 1s. Such a situation, often called the *true trigger,* results in a trigger output when both channels 1 and 2 have a digital 1 on them, as shown in Fig. C-5a. It is also possible to generate what is called a *false trigger,* as shown in Fig. C-5b, where a trigger is generated when either channel 1 or channel 2 has a 1 on it.

In computer systems functional errors of either the hardware or the software types often happen, but their effects do not become evident until several machine cycles after the error has occurred. For troubleshooting purposes it is necessary that the events preceding the detection of the error condition be examined. The pretrigger recording mode of the logic analyzer is the most useful feature of this instrument because it enables the test engineer to look back in time (prior to the event that triggered the analyzer). Pretriggering is possible because the incoming bits on each channel are loaded into the RAM chips in a *serial* fashion. Each sample clock pulse shifts the data from left to right. When the analyzer is triggered, the bits that precipitated the trigger are one or two sample clocks into the RAM shift register. All the rest of the bits to the left (in the register) contain the useful information that was captured prior to the trigger.

Some analyzers have another feature that enables the user to delay the actual triggering of the analyzer. Delaying the trigger for some time period after the triggering event has occurred, permits the user to capture and record data immediately preceding the triggering event as well as data immediately following the event. This is shown in Fig. C-6 for only two channels, but it is available on all the channels of the analyzer. The triggering delay is counted out in terms of the sample clock periods, usually up to 10,000 clock periods. (Some analyzers go even higher than this, but this feature is not available on all instruments.)

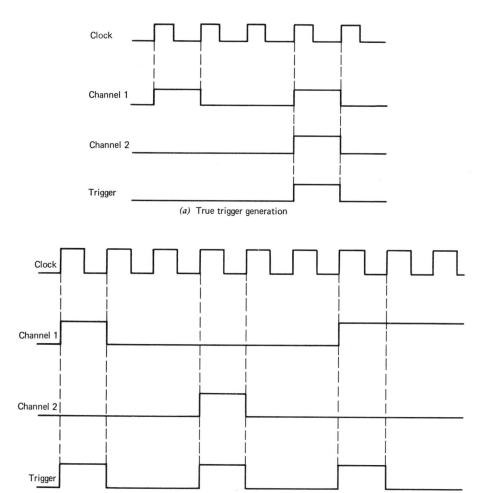

(a) True trigger generation

(b) False trigger generation

Figure C-5   True/false combination trigger.

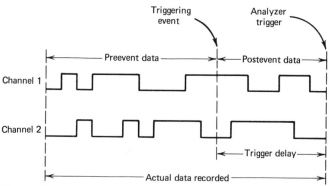

Figure C-6   Data recording with delayed trigger.

C-2.3 Storage Function

The recording or storage function is accomplished by using semiconductor RAM chips. The memory in the logic analyzer can be thought of as a FIFO (first-in, first-out) stack. The first bit loaded in each channel input is serially shifted down the register as succeeding bits come in. Eventually, the first bit is shifted out of the last bit position of each memory register. The depth of the stack represents the number of bits that can be shifted into each register in the memory. Figure C-7 shows a 4-channel, 16-deep stack.

The application of the trigger stops loading any new bits into the RAM. In Fig. C-1 notice that a 1 output from the pretrigger delay block disables AND gates A3, which prevents any new data bits from being loaded into the memory through A3 and O1. At the same time, the trigger output, 1, enables AND gate A2. This completes a recirculation path from the output of the RAM back into its input through A2 and O1. The recirculation is required for two reasons. First, most RAM chips used in analyzers are dynamic RAMS that require periodic refreshing to retain the data. Second, each channel must be read out serially in a repetitive manner for displaying the data on a CRT display. Recirculation as shown in Fig. C-1 accomplishes both goals.

In order to display and analyze complex logic problems, the RAM must be capable of acquiring data from several channels and of storing many bits on each channel. Depending on the applications involved, the RAM can be formatted in several different ways. In this case formatting refers to the number of channels and number of bits per channel. For example, a 1024-bit RAM could be formatted as 16 channels with 64 bits per channel, or it could be formatted as 8 channels with 128 bits per channel. Some analyzers offer different storage formats that can be selected by the user as needed. Also, some analyzers provide facilities for using the RAM outputs as inputs for use in other compatible digital equipment.

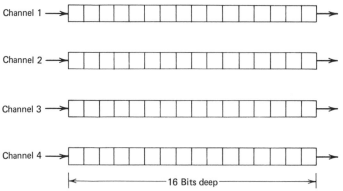

Figure C-7   Four-channel, 16-deep, FIFO stack in RAM chips (serial in, serial out).

C-2.4 Display Function

There are several ways by which the data captured and stored in the memory are displayed to the user.

1. *Light-Emitting Diodes*. This is the simplest and the least expensive method. The LEDs are arranged in a convenient order on the front panel. LEDs are not used much in today's logic analyzers.
2. *Timing Diagrams*. The binary bits captured from each channel are simultaneously displayed on a CRT as rectangular waveforms. Figure C-5 is an example of this type of display. Such a display clearly shows the timing relationships between various bits on different channels, since all channels use a common time base. Such displays are particularly useful for hardware debugging.
3. *Tabular Readout (Binary/Hexadecimal)*. The stored bits can also be displayed as tabular readouts on the CRT in truth table formats of 1s and 0s. It is also possible to display the same data in hexadecimal notations. In some instruments the data are even displayed in octal notations. These displays are especially helpful in software debugging.
4. *Mapping Displays*. The stored bits can also be presented on the CRT as a mapping display. Such a display is an overall view of the system operation and is presented on the CRT as a pattern of dots. Each dot represents 1 input word. For a specific sequence of input words, the combination of dots forms a signature that is unique to that particular group of words or a block of data. Using this method, the entire contents of a block of memory can be displayed on a CRT as a dot matrix, where each dot represents 1 word. This is accomplished by splitting the word in half. Then, through a D/A converter, the most-significant bits of the word are sent to the vertical channel of the display and the least-significant bits to the horizontal channel of the display through another D/A converter.

GLOSSARY

Absolute Value. The value of an operand independent of any algebraic sign.

Access Time. The time period measured from the instant the CPU sends an address for a readout from the memory and the instant that the contents of that memory location are available at the outputs. In case of a memory write-in, it is the time interval between the instant that the CPU is ready to send information to the memory and the instant at which it is completely written into the addressed location.

Accumulator. A register in the ALU that usually contains one operand used in an arithmetic or logical operation of the ALU and is often the destination of the result of the arithmetic or logical operation. It frequently has the capability to perform other functions such as shift, rotate, and cumulative addition (or subtraction, in some cases).

Active-High. The situation where the binary signal performs its intended function when the signal is in the high or 1 state.

Active-Low. The situation where the binary signal performs its intended function when the signal is in the low or 0 state.

Adder. A device in the ALU of a computer that performs an addition on two operands input into it.

Address. A code that uniquely identifies a memory location for either reading the information out of it or writing the information into it. It may also apply to registers in the CPU as well as to I/O ports.

Addressing Modes. The methods that specify how the address contained in a computer instruction will be used to access the ultimate desired memory or I/O register location. Common addressing modes are direct, indirect, immediate, indexed, program counter-relative, and page relative.

Algorithm. A processing procedure that always leads to the solution of a particular problem in a finite number of steps.

Analog Signals. A continuously variable signal used to represent some physical condition that can take any value. Typical examples are electrical voltages representing rotation of shafts, pressures, or temperatures.

Analog-to-Digital Converter (ADC). An interface device or circuit that converts an incoming analog signal into its equivalent digital signal.

Argument. An independent variable. In table look-up it is the number that identifies the location of the desired quantity (i.e., an address).

Arithmetic Logic Unit (ALU). The portion of the CPU that performs arithmetic and logical operations on input operands under control of the program instructions.

Arithmetic Shift. A right or left shift operation in a register that preserves the sign bit located in the most significant bit position of the word.

Architecture. The organizational structure of a computing system.

Array. A group of items arranged in a meaningful order or manner.

ASCII. American Standard Code for Information Interchange, widely used in computer and communication systems. It is a 7-bit character code.

Assembler. Software that converts assembly language program codes into machine language codes that can be utilized by the computer. Assembler translates mnemonics into equivalent binary codes and replaces names with binary equivalents. Finally, it assigns memory locations to instructions and data words.

Assembly Language. A programming language similar to English that relieves the programmer of the need to remember the bit patterns for each instruction. Assembly language instructions are translated into machine language instructions on a one-to-one basis. Alphabetical characters and numerals are used in assembly language.

Asynchronous Operation. A system operating at irregular intervals without reference to a central timing clock or source. Termination of each operation is indicated by a specific signal that initiates the next operation.

Autoindex. An index register that automatically increments or decrements every time that it is used.

Base. The radix point in a number system.

BASIC. A higher-level, procedure-oriented, language (beginners' all-purpose symbolic instruction code) widely used in microcomputer systems.

Baud. A communications measure of serial data transmission usually measured as bits per second. It also includes bits for synchronization, error checking, and framing bits (start and stop bits).

Baudot Code. A 5-bit character code widely used in communications systems and terminals, including telegraphy.

Binary-Coded Decimal (BCD). A system where decimal digits are represented by the first 10 equivalent codes using 4 binary bits in the 8421 system.

Benchmark Program. A sample program designed to compare and evaluate the performance characteristics of computers, especially the speed of performance.

Binary. A number system whose radix or base is the quantity 2. Widely used in today's digital computers, the system has two discrete states or levels that can be readily represented by electrical signals.

Bit. An abbreviation of *binary digit*. In the binary number system the bits have two possible values of 1 and 0.

Bit Manipulation. The process of examining (i.e., sampling) and changing 1 or more bits within a single word.

Bit Slice. A process whereby a section of the CPU hardware architecture is combined in parallel with other similar sections to form a complete CPU. This allows CPUs with various word lengths to be formed.

Block. A group of data words considered as a unit during processing. The words in a block are stored in successive memory locations.

Bootstrap (Bootstrap Loader). A technique for loading a program into the computer memory where the first (or first few) instruction(s) are loaded (usually manually) and then used to bring in or load the rest of the program.

Branch. A process by which the program sequence departs from the normal one-step incrementation in the program counter by inserting a new value into it. The new value is the starting address of a subroutine, which is distinct and separate from the main program. A branch may be conditional or unconditional.

Breakpoint. A location in a program, specified by the programmer, at which the computer automatically stops program execution to check progress of the data handling process and/or to locate program errors.

Buffer. Usually a register (or a group of registers) in a computer system used as intermediate storage devices between two data-handling or memory devices and/ or the CPU, having different access times or speeds. Buffers are also used for handling transfers between devices having different word formats.

Bus. A group of conducting wires that allow the parallel transfer of words between various sources and destinations within a computing system.

Byte. The basic grouping of a certain number of bits that the computer processes as a unit. The byte may or may not be different from the computer word. Most often in microprocessors, a byte refers to an 8-bit grouping of bits, regardless of the word length. For example, both 8-bit and 16-bit word length microprocessors may operate on 8-bit bytes.

Call Subroutine. The process of passing control from the main program to a subroutine.

Carry Bit. A 1 bit that is generated as a result of an add operation on the most significant bit pair of two words and used for further mathematical processing or as a status bit. In microprocessors a special flip-flop, the CARRY F/F in the status register, is set when a carry is generated.

Central Processing Unit (CPU). The portion of a computer system that controls the interpretation and execution of the program instructions. The CPU generally contains the ALU, scratch-pad registers, the program counter and the related stack, the instruction decoder, and the timing and control circuits.

Checksum. The logical sum of the data in a record. It is used as an error-checking device to guard against errors caused during transmission of data.

Clear. The process of setting all the bit positions of a register or a memory location to 0.

Clock. A timing device that emits pulses at regular time intervals; the pulses are then used to synchronize the various operations of a computing system.

COBOL. A higher-level, procedure-oriented language (common business-oriented language) widely used in business-type applications of computers.

Coding. The process of writing programs (i.e., instructions), in a language or system of codes, which can be interpreted and executed by a computing system.

Comparator. A device that compares two binary words input into it and outputs a signal or signals that indicates whether the two quantities are equal or not and, if not, which is the larger quantity and the smaller quantity.

Compiler. A program that converts a program written in a higher-level or procedure-oriented language such as BASIC, FORTRAN, or COBOL into an assembly language or machine language program.

Complement. The process of changing all 1s to 0s and 0s to 1s in a register or a memory location.

Counter. A register having the capability to store a given number, which is determined by the number of pulses input into it. In an UP counter the number is increased (incremented) by one every time a pulse is input into it. In a DOWN counter the number is decreased (decremented) by one every time a pulse is input into it.

Cross Assembler. A language translator program that runs on one type of computer and produces the machine language code for another type of computer.

Current Page. The page in memory in which the current instruction is located.

Cycle Stealing. A machine cycle stolen from the normal CPU operation for a DMA transfer operation. During the stolen cycle, the CPU is not able to access any memory location or perform an I/O transfer operation.

Cycle Time. The time interval at which a given set of fundamental operations is regularly repeated in the same sequence.

Daisy Chain. A hardware polling technique used to identify the interrupting I/O device. A signal generated by the CPU is passed from one noninterrupting I/O device to another but is blocked from propagating further when it reaches the interrupting I/O device.

Data Pointer. A register (or memory location) that holds the address of the operand, not the operand itself, to be used in instruction execution.

Data Register. A register, usually in the CPU, that holds either the incoming or outgoing data word. Primarily used as a buffer for reconciling timing differences between the faster CPU and the slower memories or I/O devices.

Debugging. The process of locating and eliminating errors in computer programs.

Decimal Adjust. A process in an arithmetic operation that converts a binary arithmetic result into an appropriate and correct decimal or BCD result.

Decoder, Instruction. A device into which coded instruction words are input that produces corresponding uncoded outputs.

Demultiplexer. A device having a single-word input capability that directs and outputs that word to one of several possible outputs as determined by the control signals to the device.

Destructive Readout (DRO). A phenomenon associated with certain memory devices in which the reading out process destroys the original contents of the addressed memory location.

Development System. A special computer system designed for developing computer programs and hardware/software interfaces for the intended system.

Diagnostic Programs. A group of programs designed for checking out the operations of specific hardware sections of a computing system.

Digital-to-Analog Converter (DAC). The interface circuitry that converts a digital word input into it (usually by a computer system) into an equivalent analog output signal.

Direct Addressing. A method of accessing either a memory location or an I/O port where the address specified in the related instruction is used as the final or ultimate address without reference to or modification by a base or index register.

Direct Memory Access (DMA). An I/O transfer method where an external controller takes control of the operation for one or more machine cycles. Data transfer between the external I/O device or auxiliary memory and the computer memory occurs without any intervention or control by the CPU.

Disable. A control process that prevents or prohibits a certain device from performing its function, such as preventing a register from outputting its contents.

Diskette. A flexible magnetic surface device used as a data storage device; often called a floppy disk.

Disk Operating System (DOS). An operating system capable of transferring data and programs between a disk and other parts of the computing system (mainly the CPU). The operating system usually is resident in the disk itself.

Dual Inline Package (DIP). A container for holding a semiconductor device or chip. The package has parallel rows of pins protruding in a perpendicular manner from the two lengthwise edges of the package.

Dynamic Memory. A semiconductor memory in which the information must be periodically rewritten or refreshed in order to retain it.

EAROM. Electrically alterable ROM. A nonvolatile semiconductor ROM that can be erased and reprogrammed any number of times, generally without being removed from the memory circuits. Has a relatively long write time.

EBCDIC. Extended binary-coded interchange code. It is an 8-bit character most often used in large computers.

Editor. A program used as an aid in preparing source programs. The editor enables the user to make modifications, additions, and deletions to the text material in the source program.

Effective Address. The ultimate or actual address to be used in accessing an I/O or a memory. The effective address could be obtained from another memory location where it is stored or by modifying the address specified in the applicable instruction.

Emulator. A microprogram that is a copy of another existing computer system.

Enable. A control process or signal that initiates and/or allows a device to perform a certain intended function, such as allowing a register to output its contents.

Encoder. A device into which uncoded signals are input that translates them and produces coded outputs.

EPROM or EROM. A programmable, read-only memory (PROM) that can be completely erased by exposure to ultraviolet light.

Execute. The process of interpreting an instruction and performing the indicated operation(s).

Fan-In. The maximum number of inputs that can be connected to a logic gate from other gates that have similar electrical characteristics.

Fan-Out. The maximum number of similar gates that a logic gate can drive at the output without being electrically overloaded.

Fetch. The process of accessing the addressed location in the memory and transferring the contents of that location into the CPU. Usually refers to reading out an instruction from the program memory.

Firmware. Software (generally microprograms) implemented in ROMs.

Fixed-Instruction Computer. A computer whose instruction set is fixed by design and manufacture of the system and is not alterable by the user, as opposed to a microprogrammable computer. The user designs the application programs using the given fixed-instruction set.

Flag. A binary bit used as an indicator to tell some later part of the program that a certain condition exists as a result of prior processing.

Flip-Flop. A bistable device that can be made to switch from one stable state to another and that will stay in that particular state until such time as it is switched again.

Floating Point. A system where numerical quantities are represented by digits (or bits) in a variable number of places and the radix point is represented by a coded exponent of a power of the radix.

Floppy Disk. See *Diskette*.

Flowchart. A graphical or pictorial representation of the major steps of work in process or of a complete program.

FORTRAN. Formula translation. A high-level, procedure-oriented programming language designed for solving scientific and engineering problems that can be expressed in algebraic notation.

Gate. A logic element whose binary output is determined by and dependent on one or more binary inputs according to some specific rules of logic.

General-Purpose Register. A register (usually in the CPU) used for a multiplicity of purposes as opposed to dedicated registers, which are used for only one specific function. In microprocessors the term is generally applied to scratch-pad memory registers into which many different words can be temporarily stored.

Hard Copy. A paper document containing printed symbols in a human language.

Hardware. The physical equipment comprising the computer system.

Hexadecimal Numbers. A number system consisting of the numerals 0, 1, . . . 9 and alphabetical characters A, B, . . . F, which represent all the possible combination codes formed by a 4-bit binary word. The decimal equivalents of these possible binary codes are 0, 1, . . . 15.

High-Impedance State. The open-circuit state in tristate logic configurations.

High-Level Languages. Programming languages in which single statements are problem or function-oriented statements that represent procedures instead of single machine codes instructions. A single statement in a high-level language could translate into several instructions or may call out subroutines. Typical examples are BASIC, COBOL, and FORTRAN.

Immediate Addressing. A method of addressing in which the operand is located in the instruction itself. In multibyte or multiword instructions, the operand is usually located in the memory location immediately following the instruction.

Implied Addressing. A method of addressing where the op code, not separate address codes, of the instruction itself specifies all the required addresses.

Indexed Addressing. A method of addressing in which the address portion in the instruction is modified by the contents of the index register to obtain the ultimate or effective address of the location to be accessed.

Index Register. A register that contains a quantity (called the modifier) that is used to modify an address.

Indirect Addressing. A method of addressing in which the address in the instruction specifies a memory location where the true or effective address of the memory location to be accessed is stored. It is a two-step addressing procedure.

Input-Output (I/O). A general term usually applied to the section of the system that handles data communications between the CPU and external peripheral devices.

Instruction. A basic command consisting of a set of bits that defines a specific computer operation to be performed by the CPU.

Instruction Cycle. The process involved in fetching, decoding, and executing the instruction.

Instruction Length. The number of words needed to construct a complete instruction. Instructions may be single-word or multiple-word instructions.

Instruction Register. A register that temporarily stores the current instruction that is being decoded and executed.

Instruction Repertoire. See *Instruction Set*.

Instruction Set. The total complement of general-purpose instructions that is available with a specific computer. Different computers have different instruction sets.

Instruction Time. The time required to fetch an instruction, decode it, and execute it. The instruction time depends on the instruction length.

Interpreter. A program that fetches an instruction and executes it immediately. It is written in a higher-level language and does not produce an object program the way an assembler or a compiler does.

Interrupt Acknowledge. A signal from the CPU to the interrupting device informing the latter that the CPU has received an interrupt request and that the service subroutine will be called out and executed on completion of the current instruction.

Interrupt Mask. A capability in the computer that allows the programmer to specify whether an interrupt request will be accepted or not.

Interrupt Service Routine. A subroutine that performs the actions required to branch away from the main program, perform the tasks required by the I/O device, and return control to the main program.

Interrupt Request. A signal from an I/O device to the computer that temporarily suspends the normal sequence of the main program and transfers control to a special subroutine that services that particular I/O device.

I/O Port. The basic addressable unit of a computer (usually a register) that provides a connection between the computer and the I/O device for transmission of data between them.

Iterative Loop. A group of instructions in a program that is repeated a number of times.

JUMP. An instruction that forces a new value into the program counter, thereby departing from the normal one-step incrementation of the address of the next instruction to be fetched. Usually a JUMP fetches the next instruction from the main program as opposed to a BRANCH, which transfers control to a subroutine. A JUMP may be either a forward or backward JUMP from the address of the current instruction.

Kilo-. A prefix meaning 1000. For example, 1 kilobit means a 1000 bits and 2 kHz means a frequency of 2000 Hz.

Label. A set of symbols or a name attached to an instruction or a statement in a program that identifies a memory address in which that instruction or statement is stored.

Language. A system for representing and communicating data and information between human beings and computer systems that contains well-defined characters and rules for combining these characters into expressions or statements.

Large-Scale Integration (LSI). A term applied to high-density, monolithic, semiconductor integrated circuits, diffused in a single silicon chip. Circuit complexity generally exceeds the equivalent of 100 ordinary logic gates.

Latch. A temporary storage device, usually a D-type or JK-type flip-flop, that is controlled by a timing pulse or signal. The binary bit inserted in a latch remains in it for a time period from one clock pulse to the next, regardless of any input changes during this time period.

Linking Loader. A loader program that loads a series of main programs and subroutines into the program memory and provides the necessary interconnections between them.

Literal. An operand that is contained in the instruction itself; often referred to as zero-level addressing.

Loader. A program that transfers either application or system programs from an input device into the computer memory.

Logic Analyzer. A test instrument capable of detecting and displaying parallel digital signals in squarewave or truth table forms.

Logical Shift. Either a right or a left shift operation in a register without any regard for the sign bit in the most-significant bit position of the register. Generally, 0s are inserted in the empty bit positions.

Logical Sum. A bit-by-bit exclusive-OR operation performed on two binary numbers or operands.

Look-Up Table. A collection of data, stored in sequential memory locations, in a form suitable for convenient and ready reference.

Loop. See *Iterative Loop*.

Low-Level Language. See *Assembly Language*.

Machine Cycle. This is the basic CPU operation cycle that indicates the time required to fetch one word of data from the memory or write it into the memory, or it could be the time required to execute one instruction.

Machine Language. The lowest-level language in which programs can be written. It specifies each instruction in binary form, ready for loading into the program memory and execution by the computer.

Macroinstruction. A source language statement expressed in symbolic form that is expanded by the assembler into one or more machine language instructions. Sometimes this translation process may involve calling out an entire subroutine.

Majority Logic. A form of combinational logical function where the single output is true only if more than one-half the total number of input signals is true.

Maskable Interrupt. See *Interrupt Mask*.

Medium-Scale Integration (MSI). A semiconductor, monolithic integrated circuit diffused in a silicon chip having the circuit complexity of between 10 and 100 ordinary logic gates.

Mega-. A prefix meaning 1 million. For instance, 2 megabits means 2 million bits.

Memory. The section of a computer that stores instructions and data words. Each stored word is assigned a unique address used by the CPU to access the contents of that particular memory location.

Memory Address Register. A dedicated register in the CPU that holds the address of the memory location to be accessed.

Memory Addressing Modes. See *Addressing Modes*.

Microassembler. An assembly program specifically designed for writing and assembling microprograms.

Microcomputer. A computer system consisting of a microprocessor chip, semiconductor memories (RAMs and ROMs), I/O chips, and other supporting logic on semiconductor chips. Usually, all components of the computer are on a single printed circuit board.

Microcontroller. A controller unit that can be microprogrammed but that has no capabilities to perform arithmetic operations.

Microinstruction. An instruction stored in the control memory of a microprogrammable machine, usually in ROM chips. It is one of the several control word signals that is part of the macroinstruction.

Microprocessor. A small computer whose CPU is fabricated on one silicon chip or, in some cases, on more than one chip. The microprocessor is one of the components in a microcomputer.

Microprogram. A program consisting of a group of microinstructions. Each group can be initiated by a macroinstruction in the main program, stored in the data memory of the computer.

Microprogrammable Computer. A computer whose internal CPU control signals are stored in a control read-only memory (CROM) as sequences of microinstructions that can be called out by macroinstructions of the main program.

Microsecond (μs). One-millionth of a second.

Mnemonics. Symbolic names or abbreviations used in instructions, usually in assembly language programming, for instructions as well as several parts of the computer such as registers, memory, and the like. Mnemonics must be translated into machine codes before they can be used. Using mnemonics, the programmer need not remember the bit patterns of each instruction.

Modem. Modulator-demodulator. A device used in serial data communications, usually over long lines. It adds or removes a carrier frequency to or from data signals, which are transmitted on high-frequency channels.

Monitor. An operating system that enables the user to enter programs, run them, and modify them as needed. It also enables the user to observe the status of the various parts of the computer system.

MOS. Metal-oxide-semiconductor device. A semiconductor fabrication process that uses field-effect transistors as active circuit elements.

Multiplexer. A device having several possible inputs that selects a specific input under control of signals and outputs that word on a single common output.

Multiprocessing. A computing system consisting of two or more processors operating out of a common memory. Such a configuration makes it possible to run as many programs as there are processors in the system simultaneously.

Nanosecond (ns). One-billionth of a second.

Negative Logic. A system of logic signals where the active state, or one, is represented by a low-level signal.

Nesting. A procedure where subroutines can be called out by other subroutines. The level of nesting is the number of subroutines that can be called out before returning control to the main program.

Nibble. A group of 4 bits operated on as a single unit. In microcomputers, 2 nibbles make a byte (for 8-bit machines).

NONDESTRUCTIVE READOUT (NDRO) Memory. A memory device in which the contents of the accessed locations are *not destroyed* during the readout process.

Nonmaskable Interrupt. An interrupt system in a computer that cannot be disabled under program control.

Nonvolatile Memory. A memory whose contents are not lost or altered when electrical power is removed from the device.

NO OP Instruction. No-operation instruction. This instruction performs no specific function. It merely increments the program counter, thereby fetching the next instruction and executing it.

Object Code. The machine language code that is output by a translating program, either an assembler or a compiler.

Object Program. The machine language program output by a translating program, an assembler, or a compiler that can be loaded into the program memory of the computer for execution.

Octal. A number system based on the radix 8. A total of 8 digits, 0 to 7, are used in the octal system, thus making it possible to express an octal digit by means of a 3-bit binary code.

Offset. A number or quantity added to another quantity, usually an address in the instruction, to obtain the true or effective memory address.

One's Complement. A system where the binary bits in a word are complemented on a bit-to-bit basis (i.e., all 1s are changed to 0s and 0s are changed to 1s).

On-Line System. A computer system in which the operation of the I/O devices is under control of the CPU. As soon as the current information is available and reflected in the I/O devices, it is introduced into the computing system for processing.

Op Code. Operating code. A code that is part of an instruction that specifies the operation to be performed during the next machine cycle.

Operand. A computer word that is being acted on or being processed. Generally applied to a datum.

Operating System. System software that controls the overall operation of a computing system, including various tasks such as memory allocation, interrupt processing, and job handling.

Overflow Bit. A bit resulting from an arithmetic operation that is in excess of the normal number of bits that the register can hold. In most microprocessors it is a status bit resulting from two's-complement arithmetic operation, which is stored in the OVERFLOW flip-flop of the status register.

Page. A subdivision of the memory by some natural group, where the page number is identified by the higher-order bits of the address and the lower-order bits identify the location within the page. In microcomputers a memory chip provides a convenient natural grouping of memory locations and is often designated as a page.

Page Zero. The first page of the memory.

Parallel Transfers. A system where all the bits in a word or a byte are transmitted simultaneously. A separate conducting line is provided for each bit.

Parity Bit. A 1-bit code appended to a word to make the total number of 1 bits even (even parity) and the total number of 1 bits odd (odd parity). Mainly used in serial transmission of digital data.

PC Board. Printed circuit board on which semiconductor chips and other components are mounted and interconnected by etched lines.

Pointer. See *Data Pointer*.

Polling. The process of determining the current status of peripherals in a computing system by examining each device sequentially. Polling can be accomplished by software or hardware. Mainly used in identifying the interrupting I/O device.

Pop. The process of removing the last inserted return address from a LIFO (last-in, first-out) stack.

Port. See *I/O Port*.

Priority Interrupt. An interrupt system in which the interrupting I/O devices are assigned hierarchical priorities. A device with higher priority can interrupt one with lower priority, but a lower-priority device cannot interrupt one with a higher priority.

Procedure-Oriented Language. See *High-Level Language*.

Program. A set of coded instructions arranged in proper sequence to perform a specific set of tasks to give the desired results.

Program Counter. A counter in the CPU that specifies the address of the next instruction to be fetched from the program memory. Normally, the program counter is automatically incremented each time an instruction is fetched.

Programmable Interface. An interface device whose logical configuration can be altered (within certain limits) under program control, making the interface flexible and therefore usable in several different applications.

Programmable Timer. A timing device that, under program control, can be configured to give different timing intervals and different timing modes.

PROM. Programmable read-only memory. An integrated-circuit memory chip that cannot be rewritten or altered during normal computer operation but can be reprogrammed off-line by the user using special equipment.

Prototyping System. A hardware system used for breadboarding a microcomputer-based product or system. Includes CPU, memory chips (ROMs and RAMs), I/O chips, and power supply. Some software, such as utility programs, are also provided, generally in ROMs.

Pseudo-Instruction. An operation code in assembly language that directs the assembler to perform some function but which does not result in machine code or a machine language instruction.

Push. The process of inserting an updated (i.e., incremented) return address in a LIFO (last-in, first-out) stack during a BRANCH operation.

Queue. Refers to an operation where data words or operands are stored in a stack, composed of either registers or memory locations, which is operated on a FIFO (first-in, first-out) basis.

RAM. Random-Access Memory. A read/write memory having the capability that any location in the memory can be addressed and accessed at the same time, regardless of its position in the memory. The contents of any desired location can be altered during normal operation of the computer.

ROM. Read-only memory. A semiconductor memory whose contents can be read out as desired without destroying them but cannot be erased or rewritten during normal computer operation. Contents can be erased and rewritten in PROMs (programmable ROMs) by means of special off-line equipment.

Real Time. Any process or computation that takes place in synchronization with events that actually occur in time.

Refresh. The process of rewriting the contents of a dynamic semiconductor memory before they are lost.

Register. A device that temporarily holds a word or a byte. Usually located in the CPU. Registers generally do have other capabilities associated with them, such as shifting or recirculation.

Relative Addressing, Page. A method of memory addressing in which the address contained in the instruction refers to the local address of the same page number as the page number in which the instruction itself is located and that is indicated in the program counter.

Relative Addressing, Page-Zero. A method of memory addressing in which the address contained in the instruction is automatically interpreted as the local address in the base page (i.e., page zero) of the memory.

Relative Addressing, Program Counter. A method of addressing in which the true or effective address is obtained by adding the address in the instruction to the address of the instruction contained in the program counter.

Relocatable Programs. Programs that can be located in any part of the memory and can be moved to other parts of the memory, in their entirety, without any alterations in the programs themselves.

Reset. A process that returns a device or a system to a known, predetermined state before it is started. As applied to registers/counters/accumulators, it generally means inserting 0s in all bit positions.

Resident Programs. Programs (such as assemblers or compilers) stored in the computer memory or some other auxiliary memory units such as disks that can run on the computer itself.

Routine. A computer program. Usually refers to a subprogram or subroutine.

RS Flip-Flop. A bistable circuit with two inputs and two outputs. A 1 signal on the SET input puts its corresponding output in the 1 state and the other output in the 0 state. A 1 on the RESET input reverses the state on the two outputs.

Scratch-pad Memory. A group of registers in the CPU or a group of locations in the memory that are used for temporarily storing intermediate or partial results of computations or logical operations in progress.

Serial Memory. A memory in which the desired location cannot be accessed randomly. In order to reach the desired location all the prior, undesired locations must be accessed first. Consequently, the access time for each location is different.

Serial Shift. An operation in which the bits of a word or byte are shifted, either right or left, 1 bit at a time.

Set. The process of inserting a logical 1 in all the bit positions of a device such as a register.

Shift Register. A digital device whose contents can be shifted either right or left, one position at a time, in synchronization with each clock pulse.

Sign Bit. The most significant bit appended to a word representing a numerical quantity. According to the widely used convention, a 0 represents a positive number and a 1 represents a negative number.

Signature Analysis. A fault-detection method used in bus-oriented digital systems in which faults are determined by examining the time histories of certain digital signals at specific nodes in the system.

Simulator (Software). A computer program that simulates the execution of a machine language program on another machine. Commonly used for testing and debugging.

Software. A collective term for computer programs.

Source Program. A computer program written in either the assembly language of the particular machine or a higher-level language such as BASIC or FORTRAN.

Space. In serial data communication systems the 0 state on the line.

Stack. A group of registers or consecutive locations in the memory used for saving the return addresses during branch operations on a LIFO (last-in, first-out) basis. Stacks can be the cascade type or use pointers for addressing purposes.

Stack Pointer. An UP/DOWN counter that is used for addressing the locations in a stack. Used during the push-pop operations in a LIFO stack.

Stand-Alone System. In microcomputers, a software development system that runs on a microcomputer without connection to another computer or a time-sharing system.

Start Bit. A single bit signal (usually a 0) used for framing the data word in an asynchronous serial data transmission system that indicates the start of the transmission.

State Code. A code that indicates what state the CPU is in in response to externally generated conditions such as interrupt requests or DMA requests.

Static Memory. Semiconductor, read/write memory chips whose contents are retained without the need for periodic refreshing or rewriting. Opposite of dynamic memory chips.

Status Register. A register in the CPU. Each bit in the register reflects the current status of some particular logic device in the CPU. The status bits in this register are used to determine and establish subsequent operations in the program such as JUMP and BRANCH.

Stop Bit(s). One or two bits (usually ones) used as framing bits for indicating the end of a transmission in asynchronous serial data transmission systems.

Strobe. A control signal that generally initiates some operation such as enabling a gate or enabling a register to perform some specific function such as reading out its contents.

Subroutine. A program that can be called out from any part of the main program as often as desired.

Synchronous Operation. An operation such as transfer of data performed in accordance with a common timing source such as a clock, which emits timing pulses at regular intervals.

Syntax. The formal rules governing the structures of statements in assembly level programming or in higher-level language programming such as BASIC.

Terminal. An I/O device through which data may be entered into a computer system or through which data may leave the computer system. For example, a CRT display, a printer, or an entry keyboard.

Time-Shared Bus. A bus in a computing system used for different purposes during the same overall time span by interspersing the activities on the bus in time.

Time Sharing. The use of a device or a circuit for more than one purpose during the same overall time span. This is accomplished by interspersing the activities of the devices or circuits in time.

Trap. An instruction that forces a program to JUMP conditionally to a specified address. Traps are used to produce breakpoints either to indicate hardware/software errors or to determine the progress of data through the system by examining the contents of certain CPU registers.

Tri-State Logic. Logic circuits and configurations having three possible states, a high, a low, and a high-impedance or inactive state that essentially results in an open-circuit state. When combined with other similar configurations, a bussing structure can be designed with tristate characteristics that can be selectively isolated from certain logic blocks in a system.

TTL-Compatible. Logic circuits and configurations that use and operate with signal voltages that are within the range of voltages used by the TTL family of logic gates, without the need for level-shifting interface circuitry.

TTL Gates. Transistor-transistor-logic family of digital circuits. A bipolar transistor family of logic circuits that is widely used in digital systems and fabricated by means of the semiconductor integrated circuit technology.

Two's Complement. A binary number obtained by adding a 1 to the one's complement of the original binary number. When the two's complement of a binary number is added to the number itself, the resulting sum is 0, with a 1 carry from the most-significant bit position.

UART. Universal asynchronous receiver/transmitter. An interface logic device used in data communication systems that makes it possible for a parallel data device, such as a computer, to transfer data back and forth with another device that can handle only serial asynchronous data.

USRT. Universal synchronous receiver/transmitter. An interface logic device used in data communication systems that makes it possible for a parallel data device, such as a computer, to transfer data to and from another device that handles data in synchronous serial form.

Utility Programs. Programs that provide basic conveniences for operations such as initiating program execution, for examining and modifying contents of memory locations or CPU registers, loading and saving programs, and setting breakpoints.

Vectored Interrupt. An interrupt I/O system where the interrupting device identifies itself to the CPU by sending its own address or unique identification code. The CPU then uses this information to call out the appropriate service subroutine and executes it.

Volatile Memory. A memory that loses the information stored in it when the power is removed. Semiconductor RAM chips are generally volatile memories.

Word. The basic group of bits that is manipulated or operated on by the computer in one cycle. These manipulations include read/write and add operations. Words can be data words or instruction words.

Word Length. The number of bits comprising the computer word. The word length is also related to the computer system's data bus width (i.e., the number of parallel wires in the data bus) and the number of bits that can be handled by the instruction and the data registers in the CPU.

Zero Bit. One of the two coefficients used in the binary number system, represented by a predefined voltage level in a computing system.

INDEX